SECOND EDITION

JUVENILE DELINQUENCY
Readings

TITLES OF RELATED INTEREST FROM PINE FORGE PRESS

Adventures in Criminal Justice Research, Revised Edition: Data Analysis for Windows 95/98 & Using SPSS7 Versions 7.5, 8.0, or Higher by George W. Dowdall, Kim Logio, Earl Babbie, and Fred Halley.

Adventures in Social Research: Data Analysis Using SPSS7 for Windows 95/98 & Version 9.0 and 10.0 With 1998 GSS Data by Earl Babbie, Fred Halley, and Jeanne Zaino.

Constructing Social Research by Charles C. Ragin.

Crime, Second Edition by Robert D. Crutchfield and Charis Kubrin.

Of Crime and Criminality: The Use of Theory in Everyday Life by Sally Simpson.

Crime and Disrepute by John Hagan.

Crime and Everday Life, Second Edition by Marcus Felson.

Criminal Justice edited by George Bridges.

Designing Surveys: A Guide to Decisions and Procedures by Ronald Czaja and Johnny Blair.

Ethnicity and Race: Making Identities in a Changing World by Stephen Cornell and Doug Hartmann.

Experimental Design and the Analysis of Variance by Robert Leik.

A Guide to Field Research by Carol A. Bailey.

How Sampling Works by Richard Maisel and Caroline Hodges Persell.

Investigating the Social World: The Process and Practice of Research, Second Edition by Russell K. Schutt.

Media/Society: Industries, Images, and Audiences, Second Edition by David Croteau and William Hoynes.

Multiple Regression: A Primer by Paul Allison.

The Politics of Injustice: Crime and Punishment in America by Katherine Beckett and Ted Sasson.

Profitable Penalties: How to Cut Both Crime Rates and Costs by Daniel Glaser.

Social Statistics for a Diverse Society, Second Edition by Chava Frankfort-Nachmias and Anna Leon-Guerrero.

The Social Worlds of Higher Education: Handbook for Teaching in a New Century by Bernice Pescosolido and Ronald Aminzade.

SECOND EDITION

JUVENILE DELINQUENCY
Readings

EDITORS

Joseph G. Weis

Robert D. Crutchfield

George S. Bridges
University of Washington, Seattle

With

Jon'a Meyer
Rutgers University

Pine Forge Press

Boston   London   New Delhi

For information:

 Pine Forge Press
A Sage Publications Company
2455 Teller Road
Thousand Oaks, California 91320
E-mail: order@sagepub.com

Sage Publications Ltd.
6 Bonhill Street
London EC2A 4PU
United Kingdom

Sage Publications India Pvt. Ltd.
M-32 Market
Greater Kailash I
New Delhi 110 048 India

Printed in the United States of America

Library of Congress Cataloging-in-Publication Data

Juvenile delinquency : readings / by Joseph G. Weis, Robert D.
    Crutchfield, and George S. Bridges [editors].— 2nd ed.
        p. cm.
    Includes bibliographical references and index.
    ISBN 0-7619-8678-2 (pbk.: alk. paper)
    1. Juvenile delinquency—United States. 2. Juvenile justice,
Administration of—United States. I. Weis, Joseph G. II. Crutchfield,
Robert D. III. Bridges, George S.
HV9104 .J835 2000
364.36'0973—dc21   00-011073

This book is printed on acid-free paper.

01   02   03   04   05   06   07   7   6   5   4   3   2   1

Publisher: Stephen D. Rutter
Assistant to the Publisher: Ann Makarias
Production Editor: Sanford Robinson
Editorial Assistant: Candice Crosetti
Typesetter: Tina Hill
Indexer: Molly Hall
Cover Designer: Ravi Balasuriya

About the Editors

Joseph G. Weis is Professor of Sociology and the Director of the Center for Law and Justice. He served for a number of years as the Director of the National Center for the Assessment of Delinquent Behavior and Its Prevention, funded by the U.S. Department of Justice, as well as a member of the Washington State Governor's Juvenile Justice Advisory Committee. He is a past editor of the journal *Criminology* and a co-author, with Michael J. Hindelang and Travis Hirschi, of *Measuring Delinquency.*

Robert D. Crutchfield is Professor of Sociology and Chair of the Department of Sociology. He served on the Washington State Juvenile Sentencing Commission and is also a former juvenile probation officer and adult parole officer. He was a deputy editor of *Criminology* and has published a number of papers on labor markets, crime, and racial and ethnic disparities in the administration of justice, including "Labor Stratification and Violent Crime."

George S. Bridges is Professor of Sociology and Associate Dean of Undergraduate Education. He has served as a staff member of the policy office of the Attorney General of the United States as well as deputy editor of *Criminology*. He has published many papers on racial biases in American law and is co-editor, with Martha Myers, of *Crime, Inequality, and Social Control.*

About the Publisher

Pine Forge Press is a new educational publisher, dedicated to publishing innovative books and software throughout the social sciences. On this and any other of our publications, we welcome your comments.

Please write to:

Pine Forge Press
A Sage Publications Company
31 St. James Ave., Suite 510
Boston, MA 02116
(617) 753-7512
E-mail: info@pfp.sagepub.com

Visit our World Wide Web site, your direct link to a multitude of online resources:

www.pineforge.com

Brief Contents

Detailed Contents

Drugs

Psychological Control, Early Identification, and Intervention

Risk Factors and Prevention

Ecology, Enculturation, and Community Organization

Cultural Deviance and Gang Work

Social Learning and Behavior Modification

Labeling, Diversion, and Radical Nonintervention

PART V: JUVENILE JUSTICE REFORM   487

Judicial Reform

The Legal Legacy

The System Legacy

Preface

A leading "crime story" over the past decade has been the declining American crime and delinquency rate. Each year the Federal Bureau of Investigation releases its Uniform Crime Reports, leading to a flurry of phone calls and interviews with criminologists by those seeking to understand the decline. But despite this downward trend in crime, politicians continue to "run against crime" at election time, and the popular media remain fascinated with "true crime" shows and news of criminal events. And, within the academy, students and teachers alike continue to spend much time and energy thinking about crime and criminals, particularly juvenile delinquents.

Though rates of adult and juvenile crime are down, no one contends that it is no longer a major problem. In the second edition to their *Crime and Justice*, Sir Leon Radzinowicz and Marvin E. Wolfgang wrote, "There can be no doubt that optimism has gone, platitudes have proven empty. We are living through a time when, more than ever before, there can be no consensus on how to tackle crime. We do not feel it our business to try to resolve the current conflicts, but we feel it our duty, in the section entitled 'The Neo-Classical Revival,' to try to reflect it." Though that now classic three-volume set was first published in 1971, those words continue to reflect the lack of consensus in our thinking about crime, delinquency, and juvenile justice. Criminologists, politicians, and the general public are no closer to consensus on how to confront the problem of crime and delinquency than we were thirty years ago. Perhaps, we are even more divided.

This lack of consensus is reflected in the answers given by criminologists and practitioners when queried about the crime rate decline. Some argue that the decline is a product of tough law enforcement, while others contend it is a result of the recent shift toward community-oriented policing. Some attribute it to the massive increases in the number of people incarcerated, while others point to shrinking drug markets that have led to less juvenile gang activity and, therefore, lower levels of drug-related violence. There are some who point to a strong economy, while others focus on demographic forces and an aging population. Of course, there are those who suggest that all or many of those explanations are needed for a complete understanding of the downward trend in crime and delinquency.

In this, the second edition of *Juvenile Delinquency*, we do not try to resolve the conflicts in the study of juvenile crime, but we do try to represent the range of debate about the causes of delinquency and approaches to preventing and controlling it. The organizing principle for the first and now this second edition of *Juvenile Delinquency* is that the literature, both the old and the new, provides an important basis for thinking about crime for professionals, students, and the general public. As a result, we have included some of the classical studies along with contemporary empirical research.

This collection of readings began in our conversations about teaching our classes at the University of Washington. We believe that students should read the actual work of scholars who study crime and delinquency. Reading the original literature is an important part of a liberal education. The public debate about crime and what to do about it will be better informed if the public is exposed to what we know, and how we have come to know it, as well as what we do not know.

Some may believe that students will be unable to appreciate articles published in scholarly journals. Some teachers believe that students will find them inaccessible or of limited appeal. We have found that when students are asked to reach a bit beyond their grasp, more often than not, they respond positively. Our experience, as well as that of our colleagues that used the first edition of *Juvenile Delinquency* in their classes, confirm that students from private liberal arts colleges, to research universities, to community colleges can read and understand scholarly papers. There are of course characteristics of some academic articles that scare some students off. Most notable among these are analytic procedures and statistics. As we did in the first edition, we have edited out much of this material, leaving the presentation of theoretical ideas and conceptualization, results, discussions, and conclusions.

Nearly all of the selections in *Juvenile Delinquency* have been used in one or more of our courses. We have included, and even emphasized, a number of theoretical pieces because they form the basis of scholarship in criminology, and also because most common-sense explanations of the causes of crime and delinquency have actually been captured in those theories. When we explain this to students we can help them to see why theory is important to criminologists and also why it can be of interest to them. The empirical pieces in this volume frequently reflect modifications and refinements in classic theories.

For the second edition we decided to continue with the format that was successful in the first edition—sections on history and definitions, measurement, correlates of delinquency, theories and related practices, and contemporary issues in juvenile justice. Throughout, we have paid attention to both historical and contemporary efforts to understand delinquency. We say that this format is successful for several reasons. First, we have been careful to listen to the comments of instructors who used the first edition. Second, we have taken into account those things that our students liked and disliked and have made changes with their critiques in mind. Third, we have received the most generous flattery: Other editors have produced volumes that copy our format.

What is new in *Juvenile Delinquency, Second Edition*?

- **Selected references.** We have added selected references to each piece. This will allow students to seek out important criminological publications cited by the authors and permit instructors to direct students in their search for additional literature to be used in class papers and assignments.
- **New articles.** We have added new articles for two reasons. First, we made changes where our colleagues, our students, or our own experience with the first edition suggested that a new piece might work better. Second, we took advantage of research and writing that has taken place since the first edition was put together. We have especially focused on trying to keep our contemporary selections contemporary.
- **Exercises and a CD-ROM.** The present edition has an optional CD-ROM that includes exercises and other opportunities for teachers to have their students work with ideas, manipulate data, and experience the discovery that makes scholarship exciting.
- **Expanded juvenile justice section.** In this edition we have added pieces to this section to provide more depth to the coverage of contemporary programs and issues in juvenile justice.

We have retained the Introduction to the first edition of *Juvenile Delinquency* prepared by Travis Hirschi. This essay sets the stage for the very best ideas from theory and research on juvenile delinquency and its control produced by criminologists over the past century. The readings represent different academic disciplines, with different theoretical and ideological orientations, and diverse ideas on the best ways to prevent and control juvenile delinquency in our society.

ACKNOWLEDGMENTS

Many persons have contributed to this volume, beyond those whose work is included in the volume itself. We are indebted to those individuals. Without their dedicated work and assistance, this edition of the book would not have been completed. We appreciate the commitment of Steve

Rutter, President of Pine Forge Press, and his editorial staff to our project and their uncompromising pursuit of excellence.

We are extremely grateful to Jon'a Meyer for her excellent contributions to this second edition, the data analysis exercises and the questions at the end of each reading. These have improved the book immeasurably.

We are also indebted to colleagues (some of whom are former students) who contributed to this volume primarily through their contributions to the first edition. Kristin Bates, Rod Engen, Randy Gainey, Eddie Pate, and Sara Steen all helped with the development of the book.

We are also deeply appreciative of the helpful comments supplied by reviewers of earlier drafts of the manuscripts, including

Q. Akin Adeseun, *Pennsylvania State University*
Mark Beaulieu, *State University of New York, Albany*
James W. Burfeind, *University of Montana*
Amy V. D'Unger, *Emory University*
Helen Taylor Greene, *Old Dominion University*
James W. Kanan, *Western Kentucky University*
Celia Lo, *University of Akron*
Daniel Preston Mears, *University of Texas, Austin*
Amie L. Nielsen, *Bowling Green State University*
Mark Stafford, *University of Texas, Austin*
Tracey Steele, *Wright State University*
Gene T. Straughan, *Lewis-Clark State College*

Despite the important comments these reviewers provided, we alone are responsible for the editing of the manuscripts and for any errors or omissions in the editing process.

Finally, we want to acknowledge the contributions our undergraduate students at the University of Washington have made to this effort. They have toiled through many earlier versions of this book, commenting on the books and our teaching over the years. We have benefited immensely from their reactions, both positive and negative. Without their insightful comments and suggestions, we would be much less effective as teachers and learners.

—THE EDITORS

Introduction

CRIME rates were down last year, continuing a trend of several years' duration. This is good news, right? Well, yes and no. It depends on your interests and purposes. Citizens presumably like to hear that the crime rate is down because they have less to fear and more to spend on things they value. But other groups may find such news unsettling and counterproductive. Politicians, the media, and even criminologists are likely to see declining crime rates as mixed blessing. A few weeks ago, I told a meeting of the League of Women Voters that I thought predictions of sharp increases in violent crime over the next 15 years were overblown, that there is good chance the violent crime rate will remain stable over the period in question. A leader of the group could not have been more candid in her response. "As a professor, you can afford to play down the crime problem. Our mission is to propose action to the legislature. How can we recommend significant legislation at the same time we argue that crime is under control?"

The point is not that some of us are interested in truth while others are interested in practice. The point is that the stand we take toward the seriousness of crime determines how we explain it, what we propose to do about it, and how we assess the adequacy of what is now being done. At the same time, it is hard to decide once and for all how serious the crime problem really is. Nowhere are these points clearer than in the area of juvenile delinquency.

This area was set aside and called juvenile delinquency to stress the youthfulness of the parties and the nonseriousness of their acts, to remind us that young people are not beyond redemption and that what they have done can be in most cases forgiven and forgotten. At the same time, a case could be made that the crime problem is largely a problem of youth crime, that youthfulness does not reduce the seriousness of an offense, and that young people are not more treatable than adults. And sure enough we tend to move back and forth between these contradictory images. Ten years ago, public and scholarly attention was focused on the hardened adult career criminal. Youth crime was pretty much ignored. Today the career criminal has been replaced by the scary teenager said willing to "pull the trigger over a leather jacket, a pair of sneakers, or a joke."

The selections in this volume return again and again to this theme, showing us the close connection between how we conceive, measure, and explain delinquency on the one hand and what we propose to do about it on the other. This close interplay between theory and practice gives the field of juvenile delinquency a dynamic tension, a level of excitement and interest rare in social science. If theory lags, if no one is saying why delinquents do it, practical programs are unguided and, in the eyes of many, dangerous. If no one is proposing and trying fresh treatment and prevention programs, the purpose of theory and research is called into question.

The selections in this volume also emphasize another source of healthy tension in the field. Theories of delinquency identify causes and thus breed optimism about solutions. Research does the same thing by isolating factors in delinquency that may be manipulated to reduce its frequency. And of course treatment and prevention programs often fairly bubble with optimism and hope about their potential accomplishments. To balance such enthusiasm, it is necessary to call on evaluators and critics, persons trained to cast a skeptical eye on the claims of theory, research, and treatment. Nowadays, both the optimist and the skeptic are well represented in the field of juvenile delinquency. It is fitting that they are also well represented in the articles in this volume.

Many topics in the field are interesting in their own right, irrespective of their ties to larger issues. These topics too are well represented. Included are articles on drugs, violence, gangs, families, boot camps, and electronic monitoring, to name only a few. Some are of traditional interest. Some are practically brand new. All illustrate the health and vigor of the field and its willingness to grapple with a social problem of abiding interest.

The number of teenagers in the population is beginning to rise and will continue to rise into the foreseeable future. Those who emphasize the contribution of youth to the crime problem and the dangers inherent in greater numbers of them advise us to "Get ready!" It is good advice. The advice from this fine collection is perhaps more balanced. I recommend it to you. Get reading.

—TRAVIS HIRSCHI

I

WHAT IS DELINQUENCY?

The History and Definitions of Delinquency

CONTRARY to what most people believe, "juvenile delinquency" as we know it today has not always existed. In fact, many criminologists agree with Platt's assertion in "The Rise of the Child-Saving Movement" that the concept of juvenile delinquency is a relatively modern legal "invention," tied to the passage of the first juvenile court law in 1899 in Illinois. That is not to say that children and young people throughout history have not committed crimes or engaged in other illegal acts. Rather, it is likely that in the past, as today, the highest rates of law violation were among the young. Nor does it mean that there were not prior laws that focused on the misbehavior of children.

As Sutton points out in "Inventing the Stubborn Child," as early as 1646 in colonial Massachusetts the "stubborn or rebellious" child law was drafted. It represents the first statute of its kind to define legal child regulation and the obligation of parents to bring their disobedient child to the attention of the court. The penalty for the young Puritan's wayward behavior was death. Capital punishment for not obeying one's parents seems harsh and barbaric by contemporary standards of child care, even though it was never actually imposed. The law was meant to send a message to parents and their children that immoral conduct, perceived as a threat to social order, would not be tolerated by anyone, even children.

It was not until the end of the nineteenth century, however, that the state of Illinois legislated the first separate juvenile court, defined the jurisdiction of the court over a variety of offenses and personal conditions, and laid the foundation for a distinct juvenile justice system, including juvenile probation and corrections. The concept and term *juvenile delinquent* had been used, often interchangeably with juvenile mendicant, vagabond, or rogue, at least as far back as the early 1800s in the United States, to describe children who broke the law and also those who resembled the homeless children, the street kids, the victims of child abuse, and the unwanted children of today. The latter, without proper parental care and supervision, were considered the juvenile delinquents of tomorrow—what we now call predelinquents or at-risk youths. Therefore, what had been an informal social category for many years was turned into a distinctly "official" legal category, with its own agencies of justice administration.

The first juvenile court law is described in the words of one of its first judges in Cook County (Chicago), Illinois, the Honorable R. S. Tuthill. The original law defined three categories of children, over whom the juvenile court could claim legal jurisdiction: the "delinquent child," who violates the law, and the "dependent child" and "neglected child," who have not committed a crime but are without proper parental care or supervision. The juvenile court is supposed to act *in loco parentis*—as a substitute guardian—and control the criminal behavior of the juvenile delinquent and prevent the conditions of dependency or neglect from causing future criminality. From the beginning, there was excitement and optimism that the new juvenile court would "save" the lives of young people in whatever kind of trouble by acting in the best interests of the child and providing personalized rehabilitation. The "traditional" juvenile court was considered as much a social welfare agency as a legal institution with the responsibility of administering justice. The original Illinois law was the blueprint for the juvenile codes that were legislated in other states. This traditional family court model remained essentially intact for about 75 years.

Most states are still committed to some version of the traditional model of juvenile justice, but a small number of states have "criminalized" the juvenile court by redefining its jurisdiction to focus primarily on juvenile criminals, changing its major purpose from the rehabilitation of the child to criminal accountability for the offense, and replacing the discretion of juvenile court judges acting in the best interest of the child with a set of rigidly structured sentencing guidelines. Rather than basing a judicial decision on the total circumstances surrounding the offense, including the characteristics of the juvenile and family, the criminalized juvenile court in Washington, as stipulated by "The Juvenile Justice Act," can only consider the current offense, the prior record, and the juvenile's age in sentencing, and the sanctions are defined by law, not by the juvenile court judge. The focus is on the offense, the appropriate punishment, and the limitation of judicial discretion, with the hope that decisions will be more "just" and juvenile delinquency controlled more effectively.

Inventing the Stubborn Child

JOHN SUTTON

IN November of 1646, the governing General Court of Massachusetts Bay passed a barrage of legislation designed to codify a unique legal structure for the colony. These laws formalized the rights and responsibilities of colony members, proscribed a variety of criminal acts, and clarified the legitimate domain of official authority. Among the laws passed at this time was a statute that made it a capital offense for a child to disobey his parents:

If a man have a stubborn or rebellious son, of sufficient years and understanding (viz.) sixteen years of age, which will not obey the voice of his Father, or the voice of his Mother, and that when they have chastened him will not harken unto them: then shall his Father and Mother being his natural parents, lay hold on him, and bring him to the Magistrates assembled in Court and testify unto them, that their son is stubborn and rebellious and will not obey their voice and chastisement, but lives in sundry notorious crimes, such a son shall be put to death.

The Puritans took the text of this statute almost verbatim from Deuteronomy 21:20-21. Taking it at face value, the "stubborn child" law was legally distinctive in three ways. It defined a special legal obligation that pertained to children, but not to adults; it defined the child's parents as the focus of that obligation; and it established rules to govern when public officials could intervene in the family and what actions they could take. It was the first statute of its kind in North America, and probably in the modern world.

Two interpretations of the meaning of this statute have been presented. One suggests that the stubborn child law is the progenitor of modern child regulation laws—"not only the root but also the trunk of many current laws governing parent-child relations." It was copied into the colonial codes of Connecticut, Rhode Island, and New Hampshire, and it remained in force in Massachusetts in substantially amended form until 1973. It served as a direct or indirect model for legislation enacted by every American state making children's misbehavior a punishable offense. It appears to foreshadow the 1838 case of *ex parte Crouse*, which legitimized state suspension of troublesome children on the basis of the medieval doctrine of *parens patriae*, and which has never been entirely repudiated.

But the bare words of this statute belie any sense of legal continuity between colonial and modern means of child control; indeed, they suggest an enormous gulf between the Puritans and ourselves in attitudes toward children's misconduct. Modern policies are framed in the language of secular experts, not Old Testament prophets; they emphasize discretion rather than dogmatic judgment and ameliorative treatment rather than punishment. The statute contains no hint of mercy, let alone of the modern notions of prevention and rehabilitation, and the fact that the penalty was never actually imposed—indeed, it was reduced by subsequent amendment—further obscures the meaning of the statute.

Thus, a second interpretation suggests conversely that there is no continuity between colo-

From *Stubborn Children: Controlling Delinquency in the United States, 1640-1981* (pp. 10-42) by J. Sutton, 1988, Berkeley: University of California Press. Copyright 1988 by the Regents of the University of California. Reprinted by permission.

nial and modern means of child regulation. According to this view, the stubborn child law was a product of an economically tenuous authoritarian society, a futile and atavistic attempt to enforce traditional authority relationships on the doorstep of the New World. The statute is seen as being primarily of instrumental significance in supporting parental control over children's labor, and more generally in assuring rigid conformity, of thought and action in future generations. Such a law, it is suggested, has no such instrumental role in a modern, pluralistic society.

In both of these interpretations, the stubborn child law is conceived narrowly, either as legal precedent or economic instrumentality; from either perspective it appears to be a slightly absurd historical curiosity. I argue that beneath the archaic language of the law lies a distinctively, precociously modern approach to social control. Seen in the wider context of colonial society, the statute exemplifies two tendencies in colonial Puritan law that presaged the emergence of a rational therapeutic model of control in the nineteenth- and early twentieth-century United States. The first of these tendencies is toward the socialization of law and the family. By this I mean that formal law chartered the family as an agent to further the values of the common-wealth. Law in Massachusetts Bay developed as a response to perceived disorder and as an affirmative statement of public policy. Its substantive goal was to sustain a community of saints through the rational allocation of responsibilities among appropriate spheres in the social order, of which the family was the most fundamental.

A second tendency of Puritan law was toward the normalization and universalization of deviance. In Puritan thought no individual, not even those of the saved elect, was immune from sin; its seeds were perceived to lie in everyone, especially untutored children. Thus, the survival of the commonwealth as a moral enterprise demanded the development of formal means of surveillance and self-regulation. In short, the argument here is that the stubborn child law can best be explained not as a means to control children's misbehavior, but as part of a larger strategy for limiting conflict and maintaining established authority.

The Puritans' dream of commonwealth was never realized, and their technology of surveillance was largely dismantled by subsequent events in colonial history. But the stubborn child law itself stayed in force in amended form until 1973, and the Puritan notion of legal child regulation was never entirely extinguished.

QUESTIONS FOR DISCUSSION AND WRITING

1. What was the stubborn child law and how was it distinctive?
2. The stubborn child law exemplifies "two tendencies in colonial Puritan law that presaged the emergence of a rational therapeutic model of control in the nineteenth- and early twentieth-century United States." What was the "substantive goal" of the first tendency?
3. In short, what is the argument against the second tendency?

The Rise of the Child-Saving Movement

ANTHONY PLATT

STUDIES of crime and delinquency have, for the most part, focused on their psychological and environmental origins. Correctional research has traditionally encompassed the relationship between prisoners and prison management, the operation of penal programs, the implementation of the "rehabilitative ideal," and, in recent years, the effectiveness of community-based corrections. On the other hand, we know very little about the social processes by which certain types of behavior come to be defined as "criminal" or about the origins of penal reforms. If we intend rationally to assess the nature and purposes of correctional policies, it is of considerable importance to understand how laws and legislation are passed, how changes in penal practices are implemented, and what interests are served by such reforms.

This chapter analyzes the nature and origins of the reform movement in juvenile justice and juvenile corrections at the end of the nineteenth century. Delinquency raises fundamental questions about the objects of social control, and it was through the child-saving movement that the modern system of delinquency control emerged in the United States. The child-savers were responsible for creating a new legal institution for penalizing children (juvenile court) and a new correctional institution to accommodate the needs of youth (reformatory). The origins of "delinquency" are to be found in the programs and ideas of these reformers, who recognized the existence and carriers of delinquent norms.

IMAGES OF DELINQUENCY

The child-saving movement, like most moral crusades, was characterized by a "rhetoric of legitimization" built on traditional values and imagery. From the medical profession, the child-savers borrowed the imagery of pathology, infection, and treatment; from the tenets of social Darwinism, they derived their pessimistic views about the intractability of human nature and the innate moral defects of the working class; finally, their ideas about the biological and environmental origins of crime may be attributed to the positivist tradition in European criminology and to antiurban sentiments associated with the rural, Protestant ethic.

MATERNAL JUSTICE

The 1880s and 1890s represented for many middle-class intellectuals and professionals a period of discovery of the "dim attics and damp cellars in poverty-stricken sections of populous towns" and of "innumerable haunts of misery throughout the land." The city was suddenly discovered to be a place of scarcity, disease, neglect, ignorance, and "dangerous influences." Its slums were the "last resorts of the penniless and the criminal"; here humanity reached its lowest level of degradation and despair.

The discovery of problems posed by "delinquent" youth was greatly influenced by the role of feminist reformers in the child-saving movement. It was widely agreed that it was a woman's business to be involved in regulating the welfare of children, for women were considered the "natural caretakers" of wayward children. Women's claim to the public care of children had some historical justification during the nineteenth century, and their role in child rearing was considered paramount. Women were regarded as better teachers than men and were also more influential in child training at home. The fact that public education also came more under the direction of women teachers in the schools increased the predominance of women in the raising of children.

Child-saving was a predominantly feminist movement, and it was regarded even by antifeminists as female domain. The social circumstances behind this appreciation of maternalism were women's emancipation and the accompanying changes in the character of traditional family life. Educated middle-class women now had more leisure time but a limited choice of careers. Child-saving was a reputable task for women who were allowed to extend their housekeeping functions into the community without denying antifeminist stereotypes of woman's nature and place.

Child-saving may be understood as a crusade which served symbolic and status functions for native, middle-class Americans, particularly feminist groups. Middle-class women at the turn of the century experienced a complex and far-reaching status revolution. Their traditional functions were dramatically threatened by the weakening of domestic roles and the specialized rearrangement of family life. One of the main forces behind the child-saving movement was a concern for the structure of family life and the proper socialization of young persons since it was these concerns that had traditionally given purpose to a woman's life. Professional organizations—such as settlement houses, women's clubs, bar associations, and penal organizations—regarded child-saving as a problem of women's rights, whereas their opponents seized upon it as an opportunity to keep women in their proper place. Child-saving organizations had little or nothing to do with militant supporters of the suffragette movement. In fact, the new role of social worker was created by deference to antifeminist stereotypes of a "woman's place."

A Woman's Place

Feminist involvement in child-saving was endorsed by a variety of penal and professional organizations. Their participation was usually justified as an extension of their housekeeping functions so that they did not view themselves, nor were they regarded by others, as competitors for jobs usually performed by men. Proponents of the "new penology" insisted that reformatories should resemble home life, for institutions without women were likely to do more harm than good to inmates. According to G. E. Howe, the reformatory system provided "the most ample opportunities for woman's transcendent influence."

Female delegates to philanthropic and correctional conferences also realized that correctional work suggested the possibility of useful careers. Mrs. W. P. Lynde told the National Conference of Charities and Correction in 1879 that children's institutions offered the "truest and noblest scope for the public activities of women in the time which they can spare from their primary domestic duties." Women were exhorted by other delegates to make their lives meaningful by participating in welfare programs, volunteering their time and services, and getting acquainted with less privileged groups. They were told to seek jobs in institutions where "the 'woman-element' shall pervade . . . and soften its social atmosphere with motherly tenderness."

Although the child-savers were responsible for some minor reforms in jails and reformatories, they were more particularly concerned with extending governmental control over a whole range of youthful activities that had previously been handled on an informal basis. The main aim of the child-savers was to impose sanctions on conduct unbecoming youth and to disqualify youth from enjoying adult privileges. As Bennett Berger has commented, "Adolescents are not made by nature but by being excluded from responsible participation in adult affairs, by being rewarded for dependency, and penalized for precocity."

The child-saving movement was not so much a break with the past as an affirmation of faith in traditional institutions. Parental authority, education at home, and the virtues of rural life were emphasized because they were in decline at this time. The child-saving movement was, in part, a crusade which, through emphasizing the dependence of the social order on the proper socialization of children, implicitly elevated the nuclear family and, more especially, the role of women as stalwarts of the family. The child-savers were prohibitionists, in a general sense, who believed that social progress depended on efficient law enforcement, strict supervision of children's leisure and recreation, and the regulation of illicit pleasures. What seemingly began as a movement to humanize the lives of adolescents soon developed into a program of moral absolutism through which youth was to be saved from movies, pornography, cigarettes, alcohol, and anything else which might possibly rob them of their innocence.

Although child-saving had important symbolic functions for preserving the social prestige of a declining elite, it also had considerable practical significance for legitimizing new career openings for women. The new role of social worker combined elements of an old and partly fictitious role—defenders of family life—and elements of a new role—social servant. Social work was thus both an affirmation of cherished American values and an instrumentality for women's emancipation.

JUVENILE COURT

The essential preoccupation of the child-saving movement was the recognition and control of youthful deviance. It brought attention to, and thus "invented," new categories of youthful misbehavior which had been hitherto unappreciated. The efforts of the child-savers were institutionally expressed in the juvenile court, which, despite recent legislative and constitutional reforms, is generally acknowledged as their most significant contribution to progressive penology.

The juvenile court system was part of a general movement directed toward removing adolescents from the criminal law process and creating special programs for delinquent, dependent, and neglected children. Regarded widely as "one of the greatest advances in child welfare that has ever occurred," the juvenile court was considered "an integral part of total welfare planning."

The juvenile court was a special tribunal created by statute to determine the legal status of children and adolescents. Underlying the juvenile court movement was the concept of *parens patriae* by which the courts were authorized to handle with wide discretion the problems of "its least fortunate junior citizens." The administration of juvenile justice differed in many important respects from the criminal court processes. A child was not accused of a crime but offered assistance and guidance; intervention in his life was not supposed to carry the stigma of criminal guilt. Judicial records were not generally available to the press or public, and juvenile court hearings were conducted in relative privacy. Juvenile court procedures were typically informal and inquisitorial. Specific criminal safeguards of due process were not applicable because juvenile proceedings were defined by statute as civil in character.

The original statutes enabled the courts to investigate a wide variety of youthful needs and misbehavior. As Joel Handler has observed, "The critical philosophical position of the reform movement was that no formal, legal distinctions should be made between the delinquent and the dependent or neglected." Statutory definitions of delinquency encompassed (a) acts that would be criminal if committed by adults; (b) acts that violated county, town, or municipal ordinances; and (c) violations of vaguely defined catch-alls—such as "vicious or immoral behavior," "incorrigibility," and "truancy" which "seem to express the notion that the adolescent, if allowed to continue, will engage in more serious conduct."

The juvenile court movement went far beyond a concern for special treatment of adolescent offenders. It brought within the ambit of governmental control a set of youthful activities that had been previously ignored or dealt with on an informal basis. It was not by accident that the behavior selected for penalizing by the child-savers—sexual license, drinking, roaming the streets, begging, frequenting dance halls and movies, fighting, and being seen in public late at night—was most directly relevant to the children of lower-class migrant and immigrant families.

The juvenile court was not perceived by its supporters as a revolutionary experiment, but rather as a culmination of traditionally valued practices. The child-saving movement was "antilegal" in the sense that it derogated civil rights and procedural formalities while relying heavily on extralegal techniques. The judges of the new court were empowered to investigate the character and social life of predelinquent as well as delinquent children; they examined motivation rather than intent, seeking to identify the moral reputation of problematic children. The requirements of preventive penology and child-saving further justified the court's intervention in cases where no offense had actually been committed, but where, for example, a child was posing problems for some person in authority such as a parent or teacher or social worker.

The Personal Touch

Judges were expected to show the same professional competence as doctors and therapists. Juvenile court judges had to be carefully selected for their skills as expert diagnosticians and for their appreciation of the "helping" professions. Miriam Van Waters, for example, regarded the juvenile court as a "laboratory of human behavior" and its judges as "experts with scientific training and specialists in the art of human relations." It was the judge's task to "get the whole truth about a child" in the same way that a "physician searches for every detail that bears on the condition of a patient."

The child-savers' interest in preventive strategies and treatment programs was based on the premise that delinquents possess innate or acquired characteristics which predispose them to crime and distinguish them from law-abiding youths. Delinquents were regarded as constrained by a variety of biological and environmental forces so that their proper treatment involved discovery of the "cause of the aberration" and application of "the appropriate corrective or antidote." "What the trouble is with the offender," noted William Healy, "making him what he is, socially undesirable, can only be known by getting at his mental life, as it is an affair of reactive mechanisms."

The use of terms like "unsocialized," "maladjusted," and "pathological" to describe the behavior of delinquents implied that "socialized" and "adjusted" children conform to middle-class morality and participate in respectable institutions. The failure empirically to demonstrate psychological differences between delinquents and nondelinquents did not discourage the child-savers from believing that rural and middle-class values constitute "normality." The unique character of the child-saving movement was its concern for predelinquent offenders—"children who occupy the debatable ground between criminality and innocence"—and its claim that it could transform potential criminals into respectable citizens by training them in "habits of industry, self-control, and obedience to law." This policy justified the diminishing of traditional procedures in juvenile court. If children were to be rescued, it was important that the rescuers be free to provide their services without legal hindrance. Delinquents had to be saved, transformed, and reconstituted. "There is no essential difference," said Frederick Wines, "between a criminal and any other sinner. The means and methods of restoration are the same for both."

THE REFORMATORY SYSTEM

It was through the reformatory system that the child-savers hoped to demonstrate that delinquents were capable of being converted into law-abiding citizens. The reformatory was initially developed in the United States during the middle of the nineteenth century as a special form of prison discipline for adolescents and young adults. Its underlying principles were formulated in Britain by Matthew Davenport Hill, Alexander Maconochie, Walter Crofton, and Mary Carpenter. If the United States did not have any great penal theorists, it at least had energetic penal administrators who were prepared to experiment with new programs. The most notable advocates of the reformatory plan in the United States were Enoch Wines, Secretary of the New York Prison Association; Theodore Dwight, the first dean of Columbia Law School; Zebulon Brockway, Superintendent of Elmira Reformatory in New York; and Frank Sanborn, Secretary of the Massachusetts State Board of Charities.

The reformatory was distinguished from the traditional penitentiary by its policy of indeterminate sentencing, the "mark" system, and "organized persuasion" rather than "coercive restraint." Its administrators assumed that abnormal and troublesome individuals could become useful and productive citizens. Reformatories, unlike penitentiaries and jails, theoretically repudiated punishments based on intimidation and repression. They took into account the fact that delinquents were "either physically or mentally below the average." The reformatory system was based on the assumption that proper training can counteract the impositions of poor family life, a corrupt environment, and poverty while at the same time toughening and preparing delinquents for the struggle ahead. "The principle at the root of the educational method of dealing with juvenile crime," wrote William Douglas Morrison, "is an absolutely sound one. It is a principle which recognizes the fact that the juvenile delinquent is in the main, a product of adverse individual and social conditions."

To Cottage and Country

The trend from congregate housing in the city to group living in the country represented a signif-

icant change in the organization of penal institutions for young offenders. The family or cottage plan differed in several important respects from the congregate style of traditional prisons and jails.

The new penology emphasized the corruptness and artificiality of the city; from progressive education, it inherited a concern for naturalism, purity, and innocence. It is not surprising, therefore, that the cottage plan also entailed a movement to a rural location. The aim of penal reformers was not merely to use the countryside for teaching agricultural skills. The confrontation between corrupt delinquents and unspoiled nature was intended to have a spiritual and regenerative effect. The romantic attachment to rural values was quite divorced from social and agricultural realities. It was based on a sentimental and nostalgic repudiation of city life. Advocates of the reformatory system generally ignored the economic attractiveness of city work and the redundancy of farming skills.

The "new" reformatory suffered, like all its predecessors, from overcrowding, mismanagement, "boodleism," understaffing, and inadequate facilities. Its distinctive features were the indeterminate sentence, the movement to cottage and country, and agricultural training. Although there was a decline in the use of brutal punishments, inmates were subjected to severe personal and physical controls: Military exercises, "training of the will," and long hours of tedious labor constituted the main program of reform.

SUMMARY AND CONCLUSIONS

The child-saving movement was responsible for reforms in the ideological and institutional control of "delinquent" youth. The concept of the born delinquent was modified with the rise of a professional class of penal administrators and social servants who promoted a developmental view of human behavior and regarded most delinquent youth as salvageable. The child-savers helped to create special judicial and correctional institutions for the processing and management of "troublesome" youth.

There has been a shift during the past 50 years or so in official policies concerning delinquency. The shift has been from policies emphasizing the criminal nature of delinquency to the "new humanism" which speaks of disease, illness, contagion, and the like. It is essentially a shift from a legal to a medical emphasis. The emergence of a medical emphasis is of considerable significance since it is a powerful rationale for organizing social action in the most diverse behavioral aspects of our society. For example, the child-savers were not concerned merely with "humanizing" conditions under which children were treated by the criminal law. It was, rather, their aim to extend the scope of governmental control over a wide variety of personal misdeeds and to regulate potentially disruptive persons. The child-savers' reforms were politically aimed at lower-class behavior and were instrumental in intimidating and controlling the poor.

The child-savers made a fact out of the norm of adolescent dependence. "Every child is dependent," wrote the Illinois Board of Charities in 1899, "even the children of the wealthy. To receive his support at the hands of another does not strike him as unnatural, but quite the reverse." The juvenile court reached into the private lives of youth and disguised basically punitive policies in the rhetoric of "rehabilitation." The child-savers were prohibitionists, in a general sense, who believed that adolescents needed protection from even their own inclinations.

The basic conservatism of the child-saving movement is apparent in the reformatory system which proved to be as tough-minded as traditional forms of punishment. Reformatory programs were unilateral, coercive, and an invasion of human dignity. What most appealed to correctional workers were the paternalistic assumptions of the "new penology," its belief in social progress through individual reform, and its nostalgic preoccupation with the "naturalness" and intimacy of a preindustrial way of life.

The child-saving movement was heavily influenced by middle-class women who extended their housewifely roles into public service. Their contribution may also be seen as a "symbolic crusade" in defense of the nuclear family and their positions within it. They regarded themselves as moral custodians and supported programs and institutions dedicated to eliminating youthful immorality. Social service was an instrumentality for female emancipation, and it is not too unreasonable to suggest that women advanced their own fortune at the expense of the dependency of youth.

QUESTIONS FOR DISCUSSION AND WRITING

1. How may child-saving be "understood as a crusade which served symbolic and status functions for native, middle-class Americans, particularly feminist groups"?
2. On what premise was the child-savers' interest in preventive strategies and treatment programs based?
3. Rather than merely being concerned with " 'humanizing' conditions under which children were treated by the criminal law," what was the aim of the child-savers?
4. What does the author conclude motivated the child-savers who were mostly middle-class women?

The Juvenile Court Law in Cook County, Illinois, 1899

HON. R. S. TUTHILL

ILLINOIS has claimed and in many respects has justly claimed the right to be classed with the advanced states of the Union. Yet a deplorable condition with respect to the treatment of children has existed in the state from its organization up almost to the present time. This condition in Cook County is stated in moderate language in the official reports of grand juries, month after month, in substantially these words:

There is at present in this county no proper place for the detention or final commitment of youthful offenders. We have no institution where friendless children of tender age, who have been arrested for offenses against the law, can be sent, educated, and possibly saved from a criminal career. A commitment to the Glenwood School under sentence for crimes committed is not allowed, as that institution is simply for incorrigible children. We call attention to the fact that there are at present confined in our county jail, children of eleven, twelve, thirteen, and fourteen years of age, where they are exposed to the evil association of older criminals.

Indeed, in the county jail, we found children of nine years of age, who had been bound over to the grand jury by incompetent or corrupt justices of the peace, in disregard of the fact that the laws of Illinois recognize no capacity for criminality in a child of that age.

This condition, especially in Cook County, grew worse from year to year, until at length the people of the state awakened to the fact that the state by the inadequacy of its laws and failure to care for these children who were without proper parental care was creating—breeding as it were—an army of criminals who in a short time would be its open and avowed enemies. An appeal was made to the General Assembly at its last session for relief. A law was prepared as a result of extended consideration of the subject by men and women of all creeds and political affiliations and was submitted for enactment. It was, in the form originally agreed upon, probably as well considered, as wise, and humane a measure as was ever presented to the lawmaking body of the state. The Bar Association of Chicago composed of the ablest and best members of our metropolitan bar was active in the preparation of the bill and gave its powerful influence toward its enactment. The good women of the state, always quick and earnest in everything which tends to the proper care of children, were leaders in the movement, laboring in season and out of season to induce the representatives of the people by the passage of this bill to place Illinois *primus inter pares* in respect to provisions made for the exercise of this highest duty of a state—a civilized state—to stand *in loco parentis,* to be a parent to all the neglected and delinquent children of the state. It is to be regretted that various antagonistic interests made themselves manifest and opposed the bill with such mistaken pertinacity as that some

Tuthill, R. S. 1900. "The Juvenile Court Law in Cook County, Illinois, 1899." In *Proceedings of the Illinois Conference of Charities*, November 1900, Springfield, Illinois, pp. 10, 12-14.

of the most essential features in it were per force dropped.

Yet, what is known as the Juvenile Court Law became the law of Illinois, going into effect July 1, 1899.

The law made it the duty of the judges of the circuit court in Cook County to designate one of their number to preside in this new branch, which for convenience was designated as the Juvenile Court. This designation was promptly made. The duty of inaugurating the work was placed upon me.

There are three classes of children mentioned in the law as coming within its purview. First is the "dependent child" and second, the "neglected child," which classes are defined to mean

any child who for any reason is destitute or homeless or abandoned; or dependent upon the public for support; or has not proper parental care or guardianship; or who habitually begs or receives alms; or who is found living in any house of ill-fame or with any vicious or disreputable persons; or whose home by reason of neglect or depravity on the part of its parents, guardian, or other person in whose care it may be, is an unfit place for such child; and any child under the age of eight years who is found peddling or selling any article or singing or playing any musical instrument upon the street or giving any public entertainment.

Third is the "delinquent child," which it is declared "shall include any child under the age of sixteen years who violates any law of this State, or city or village ordinance" and "who is not now or hereafter an inmate of a state institution or any training school for boys or industrial school for girls." Section 5 of the law has this provision: "Pending the final disposition of any case, a child may be retained in the possession of the person having the charge of the same or may be kept in *some suitable place* provided by the city or county authorities."

Section 11 provides: "No court or magistrate shall commit a child under the age of twelve years to a jail or police station."

Here was an immediate difficulty inasmuch as neither city nor county had a place of detention such as the law contemplated for the children brought under this operation.

The county had prior to the enactment of the law cared for the dependent and neglected children in a building at the county hospital used for the temporary detention of insane persons. A more serious difficulty was to secure a place other than the jail or police station of the city for the detention, pending the hearing of the delinquent. The generous action of the Board of Directors of the Illinois Industrial Association gave the use of their cottage for this purpose. This has since served as a detention home.

The law makes provision for the appointment by the court of probation officers. It declares that "it shall be the duty of the said probation officer to make such investigation as may be required by the Court; to be present in Court in order to represent the interest of the child when the case is heard; to furnish to the Court such information and assistance as the judge may require; and to take such charge of any child before and after trial as may be directed by the Court."

Printed instructions are given to each probation officer when appointed.

INSTRUCTION TO PROBATION OFFICERS

In appointing probation officers, the court places a special reliance upon the faithfulness and wisdom of the persons so designated. There is no more important work than that of saving children, and much will depend upon your faithfulness.

This appointment is made under the provision of the law, enacted by the Legislature of 1899. Your attention is particularly called to the last section of that act, which declares the purpose of the law as follows:

This act shall be liberally construed to the purpose that its end may be carried out to wit: That the care, custody, and discipline of a child shall approximate as nearly as may be that which should be given by its parents, and in all cases where it can be properly done, the child be placed in an approved family home and become a member of the family by legal adoption or otherwise.

It will be the endeavor of the court to carry out both the letter and the spirit of this act, and to this end the court will have in mind the following considerations in order named:

1. *The welfare and interests of the child.* It is the desire of the court to save the child from neglect and cruelty, also to save it from the danger of becoming a criminal or a dependent.
2. *The welfare of the community.* The most practical way of lessening the burdens of taxations and the loss of property through the ravages of the crime class is by the prevention of pauperism and crime. Experience proves that the easiest and most effective way of doing this is by taking hold of the children while they are young—the younger the better.
3. *The interests and feelings of parents and relatives.* It is right and necessary that parental affection should be respected, as far as this can be done without sacrificing the best interests of the child and without exposing the community to unnecessary damage.

Dependents and Delinquents

The law divides the children into two classes, dependents and delinquents. Cases of both classes will be referred to you (a) for investigation pending action of the court, (b) for temporary supervision pending action of the court, and (c) for supervision after action by the court.

INVESTIGATION
When cases are referred for investigation, you will be expected to make personal inquiry into the facts of the case, with the view to assist the court in deciding what ought to be done. To this end, it will be necessary to record the history and the circumstances of the child as fully as possible, and blanks will be provided for this purpose. The court will desire to ascertain the character, disposition, and tendencies and school record of the child; also, the character of the parents and their capability for governing and supporting the child, together with the character of the home as to comforts, surroundings, inmates, and so on.

This information will be obtained in your own way, from the child, from the parents, neighbors, teachers, clergymen, police officers, and from the records of the poor department, the police department, and the various charitable agencies.

The court will wish to determine, from these inquiries, whether the child should be separated from the parents, guardian, or custodian, and if so, whether it should be committed to the care and guardianship of some individual or to some suitable institution. The court will not ordinarily separate children from their parents unless (a) the parents are criminals, (b) the parents are vicious or grossly cruel, (c) the parents are entirely unable to support the children, or (d) the home is in such condition as to make it extremely probable that the child will grow up to be vicious or dependent.

TEMPORARY CARE
The law forbids the keeping of any child in any jail or police station. A place of detention for children under the care of the court will be provided, but it is the desire of the court to avoid congregating children even in this temporary home. Whenever practicable, therefore, the child will be left in the care of the parents or of some suitable family, under the supervision of the probation officer, pending the final action of the court. In your investigations, you will have in mind the question whether the child can be suitably cared for in his own home, and, if not, whether a suitable temporary home can be secured without expense.

SUPERVISION AFTER ACTION OF THE COURT
The law makes it the duty of the court, as far as possible, to locate its young wards, both dependents and delinquents, in family homes.

When practicable, the child will be remanded to its parents, or will be placed directly in the family of some suitable citizen. In such cases, the probation officer will be expected to maintain a special oversight of the child, either by personal visits at frequent intervals or by written report from parents or custodian. All visits to wards of the court will be reported on blanks provided for that purpose.

The probation officer feature is in my judgment the keystone which supports the arch of this law, an arch which shall be as a rainbow of hope to all who love children and who desire that all children shall be properly cared for.

QUESTIONS FOR DISCUSSION AND WRITING

1. What did Cook County finally realize?
2. What is a neglected child?
3. What three considerations will the juvenile court have in mind?

Title 13, Revised Code of Washington: The Juvenile Justice Act, 1994

13.40.010 Short Title—Intent—Purpose

(1) This chapter shall be known and cited as the Juvenile Justice Act.

(2) It is the intent of the legislature that a system capable of having primary responsibility for, being accountable for, and responding to the needs of youthful offenders, as defined by this chapter, be established. It is the further intent of the legislature that youth, in turn, be held accountable for their offenses and that both communities and the juvenile courts carry out their functions consistent with this intent. To effectuate these policies, the legislature declares the following to be equally important purposes of this chapter:

(a) Protect the citizenry from criminal behavior;
(b) Provide for determining whether accused juveniles have committed offenses as defined by this chapter;
(c) Make the juvenile offender accountable for his or her criminal behavior;
(d) Provide for punishment commensurate with the age, crime, and criminal history of the juvenile offender;
(e) Provide due process for juveniles alleged to have committed an offense;
(f) Provide necessary treatment, supervision, and custody for juvenile offenders;
(g) Provide for the handling of juvenile offenders by communities whenever consistent with public safety;

From the Revised Code of Washington: *The Juvenile Justice Act*, 1994.

(h) Provide for restitution to victims of crime;
(i) Develop effective standards and goals for the operation, funding, and evaluation of all components of the juvenile justice system and related services at the state and local levels; and
(j) Provide for a clear policy to determine what types of offenders shall receive punishment, treatment, or both, and to determine the jurisdictional limitations of the courts, institutions, and community services.

13.40.020 Definitions

For the purposes of this chapter: "Serious offender" means a person fifteen years of age or older who has committed an offense which if committed by an adult would be:

(a) A Class A felony, or an attempt to commit a Class A felony;
(b) Manslaughter in the first degree; or
(c) Assault in the second degree, extortion in the first degree, child molestation in the second degree, kidnapping in the second degree, robbery in the second degree, residential burglary, or burglary in the second degree, where such offenses include the infliction of bodily harm upon another or where during the commission of or immediate withdrawal from such an offense the perpetrator is armed with a deadly weapon or firearm.

"Criminal history" includes all criminal complaints against the respondent for which, prior to the commission of a current offense:

(a) The allegations were found correct by a court. If a respondent is convicted of two or more charges arising out of the same course of conduct, only the highest charge from among these shall count as an offense for the purposes of this chapter; or

(b) The criminal complaint was diverted by a prosecutor pursuant to the provisions of this chapter on agreement of the respondent and after an advisement to the respondent that the criminal complaint would be considered as part of the respondent's criminal history.

"Juvenile," "youth," and "child" mean any individual who is under the chronological age of eighteen years and who has not been previously transferred to adult court.

"Juvenile offender" means any juvenile who has been found by the juvenile court to have committed an offense, including a person eighteen years of age or older over whom jurisdiction has been extended.

"Middle offender" means a person who has committed an offense and who is neither a minor or first offender nor a serious offender.

"Minor or first offender" means a person sixteen years of age or younger whose current offense(s) and criminal history fall entirely within one of the following categories:

(a) Four misdemeanors;

(b) Two misdemeanors and one gross misdemeanor;

(c) One misdemeanor and two gross misdemeanors;

(d) Three gross misdemeanors;

(e) One Class C felony except manslaughter in the second degree and one misdemeanor or gross misdemeanor;

(f) One Class B felony except: Any felony which constitutes an attempt to commit a Class A felony; manslaughter in the first degree; assault in the second degree; extortion in the first degree; indecent liberties; kidnapping in the second degree; robbery in the second degree; burglary in the second degree; residential burglary; vehicular homicide; or arson in the second degree. For purposes of this definition, current violations shall be counted as misdemeanors.

"Offense" means an act designated a violation or a crime if committed by an adult under the law of this state, under any ordinance of any city or county of this state, under any federal law, or under the law of another state if the act occurred in that state.

13.40.0351 Equal Application of Guidelines and Standards

The sentencing guidelines and prosecuting standards apply equally to juvenile offenders in all parts of the state, without discrimination as to any element that does not relate to the crime or the previous record of the offender.

13.40.0354 Computation of Current Offense Points

The total current offense points for use in the standards range matrix of schedules D-1, D-2, and D-3 are computed as follows:

(1) The disposition offense category is determined by the offense of conviction. Offenses are divided into 10 levels of seriousness, ranging from low (seriousness level E) to high (seriousness level A+); see Schedule A, RCW.

(2) The prior offense increase factor is summarized in Schedule B, RCW. The increase factor is determined for each prior offense by using the time span and the offense category in the prior offense increase factor grid. Time span is computed from the date of the prior offense to the date of the current offense. The total increase factor is determined by totaling the increase factors for each prior offense and adding a constant factor of 1.0.

(3) The current offense points are summarized in Schedule C, RCW. The current offense points are determined for each current offense by locating the juvenile's age on the horizontal axis and using the offense category on the vertical axis. The juvenile's age is determined as of

the time of the current offense and is rounded down to the nearest whole number.

(4) The total current offense points are determined for each current offense by multiplying the total increase factor by the current offense points. The total current offense points are rounded down to the nearest whole number.

(5) All current offense points calculated in schedules D-1, D-2, and D-3 shall be increased by a factor of 5% if the offense is committed by a juvenile who is in a program of parole under this chapter.

13.40.070 Complaints—Screening— Filing Information—Diversion

(1) Complaints referred to the juvenile court alleging the commission of an offense shall be referred directly to the prosecutor. The prosecutor, upon receipt of a complaint, shall screen the complaint to determine whether

(a) The alleged facts bring the case within the jurisdiction of the court; and

(b) On a basis of available evidence there is probable cause to believe that the juvenile did commit the offense.

(2) If the identical alleged acts constitute an offense under both the law of this state and an ordinance of any city or county of this state, state law shall govern the prosecutor's screening and charging decision for both filed and diverted cases.

13.40.080 Diversion Agreement—Scope— Modification—Limitations—Divertee's Rights— Diversionary Unit's Powers and Duties

(1) A diversion agreement shall be a contract between a juvenile accused of an offense and a diversionary unit whereby the juvenile agrees to fulfill certain conditions in lieu of prosecution. Such agreements may be entered into only after the prosecutor, or probation counselor pursuant to this chapter, has determined that probable cause exists to believe that a crime has been committed and that the juvenile committed it. Such agreements shall be entered into as expeditiously as possible. The juvenile shall be advised that a diversion agreement shall constitute a part of the juvenile's criminal history.

13.40.110 Hearing on Question of Declining Jurisdiction

(1) The prosecutor, respondent, or the court on its own motion may, before a hearing on the information on its merits, file a motion requesting the court to transfer the respondent for adult criminal prosecution and the matter shall be set for a hearing on the question of declining jurisdiction. Unless waived by the court, the parties, and their counsel, a decline hearing shall be held where

(a) The respondent is fifteen, sixteen, or seventeen years of age and the information alleges a Class A felony or an attempt, solicitation, or conspiracy to commit a Class A felony; or

(b) The respondent is seventeen years of age and the information alleges assault in the second degree, extortion in the first degree, indecent liberties, child molestation in the second degree, kidnapping in the second degree, or robbery in the second degree.

(2) The court after a decline hearing may order the case transferred for adult criminal prosecution upon a finding that the declination would be in the best interest of the juvenile or the public. The court shall consider the relevant reports, facts, opinions, and arguments presented by the parties and their counsel.

(3) When the respondent is transferred for criminal prosecution or retained for prosecution in juvenile court, the court shall set forth in writing its finding which shall be supported by relevant facts and opinions produced at the hearing.

13.40.140 Juveniles Entitled to Usual Judicial Rights—Notice of—Open Court—Privilege Against Self-Incrimination—Waiver of Rights, When

(1) A juvenile shall be advised of his or her rights when appearing before the court.

(2) A juvenile and his or her parent, guardian, or custodian shall be advised by the court or its representative that the juvenile has a right to be represented by counsel at *all* critical stages of the proceedings. Unless waived, counsel shall be provided to a juvenile who is financially unable to obtain counsel without causing substantial hardship to himself or herself or the juvenile's family, in any proceeding where the juvenile may be subject to transfer for criminal prosecution, or in any proceeding where the juvenile may be in danger of confinement. The ability to pay part of the cost of counsel does not preclude assignment. In no case may a juvenile be deprived of counsel because of a parent, guardian, or custodian refusing to pay therefor. The juvenile shall be fully advised of his or her right to an attorney and of the relevant services an attorney can provide.

(3) The right to counsel includes the right to the appointment of experts necessary, and the experts shall be required pursuant to the procedures and requirements established by the Supreme Court.

(4) Upon application of a party, the clerk of the court shall issue, and the court on its own motion may issue, subpoenas requiring attendance and testimony of witnesses and production of records, documents, or other tangible objects at any hearing, or such subpoenas may be issued by an attorney of record.

(5) All proceedings shall be transcribed verbatim by means which will provide an accurate record.

(6) The general public and press shall be permitted to attend any hearing unless the court, for good cause, orders a particular hearing to be closed. The presumption shall be that all such hearings will be open.

(7) In all adjudicatory proceedings before the court, all parties shall have the right to adequate notice, discovery as provided in criminal cases, opportunity to be heard, confrontation of witnesses except in such cases as this chapter expressly permits the use of hearsay testimony, findings based solely upon the evidence adduced at the hearing, and an unbiased factfinder.

(8) A juvenile shall be accorded the same privilege against self-incrimination as an adult. An extrajudicial statement which would be constitutionally inadmissible in a criminal proceeding may not be received in evidence at an adjudicatory hearing over objection. Evidence illegally seized or obtained may not be received in evidence over objection at an adjudicatory hearing to prove the allegations against the juvenile if the evidence would be inadmissible in an adult criminal proceeding. An extrajudicial admission or confession made by the juvenile out of court is insufficient to support a finding that the juvenile committed the acts alleged in the information unless evidence of a corpus delicti is first independently established in the same manner as required in an adult criminal proceeding.

(9) Waiver of any right which a juvenile has under this chapter must be an express waiver intelligently made by the juvenile after the juvenile has been fully informed of the right being waived.

(10) Whenever this chapter refers to waiver or objection by a juvenile, the word juvenile shall be construed to refer to a juvenile who is at least twelve years of age. If a juvenile is under twelve years of age, the juvenile's parent, guardian, or custodian shall give any waiver or offer any objection contemplated by this chapter.

13.40.150 Disposition Hearing

In disposition hearings all relevant and material evidence, including oral and written reports, may be received by the court and may be relied upon to the extent of its probative value, even though such evidence may not be admissible in a hearing on the information. The youth or the youth's counsel and the prosecuting attorney shall be afforded an opportunity to examine and controvert written reports so received and to cross-examine individuals making reports when such individuals are reasonably available, but sources of confidential information need not be disclosed. The prosecutor and counsel for the juvenile may submit recommendations for disposition.

13.40.240 Construction of RCW References to Juvenile Delinquents or Juvenile Delinquency

All references to juvenile delinquents or juvenile delinquency in other chapters of the Revised Code of Washington shall be construed as meaning juvenile offenders or the commitment of an offense by juveniles as defined by this chapter.

QUESTIONS FOR DISCUSSION AND WRITING

1. The first section provides "equally important purposes." How do they differ from the 1899 juvenile court in Cook County that was discussed in the previous chapter by the Hon. R. S. Tuthill?
2. What is a decline hearing and when is it held?
3. When is a juvenile entitled to counsel?

II

HOW IS DELINQUENCY MEASURED?

The Observation and Measurement of Delinquency

IF you ask people whether juvenile delinquency is a growing menace to society, most will offer the opinion that it is a bigger and worse problem than it used to be. If you ask them who is responsible for the apparent increases in juvenile crime, they will most likely describe juvenile offenders who live in the city and are poor, minority-group members of gangs who deal in drugs and violence.

Those public perceptions of the magnitude and characteristics of juvenile delinquency are often wrong simply because they are usually based on unreliable and inaccurate information, collected unsystematically from a variety of unofficial sources, including personal experiences, the media, conversations with friends, the sound bites of politicians, and other sources of "impressions." Criminology cannot rely on such subjective "measures" of the volume and nature of juvenile offenses or offenders. The scientific study of juvenile delinquency requires rigorous, objective, systematic, and accurate observation or measurement. To develop more valid explanations of delinquent behavior and more effective control and prevention efforts, we need to identify and describe the "facts" about juvenile delinquency as precisely as possible.

Criminologists have used a variety of data sources and measurement techniques to study juvenile delinquency, including (a) the "official records" of the police, the juvenile court, and juvenile corrections as well as the education and mental health systems; (b) the "self-reports" of individuals in response to survey questions asking about their involvement in delinquent behaviors; (c) the survey reports of "victims" of crime about the nature of their victimizations and the characteristics of the known offenders; (d) the information provided by "informants," whether a peer, teacher, parent, or other who knows the juvenile well enough to report on his or her involvement in delinquency; and (e) "field observations," typically of delinquent groups or gangs in natural settings, meaning on the street and in the community. There are advantages and disadvantages to each of these methods of measuring delinquency, but there are two that are used most often in research by criminologists—official records and self-report surveys.

Before the emergence of the self-report technique in the late 1950s as a viable alternative to police records of "arrest" or to juvenile court records of "referral," official records were the preferred and most used source of data on juvenile delinquency. The Uniform Crime Reports of the FBI, an annual compilation of national arrests and offenses known to the police departments in most jurisdictions of the United States, has been used for years to describe the "national picture" of crime, including juvenile involvement.

There have also been innumerable "local" studies using police agency or juvenile court data. One of the very best was conducted by Wolfgang and colleagues—the Philadelphia birth cohort study of juvenile delinquency. Using official record data from this project, primarily the "offenses known" to the police, Tracy describes the "Prevalence, Incidence, Rates, and Other Descriptive Measures" that can, and should, be derived and calculated from official record data as well as from other quantitative data sources. To many criminologists, the distinction between "prevalence" measures (e.g., the percentage of a group that has at least one police contact) and "incidence" measures (e.g., the average frequency of police contacts in the group, among only those who have contacts, or for each individual) is critical to an accurate description of juvenile delinquency because depending on how one "counts it," the description of delinquent acts, of delinquents, and of their correlates may vary.

Ideally, different measures will produce the same picture of juvenile delinquency, particularly of the personal and sociodemographic characteristics (e.g., sex, age, race, and social class) of those juveniles involved in delinquency and of other factors (e.g., family relationships, school experiences, peer influence, and gang membership) that may be associated with and "cause" delinquent involvement. Unfortunately, studies using different measures often produce different descriptions of juvenile delinquency. This became apparent and a critical methodological issue with the advent of self-report studies, most of which have shown that (a) there is a substantial amount of "unrecorded" juvenile delinquency and (b) many of the strong correlates of "official delinquency" (e.g., social class and race) are much weaker correlates of self-reported delinquency.

Of course, the supporters of each method have claimed that their preferred data source is superior and that the other measure simply does not produce accurate information about the distribution of delinquency. Surprisingly, there have not been many attempts by criminologists to sort out and resolve the issue of the relative validity and reliability of each method or the apparent discrepancies produced by official versus self-report measures. The most comprehensive empirical assessment of the comparative accuracy of the two competing methods of measuring delinquency was conducted by Hindelang, Hirschi, and Weis. An excerpt from their book, *Measuring Delinquency,* "The Accuracy of Official and Self-Report Measures of Delinquency," compares the two techniques and concludes that self-reports are both reliable and valid measures of juvenile involvement in the types of crime that typically lead to juvenile arrests. They also conclude, therefore, that data produced by self-report studies can be used with at least as much confidence as, and probably more than, official records in research on the correlates of juvenile delinquency.

There may be convincing evidence that self-report measures are trustworthy, but there is still another threat to their utility. Cernkovich, Giordano, and Pugh note that an important group of respondents is usually absent from self-report surveys—chronic offenders, particularly those frequent and serious offenders who have had many contacts with the juvenile justice system, including institutionalization. By including this type of juvenile delinquent in their study, along with a general youth population sample as is done in most self-report surveys, and by comparing their respective self-reported delinquency, they showed that the chronic offender far outstrips all others in overall frequency and seriousness of involvement. In addition, they have characteristics that are sufficiently different from those of other self-reported delinquents that the authors conclude that there needs to be "a return to the study of official delinquents, research subjects virtually abandoned with the advent of the self-report methodology some 30 years ago."

Prevalence, Incidence, Rates, and Other Descriptive Measures

PAUL E. TRACY, Jr.

ONE of the most fundamental tasks that must be accomplished in the very beginning of any statistical analysis of research data is to specify and investigate the distribution of the particular phenomenon of interest in the study population or sample. In the most simple, general terms, a researcher needs to know (a) how many persons in the study possess the trait being investigated? and (b) how much of the trait do these people have?, or stated another way, how often do these persons exhibit the trait? The former measure, which is qualitative and which concerns the classification of the population usually into two groups—those subjects that have the trait versus those persons that do not—is known as *prevalence*. The latter measurement, which is quantitative and which is concerned with counting the number of times that the trait is observed, is known as *incidence*. These two measures, prevalence and incidence, are the fundamental raw material of any social science research involving human subjects, regardless of whether the research is testing a social science theory, evaluating a particular treatment program, or merely exploring and describing a set of data.

Although these concepts are very basic and must be examined before any sophisticated multivariate statistical procedures are applied to the data, it is surprising to see how often these concepts are confused or even neglected alto-gether. The problem surrounding prevalence and incidence is especially acute in criminal justice research, where the focus of the research concerns the criminal element in the population and the number of offenses committed by these persons or the number of arrests or convictions that they have. Because of the distributional nature of crime and criminals, we know that the prevalence of crime in a study population is often rare and will usually characterize only a small number of the subjects—most people have never been arrested or convicted of a crime. Likewise, the incidence of crime is usually skewed and unevenly distributed, thus indicating varying criminal involvement levels among the subset of the population that is criminal—some offenders commit only one offense, others accumulate a few offenses, while still others commit many crimes.

This situation is further complicated by the fact that both prevalence and incidence measures in criminal justice are very often related to many sociodemographic characteristics of the subjects, such as sex, race, age, and social class. Thus, the extent to which there is variation in a study population in terms of sociodemographic factors (i.e., more males than females or more whites than nonwhites), there will be natural variation in the prevalence and incidence of crime that is directly related or attributable to these factors.

The goal of this chapter, then, is to elucidate the concepts of prevalence and incidence and to show why various types of descriptive statistical measures must be calculated in order to understand properly the group differences that are

From *Measurement Issues in Criminology* (pp. 51-77) K. Kempf, editor, 1990, New York: Springer-Verlag. Copyright 1990 by Springer-Verlag New York, Inc. Reprinted by permission.

exhibited in the number of persons that can be classified as offenders and the frequency of criminal offenses committed by these offenders. In order to place the presentation in a real-life research context, all of the analyses will be based upon data that were collected from an actual research project that the author has been involved in for over 10 years. Thus, none of the results that are reported in tables or presented in figures have been orchestrated or constructed in order to support the issue being presented. The data being analyzed are real.

A particular style of analytical method will be employed throughout the presentation. This method, often referred to as *elaboration*, starts with a basic bivariate relationship of one independent variable and one dependent, or criterion, variable and then introduces other independent variables in a process designed to detect spurious relationships and interactive or contingent associations. At each step of the presentation, we will be concerned with the nature of the research issue before us, the reason for the particular analysis being conducted, and the effect of analyzing the data in a particular way.

THE DATA

The 1958 Philadelphia Birth Cohort is a longitudinal research project that has been investigating the delinquency and adult criminal careers of a large group of subjects since 1977. Through the use of Philadelphia, Pennsylvania, public and parochial/private school records, a cohort of persons, born in 1958, who had continuous residence in Philadelphia at least from the ages of 10 through 17, was identified. The 1958 birth cohort is composed of 27,160 subjects. The birth cohort contains 13,160 males and 14,000 females. The distributions by sex and race shows that 6,216 males and 6,637 females are white, while 6,944 males and 7,363 females are nonwhite. The measure of socioeconomic status (SES) that was used consisted of a factor analysis of Philadelphia census tract variables. For present purposes, we have dichotomized SES into low versus high, which produces the fol-

lowing breakdowns: for males—6,414 low SES and 6,746 high SES; for females—6,948 low SES and 7,052 high SES.

The delinquency data were collected from the Juvenile Aid Division of the Philadelphia Police Department and from the Juvenile Court Division of the Court of Common Pleas for Philadelphia. The juvenile offense data represent all police contacts experienced by a cohort member, whether or not the offense resulted in official arrest processing or whether the case was referred to the juvenile court. Thus, we have available for our analyses a sense of delinquency measures: (a) offender status (delinquent vs. nondelinquent); (b) offender status by arrest category (e.g., one time vs. recidivist); (c) number of offenses committed; (d) type of offenses committed; (e) age at onset of delinquency; and (f) age at offense for each delinquent act.

PREVALENCE

Our first task in the analysis of the delinquency data of the 1958 birth cohort is to investigate the prevalence of juvenile delinquency. Table 1 displays simple counts of the number of subjects that were not recorded as delinquent, the number that were classified as delinquent in the police files, and the total number of subjects. These data are given for females and males in the top portion of the table and for males by race and SES in the bottom portion.

When we examine just the frequency counts in Table 1, we note first that a total of 1,967 females in the cohort were delinquent compared to 4,315 males.

The essential problem with comparing the absolute frequencies of an observed trait or status is that such counts ignore the total number of cases in each group (e.g., males vs. females, whites vs. nonwhites) eligible to occupy the status or exhibit the particular trait. When the total number of cases in the comparison groups are equal, then the frequencies can be compared directly. When the comparison groups differ in size, however, we need to take explicitly into

TABLE 1

Breakdown of nondelinquents, delinquents, and subjects by sex, and breakdown by race and socioeconomic status for males.

Category		Nondelinquents	Delinquents	Subjects
Females	No.	12,033	1,967	14,000
	%	86.9	14.1	100.0
Males	No.	8,845	4,315	13,160
	%	67.2	32.8	100.0
White males	No.	4,804	1,412	6,216
	%	77.3	22.7	100.0
Nonwhite males	No.	4,041	2,903	6,944
	%	58.2	41.8	100.0
Low-SES males	No.	3,711	2,703	6,414
	%	57.9	42.1	100.0
High-SES males	No.	5,134	1,612	6,746
	%	76.1	23.9	100.0

Note: Percentages are row percents.

account the size difference. Thus, in our example concerning delinquency prevalence, we need a general measure that takes into account the number of persons classified as delinquent and the number of persons at risk for delinquency. What we need simply is the *proportion* or *percentage* of delinquents in the two groups.

The proportion and the percentage are methods of standardizing a frequency distribution for the size of the groups being studied. The proportion is computed by dividing the frequency of delinquency by the number of persons at risk (proportion = frequency of delinquents ÷ number of subjects). The percentage is perhaps a more familiar measure and is just another way of expressing the frequency occurrence of a status or trait per 100 cases of subjects. The percentage is computed by dividing the frequency of delinquency by the number of subjects and then multiplying by 100 (percentage = frequency of delinquents ÷ number of subjects × 100). Table 1

gives the appropriate percentages for the frequency counts of delinquency.

Table 1 indicates that about 14% of the females in the cohort compared to about 33% of the males were processed or recorded as delinquent by the Philadelphia police. These are the appropriate prevalence measures for our purposes. They indicate, regardless of the size of the male and female groups, the relative prevalence of delinquency. Further, these measures are directly comparable and allow us to compute a male to female ratio, which indicates that males were 2.3 times more likely to be delinquent than their female counterparts.

Now that we have established the need to examine percentages, or proportions, rather than just frequency counts, we can begin our discussion of two of the major correlates of delinquency prevalence—race and SES. These data are given in the bottom portion of Table 1 for the males in the 1958 cohort. The results shown pertain to two separate bivariate associations—

TABLE 2

Number and percentage of delinquents and nondelinquents by socioeconomic status controlling for race for males.

Category		Nondelinquents	Delinquents	Subjects
Males	No.	8,845	4,315	13,160
	%	67.2	32.8	100.0
White males				
Low SES	No.	881	437	1,318
	%	66.8	33.2	100.0
High SES	No.	3,923	975	4,898
	%	80.1	19.9	100.0
Nonwhite males				
Low SES	No.	2,830	2,226	5,096
	%	55.5	44.5	100.0
High SES	No.	1,211	637	1,848
	%	65.5	34.4	100.0

Note: Percentages are row percents.

race and delinquency status (i.e., nondelinquent vs. delinquent) and SES and delinquency status. When we first look at the data by race, we note that 1,412 cases or about 23% of the 6,216 white males were delinquent compared to 2,903 cases or about 42% of the 6,944 nonwhite males. Similarly, we note that 42% of the low-SES males were delinquent compared to about 24% of the high-SES males.

The results displayed in Table 1 would seem to indicate that delinquency status is strongly related to both the race and the SES of the cohort member. That is, nonwhites and low-SES cohort subjects have a higher prevalence of delinquency. Before we accept the validity of these observations, however, we need to establish that the relationships are genuine and not spurious. That is, we need to know (a) whether nonwhites are more delinquent than whites not just because they also happen to be disproportionately of lower SES and (b) whether low-SES persons in the cohort are more delinquent than their high-SES counterparts not just because

low-status persons are more likely to be nonwhite. In effect, we need to know whether the race effect holds regardless of SES and whether the SES effect holds regardless of race.

In order to determine the proper inferences from the data, we need to consider all three variables at once—the two independent variables (race and SES) and the dependent variable (delinquency status)—in what is known as a multiway cross-tabulation, or contingency table. In such a table, we examine one of the independent variables while *holding constant or controlling for* the other. In order to do this, we examine the two levels of SES for each race category separately, and we examine the two race categories for each SES level separately. A basic layout of this approach is given in Table 2.

These data indicate that among white males there is a moderate but definite SES effect—low-SES subjects show a higher prevalence of delinquency than do high-SES subjects (33.2% vs. 19.9%). Similarly, among nonwhite males, there is a weaker but definite SES effect, with low

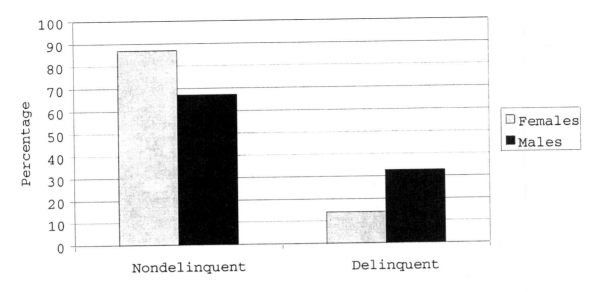

FIGURE 1 *Delinquency status percentages by sex.*

status (44.5%) showing a higher prevalence of delinquency than high status (34.4%).

If we were to focus instead on the race/delinquency relationship while controlling for SES, we would compare whites versus non-whites at each SES level. These comparisons are as follows. Among low-SES subjects, there is a moderate race effect—33% of whites were delinquent versus 45% of nonwhites. At the level of high SES, there is a stronger race effect—20% of whites were delinquent versus 34% of nonwhites.

These particular results of our real-life analyses have indicated neither (a) a spurious relationship (between race and delinquency status, or between SES and delinquency status) nor (b) a conditional, or contingent, association.

Since we are primarily interested in the prevalence of delinquency, we should consider an alternative method of displaying our results. It is sometimes more effective to use figures rather than tables because figures can immediately present and emphasize the results one is primarily interested in showing the reader.

Thus, for example, we might present our original male versus female prevalence data as

shown in Figure 1. Figure 1 is known as a histogram or vertical bar chart. The vertical, or *y*, axis reports the percentage of cases that fall into the particular groups that are shown on the horizontal, or *x*, axis. With the histogram, we can see quite immediately that the prevalence of delinquency varies considerably by sex. Males are much more likely to be delinquent, and females are much more likely to be non-delinquent.

INCIDENCE

We previously defined incidence as a quantitative measure that counts the number of times that offenders exhibit the trait of delinquency. In other words, regardless of the number of persons that occupy the status of delinquent, we need to investigate how many times offenders exhibit delinquent behaviors. This simple definition needs to be expanded now to reflect the two basic components of incidence—extent and the *character* of delinquency. The extent of delinquency pertains to the number, or frequency, of the sum total of delinquent acts committed by the offenders in the birth cohort. On the other hand, the character of delinquency incorporates a counting process, but it also includes first classifying or grouping offenses into meaningful categories and then counting them.

There were a total of 15,248 delinquent acts charged to the 4,315 male delinquents in the cohort. These delinquency data are displayed by specific offense type and by race in Table 3. Our interest in analyzing these data is to compare the relative incidence of delinquency between nonwhites and whites. First, concerning the extent of delinquency, let us look at the two N columns, which show the number, or frequency, of offenses committed by each race group. We see, for example, that overall nonwhites committed 11,340 offenses compared to 3,908 for whites, and we also see that the former committed 1,210 robberies compared to 80 for the latter.

As we learned in our discussion above concerning prevalence, we cannot just compare frequency distributions directly, when the underlying sizes of the populations are different. Thus, nonwhites could have a greater extent of delinquency, not because the offenders were more delinquent, but rather, because (a) there were more subjects to become delinquent in the first place and (b) more delinquents did emerge among the nonwhite group.

In the case of prevalence, we used percentages as the means of standardizing our frequency distributions. Can we do the same thing to compare the relative extent of delinquency for nonwhites versus whites? Table 3 gives the percentage of each offense type out of the total offenses for each race. We see that robbery accounts for 10.7% of nonwhite delinquencies (1,210 ÷ 11,340) and 2.1% of white delinquencies (80 ÷ 3,908). Here, the frequencies are very different with a ratio of about 15 to 1, and the percentages are very different but with a smaller ratio of about 5 to 1.

The problem with comparing the nonwhite and white percentages to reveal differences in the extent of delinquency is that the percentages do not remedy or remove differences in the size of the two subject groups, the number of offenders in each group, and the vastly different total

number of offenses committed by the offenders in the two groups. These percentages do not allow us to compare whites versus nonwhites in terms of the extent of delinquency; they only permit us to compare the role that various offense types play for each group. Thus, using percentages we can suggest that robbery, with 10.7% for nonwhites versus 2.1% for whites, is more characteristic of nonwhite delinquency than white delinquency. This, however, pertains to the character component of incidence and still does not address our need to investigate the relative extent of delinquency.

The answer to our problem is to compute delinquency rate statistics. Rates are widely used measures in social science research. A rate is based on the number of actual cases of a phenomenon compared to the number of possible cases. A rate is also expressed in terms of some unit of population, like per capita (one person), per 1,000, per 10,000, or per 100,000. For our purposes, we will use 1,000 as the relevant unit of population because we have a cohort population that is in this unit rather than tens of thousands of subjects; we have 13,160 males divided into 6,944 nonwhite males and 6,216 white males. Then,

$$\text{delinquency rate} = \frac{\text{number of delinquent acts}}{\text{number of subjects in group}} \times (1{,}000)$$

Table 3 gives the various delinquency rates for nonwhites and whites in the cohort. With these rates, we can compare the two groups regarding the extent of delinquency for total offenses, specific offense types, and various offense classifications. We see that, overall, nonwhites have a delinquency rate of 1,633.1 offenses per 1,000 subjects, which is about 2.6 times higher than the white offense rate of 628.7 delinquencies per 1,000 subjects. We note also that for all of the 30 specific offenses listed, the nonwhite delinquency rate is higher than the white rate except for three offenses—drunk driving, liquor laws, and hospital cases. Some of the nonwhite rates are very much higher than those for their white counterparts, while

TABLE 3

Number, percentage, and rate of delinquent offenses by race for males.

Offense	Nonwhite			White		
	N	%	Rate	N	%	Rate
Homicide	51	0.5	7.3	4	0.1	0.6
Rape	92	0.8	13.2	9	0.2	1.4
Robbery	1,210	10.7	174.3	80	2.1	12.9
Aggravated assault	458	4.0	66.0	103	2.6	16.6
Burglary	1,261	11.1	181.6	412	10.5	66.3
Larceny	1,304	11.5	187.8	367	9.4	59.0
Auto theft	458	4.0	66.0	182	4.7	29.3
Simple assault	504	4.4	72.6	194	4.9	31.2
Arson	27	0.2	3.9	15	0.4	2.4
Forgery	3	0.0	0.4	—	—	—
Fraud	4	0.0	0.6	2	0.1	0.3
Stolen property	41	0.4	5.9	28	0.7	4.5
Vandalism	528	4.7	76.0	285	7.3	45.8
Weapons	95	3.5	56.9	62	1.6	10.0
Prostitution	8	0.1	1.2	3	0.1	0.5
Sex offense	37	0.3	5.3	29	0.7	4.7
Drug offense	467	4.1	67.3	247	6.3	39.7
Gambling	7	0.1	1.0	1	0.0	0.2
Drunk driving	5	0.0	0.7	35	0.9	5.6
Liquor laws	77	0.7	11.1	134	3.4	21.6
Drunkenness	94	0.8	13.5	72	1.8	11.6
Disorderly	1,089	9.6	156.8	748	19.1	120.3
Vagrancy	27	0.2	3.9	8	0.2	1.3
Suspicious person	73	0.6	10.5	24	0.6	3.9
Traffic	39	0.3	5.6	30	0.8	4.8
Hospital cases	—	—	—	1	0.0	0.2
Investigations	33	0.3	4.8	9	0.2	1.4
Disturbance	3	0.0	0.4	1	0.0	0.2
Missing person	134	1.2	19.3	70	1.8	11.3
All others	2,911	25.7	419.2	753	19.3	121.1
Total offenses	11,340	100.0	1,633.1	3,908	100.0	628.7
UCR index	4,834	42.6	696.2	1,157	29.6	186.1
UCR nonindex	6,506	57.4	936.9	2,751	70.4	442.6
UCR violent	1,811	37.5	260.8	196	16.9	31.5
UCR property	3,023	62.5	435.3	961	83.1	154.6

Note: Percentages are column percents. UCR = Uniform Crime Reports.

others are similar; the point remains that the extent of delinquency is much greater for nonwhites than whites.

Another way to examine the extent component of incidence is to focus explicitly on the delinquent individuals in the nonwhite and white subgroups and the offenses they have committed. Although we cannot examine absolute frequencies or percentages, we can try to find a single measure that is typical of the nonwhite and white delinquency data. For this measure, we need a statistic that incorporates the number of delinquents and the number of delinquencies into a measure that is comparable across groups. What we need is a measure of *central tendency,* and for quantitative data like offenses, what we need is the arithmetic mean. For us, the mean is simply the sum of the offenses committed by a particular group divided by the number of individuals responsible for these offenses, namely, the number of delinquents.

The 11,340 nonwhite delinquencies were committed by 2,903 nonwhite delinquents, while the 3,908 white offenses were committed by 1,412 white offenders. These numbers produce a mean for nonwhites (3.91) that is greater than the mean for whites (2.77). We could also examine the mean number of offenses for specific groups of offenses, like violent crimes, robbery, burglary, or larceny/vehicle theft. Because the nonwhite means for these offense groups or types are higher than those for whites, we could conclude that, on average, nonwhite delinquents commit more offenses than their white counterparts, or we could say that nonwhite delinquency is more extensive than white delinquency.

COMBINING PREVALENCE AND INCIDENCE

Although essential in most respects, the data pertaining to the prevalence and incidence of delinquency in the birth cohort do not permit as precise a comparison as we might desire of the delinquent behavior across the two subgroups of whites and nonwhites. That is, comparing just the proportions of subjects who fall into the nondelinquent versus delinquent category ignores the fact that some delinquents commit one offense, while others commit two or three or more offenses. Thus, we need to focus on a more precise measure of delinquency status, which we shall call *delinquent subgroups.* Moreover, relying solely on the incidence of the delinquencies ignores the question of just what percentage of the delinquents are responsible for the various offenses. Thus, here, we need to focus on the incidence of delinquency across the various delinquent subgroups or categories.

In other words, what we will examine next are results that will take into account or combine both the various levels of delinquency prevalence and the frequency, or incidence, of the delinquencies committed. First, we will examine the classification of delinquents into three basic categories—one-time offenders, two-to-four-time recidivists (called nonchronic delinquents), and five-or-more-time recidivists (called chronic delinquents). Second, we will look at the number of offenses that can be attributable to these three levels, or categories, of delinquency status. With these two analyses, we will be better able to see any differences between whites and nonwhites in both the level of delinquency status and the degree of delinquency represented by these delinquent subgroups.

Table 4 reports the delinquency status categories in two ways for nonwhites and whites. In the top portion of the table, with respect to total delinquents, we see that nonwhites are less likely than whites to be one-time offenders (37% vs. 52%), and they are more likely to be recidivists either with two to four offenses (37% vs. 33%) or with five or more offenses (27% vs. 15%). When we ignore the one-time offenders and use just the recidivists as the percentage base in the bottom of Table 4, we again see a distinct race effect. Among nonwhite recidivists, about 58% are classified as nonchronic, while about 42% are chronic. On the other hand, for whites, the percentage for nonchronic recidivists (69%) is higher, and the percentage for

TABLE 4

Number and percentage of delinquents by frequency category and race for males.

Delinquency Category		Nonwhite	White	Both
Delinquents	No.	2,903	1,412	4,315
One-time offender	No.	1,071	733	1,804
	%	36.9	51.9	41.8
Two- to four-time recidivist	No.	1,059	470	1,529
	%	36.5	33.3	35.4
Five- or more-time recidivist	No.	773	209	982
	%	26.6	14.8	22.7
Recidivists	No.	1,832	579	2,511
Two- to four-time recidivist	No.	1,059	470	1,529
	%	57.8	69.2	60.9
Five- or more-time recidivist	No.	773	209	982
	%	42.2	30.8	39.1

Note: Percentages are column percents of the total number of delinquents and then the total number of recidivists.

chronic recidivists (31%) is lower than the nonwhite data.

Therefore, we find that over one-quarter of nonwhite delinquents and about 4 out of 10 nonwhite recidivists may be classified as chronic delinquents by virtue of having committed five or more offenses.

Figure 2 is a horizontal bar chart that displays the delinquent subgroup and offense data by race. The chart shows quite effectively the tabular results discussed above. In the top segment of the chart, we note that the nonwhite chronic delinquents represent 26.6% of the delinquents, but this chronic subgroup committed 64.6% of all the nonwhite delinquency. The white chronic subgroup represents a smaller percentage (14.8%), and consequently, the share of white delinquency committed by the chronic subgroup (49%) is less than for nonwhites.

In this section we have seen, therefore, that using either prevalence or incidence separately to describe and compare the relative delinquency committed by whites and nonwhites

does not portray the complete picture. Instead, we classified prevalence into three basic levels—one-time delinquents, nonchronic recidivists, and chronic recidivists—and examined the overall incidence data belonging to these delinquent subgroups. As before, we used simple percentages to reveal whether whites and nonwhites differ (a) in the distribution of delinquent subgroups and (b) in the share of overall delinquency committed by these subgroups. A chronic delinquent effect was evident in the data, and this effect was more pronounced for nonwhites than whites.

SUMMARY

We have examined two of the most basic descriptive concepts in criminal justice research—prevalence and incidence. We may summarize our efforts as follows.

First, we have seen that prevalence is a measure that pertains to the subgroup in a popula-

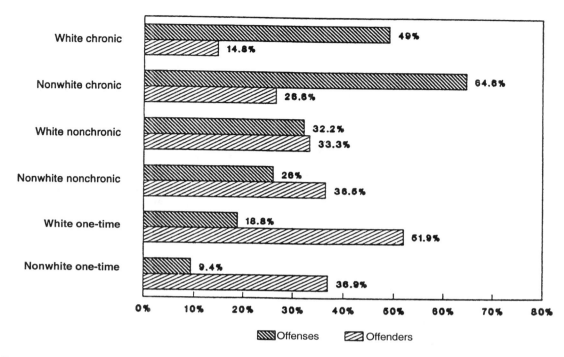

FIGURE 2 *Percentages of offenders and offenses by race for males.*
Source: Tracy et al. (1985).

tion or study sample that must be classified as delinquent or criminal by virtue of an arrest or conviction record or some other measurement of criminality. Thus, initially, prevalence is a qualitative variable that classifies subjects into the status of offender versus nonoffender.

Second, we have also learned that incidence pertains to a measurement of the offenses committed or the arrests or convictions recorded for the delinquent or criminal subgroup. Further, it was pointed out that the incidence concept subsumes two components—the extent of offenses and the character or seriousness of the offenses. Incidence, therefore, unlike prevalence, is primarily a quantitative concept that pertains to the frequency of offenses committed by offenders. In other words, incidence is the number of times that each subject may be classified as delinquent or criminal.

Third, we have further seen that, because the prevalence concept does not necessarily refer to

only a dichotomous attribute of offender versus nonoffender, we must incorporate the concepts of prevalence and incidence into a more definitive measure that we called delinquent subgroups. The delinquent subgroup measure is a classification of offenders into frequency levels such as one-time offender, nonchronic recidivist, and chronic recidivist. By using a measure such as the delinquent subgroups, we are able to differentiate the presence of the high-rate offender across various subgroups of our study sample.

Throughout our discussions of statistical measures, we have emphasized the fact that it is not appropriate to just compare raw numbers or frequencies. Because the size of subgroups can be expected to differ in a study sample, the frequency distributions must be standardized so that the statistics will be comparable. We thus showed that the percentage, the rate, and the mean are simple descriptive measures that are easily computed and that allow the researcher to compare prevalence or incidence across subgroups such as males versus females or whites versus nonwhites.

Finally, we have demonstrated that both tables and figures have a place in the presentation of results. Tables are effective when more than one statistical measure is being reported or when sets of exact scores should be given. On the other hand, figures, such as histograms and bar charts, are very effective for displaying descriptive measures when the interest is in highlighting particular relationships, especially comparative differences across groups. Line charts are essential in depicting data trends over time.

In conclusion, one final cautionary note is necessary. There is a tendency in social science research today, especially with the availability of microcomputers and statistical software packages, to apply very sophisticated statistical models and multivariate analytical procedures to research data. In many instances, these highly advanced procedures are desirable, if not absolutely necessary. Despite this tendency, there is no substitute for a thorough descriptive analysis of one's data accompanied by a well-conceived presentation of tables and figures. The most simple analyses, effectively displayed, are often the most convincing and communicative to the reader.

QUESTIONS FOR DISCUSSION AND WRITING

1. What are the differences between prevalence and incidence?
2. What is the "essential problem with comparing the absolute frequencies of an observed trait or status," and what measures take "into account the number of persons classified as delinquent and the number of persons at risk for delinquency"?
3. What do we need to know before we "accept the validity of these observations"? What does a multiway cross-tabulation, or contingency table, do?
4. What is the formula for incidence and how does it differ from the previously mentioned formula?
5. In the summary, the author discusses a "delinquent subgroup measure." What is it, and what does it allow us to do?

The Accuracy of Official and Self-Report Measures of Delinquency

MICHAEL J. HINDELANG
TRAVIS HIRSCHI
JOSEPH G. WEIS

WE examine evidence on the reliability and validity of self-report measures of delinquency. The absence of measures of reliability and validity of self-report instruments in many studies has promoted the view that such instruments are unreliable and invalid. Clearly, the reliability and validity of self-report instruments deserve careful consideration.

The literature and our extensive analyses of both official and self-report data collected on 1,600 youths in Seattle show clearly that self-reports of delinquent involvement are reliable. In short, although many self-report researchers may not have assessed the reliability of their instruments, there appears to be some empirical justification for this stance in light of the fact that no study examining the reliability of self-report instruments reports coefficients inadequate by prevailing standards. To the contrary (with the exception of test-retest results over a number of years), self-report items appear to behave with notable consistency. If self-report measurement is flawed, it is not here, but in the area of validity.

Many pitfalls await the student of delinquency who would attempt to establish the validity of the self-report method of measuring

From *Measuring Delinquency* (pp. 75-84, 88-114) by M. Hindelang, T. Hirschi, and J. Weis, 1981, Newbury Park, CA: Sage Publications. Copyright 1981 by Sage Publications, Inc. Reprinted by permission.

crime. It is true that, as we have seen, most students of delinquency purport to be measuring the same thing with self-reports that valid official statistics would also measure—that is, the commission of criminal acts. Official statistics, of course, do not claim to measure all criminal acts. Thus, the stage is set for confusion: The two techniques are said to measure the same thing, but there is really only a meager attempt in most self-report studies to bring the two definitions strictly into line with each other.

Let us see if we can set up some rational strategies that self-report researchers might follow and the validation problems these strategies would entail.

1. *The goal of self-report research is to construct a measure of delinquency identical to the measure of delinquency explicit in official definitions and implicit in official procedures, but without the omissions, mistakes, and biases of official measurement (Identical concept).*

Attainment of this goal would allow the researcher to treat discrepancy between self-report and official measures as evidence of the magnitude of "error" in official measures; it would allow confident assertions about bias, discrimination, and prejudice in official procedures; it would allow statements about change in the volume of crime independent of and superior to estimates of such change provided by official statistics.

2. *The goal of self-report research is to test theories of delinquency (Theoretical).* In this strategy, self-report measures of delinquency must reflect the definition of delinquency implicit in the theory at issue. It is unlikely that a single self-report measure will be sufficient since each theorist must be free to define delinquency in the process of explaining it. Restricting research to a single measuring device would inhibit the growth of new theories and would lock the field into a rigid pattern of social reporting or accounting.

This approach would not necessarily allow the researcher to treat discrepancy between self-report and official measures as evidence of "error" on either side. Discrepancy could (and indeed often would) simply reflect differences in definitions of the phenomenon.

A practical analog to the theoretical strategy might be stated as follows:

3. *The goal of self-report research is to construct a measure of delinquency that reflects the incidence and prevalence of socially harmful acts in the population (Social Indicator).*

CORRELATIONAL VALIDITY

For those researchers adopting a definition of delinquency identical to that explicit in legal codes and implicit in juvenile justice procedures, a variety of official measures are available for validation purposes. These measures include self-reports of police contacts, offenses known to the police, police and court contacts, court appearances, and court convictions. Several critics have asserted that using such official criteria is at least paradoxical and at most an admission of the superiority of official records.

Actually, such procedures are standard in all validation efforts in the social sciences where an instrument that is hoped to be an improvement over existing instruments is being devised. Given the history of criticism of official data and the range and volume of defects allegedly present in them, one would expect a good self-report instrument to fall closer to the discriminant end of the continuum—that is, to show weak to moderate associations with the official criterion. Although a weak association is perhaps expected from self-report criticisms of official data, it is also the case that a good self-report instrument should be able to identify as delinquent virtually all of those with official records since the validity of such "records" is questioned only from a radical self-report perspective. In other words, the lower limit of the association between self-report and official measures is fixed by virtual agreement on the basic accuracy of positive identification of delinquents through official procedures. Disagreement thus revolves around the extent to which those *without* official records also have engaged in delinquent activities sufficiently serious to warrant official action.

The validity of self-reports among those lacking official records can be investigated in a variety of ways. In fact, before proceeding further, it may be useful to diagram and list the various pieces of information and potential validity coefficients available to the researcher interested in the measurement of delinquent behavior (Figure 1). The numbers in Figure 1 identify sets of relations among measures of delinquency distinguished by the source of the information and the method of measurement producing it. As is apparent from the figure, a large variety of information is potentially available on the delinquent behavior of individuals.

Ideally, all of it would be used in constructing an index of delinquent behavior. Unfortunately, however, much of this information is too expensive and time-consuming for ordinary research purposes. Therefore, it is necessary to select some limited set of information and base decisions about its validity as an index of delinquency on previously established relations. In this context, our discussion will focus on the links among the various indicators. In the course of this discussion, it is essential to remember that delinquent behavior, an unobserved variable, is the object of ultimate interest.

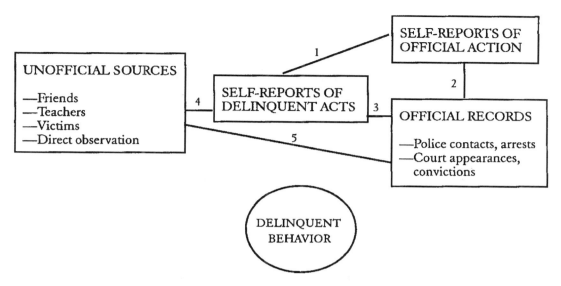

FIGURE 1 *Validation strategies in self-report research.*

All of the other variables shown in Figure 1 are imperfect or incomplete *indicators* whose interrelations shed light on each indicator and its validity as a measure of delinquent behavior.

Coefficients in Group 1 refer to the links between self-reports of delinquent acts and self-reported contacts with the juvenile justice system. Although a relatively weak form of validation, since both measures employ the same (self-report) method, these relations are potentially valuable in that they identify respondents who may have had contact with the system but who, for a variety of reasons (e.g., poor record keeping, informal disposition, and geographic mobility) do not appear (or are not located) in official records. Link 1 coefficients are especially interesting when considered in combination with Link 2 coefficients.

Insofar as official records are an incomplete accounting of the activities of officials, self-reports of official contact can help fill the gaps in such records. The adolescent reporting having been picked up by the police may or may not have a police record. The magnitude of Link 2 coefficients helps establish the validity of the

basic (official) criterion. To the extent that these coefficients vary depending on the characteristics of the child—for example, the police may be much more likely to accord informal dispositions to younger adolescents—we may be able to account for *apparent* differential validity in the basic self-report instrument.

Coefficients in Group 3 are of course usually taken as the primary source of information on the validity of self-report scales. Link 3 associations in theory summarize two unobserved associations, one between delinquent behavior and self-reported delinquency and another between delinquent behavior and official records. In practice, Link 3 correlations may be inflated by contamination of self-reports by experiences in the juvenile justice system that heighten recall of the associated offense.

Coefficients in Group 4 link self-reports to a variety of measures of delinquency constructed independent of official records. Although some of these unofficial measures (e.g., teachers' ratings) may be contaminated by the actions of juvenile justice officials, their variety attests to the fact that the self-report researcher seeking answers to the validity question is by no means restricted to speculation about tendencies of children to exaggerate or conceal their offenses.

Although the coefficients in Group 5 bear only indirectly on the validity of self-reports, they bear directly on the validity of two major sets of criterion variables. Thus, were self-report and official measures uncorrelated (3), a positive correlation between unofficial and official sources of information (5) would confirm that the self-report measure was partially invalid (depending on the magnitude of 4).

As is obvious from Figure 1, one should not expect all validation efforts to produce identical results, nor should one expect unequivocal answers to the "validity" question. Validity coefficients can be expected to vary by the method of measurement employed, by sample composition (e.g., age, sex, and race), and among various method-sample combinations. For example:

1. The younger the sample, the rarer the official record and the more ambiguous the behavior (self-) reported; therefore, the lower the correlation anticipated.
2. The more mobile the sample and the larger the number of jurisdictions covered, the weaker the official criterion and the lower the anticipated correlation.
3. The less literate the sample, the more questionable the use of questionnaires as opposed to interviews; therefore, the lower the anticipated correlation between self-report questionnaires and official measures.

Strangely enough, few of these considerations have been addressed either conceptually or empirically in the self-report literature. Validity is assumed to be undifferentiated with respect to such dimensions.

Parenthetically, Figure 1 reminds us that although self-report researchers may implicitly adopt a strategy I approach, according to which their conceptual definition of delinquency is identical to that embodied in official records, their validation efforts may focus on unofficial criteria. The net effect may be to pull the *operational* definition of delinquency away from the legal criterion. Insofar as this operational definition proves valid by unofficial criteria, there will be a tendency to treat weak correlations with official measures as evidence of the *invalidity of the official criterion*. In any event, there has been little effort on the part of self-report researchers to maximize the agreement between their operational definition and that employed by officials. As a result, while the association between self-reported and official delinquency is not expected to be strong, we would expect the association actually observed to be unnecessarily or spuriously low because self-report researchers rarely select items with official procedures in mind. They do, however, frequently attend to the adequacy with which officially recorded contacts are admitted in the self-report situation. Admission of known offenses, as suggested earlier, is a necessary condition for valid self-reports. Whether it is a sufficient condition, as often seems to be assumed, is another question. We now turn to the research literature and the Seattle data bearing on the correlational validity of self-report measures, organized by the links depicted in Figure 1.

LINK 1: SELF-REPORTED DELINQUENCY AND SELF-REPORTED OFFICIAL DELINQUENCY

Many studies have included self-reports of police contacts, in most cases presumably as alternative self-report indicators of official delinquency. These correlations are often among the strongest in the data sets, with Pearson's r's for the correlation between global self-report scales and the single item "have you ever been picked up by the police" often on the order of .4 (Hindelang's Somerville data set) to .5 (Richmond Youth Project, white males only).

The indicators of *self-reported official contacts* used in the Seattle study are (a) number of times the respondent had been picked up by the police, (b) number of times the respondent has been referred to court by the police, and (c) a composite index made up of five items in addition to those already mentioned.

TABLE 1

Weighted Seattle correlations (gamma) between official measures of delinquency and self-reports of official contacts.

Self-Reported Official Contacts	Official Measures					
	Delinquency Status[a]		Major Offenses on Record[b]		Referrals to Court[c]	
	Males[d]	Females[e]	Males[d]	Females[e]	Males[d]	Females[e]
Number of times picked up by police	.68	.67	.69	.51	.63	.67
Number of times referred to court by the police	.86	.82	.80	.63	.82	.85
Self-reported official contacts index	.75	.75	.73	.63	.73	.79

a. Coded (1) nondelinquent, (2) police delinquent, (3) court delinquent.
b. Number of major offenses found in police and court records coded (0) none, (1) one, (2) two or more.
c. Number of referrals to juvenile court found in search of court records coded (0) none, (1) one, (2) two or more.
d. N ranges from 1,120 to 1,194.
e. N is 395.

The indicators of *self-reported delinquent behavior* are (a) an ever variety scale based on the number of distinct acts the respondent reported ever having committed and (b) the four last year frequency subscales derived from cluster analyses of self-report responses (serious, general, drug, and family/school).

Among males, the ever variety scale is the best predictor of (self-reported) official behavior, producing gammas in the range of .62 to .70. In the two sex groups as a whole, the self-report cluster consisting of serious offenses does even better than the ever variety measure in predicting (self-reported) official action. In both sex groups, the indexes most closely related to standard self-report measures of delinquency (the general and the family/school factors) do less well in predicting the official contacts reported by the respondent.

LINK 2: SELF-REPORTED OFFICIAL DELINQUENCY AND OFFICIAL POLICE AND COURT RECORDS

Overall, the literature suggests that only a small portion of those with official records fail to disclose them and very few without official records claim to have them. All available studies show that most of those with official records can be identified through self-reports. What is the magnitude of the association between these measures? Table 1 shows the correspondence (gamma) between police records and responses to the question "Have you ever been picked up by the police?" by sex in the Seattle data (Link 2). The associations between these self-report and official indicators of official contacts are very high, with gammas ranging from .63 to .86 among males and from .51 to .85 among females.

TABLE 2

Weighted Seattle correlations (gamma) between self-report and official measures of delinquency (Link 3), by sex.

	Official Measures					
	Delinquency Status		Major Offenses on Record		Referrals to Court	
Self-Report Measures of Delinquency	Males[a]	Females[b]	Males	Females	Males	Females
Ever Variety	.55	.57	.55	.54	.54	.63
Serious Ever Variety	.55	.54	.56	.55	.56	.66
General Ever Variety	.47	.33	.48	.34	.46	.34
Drug Ever Variety	.44	.49	.42	.44	.41	.50
Family-School Ever Variety	.47	.57	.47	.53	.44	.67
RYP Standard Index	.50	.41	.50	.43	.48	.49
RYP Recency Index	.40	.39	.39	.43	.35	.25

a. *N* ranges from 1,132 to 1,214.
b. *N* is 395.

The data thus indicate that while the relations between official records and self-reports of official contact are not as strong as might be suggested by reverse record check research, they are large enough to offer validational support to both measures. Before discussing these data further, let us examine research bearing on Link 3.

LINK 3: SELF-REPORTED DELINQUENCY AND OFFICIAL POLICE AND COURT RECORDS

Table 2 summarizes the Link 3 validity coefficients in the Seattle data. As would be expected from the Link 1 coefficients, the self-report measures that best predict official measures of delinquency for both males and females are the ever variety index based on all 63 items in our delinquency scale and the serious ever variety measure.

Validity coefficients vary systematically by race. In all the comparisons, the validity coefficients for white males are markedly higher than those for black males. Among females, the race differences are, in contrast, small or nonexistent.

These data confirm earlier concerns about differential validity by ethnicity and sex, to which we will give more attention subsequently. While it may not be difficult to construct self-report instruments that are similarly valid for males and females, the same is not true across racial groups. Among males, for all of the self-report factors and for the ever variety scale, there are substantial differences in validity coefficients by race regardless of the official criterion used. In some cases, the coefficients for blacks suggest that the self-report measure is only marginally valid.

LINK 4: SELF-REPORTED DELINQUENCY AND UNOFFICIAL SOURCES

Very few studies of concurrent validity available in the literature use criteria other than official records. Erickson and Smith assessed the accuracy of self-reported admissions of deviant behavior by recording actual cheating in a hidden manner and by then administering a confessional instrument concerning this cheating; 118 college students were given a chance to change their answers on an exam by correcting their own tests, not knowing that the exams had been previously scored. After correcting for arithmetic errors in the self-scoring section, a measure of actual cheating was computed by subtracting the previous official scores from the scores computed by the students. A week and one-half later the test scores were returned along with an apparently anonymous questionnaire concerning general deviance. Along with questions about traffic violations and petty theft were questions dealing with deviance in an academic setting. One of the questions specifically asked if the individual had cheated on the last exam in the course. Cheating "included copying from another's paper, using cheat sheets, stealing exams before tests, and changing scores if allowed to grade one's own test." A hidden marking system on the self-report questionnaire allowed matching of self-reports and actual cheating scores.

Of the male sample ($N = 50$), 54% and of the female sample ($N = 68$), 35% actually cheated on the exam. Of those students who cheated, 30% of the males and 17% of the females admitted this activity on the anonymous questionnaire. Had self-reports been used exclusively as the measure of cheating on the exam, 16% of the males and 6% of the females would have been categorized as cheaters. The relationship between actual cheating and self-reported cheating was .30.

Our investigation of Link 4 validity coefficients is limited to self-reports of respondents concerning the delinquency of siblings and friends. Although ideally the measures would be produced by independent methods, the coefficients allow us to examine the relative validity of our self-report measures since all of these coefficients share a common method effect. As is by now expected, the ever variety and serious measures appear to be the most valid measures of delinquency when judged against the two criteria shown.

LINK 5: UNOFFICIAL SOURCES AND OFFICIAL RECORDS

Although Link 5 coefficients do not intersect with self-reports of delinquent behavior, they are of utility—just as are the Link 2 coefficients—in helping to establish the validity of the criterion. Those we examined contain items encountered earlier in Link 4. Measures of siblings and of friends picked up by the police are related to official delinquency status, major offenses on records, and the number of referrals to juvenile court. As with Link 4 coefficients, "best friends" is the better predictor of official status, with gammas ranging from .38 to .44 for males and from .31 to .42 for females. By comparison, Link 5 coefficients are, as expected, not as large as Link 4 coefficients.

One final test of validity involves comparison of the behavior of alternative measures of the same concept when they are correlated with outside variables. If two variables are measures of the same concept, they should be correlated with other variables to substantially the same extent. This issue is not explored here but is in detail in *Measuring Delinquency* by the authors.

CONCLUSION

The picture emerging from this discussion of reliability and validity is familiar to people knowledgeable about social science research. Assertions about "mindless *de novo* instrumentations" and "knowledge bases that do not in fact exist" are no more justified than self-report-based quantitative estimates of the extent of bias in police data.

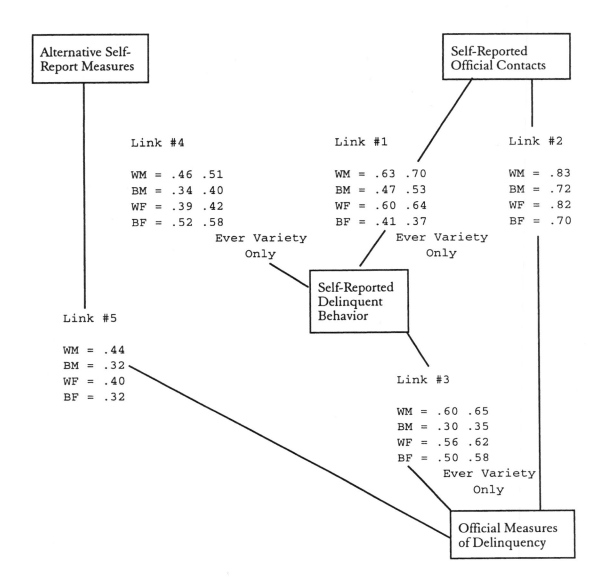

FIGURE 2 *Mean gammas for the relationship among various indicators of delinquency, by race and sex. Seattle study; weighted data.*

Figure 2 summarizes the relevant validity coefficients, many of which have been presented throughout this chapter. These average coefficients suggest, first, that self-reports of official action—such as the number of times referred to juvenile court—show quite high overall correlations with actual records of official delinquent activity (Link 2); these coefficients do not vary greatly by sex, but overall, blacks have somewhat lower coefficients than whites. Second, Links 1 and 3—two links of historical importance in establishing the validity of self-report instruments—produce coefficients that are smaller on average than Link 2 coefficients.

Again, there is a small mean gamma difference across sex and a somewhat larger difference across race. The Link 3 coefficient for black males is considerably lower than that for all other groups. Third, Links 4 and 5 are clearly of much less importance than Links 1, 2, and 3. Nonetheless, these mean gamma values indicate that there is some correspondence between our unofficial sources and self-reports of delinquency and between the former and official records.

If the various indicators of the variables in Figure 2 are accepted, and if the mean gammas are acceptably high, the self-report method appears to behave reasonably well when judged by standard criteria available to social scientists. By these criteria, the difficulties in self-report instruments currently in use would appear to be surmountable; the method of self-reports does not appear from these studies to be fundamentally flawed. Reliability measures are impressive and the majority of studies produce validity coefficients in the moderate to strong range.

Such a conclusion about reliability and validity may justify analysis of the substantive correlates of the variable in question, but it does not justify failure to pursue efforts to improve the quality of its measurement.

QUESTIONS FOR DISCUSSION AND WRITING

1. What are three possible goals of self-report research? How would attaining each goal allow the researcher to treat discrepancy in the first two measures?

2. The authors state that "it is essential to remember that delinquent behavior, an unobserved variable, is the object of ultimate interest." What are the other variables shown in Figure 1? What do you think they mean? What are some examples demonstrating why the indicators are imperfect?

3. How strong are the associations between self-report and official indicators of official contacts for "Link 2"?

4. What percentage of males and females cheated on the exam discussed for Link 4? What percentage of each gender admitted cheating? What was the relationship between "actual cheating and self-reported cheating"?

Chronic Offenders:
The Missing Cases in Self-Report Delinquency Research

STEPHEN A. CERNKOVICH
PEGGY C. GIORDANO
MEREDITH D. PUGH

IN the late 1950s and early 1960s, the number of studies of delinquency relying on official statistics or incarcerated samples declined while the number of self-report surveys using community or school samples rose. The major reason for this transformation was the recognition that samples of official delinquents are inherently biased, while self-report surveys of the general youth population are more representative and therefore more appropriate for the study of delinquent behavior. This development has been useful, but the research still is flawed. Although criminologists have developed increasingly superior self-report scales and have implemented rather sophisticated sampling designs, the reliance on general youth samples has resulted in a serious underrepresentation in these studies of what we term serious chronic offenders. Serious chronic offenders are those youth involved in serious and repeated violations of the law who are most visible to the police and courts and who are feared most by the community itself.

In order to gauge the upper limits of delinquent behavior found in our general youth sample, we used an institutional sample as a comparison group. Our data challenge the underlying assumption of much self-report research that there is no behavioral difference between institutionalized offenders and those delinquents who manage to avoid contact with the official system. The data lead us to conclude that institutionalized youth are not only more delinquent than the "average kid" in the general youth population but also considerably more delinquent than the *most delinquent* youth identified in the typical self-report survey. We contend that incarcerated youth are institutionalized not merely because they are victims of system bias and differential processing (although these factors certainly are involved to some unknown extent), but primarily because they persist in committing serious offenses.

Arguably, any comparisons between institutionalized and noninstitutionalized offenders are inappropriate because they involve comparing "apples and oranges." Yet previous self-report research based upon samples of apples (the general youth population) has been used to generalize to the population of oranges (chronic offenders). We assert that the validity of such generalizations is questionable because of the omission or underrepresentation of chronic offenders in general youth samples. The result is a serious gap between delinquency as it is defined for research purposes and delinquency as it is officially encountered.

BACKGROUND

Assume there is a relatively small but identifiable group of chronic offenders who account for the vast majority of serious delinquent acts. An important question emerging out of this assumption is the kind of sample which should be drawn to study delinquency. The alternatives are (a) a sample that is representative of the general youth population, which allows an examination of the epidemiology of delinquency and of the typical delinquent, or (b) one that concentrates on, or at least includes, sufficient numbers of chronic offenders, those atypical delinquents about whom the community and justice system are most concerned. Both objectives appear worthwhile and certainly are not mutually exclusive. Nevertheless, self-report researchers generally have opted for the first kind of sample, excluding chronic offenders.

But delinquency researchers also should be interested in the extreme case—the chronic offender. Although this has become increasingly apparent among criminologists, it typically has been assumed that since general youth samples represent such a broad range of youth, chronic offenders must, as a function of good sampling, be included as well. We contend that these offenders will not be included in very large numbers, if at all, as an automatic function of sound sampling techniques. While it may appear—relative to others in such samples—that such a group has been located, we believe this is rarely the case.

In addition to sampling problems, a number of characteristics of self-report delinquency (SRD) scales mitigate against measuring adequately the behavior of those small numbers of chronic offenders who are included in general youth samples. Five problems have contributed to inaccurate measurement: lack of item representativeness, item overlap, nonactionable items, nonspecifiable items, and response format and coding conventions.

A major criticism of SRD instruments concerns the representativeness of the items that comprise the measures. Most self-report inventories overrepresent relatively nonserious and trivial offenses while underrepresenting truly serious infractions. Item representativity is only one of several important criteria for evaluating SRD measures. The items that comprise these scales also should be nonoverlapping, actionable, and specifiable. Overlapping items result in inaccurate estimates of offense frequencies because of duplicate counts of certain events. Furthermore, since overlapping items lead to inflated delinquency scores, they may also result in the false identification of some youth as chronic offenders.

Actionable items specify behaviors that ordinarily would warrant official action. Perhaps survey measures of delinquency must include a high proportion of minor offenses, but it is problematic when an overabundance of items reflect events that typically would not call for an official response from recognized authorities. This concentration on minor offenses ignores major forms of delinquency and fails to differentiate chronic offenders from more conventional delinquents.

Specifiable items indicate behaviors in sufficient detail for classification as status offenses, misdemeanors, or felonies. For example, many SRD inventories ask respondents if they have "stolen money or other things from their parents or other members of their family." Aside from overlapping with other standard items inquiring about stealing, this item fails to provide information sufficient to distinguish between petit theft and grand theft; as a result, the distinction between minor and major offenses, and between minor and major offenders, is again blurred.

A final characteristic of SRD scales which has caused measurement difficulties is the response formats typically used. Such frequently used normative formats as *often, sometimes, occasionally, never* are subject to a wide range of interpretation by subjects and are imprecise. Similarly, such formats as the popular *never, once or twice, three times or more* are inexact and fail to measure adequately variation at the high-frequency end of the delinquency continuum. By placing all high-frequency offenders in the *three times or more* category, researchers cannot make meaningful distinctions between chronic offenders and other norm-violating youth, or among chronic offenders themselves.

RESEARCH DESIGN

The two data sources for this study are (a) a sample of all youth 12 through 19 years of age living in private households in a large north-central standard metropolitan statistical area; and (b) a sample of the populations of three male juvenile institutions within the same state, and the entire population of the only female juvenile institution in the state. In order to obtain a cross section of neighborhood youth between 12 and 19 years of age geographically dispersed throughout the metropolitan area, we used a multistage modified probability sample design.

We successfully completed 942 neighborhood interviews. The institutional portion of the data was derived from 254 personal interviews. Our SRD scale was based on items selected from the Elliott and Ageton inventory and chosen so that they would be nonoverlapping, actionable, reasonably specifiable, and representative of the full range of delinquent involvements. Subjects indicated how many times during the past year they had committed each act.

ANALYSIS AND FINDINGS

Our analysis begins with the construction of an offender index based on the qualitative distinction between major and minor offenses. We consider the 81 juveniles who reported no major offenses (felonies) and no minor offenses (misdemeanors) to be *nonoffenders.* Those 333 juveniles who reported no major offenses and a low rate of minor offenses are *low-frequency minor offenders.* The next level of more serious delinquent involvement includes the 222 juveniles who reported no major offenses and a high rate

of minor offenses; these were the *high-frequency minor offenders.* Of the 306 adolescents reporting any major offense involvement, the vast majority (68%) also reported a high rate of involvement in minor offenses. Our assumption that seriousness of offense is more salient than frequency of offense permits a functional reduction of the table by collapsing the three columns (none, low-frequency minor, and high-frequency minor) for rows 2 and 3 (low-frequency major and high-frequency major) so that the 178 cases become *low-frequency major offenders,* and the 128 cases become *high-frequency major (i.e., chronic) offenders.*

The data in Table 1 lead to several important conclusions. First, there are a significant number of youth reporting virtually no delinquency involvements. This finding is consistent with other surveys and contradicts the common assumption of sociologists and criminologists that delinquency is universal. Second, there are a substantial number of youth with high rates of minor-offense involvement who refrain, however, from participation in serious delinquent activities. This suggests that there is an important empirical difference between youth who commit major offenses and those who commit only minor offenses—even if the latter are involved in many minor violations. Third, the vast majority of high-frequency major offenders also report high rates of participation in minor offenses. While there are only 128 of these youth (representing less than 14% of the neighborhood sample), they account for almost 95% of all the major offenses reported by the non-institutionalized respondents.

In the next stage of the analysis, we examine the extent to which our offender groups prompted official reactions to their misbehavior. We are especially interested in whether those youth identified as high-frequency major offenders in the neighborhood sample are the youth who come to the attention of local authorities more frequently than others. To investigate this question, we constructed three societal reaction indices, two official and one informal. The informal reaction index was created by asking the respondents whether they had been

TABLE 1

Cross-classification of neighborhood youth on major and minor offense subscales.

Major Offenses	Minor Offenses			
	None	Low Frequency[a]	High Frequency[a]	Totals
None	81	333	222	636
Low frequency[b]	0	80	98	178
High frequency[b]	0	18	110	128
Totals	81	431	430	942

a. Low frequency = 1-47 minor offenses; high frequency = 48 or more minor offenses. This is the median cutoff for those reporting any minor offense involvement in the neighborhood sample. Those reporting no minor offenses were excluded from the calculation of the median.
b. Low frequency = 1-4 major offenses; high frequency = 5 or more major offenses. This is the median cutoff for those reporting any major offense involvement in the neighborhood sample. Those reporting no major offenses were excluded from the calculation of the median.

grounded by their parents during the past year. The first official contact index probed sanctioning by school authorities and asked respondents if they had been sent to their principal's office for disciplinary action or had been suspended or expelled from school in the past year. The second official index was based on responses to questions which asked whether subjects had been apprehended by the police, appeared in juvenile court, or had been placed on probation or institutionalized in the past year.

The data presented in Table 2 indicate uniformly linear increases across the five offender groupings for each of the sanction categories. Especially interesting are the differences between the high-frequency major offenders and high-frequency minor offenders, where the ratios are at least 2:1 for most of the sanction categories. This is consistent with our assumption that seriousness of offense is more important than frequency in eliciting societal reactions to delinquent behavior.

High-frequency major offenders report the greatest contact with official control agencies; therefore, this group should contain the most

likely candidates for institutionalization. To the extent that the sanctioning process acts accordingly, we would expect the majority of institutionalized youth to be high-frequency major offenders. The data in Table 3 address this issue and are based on the theory of *known group validity:* Groups known to differ in official delinquency status should also differ in the same ways on self-report measures. A good self-report index should be able to identify as delinquent, for example, all individuals who currently are confined in state institutions.

Low-frequency minor offenders are the largest offender group in the neighborhood sample (35.4%) but comprise less than 3% of the institutional sample. Similarly, while high-frequency minor offenders constitute almost 24% of the neighborhood sample, they make up less than 7% of the institutionalized sample. Furthermore, while only 13.6% of the neighborhood youth are high-frequency major offenders, 80% of the institutionalized youth are. Finally, less than 11% of the institutional sample is composed of low-frequency major offenders. Thus, the surest route to institutionalization is to

TABLE 2

Percentage of neighborhood youth reporting parental, school, and official sanctions.

	Non-offenders (n = 81)	Low-Frequency Minor Offenders (n = 333)	High-Frequency Minor Offenders (n = 222)	Low-Frequency Major Offenders (n = 178)	High-Frequency Major Offenders (n = 128)
Parental sanctions					
Grounded by parents	43.2	45.9	50.9	56.2	56.3
School sanctions					
Sent to principal's office	28.8	40.0	45.4	64.8	70.4
Suspended from school	16.3	17.6	25.2	34.1	37.6
Expelled from school	0.0	2.1	2.8	5.7	7.2
Official sanctions					
Picked up by police	0.0	3.3	7.2	8.4	17.2
Appeared in juvenile court	1.2	4.5	8.1	9.0	18.0
Placed on probation	0.0	1.8	2.7	5.6	10.2
Institutionalized	0.0	0.6	1.4	3.4	7.0

achieve a *high frequency* of committing major offenses. Minor offenses may be troublesome and may lead to official contacts, but they apparently are not sufficient provocation for institutionalization.

The data presented in Table 3 do not imply that the high-frequency major offenders in our neighborhood survey are comparable to institutionalized youth. Indeed, the data also show that there are major differences between the youth in the neighborhood sample and those who are institutionalized.

The various comparisons of the offenders, whether on the basis of specific offense or offense type, among males or females, indicate that with virtually no exceptions the institutional offenders are significantly more delinquent than their neighborhood counterparts. For example, among males, 31% of the neighborhood high-frequency major offenders report involvement in grand theft while 91% of the institutional offenders admit such involvement.

Thus, even when we isolate a group of *apparent* chronic offenders in a general youth sample, their levels of involvement do not approach the rates of institutional offenders.

Even when we isolate a group of offenders who appear to be chronic delinquents relative to the other youth in a *general youth sample,* the level of their involvement pales in comparison to that of institutionalized chronic offenders. This is the basis for our contention that the typical self-report survey, based on either a school or neighborhood sample, is unlikely to discover more than a handful of the kind of chronic offenders generally processed by official agencies.

Only 23 of the neighborhood high-frequency major offenders (2.4% of the neighborhood sample) had appeared in juvenile court during the past year, 13 had been on probation, and 9 had been institutionalized for their delinquency. To the extent that official reactions such as these are important correlates of chronic delinquency, this hardly represents a sufficient number of

TABLE 3

Known group validity test for offender index.

	Official Status	
Offender Index	Neighborhood	Institution
Nonoffender	8.6	0.0
Low-frequency minor offender	35.4	2.4
High-frequency minor offender	23.6	6.9
Low-frequency major offender	18.9	10.6
High-frequency major offender	13.6	80.0
Totals	942	245
Gamma = .88		

youth on which to base any analysis. Yet the assumption contradicted by these data—that chronic offenders are represented in reasonable numbers in general youth samples—is commonplace in the self-report literature.

Next, we examined how this small group (neighborhood high-frequency major offenders who have appeared in court, been on probation, or institutionalized) compares with institutionalized chronic offenders. Differences in mean levels of involvement between the two groups are significant for more than 70% of the 27 delinquent acts comprising our SRD scale, with the institutionalized youth reporting the highest rates.

Clearly, even this very "select" group of neighborhood offenders is not comparable to the chronic offenders identified in our institutional sample. Even though chronic offenders can be defined apart from official reactions to their behavior, it is clear that very few of the neighborhood youth are the kinds of offenders who come to the attention of the authorities, and even those few who do are significantly less delinquent than their institutional counterparts.

CONCLUSION

While criminologists always have recognized the existence of chronic offenders, researchers rarely have taken the steps necessary to ensure the inclusion of these youth in their samples. The inclusion of official delinquents in adolescent samples has not only been defined as inappropriate, owing to various processing biases, but also as unnecessary because of the "complete" coverage of self-report surveys of the general youth population.

This focus on samples of the general youth population has resulted in many important insights about adolescents and their misbehavior. This is a reasonable and useful focus, and such research should continue. It also is important to locate the chronic delinquent offender, to compare the behavior of this youth with that of others along the behavioral continuum, and to identify those factors and processes that lead to this extreme level of delinquency involvement. We believe that such a focus will necessitate a return to the study of official delinquents, research subjects virtually abandoned with the advent of the self-report methodology some 30 years ago. While commentators repeatedly have emphasized the hazards of using institutional or other official and quasi-official samples, we believe that these kinds of samples can locate, in a practical manner, a meaningful number of chronic offenders upon which to base criminological research.

A major assumption among many SRD researchers is that official delinquents are no different from adolescents located at various other points along the delinquency continuum. We have argued, however, that the validity of this assumption is questionable. Chronic offenders are involved in significantly more serious and more frequent delinquent activity than are the adolescents typically identified in self-report surveys of the general youth population. While criminologists should be cognizant of the extralegal biases that affect the probability of arrest, referral to court, and institutionalization for various segments of the population, they also should recognize that the major reason most adolescents come to the attention of the justice system is because they are persistent and serious offenders. This does not imply that chronic offenders are somehow intrinsically different from other youth in social background or personality. Many of their behaviors and the frequency with which they are committed, however, do differ from those of the average adolescent.

QUESTIONS FOR DISCUSSION AND WRITING

1. What is a "major criticism of SRD instruments," and why is it a problem?
2. Low-frequency minor offenders were the "largest offender group in the neighborhood sample," but how common were they in the institutionalized sample? What other differences appeared? What did the authors find was "the surest route to institutionalization"?
3. What happens "even when we isolate a group of offenders who appear to be chronic delinquents relative to the other youth in a general youth sample"?

Data Analysis Exercise

████████████████

A Look at Incidence and Prevalence of Delinquency

Welcome to the world of data analysis! In the data analysis exercises, we will be exploring some of the ideas we have read about in this book. This first exercise is designed to introduce you to the student version of the Statistical Package for the Social Sciences (SPSS) and to allow you to do some data exploring. The setup of these exercises is consistent throughout the book. After completing a number of guided activities, you will be able to conduct similar analyses on your own. There are three homework assignments at the conclusion of each exercise. The first is a general assignment that asks questions about the guided activities. The second assignment (Further Exploration) is designed to facilitate further exploration of the researched relationships. The third assignment (On Your Own) allows you to expand on the material and further extend your understanding of the theories about which you have read. In short, these exercises add a "hands-on" component to the study of juvenile delinquency. Our first exercise involves using Wave I data from the National Youth Survey (Elliott, 1994) to examine the incidence and prevalence of juvenile delinquency, as discussed in Part I of the book.

DESCRIPTION OF THE DATA SET

In 1977, a team of researchers administered the first wave of the National Youth Survey (NYS) that asked youths about their activities in 1976. One major benefit of the NYS is that it involves a representative sample of youths, so we can generalize findings from the NYS to the population as a whole, at least the population in 1976 since that is the time frame for the data. *Representative* means that the sample is similar to the population from which it was drawn.

Consider a brief example: I have decided, because writing exams is so difficult, that I should instead randomly assign grades to my students through use of a lottery system. I will randomly pull from a hat 10 names and give those students A's and give B's to the next 10 students, and so on. Under this scheme, those students who receive A's will be no different from the other students in my classes, including those who receive F's. Unfortunately, when assigning grades, we do not really want representative samples; we want the students who study hard and master the material to get the A's! Therefore, maybe I will not try for a representative sample of A's.

Representativeness is a goal in research sampling because it allows us to generalize our findings beyond our sample. If I was doing a survey of juveniles who had been tried as adults, for example, my findings would not generalize, or be true for, juveniles as a whole. The NYS, however, used a representative sample so we can say that the findings obtained using the NYS generalize or are true for American juveniles as a whole at the time of the survey. That makes the NYS an ideal data set to use when studying juvenile delinquency.

The NYS was a comprehensive survey that asked juveniles about their attitudes toward and participation in deviant acts. The survey also queried the youths and their parents or guardians about the youths' home lives, friends, and work and school activities. Although the youths were followed into adulthood with yearly surveys, we only use the first wave, obtained when the youths were 11 to 17 years old. I have made changes to this data set to make it ready for our use.[1] You will find that the subsets included on the data disk that came with your book allow you to explore many relationships.

SPSS for Windows is not very difficult to operate, even if you have never used a computer before. One essential concept is coding. Coding is actually a form of translation from "Computerese" to English because most humans do not think in terms of numbers. In computer language, strings of numbers are used. Thus, if the number "2" were coded to mean "Female," then the computer would read the "2" and tell the researcher that a given respondent answered "Female." Researchers need codebooks to be able to make the computer understand what they want to do and also to decipher the results that the computer generates.

Consider a coding example from the NYS, respondent's sex, which has three possible answers: Male, Female, or No Response (a respondent could have chosen not to answer the question at all). If a respondent was male, the response was coded "1." Females were coded "2." If the respondent did not answer the question at all, the response was left blank. Luckily, we do not have to worry too much about coding because labels are already included to make the data we will be using more easy to work with. If the labels were not included in the file, we would need a codebook that would help us decipher the computer's printouts. For now, we can put the idea of coding on the back burner because we will not need to use codes unless we use the Data Editor or try to transform the data (e.g., by recoding a variable into smaller categories). If you open the Data Editor, you will see all the numbers that SPSS uses to generate its outputs. SPSS pairs those numbers with the labels assigned by the researchers to make the printouts you will soon be generating.

Before we start, we will need to load up the data set and get ready to run our numbers. To do this, launch/run SPSS and click **OK** to **open an existing file** (bold words indicate commands that you need to click on). When given the opportunity, click on "JDPREV1" to open the data set. If you do not see it listed, you might have to locate the subdirectory in which JDPREV1 is located. You will notice that a "viewer" is opened, with a tool bar along the top, a navigator along the left-hand side, and a large window for outputs. Right now, all it says is that it opened the JDPREV1 data set (the SAV extension merely identifies the data set as being in SPSS for Windows format).

GETTING A HANDLE ON THE DATA

Usually, we would take a quick look at some demographic factors before getting into any serious analyses, but we are going to postpone that until the next exercise, which will examine the correlates of juvenile delinquency. Instead, we will focus on "getting a handle" on the types of delinquent acts reported by the respondents (i.e., the youths) so that we better understand where our data came from. I included all the delinquent acts that the youths were asked about in the NYS, ranging from minor misdeeds such as ditching school to serious crimes such as aggravated assault. The researchers included a good range of delinquent acts, which I divided into eight groups:

- TOTDAMP: total property damage offenses. This category includes intentional damage to property owned by one's family (DAMFAMP), intentional damage to school property (DAMSKLP), and intentional damage to other property (DAMOTHP).[2]
- TOTTHFT: total theft-related offenses. This category includes vehicle theft (THFTVEH); theft of items worth $50.00 or more (THEFT50); theft of items worth $5.00 to $50.00 (THFT5_50); theft of items worth less than $5.00 (THFT5L); theft of money or other things from one's family (THFTFAM$); theft of items such as coats at school (THFTSKL); buying or selling stolen property (THFTFENC); theft of services by avoiding payment for movies, bus rides, and so on (THFTNOPY); and taking a vehicle for joyriding (THFTJOYR).[3]
- TOTVIO: total violent offenses. This category includes violently attacking someone with the intent to kill or seriously injure him or her (VIOATAKS); participation in gang fights (VIOGANGF); sexual assaults on others (VIOSEX_A); hitting teachers (VIOTEACH), parents (VIOPARNT), or students (VIOSTUDS); using violence to take things away from students

(VIOFORCS), teachers (VIOFORCT), or others (VIOFORCO); and throwing objects such as rocks at cars or people (VIOTHROW).[4]

- TOTSTAT: total status offenses. This category includes running away (STATRUNW), lying about one's age to gain admittance or to buy something such as liquor (STATLIE), engaging in sexual intercourse (STATSEX), consuming alcohol (STATALCO), and buying or providing liquor to a minor (STATBUYL).[5]
- TOTDRUG: total drug use offenses. This category includes using marijuana (DRUGMJ), using hallucinogens (DRUGHALL), using amphetamines (DRUGAMPH), using barbiturates (DRUGBARB), using heroin (DRUGHER), and using cocaine (DRUGCOC).[6]
- TOTDRGS: total drug sales offenses. This category includes selling marijuana (DRGSELMJ) and selling hard drugs (DRGSELHD).
- TOTOTH: total other offenses. This category includes carrying a hidden weapon (OTHHIDNW), burglary of a building to steal or just look around (OTHBURG), prostitution (OTHPROST), hitchhiking where illegal (OTHHITCH), disorderly conduct (OTHDISOR), being drunk in public (OTHDRNK), and making obscene phone calls (OTHOBS_C).[7]
- TOTSKL: total school-related delinquency. This category includes cheating at school (SKLCHEAT), ditching (SKLDITCH), and being suspended from school (SKLSUSP).

I chose these categories simply by putting the delinquent acts into groups with similar acts. You might not believe these are the best categories (e.g., you might believe burglary belongs in the theft category),[8] but they are a start. One of the strengths of SPSS is that you can quickly make categories of your own; if you decide, for example, to divide the delinquent actions into two categories, those with a clear crime victim (e.g., assault) and those that lack a clear victim (e.g., underaged drinking), you could do so in just a few minutes. Categorizing variables like this helps us analyze them without having to examine each variable (in this case, each individual delinquent act) by itself. I also created a catchall variable (TOTANY), which includes all of the delinquent acts combined into one variable. This combined measure will allow us to easily examine overall delinquency and make comparisons within groups (e.g., determining which gender commits more delinquent acts).

Think back to the readings in Part II of the book. On the basis of those articles, for which delinquent acts do you expect to see higher percentages (prevalence)? You probably expect a sizable number of youths committing minor acts and few youths engaging in the very serious crimes. Let's see what happens. We will start with just one deviant act. The article by Hindelang, Hirschi, and Weis describes a study in which a research team found that cheating on college exams was fairly common (54% of males and 35% of females cheated when given the opportunity), but that disclosure of that deviance was less common (6% of females and 16% of males said they had cheated when later asked on a confidential survey). Let's see how the NYS youths compare. To do this, run a frequency of SKLCHEAT. That table appears after the directions for running frequencies in SPSS.

Box 1: How to Run Frequencies in SPSS

1. Click on **Analyze** (on the tool bar along the top of your screen), then **Descriptive Statistics,** and then **Frequencies.**
2. Highlight the variables you want, one at a time or in groups by holding down your right mouse button and dragging your mouse pointer down until you have highlighted the whole group. If you want to pick variables further down on the list, simply hit the scroll button to move around the list. To read a whole label, merely position your mouse over the visible part of the label, and you will be able to read the entire label with its variable name in parentheses at the end of the text. The variables are listed in order by variable name, but the variable labels are shown in the listing on the left-hand side of the dialog box, making it a tad tricky to negotiate the list. Do not worry; you will get the hang of it.
3. Click on the arrow to the right of the variable list to move your selection into the right-hand box labeled "Variable(s)." You will get frequencies for each variable listed in this box.
4. Continue selecting variables until you have all the ones you want in the "Variable(s)" box.
5. If you accidentally include a variable you do not want, highlight its name and click on the arrow to move it back into the variable list. Notice that the direction of the arrow indicates the box into which your selection will be moved.
6. Click on the **OK** button in the upper right-hand corner of the command box to run your frequencies. You will notice that your frequencies appear in the large viewer window.

Box 2: Step-by-Step Example: Running Frequencies

1. Click on **Analyze,** then **Descriptive Statistics,** and then **Frequencies.**
2. Highlight "Y1-247: FREQUENCY (V412) (SKLCHEAT)," and then click on the arrow.
3. Click **OK** to run the frequency table.

You can look at frequency tables in the viewer by using the scroll bars on the right-hand side and bottom of the viewer window, or you can use the handy SPSS student version navigator along the left-hand side of the viewer window. Simply click on the output you want and then you are instantly there (Table 1).

The first thing many students notice about the frequencies produced by SPSS is the columnar format in which they are printed. Do not let this overwhelm you. The first column contains the value labels for the variable we want

TABLE 1

Frequency of SKLCHEAT.

Y1-247: Frequency (v412)

		Frequency	Percent	Valid Percent	Cumulative Percent
Valid	0	761	50.7	50.7	50.7
	1	216	14.4	14.4	65.1
	2	210	14.0	14.0	14.0
	3	79	5.3	5.3	84.4
	4	40	2.7	2.7	87.1
	5	52	3.5	3.5	90.5
	6	17	1.1	1.1	91.7
	7	5	0.3	0.3	92.0
	8	4	0.3	0.3	92.3
	9	11	0.7	0.7	93.0
	10	24	1.6	4.6	94.6
	11	1	0.1	0.1	94.7
	12	8	0.5	0.5	95.2
	13	2	0.1	0.1	95.3
	14	1	0.1	0.1	95.4
	15	14	0.9	0.9	96.3
	20	11	0.7	0.7	97.1
	22	2	0.1	0.1	97.2
	23	1	0.1	0.1	97.3
	24	1	0.1	0.1	97.3
	25	3	0.2	0.2	97.5
	30	7	0.5	0.5	98.0
	33	1	0.1	0.1	98.1
	35	4	0.3	0.3	98.3
	36	4	0.3	0.3	98.6
	40	4	0.3	0.3	98.9
	50	6	0.4	0.4	99.3
	52	3	0.2	0.2	99.5
	70	1	0.1	0.1	99.5
	71	1	0.1	0.1	99.6
	72	1	0.1	0.1	99.7
	100	1	0.1	0.1	99.7
	116	1	0.1	0.1	99.8
	119	2	0.1	0.1	99.9
	200	1	0.1	0.1	100
	Total	1500	100.0	100.0	

to study, one for each category (e.g., Male and Female). In the case of SKLCHEAT, the labels are the actual number of times the youths reported cheating; for example, the first line contains those students who said they had not cheated during the past year (i.e., they cheated "0" times), the line labeled "1" contains those who had cheated once, the line labeled "2" contains those who reported cheating on two occasions, and so on. Categories that have been coded as missing appear at the bottom of the frequency table so that we can see which categories have been coded as missing and how many respondents fall into each of these categories (although there are none for any of the delinquent acts included in this subset of data, you will see missing categories for some of the variables used in later exercises). Missing cases are those for which no data are included for a variable for a particular individual, usually because the respondent did not answer the question for some reason. Below the frequency table appears a summary of the "valid" cases, which are those that will be included in any analyses we complete.

The second column contains the frequency, or number, of cases that are classified into each category (e.g., 761 of the 1,500 respondents in this sample reported that they had not cheated during the prior year, 216 said they had cheated once, 210 reported cheating on two occasions, etc.).

The third column contains the percentage of cases classified into each category (e.g., 50.7% of the 1,500 respondents in this sample reported that they had not cheated during the prior year). This is sometimes called the "raw percent" because it has not been transformed in any way.

The fourth column presents the "valid percent," which is the percentage of all cases for which data exist. To illustrate, consider that I polled my class last week about whether they would like to get an A in my course. Every student in the room agreed, but only half of my students were in class that day due to bad weather. The raw percent of my students who said they wanted an A would be 50% (because only half were in the room so only half could say they wanted an A), but the valid percent would be 100% (since everyone who answered the question wanted an A). When we are looking at frequencies of variables that have missing data, we need to be careful that we use the appropriate percentage. Because none of the variables used in the exercise have missing cases, the raw percents and valid percents will be the same.

The final column contains the cumulative percent. This percent shows the percentage of cases classified into all the value categories up to and including the value category in question. To illustrate cumulative percentages, look briefly at the table for SKLCHEAT. The table shows that 50.7% of the respondents said they had not cheated during the past year, 65.1% of the respondents had cheated once or less (50.7% + 14.4% = 65.1%), 79.1% had cheated on two or fewer occasions (50.7% + 14.4% + 14.0% = 79.1%), and so on until we learn that 100% (all) of the respondents cheated 200 or fewer times during the past year. Take a quick look at the frequency distribution, and find out what percentage of individuals cheated on 12 or fewer occasions. If you say 95.2%, you are able to interpret cumulative percentages. Cumulative percentages are most useful when the variable in question has many sequential categories such as the number of times someone cheated during the past year. Cumulative percentages are meaningless when used with nominal data (i.e., data that cannot be rank ordered, such as sex or race).

From the frequency table, we can see that about half of our sample cheated during the past year in varying amounts (incidence). The vast majority of the cheaters did so on 6 or fewer occasions, but a few cheated 100 or more times. Cheating is interesting, but let's look at some of the other delinquent acts in the data set. To do this, use the directions in Box 1 to run frequency tables for the following set of acts, chosen from among all of those included in the study: vehicle theft (THFTVEH), selling hard drugs (DRGSELHD), theft of money or other things from one's family (THFTFAM$), engaging in gang fights (VIOGANGF), throwing objects at people or cars (VIOTHROW), ditching school (SKLDITCH), and all of the combined category measures (TOTDAMP, TOTTHFT, TOTVIO, TOTSTAT, TOTDRUG, TOTDRGS, TOTOTH, TOTSKL, and TOTANY). To make sure you are on the right track, the frequency tables for two of these delinquent acts (THFTVEH and DRGSELHD) are replicated in Tables 2 and 3. The other tables will only be summarized since they are too long to print here due to the varying levels of incidence for each delinquent act.

From the frequency tables, we can see that very few individuals in our sample had stolen vehicles during the past year; in fact, fewer than 1% engaged in this crime. The same applies to the other serious offense, selling hard drugs. The moderately serious crimes are much more diverse, however, with more than 15% (100% – 84.2% = 15.8%) having stolen money or other things from their families during the past year, and more than 10% (100% – 88% = 12%) having engaged in a gang fight. The less serious delinquent acts seem to be more common, with nearly half (100% – 52.5% = 47.5%) throwing rocks at others and more than one third (100% – 69.9% = 30.1%) ditching school.

When we turn our attention to the combined measures, we see that the sample was likely to engage in some form of delinquency. If you look at the long frequency table for TOTANY, you should first notice that only 12.1% of the sample had not committed any of the deviant acts during the prior year. The rest reported engaging in at least one delinquent act. Also notice that as the amount (incidence) of deviant actions increases, the percentage of youths at those levels becomes increasingly smaller. In fact, although one third (32.9%) of the sample completed 4 or fewer delinquent acts during the past year, just over half of the sample (50.8%) engaged in 10 or fewer acts during the past year. Then the percentages start declining. When we consider the chronic offenders, such as those who average more than 1 delinquent act per week (look at the cumulative average for 53 acts, then subtract that amount from 100%), we see that only about 20% of the youths engage in that amount of delinquency. Although some of the youths engage in 150 or more deviant acts a year, they constitute less than 10% of the sample. Then, way off the delin-

TABLE 2

Frequency of THFTVEH.

Y1-219: Frequency (v384)

		Frequency	Percent	Valid Percent	Cumulative Percent
Valid	0	1488	99.2	99.2	99.2
	1	7	0.5	0.5	99.7
	2	4	0.3	0.3	99.9
	8	1	0.1	0.1	100.0
	Total	1500	100.0	100.0	

TABLE 3

Frequency of DRGSELHD.

Y1-263: Frequency (v428)

		Frequency	Percent	Valid Percent	Cumulative Percent
Valid	0	1490	99.3	99.3	99.3
	1	4	0.3	0.3	99.6
	2	2	0.1	0.1	99.7
	3	1	0.1	0.1	99.8
	7	1	0.1	0.1	99.9
	12	1	0.1	0.1	99.9
	321	1	0.1	0.1	100.0
	Total	1500	100.0	100.0	

quency charts are 15 youths (1% of the total sample) who committed 1,000 to 2,000 delinquent acts and 1 serious chronic offender who reports engaging in 3,790 acts during the previous year (that is an average of more than 10 deviant actions a day). Of course, some of these 16 "high achievers" may have exaggerated their rates of offending, but we know from the readings in Part II of this book that self-report research is actually rather accurate.

Looking at the other combined measures, we see that status offenses are fairly common, with 56.8% (100% – 43.2%) of the youths admitting to committing at least one during the past year. Thefts and damaging property are approximately equally as likely, with 38.9% of the youths reporting that they engaged in one or more types of theft and 35.7% damaging some form of property. Very few (4.3%) of the youths engaged in drug sales, but 17.3% reported using drugs during the past year. Due in part to the high numbers of disorderly conduct offenses, 43.4% engaged in "other" offenses. School-related deviance was high, with 59.5% engaging in some form of it. Perhaps most surprising, however, is the finding that two thirds (66.8%) of the youths admitted to engaging in violence—due in part, by the way, to the fact that almost half (47.5%) had thrown rocks or other objects at cars or people, and a nearly equal number (47.7%) had hit other students. Remember from the description of the data set that the NYS is representative of American youth so that we can generalize from our findings to youth in general (at least those in 1976). If we consider our findings with respect to the combined measures to be representative of American youth, we cannot say that most juveniles lead completely delinquency-free lives, nor can we state that the majority of youths are high-rate offenders. Instead, the majority of youths appear to engage in 10 or fewer delinquent acts a year (remember our findings from the TOTANY measure), most of which are not serious.

I encourage you to run frequencies for the other delinquent acts so that you can get a better handle on the data. You will be doing this in the Further Exploration section.

MEANS AND RATES OF DELINQUENCY

Now that you have run some frequencies, it is time to discuss a few other descriptive measures. Means and rates are two useful measures for studying crime. SPSS will compute one for you, and the other is easily computed from statistics that SPSS will provide for you. The best way to remember the definition of *mean* is to realize that mean is simply a fancy word for "average." To calculate a mean number of delinquent acts, you divide the total number of delinquent acts committed by your sample by the number of people in your sample. Therefore, if you had a sample of 10 youths who had committed seven shoplifting incidents between them, the mean shoplifting rate would be 7/10 = 0.7 (which means that, on average, each youth shoplifted 0.7 times). You can also use SPSS to generate means for you; to do this, follow the directions in Box 3. Box 3 also includes directions to generate the statistics you will need to calculate delinquency rates.

To calculate a rate, use the following formula: Delinquency rate = (number of delinquent acts/number of subjects in group) × 1,000. Back to our sample of 10 youths who had shoplifted seven times between them. The rate of shoplifting would be 7/10 × 1,000 = 0.7 × 1,000 = 700. When we are using a sample of 10, it is pretty easy to sum up the number of delinquent acts. When samples are larger, however, it is much more difficult to sum them by hand. For this reason, we will use SPSS to calculate the sums for us, as shown in Box 3.

Look at the row for TOTANY (it is toward the bottom of the list). The mean number of delinquent actions per youth was 67.74. This does not mean that every youth committed exactly 67.74 deviant actions. Instead, it means that

---

Box 3

How to Run Descriptives in SPSS

1. Click on **Analyze** (on the tool bar along the top of your screen), then **Descriptive Statistics,** and then **Descriptives.**
2. Highlight the variables you want, one at a time or in groups by holding down your right mouse button and dragging your mouse pointer down until you have highlighted the whole group. If you want to pick variables further down on the list, simply hit the scroll button to move around the list. To read a whole label, position your mouse over the visible part of the label, and you will be able to read the entire label with its variable name in parentheses at the end of the text. The variables are listed in order by variable name, but the variable labels are shown in the listing on the left-hand side of the dialog box, making it a tad tricky to negotiate the list. Do not worry; you will get the hang of it.
3. Click on the arrow to the right of the variable list to move your selection into the right-hand box labeled "Variable(s)." You will get descriptives for each variable listed in this box.
4. Continue selecting variables until you have all the ones you want in the "Variable(s)" box.
5. If you accidentally include a variable you do not want, highlight its name and click on the arrow to move it back into the variable list. Notice that the direction of the arrow indicates the box into which your selection will be moved.
6. Click on the **Options** button in the lower right-hand corner of the command box. Put a check in the "Sum" box, and then click **Continue.**
7. Click on the **OK** button in the upper right-hand corner of the command box to run your descriptives. Notice that your descriptives appear in the large viewer window.

Box 4

Step-by-Step Example: Running Descriptives

1. Click on **Analyze,** then **Descriptive Statistics,** and then **Descriptives.**
2. Highlight "TOTANY," and then click on the arrow. Also click on the other combined measures to move them into the box: TOTDAMP, TOTTHFT, TOTVIO, TOTDRUG, TOTDRGS, TOTSTAT, TOTOTH, and TOTSKL. Finally, add all the individual delinquent acts from DAMFAMP to SKLSUSP into the box.
3. Click on the **Options** button in the lower right-hand corner of the command box. Put a check in the "Sum" box, and then click **Continue.**
4. Click **OK** to run the descriptives.

---

some youths committed fewer and some committed more, but the average per youth statistic is 67.74. Skip across the columns to the last two columns, "sum" and "valid n." To get the rate, divide the sum by the valid n and multiply by 1,500: $101{,}613 / 1{,}500 \times 1{,}000 = 67.74 \times 1{,}000 = 67{,}742$. Did you notice something about the average and the first part of the rate formula? You probably noticed that the numbers are the same; this is because the first part of the rate formula is the same as the average (sum of acts divided by sample size). To save time, then, you could just multiply the average by 1,000 to get the rate per 1,000 cases.

You might also look at the minimum and maximum for each variable. The minimums are all zero (for youths who did not engage in that form of delinquency during the past year), but the maximums vary widely by action. The highest number of vehicles stolen by any one juvenile was eight (look at THFTVEH), but the highest number of objects thrown at people or cars by one juvenile was 900 (look at VIOTHROW). Take a moment to look at the minimums and maximums for the combined measures. For TOTANY, we see our most delinquent youth, who topped out with 3,790 delinquent acts, but the other maximums are much lower.

Now, turn your attention to the means. Because they are adjusted by the valid n for each act, they are directly comparable. Although one chronic offender could make the maximum acts look very high, it takes more chronic offenders to boost the average. This is not to say that the average is immune from the effects of cases on the extremes, called outliers in statistical parlance. To illustrate, consider my technology and criminal justice class. For a typical class of students, the average family income was approximately $40,000. When Bill Gates came to guest lecture last week, however, the average income of the people in the classroom skyrocketed to more than $1 million dollars each. This does not mean the students all got scholarships from the Bill and Melinda Gates fund; it simply means that Bill Gates's superhigh annual income drove the average way beyond any but his own income. For this reason, sometimes researchers talk about excluding outliers from their statistics; in cases such as this one, such an approach is a good idea.

EXPLORATION WITH CROSS-TABULATION TABLES

Now, let's run some analyses to further explore the incidence and prevalence of juvenile delinquency. For this exercise, we will break out, by gender, recoded versions of the nine combined measures. Before we do this, however, run a frequency table for MALE[9] to determine how it is distributed; we need to ensure that there are enough cases in each category to make our analyses worthwhile. If there are very few cases, statistical analyses are not valid. For example, if there were only a few girls in the data set, any tables run on such a

TABLE 4

Frequency of male.

MALE

		Frequency	Percent	Valid Percent	Cumulative Percent
Valid	Female	705	47.0	47.0	47.0
	Male	795	53.0	53.0	100.0
	Total	1500	100.0	100.0	

variable would be invalid due to small cell sizes. Table 4 is the frequency table for MALE.

As you can tell, about half ($n = 795$, 53.0%) of the sample was male; the remaining 47% ($n = 705$) of the individuals were female (note that there were no "missing cases" or cases of youths who failed to provide a gender to the researchers). The articles in Part II (e.g., see Table 1 of Paul Tracy's article) note that females appear to commit fewer delinquent acts than males, so let's see if this is true for our representative sample of youth.

Now, we will determine if gender plays a role in the likelihood of engaging in delinquent acts, as discussed in the readings. A good technique for examining differences between groups is the cross-tabulation table. You have seen many of these before but may not have known the name for them. When you see political polls broken down by party or gender, you are actually examining cross-tabulation tables. Most cross-tabulation tables, including all the ones we will look at in this chapter's exercises, present two variables: One variable appears at the top of the table, and the other variable appears on the left-hand side.

Cross-tabulation tables are easy to make. Just follow the directions in Box 5. To make our first table, follow the directions in Box 6.

Yikes! The resulting table is nothing but cell after cell after cell. Even I would not be able to interpret that mess. We have just committed a common error in the making of cross-tabulation tables—using variables with too many categories to allow us to do meaningful analysis. Sure, we could poke around from cell to cell and say "Well, males were more likely to commit six delinquent acts [look at the row labeled 6, and compare the percentages for males and females to determine which is higher], but females were more likely to commit five offenses" (compare the percentages for row 5). Instead of forcing you to engage in this statistically useless (and dangerous, too, since you could easily reach the wrong conclusions) activity, I recoded all the combined measures into new variables because the original versions had too many categories to allow for worthwhile cross-tabulation tables. The recoded versions (relabeled DIDANY, DIDSTAT, etc.) have only two categories: 0 if the youth did not report engaging in the activity, and 1 if the youth reported committing the delinquent act at least once. Notice that we have now formally moved from examining incidence (the amount of delinquency committed by the target population) to examining prevalence (the percentage of the target population that engages in delinquent acts).

To make some useful tables, follow the directions in Box 7.

The first three frequency tables are replicated here, and an explanation of each is provided. The remaining tables are only described. Table 5 is the table for MALE → DIDANY; the statistics appear below the table. Note the higher percentage of males compared to females who admitted they had committed at least one delinquent act.

Box 6

Step-by-Step Example: Running Cross-Tabulation Tables

1. Click on **Analyze,** then **Descriptive Statistics,** then **Crosstabs.**
2. Highlight "TOTANY," and then click on the arrow beside the "Row(s)" box. This is our dependent variable.
3. Highlight "MALE," and then click on the arrow beside the "Column(s)" box. This is our independent variable.
4. Click on the **Statistics** button at the bottom of the command box, then put a check mark in the box labeled "Phi and Cramer's V," and then click **Continue** to return to the command box.
5. Click on the **Cells** button at the bottom of the command box, then put a check mark in the box labeled "Column," and then click **Continue** to return to the command box.
6. Click **OK** to run the cross-tabulation table.

Box 7

Step-by-Step Example: Running Cross-Tabulation Tables

1. Click on **Analyze,** then **Descriptive Statistics,** and then **Crosstabs.**
2. Highlight "DIDANY," and then click on the arrow beside the "Row(s)" box. This is our first dependent variable.
3. Highlight "DIDDAMP," and then click on the arrow beside the "Row(s)" box. This is our second dependent variable.
4. Highlight "DIDTHFT," and then click on the arrow beside the "Row(s)" box. This is our third dependent variable.
5. Highlight "DIDVIO," and then click on the arrow beside the "Row(s)" box. This is our fourth dependent variable.
6. Highlight "DIDSTAT," and then click on the arrow beside the "Row(s)" box. This is our fifth dependent variable.
7. Highlight "DIDDRUG," and then click on the arrow beside the "Row(s)" box. This is our sixth dependent variable.
8. Highlight "DIDDRGS," and then click on the arrow beside the "Row(s)" box. This is our seventh dependent variable.
9. Highlight "DIDOTH," and then click on the arrow beside the "Row(s)" box. This is our eighth dependent variable.
10. Highlight "DIDSKL," and then click on the arrow beside the "Row(s)" box. This is our ninth dependent variable. This means that we will get nine separate tables, one for each dependent variable.
11. Highlight "MALE," and then click on the arrow beside the "Column(s)" box. This is our independent variable.
12. Click on the **Statistics** button at the bottom of the command box, then put a check mark in the box labeled "Phi and Cramer's V," and then click **Continue** to return to the command box.
13. Click on the **Cells** button at the bottom of the command box, then put a check mark in the box labeled "Column," and then click **Continue** to return to the command box.
14. Click **OK** to run the cross-tabulation table.

TABLE 5

MALE → DIDANY cross-tabulation.

Crosstab

			MALE		Total
			Female	Male	
DIDANY	0	Count	120	61	181
		% within MALE	17.0%	7.7%	12.1%
	1	Count	585	734	1319
		% within MALE	83.0%	92.3%	87.9%
Total		Count	705	795	1500
		% within MALE	100.0%	100.0%	100.0%

Symmetric Measures

		Value	Approx. Sig.
Nominal by	Phi	.143	.000
Nominal	Cramer's *V*	.143	.000
N of valid cases		1500	

a. Not assuming the null hypothesis.
b. Using the asymptotic standard error assuming the null hypothesis.

From Table 5, we learn that 92.3% of the males reported committing at least one delinquent act during the previous year compared to 83.0% of females. The difference between the two percentages is 9.7%, so the finding is potentially interesting (had the percentage been only a few percent, we would say the difference is negligible). We might have a real finding, but we need to examine the statistics to ensure that this finding is not due to chance or random fluctuations in our data. The phi value is .14, which means that we can predict delinquency 14% better when we know a respondent's gender. Alternatively, we can say that 14% of the variance in delinquency can be explained by gender. We can classify the strength of a relationship based on the absolute value of the phi value (remember from your math classes that all you do to get an absolute value is drop the minus sign if there is one so that the number is always positive). One rule of thumb is that a phi lower than .10 indicates a weak relationship, a phi between .10 and .30 indicates a moderate relationship, and a phi larger than .30 indicates a strong relationship (Cramer's *V* is interpreted in the same way). In the case of MALE and TOTANY, the relationship would be considered moderate. We used phi for this table rather than Cramer's *V* because the table is a 2×2 table (i.e., it has two columns and two rows, excluding the Total column and row).

From the Approx. Sig. column, we can see that the phi value is significant at the .000 level. (Note: This is not zero; the computer rounded it off to .000, but it

TABLE 6

MALE → DIDDAMP.

Crosstab

			MALE		Total
			Female	Male	
DIDDAMP	0	Count	531	433	964
		% within MALE	75.3%	54.5%	64.3%
	1	Count	174	362	536
		% within MALE	24.7%	45.5%	35.7%
Total		Count	705	795	1500
		% within MALE	100.0%	100.0%	100.0%

Symmetric Measures

		Value	Approx. Sig.
Nominal by	Phi	.217	.000
Nominal	Cramer's *V*	.217	.000
N of valid cases		1500	

a. Not assuming the null hypothesis.
b. Using the asymptotic error assuming the null hypothesis.

is probably a number such as .0001.) Significance values sound scarier than they are in reality. All they do is alert the researcher (you) to the possibility that his or her findings are due to chance rather than due to a real relationship between two variables. Significance ranges from 0 to 1. A significance value of 1 means there is a 100% chance the finding is due to chance, so it cannot be trusted. A significance value of 0 means there is almost no chance the finding is due to chance, so it can be trusted. Very few relationships have significance values of 1 or 0, however, so researchers had to develop a scale so that they could determine when they could trust their findings. Many years ago, they decided that they would accept any finding with a significance level of .05 or lower because that would mean there is only a 5% (or lower) chance that the finding is due to chance or coincidence. In our MALE → DIDANY cross-tabulation, there is almost no chance that our observed relationship (i.e., that males commit more delinquent acts than females) is due to coincidence.

Table 6 is the table for MALE → DIDDAMP; the statistics appear below the table. Notice the higher number of males compared to females who said they had damaged property.

Notice that males are almost twice as likely as females to report having damaged property (45.5% of males vs. 24.7% of females). The difference between the two percentages is 20.7%; therefore, the finding is potentially interesting. The phi value is –.21, indicating that we can predict the likelihood of

TABLE 7

MALE → DIDTHFT.

Crosstab

			MALE		Total
			Female	Male	
DIDTHFT	0	Count	490	427	917
		% within MALE	69.5%	53.7%	61.1%
	1	Count	215	368	583
		% within MALE	30.5%	46.3%	38.9%
Total		Count	705	795	1500
		% within MALE	100.0%	100.0%	100.0%

Symmetric Measures

		Value	Approx. Sig.
Nominal by	Phi	.162	.000
Nominal	Cramer's V	.162	.000
N of valid cases		1500	

a. Not assuming the null hypothesis.
b. Using the asymptotic standard error assuming the null hypothesis.

engaging in property damage 21% better when we know a respondent's gender, and the significance level is again .000. According to the phi value, this relationship would be considered moderate. This cross-tabulation shows that gender and likelihood of engaging in property damage are related.

Now, it is your turn to examine and interpret the remaining tables. The easiest way is to examine each value of the dependent variable individually. Therefore, in the MALE → DIDTHFT cross-tabulation (Table 7; notice the higher percentage of males compared to females who admitted theft-related offenses), you should examine the percentages of individuals who said they had stolen something during the past year. First, note what percentage of males said they had stolen something and then the percentage of females who had done so. Do the percentages differ? If so, is the difference substantial enough to warrant our interest? What is the phi value? Is the finding significant or meaningful? If you have problems with this table, go over the first two cross-tabulation tables, using the text to check your work.

Now, look at the MALE → DIDVIO cross-tabulation table and interpret it. What percentage of the males said they had engaged in violent offenses? What percentage of females? Do the percentages differ? If so, is the difference substantial enough to warrant our interest? What is the phi value? Is the finding significant or meaningful?

What about the MALE → DIDSTAT cross-tabulation table? What percentage of the males said they had committed status offenses? What percentage of females? Do the percentages differ? Although it is less of a difference than that for the previous variables, is the difference substantial enough to warrant our interest? What is the phi value? Is the finding significant or meaningful? Note that .004 is well within the statistically significant range (since it is less than .05).

Now, look at the MALE → DIDDRUG cross-tabulation table and interpret it. What percentage of the males said they had sold drugs? What percentage of females? Do the percentages differ? If so, is the difference substantial enough to warrant our interest? Note that the percentages do not differ as much as they did for the previous variables; this is an example of a negligible difference. A difference of 3.5% is not sufficient to conclude that one gender is more or less delinquent than the other. What is the phi value? Is the finding significant or meaningful (in other words, do we consider the significance level of .07 to signal a statistically important finding)? This one is tricky. Although .07 seems close to .05, most researchers would consider this nonsignificant because it does not meet the important significance cutoff. A few researchers call these "close-call" significance levels "trending," and they tell the reader the exact value so that he or she knows it was a close call and can determine how much weight to accord to the findings. Either way, however, the relationship is weak because the phi value is less than .10. As a general rule, in no circumstances are significance levels higher than .10 considered to signal significant findings. We will play by the more common conservative rules and say this finding is not significant.

Now, look at the MALE → DIDDRGS cross-tabulation table and interpret it. What percentage of the males said they had sold drugs? What percentage of females? Note that the percentages are smaller but may still be compared. Do the percentages differ? If so, is the difference substantial enough to warrant our interest? What is the phi value? Is the finding significant or meaningful?

Now, look at the MALE → DIDOTH cross-tabulation table and interpret it. What percentage of the males said they had engaged in offenses other than those contained within the previously analyzed combined measures? What percentage of females? Do the percentages differ? If so, is the difference substantial enough to warrant our interest? What is the phi value? Is the finding significant or meaningful?

Finally, look at the MALE → DIDSKL cross-tabulation table. What percentage of the males said they had committed school-related deviant acts? What percentage of females? Do the percentages differ? Although it is less of a difference than for the previous variables, is the difference substantial enough to warrant our interest? What is the phi value? Is the finding significant or meaningful (in other words, do we consider the significance level of .06 to signal a statistically important finding)? This one is even trickier than DIDDRUG because it is even closer to .05, but we will still say it is not significant because it does not meet the important significance cutoff. Extremely close calls such as this make researchers' lives more difficult due to the absence of absolute guidelines.

POINTS TO PONDER: Having examined the nine cross-tabulation tables, what can we say about the influence of gender on the likelihood of engaging in delinquent acts?

FURTHER EXPLORATION

What are the incidence levels for the other individual crimes? Maybe you want to determine which delinquent act under status offenses contributed to the high incidence level for that category. For the Further Exploration homework assignment, pick five delinquent acts and run frequency tables for them like we did previously to further explore prevalence and incidence levels.

ON YOUR OWN

Now that we have explored the combined measures of juvenile delinquency, and broken them down by gender, examine some of the individual delinquent acts. Perhaps you want to know if males are more likely than females to engage in teen sex (STATSEX) or if females are more likely than males to steal items worth less than $5.00. Run analyses for these two variables and two additional ones of your choice. While you are exploring the breakouts by gender, think about the readings and how they help predict which gender is more likely to commit delinquent acts.

NOTES

1. The original National Youth Survey Wave I data included 500 variables for 1,725 individuals. Because the student version of SPSS will only accommodate 1,500 cases, the data for this exercise in this book do not include youths who were not either white or black (76 Chicanos, 8 Native Americans, 17 Asians, and 3 nonresponders), the 94 youths who did not have comparison data completed by a parent or stepparent, and the 35 youths who failed to answer at least one of the self-reported delinquency questions. This left precisely 1,500 cases. Also, the student version of SPSS can only handle 50 variables, so many interesting variables had to be deleted from the data set. If you are interested in obtaining the entire data set, you may do so by contacting the Inter-University Consortium for Political and Social Research (ICPSR; a quick Web search for ICPSR will result in a link to their homepage from which the entire data set may be downloaded free of charge). The variable names (i.e., short descriptors, up to 8 characters in length, that are assigned to each vari-

able) have been changed to make the data more student friendly, but the original names have been appended to the variable labels (i.e., longer descriptions, up to 40 characters in length, that are associated with each variable) for those students who wish to obtain and work with the full data set. For example, V386 (one of the variables in the original data set) has been renamed THEFT50 to make the name more descriptive, and the original name has been moved to the end of the variable label (i.e., THEFT50's variable label became "Y1-221 FREQUENCY (V386)"). Be warned that a few errors occur in the original data set, such as mislabeled variables, but these flaws have been corrected in the versions you will be using in the exercises.

2. Due to the file size limitations imposed by SPSS (i.e., a 50-variable limit), the individual property damage measures are not included in JDPREV1; see JDPREV2 for these variables.

3. Due to the file size limitations imposed by SPSS (i.e., a 50-variable limit), THFTFENC, THFTJOYR, THFTNOPY, and THFTSKL are not included in JDPREV1; see JDPREV2 for these acts.

4. Due to the file size limitations imposed by SPSS (i.e., a 50-variable limit), VIOFORCS, VIOFORCT, and VIOFORCO are not included in JDPREV1; see JDPREV2 for these acts.

5. Due to the file size limitations imposed by SPSS (i.e., a 50-variable limit), the only individual act from this category that is included in JDPREV1 is STATSEX; see JDPREV2 for the other acts.

6. Due to the file size limitations imposed by SPSS (i.e., a 50-variable limit), the individual drug use measures are not included in JDPREV1; see JDPREV2 for these variables.

7. Due to the file size limitations imposed by SPSS (i.e., a 50-variable limit), the individual delinquent acts are not included in JDPREV1; see JDPREV2 for these variables.

8. I included burglary in the "other" category because the survey question asked if the youths had broken into a building to steal or just look around; therefore, some of the burglaries were not committed in anticipation of gaining access to items to steal.

9. To make the analyses easier, I recoded the variable so that males are coded as 1 and females are coded as 0.

REFERENCE

Elliott, D. (1994). National Youth Survey [United States]: Wave I, 1976 [Computer file]. ICPSR version. Boulder: University of Colorado, Behavioral Research Institute [producer], 1977. Ann Arbor, MI: Inter-University Consortium for Political and Social Research [distributor], 1994.

Homework for Part II: General Questions
Incidence and Prevalence of Delinquency

Name: _____   Date: _____

Directions: Complete the following exercises by filling in the blanks or circling the appropriate responses. A couple of answers have been filled in for you to make sure you are on the right track.

GETTING A HANDLE ON THE DATA

1. In the 1976 NYS sample, 761 youths had not cheated in school (SKLCHEAT) during the year, and they comprise _____% of the sample. _____ (_____%) of the youths had cheated once during the year and _____ (_____%) had cheated twice. _____% had cheated on 24 or fewer occasions (HINT: check the cumulative percent for this last one). The highest number of times any one youth cheated in school was 200, and a total of _____ youths cheated 100 or more times.

2. In the 1976 NYS sample, 1,488 youths had not stolen vehicles (THFTVEH) during the year, and they comprise _____% of the sample. _____ (_____%) of the youths had stolen one vehicle, _____ (_____%) had stolen two vehicles, and _____ (_____%) had stolen eight vehicles.

3. In the 1976 NYS sample, _____ youths had not sold hard drugs (DRGSELHD) during the year, and they comprise _____% of the sample. _____ (_____%) of the youths had sold hard drugs once during the year, 2 (_____%) had sold them twice, _____ (_____%) three times, _____ (_____%) seven times, _____ (_____%) twelve times, and _____ (_____%) had sold drugs on 321 occasions during the past year.

4. In the 1976 NYS sample, _____ youths had not engaged in gang fights (VIOGANGF) during the past year, and they comprise _____% of the sample. _____ (_____%) of the youths had engaged in gang fights once during the year, 49 (_____%) had engaged in two gang fights, _____ (_____%) had engaged in three gang fights, and _____ (_____%) had engaged in four or more gang fights during the past year.

5. In the 1976 NYS sample, _____ youths had not thrown objects at people or cars (VIOTHROW) during the past year, and they comprise _____% of the sample. _____ (_____%) of

the youths had done this once during the year, _____ (_____%) had done it twice, _____ (_____%) had done it three times, and _____ (_____%) had thrown objects at people or cars four or more times during the past year.

6. In the 1976 NYS sample, _____ youths had not ditched school (SKLDITCH) during the past year, and they comprise _____% of the sample. _____ (_____%) of the youths had done this once during the year, _____ (_____%) had done it twice, _____ (_____%) had done it three times, and _____ (_____%) had ditched school four or more times during the past year.

7. Complete the following table using the information from the frequency tables for the combined category measures:

Variable	Number and % Not Engaging in Act	Number and % Engaged in Act 1-3 Times	Number and % Engaged in Act 4-12 Times	Number and % Engaged in Act 13-52 Times	Number and % Engaged in Act 53+ Times
TOTANY					
TOTDAMP	964 (64.3%)				
TOTTHFT					
TOTVIO					
TOTSTAT					
TOTDRUG					
TOTDRGS					
TOTOTH					
TOTSKL					

MEANS AND RATES OF DELINQUENCY

1. Complete the following table using the information from the Descriptives statistics:

Variable	Mean/Average	Rate per 1,000
TOTANY	67.74	67,740
TOTDAMP		
TOTTHFT		
TOTVIO		
TOTDRUG		
TOTDRGS		
TOTSTAT		
TOTOTH		
TOTSKL		

EXPLORATION THROUGH CROSS-TABULATION TABLES

1. In the 1976 NYS sample, there were <u>795</u> males, and they comprise _____% of the sample. There were _____ females; they were _____% of the sample. This division *is/is not* roughly equal.

2. In the MALE → DIDANY cross-tabulation, <u>734</u> (_____%) of the male respondents said they had committed any delinquent acts during the past year compared to _____ (_____%) of the female respondents. The difference between the two percentages is _____%, which appears to be *negligible/potentially interesting*. The *phi/Cramer's V* value is _____, which means that we can do _____% better predicting general delinquency when we know a respondent's gender. This relationship is *weak/moderate/strong*. The approximate significance is _____, which means there is a <u>negligible</u> % that the relationship between MALE and DIDANY is due to chance. (Note: When SPSS says the significance is .000, we label it "negligible" rather than "zero" because we recognize there is an infinitesimal possibility of error due to chance.) This relationship *is/is not* statistically significant.

In articles in Part II, Paul Tracy and the other authors found that *males/females* were more likely to engage in delinquency. The relationship between gender and delinquency found using the 1976 NYS data *is similar to/differs greatly from* the findings regarding gender reported by the authors in Part II.

3. In the MALE → DIDDAMP cross-tabulation, <u>362</u> (_____%) of the male respondents said they had damaged property during the past year compared to _____ (_____%) of the female respondents. The difference between the two percentages is _____%, which appears to be *negligible/potentially interesting*. The *phi/Cramer's V* value is _____, which means that we can do _____% better predicting property damage when we know a respondent's gender. This relationship is *weak/moderate/strong*. The approximate significance is _____, which means there is a <u>negligible</u> % that the relationship between MALE and DIDDAMP is due to chance. This relationship *is/is not* statistically significant.

   The relationship between gender and delinquency (measured by property damage) found using the 1976 NYS data *is similar to/differs greatly from* the findings regarding gender reported by the authors in Part II.

4. In the MALE → DIDTHFT cross-tabulation, _____ (_____%) of the male respondents said they had committed any thefts during the past year compared to _____ (_____%) of the female respondents. The difference between the two percentages is _____%, which appears to be *negligible/potentially interesting*. The *phi/Cramer's V* value is _____, which means that we can do _____% better predicting participation in theft when we know a respondent's gender. This relationship is *weak/moderate/strong*. The approximate significance is _____, which means there is a _____ % that the relationship between MALE and DIDTHFT is due to chance. This relationship *is/is not* statistically significant.

   The relationship between gender and delinquency (measured by theft) found using the 1976 NYS data *is similar to/differs greatly from* the findings regarding gender reported by the authors in Part II.

5. In the MALE → DIDVIO cross-tabulation, _____ (_____%) of the male respondents said they had engaged in violent acts during the past year compared to _____ (_____%) of the female respondents. The difference between the two percentages is _____%, which appears to be *negligible/potentially interesting*. The *phi/Cramer's V* value is _____, which means that we can do _____% better predicting participation in violence when we know a respondent's gender. This relationship is *weak/moderate/strong*. The approximate signifi-

cance is _____, which means there is a _____ % that the relationship between MALE and DIDVIO is due to chance. This relationship *is/is not* statistically significant.

The relationship between gender and delinquency (measured by violence) found using the 1976 NYS data *is similar to/differs greatly from* the findings regarding gender reported by the authors in Part II.

6. In the MALE → DIDSTAT cross-tabulation, _____ (_____%) of the male respondents said they had committed any status offenses during the past year compared to _____ (_____%) of the female respondents. The difference between the two percentages is _____%, which appears to be *negligible/potentially interesting*. The *phi/Cramer's V* value is _____, which means that we can do _____% better predicting participation in status offenses when we know a respondent's gender. This relationship is *weak/moderate/strong*. The approximate significance is _____, which means there is a _____ % that the relationship between MALE and DIDSTAT is due to chance. This relationship *is/is not* statistically significant.

The relationship between gender and delinquency (measured by status offenses) found using the 1976 NYS data *is similar to/differs greatly from* the findings regarding gender reported by the authors in Part II.

7. In the MALE → DIDDRUG cross-tabulation, _____ (_____%) of the male respondents said they had used drugs during the past year compared to _____ (_____%) of the female respondents. The difference between the two percentages is _____%, which appears to be *negligible/potentially interesting*. The *phi/Cramer's V* value is _____, which means that we can do _____% better predicting drug use when we know a respondent's gender. This relationship is *weak/moderate/strong*. The approximate significance is _____, which means there is a _____ % that the relationship between MALE and DIDDRUG is due to chance. This relationship *is/is not* statistically significant.

The relationship between gender and delinquency (measured by using drugs) found using the 1976 NYS data *is similar to/differs greatly from* the findings regarding gender reported by the authors in Part II.

8. In the MALE → DIDDRGS cross-tabulation, _____ (_____%) of the male respondents said they had sold drugs during the past year compared to _____ (_____%) of the female respondents. The difference between the two percentages is _____%, which appears to be *negligible/potentially interesting*. The *phi/Cramer's V* value is _____, which means that we can do _____% better predicting drug sales when we know a respondent's gender. This rela-

tionship is *weak/moderate/strong*. The approximate significance is _____, which means there is a _____ % that the relationship between MALE and DIDDRGS is due to chance. This relationship *is/is not* statistically significant.

The relationship between gender and delinquency (measured by drug sales) found using the 1976 NYS data *is similar to/differs greatly from* the findings regarding gender reported by the authors in Part II.

9. In the MALE → DIDOTH cross-tabulation, _____ (_____%) of the male respondents said they had committed "other" offenses (i.e., those not classified into the other categories) during the past year compared to _____ (_____%) of the female respondents. The difference between the two percentages is _____%, which appears to be *negligible/potentially interesting*. The *phi/Cramer's V* value is _____, which means that we can do _____% better predicting engaging in "other" delinquency when we know a respondent's gender. This relationship is *weak/moderate/strong*. The approximate significance is _____, which means there is a <u>negligible</u> % that the relationship between MALE and DIDOTH is due to chance. This relationship *is/is not* statistically significant.

The relationship between gender and delinquency (measured by "other" offenses) found using the 1976 NYS data *is similar to/differs greatly from* the findings regarding gender reported by the authors in Part II.

10. In the MALE → DIDSKL cross-tabulation, _____ (_____%) of the male respondents said they engaged in school-related delinquency during the past year compared to _____ (_____%) of the female respondents. The difference between the two percentages is _____%, which appears to be *negligible/potentially interesting*. The *phi/Cramer's V* value is _____, which means that we can do _____% better predicting school-related delinquency when we know a respondent's gender. This relationship is *weak/moderate/strong*. The approximate significance is _____, which means there is a _____ % that the relationship between MALE and DIDSKL is due to chance. This relationship *is/is not* statistically significant.

The relationship between gender and delinquency (measured by school-related delinquency) found using the 1976 NYS data *is similar to/differs greatly from* the findings regarding gender reported by the authors in Part II.

11. Overall, we can say our findings regarding the relationship between gender and delinquency *are/are not* consistent with prior research.

Homework for Part II: Further Exploration
Incidence and Prevalence of Delinquency

Name: _____ Date: _____

TASK: Run frequencies for at least five delinquent acts.

Directions: Complete the following exercises by answering the questions.

NOTE: Please print out and include your tables with these questions so your work can be graded.

FURTHER EXPLORATION

1. Which delinquent acts did you choose to explore with frequency tables?

2. Complete the following table using information from your frequency tables. You will have to add some frequencies together to fill in the table. If you ran more than five frequencies, there are additional rows in the table so you may fill in the values for your other delinquent acts.

Delinquent Act Type	% of Youth Not Engaging in the Act	% of Youth Engaging in the Act Once or Twice	% of Youth Engaging in the Act 3-50 Times	% of Youth Engaging in the Act 51 or More Times

3. What can you say about the prevalence and incidence of delinquency based on your frequency tables?

Homework for Part II: On Your Own
Incidence and Prevalence of Delinquency

Name: _____   Date: _____

TASK: Look at some of the individual delinquent acts to include other actions that might be related to gender (e.g., STATSEX and THFT5L).

Directions: Complete the following exercises by answering the questions.

NOTE: Please print out and include your tables with these questions so your work can be graded.

ON YOUR OWN

1. Which two delinquent acts did you select as dependent variables and why did you choose those two? Try to tie your reasoning to the readings (e.g., do the readings suggest that males or females might be more likely to engage in a particular delinquent act?).

2. How did MALE affect your first dependent variable? Make sure to provide a description that includes the percentages, phi or Cramer's *V* value, the strength of the relationship, and the significance value.

3. How did MALE affect your second dependent variable? Make sure to provide a description that includes the percentages, phi or Cramer's V value, the strength of the relationship, and the significance value.

4. Try to suggest an explanation, grounded in the readings, for the findings you found for your two dependent variables.

III

WHO ARE THE DELINQUENTS?

The Distribution and Correlates of Delinquency

IT is a common observation that boys get into trouble more often than girls. A criminologist can infer that one's biologically determined sex is "associated" with involvement in delinquency. Sexual identity—the condition of being male or female—is a "correlate" of delinquent behavior. There are many other correlates that have been identified through empirical research on the distribution of juvenile delinquency. Most are weak correlates, but some have been identified consistently over many studies as strong correlates, meaning that there is a large and likely significant statistical association between the variable and delinquency. Theories should attempt to explain these "facts" of juvenile delinquency—that is, the observed correlates. For example, why and how are boys more delinquent than girls?

In a general sense, the correlates describe the distribution of characteristics that distinguish, in relative terms, delinquents from nondelinquents. Among those correlates identified consistently as strong, important variables to take into account in explanations of delinquency, there are three physical characteristics that vary with levels of involvement in delinquency—sex, age, and race. As Hindelang's self-report study, "Age, Sex, and the Versatility of Delinquent Involvements," shows, boys are more frequently involved in juvenile delinquency than girls, particularly in the most serious property and violent offenses. Girls, however, commit the same crimes as boys, with the same pattern of involvement. That is, boys and girls are both versatile, rather than specialized, offenders. He also reports a common finding that among juveniles, delinquency is positively related to age—as children get older, they get into more serious trouble. Many studies have observed that involvement in crime increases throughout the teen years, peaking at about age 17 and decreasing dramatically thereafter. Also, Huizinga and Elliott, in "Juvenile Offender Prevalence, Incidence, and Arrest Rates by Race," explore the many complexities of the apparently strong relationship between race and delinquency. The highest rates of incarceration, arrest, and self-reported delinquency are found among nonwhites, particularly African and Hispanic Americans, but the original observed differences in delinquent behavior cannot account for the much larger race differences in incarceration.

Another important variable, a juvenile's social class of origin, has played a central role in most contemporary sociological theories of juvenile delinquency. For many years, it has been observed that the highest rates of "official" delinquency are among juveniles from the lower class, particularly those that live in the poorest and most deteriorated neighborhoods. This correlation was replicated many times over in a variety of studies, until it took on the status of a taken-for-granted "axiom" about juvenile delinquency—that is, until self-report studies, with few exceptions, began to find equally consistently that social class was not a strong correlate but rather a weak to nonexistent one. The paper by Weis, "Social Class and Crime," attempts to address the question of whether there is a meaningful relationship between class and delinquency by reanalyzing data from the Seattle Youth Study, taking into account the criticisms of the self-report technique and examining the impact of the social class of the individual on delinquency within different social class contexts. In general, a juvenile's social class of origin is a weak correlate of involvement in delinquent behavior, certainly not robust enough to support theories that depend on the impact of class on crime.

The work of Entner Wright, Caspi, Moffitt, Miech, and Silva, on "Reconsidering the Relationship Between SES and Delinquency," suggests why this weak correlation exists. They propose that socioeconomic status (SES) has both a negative and positive effect on delinquency—that is, lower SES increases involvement in delinquency through heightened strain and frustration and diminished educational and occupational opportunities, whereas higher SES leads to delinquency through increased risk taking and empowerment and weakening conventional values. They conclude that the empirical findings of an insignificant SES/crime correlation are supported, as are the lower-class-specific theories that depend on a meaningful negative relationship.

There are other correlates that are less controversial and for which there is much less disagreement regarding the evidence and their importance in describing and understanding juvenile delinquency. Most criminologists agree that family experiences, school performance, peer influences including gang membership, and involvement with drugs are all associated with juvenile delinquency.

Wells and Rankin focus on the role of the family in delinquency in "Families and Delinquency: A Meta-Analysis of the Impact of Broken Homes." From their systematic, quantitative analysis of the literature, they conclude that the structure of the family is not nearly as important as most people believe, but the nature and quality of the relationships within the family, whether "broken" or not, are a critical influence on childrens' behavior.

It is common knowledge that kids who do not do well in school are more likely to get into trouble, both in and out of school. Research has shown that school performance, whether grades, standardized achievement tests, attendance, or other indicators of academic achievement, is a strong correlate of delinquency. Thornberry, Moore, and Christenson examine "The Effect of Dropping Out of High School on Subsequent Criminal Behavior" and conclude that juveniles who are "failures" at school are more likely to be involved in juvenile delinquency while still in school as well as after leaving it. That is, poor school performance predicts current and future higher rates of trouble.

When parents find out that their child has gotten into trouble with the law, they often leap to the conclusion that it only happened because of the influence of their child's friends. In other words, peer pressure is responsible for the criminal behavior of an otherwise model child. Research shows that there is a very strong relationship between negative peer influence and involvement in juvenile delinquency. In fact, the empirical evidence suggests that it may be a better predictor of delinquency than any of the common correlates of involvement. Warr's research on the interactions among "Age, Peers, and Delinquency" shows that the nature and effects of peer influence (exposure to delinquent peers, time spent with peers, and loyalty to peers) change as youths get older, becoming more influential and mirroring the age distribution of involvement in delinquency. This expanding negative peer influence is sufficiently strong that it renders the effects of age on self-reported delinquency insignificant. That is, the substantial increases in delinquency over the teen years can be accounted for by the ever-expanding social influence of friends and associates on delinquent behavior.

Of course, the prototype for negative peer influence is the delinquent gang. Gangs are the collective personification of the danger and threat of juvenile delinquency. Even though gang-related crime is a small portion of the overall delinquency problem, it produces disproportionate public concern and fear. Whether it is the more than 1,000 gangs observed by Thrasher in Chicago in the 1920s or the Bloods and Crips in South Central Los Angeles today, identified groups of delinquents have occupied a featured spot in the public's consciousness and the criminologist's research. Miller may have done more empirical research on delinquent gangs than any other social scientist. In "Violent Crimes in City Gangs," he describes the results of an intensive observational study of many gangs in the Boston area. He concludes that they are not as violent as people believe or fear.

This was before the appearance and proliferation of "crack" cocaine and automatic/semiautomatic weapons among young people, however, particularly in the inner cities of America. Things certainly have changed, but perhaps not as much as most people believe. The major difference is the introduction of guns into the everyday arsenal of weapons that gang members have at their disposal and the greater chance, therefore, that someone will be hurt badly or killed when there is a conflict. Most "modern" gang members, like those observed by Miller more than 30 years ago, do not deal drugs, shoot people, or even engage in serious violent acts. That does not mean that gangs do not attract juvenile delinquents or reinforce their involvement in serious, violent crime. Without a doubt, they do both—but not to the extent that the public believes. After all, the kind of person with greatest risk of becoming a victim of gang violence—whether a drug deal gone sour or a drive-by shooting—is another gang member, even of one's own gang, or an associate or wannabe.

The research of Winfree, Bäckström, and Mays, which is based on self-reports of delinquency rather than on field observations, shows that gang membership affects involvement in group-context personal crimes—offenses committed with the group or under its direct influence—but not in property or more general personal crimes. That is, as one might expect, the delinquency of gang members is most different from that of nongang members when their crimes include collective participation in more typically violent interpersonal acts.

Finally, Fagan, Weis, and Cheng, in "Delinquency and Substance Use Among Inner-City Students," show that there are mistaken beliefs about the extent and nature of drug use in high-crime-rate neighborhoods of our cities. The relationship between drug use and involvement in crime is not simple or direct, with one causing the other. Rather, as with gangs and violence, the research evidence calls into question what many people think they know about the connection between drug use and delinquency.

AGE, SEX, AND VERSATILITY

Age, Sex, and the Versatility of Delinquent Involvements

MICHAEL J. HINDELANG

THERE has been substantial disagreement as to whether delinquent actors generally engage in a wide variety of delinquent acts (i.e., tend to be versatile in their delinquent behavior) or whether they engage in only a very limited variety of delinquent acts (i.e., tend to be specific in their delinquent behavior). The question has also been raised as to whether versatility or specificity varies as a function of the age and sex of the delinquent participants.

In addition to the polemics surrounding the specialization-versatility argument, there have been differing views concerning the relationship between the sex of the actor and the type of delinquent involvement. When official statistics have been examined, it has been argued that there is a cleavage between male and female delinquency; specifically, female delinquency has often been viewed as revolving around "sex" delinquency while male delinquency has been viewed as centering largely around property offenses. Studies using self-report methods have found female delinquents to be more diversified and to be somewhat more similar to male delinquents than official statistics would indicate.

The major aims of the present study are to examine the interrelationships of a variety of self-

From "Age, Sex, and the Versatility of Delinquent Involvements" by M. Hindelang, 1971, *Social Problems 18*, pp. 522-535. Copyright 1971 by the Society for the Study of Social Problems. Reprinted by permission.

reported delinquent activities and to discover the extent to which these interrelationships vary by age and sex in a sample of middle-class to lower-middle-class respondents. The 950 students enrolled in a Catholic coeducational high school in Oakland, California, comprised the population. The 820 students present on the day during which the test battery was administered can be, for the purposes of the present study, viewed as a representative sample of students enrolled in the school. The 24 self-reported delinquency items made up one section of the test battery administered. The 346 males and 474 females present for testing yielded 319 and 444 usable questionnaires, respectively.

For each of the 24 activities listed in Table 1, the respondents were asked to report the number of times in the last year they had engaged in the act. It can be seen from this table that the percentage of respondents who report engaging in each activity—especially among the females—is generally not large.

Among the males, more than half of the respondents report having engaged at least once in cheating on school examinations, drinking, promiscuous sexual behavior, fistfighting, theft of items worth less than $10.00 in value, and vandalism doing less than $10.00 damage; among the females, more than one fifth of the respondents report having engaged at least once in cheating on school examinations, drinking, theft of items worth less than $10.00 in value,

TABLE 1

Male and female self-reported delinquent involvements.

	Percentage Engaging in Act One or More Times			Frequency of Delinquent Involvement					Each Act's Percentage of Total Number of Acts Committed by the Group	
	A	B	C	D	E	F	G	H	I	J
	Male	Female	Ratio	Male		Female		p	Male	Female
				Mean	S.D.	Mean	S.D.			
1. Theft less than $10.00	53.45	26.27	2.03	2.52	3.29	.91	2.05	.01	9.03	8.37
2. Theft greater than $10.00	19.02	4.58	4.15	.59	1.68	.14	.84	.01	2.10	1.23
3. Property destruction (< $10)	51.31	16.35	3.13	1.68	2.45	.41	1.23	.01	6.05	3.80
4. Property destruction (> $10)	23.78	7.72	3.08	.68	1.75	.21	1.03	.01	2.45	1.92
5. Drinking alcohol	63.61	42.79	1.48	3.83	3.88	2.13	3.17	.01	13.73	19.52
6. Getting drunk	39.42	17.44	2.26	1.43	2.57	.37	1.09	.01	5.16	3.38
7. Individual fistfights	56.03	21.64	2.58	2.09	2.72	.56	1.46	.01	7.52	5.12
8. Gang fistfights	25.82	6.27	4.11	.73	1.80	.17	.87	.01	2.61	1.57
9. Carrying a concealed weapon	33.23	10.13	3.28	1.66	3.09	.37	1.47	.01	5.98	3.42
10. Individual weapon fights	11.08	4.10	2.70	.22	.85	.09	.60	.05	0.79	0.82
11. Gang weapon fights	8.47	2.90	2.92	.19	.96	.07	.58	.05	0.68	0.69
12. Gambling	16.34	3.86	4.23	.71	2.08	.14	.81	.01	2.56	1.26
13. Using marijuana	26.15	14.50	1.80	1.40	2.95	.69	2.08	.01	5.04	6.30
14. Sniffing glue	10.75	6.75	1.58	.29	1.22	.21	1.06	n.s.	1.06	1.92
15. Using LSD, methedrine, or mescaline	7.50	4.86	1.54	.27	1.30	.17	.96	n.s.	0.99	1.50
16. Using heroin	4.27	2.90	1.47	.10	.76	.09	.73	n.s.	0.36	0.84
17. Shaking down others for money	9.45	3.15	3.00	.20	.79	.09	.65	.05	0.73	0.80
18. Promiscuous sexual behavior	58.22	11.96	4.86	2.32	3.47	.47	1.68	.01	8.19	4.24
19. Drag racing on street	45.17	22.49	2.01	2.63	3.62	1.10	2.48	.01	6.71	7.27
20. Driving under the influence	21.20	6.36	3.33	.79	2.08	.21	1.07	.01	2.01	1.39
21. Hit-and-run accidents	9.73	7.00	1.39	.21	.87	.19	.97	n.s.	.53	1.26
22. Cheating on exams	71.76	59.67	1.20	3.52	3.53	2.25	2.75	.01	8.93	14.91
23. Using false ID	23.86	15.29	1.56	.95	2.15	.48	1.50	.01	2.42	3.16
24. Cutting school	40.56	24.75	1.63	1.73	2.88	.80	1.95	.01	4.40	5.30
									100%	100%
									(8,315)	(4,527)
	N = 319	N = 444		N = 319		N = 444				

cutting school, drag racing, and fistfighting. For all activities, the percentage of males involved exceeds the percentage of females involved; the ratios are largest for promiscuous sexual behavior, gambling, theft of items worth more than $10.00, and group fistfighting; the ratios are smallest for cheating on school examinations; hit-and-run accidents; heroin use; drinking; using LSD, methedrine, or mescaline; using false ID; and sniffing glue.

Across all 24 activities, the mean male to female ratio was 2.56—less than figures from official sources.

The offenses admitted with the greatest frequency are drinking alcoholic beverages, cheating on school examinations, minor theft, street drag racing, fistfighting, and truancy; those offenses admitted with the least frequency are heroin use, shaking down others, individual weapon fighting, and gang fighting with a weapon. Using either the percentage involved or mean frequency of involvement as the criterion, the offenses most often engaged in are those which are considered petty and which would not most often entail arrest unless persistent.

Table 1 (column H) also shows the probabilities of chance differences between the mean ranks of reported frequencies of delinquent involvement of the males and females. Although the females report markedly less delinquent involvement, the pattern of female delinquency is strikingly similar to that of the males. Within each sex group, the rank order of the mean frequencies of delinquent involvements is nearly identical—the rank-order correlation coefficient for the two groups is .925 ($p < .001$). This finding is certainly inconsistent with the proposition that male and female delinquencies are dissimilar in content. The activities most frequently engaged in by the males are, by and large, the activities most frequently engaged in by the females. It appears to be primarily the frequency of the activities and not the focal activities themselves which differentiates male and female delinquent involvement in this sample.

In order to examine the relationship of the delinquent activities to each other, the complete matrix of intercorrelations was computed for the males and females. Among the females, 244 out of the 276 correlation coefficients are significantly and positively related to each other ($p < .01$). Among the males, 189 out of the 276 correlation coefficients are significantly and positively related to each other ($p < .01$). These findings, that among the females 89%, and among the males 65%, of these quite diverse behaviors are significantly related to one another, give limited support to the contention that the delinquent behavior of this sample is relatively versatile. If delinquent involvements were very specialized, one would expect to find a larger proportion of the correlations to be independent of each other. It is interesting to note that for the males the more innocuous acts tend to be better predictors of the remaining acts than the more serious acts; for the females, this situation is reversed. This is perhaps an artifact of the condition that female delinquency in this sample is more an "all or none" phenomenon than is male delinquency. Independent samples are now being used to more thoroughly investigate this circumstance.

Cohen and Short have suggested that delinquent subcultures may evolve from more versatile behaviors to more specialized behaviors as a function of age. If this is true, then one would expect a decrease in the mean intercorrelation coefficient as age increases. That is, the strength of each item's relationships with two or three other items of similar content would increase, but that item's correlation with the remaining items would decrease. For example, if fighting behaviors became specialized with age, the intercorrelations among individual fistfighting, group fistfighting, carrying a weapon, individual weapon fighting, and group weapon fighting might be expected to increase, while the correlation of these items with other types of delinquent behaviors would be expected to decrease; if specialization increases, the net effect should be a decrease in the mean intercorrelation, when the number of items constituting the speciality (e.g., fighting-related items) is small relative to the number of remaining items. This is true because although the intercorrelations of a few items increase, the intercorrelations of many items decrease.

Both the male and the female respondents were separated into two groups according to their grade in school—a freshman-sophomore group and a junior-senior group. Then within these older and younger groups, for both sexes the intercorrelations for the delinquent activities were again computed. Using either the mean correlation coefficient or the mean communality as a criterion, within each grade group the activities of the females have relatively more generality than the activities of the males. Also, by either criterion, there is no evidence of an increase in specialization with the increase in age. Thus, these data do not support the view that the delinquencies committed by older subjects are more specialized than those committed by younger subjects.

These data are generally consistent with those of Short and Strodtbeck in finding a lack of independence among different types of delinquent involvement. The intercorrelations of the delinquent activities, as well as the intercorrelations of clusters of delinquent activities, argue against the existence of specialized or "pure" delinquent subcultures.

SUMMARY AND CONCLUSIONS

1. The mean frequency of male delinquency is significantly greater than that of female delinquency for all activities except hit-and-run accidents and nonmarijuana drug activities. This finding is consistent with the stereotypic view of the relative incidence of male and female delinquent involvement.

2. Across all activities, the mean ratio of males to females engaging in the act at least once is 2.56. The ratios of male to female involvement are, in general, substantially smaller than official sources indicate.

3. The pattern of female delinquent involvement, although at a reduced frequency, parallels quite closely the pattern of male delinquency; when the mean frequencies of delinquent involvement are ranked for both the males and the females, the rank-order correlation coefficient is found to be .925, which indicates that the most and least frequent activities among the males and females are nearly identical. This finding is at odds with the conception of female delinquents as engaging primarily in "sex" delinquencies.

4. The intercorrelations of the 24 diverse delinquent activities suggests that delinquent involvement is more a generalized than a specialized phenomenon. Among the females, delinquent involvement was found to have more generality than among the males.

5. When the activities were clustered, the correlations among clusters were also indicative of a generalized rather than a specialized delinquent involvement.

6. By analyzing the correlation matrices for four sex-grade subsamples, it was found that the correlation coefficients did not vary substantially across age among either the males or females, which suggests that specialization in delinquent involvement does not increase with age.

7. In interpreting the findings of the present study, the reader should again be reminded that the respondents were drawn from a Catholic high school, and hence the generality of the results is limited to comparable populations; likewise since the respondents are not primarily lower class, and since they have not been shown to be gang delinquents, the findings cannot be directly used to evaluate many of the theoretical propositions referred to above.

QUESTIONS FOR DISCUSSION AND WRITING

1. What percentage of males and females report "having engaged at least once in cheating on school examinations, drinking, promiscuous sexual behavior, fistfighting, theft of items worth less than $10.00 in value, and vandalism doing less than $10.00 damage"? What is true about the percentage of males versus the percentage of females involved?

2. What does column H of Table 1 show and how do the authors interpret this finding?

3. Look over Table 1. What are the top five delinquent acts for males (include the percentages engaging in each)? For females? Where is this sample drawn from (i.e., are these inner-city ghetto school students)?

Juvenile Offender Prevalence, Incidence, and Arrest Rates by Race

DAVID HUIZINGA

DELBERT S. ELLIOTT

Mᴏsᴛ of the data used in this report are taken from the National Youth Survey (NYS), an ongoing, projected longitudinal study of delinquent behavior, alcohol and drug use, and problem-related substance use in the American youth population. To date, six waves of data have been collected on this national youth panel covering the period from 1976 to 1983. The NYS employed a probability sample constructed to be representative of the 11- to 17-year-old population of the continental United States in 1976.

Annual involvement in delinquent behavior and substance use was self-reported by members of the youth panel in confidential, personal (face-to-face) interviews. In most instances, these interviews occurred in the respondent's home. If the situation at home was such that privacy could not be guaranteed, arrangements were made to conduct the interview in some other setting where privacy was assured.

The self-reported delinquency (SRD) measure was constructed as a parallel measure to the FBI's Uniform Crime Reports (UCR) arrest measure. All UCR offense categories involving more than 10% of the reported juvenile arrests

between 1972 and 1974 were included in the initial SRD measure. A number of additional offenses classified in UCR reports as "other offenses" were included as this offense class accounts for approximately 15% of juvenile arrests each year. The resulting set of 47 items (offenses) includes all but one of the UCR Part I offenses (homicide is excluded); 75% of all Part II offenses; and a wide range of "other" offenses—primarily misdemeanors and status offenses. The vast majority of items involve a violation of criminal statutes.

Respondents were asked how many times during the preceding calendar year they committed each offense. In general, the NYS delinquency measures have acceptable levels of reliability and validity. Although there is some concern about levels of underreporting of delinquent behaviors by blacks, the size of this potential error does not affect the basic conclusions presented in this chapter.

In 1979-1980 and in 1984-1985, a search of police records was completed for each respondent in each location where the respondent lived between 1976-1979 and 1976-1983, respectively. Over 90% of all the respondent/agency record checks were completed. For all youth with one or more arrest records, the date of arrest, description of offense, and ancillary information was collected. An individual arrest history that

From "Juvenile Offender Prevalence, Incidence, and Arrest Rates by Race" by D. Huizinga and D. Elliott, 1987, *Crime and Delinquency 33*, pp. 206-223. Copyright 1987 by Sage Publications, Inc. Reprinted by permission.

included all reported arrests was subsequently constructed.

FINDINGS

Before examining differences in delinquent behavior, it is useful to examine the relationship between involvement in delinquent behavior, frequency of arrest, frequency of referral to juvenile court, and the frequency of incarceration. Combining information from the NYS, UCRs, and other sources, very rough estimates of the rates of penetration into different levels of the juvenile justice system can be obtained. Only about 24% of those committing offenses for which they could be arrested are in fact arrested. Of those arrested, approximately 64% are referred to juvenile or adult court, and of those referred to court only about 2% to 10% are incarcerated. Thus, there are several stages between delinquent behavior and incarceration, and only a very small proportion of active offenders are ever incarcerated.

There is a large proportion of offenders (84%) who are never arrested. Not all crimes are reported or known to the police, and not all crimes that are known result in an arrest. As a result, there is a large amount of "hidden crime" not contained in arrest data.

In addition, persons arrested may not be representative of offenders in general. That is, arrestees may not provide an adequate representation of the kinds of active offenders that exist in the population and may provide a biased representation in terms of either delinquency involvement, race, or other characteristics. Given the difficulties in using arrest data to examine the delinquent behavior of individuals and of different groups, a second option is the use of self-report studies, such as the NYS, described earlier. These studies are similar to opinion polls and ask people directly about their offense behavior. Although there is some question about whether people will be honest and report violations they have committed, the evidence indicates that they will report such behaviors as long as their answers are protected by anonymity and confidentiality. For example, offenses recorded in police records are usually reported in self-report surveys.

Using data from the NYS, the prevalence rates by racial groups for measures of general delinquency, UCR index offenses, felony assault, and felony theft are given in Table 1 for each of the years 1976 through 1980. The General Delinquency Scale includes less serious offenses (minor theft, minor assault, property damage, and so on), status offenses, and serious offenses (felony theft, felony assault, robbery, and so forth). Index offenses include all UCR Part II offenses except homicide and minor larcenies. Felony assault includes aggravated assaults, sexual assaults, and gang fights; and felony theft includes grand theft, auto theft, burglary, and possession of stolen goods. Because the same individuals are followed over time in NYS youth panel, the age range changes from 11 to 17 in 1976 to 15 to 21 in 1980.

As seen in Table 1, in comparison with other racial groups, a slightly larger proportion of blacks report involvement in general delinquency offenses in most years. Both blacks and Hispanics report slightly higher rates than whites in involvement in index offenses, and, in general, minority groups have larger proportions reporting involvement in felony assaults. Findings about felony thefts are mixed, with whites exceeding other groups in several years. Few of the differences between racial groups are statistically significant, however. There is no consistency across years such that any one racial group reports statistically higher rates in a majority of years.

Given these findings, it does not appear that differences in incarceration rates between racial groups can be explained by differences in the proportions of persons of each racial group that engage in delinquent behavior. Even if the slightly higher rates for more serious offenses among minorities were given more importance than is statistically indicated, the relative proportions of whites and minorities involved in delinquent behavior could not account for the observed difference in incarceration rates.

TABLE 1

Prevalence rates by ethnicity (percentage of persons).

	Age: 11–17 Year: 1976	12–18 1977	13–19 1978	14–20 1979	15–21 1980	11–17 1976	12–18 1977	13–19 1978	14–20 1979	15–21 1980
	General delinquency					*Index offenses*				
White	67	64	64	65	65	19	16	14	13	12
Black	70	67	70	73	72	29	20	16	20	13
Hispanic	65	69	56	63	59	24	23	17	24	13
Other	56	48	42	48	48	19	22	9	16	12
				*	*	**			**	
	Felony assault					*Felony theft*				
White	15	12	10	10	9	12	12	11	9	9
Black	12	17	11	16	9	14	10	8	7	8
Hispanic	20	23	16	18	13	8	9	13	9	8
Other	19	15	15	12	8	7	14	15	12	16
	**			**						

*Significant at .05 level; **significant at .01 level.

TABLE 2

Offender incidence rates by ethnicity (average number of offenses per offender).

	Age: 11–17 Year: 1976	12–18 1977	13–19 1978	14–20 1979	15–21 1980	11–17 1976	12–18 1977	13–19 1978	14–20 1979	15–21 1980
	General delinquency					*Index offenses*				
White	28.0	25.0	27.2	32.2	33.0	4.8	10.6	5.1	6.5	5.0
Black	35.8	32.2	30.4	33.3	38.0	5.2	10.4	4.0	6.9	4.6
	Felony assault					*Felony theft*				
White	2.7	4.9	3.0	4.3	3.4	6.1	6.8	4.7	6.7	4.6
Black	4.6	5.6	2.1	4.2	2.2	3.0	17.9	7.3	5.0	6.3

Although the proportion of persons engaging in delinquent behavior is not substantially different by race, another behavioral possibility that might account for differences in incarceration rates is the difference in the frequency at which active offenders commit delinquent acts. For example, if each minority offender committed twice as many offenses of a particular type as a white offender and the arrest probability is constant for each offense, then minorities would be twice as likely to be arrested and, presumably, incarcerated.

To examine this possibility, Table 2 contains offender incidence rates (average number of offenses per offender) for race. Blacks report slightly higher rates for general delinquency,

TABLE 3

Arrest rates by severity of offense by race.

Most Serious Reported Offense	Percentage of Group That Are Offenders		Most Serious Arrest					
			Percentage of Offenders Arrested for Nonindex Offense		Percentage of Offenders Arrested for an Index Offense		Percentage of Offenders Arrested for Any Offense	
Nonindex offenses								
White	52.7		13.1		0.5		13.6	
Black	44.8		6.1		3.7		9.9	
Other	47.1	n.s.	9.0	n.s.	0.0	.05	9.0	n.s.
Index offenses								
White	34.9		23.9		5.9		29.8	
Black	44.8		14.8		13.5		28.3	
Other	35.7	n.s.	20.0	n.s.	12.0	.10	32.0	n.s.
Any offense								
White	87.7		17.4		2.7		20.1	
Black	89.5		10.5		8.6		19.1	
Other	82.9	n.s.	13.7	n.s.	5.1	.01	18.9	n.s.

Note: Level of statistical significance between groups is given at bottom of each column; n.s. = not significant.

but none of these differences or any of the differences for any other delinquency scale or year is statistically significant. Thus, it appears that there are essentially no consistent differences between white and black offender incidence rates and that such differences could not explain the observed differences in arrest or incarceration rates.

Overall, these findings suggest that there are few if any substantial and consistent differences between the delinquency involvement of different racial groups. This finding relative to prevalence rates is not unique. Other large-scale self-report studies of delinquency have reached similar conclusions.

There are no earlier national estimates of individual offending rates, but the NYS data suggest there are no racial differences in this measure of offending either. As a result, it does not appear that differences in delinquent behavior can provide an explanation for the observed race differential in incarceration rates.

If differences in delinquent behavior do not explain the differential in incarceration rates, then differences in official responses to offenders/offenses (i.e., arrest rates, rates of referral to juvenile court, and court processing) would seem likely candidates to explore as major determinants of the differential in incarceration rates. Using data from the NYS, some preliminary findings about arrest rates within racial groups were obtained. These data combine information from the first five waves of the NYS (1976-1980) and are provided in Table 3. It must be emphasized that these data are very preliminary. More detailed analyses are currently under way within the NYS but are not yet available. Still, these preliminary analyses reveal some interesting relationships.

It should first be noted that although there are some sizable differences between racial groups in the percentage of offenders, percentage arrested for nonindex offenses, and percentage arrested for any offense, none of these differences are statistically significant ($p < .05$). Statistically significant differences are found, however, between different racial groups in the percentage of offenders arrested for index offenses. Among less serious, nonindex offenders, blacks have a significantly higher chance of being arrested for an index offense. The rates are approximately in a 7 to 1 ratio. For the more serious index offenders, both black and other minority offenders have significantly higher arrest rates for index offenses, with approximately a 2 to 1 ratio for minority groups as compared to whites. These translate to an overall arrest rate for serious offenses among minority groups that is approximately two to three times that of whites. Thus, it would appear that among minority offenders the "risk" of being apprehended and charged with an index offense is substantially and significantly higher than it is for whites who report involvement in the same kinds of offenses.

There are several explanations for this finding. As one possibility, minority arrestees charged with an index offense may be more delinquent than their white counterparts. An examination of the mean general delinquency and index offense scales among index arrestees by racial group did not support this contention, however. Another possibility is that minority offenders may more frequently commit offenses that involve greater physical injury to victims or the use of weapons, and thus when apprehended have a greater chance of being charged with a more serious offense. An examination of this possibility indicated that there were essentially no racial differences in the severity of offenses as indicated by these factors. Among other explanations are factors affecting the probability of apprehension and the probability of being charged with an index offense after apprehension, police surveillance practices, and offender demeanor. Consideration of these explanations is beyond the scope of this chapter.

CONCLUSION

The preliminary finding of higher arrest rates for serious offenses among minority group offenders provides an indication of factors that may influence the differential incarceration rate among racial groups. Although studies that control for arrest history commonly find little evidence of racial bias in juvenile justice system processing, the information presented suggests that bias may exist in the nature of the offense charged at the time of arrest, a factor related to justice agency decision making. Minorities appear to be at greater risk for being charged with more serious offenses than whites involved in comparable levels of delinquent behavior, a factor that may eventually result in higher incarceration rates among minorities. However, as indicated earlier, there are several steps between arrest and incarceration. A more complete understanding of why a disproportionate number of minorities are incarcerated will likely require longitudinal information about delinquent behavior patterns, arrests, and factors surrounding arrests, referrals to court, court processing, and sentence decisions.

Of particular importance may be the relationship between social class, race, and juvenile justice system processing. Because the majority of minority individuals are in the lower socioeconomic class (NYS data estimates that approximately 73% to 75% of minority youth are in the lower social classes as measured by Hollingshead Index of Social Position), it is possible that social class and social conditions may affect the ability to avoid apprehension, the ability to avoid arrest if apprehended, the presence of parental and legal support at both arrest and court-processing stages, and general demeanor at points of contact with the juvenile justice system. In addition, there are indications of differences in offending rates among social classes so that offending rates may be a class-linked but not race-linked phenomenon. Clearly, additional information is required to examine factors affecting incarceration rates more completely.

In conclusion, a summary of the findings would suggest that differences in incarceration rates among racial groups cannot be explained by differences in offense behavior among these groups. The assertion that differential incarceration rates stem directly from differences in delinquency involvement is not supported by these analyses. There is some indication of differential arrest rates for serious crimes among the racial groups, but further investigation of the relationship of race to arrest and juvenile justice system processing is required if reasons underlying the differences in incarceration rates are to be more fully understood.

QUESTIONS FOR DISCUSSION AND WRITING

1. What is the NYS and why is it believed to be representative of the 11- to 17-year-old population of the continental United States in 1976?
2. What does a comparison of the racial groups in Table 1 show? Given these findings, what do the authors conclude?
3. What may be of "particular importance" and why might this be true?

CLASS

Social Class and Crime

JOSEPH G. WEIS

MORE research and theoretical attention has been devoted to the role of social class in the etiology of crime than to any other variable. The empirical relation between social class and criminal behavior was first established with ecological correlations and official crime data, while the theoretical relation has been made a central etiological dynamic in most major theories of crime, including strain, conflict, cultural deviance, and labeling perspectives. With the notable exception of control theory, contemporary theories of crime depend on a robust, significant, and meaningful negative correlation between social class and crime. According to some scholars, this relationship is a "thoroughly documented" fact; to others, its documentation as a predominant correlate is inconsistent, weak, and unconvincing.

There are two critical research issues regarding the apparently elusive correlation between social class and crime. The first was raised by the startling finding of Short and Nye of no relationship between self-reported delinquent behavior and parents' socioeconomic status (SES). The second issue was raised by the recent work of Hindelang, Hirschi, and Weis on the measurement of crime, particularly on the discrepancy between correlations produced by different measurement methods. If there is a negative correlation between social class and crime, is it found in both official and self-report measures of crime? Discrepant correlations may reflect empirical reality or inadequate measurement.

The controversy surrounding these research issues continues, but most research is incapable of assessing them because studies typically rely on only one measure of crime, either official data or self-reports, precluding a direct comparison of the correlations generated by each measurement method on the same sample. Usually, it is assumed that there is a strong inverse relation between class and official crime and the self-report estimates are compared with this standard. However, this relationship was established with ecological correlations that tend to overestimate substantially individual-level correlations. And it is not clear that there is, indeed, a relationship between social class and official measures of crime.

Two meta-analyses of the class-crime relationship come to opposite conclusions regarding the correlation between social class and official crime measures. Tittle et al. report no important relationship, while Braithwaite concludes in a later review that there is some evidence to support an official crime-class correlation. Finally, when one examines those studies using individual-level official data only, the relationship between social class and official delinquency is weakly negative to nonexistent. A more recent longitudinal study of a cohort of 7,719 boys in Stockholm also reports no important individual-level relationship between a family's social position and a boy having a police record.

Self-report studies typically also report no relationship between individual-level measures of self-reported crime and class. However, there is a recent exception to the trend in reported findings of self-report studies. Elliott and Ageton report from analyses of the National Youth Survey (NYS) probability sample of approximately 1,500 youths that there is a moderate inverse relationship between SES and serious "person crimes" and serious "property crimes," particularly for the former among black youths. Later analyses of the panel for 1976 to 1980 show small to moderate class differences in prevalence and incidence for serious crimes, and the relationship is stronger for incidence than prevalence scales.

The small number of studies that are capable of assessing rigorously the discrepancy between social class and official and self-report measures of crime show somewhat mixed results. Of the five major studies reviewed by Hindelang, Hirschi, and Weis that have both individual-level official and self-report measures on the same sample, all showed convergent estimates of the correlation between social class *and* official and self-reported crime. Four of these studies reported convergence around no relationship, while only one showed convergent estimates of a small inverse relationship.

Two other major studies report convergent correlations. In an important reanalysis of the follow-up interview data from the Philadelphia cohort study, Thornberry and Farnworth report that there is no important relationship between status, as measured primarily by educational attainment, and criminal involvement, whether measured by self-report interview or official police arrest data, when the cohort members were *juveniles*. However, there was a significant inverse relationship between status and both official and self-reported crime when the cohort members were *adults*. That is, convergent estimates of the class-crime relationship are produced for juveniles and adults, but they are in different directions. Apparently, the effect of social class varies by age status—one should not assume that the operation of social class is the same at 15 as it is at 25.

Finally, Hindelang et al. propose that the alleged discrepancy between self-report and official measures for social class, as well as for gender and race, becomes "illusory" when standard but critical methodological considerations are taken into account, particularly comparisons of results by level of measurement and by the domain, content, and seriousness of criminal behavior. If the data are properly analyzed by comparing individual-level measures of both official and self-reported crime with individual-level measures of class, and the types and seriousness of crimes compared are the same, the alleged discrepancy for social class is resolved. A comprehensive empirical test of these hypotheses shows that there is a very weak, insignificant relationship with SES when one controls for level of measurement and compares individual-level data on both variables. It seems that no matter how one measures, scores, or scales the data there are small, typically negative relations between social class and juvenile crime, whether official or self-report. The correlations (gamma) range from −.01 to −.08 between occupation of principal wage earner and the self-reported delinquency prevalence scales (Total, Serious Crime, General Delinquency, Drug Use, Family-School Offenses) and the total official offenses index. In short, there is not the kind of robust relationship between social class and either self-reported or official juvenile crime that most contemporary theories of crime propose should exist.

THE CURRENT STUDY

These results are perplexing because a few rigorous studies report a moderate inverse relation between social class and self-reported crime (e.g., Elliott et al.), while more equally rigorous studies show an absent to weak inverse relation for *both* self-report and official measures (e.g., Hindelang et al.). In an effort to clarify the current confusion, analyses of the social class and juvenile crime relationship in the Seattle Youth Study (SYS) data set will be carried further than reported in Hindelang, Hirschi, and Weis. The continuing search for the elusive correlation between social class and crime will focus on methodological and substantive factors that might produce a meaningful correlation.

First, given the apparent success in finding an inverse relationship between class and delinquency in the NYS, the procedures used by Elliott et al. will be replicated as closely as possible. In addition to the same methodological adjustments (same level of measurement, domain, content, and seriousness of offenses) recommended by Hindelang et al., they offer the additional suggestions that the proper analysis of self-report data should include more attention to scoring and scaling of items. Specifically, Elliott et al. argue that the reported frequency of illegal acts should not be restricted in the scoring of individuals and that the unique properties and contributions of individual crimes that may be related to social class (or other variables) not be masked or lost in global scales of delinquency.

Accordingly, these analyses will also use unrestricted incidence rather than prevalence scores of criminal involvement during the past year; NYS scales will be replicated in scale analyses; item analyses will be performed, particularly for those crimes that are included in the NYS scales; and the analytic procedures and statistics used by Elliott et al. will be employed in the current analyses. Perhaps these additional methodological refinements will generate correlations in the SYS similar to those discovered in the NYS.

Second, if replicating the technical tinkering with the self-report measurement method does not also replicate the elusive inverse correlation, one of a number of substantive factors—particularly potential "ecological context" effects—will be explored that may help specify the relation between social class and crime.

The data to be analyzed were collected during the 1978-1979 academic year in Seattle, Washington, on a random sample of over 1,600 youths, stratified by sex, race (black, white), SES (high, low), and delinquency status (nondelinquent, police record, court record). Both official records of police and court contact and self-reports of involvement in 69 "chargeable offenses" were collected on the sample, as well as other demographic and social information. Males, blacks, lower SES, and official delinquents were oversampled in order to facilitate analysis on those variables of etiological and methodological interest that are often underrepresented in general random or probability samples. The data were collected within a quasi-experimental design to assess the effects of different measurement methods on estimates of the prevalence, incidence, and, particularly, correlates of juvenile crime.

In order to replicate the procedures used in the analysis of the NYS, one social class scale and two sets of self-reported delinquency scales were simulated with the SYS data. Following Elliott and Ageton, a set of *offense-category* scales was constructed, and following Elliott and Huizinga, a set of *offense-specific* scales was constructed (Table 1). In total, 37 of the 69 self-report items in the Seattle data are included in these various scales; they also serve as the basis of the item-by-item analyses. The scales are past-year *incidence* scales, computed by adding frequency responses to the question "How many times in the past year have you . . . ?" The incidence reported for an item is not restricted or truncated in any meaningful way—the reported frequency of involvement for a crime may range from 0 to 998. There were only a few items for a few respondents with higher frequencies, and the variance with the given range should be sufficient to show a relationship if it exists.

The three social class categories used in the analyses of the NYS were simulated by converting the SYS occupational and educational codes into their equivalents in the Hollingshead Two-Factor Index of Social Position. Following the Hollingshead scoring procedures, as did the NYS analyses, a social position score was computed for each member of the sample, who was then assigned to the corresponding middle-, working-, or lower-class category. Apparently, social class has been trichotomized in order to facilitate comparisons based on group means and differences (e.g., ANOVA, t test), rather

TABLE 1

Comparison of self-reported delinquency scale items.

National Youth Survey (NYS)	Seattle Youth Study (SYS)

Offense—specific

Felony assault
   Aggravated assault   Seriously injured victim
   Sexual assault   Forced sex
   Gang fights   Jumped and beat up someone

Minor assault
   Hit teacher   Hit teacher
   Hit parents   Hit parents
   Hit students   Picked fight with stranger

Robbery
   Strongarmed students   Robbery with weapon
   Strongarmed teachers   Strongarm robbery
   Strongarmed others

Felony theft
   Bought stolen goods   Bought stolen goods
   Stole something greater than $50   Shoplift greater than $50
   Stole motor vehicle   Broke into car
   Broke into buildings/vehicle   Burglary
                                                           Breaking and entering

Minor theft
   Joyriding   Took car
   Stole something less than $5   Shoplifting less than $2
   Stole something $5–$50   Shoplifting $10–$50

Damaged property
   Damaged family property   Broke up furniture
   Damaged school property   Broke school windows
   Damaged other property   Broke car windows
                                                             Broke windows/empty building
                                                           Slash seats
                                                           Destroy mailboxes
                                                           Destruction at construction site

Drug use   (Hard drug use)
   Hallucinogens   LSD, PCP, mescaline
   Barbiturates   Barbiturates
   Heroin   Heroin
   Cocaine   Cocaine
   Amphetamines

(continued)

TABLE 1   (Continued)

National Youth Survey (NYS)	Seattle Youth Study (SYS)
Offense category	
Illegal services	(Selling drugs)
Sold hard drugs	Sold illegal drugs
Sold marijuana	
Prostitution	
Public disorder	(Disorderly conduct)
Hitchhiked illegally	Carried weapon
Disorderly conduct	Smoked marijuana
Public drunkenness	High/drunk at school
Panhandled	
Obscene calls	
Status offenses	
Runaway	Runaway
Skipped classes	Cut school
Lied about age	Drank beer/wine
Sexual intercourse	Drank hard liquor
Person crimes	
Aggravated assault	Seriously injured victim
Gang fights	Jumped and beat up victim
Hit teacher	Hit teacher
Hit parent	Hit parent
Hit students	Picked fight with stranger
Sexual assault	Forced sex
Strongarmed students	Robbery with weapon
Strongarmed teachers	Strongarm robbery
Strongarmed others	
General theft	(Property crimes)
Stole something greater than $50	Shoplifted greater than $50
Stole something less than $5	Shoplifted less than $2
Stole something $5–$50	Shoplifted $10–$50
Bought stolen goods	Bought stolen goods
Joyriding	Took car
Stole motor vehicle	Broke into car
Broke into buildings/vehicle	Breaking and entering
	Burglary
	Sell stolen goods
	Stole from desk, locker
	Broke car windows
	Broke school windows
	Broke windows, empty building
	Broke up furniture
	Slashed seats
	Destroyed mailboxes
	Destruction at construction site

TABLE 2

Self-reported delinquency scales by ecological measures of class: National Youth Survey scales, census tract-level measures of class, Pearson correlations.

	Middle Class[a]	Median Family Income	Families Below Poverty	Residents Below Poverty	Families Receiving Welfare	Black
Total SRD	.04	.06*	−.02	−.02	−.01	−.04
Person crimes	.01	.01	.01	.02	.00	.02
Property crimes	.02	.07*	−.04	−.04	.01	−.04
Selling drugs	.02	.03	−.02	−.02	−.01	.01
Disorderly conduct	.03	.04	.00	−.01	.01	−.01
Hard drug use	.01	.00	−.01	.00	.00	−.02
Status offenses	.05*	.04	−.02	−.01	−.02	−.05*

a. Middle class refers to percentage employed in managerial or professional occupations.
*$p < .05$.

than those based on individual attributes and difference (e.g., correlation).

Using these simulated scales, the original SYS scales, and individual delinquency items, the analyses reported here will attempt to discover and specify, once again, the relation between social class and juvenile crime.

ECOLOGICAL MEASURES OF CLASS

As reported by Hindelang, Hirschi, and Weis, ecological measures of social class do not show even a moderate relation with either self-report or official measures of juvenile crime. The largest gamma (−.17) is between official delinquency and social status as measured by median income of the census tract in which respondents live. The relations with the self-reported delinquency prevalence scales (Total, Serious Crime, General Delinquency, Drug Use, Family-School Offenses) are even smaller, ranging from .01 to −.06. When additional ecological measures of social class (percentage of families below the poverty level; percentage of residents below the poverty level; percentage of labor force "middle class" or in managerial and pro-

fessional occupations; percentage of families receiving welfare; median income of families) are examined for their relation with other delinquency scales—the NYS self-report scales (Person, Property, Illegal Service, Public Disorder, Hard Drug Use, Status Offenses)—the relationship is virtually the same (Table 2). For example, the largest correlation (.07) is between property crimes and median family income. The strongest relation among whites is between total offenses and median family income (.06), whereas for blacks it is between person crimes and median family income (−.06). And the other four ecological measures show similar weak relations with these self-reported delinquency scales.

The relations with the three official measures of delinquency—Police Contacts Ever, Police Contacts Past Year, Juvenile Court Referrals Ever—also show weak but slightly larger coefficients. For example, the strongest relation for the total sample is between percentage families on welfare with police contacts ever (.10); the highest for whites (.07) and blacks (12) are also with police contacts ever. Apparently, as the percentage of welfare families in a census tract increases, there is a weak relationship with police contacts.

TABLE 3

Self-reported delinquency scales by individual-level measures of class: National Youth Survey scales, individual-level measures of class, Pearson correlations.

	Father's Education	Father's Occupation	Father's Employment	Father's SES	Mother's Education	Mother's Occupation	Mother's Employment	Mother's SES
Total SRD	−.07*	.04	−.07*	−.02	−.03	−.03	−.06*	−.02
Person crimes	−.01	−.02	.00	−.05*	−.01	.00	−.02	.00
Property crimes	−.04	.02	−.04	−.01	−.06*	.02	.01	.02
Selling drugs	−.02	−.02	.00	.01	.01	−.01	.02	−.02
Disorderly conduct	−.07*	.03	−.07*	−.02	−.01	−.03	−.07*	−.03
Hard drug use	−.02	.00	−.01	.00	.00	.01	−.02	.01
Status offenses	−.02	.02	−.05*	.01	−.02	−.03	−.04	.00

*$p < .05$.

Overall, these additional analyses of the relation between a variety of ecological measures of class and a variety of self-report and official measures of juvenile crime confirm Hindelang, Hirschi, and Weis. But the data suggest that there may be ecological factors that affect the social class-official delinquency relation. This may be associated with the ecological contexts within which different types of youths reside—this possibility will be explored later.

INDIVIDUAL MEASURES OF CLASS

At the individual level of measurement of both social class and self-reported and official delinquency, there are, again, uniformly small and typically negative correlations that range from −.01 to −.08 between occupation of principal wage earner and the SYS self-report and official delinquency scales. When one goes beyond these analyses and (a) uses the same SYS plus the NYS self-report scales but scored for incidence or the total unrestricted frequency within

the past year; (b) examines each of the three official delinquency indexes (Police Contacts Ever, Police Contacts Past Year, Juvenile Court Referrals Ever); (c) does an item-by-item analysis of the self-reported delinquency items; and (d) examines each of their (a, b, c) relationships with social class separately with a variety of indicators of SES, including father's education, father's occupation, mother's education, mother's occupation, father employed, mother employed, father's SES, and mother's SES, one *still* finds consistently weak to nonexistent relations that at times are in the wrong direction.

Beginning with the SYS self-reported delinquency scales, the strongest relation is −.09 between family-school offenses and father's education. The relations between the NYS scales and the eight individual-level measures of class are also consistently weak and negative, ranging from .04 to −.07 (Table 3). For the three SYS official delinquency indexes, the relations are similarly weak. The strongest relation (−.08) is between juvenile court referrals ever and father's education. Finally, an item-by-item

TABLE 4

Self-reported delinquency scales by father's SES: National Youth Survey scales and SES categories, mean standardized scale scores, one-way analysis of variance.

Class	N	$\overline{X}$	SD	N	$\overline{X}$	SD	N	$\overline{X}$	SD	N	$\overline{X}$	SD
	Total SRD			*Person Crimes*			*Property Crimes*			*Selling Drugs*		
Lower	383	−.130	12.118	444	.218	4.473	417	.204	8.058	452	.008	1.019
Working	253	−.151	14.996	299	−.018	4.618	283	.064	7.067	303	.014	1.044
Middle	277	−.213	11.243	304	−.194	2.736	292	−.369	4.500	306	.100	1.482
F	.004			.560			.557			.210		
p	.996			.571			.573			.811		
	Disorderly Conduct			*Hard Drug Use*			*Status Offenses*					
Lower	432	−.129	1.706	450	.036	3.116	422	−.032	2.387			
Working	290	.032	2.337	311	−.179	.766	297	−.058	2.584			
Middle	307	.050	2.274	314	.104	3.650	307	.182	3.151			
F	.891			1.224			1.686					
p	.410			.295			.186					

analysis of the 69 self-reported criminal acts also produces consistently weak correlations with each indicator of social class. The strongest relation for the total sample is −.08 for skipping school and mother's education; among whites the largest correlation is −.09 between skipping school and mother's education, while for blacks it is .17 between purse/wallet theft and mother's SES.

Overall, these findings from correlational analyses further substantiate a systematically weak relationship between a variety of measures of social class and (a) a variety of self-reported delinquency incidence scales, (b) a variety of official crime indexes, and (c) a number of self-report items, all at the individual level of measurement. These findings also provide more evidence that there is no discrepancy in the correlation between social class and official or self-report measures of crime.

Given that Elliott and Ageton were able to tease out an inverse relation between social class and predatory person crimes, especially among blacks, by analyzing group differences in juvenile crime, it may be possible to discover similar relations in the SYS data by replicating their procedures.

ANALYSIS OF SOCIAL CLASS GROUP DIFFERENCES

Analyses of variance on the relationship between the NYS self-reported delinquency scales and tripartite social class categories support the findings of the prior correlational analyses. Using mean standardized scores on the offense-category scales and class divisions based on father's SES, there are no significant or meaningful relationships between social class and self-reported delinquency (Table 4).

The SYS data once again allow similar analyses of variance on the relation between class and official delinquency. Here there is one significant relation ($f = 3.115$; $p = .05$) between police contacts ever and father's occupation among the many differences compared. This is a significant but small correlation, which may reflect the large size of the total sample. This artifactual quality is supported by the absence of significant relations between official delinquency and social class among whites and blacks. And analyses of variance show that there are no statistically significant relations between self-reported delinquency and class among the official delinquents in the sample who have police and juvenile court records. It seems that even among the "most delinquent" members of the sample there is a consistently weak correlation. Given the hundreds of differences computed, it is difficult to know if this is a meaningful or "chance" significant difference. It is definitely not part of a consistent pattern of inverse relationships between social class and crime.

Following Elliott and Huizinga, social class group differences on offense category scales, offense-specific scales, and individual delinquency items were analyzed using pooled variance t tests. The comparisons were performed for the entire sample, white males, and black males. For the entire sample and black males, there are no significant differences among any of the three social class groups on all of the self-reported offense-category and offense-specific scales. Among white males, there are no significant differences on any of the offense category scales, but there is one significant difference between the middle and lower class on one of the offense-specific scales—damaged property. Here, the lower-class boys are more involved than middle-class boys in damaging property. Overall, this means that there is one significant difference among the 108 comparisons of the 12 self-reported delinquency scales by the three social class categories for the three groups of respondents. This could be a random significant finding.

The results of the item analysis are more mixed. For the entire sample, there are six significant differences in the expected direction between the social class groups on four crimes—robbery with a weapon, jumped and beat someone up, shoplifting greater than $50, and breaking windows in an empty building. These four crimes are among the most serious of the 37 self-reported offenses tested. They involve violent crimes against the person and high-value crimes against property. And the largest number of significant differences (four) on these crimes are between middle- and lower-class youths, findings similar to those reported by Elliott et al.

These results must be placed within the appropriate analytic context—the six statistically significant differences represent less than 5% of all 111 comparisons made and each has a small t value (ranging around 2.0) that is just above the cutoff point for significance given the sample size. Additionally, the same tests performed separately for white males and black males provide a broader perspective on these findings. Among the white males, there are also six significant differences in the expected direction. Lower-class boys are more involved than middle-class boys in robbery with a weapon, shoplifting greater than $50, breaking windows in an empty building, and the use of hard drugs. Lower-class boys are more involved than working-class boys in taking a car and breaking windows in an empty building. Among the black males, there is only one significant difference between middle- and lower-class boys on breaking windows in an empty building.

Again, the differences between middle- and lower-class youths are most prominent, and for the more serious crimes, as one would expect. However, these additional comparisons contribute to a total of only 13 significant social class differences among 333 comparisons—representing less than 4% of the total and, perhaps, random differences. However, the apparently more regular middle- versus lower-class differences on similar serious crimes suggest that the differences are not random, particularly for the entire sample and white males. But the almost virtual absence of class differences among black males supports the overall perception of a weak, unsystematic class effect.

If social class affects involvement in only a small number of certain types of crime among only certain types of offenders (and it is not clear from the data that this is so), the evidence from these analyses of social class group differences lends support to the conclusion of the correctional analysis that there is no meaningful relationship between social class and crime. Most theories of crime and their validation research require a stronger, more systematic, and perhaps more pervasive class effect. In short, social class should be doing more etiological work than the evidence shows.

ECOLOGICAL CONTEXT EFFECTS: CENSUS TRACTS AND NEIGHBORHOODS

It is somewhat disturbing that the agreed-upon standard methodological adjustments that need to be applied to these data comparisons (same level of measurement, same domain of criminal acts, more sensitive scoring and scaling procedures) do not go far enough in generating a meaningful relationship between social class and crime. Even type of sample design does not seem to generate predictable relationships; for example, the two national probability samples of youth generate different relationships between self-reported delinquency and class, and the earlier NYS data show convergence around no relationship. More "substantive" adjustments may need to be considered. For example, the fact that some self-report studies report no relationship between social class and crime, while others do, suggests that social class may operate in different ways in different ecological contexts, whether social area, neighborhood, community, or city.

Theoretically, ecological context should affect the relationship between social class and crime—it provides the social milieu within which the daily, direct effects of those social, economic, and educational factors and relationships that make up "social class" are experienced as one grows, lives, and works. Where and among whom one experiences these effects should make a difference, perhaps even in relationship to one's criminal behavior. To see if ecological context does affect the influence of social class, one needs to examine the individual-level class-crime relation within different ecological contexts—for example, within a variety of neighborhoods in a city. The SYS data are unique in that both self-report and official crime measures can be used in this type of analysis because both can be linked to census tract through the address of respondents.

Beginning with census tract ecological contexts, the results once again show inconsistent weak negative relations. By trichotomizing the census tracts ($N = 120$) on each of six ecological variables (percentage of families below the poverty level; percentage of residents below poverty level; median income of families; percentage of families receiving welfare; percentage black; employment rate), one can look at the relation between the NYS self-report scales and the eight social class indicators within each type of census tract ecological context. For example, for those respondents who live in census tracts where there is a small percentage (0-3%) of families below the poverty level (low-poverty census tracts), the strongest relation between class and self-reported delinquency is –.11, between disorderly conduct and mother's employment status. In the medium-poverty census tracts (4-10% of families below poverty level), it is between disorderly conduct and father's SES (–.08). In the high-poverty census tracts (11-40% of families below poverty level), the largest correlation is –.12, between property crimes and mother's education. These correlations are certainly in the right direction, but they are weak and, perhaps most important here, there is really no difference by type of census tract ecological context. The same analyses were also done for each of the other five census tract characteristics with similar results.

"Census tract" is really too small an ecological context to have much social meaning or impact on the lives of its residents. "Neighborhood" may be a more powerful social context for generating, or at least reinforcing and maintaining, class effects on criminal behavior, as well as on other phenomena. Seattle has 14 neighborhoods that are linked with its "Seven Hills" and other identifiable areas in the city, each with its own name and identity, which are well recognized and even institutionalized on the maps of the city's Office of Community Development. These 14 neighborhoods were divided into three groups based on the median income of families within their constituent census tracts, and then *within* each neighborhood context (high, middle, low) the relations between both the seven NYS self-report scales and three SYS official delinquency indexes and the eight social-class indicators were examined.

For the total sample, nearly all correlations are not significant. The strongest relations with self-reported delinquency within the three types of neighborhoods, from high- to middle- to low-median income, are –.12, –.10, and –.14. The strongest relations with official delinquency are similar: –.07, –.11, and –.13. These findings basically replicate the earlier Hindelang et al. work, and the earlier analyses here—there is still a weak negative relation between social class and crime within high-, middle-, and low-SES neighborhoods, *and* there is still no discrepancy between the self-report and official correlates of social class. Of some interest are the apparently stronger relations between both parents' education and delinquency within the middle-income neighborhoods. The middle-class value of education may have, one might hypothesize, a more substantial effect than other indicators of social class in those neighborhoods and among those families where education is important to occupation and socialization of children. In short, different components of social class may affect crime in different ways in different ecological contexts.

CONCLUSION

Most theories of criminal behavior are constructed around the assumption of a strong negative correlation between social class and crime. However, the empirical evidence shows that there is not the kind of meaningful inverse relationship between social class and both official and self-report measures of crime that are required for their empirical validation. To the contrary, extended analyses of the SYS data show that there is a systematically weak relationship, no matter how one measures, scales, or scores the data. The replication of analytic procedures used by Elliott et al. in their discovery of an inverse relationship in the NYS data—unrestricted incidence scales, item analysis, tests of group differences—did not produce the same results. Except for a small number of social class group differences on a few self-report items, these findings support the general conclusion that there is a systematically weak relationship between social class, measured by a number of different indicators, and a variety of self-reported delinquency incidence scales, a number of official crime indexes, and a large number of self-reported crime items, all at the individual level of measurement. The findings also provide more evidence for convergence, rather than discrepancy, in the correlation between social class and official and self-report measures of crime. Perhaps, social class as a correlate of crime is not so elusive after all—it may simply not exist as proposed or assumed by criminological theorists and researchers.

QUESTIONS FOR DISCUSSION AND WRITING

1. As reported by Hindelang, Hirschi, and Weis's ecological measures of social class, how strong are relationships between ecological measures of social class and self-report or official measures of juvenile crime?
2. Overall, what do the findings regarding individual measures of class substantiate?
3. Around what assumption are most theories of criminal behavior constructed, and what is the reality?

Reconsidering the Relationship Between SES and Delinquency: Causation but Not Correlation

BRADLEY R. ENTNER WRIGHT
AVSHALOM CASPI
TERRIE E. MOFFITT
RICHARD A. MIECH
PHIL A. SILVA

SOCIOECONOMIC status (SES) has played a dominant role in the history of sociological explanations of delinquency. Various sociological theories hold that low SES brings about individuals' participation in delinquency through a variety of causal mechanisms. This assumed negative effect of SES upon delinquency fits researchers' intuition as well as general public opinion. There is a problem, though. Empirical studies consistently have found weak or nonexistent correlations between individuals' socioeconomic background and their self-reported delinquent behavior. This has created a peculiar mismatch between theory and empirical research: Do low levels of SES cause high levels of delinquency, as per theory, or are the two only weakly correlated or noncorrelated, as per empirical findings? The answer given in this article is yes to both questions, and our explanation hinges on the idea that causation does not necessarily denote statistical correlation.

We develop our approach to this issue with three propositions: (a) The effect of SES upon delinquency is primarily indirect, operating through various causal mediators; (b) through some mediators, such as those identified in classical criminological theories, low SES causes high levels of delinquency; and (c) through other mediators, such as those identified in power control theory and social-psychological theories of conformity, high SES causes high levels of delinquency. Taken together, these propositions suggest that the coexisting negative and positive effects of SES upon delinquency cancel each other out across individuals, thus attenuating any overall correlation between the two phenomena. We test these propositions by identifying a series of social-psychological characteristics that link SES and delinquency, both negatively and positively. These social-psychological mediators allow for analysis of the various effects of SES upon delinquency.

STUDIES OF SES AND DELINQUENCY

Given the theoretical centrality of SES in explanations of delinquency, a rather significant empirical problem has arisen: Studies have found that general measures of SES and delinquency are often, and perhaps usually, not correlated. This counterintuitive finding was initially discovered in the first studies of self-reported measures of delinquency. Since then, most studies of this issue have found the same null relationship between omnibus measures of SES and delinquency.

This robust null finding has obvious theoretical implications. If SES and delinquency are not highly associated in empirical data, should they be so in theories? Without SES, some theories of delinquency would lose their conceptual underpinning; thus, the relationship between the two is of central theoretical importance.

One response to this theoretical quandary has been to recast the SES-delinquency issue as one of specification: In which circumstances are SES and delinquency most strongly correlated? This approach, however, suffers several problems. Empirically, a review of the specification literature found no consistent support for any of the most commonly hypothesized specifying conditions. Conceptually, this approach to the SES-delinquency issue suffers from an inherent loss of parsimony, for the single theoretical relationship between general measures of SES and crime fragments into many relationships between types of measures across groups of people across settings.

RECONSIDERING THE SES-DELINQUENCY RELATIONSHIP

In this article, we return to the general relationship between SES and delinquency and offer an explanation for why individuals' SES and delinquency are not, and in fact should not be, strongly correlated.

The Link Between SES and Delinquency Is Indirect

Our first proposition is that the effect of SES upon delinquency is primarily indirect and operates through various mediating variables. Individuals' SES alters a variety of life contexts and chances, such as neighborhoods, local environmental conditions, cultures, economic opportunities, family conditions, peer networks, attitudes, and behaviors. These factors, in turn, can have more proximal effects upon delinquency, thus linking SES to delinquency. In this article, we focus on social-psychological mediators such as attitudes, values, and personal traits.

Low SES Causes Delinquency

Our second proposition is that low SES can increase individuals' propensity for delinquency through various causal mediators; that is, SES has a negative effect on delinquency. Various criminological theories have negatively linked, either explicitly or implicitly, SES and delinquency through social-psychological mediators. For example, Merton's strain theory holds that crime results when a society strongly emphasizes culturally valued goals without providing the corresponding culturally approved means with which to achieve those goals. This produces strain in individuals, which is assumed to be most prevalent among those in the lower socioeconomic classes because they possess the fewest social and economic opportunities. Therefore, financial strain can explain a negative link between SES and delinquency. Other negative linkages implicated in contemporary theories have low SES producing crime via heightened aggression and alienation and lessened educational and occupational aspirations, social closeness, and self-control.

High SES Causes Delinquency

Our third proposition proposes the opposite of the second proposition: High SES can increase individuals' propensity for delinquency through various causal mechanisms; that is, SES has a positive effect on delinquency. This seemingly counterintuitive idea is found in several criminological and social-psychological theories, most notably power control theory. This theory posits several positive connections between social class and delinquency. One connection is through risk taking. Risk taking is especially encouraged among the upper classes as a means to enhance upward social mobility; however, it has the unintended negative consequence of fostering juvenile delinquency. Another positive connection is through social power. Individuals in the upper levels of society have more social power and thus may with impunity hold attitudes that are conducive to crime. They see themselves as above society's precepts, they have more resources with which to respond to any negative societal reactions to their deviance, and they assess themselves as being at relatively low risk of detection and punishment for their deviant acts. Thus, increased social power and decreased risk of detection for criminal activities can positively link SES and delinquency.

Causation but Not Correlation

Combining these three propositions, we expect that SES has both negative and positive indirect effects on delinquency. If this is the case, the negative and positive effects would cancel each other, resulting in either a weak or nonexistent correlation between measures of SES and delinquency across individuals in the population. A statistical truism holds that correlation does not necessarily denote causality. Indeed, the reverse is equally true: Causation does not necessarily denote correlation. We hypothesize that such is the case here. Through some social-psychological characteristics individuals' *low* SES produces high levels of delinquency, and through others *high* SES produces delinquency. Thus, we expect many causal connections, but little correlation, between individuals' SES and their self-reported delinquency.

Conceptual Model

We illustrate our conceptual model in Figure 1. High SES *decreases* delinquency through some social-psychological mediators, including less financial strain, less aggression, less alienation, high educational and occupational aspirations, social closeness, and self-control. High SES *increases* delinquency through other mediators, including taste for risk, social power, less perceived risk of detection, and less conventional values. The coexistence of these negative and positive links, we believe, explains the lack of strong empirical correlations between SES and delinquency in the population.

We analyze this conceptual model in three steps. First, using data described below, we assess the zero-order association between standard measures of SES and delinquency. Second, we estimate a series of regression equations that isolate the separate negative and positive effects of SES on delinquency. Third, to test the sensitivity of our findings, we replicate our analyses with alternative measures of SES and delinquency.

DATA AND MEASURES

The data used to test these hypotheses come from the Dunedin Multidisciplinary Health and Development Study. Subjects in this study were members of an unselected birth cohort that has been studied extensively since birth. Briefly, the study is a longitudinal investigation of the health, development, and behavior of a complete cohort of children born between April 1, 1972, and March 31, 1973, in Dunedin, New

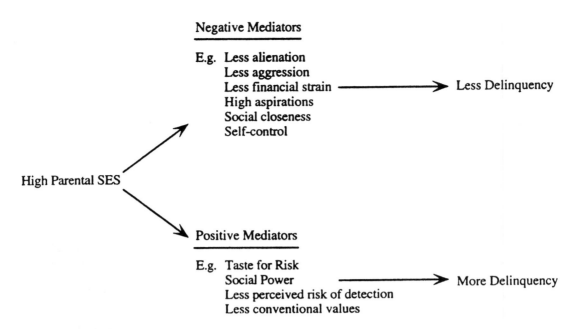

FIGURE 1 *Conceptual model of the effects of parental SES on delinquency.*

Zealand, a city of approximately 120,000 people. Data were collected at birth and at age 3 for 1,037 study members (52% males and 48% females—91% of the eligible births). This base sample has been reassessed with a diverse battery of psychological, medical, and sociological measures at ages 5, 7, 9, 11, 13, 15, 18, and 21. Overall, the study has enjoyed high rates of participation at each wave. At the most recent wave, age 21 in 1993 and 1994, 992 (97.3%) of the study members participated.

Measuring Social Class and Delinquency

This study capitalizes on the longitudinal nature of the Dunedin study by using parental SES during childhood and early adolescence (birth through age 15) to predict delinquency in late adolescence and early adulthood (ages 18-21) as mediated by social-psychological characteristics measured at age 18.

The SES of study members' families was measured with a 6-point scale assessing parents' occupational status. The scale places each

occupation into one of six categories based on the educational levels and income associated with that occupation in data from the New Zealand census. The variable used in our analyses, Parental SES, is the average of the highest SES level of either parent across the interviews from the study member's birth through age 15. This variable reflects the socioeconomic conditions experienced by study members while they grew up. For our sensitivity analyses, we analyzed two additional measures of social class. Parental Education was measured with a 3-point scale indicating parents' highest level of education (university degree, a high school or a vocational degree, or did not finish high school) when the study member was age 15. Family Income (in units of $10,000 NZ) was also measured at age 15.

Delinquency was measured at age 21 with a private, self-reported delinquency interview. This variable, Delinquency at Age 21, indicates how many different illegal acts the study members committed at least once in the 12 months prior to their age 21 interview. To be clear, this is a variety scale (i.e., how many types of acts), not a frequency scale (i.e., how many times acts were committed). The 48 individual items comprising this variety scale represent a wide range of offenses, including theft, burglary, assault, fraud, and drug offenses.

For our sensitivity analyses, we analyzed three additional measures of delinquency. Frequency of Delinquency at age 21 is a frequency scale of the total number of illegal acts, regardless of the type of act, that were self-reported at the age 21 interview. Self-reported Delinquency at Age 18, like the age 21 measure, is a variety score of self-reported delinquent acts. Index Offenses at age 21 is a scale of index offenses. Taken from the general self-report delinquency questionnaire, it includes aggravated assault, gang fights, stole motor vehicles, stole something worth more than $50, broke into a building or vehicle, and strong-armed theft.

Measuring Social-Psychological Mediating Variables

We use 11 social-psychological mediating variables to link Parental SES to Delinquency, variables commonly implicated in contemporary theories. Seven of these mediating variables use measurement scales developed from the Multidimensional Personality Questionnaire (MPQ). Each MPQ scale is composed of about 20 true-false items.

Of the negative mediating variables, the variable Self-Control is based on self-reported and informant data. The self-reported data come from the "control" scale of the MPQ. A high score on this scale indicates that study members had a propensity to be reflective, cautious, careful, planful, and not impulsive. The informant data come from a reverse-coded single-item measure for which informants assessed on a 3-point scale the extent to which they thought study members had problems with impulsivity, such as rushing into things without thinking about what might happen. The variable Social Closeness is also an MPQ scale. Study members with high scores on this scale said that they were sociable, liked other people, and turned to others for comfort. The variables Educational Aspirations and Vocational Aspirations measured study members' aspirations for their educational and occupational careers. Educational Aspirations was measured at age 15 and then updated at age 18, and it records study members' estimate of when they expected to leave school. Vocational Aspirations was measured at age 18, and it records what sort of work the study members hoped to be doing at age 25. The variable Aggression, like Self-Control, uses both self-reported and informant data. The self-reported data are an MPQ scale. Study members with high scores on this scale were those who said they would hurt others for their own advantage and would frighten and cause discomfort for others. The informant data come from a single-item measure in which informants assessed on a 3-point scale the extent to which study members had problems with aggression, such as fighting or controlling anger. The variable Alienation is an MPQ scale. Study members with high scores on it said that they felt mistreated, victimized and betrayed by others, and the target of false rumors. The variable Financial Strain is a combination of three separate measures. Using 3- and 4-point scales, study members reported how difficult it was for them to support themselves/their families financially at the time of the interview, how worried they were about inadequate income or poverty in the future, and how unhappy they were with their standard of living.

Of the positive mediating variables, the variable Taste for Risk is a reverse coding of the MPQ scale labeled "harm avoidance." Study members with high scores were those who preferred exciting, dangerous activities over safe, tedious activities. The variable Social Power is an MPQ scale called "social potency." High-scoring study members were those who said that they were forceful and decisive in social situations and were fond of influencing others and of leadership roles. The variable Low Perceived Risk of Detection is the average of four separate items. In each of them study members were asked, hypothetically, how many times they thought that they would get caught (from 0 to

10) if they committed a certain crime on 10 different days. The four crimes queried about were shoplifting, stealing a car, breaking into a place to steal something, and using a stolen bank card to get money. The final variable, Conventional Values, is an MPQ scale called "traditionalism." Study members with high scores were those who desired a conservative social environment and strict moral standards.

RESULTS

We present three empirical tests in this section. First, we tested if there was any statistical association between SES and delinquency. Second, we tested for the existence of *both* a negative and a positive effect of SES on delinquency. Third, we retested these negative and positive effects using alternative measures of SES and delinquency.

The Lack of Correlation Between SES and Delinquency

The simple correlation between socioeconomic status (Parental SES) and delinquency (Delinquency at Age 21) among study members was $r = -.02$ and not statistically significant. It is possible, however, that the relationship between SES and delinquency is not linear and therefore would not be detected with a simple correlation. Specifically, it has been suggested that individuals in the upper and lower strata of society have the highest proportional involvement in criminal offenses, and that the middle strata has the lowest. This would imply a U-shaped relationship between SES and delinquency.

To test for this possibility, we plotted levels of delinquency as a function of SES for groups of study members. Visual inspection suggests that no significant statistical relationship was present between Parental SES and Delinquency at Age 21, for levels of self-reported delinquency were constant across all levels of SES. Thus, we found here what so many previous studies have

found and what is the counterintuitive social fact that is the stimulus for this article: There appears to be no empirical association between general measures of SES and delinquency.

The Negative and Positive Effects of SES on Delinquency

We hypothesized that the above lack of association results from SES having a negative and a positive effect on delinquency that cancel each other out. We tested this hypothesis with social-psychological mediating variables that link SES to delinquency.

Table 1 presents the simple correlations between SES, delinquency, and 11 social-psychological mediating variables. The correlations between SES and the mediating variables were mostly statistically significant. The study members who grew up in high-SES families were less alienated, reported less financial strain, were less aggressive, and had higher educational and occupational aspirations. In addition, they reported a greater taste for risk taking, more social potency, and fewer conventional values. The study members who committed the most delinquency were those who reported more financial strain, were more aggressive, were more alienated, had lower educational and occupational aspirations, had less social closeness, and had less self-control. In addition, they reported a greater taste for risk, more social potency, lower perceived risk of detection of crimes, and fewer conventional values.

These correlations support the hypothesized relationships summarized in Figure 1. To test more directly the effects of SES upon delinquency, we regressed delinquency upon SES and various combinations of the social-psychological mediating variables.

As with the correlations in Table 1, these zero-order estimates were all statistically significant except for Parental SES. This insignificant zero-order Parental SES coefficient represents a baseline with which to compare the coefficients in the remaining equations.

TABLE 1

Correlations of socioeconomic status and delinquency with social-psychological mediating variables.

Mediating Variables	Parental SES	Delinquency
Socioeconomic status		
Parental SES		−.02
Variables through which low SES is hypothesized to increase levels of delinquency		
Financial strain	−.11***	.21***
Aggression	−.15***	.49***
Alienation	−.18***	.23***
Educational aspirations	.33***	−.18***
Vocational aspirations	.25***	.25***
Social closeness	.05	−.22***
Self-control	.05+	−.37***
Variables through which high SES is hypothesized to increase levels of delinquency		
Taste for risk	.12***	.29***
Social power	.15***	.16***
Low perceived risk of detection	.06+	.23***
Conventional values	−.07*	−.38***

$+p < .10$; $*p < .05$; $***p < .001$.

The [analysis] next regressed delinquency upon SES plus the social-psychological mediators through which high SES is hypothesized to increase levels of delinquency. By empirically modeling the positive effects (i.e., including them in the regression equation), we leave resident in the SES measure its negative effect. This isolates and estimates the negative effect of SES on delinquency. The four hypothesized positive mediators were in the expected direction and were statistically significant. The estimated effect of Parental SES on delinquency, net of these mediators, was statistically significant and *negative*. That is, when controlling for the positive mediators of the SES-delinquency relationship, higher levels of SES predicted significantly *lower* levels of delinquency.

The [analysis] next regressed delinquency on SES plus the social-psychological mediators through which high SES is hypothesized to decrease levels of delinquency. This model tested for the positive effect of SES on delinquency. In this equation, all seven hypothesized negative mediators had effects in the expected direction and five of them were statistically significant. By empirically modeling the negative effects (i.e., including them in the regression equation), we isolate and estimate the positive effect of SES on delinquency. The estimated effect of Parental SES on delinquency, net of these mediators, was statistically significant and *positive*. That is, when controlling for the negative mediators of the SES-delinquency relationship, higher levels of SES predicted significantly *higher* levels of delinquency.

The final [analysis] regressed delinquency on SES plus all 11 of the social-psychological mediating variables. Here, the estimated effect of Parental SES was statistically insignificant. This demonstrates that the various causal mechanisms linking SES to delinquency cancel each other out. That is, when controlling for all of the mediating variables, we got the same result as when not controlling for any of them (e.g., with a simple correlation): no statistical association between SES and delinquency.

Alternative Measures of SES and Delinquency

We tested the sensitivity of our analyses to different specifications of SES and delinquency by rerunning the analyses five times—twice with different measures of SES and three times with different measures of delinquency. Each time the same pattern emerged. Socioeconomic status had a positive indirect effect on delinquency through some mediators and a negative indirect effect through others.

Our first two reanalyses used alternative specifications of SES—parental education and family income, and these two variables produced results nearly identical to those found with parental occupational status. Neither parental education nor family income had a statistically significant zero-order association with delinquency at age 21. Both, however, had statistically significant *negative* effects on delinquency when the positive mediating variables were included (i.e., variables Taste for Risk through Conventional Value), and both had statistically significant (or near significant) *positive* effects when we controlled for the negative mediating variables (i.e., Financial Strain through Self-Control).

Our next three reanalyses used alternative specifications of delinquency—frequency of delinquent acts at age 21, variety of delinquent acts at age 18, and index offenses at age 21. The frequency scale showed a nearly identical pattern of findings as did the corresponding age 21 variety scale. The remaining two measures of delinquency had weak, but statistically significant, negative zero-order associations with parents' occupational status. These negative associations increased in magnitude when we controlled for the "positive" mediating variables, and they attenuated to statistical insignificance when we controlled for the "negative" mediating variables.

To summarize, these alternative measures of SES and delinquency show the same pattern of findings as our initial analyses: SES had both negative and positive indirect effects on delinquency through social-psychological mediators. When there was an initially insignificant statistical relationship between SES and delinquency, these indirect effects could make it significantly negative or positive. When there was an initially weak relationship, these indirect effects could magnify or nullify it.

SUMMARY AND DISCUSSION

In this article we have reexamined the relationship between SES and delinquency. While various classical theories of delinquency have posited a negative relationship between the two, empirical studies have found little statistical association between them. How can this apparent disparity between theory and data be explained? Drawing on recent theoretical insights, we propose that SES has a negative effect on delinquency through some mediators, that SES has a positive effect on delinquency through other mediators, and that these negative and positive effects coexist and can cancel each other out. As a result, there can be many causal links between SES and delinquency but little overall correlation.

Our empirical analyses support this proposed explanation. From previous criminological and social-psychological research, we identified 11 social-psychological characteristics that negatively and positively mediate the effect of parental SES on adolescent delinquency. By selectively controlling for these mediators, we isolated and estimated the negative and positive effects of SES on delinquency, and they were statistically significant.

This article, then, reconciles theories and empirical studies of SES and delinquency, for we find that SES both has a negative effect on delinquency and is not highly correlated with it. The missing piece to this puzzle is the existence of a positive effect as well.

QUESTIONS FOR DISCUSSION AND WRITING

1. What two alternative questions do the authors ask, and what answers does the article give?
2. What three propositions do the authors present, and what do they expect when they combine them?
3. How did the authors test the sensitivity of their analyses to different specifications of SES and delinquency?

FAMILY

Families and Delinquency: A Meta-Analysis of the Impact of Broken Homes

L. EDWARD WELLS

JOSEPH H. RANKIN

THE topic of broken homes has been a central part of delinquency theory since the emergence of criminology in the nineteenth century. Indeed, the "defective" or incomplete family constitutes one of the most common and enduring themes in the modern attempt to explain juvenile delinquency. Consistent with the primacy and persistence of the broken home as a concept in criminological analysis, an extensive research literature involving hundreds of studies has accumulated.

Although the empirical evidence on broken homes and delinquency is large and diverse, it is surprisingly incomplete and disappointingly inconclusive. The dozens of studies yield little accumulation of well-documented knowledge. Since the basic aim of science is to develop knowledge cumulatively across many fallible, repeated studies, our concern in this chapter is the development of a systematic, quantitative, integrative assessment of existing research on the relation between broken homes and delinquency.

The traditional approach to assessing and synthesizing a body of research is the "narrative research review." This entails a careful subjective summary of prior studies in which the following occurs: A number of studies are identified, the features of these studies are described and evaluated, and the results are interpreted and synthetically combined. Such reviews rely heavily on the interpretation and judgment of the reviewers regarding the description of findings, their magnitudes, and how they may be combined into a general, unitary conclusion. Although all reviews reflect some of the authors' biases and preconceptions, the biases in narrative review are implicit, an unspecified part of a verbal summary, and thus difficult to "factor out" in any systematic way.

A more rigorous method for synthesizing a collected body of research is *meta-analysis*, using recently developed quantitative methods to systematically summarize and analyze the results of multiple independent studies of a topic. This strategy treats the findings of prior studies as empirical data points in a new, second-order analysis, resulting in a statistical summary of prior studies that is more precise, quantitative, objective, and replicable than the traditional narrative review. Thus, the intent of this chapter is to apply meta-analysis methodology to a systematic analysis of the available "broken homes" research.

META-ANALYSIS OF THE BROKEN HOMES RESEARCH

The present study applies meta-analysis procedures to the structural issue of broken homes as a predisposing or causal variable in juvenile delinquency and crime. Although the scope of our analysis is limited by omitting several other relevant family factors, we adopt this specific focus on the broken homes variable for several reasons.

First, the topic of broken homes is "ripe" for such an analysis. Despite a great deal of research over the past eight decades, we lack clear, quantitative summaries of how broken homes relate systematically to juvenile delinquency, controlling for such variables as age, sex, race of children, and family circumstances. At the same time, the literature evinces the general belief that this information already exists and that research has already settled the issue. That impression can readily stifle and misinform additional research.

A second consideration for examining this specific topic is its amenability to meta-analysis. Allowing for variations in its substantive elaboration, the idea of broken homes nonetheless entails a variable with relatively clear conceptualization and measurement, especially when compared to other family process variables such as attachment, identification, or discipline. Indeed, broken homes are conceptualized similarly across different disciplines and are operationalized in fairly standard ways that allow for empirical comparability across studies. Such considerations are important, since meta-analysis is a method to resolve *empirical* inconsistencies and ambiguities rather than a means to resolve theoretical disagreement and confusions over conceptual terms.

Our meta-analysis addresses the following questions about broken homes in the etiology of juvenile delinquency:

Total effect: What is the overall association between parental absence (broken homes) and juvenile delinquency? What is the magnitude of this effect? Is it statistically significant?

Variability: How much variation occurs in the pattern of effects across different studies?

Covariation: To what extent does the relation between broken homes and delinquency vary according to methodological factors (type of sample, type of measurements, historical location of the study, theoretical orientation of the researcher) and substantive factors (different types of delinquent behavior; age, sex, race, and social class of the juveniles; social context of the sample)?

RESULTS

An overview of the major characteristics of the 50 studies included in this meta-analysis reveals considerable variation among the studies in their basic characteristics and general findings (Table 1).

The last column (9) in Table 1 reports the broken home effect (correlation) coefficients for *overall* delinquency indexes. These are coefficients that were reported in the original study or were computed by us from statistical information provided in the study. If results were reported separately for black and white youths or for boys and girls, we averaged the separate scores to provide an overall sample estimate.

The coefficients in Table 1 show substantial variation from a low value of .005 to as large as .50. For most of the studies, broken homes (or family structure) has a consistent and reliable association with juvenile delinquency, ranging between .05 and .15. While this seems fairly modest in size for correlation coefficients, we note that the phi coefficient can be usefully interpreted as percent difference in outcomes between the two categories of the independent variable. A phi coefficient of 0.15 means a 15% difference in delinquency between intact and

TABLE 1

Summary of studies in meta-analysis.

(1) Study Reference	(2) Year (Data)	(3) Disci- pline	(4) Sample Type	(5) Sample Size	(6) Delinq. Meas.	(7) Sex Comp.	(8) Racial Comp.	(9) Effect Coeff.
Austin (1978)	1965	Cr	LP	4077	SR	B/G	B/W	.010
Biron & LeBlanc (1977)	1973	PM	LP	326	SR	B/G	W	.210
Blakely et al. (1974)	1969	PM	OC	87	OR	B/G	—	.344
Browning (1960)	1959	Cr	OC	120	OR	B	B/W	.297
Burt (1929)	1925	PM	OC	597	OR	B/G	—	.314
Canter (1982)	1977	Cr	GP	1725	SR	B/G	B/W	.112
Carr-Saunders et al. (1942)	1939	Cr	OC	3946	OR	B	—	.154(B)
Dentler & Monroe (1961)	1960	Cr	CN	912	ST	B/G	W	—
Dornbusch et al. (1985)	1970	DP	GP	6710	ST	B/G	B/W	.112
Douglas et al. (1966)	1963	Cr	GP	2402	OR	B	B/W	.060(B)
Ensminger et al. (1983)	1976	PM	CN	695	SR	B/G	B	.076
Glueck & Glueck (1950)	1940	Cr	OC	1000	OR	B	B/W	.262
Goldstein (1984)	1969	DP	GP	6287	ST	B/G	B/W	.068
Gove & Crutchfield (1982)	1978	Cr	LP	620	RP	B/G	B/W	.110
Gregory (1965)	1957	PM	LP	11121	OR	B/G	B/W	.072
Hennessy et al. (1978)	1975	Cr	CN	1240	SR	B/G	W	—
Hirschi (1969)	1965	Cr	LP	1810	SR	B	B/W	.041(B)
Hodgkiss (1933)	1930	Cr	OC	724	OR	G	—	.220(G)
Johnson (1986)	1975	Cr	LP	734	SR	B/G	B/W	.095
Kalter et al. (1985)	1972	PM	GP	1395	SR	G	B/W	—
Koller (1971)	1968	PM	OC	222	OR	G	—	.500(G)
Matsueda & Heimer (1987)	1965	Cr	LP	2589	SR	B	B/W	—
McCarthy et al. (1982)	1975	DP	CN	1605	CP	B/G	B/W	—
McCord (1982)	1978	Cr	CN	201	OR	B	B/W	.035(B)
Mednick et al. (1987)	1985	PM	LP	423	OR	B	W	.149(B)
Merrill (1947)	1935	MF	OC	600	OR	B/G	—	.254
Monahan (1957)	1954	Cr	OC	36275	OR	B/G	B/W	.123
Morris (1964)	1961	Cr	OC	224	OR	B/G	—	.242
Nye (1957)	1955	MF	LP	780	SR	B/G	W	.072
Nye (1958)	1955	Cr	LP	2343	SR	B/G	W	.079
Offord (1982)	1973	PM	OC	146	OR	B	—	.212(B)
Offord et al. (1979)	1975	PM	OC	118	OR	G	—	.444(G)
Peterson & Zill (1986)	1981	MF	GP	1080	CP	B/G	B/W	.254

(continued)

TABLE 1   (Continued)

(1) Study Reference	(2) Year (Data)	(3) Discipline	(4) Sample Type	(5) Sample Size	(6) Delinq. Meas.	(7) Sex Comp.	(8) Racial Comp.	(9) Effect Coeff.
Rankin (1983)	1972	Cr	GP	2242	SR	B/G	B/W	—
Rickel & Langner (1985)	1975	DP	LP	732	CP	B/G	B/W	.245
Robins & Hill (1966)	1950	PM	LP	295	OR	B	B	.005(B)
Slawson (1926)	1925	Cr	OC	4847	OR	B	—	.147(B)
Slocum & Stone (1963)	1959	MF	CN	3242	SR	B/G	W	.156
Smith & Paternoster (1987)	1981	Cr	LP	1383	SR	B/G	B/W	.098
Spergel (1965)	1963	Cr	CN	131	SR	B	B	.154
Steinberg (1987)	1985	DP	CN	865	CP	B/G	W	.043
Toby (1957)	1929	Cr	OC	8953	OR	B	B/W	.114
Tolan & Lorian (1988)	1985	DP	CN	337	SR	B	W	.150
Van Voorhis et al. (1988)	1980	Cr	CN	152	SR	B/G	W	.110
Wadsworth (1979)	1963	DP	GP	2190	OR	B/G	W	.068(B)
Weeks (1940)	1937	Cr	OC	837	OR	B	—	.147(B)
Weeks & Smith (1939)	1935	Cr	OC	2445	OR	B	—	.114(B)
Wells & Rankin (1985)	1972	Cr	GP	1395	SR	B/G	B/W	.072
West & Farrington (1973)	1963	Cr	GP	411	OR	B	—	.132(B)
Wilkinson (1980)	1975	Cr	LP	3267	SR	B/G	B/W	.070

Note: Column (3): Disciplinary Orientation; Cr = criminology; MF = marriage and family study; DP = developmental psychology; PM = psychiatric/medical. Column (4): Sample Type; GP = general probability sample; LP = local probability sample; CN = convenience sample; OC = official/institutional "contrived" sample (official delinquent group + nondelinquent control group). Column (6): Delinquency Measurement; OR = official record data; SR = self-report measure of delinquent behaviors; ST = self-reported trouble with authorities; RP = rating by parents. Column (7): Gender Composition; B = boys-only sample; G = girls-only sample; B/G = boys and girls mixed sample. Column (8): Race/Ethnic Composition; B = black-only sample; W = white-only sample; B/W = black and white combined sample. Column (9): Effect Coefficients; coefficients reported are correlations (*r*, phi, point-biserial, or eta). Coefficients with a (B) next to them indicate estimated effects based on a boys-only sample. Coefficients with a (G) next to them indicate estimated effects based on a girls-only sample.

broken families. We note also that the coefficients larger than 0.3 resulted from studies using a more "clinical" (medical/psychiatric) orientation with small, nonrepresentative, contrived-comparison samples measuring delinquency through official court or institutional records. Excluding these four studies lowers the average effect size somewhat from .153 to .129.

Recognizing the complexity and heterogeneity of delinquency, numerous researchers argue that the impact of family structure is significant only for particular forms of juvenile misbehavior—especially the less serious, "acting out" forms of deviance. For more serious offenses that reflect more systematic personal and peer involvement, the impact of family structure may be much weaker or even negligible. The impact of family structure does seem to depend on the type of delinquency. The largest correlations with broken homes occur for status offenses, drug use (mainly marijuana) having the second highest average coefficient, and violence having the lowest. Even with weighting, the association between broken homes and type (or seriousness) of delinquency remains significant, and the relative ordering of effect sizes across different kinds of delinquency is the same.

Of the six studies which reported racial comparisons, three reported finding no black-white differences (including two large national surveys), two reported stronger effects for white youths, and one reported a stronger effect of broken homes for black youth. The comparisons by sex are also equivocal, although the effect of broken homes on boys may be slightly stronger. The age of the child at family breakup is prominently mentioned in the clinical and child development literatures yet the age comparisons (reflecting child's age when the breakup occurred) indicates that six of the nine studies reported finding no significant differences in the effect of broken homes on delinquency between younger and older children. The three studies that found stronger broken home effects for younger children all analyzed official delinquency records. There is no clear evidence that the relationship between broken homes and delinquency is differentially affected by the child's age at the time of parental separation.

A widespread belief in both the delinquency and child development literatures is that families broken by divorce are more harmful than families broken by the death of a parent, since the former are attended by much more hostility, resentment, and conflict. Eight of the studies reported such comparisons. Half of these studies found the association between broken homes and delinquency to be significantly stronger for families broken by divorce.

A distinct but related question concerns the replacement of absent parents with stepparents. A common position holds that stepparents may in fact increase the detrimental effect of broken homes on delinquent behavior, since the stepparent commonly adds new conflicts to those already present in the home. Seven studies reported comparisons between reconstituted families (with stepparents) and single-parent families. Overall, stepparents do not add measurably to the negative association between broken families and delinquency.

Are the differences in the broken homes/delinquency findings due to methodological variations among the studies, or are they the result of substantive variations among families and social contexts? With only 50 studies, very detailed or elaborate analyses are not possible. However, we did examine the following bivariate effects: period of data collection, sample size, type of sample, disciplinary orientation of the research, and type of delinquency measurement.

No major historical shifts in the magnitude of the broken home-delinquency correlation are evident. The slight tendency for earlier studies (1920-1949) to report somewhat higher associations than more recent studies is due to the reliance of earlier research on official delinquency ("contrived") samples and official record measurements.

There is a strong inverse relation between sample size (categorized into five levels for comparison purposes) and the size of the effect coefficient (eta = .500). The largest coefficients appear in the smallest (statistically least reliable) and generally most unrepresentative samples. The size of the coefficients declines as samples become larger and more representative. The standard errors of the estimated effects are also much smaller for the larger studies, indicating more consistency between studies.

Coefficients based on official record data are substantially higher than those based on self-reports. This may reflect some bias in official processing of juveniles from "broken" or unconventional family situations. Studies with a medical/psychiatric orientation mainly rely on clinically oriented measures of juvenile deviance that reflect general "conduct problems." The coefficients for such measures also show higher levels of correlation, indicating that while they have some common content with standard measures of juvenile delinquency, they are not equivalent.

Studies within the medical/psychiatric orientation show a higher average correlation between broken homes and delinquency than do studies within the other disciplines, since medical/psychiatric studies commonly use small, "contrived" samples of officially or clinically identified delinquents. Thus, the disciplinary variations reflect mainly methodological differences in research procedure rather than theoretically meaningful variations in substance.

The final aspect of our data analysis provides a statistical answer to the question, "How much of the variation in the correlation between broken homes and delinquency is due to methodological rather than substantive factors?" These results suggest that, allowing for some normal sampling variation among studies, almost all of the variation in reported effects across studies is a result of methodological rather than substantive features. Thus, anyone attempting to draw conclusions from earlier studies should note the large contributions by theoretically irrelevant, extraneous methodological variables to the research.

DISCUSSION

Overall, what have this survey and meta-analysis of 50 published studies dealing with broken homes and juvenile delinquency shown? Does it simply confirm statistically what was already known (or at least believed)? While partly true, recall that prior "knowledge" on broken homes and delinquency contained contradictory predictions and conclusions. The intent of our meta-analysis was not to disprove what people already knew but rather to provide a systematic, cumulative, and empirically grounded evaluation of that knowledge using available research.

Our meta-analysis was not restricted to a specific sample or measurement procedure; rather, it applied across a range of studies and research procedures. Our results can be grouped into substantive and methodological findings.

Substantively, we found the following across the 50 studies reviewed:

1. No clear historical shift is apparent such that incomplete families have less impact now than in earlier decades (when the family was ostensibly more important). Rather, any impact of family structure on juvenile delinquency appears stable.
2. The effect of intact versus "broken" families is a consistent and real pattern of association, showing a bivariate correlation with delinquency of .10 to .15. In the case of phi coefficients, this means that the prevalence of delinquency in broken homes is 10% to 15% higher than in intact homes.
3. The correlation between broken homes and juvenile delinquency is stronger for minor forms of juvenile misconduct (status offenses) and weakest for serious forms of criminal behavior (such as theft and interpersonal violence).
4. The type of family break does seem to affect juvenile delinquency. The association with delinquency is slightly (albeit not significantly) stronger for families broken by divorce or separation than by death of a parent.
5. There are no consistent or appreciable differences in the impact of broken homes between girls and boys or between black youths and white youths.
6. There are no consistent effects of the child's age at breakup on the negative effects of the separated family.
7. There is no consistent evidence of the often-cited negative impact of stepparents on juvenile delinquency. Apparently, stepparents do not make a problematic family situation worse, at least in terms of controlling the children.

Methodologically, we found that the procedural features of previous research efforts had a substantial influence on the patterns of findings. Indeed, the methods component of variance in effects dominated over substantively meaningful components. Specifically, we found the following:

1. Use of an "official-contrived" sample of delinquents/nondelinquents superficially inflates the correlation between family structure and delinquency. Such samples produce fairly uninformative findings of limited generalizability. Large probability samples of general populations consistently produce more modest correlation coefficients.

2. Use of official record or institutional data to measure delinquency results in a significantly higher (inflated) correlation between broken homes and delinquency compared to self-reported measurements.

3. There is an inverse, monotonic relationship between sample size and reported effect size, where the most substantial correlations are produced by the smallest, least reliable, and least representative studies. This underlines the importance of weighting for sample size when estimating summary effect coefficients.

QUESTIONS FOR DISCUSSION AND WRITING

1. What is the basic aim of science, and what is the traditional approach to assessing and synthesizing a body of research?
2. What is a more rigorous method for synthesizing a collected body of research, and how is that method better than the traditional approach?
3. Does the "impact" of family structure seem to depend on the type of delinquency?
4. Substantively, what did the authors find?

SCHOOL

The Effect of Dropping Out of High School on Subsequent Criminal Behavior

TERENCE P. THORNBERRY
MELANIE MOORE
R. L. CHRISTENSON

THE relationship between school failure and criminal behavior is a recurrent theme in theories of delinquency. Eventual dropouts have been found to have considerably higher rates of delinquency during high school than do graduates, a finding consistent both with conventional wisdom and most theories of delinquency. However, what is not clear either theoretically or empirically is the effect that dropping out of high school has on subsequent criminal behavior.

Strain and control theories offer divergent assessments of the relationship between school and delinquency, especially for lower-class youths. In the former, school is a source of failure and frustration which increases delinquent conduct; in the latter, it is a source of social control which decreases delinquent conduct. According to strain theory, because dropping out eliminates the source of frustration brought about by failure in the school, criminal conduct should decline sharply following dropout. According to control theory, however, because dropping out reduces institutional control, criminal behavior should increase.

Dropouts and Later Criminality

Although these theories offer contradictory predictions about the relationship between dropping out and delinquency, both enjoy some degree of empirical support. The most influential investigation of the relationship between dropping out and delinquency, Elliott and Voss's panel study, is clearly supportive of strain theory. However, other studies which extend the follow-up period until subjects are in their mid-20s report findings more consistent with a social control perspective. Polk et al. report that during the early 20s dropouts have consistently higher rates of criminality than do graduates.

In general, therefore, while these two sets of empirical studies report contradictory results, they also emphasize different consequences of dropping out. Elliott and Voss report that dropping out has a rather immediate dampening effect on delinquency, while Polk et al. report that in the long run dropping out has an enhancing effect on criminal involvement. Thus, empirical evidence on the relationship between dropping out and later criminal behavior is equivocal and does not provide clear support for either strain or control theory.

METHODOLOGY

The present study reevaluates the association between dropout status and later criminal involvement, examining both short-term and long-term effects and controlling for the influence of both age and postschool experiences. To do so, it uses longitudinal data from a 10% sample of the Philadelphia birth cohort of 1945. The cohort consists of all males ($N = 9,945$) born in that year who resided in Philadelphia from at least the age of 10 to the age of 18. The members of the 10% sample were the focus of a follow-up study that extended the observation period to age 25. For the entire sample ($N = 975$), complete arrest histories are available, and in addition, attempts were made to interview all members of the sample.

Variables for Analysis

The measure of the independent variable, dropout status, is based on responses to interview items in which each subject reported his educational attainment. Subjects are divided into high school dropouts, those who report completing less than 12 years of schooling, and high school graduates, those who report completing 12 or more years. For most analyses, dropouts are further divided into groups based on the age at which they left high school.

The dependent variable, criminal involvement, is measured by the number of times each subject was arrested. These data are arrayed in annual intervals so that criminal involvement both before and after dropout can be compared.

Four additional variables are included in analysis: race, social status of origin, marital status, and unemployment.

RESULTS

Examination of the mean number of arrests at each age from 13 to 25, for all high school dropouts, three subgroups based on the age at dropout, and all high school graduates and graduates who did not continue on to college, produces little support for the strain hypothesis that dropping out of school has a short-term dampening effect on criminal behavior. For two of the age-at-dropout groups, those who dropped out at 16 and at 18, the mean number of arrests are higher in the year following dropout than in the preceding year. For those who dropped out at age 17, the percentage decrease in arrests from 17 to 18, 22%, is less than the comparable percentage decrease for all graduates, 55 percent, and for graduates who did not attend college, 74%. There does not appear to be an immediate reduction in criminal involvement following dropping out.

When analysis addresses the long-term impact of dropping out, results indicate that dropping out of high school is positively related to adult criminal involvement. For high school graduates, arrest rates drop sharply from age 16 to age 18 and reach a point of stability at approximately 19 years of age. Indeed, after age 18 the rates do not exceed .06 for all graduates or .08 for graduates who did not attend college. For dropouts, however, these rates do not exhibit the same precipitous drop in the late teenage years. They decline rather gradually throughout the early 20s, and it is not until age 22 or 23 that the rates converge with those of the graduates and reach a point of stability. Even at these ages, however, dropouts are arrested more frequently than are graduates. Thus, rather than reducing criminal involvement, dropping out of high school tends to be related to high rates of crime throughout the early 20s.

Although dropping out appears to have a long-term enhancing effect on later criminal involvement, all groups' criminal behavior declines substantially throughout the early 20s. It is necessary, therefore, to determine if dropout status has a significant effect once the dampening influence of age is controlled. Age has a negative effect on criminal involvement as expected. Controlling for the influence of age, dropout status has a significant positive effect on crime rates throughout these years. Thus, dropping out is positively related to criminal involvement even when the general decline produced by the age distribution is held constant.

In general, therefore, results of this analysis offer little support for a strain model interpretation of the association between dropping out of high school and subsequent criminal involvement; dropouts exhibit neither a short-term nor long-term reduction in criminal activity. These results are, however, quite consistent with a control perspective which suggests that criminal behavior should remain high following the reduction in social control represented by dropping out of school. Even controlling for the influence of age, dropout status is found to be positively related to later criminal behavior.

Controlling for Social Status and Race

Holding constant social status of origin and race does not alter the basic finding of this analysis. At all ages, both before and after dropping out, high school dropouts have higher rates of criminal involvement than do graduates. Of particular interest, given strain theory's class-specific predictions, are the results for blue-collar subjects and blacks. In both cases, analysis indicates that dropping out is not followed by a substantial reduction in criminal involvement. On the contrary, dropping out is positively related to later crime for these subjects.

Postschool Experiences

The final analysis examines the postschool experiences of these subjects to see if dropping out has an independent effect on later crime or if the effect is primarily due to different experiences of dropouts and graduates. Following Elliott and Voss's design, the influences of marital status and unemployment status are examined.

Results of this analysis indicate that, at all four ages, high levels of unemployment are positively associated with criminal behavior. For marital status, however, the regression coefficients are close to zero and do not attain statistical significance at any age. Finally, dropout status exerts the expected positive effect on adult crime, even when the influence of marriage and employment are held constant. From ages 21 to 23, the regression coefficients for dropout status are positive and significant while at the last age studied, 24, the coefficient is not significantly different from zero. The latter finding is consistent with earlier results which indicate that arrest rates for dropouts and graduates converge by the mid-20s. Overall, therefore, these results indicate that dropout status does have a positive impact on criminal involvement, especially during the early 20s, even when appropriate postschool experiences are held constant.

CONCLUSION

One ineluctable conclusion emerged: Dropping out of high school is positively associated with later criminal activity. Unlike Elliott and Voss, we do not find an immediate dampening effect of dropping out on criminal involvement. Indeed, for two of the three age-at-dropout groups, criminal behavior increased in the year following departure from school. Moreover, dropping out of high school was also found to have a positive long-term effect on criminal behavior. Throughout the early 20s, dropouts have consistently higher rates of arrests than do graduates, and it is not until the mid-20s that the rates for the two groups begin to converge. These findings are also observed for minority group subjects and those from blue-collar backgrounds, the groups of particular interest to strain theory. Finally, dropout status was also found to have a significant positive effect on crime when the postschool experiences of marriage and employment are controlled. In general, therefore, results of this analysis are quite consistent with the theoretical expectations of social control theory; dropping out has a positive effect on subsequent arrest even when age and postschool experiences are controlled.

QUESTIONS FOR DISCUSSION AND WRITING

1. How do strain and control theories differ in their assessments of the relationship between school and delinquency? Do they both "enjoy some degree of empirical support"?
2. Which of the two theories does the authors' analyses support?
3. What happened to the relationship when "the general decline produced by the age distribution was held constant"? What happened when the authors held constant "social status of origin and race"? What about "when appropriate postschool experiences" were controlled?

Age, Peers, and Delinquency

MARK WARR

A decade ago, Hirschi and Gottfredson advanced strong and controversial ideas, most notably the assertion that the age distribution of crime is historically, culturally, and demographically invariant. Another equally strong assertion was that "the age distribution of crime cannot be accounted for by any variable or combination of variables currently available to criminology."

The difficulties that arise in explaining the association between age and crime are daunting. Chief among them is the fact that any explanation must account for seemingly contrary phenomena, that is, the rapid onset *and rapid desistance* from crime that, for most offenses, is centered in the middle to late teens. In addition, the age gradient of crime is so steep that it requires from any explanation rather profound age-related changes in the explanatory variables.

This paper examines a quintessentially sociological theory of delinquency—Sutherland's theory of differential association—and evaluates its ability to explain the age distribution of crime. The analysis is fitting because Sutherland's theory was among the first major sociological theories of crime, and it helped to anchor criminology within the discipline of sociology.

DIFFERENTIAL ASSOCIATION

Sutherland's theory of differential association locates the source of crime and delinquency in the intimate social networks of individuals. Emphasizing that criminal behavior is learned behavior, Sutherland argued that persons who are selectively or differentially exposed to delinquent associates are likely to acquire that trait as well.

Although Sutherland did not limit his theory to peer influence, tests of the theory have conventionally examined the correlation between self-reported delinquency and the number of delinquent friends reported by adolescents. That association has proven to be among the strongest in delinquency research, and it is one of the most consistently reported findings in the delinquency literature. Let us consider several aspects of peer relations that are consistent with Sutherland's general intentions as well as our immediate interest in age. These include (a) differential *exposure* to delinquent peers, meaning the number of delinquent peers reported by respondents at different ages, (b) *time* spent in the company of peers, (c) the *importance of friends* to respondents, and (d) respondents' *commitment or loyalty* to their own particular set of friends. After first describing the age distributions of these variables, the discussion turns to their capacity to explain the age distribution of crime.

DATA AND METHODS

The data for this study come from the National Youth Survey (NYS). The NYS is a longitudinal study of a national probability sample of 1,726 persons aged 11-17 in 1976. Five consecutive annual waves of the survey were conducted from 1976 through 1980, and these five are used in this analysis.

The NYS is especially well suited for this analysis because it contains a unique set of carefully constructed questions about delinquent peers. Unlike most conventional questions about peers, the NYS questions refer to specific, concrete persons rather than some ill-defined set of friends. That is, respondents were asked to name individually the friends they "ran around with," and they were specifically instructed to think of those persons in subsequent questions. To maximize the age range as well as the N for each age group, all 5 years of the NYS data were pooled, producing a composite sample of 8,625 persons aged 11-21.

FINDINGS

Age and Exposure to Delinquent Peers

The first portion of the analysis examines age-related changes in respondents' relation with and attitudes toward their peers. If peer influences account in any way for the age distribution of crime, then we must expect to observe substantial and rapid changes in peer variables across age groups. Consider, first, exposure to delinquent peers, that is, the number of delinquents within the respondent's immediate circle of friends.

The absolute level of exposure to delinquent peers is heavily contingent on the seriousness of the act. Whereas a majority of respondents reported that at least some of their friends used alcohol, cheated, committed vandalism or other comparatively petty acts, no more than 20% report that any of their friends have committed burglary or serious thefts or sold hard drugs, even at the peak ages of peer involvement.

The evidence points to an initial conclusion. During their early life, individuals frequently undergo rapid and enormous changes in exposure to delinquent peers, from a period of relative innocence in the immediate preteen years to a period of heavy exposure in the middle-to-late teens. This intense exposure to delinquent peers begins to decline, however, for many, but not all offenses as individuals leave their teens and enter young adulthood. Age-related changes in the importance of peers, the amount of time spent in their company, and loyalty to peers are substantial enough that they can reasonably be expected to exert strong, even profound, effects on the behavior of adolescents. And like the age distribution of crime itself, the role of peers is transitory, rising and falling quickly during a relatively brief period of life.

Regression Models

The analysis now turns to a direct test of differential association and its capacity to explain the age distribution of crime. In each of the models to be examined, the dependent variable is the self-reported incidence of the delinquent act (SRD), measured by the question "How many times in the last year have you [offense]?" Responses were coded as raw frequencies and as rates (number per day, week, or month), and for present purposes raw frequencies are used.

Time spent with delinquent friends and commitment to delinquent friends have statistically significant effects on self-reported behavior for all six offenses [alcohol, marijuana, petty theft, burglary, cheating, major theft], but the importance placed on social activities is statistically significant in only two instances (alcohol and cheating).

Let us turn attention now to some additional questions concerning peer influence. For example, does the age at which adolescents first acquire delinquent friends have any relevance for later delinquency? Do adolescents tend to alternate between delinquent and nondelinquent friends over time, or do their friendships display greater consistency?

The NYS data permit answers to such questions, but they do so within certain limitations. One limitation is the common problem of censoring. Respondents who were young (e.g., age 11) at the initial wave of the survey can be traced through the early years of their adolescence, but the same data are not available for respondents who were older at the initial wave of the survey (e.g., age 17). Also, because the NYS contains five annual waves of data, any one cohort can be traced only over a span of 5 years. And because a single cohort will be followed over time, the N's available for analysis are much smaller (less than 200) than those for the pooled data.

Patterns of Delinquent Friendship

Consider, first, patterns of delinquent friendships over time. Because respondents are unlikely to have acquired delinquent friends before the age of about 13, the analysis focuses on respondents aged 13 at wave 1 and traces them through the age of 17 (at wave 5). If delinquent friends are treated as a binary characteristic of respondents at each age (i.e., present or absent), there are $2^5 = 32$ possible patterns of delinquent friendships over a 5-year interval. Table 1 displays these 32 patterns, with a 1 denoting the presence of delinquent friends at each age and a 0 denoting their absence. Beside each pattern is its observed frequency (expressed as a percentage of the total) in the 13 through 17 cohort. The analysis is limited to four offenses (alcohol, marijuana, cheating, and petty theft) because of extremely small N's for burglary and grand theft.

The patterns of most immediate interest, however, are those indicated with an asterisk. A close look at those patterns shows that they represent a special ordering or sequence of friendships. That is, delinquent friends, once acquired, are not lost in subsequent years. This phenomenon, which might be called "sticky friends," is crucial to understanding these data. Although the five sticky-friends patterns constitute only 15.6% of the 32 possible patterns, together they account for 56.5% of the observed

cases, and about two thirds (67.1%) of those with delinquent friends (that is, excluding pattern 32).

Much the same pattern obtains for marijuana use, although a sizable minority of respondents (42.9%) never had friends who smoked marijuana during this period. Consequently, the sticky-friends patterns include only 37.5% of all cases, but they again constitute nearly two thirds (65.7%) of those who had delinquent friends at some age. Cheating also demonstrates this phenomenon, although to a lesser degree—45.4% of those with delinquent friends fall into the sticky patterns. For theft, however, the sticky pattern is weak; only about a third (31.3%) of respondents with delinquent friends fit the pattern.

These data, then, demonstrate a general, though far from universal, tendency for adolescents to retain delinquent friends once they have been acquired.

Priority and Duration

Recall that Sutherland stipulated priority and duration as two critical elements of differential association. Hence, exposure to delinquent influences in early life has a lasting influence on behavior, and exposure to delinquent influences over prolonged periods has a greater effect than exposure over more limited periods.

The NYS data provide an opportunity to examine the effect of both priority and duration. Concentrating once again on the period from age 13 through age 17, priority was measured as the number of years prior to age 17 at which respondents first reported delinquent friends (again using a binary measure of delinquent friends). Priority thus assumes a score of 0-4. Duration was calculated as the total number of years in which the respondent reported having delinquent friends, and ranges from 1 to 5. Because duration and priority have meaning only for persons who have delinquent friends, the analysis is limited to that subset of respondents.

Now consider the relation between duration and priority. Although these parameters are

TABLE 1

Age patterns of delinquent friendships for four offenses.

	Age					Offense			
	13	14	15	16	17	Alcohol	Marijuana	Cheating	Theft < $5
1	1	1	1	1	1*	13.0	5.4	18.5	3.3
2	1	1	1	1	0	1.1	0.0	3.4	1.1
3	1	1	1	0	1	0.0	0.0	1.7	0.6
4	1	1	1	0	0	0.0	0.5	2.2	0.6
5	1	1	0	1	1	1.6	0.0	1.7	0.0
6	1	1	0	1	0	0.5	0.5	0.0	0.6
7	1	1	0	0	1	0.5	0.0	1.1	0.6
8	1	1	0	0	0	0.0	0.0	2.2	2.2
9	1	0	1	1	1	4.3	1.6	4.5	0.6
10	1	0	1	1	0	0.0	0.0	1.1	0.0
11	1	0	1	0	1	0.0	0.0	1.1	0.0
12	1	0	1	0	0	0.0	0.5	0.0	0.0
13	1	0	0	1	1	0.5	0.5	2.2	0.0
14	1	0	0	1	0	0.5	0.0	0.6	2.2
15	1	0	0	0	1	0.5	0.0	1.7	0.6
16	1	0	0	0	0	1.6	0.5	1.1	3.3
17	0	1	1	1	1*	10.9	8.7	9.0	2.2
18	0	1	1	1	0	1.1	1.6	1.1	0.0
19	0	1	1	0	1	1.1	1.1	0.6	0.0
20	0	1	1	0	0	0.5	1.1	1.1	1.1
21	0	1	0	1	1	3.8	0.5	1.7	1.1
22	0	1	0	1	0	0.0	0.0	0.6	0.6
23	0	1	0	0	1	1.1	0.5	1.7	0.6
24	0	1	0	0	0	0.0	0.5	3.4	3.3
25	0	0	1	1	1*	12.0	4.9	5.6	1.7
26	0	0	1	1	0	2.7	3.8	2.8	1.1
27	0	0	1	0	1	2.2	1.1	1.7	2.8
28	0	0	1	0	0	1.1	1.6	3.4	2.8
29	0	0	0	1	1*	10.3	9.8	1.7	1.7
30	0	0	0	1	0	2.7	3.3	3.9	2.8
31	0	0	0	0	1*	10.3	8.7	3.9	3.9
32	0	0	0	0	0	15.8	42.9	14.6	59.1
						100%	100%	100%	100%
					(N)	(184)	(184)	(178)	(181)

*Sticky-friends patterns.

logically distinct, they are not, as it happens, empirically distinct. That is, the two parameters are rather strongly correlated across individuals (from .48 to .82 among the four offenses). Why? The answer lies in the sticky-friends phenomenon observed earlier. Because those who acquire delinquent friends are likely to retain them, those who acquire such friends at younger ages (greater priority) will tend to have longer histories of delinquent friendship (greater duration). Hence, the two elements cannot be regarded as entirely orthogonal components of differential association.

The correlation between priority and duration suggested that it might be difficult to distinguish their effects on delinquency, but analyses show otherwise—the regression of self-reported delinquency at age 17 on priority and duration for each of the four offenses. In all four instances, duration has a substantial and statistically significant effect on delinquency. The coefficient for priority is also significant in three of the four cases, but in all four cases the coefficient is *negative*. The meaning of the models can thus be stated simply: The cumulative number of years in which an adolescent has delinquent friends has a positive effect on his or her current behavior. But among adolescents with the same duration of delinquent friendships, those who acquired delinquent friends *most recently* are those who are most prone to delinquency.

DISCUSSION AND CONCLUSION

The results provide mixed support for Sutherland's arguments about priority and duration. Although the duration of delinquent friendships operates as suggested, the priority of delinquent friendships acts in precisely the opposite fashion: Recent rather than early friends have the greatest effect on delinquency. This finding may surprise some, but it is surely more consistent with modern social learning theory, with its emphasis on reinforcement, extinction, and modeling or imitation.

Aside from priority and duration, the findings concerning "sticky friends" should be of general interest to criminologists. The sticky-friends phenomenon may reflect the normal process of homophily, heightened perhaps by the special camaraderie that comes from sharing illicit adventures. It is premature at this point to attach any definite interpretation to the phenomenon, especially when the domain to which it applies (i.e., offenses and persons) is not well established. But the matter clearly deserves further scrutiny.

Now recall the major issue of this paper, that the age distribution of crime cannot be explained by any variables known to criminology. The analysis presented herein shows that when measures of peer influence are held constant, the association between age and crime is substantially weakened and, for some offenses, disappears entirely. Instead of an impenetrable conundrum, the age-crime relation appears to be at least partially explicable by variables from differential association theory.

This conclusion is likely to be challenged on several grounds, and some of those objections deserve mention. The analysis covers a relatively small number of offenses, and none of the offenses is a violent offense. In addition, the explanatory variables largely fail to explain age variation in one of those offenses—cheating on school tests. There are several possible explanations for this anomaly. Although the analysis concentrated exclusively on peer influence, the relevant reference group when it comes to academic performance may well be *parents* rather than peers. That is, it seems much more likely that students cheat in order to win the approval of their parents rather than their peers. Another potential explanation comes from strain theory. Students with high aspirations and expectations for college would be expected under the theory to be the least delinquent and the least susceptible to delinquent peers. But those same students also have the greatest motivation to cheat in school in order to realize their goals. Hence, delinquent peers may have less relevance for cheaters than for other types of offenders. Whatever the explanation, the point is that differential association cannot explain the age distribution of all offenses.

Another possible objection is a conventional criticism of differential association theory (or tests thereof), that is, the issue of causal order. Rather than reflecting the influence of peers, it is argued, the association between delinquent peers and self-reported delinquency may simply express the tendency of delinquents to select persons like themselves as friends.

A growing body of longitudinal studies points to a more complex sequential, reciprocal process: Adolescents are commonly introduced to delinquency by their friends and subsequently become more selective in their choices of friends. This position is consistent with the sticky-friends phenomenon reported earlier, although it is not the only explanation for it. Still, even if the causal order assumed in this analysis is incorrect, it nonetheless remains true that the introduction of peer variables largely obviates the effects of age in the models examined. If differential selection of peers accounts for the age distribution of crime, so be it.

A final possible criticism of the findings is that they reflect nothing more than a spurious association. That is, peer delinquency explains the age distribution of delinquency because respondent's delinquency and friends' delinquency share a common association with age. That conclusion, however, is contradicted by the analysis. Recall that when age and peer behavior are introduced into the same equation, it is age—not peer behavior—that is rendered insignificant. Consequently, it is difficult to avoid the conclusion that it is *age* that is spuriously associated with delinquency.

If differential association does at least partially explain the age distribution of crime, it still does not resolve all questions. For example, if adolescents learn delinquent attitudes or behaviors from their friends, where do those attitudes or behaviors ultimately originate?

At the very least, this analysis suggests that it is premature to reject differential association as an explanation for the age distribution of crime. Rejecting a correct theory is no less serious than affirming a false one, and the evidence against differential association is simply insufficient at this time to justify rejection. The social character of crime, after all, is as persistent a feature as the age distribution of crime, and the two phenomena may be more closely related than criminologists have previously realized.

QUESTIONS FOR DISCUSSION AND WRITING

1. What four aspects of peer relations consistent with Sutherland's general intentions did the author consider?
2. To what initial conclusion does the evidence point?
3. What are "sticky friends," and what tendency do they demonstrate?
4. How can the meaning of the models "be stated simply"? How do the results provide mixed support for Sutherland's arguments about priority and duration?

GANGS

Violent Crimes in City Gangs

WALTER B. MILLER

THE 1960s have witnessed a remarkable upsurge of public concern over violence in the United States. The mass media flash before the public a vivid and multivaried kaleidoscope of images of violence. Little attention is paid to those who question the assumption that the United States is experiencing an unparalleled epidemic of violence, who point out that other periods in the past may have been equally violent or more so; that troops were required to subdue rioting farmers in 1790, rioting tax protesters in 1794, rioting laborers in the 1870s and 1880s, and rioting railroad workers in 1877; that race riots killed 50 people in St. Louis in 1917 and erupted in 26 other cities soon after; that 57 whites were killed in a slave uprising in 1831; that the Plug Uglies, Dead Rabbits, and other street gangs virtually ruled parts of New York for close to 40 years; that rival bootleg mobs engaged in armed warfare in Chicago and elsewhere during the Capone era; and that the number killed in the 1863 draft riots in New York was estimated at up to 1,000 men. Nevertheless, however much one may question the conviction that the United States today is engulfed in unprecedented violence, one can scarcely question the ascendancy of the *belief* that it is. It is this belief that moves men to action—action whose consequences are just as

real as if the validity of the belief were incontrovertible.

Close to the core of the public imagery of violence is the urban street gang. The imagery evokes tableaux of sinister adolescent wolf packs prowling the darkened streets of the city intent on evil-doing, of grinning gangs of teenagers tormenting old ladies in wheelchairs and ganging up on hated and envied honor students, and of brutal bands of black-jacketed motorcyclists sweeping through quiet towns in orgies of terror and destruction. The substance of this image and its basic components of human cruelty, brutal sadism, and a delight in violence for its own sake have become conventionalized within the subculture of professional writers. The tradition received strong impetus in the public entertainment of the early 1950s with Marlon Brando and his black-jacketed motorcycle thugs, gathered momentum with the insolent and sadistic high-schoolers of *The Blackboard Jungle,* and achieved the status of an established ingredient of American folklore with the Sharks and Jets of the *West Side Story.*

What is the reality behind these images? Is the street gang fierce and romantic like the Sharks and Jets? Is it a tough but good-hearted bunch of rough-and-ready guys like the "Gang That Sang Heart of My Heart"? Or is it brutal and ruthless like the motorcyclists in *The Wild Ones?* In many instances where an area of interest engages both scholars and the public, most of the public embrace one set of conceptions and most scholars, another. This is not so in the case

From "Violent Crimes in City Gangs" by W. Miller, 1966, *Annals of the American Academy of Political and Social Science, 364,* pp. 96-112. Copyright 1966 by The American Academy of Political and Social Science. Reprinted by permission.

of the street gang; there is almost as much divergence within the ranks of scholars as there is between the scholars and the public.

What is the reality behind these differences? The question is readily raised, but is not, unfortunately, readily answered. There exists in this area of high general interest a surprising dearth of reliable information. It is quite possible that discrepancies between the statements of scholars arise from the fact that each is referring to different kinds of gangs in different kinds of neighborhoods in different kinds of cities. We simply do not know. Lacking the information necessary to make general statements as to the nature of violence in the American city gang, it becomes obvious that one major need is a series of careful empirical studies of particular gangs in a range of cities and a variety of neighborhoods. The present chapter is an attempt to present such information for one inner-city neighborhood, "Midcity," in a major eastern city, "Port City." In the present report "violent crimes" are defined as legally proscribed acts whose primary object is the deliberate use of force to inflict injury on persons or objects, and, under some circumstances, the stated intention to engage in such acts.

CIRCUMSTANCES AND METHODS OF STUDY

Conclusions presented in subsequent sections are based on the research findings of an extensive study of youth gangs in Midcity, a central-city slum district of 100,000 persons. Information was obtained on some 150 corner gangs, numbering about 4,500 males and females, aged 12 to 20, in the middle and late 1950s. Selected for more detailed study were 21 of these gangs numbering about 700 members; selection was based primarily on their reputation as the "toughest" in the city. Study data of many kinds were obtained from numerous sources, but the great bulk of data was derived from the detailed field records of workers who were in direct daily contact with gang members for periods averaging 2 years per gang. Seven of these

gangs, numbering 205 members (four white male gangs, one Negro male, one white female, one Negro female) were subject to the most intensive field observation and are designated "intensive observation" gangs. Findings presented here are based primarily on the experience of these seven, along with that of 14 male gangs numbering 293 members (including the five intensive-observation male gangs) whose criminal records were obtained from the state central criminal records division.

Detailed qualitative information on the daily behavior of gang members in 60 "behavioral areas" (e.g., sexual behavior, family behavior, and theft) was collected and analyzed; however, the bulk of the findings presented here will be quantitative in nature, due to requirements of brevity. Present findings are based primarily on three kinds of data: (a) field-recorded behavior—all actions and sentiments recorded for the seven intensive-observation gangs which relate to assault ($N = 1,600$); (b) field-recorded crimes—all recorded instances of illegal acts of assault and property damage engaged in by members of the same gangs ($N = 228$); and (c) court-recorded crimes—all charges of assaultive or property damage offenses recorded by court officials for members of the 14 male gangs between the ages of 7 and 27 ($N = 138$).

THE PATTERNING OF VIOLENT CRIMES IN CITY GANGS

Study data make it possible to address a set of questions central to any consideration of the reality of violent crime in city gangs. How prevalent are violent crimes, both in absolute terms and relative to other forms of crime? What proportion of gang members engage in violent crimes? Is individual or collective participation more common? Are those most active in such crimes more likely to be younger or older? White or Negro? Male or female? Higher or lower in social status? What forms do violent crimes take, and which forms are most prevalent? Who and what are the targets of violent crimes? How serious are they? How does violence figure in the daily lives of gang members?

The following sections present data bearing on each of these questions, based on the experience of Midcity gangs in the 1950s. The first section bears on the last of the questions just cited: What was the role of assaultive behavior in the daily lives of gang members?

Assault-Oriented Behavior

Approximately 1,600 actions and sentiments relating to assaultive behavior were recorded by field-workers during the course of their work with the seven intensive-observation gangs—a period averaging 2 years per gang.

This number comprised about 3% of a total of about 54,000 actions and sentiments oriented to some 60 behavioral areas (e.g., sexual behavior, drinking behavior, theft, and police-oriented behavior). Assault-oriented behavior was relatively common, ranking ninth among 60 behavioral areas. A substantial portion of this behavior, however, took the form of words rather than deeds; for example, while the total number of assault-oriented actions and sentiments was over two and a half times as great as those relating to theft, the actual number of "arrestable" incidents of assault was less than half the number of theft incidents. This finding is concordant with others which depict the area of assaultive behavior as one characterized by considerably more smoke than fire.

About one half (821) of the 1,600 actions and sentiments were categorized as "approved" or "disapproved" with reference to a specified set of evaluative standards of middle-class adults; the remainder were categorized as "evaluatively neutral." There were approximately 30 disapproved assault-oriented actions for every instance of arrestable assault, and 5 instances of arrestable assault for every court appearance on assault charges. Males engaged in assault-oriented behavior far more frequently than females (males, 6.3 events per month; females, 1.4), and younger males more frequently than older.

Separate analyses were made of behavior oriented to "individual" assault (mostly fights between two persons) and "collective" assault (mostly gang fighting). With regard to individual assault, the number of actions and the number of sentiments were approximately equal (181 actions, 187 sentiments); in the case of collective assault, in contrast, there was almost twice as much talk as action (239 sentiments, 124 actions). Sentiments with respect both to individual and collective assault were supportive of disapproved behavior, but collective assault received less support than individual. Behavior *opposing* disapproved assault showed an interesting pattern; specific actions aimed to inhibit or forestall collective assault were over twice as common as actions opposing individual assault. Gang members thus appeared to be considerably more reluctant to engage in collective than in individual fighting; the former was dangerous and frightening, with uncontrolled escalation a predictable risk, while much of the latter involved relatively mild set-to's between peers within the "controlled" context of gang interaction.

Assault-oriented behavior, in summary, was relatively common, but a substantial part of this behavior entailed words rather than deeds. Both actions and sentiments ran counter to conventional middle-class adult standards, with these two levels of behavior concordant in this respect. Insofar as there did exist an element of assault-inhibiting behavior, it was manifested in connection with collective rather than individual assault. This provides evidence for the existence within the gang of a set of "natural" forces operating to control collective assault, a phenomenon to be discussed further.

Frequency of Violent Crime

The wide currency of an image of violence as a dominant occupation and preoccupation of street gangs grants special importance to the question of the actual prevalence of violent crimes. How frequently did gang members engage in illegal acts of assault and property damage? Members of the five intensive-observation male gangs, on the basis of field records of known offenses, were involved in violent crimes at a rate of somewhat under one offense for each two boys per 10-month period, and the 14 male gangs, on the basis of court-recorded offenses, were charged with violent crimes at a rate of somewhat under one charge for each two boys during the 12-year period from ages 7 through 18.

The figures would indicate that violence and violent crimes did not play a dominant role in the lives of Midcity gangs. The cumulative figures taken alone—228 known offenses by 155 boys during a period of approximately 2 years, and 138 court charges for 293 boys during a 12-year age span—would appear to indicate a fairly high "absolute" volume of violent crime. If, however, the volume of such crime is compared with that of other forms with "violent" behavior, both actional and verbal, comprising less than 4% of all recorded behavior, field-recorded violent offenses comprising less than one quarter of all known offenses, and court charges of violent crimes less than one fifth of all charges, violence appears neither as a dominant preoccupation of city gangs nor as a dominant form of criminal activity. Moreover, one should bear in mind that these rates apply to young people of the most violent sex, during the most violent years of their lives, during a time when they were members of the toughest gangs in the toughest section of the city.

Findings relating to race run counter to those of many studies which show Negroes to be more violent than whites and to engage more actively in violent crimes. Comparing similar status white and Negro gangs in Midcity shows that racial differences were relatively unimportant, and that, insofar as there were differences, it was the whites rather than the Negroes who were more likely both to engage in and to be arrested for violent crimes. White gang members engaged in field-recorded acts of illegal violence twice as often as Negro gang members and were charged in court one and a half times as often. These data, moreover, do not support a contention that Negroes who engage in crime to

a degree similar to that of whites tend to be arrested to a greater degree. Court data, however, show that the Negro boys, with a higher rate of field-recorded crime, have a slightly lower rate of court-recorded crime. An explanation of these findings cannot be undertaken here; for present purposes it is sufficient to note that carefully collected data from one major American city do not support the notion that Negroes are more violent than whites at *similar social status levels,* nor the notion that high Negro arrest rates are invariably a consequence of the discriminatory application of justice by prejudiced white policemen and judges.

Was there any relationship between the age of gang members and their propensity to engage in violent crimes? The data indicate quite clearly that involvement in violent crimes was a relatively transient phenomenon of adolescence and did not presage a continuing pattern of similar involvement in adulthood. It should also be noted that these findings do not support an image of violent crimes as erratically impulsive, uncontrolled, and unpredictable. The fact that the practice of violent crime by gang members showed so regular and so predictable a relationship to age would indicate that violence was a "controlled" form of behavior—subject to a set of shared conceptions as to which forms were appropriate, and how often they were appropriate, at different age levels.

What proportion of gang members engaged in assaultive crimes? During the 2-year period of field observation, 53 of the 205 intensive-contact gang members (26%) were known to have engaged in illegal acts of assault—50 out of 155 males (32%), and 3 out of 50 females (6%). While there is little doubt that some gang members also engaged in assaultive crimes that were known neither to field-workers nor officials, the fact that three quarters of the gang members and two thirds of the males were not known to have engaged in assaultive crimes during the observation period and that 88% of the males and 100% of the females did not appear in court on charges of assaultive crimes strengthens the previous conclusion that assault was not a dominant form of gang activity.

A related question concerns the relative prevalence of individual and collective assault. One image of gang violence depicts gang members as cowardly when alone, daring to attack others only when bolstered by a clear numerical superiority. Study data give little support to this image. Fifty-one percent of recorded assault incidents involved either one-to-one engagements or engagements in which a single gang member confronted more than one antagonist. A good proportion of the targets of collective assault were also groups rather than individuals. Some instances of the "ganging-up" phenomenon did occur, but they were relatively infrequent.

What was the character of violent crime in Midcity gangs? In three quarters of all incidents, participants on both sides were peers of the same sex. In 60% of the incidents, gang members acted in groups; in 40%, as individuals. Fifty-one percent of the incidents involved collective engagements between same-sex peers. The most common form was the collective engagement between members of different gangs; it constituted one third of all forms and was three times as common as the next most common form. Few of these engagements were full-scale massed-encounter gang fights; most were brief strike-and-fall-back forays by small guerrilla bands. It should be noted that those forms of gang assault which most alarm the public were rare. No case of assault on an adult woman, either by individuals or groups, was recorded. In three of the four instances of sexual assault on a female peer, the victim was either a past or present girlfriend of the attacker.

The character of violent crimes acted on by the courts parallels that of field-recorded crimes. About one third of all assault charges involved the threat rather than the direct use of force. The most common charge was assault and battery, including, primarily, various kinds of unarmed engagements such as street fighting and barroom brawls. The more serious forms of assaultive crime were among the less prevalent: armed assault, 8%; armed robbery, 5%; sexual assault, 4%. Not one of the 293 gang members appeared in court on charges of either murder or manslaughter between the ages of 7 and 27.

The use of weapons and the inflicting of injury are two indications that violent crimes are of the more serious kind. Weapons were employed in a minority of cases of assault actual or threatened, figuring in 16 of the 88 field-recorded offenses, and about 55 of the 187 court offenses. In none of the 88 incidents was a firearm of any description used. The bulk of assaultive incidents, then, involved the direct use of the unarmed body; this finding accords with others in failing to support the notion that gang members engage in assault only when fortified by superior resources.

What categories of person were targets of gang assault, and what kinds of physical objects were targets of damage? One image of gang violence already mentioned sees the act of "ganging up" on solitary and defenseless victims as a dominant gang practice; another sees racial antagonism as a major element in gang violence.

Of 77 targets of assault whose identity was known, a substantial majority (73%) were persons of the same age and sex category as the gang members, and a substantial majority (71%), of the same race. One half of all targets were peers of the same age, sex, and race category. There was no recorded instance of collective assault on a child, on old men or women, or on females by males. There was no instance of an attack on a white female by a Negro male.

These data thus grant virtually no support to the notion that favored targets of gang attacks are the weak, the solitary, the defenseless, and the innocent; in most cases assaulters and assaultees were evenly matched; the bulk of assaultive incidents involved contests between peers in which the preservation and defense of gang honor was a central issue.

An important form of gang violence is the gang fight; fiction and drama often depict gang fighting or gang wars as a central feature of gang life (e.g., *West Side Story*). The Midcity study conceptualized a fully developed gang fight as involving four stages: initial provocation, initial attack, strategy-planning and mobilization, and counterattack. During the study period, members of the intensive-observation gangs participated in situations involving some combination of these stages 15 times. Despite intensive efforts by prowar agitators and elaborate preparations for war, only one of these situations eventuated in full-scale conflict; in the other 14, one or both sides found a way to avoid open battle.

A major objective of gang members was to put themselves in the posture of fighting without actually having to fight. The gangs used a variety of techniques to maintain their reputation as proud men, unable to tolerate an affront to honor, without having to confront the dangerous and frightening reality of massed antagonists. Among these were the "fair fight" (two champions represent their gangs a la David and Goliath); clandestine informing of police by prospective combatants; reluctantly accepting mediation by social workers.

Despite the very low ratio of actual to threatened fighting, a short-term observer swept up in the bustle and flurry of fight-oriented activity, and ignorant of the essentially ritualistic nature of much of this activity, might gain a strong impression of a great deal of actual violence. In this area, as in others, detailed observation of gangs over extended periods revealed that gang fighting resembled other forms of gang violence in showing much more smoke than fire.

THE PROBLEM OF GANG VIOLENCE

The picture of gang violence which emerges from the study of Midcity gangs differs markedly from the conventional imagery as well as from that presented by some scholars. How is this difference to be explained? The most obvious possibility is that Midcity gangs were somehow atypical of gangs in Port City, and of the "true" American street gang. In important respects, the gangs were not representative of those in Port City, having been selected on the basis of their reputation as the toughest in the city, and were thus more violent than the average Port City gang. The possibility remains, in the absence of information equivalent in scope and detail to that presented here, that Port City gangs were atypical of, and less violent than,

gangs in other cities. I would like in this connection to offer my personal opinion, based on 10 years of contact with gang workers and researchers from all parts of the country, that Midcity gangs were in fact quite typical of tough gangs in Chicago, Brooklyn, Philadelphia, Detroit, and similar cities and represent the reality of gang violence much more accurately than "The Wild Ones" or the Egyptian Kings, represented as the prototypical "violent gang" in a well-known television program.

Even if one grants that actual city gangs are far less violent than those manufactured by the mass media and that the public fear of gangs has been unduly aroused by exaggerated images, the problem of gang violence is still a real one. However one may argue that all social groups need outlets for violence and that gang violence may serve to siphon off accumulated aggression in a "functional" or necessary way, the fact remains that members of Midcity gangs repeatedly violated the law in using force to effect theft, in fighting, and in inflicting damage on property as regular and routine pursuits of adolescence. *Customary* engagement in illegal violence by a substantial sector of the population, however much milder than generally pictured, constitutes an important threat to the internal order of any large urbanized society, a threat which must be coped with. What clues are offered by the research findings of the Midcity study as to the problem of gang violence and its control?

First, a brief summary of what it *was*. Violence as a concern occupied a fairly important place in the daily lives of gang members, but was distinguished among all forms of behavior in the degree to which concern took the form of talk rather than action. Violent crime as such was fairly common during middle and late adolescence, but relative to other forms of crime, was not dominant. Most violent crimes were directed at persons, few at property. Only a small minority of gang members was active in violent crimes. Race had little to do with the frequency of involvement in violent crimes, but social status figured prominently. The practice of violent crimes was an essentially transient phenomenon of male adolescence, reaching a peak at the age when concern with attaining adult manhood was at a peak. While the nature of minor forms showed considerable variation, the large bulk of violent crime in Midcity gangs consisted in unarmed physical encounters between male antagonists either in the classic form of combat skirmishes between small bands of warriors or the equally classic form of direct combative engagement between two males.

Next, a brief summary of what it was *not*. Violence was not a dominant activity of the gangs nor a central reason for their existence. Violent crime was not a racial phenomenon—either in the sense that racial antagonisms played a major role in gang conflict, or that Negroes were more violent, or that resentment of racial injustice was a major incentive for violence. It was not "ganging up" by malicious sadists on the weak, the innocent, the solitary. It did not victimize adult females. With few exceptions, violent crimes fell into the "less serious" category, with the extreme or shocking crimes rare.

One way of summarizing the character of violent crime in Midcity gangs is to make a distinction between two kinds of violence—"means" violence and "end" violence. The concept of violence as a means involves the notion of a resort to violence when other means of attaining a desired objective have failed. Those who undertake violence in this context represent their involvement as distasteful but necessary—an attitude epitomized in the parental slogan, "It hurts me more than it does you." The concept of violence as an end involves the notion of eager recourse to violence for its own sake epitomized in the mythical Irishman who says, "What a grand party! Let's start a fight!" The distinction is illustrated by concepts of two kinds of policeman—the one who with great reluctance resorts to force in order to make an arrest and the brutal policeman who inflicts vio-

lence unnecessarily and repeatedly for pure pleasure. It is obvious that "pure" cases of either means- or end-violence are rare or nonexistent; the purest means-violence may involve some personal gratification, and the purest end-violence can be seen as instrumental to other ends.

In the public mind, means-violence is unfortunate but sometimes necessary; it is the spectacle of end-violence which stirs deep indignation. Much of the public outrage over gang violence arises from the fact that it has been falsely represented, with great success, as pure end-violence ("senseless," "violence for its own sake") when it is largely, in fact, means-violence.

What are the ends toward which gang violence is a means, and how is one to evaluate the legitimacy of these ends? Most scholars of gangs agree that these ends are predominantly ideological rather than material, and revolve on the concepts of prestige and honor. Gang members fight to secure and defend their honor as males; to secure and defend the reputation of their local area and the honor of their women; to show that an affront to their pride and dignity demands retaliation. Combat between males is a major means for attaining these ends.

It happens that great nations engage in national wars for almost identical reasons. It also happens, ironically, that during this period of national concern over gang violence our nation is pursuing, in the international arena, very similar ends by very similar means. At root, the solution to the problem of gang violence lies in the discovery of a way of providing for men the means of attaining cherished objectives—personal honor, prestige, defense against perceived threats to one's homeland—without resort to violence. When men have found a solution to this problem, they will at the same time have solved the problem of violent crimes in city gangs.

QUESTIONS FOR DISCUSSION AND WRITING

1. "In summary," what do the authors say about assault-oriented behavior?
2. How frequently did gang members engage in illegal acts of assault and property damage?
3. What proportion of gang members engaged in assaultive crimes?
4. Did the authors find support for "the notion that favored targets of gang attacks are the weak, the solitary, the defenseless, and the innocent"?

Social Learning Theory, Self-Reported Delinquency, and Youth Gangs

L. THOMAS WINFREE, JR.
TERESA VIGIL BÄCKSTRÖM
G. LARRY MAYS

G ANG researchers typically describe the "costs" and "rewards" of gang behavior and the social context—complete with initiation rituals—in which one becomes a full-fledged member; concurrently, they describe the gang's primacy for its members, the intensity that terms like "the hood" or *"mi barrio"* have for many gang members, and the priority of loyalty to the gang, a loyalty bordering on that normally expressed for one's family. That is, without specifically mentioning either differential association theory or social learning theory, many observes of the gang scene, but especially the subcultural/cultural transmission writers, have used the basic terminologies and causal processes of both theories to describe and explain the gang problem. We believe, therefore, that elements of social learning theory hold much promise for providing insights into the process of becoming and continuing as a gang member. To this end, we address the following question: To what extent are attitudes toward gangs and gang activity, social reinforc-

ers and punishers, and differential associations linked to self-reported gang involvement and gang-related delinquency? Before addressing this question, however, an examination of the ties between social learning theory and youth gangs is in order.

SOCIAL LEARNING THEORY AND YOUTH GANGS: CONCEPTUAL LINKS

Akers's variant of social learning theory represents a merger of Sutherland's differential association theory and operant conditioning. The theory not only specifies the general social learning mechanisms by which the rationalizations, norms, rules, and motivations of non-normative behavior are learned but it also specifies the roles of positive and negative social mechanisms, all of which work to condition the "learner" toward or away from crime. An important element in social learning theory is instrumental conditioning. Behavior is "acquired or conditioned by the effects, outcomes, or *consequences* it has on the person's environment." The primary processes by which instrumental conditioning are achieved are reinforcement and punishment. Behavior is said to be reinforced when repeated episodes are met with a response by others that influences the actor to engage in the behavior again under similar circumstances; as a result, the behavior increases. Behavior is punished when the response of others is such that the actor is discouraged from engaging in the conduct again in similar circumstances; as a result, the behavior decreases. This description of rewards and punishments is nearly identical to those provided by qualitative gang research. Gang members reward certain behaviors in their peers and punish others.

Delinquent conduct is more likely to ensure when young people develop, through reinforcements and punishments, definitions favorable rather than unfavorable to delinquency. For example, defending the neighborhood or the gang's honor—by whatever means necessary—is a discriminative stimuli with high moral authority.

Another point of convergence with Sutherland is found in differential associations, perhaps the single most important explanatory variable. The concept of differential associations—typically operationalized as the proportion of one's best friends that engages in some illicit act—has a natural linkage to gang research. Gangs typically do not encourage active members to have friends, especially close friends, outside of the gang. We suspect that the ties between differential associations and both gang membership and self-reported juvenile misconduct should be as strong as that previously reported between drug-using peers and self-reported illicit drug use. The greater the proportion of one's best friends who are youth-gang members, the greater the social forces impelling the youth to become a gang member.

DATA AND MEASURES

Sample

In early 1991, two independent public school districts in a single southern New Mexico county were approached about a survey of gang-related activities. After much negotiation, the administrators of three area schools agreed

to a limited, stratified random sample of 9th- and 11th-grade students. This research reports on the 9th-grade students only, of which there were approximately 1,000 in attendance at the three schools; 197 individuals formed the final sample for this study.

Nearly two thirds of the youths (62.9%) attended two rural junior high schools located within a few miles of the Mexican border and characterized by a high Mexican-American population. The remaining students (37.1%) lived in a city of 62,000 residents some 20 miles northwest of the rural school district. The final ratio of males to females was 2.3 to 1, slightly lower than called for by the sampling protocol: There were 138 males and 59 females. Three fourths of the sample was Spanish surnamed. Among the remaining students there were very few African and Asian-Americans; Anglos—an indigenous term used to refer to all non-minorities—accounted for 80% of the remaining students. The average student was 15.5 years of age, and the range was 12 to 16 years. Again, with the exception of oversampling males, these statistics suggest that the sample was representative of the communities.

Measures

DELINQUENCY

We employed a self-report delinquency (SRD) inventory. Each respondent was asked to indicate his or her involvement in a list of 22 different activities. The current study focuses on serious youthful misconduct; consequently, 7 self-reported behaviors, including general status offenses (e.g., running away from home, curfew breaking), school-based nonnormative conduct (e.g., skipped school, been suspended from school), and minor misconduct (e.g., spreading rumors about another youth), were dropped from the analysis.

The respondents were asked to indicate, using the following fixed categories, how often they had "broken these rules" since leaving the 8th grade: (1) never, (2) 1 or 2 times, (3) 3 to 5 times, (4) 6 to 10 times, (5) more than 10 times.

We also elected to focus on the level of criminal involvement as opposed to the specific rates of offending. To this end, we assigned a value of "1" to each offense for which the self-reported offending exceeded "once or twice." Individuals who did not report any offending or reported involvement only once or twice were accorded a value of "0." Next, the 15 offenses were grouped into five composite indices: (a) Theft Crimes (taken things worth less than $2; taken things worth between $2 and $50; taken things worth over $50); (b) Other-Property Crimes (borrowed someone's car without his or her permission; destroyed public property; destroyed private property); (c) General Personal Crimes (had a fistfight with one other person; "beat up" on kids who had not done anything to you; hurt or inflicted pain on someone else to see them squirm); (d) Drug-Related Crimes (bought or drank beer, wine, or liquor; used illegal drugs like marijuana or cocaine; sold illegal drugs like marijuana or cocaine); and (e) Group-Context Personal Crimes (taken part in a fight involving more than two people where only fists were used; taken part in a fight involving more than two people where weapons other than fists were used; shot at someone because you were told to by someone else). Using this procedure, the composite scores reflected how many of the offense-specific crimes the youth reported committing three or more times.

GANG MEMBERSHIP

We employed a combination of the self-definitional and criterion methods to determine whether the youth was a *youth gang member*. The instrument included a series of questions related to the respondents' gang involvement. At one point, we asked the following question: "Have you ever been in a gang?" There were three additional criteria that the gang had to possess before we included the youth as a present or former gang member. First, there had to be a group name and at least one of the following cultural elements: (a) an initiation, (b) a specific leader or leaders, and (c) gang "nicknames" for members. Second, the gang had to employ at least one of the following symbols: (a)

"colors," (b) tattoo(s), (c) hand signs, or (d) jewelry. Finally, we asked the youths to rank the five most important activities engaged in by the gang. To qualify as a youth gang, at least one illicit activity (i.e., sex, drugs, or drinking) or one illegal activity (i.e., fighting, committing crimes, or vandalism) had to appear on this list. By this restrictive definitional process, we identified 36 current or former gang members, or 18.3% of the sample of ninth-grade students in the three schools surveyed.

SOCIAL LEARNING MEASURES

Differential Associations. We defined *differential association* as the proportion of one's best friends (i.e., reflecting the intensity dimension) who were involved in gang activity, and measured it by the following question: "About how many of your *best friends* are gang members?" We provided the following response categories for our first measure of differential associations, peer gang members: (a) none or almost none, (b) less than half, (c) more than half, and (d) all or almost all. Most of the students sampled (53.3%) had no friends who were gang members.

The second aspect of differential associations, often tied to the construct of norm qualities, is defined as the perceived values of one's significant others and parents. *Norm qualities* traditionally have been defined as either prescriptive (telling you what to do) or proscriptive (telling you what not to do). More recently, additional aspects of norm qualities have been included in studies of misconduct: Ascriptive norms fail to provide guidance on matters of moral decision making, and permissive norms may not only approve of certain forms of misconduct but may even encourage participation.

In the present context, both the norm qualities of significant-other adults and peers were measured. The following question tapped the permissiveness of significant-other adult norm qualities: "What is the attitude toward gangs of most of the adults whose opinions you value or think are important?" The youths were asked to select one of the following responses: (a) strongly disapprove, (b) disapprove, (c) depends on the circumstances, (d) approve, and (e) strongly approve. The identical question was asked about ". . . teenagers whose opinions you value or think are important." As a general observation, the youths surveyed reported higher levels of peer approval than adult approval.

Differential Reinforcements. Social reinforcers constitute a major component of Akers's variant of social learning theory. Reinforcers are either positive (a reward is received) or negative (a punisher is removed). Similarly, social learning theory places considerable emphasis on the role of punishers to extinguish the behavior.

We asked the subjects to review two lists of what were arbitrarily defined as good and bad things associated with gang membership. The good things included the following: (a) be "cool" (positive social reinforcer), (b) feel successful (positive social reinforcer), (c) be more like someone else (positive social reinforcer), (d) for the excitement (positive nonsocial reinforcer), and (e) for the money (positive nonsocial reinforcer). The list of bad things included the following: (a) get in trouble with the police (negative social punisher), (b) get in trouble with my parents (negative social punisher), (c) lose friends (negative social punisher), (d) feel guilty (negative social/nonsocial punisher), and (e) get hurt (negative nonsocial punisher). The respondents were asked to check those outcomes that they believed could or would happen to gang members. For the purposes of this analysis, we assigned a value of –1 to all punishers and +1 to all reinforcers checked by the students and summed across the 10 items.

The second set of differential reinforcers measures reflected the probable rewarding and punishing reactions of friends and family members when faced with the prospect that the respondent was a gang member. To measure *parents' reactions*, we asked the following question: "What would your parents or guardians most likely do if they thought you were a member of a gang?" Respondents were asked to select one of the following possible responses: (a) encourage you, (b) disapprove but do nothing, (c) scold or punish you, (d) kick you out of the house, and (e) turn you over to the police. In addition, they could give other possible reactions. This latter group, along with the five other responses, was collapsed into a continuum that include negative responses (–1), neutral responses (0), and positive responses (+1). In order to obtain *peers' reactions*, the identical question was asked about ". . . the teenagers whose opinions you value or think are important." As a general observation, the youths surveyed reported more negative reactions among their parents and guardians than was the case for peers.

Differential Definitions. The expression of pro-deviance attitudes has been used in a number of studies to measure differential definitions. Deviant behavior is more likely to result when individuals develop definitions that are favorable rather than unfavorable to that behavior. The pro-deviance differential-definition measure used in this study was grounded in the "gang experience." The subjects were asked whether they disapproved, neither approved nor disapproved, or approved of the following: (a) having friends in gangs, (b) being in a gang yourself, (c) taking part in illegal gang activities such as fights, and (d) doing whatever the gang leaders tell you to do. The higher the scale score, the more progang the attitude.

DESIGN OF THE ANALYSIS

As a result of the variable operationalizations, we employed two different analytic techniques: logistic regression and ordinary least squares regression. First, we were interested in whether the youth had ever been involved in a gang. Our intent was to demonstrate that, knowing certain information about all members of our study, we could predict group membership.

Second, we were interested in the level of youthful involvement in five types of criminal conduct: theft crime, joyriding/destruction crime, personal crime, drug-related crime, and group-context crime. We employed z-score transformations for the measures of delinquency. Thus, using ordinary least squares (OLS) regression, we provide a test of the linkages between social learning theory, gang involvement, and five forms of illegal behavior whereby the unstandardized coefficients can be compared across all forms of illegal behavior.

RESULTS

Youth Gang Membership:
Predicting Involvement in Gangs

The logistic regression equations address the first part of the research question: To what extent is the level of self-reported gang involvement linked to personal-biographical characteristics, social reinforcers, social punishers, attitudes toward gangs and gang activity, and differential associations? It would appear that, although Hispanics and males are more likely to be gang members than nongang members, we should not make too much of this conclusion.

Gang members, more than uninvolved youths, exhibit differential associations (i.e., peers in gangs). It would appear that knowing something about one's friends' involvement in gangs is a better predictor of a youth's own gang involvement than are considerations such as race, sex, or residence pattern. Interestingly, neither the norm qualities of peers nor significant-other adults are important in distinguishing gang members from those who eschew such groups.

Knowing the extent to which a youth possesses progang attitudes provides the single best method of discriminating between gang and nongang youth. This variable alone is a better discriminator than either differential associations or differential reinforcements. Simply put, youth possessing progang attitudes are very likely to be youth-gang members.

Juvenile Crime: Predicting Crime-
Specific Offense Involvement

Given the literature on "gang-related" criminal activity, we suspect that the social learning variables will be of greatest importance for offenses committed in a group context and less so for the more garden-variety SRD offenses. Moreover, the key social learning variables are all grounded in the "gang experience." It is possible that involvement in these other nongroup-context activities is also related to gang membership or social learning factors or both.

THEFT-CRIME OFFENDING

Three variables make significant contributions to the prediction of theft crimes. Specifically, theft crimes are highest among urban, male youths with progang attitudes. This form of offending is not linked in any significant way to the remaining personal-biographical variables or social learning variables. In particular, it is not linked to gang membership. Although possession of the same generally negativistic attitudes as gang members helps us understand this form of offending, gang membership is not critical.

OTHER-PROPERTY CRIME OFFENDING

Higher instances of other-property crimes, including joyriding and vandalism, were reported by males and urban residents than by females and those subjects in rural areas. Like theft crimes, other-property crime offending was tied to the possession of progang attitudes. The relative and absolute contributions of this variable to the other-property crime solution are virtually identical to those reported for theft crime.

PERSONAL-CRIMES OFFENDING

Attitudinally, high personal-crimes offending is best understood in terms of progang attitudes. However, no other social learning variable made a significant impact. Two personal-biographical variables did come into play: Gender exhibited a significant link, with males reporting more instances of offending than females, and Spanish-surnamed youth reported significantly lower levels of offending than other youths.

DRUG-RELATED CRIME

Some different forces appear to be at work. For example, adult approval is inversely and significantly related to offending: The lower the significant-other adult approval of gangs and gang behavior, the greater the offending. We suspect that this observation is related to the fact that those who engage in a wider variety of drug-related offenses also know that the significant-other adults in their lives would disapprove of such conduct. This knowledge, however, does not equate to lower levels of criminal involvement. What we could be seeing is a problem with the time-order sequencing of the data: Those youths who already engage in higher levels of offending also view parental approval with disdain. What is interesting about this finding is its crime-specific nature: It only appears for drug-related offenses. For their part, progang attitudes contribute roughly twice as much to the explained variance as does adult approval: Youths with high progang attitudes also exhibit higher levels of involvement in drug-related crime.

Only place of residence among the personal-biographical variables makes a significant contribution to the regression equation. Its contribution lies above both the reinforcers/punishers index or adult approval and below gang attitudes. Thus, it would appear that to a far greater extent than for any other offense, drug-related offenses may be part of a larger urban crime phenomenon, perhaps even a reflection of the absolute opportunity to buy, sell, and use drugs, including alcohol.

GROUP-CONTEXT PERSONAL CRIMES

Group-context offenses have two main characteristics that together distinguish them from the previous crime indexes. First, they are violent crimes, ranging from various forms of assault to attempted murder. Second, the offenses are by definition either committed in a group setting or at the command of someone else. For example, the two fight scenarios, one with only fists and the other with weapons other than fists, both involve more than two participants;

the third offense, shooting at someone, occurred because of a third party's command or order.

First, being male is not only significantly linked to the conduct, but the coefficient equals the best this variable achieved. Thus, with the exception of drug-related crimes in which gender is relatively unimportant, males reported higher levels of involvement in theft crimes, personal crimes, other-property crimes, and group-context personal crimes.

Second, urban residence pattern makes a significant contribution; however, its contribution is more like that reported for theft and other-property crime than for drug-related crime. Thus, to the extent to which group context is a proxy measurement of "gang-related" crime, illicit gang activity is significantly more likely to occur in an urban setting than a rural one. The relative impact of this variable, however, is between one half and one third of the other significant factors, including gender.

Finally, group-context personal crimes exhibited strong and significant ties to gang attitudes and, for the first time, both differential associations and gang membership. Progang attitudes and differential associations make very similar contributions to the explained variance. Higher levels of involvement are associated with progang attitudes and higher proportions of gang-member peers. Gang membership makes roughly half the contribution of either of these social learning variables. Clearly, gang members are more likely to report higher levels of group offending.

SUMMARY AND DISCUSSION

This research takes a somewhat unique approach to the study of delinquency by applying social learning theory concepts to youth gang membership and related juvenile misconduct. Specifically, we began with the premise that involvement in youth gangs can be understood in terms of social learning theory. Indeed, this was the case: Gang members were distinguishable from nongang youths more in terms of variables derived from social learning than personal-biographical characteristics, including ethnicity, gender, and place of residence.

The level of involvement in offense-specific crimes, including theft crimes, general personal crimes, other-property crimes, and group-context personal crimes, constituted our second focus. We found that three variables were consistently and significantly related to the level of self-reported misconduct. Respondents who had higher identification with progang attitudes, which are by definition antisocial and antilegal, reported more misbehaving. Second, except for personal crimes, city youths reported higher levels of offending than rural youths. Finally, with the exception of drug-related offenses, males were more likely than females to report higher levels of SRD.

Three sets of findings are of particular interest to the question of social learning theory's viability to gang research. First, differential associations, gang attitudes, *and* active gang membership all made significant contributions only in the case of group-context personal crime. This finding configures well with the social learning perspective: This crime type consists of offenses that are committed with a group or at the behest of others. Reinforcing this view is the observation that this offense subscale is the only one in which membership in a gang exhibits a direct and independent link to the rate of offending. Second, along with other recent reports on youth gangs, we did not find a link between gang membership and theft or general personal crimes. Finally, variables derived from social learning performed differently depending on the form of offending. Peer norm qualities and both peer and parental reactions revealed virtually nothing about youthful offending, or, for that matter, about gang membership. Drug-related and group-context crimes, the two forms of offending that exhibited the closest empirical ties to social learning theory, involved different combinations of social learning variables: Drug-related offending was understood largely in terms of the reinforcers/punishers index, adult approval, and progang attitudes; group-context offending added differential associations and youth-gang mem-

bership to progang attitudes, while exhibiting no significant ties to the punishers/reinforcers index or to adult approval. In short, only progang attitudes exhibited consistent insights into youthful misconduct.

We also believe that the analyses contain several noteworthy theoretical and policy implications. First, applying a theory not normally associated with gangs proved substantively and theoretically fruitful. We suggest that the youths in our sample viewed gang behavior much like their peers in other tests of social learning theory have viewed their youthful misconduct, but perhaps with greater connectivity owing to the social nature of gangs. Second, this research runs counter to the conventional police truism that gang members are heavily involved in theft crimes. Along these same lines, although gang members appear to be no more likely than nongang youths to engage in general personal crimes, they are more likely to engage in group-context violence, much of which typically takes the form of intergang or intergroup confrontations. Besides emphasizing the social roots of gangs, this finding may mean that youths predisposed to personal assault crimes may be recognized (and perhaps even recruited) by gangs for their fighting and risk-taking behaviors (i.e., fearlessness), a conclusion supported by other gang researchers.

The fact that gangs are prevalent in the schools surveyed, as determined by independent examinations of school and police records, might explain why "gang attitudes" have effects, even when gang membership's effects are largely limited to group-context personal crimes or crimes of aggression generally. Definitions favorable to misconduct may be more prevalent in an environment where gang members exist than where they do not exist because such definitions may be learned through modeling or other vicarious experiences. Furthermore, this suggestion raises a policy implication: Reducing gangs may reduce crime not only by limiting crime by gang members but also by diminishing the power of "gang reinforcers" (progang attitudes) on nongang members.

QUESTIONS FOR DISCUSSION AND WRITING

1. What are the primary processes by which instrumental conditioning is achieved? When is behavior said to be reinforced? When is it punished?
2. How did progang attitudes affect gang membership?
3. What three variables were consistently and significantly related to the level of self-reported misconduct?

DRUGS

Delinquency and Substance Use Among Inner-City Students

JEFFREY FAGAN
JOSEPH G. WEIS
YU-TEH CHENG

RESEARCH PROBLEM

There is a renewed interest in the drug-crime relationship, especially in the prediction and control of crime through knowledge of substance use. This study provides empirical evidence on the patterns of self-reported drug use and delinquency in urban areas with very high rates of serious juvenile crime. The study provides epidemiological data to estimate the incidence and prevalence of delinquency and drug use among adolescents in inner-city neighborhoods. It examines the extent to which involvement in drug use and delinquency overlap, leading to a typology of delinquent behavior, with patterns of drug use established within types. The study also tests contemporary theoretical explanations of substance use and delinquency. The social correlates that differentiate various patterns of the two kinds of behaviors are identified to determine if separate explanations of drug use and delinquency vary by delinquent type and severity of use.

Fagan, Jeffrey, Joseph G. Weis, and Yu-Teh Cheng. 1990. "Delinquency and Substance Use Among Inner-City Students." *Journal of Drug Issues* 20:351-402.

CONTEMPORARY THEORETICAL EXPLANATIONS

Social control and social learning have been prominent, if not dominant, theories of deviance for nearly two decades. Recent integrations of Hirschi's social control and Akers's social learning theories have been applied to both delinquency, drug use, and the joint behaviors, respectively. This particular theoretical integration has rarely been applied to explain the intersection of drug use and delinquency, and has never been tested under the sampling conditions found in this study.

Social control theory proposes that when social controls are weak, deviant conduct is more likely to occur. That is, when the moral bond that ties people to each other and to social norms is broken, restraints on antisocial behavior are ineffective. Integrations of control and social learning theories attempt to explain the processes that strengthen or weaken social bonds, and, in turn, facilitate the "learning" of criminal values and behaviors. This describes a socialization process where weak social bonds are developed and delinquent socialization becomes the strongest learning influence.

Recent theoretical integrations specify both the domains of socialization and the temporal sequence of their influence. Weis and Hawkins, in the *social development model,* suggest that the social bond develops incrementally in the contexts where the most salient socialization occurs: family, school, peer associations, and community. Fagan and Jones propose that both positive and negative bonds can develop through socialization experiences in family or school among peers, and in the community. The temporal sequence suggests that there is a cumulative effect of positive and negative bonding across domains. Thus, positive socialization in the family influences bonding to school and, later, toward acceptance of law-supporting attitudes and selection of peers.

The theoretical model in this study proposes that the elements of the social bond are strengthened or weakened through socialization experiences in each domain, the family, school, peer groups, and the community. The model also examines neighborhood influences on delinquency and substance use, a departure from earlier theoretical integrations which have neglected the influence of youths' perceptions of neighborhood norms on illegal behavior.

DATA AND METHODS

Samples and Data Collection

A general population sample was drawn from students in four inner-city, high-crime neighborhoods. Student samples were drawn from randomly selected classrooms in each school. The survey questionnaire included demographic items, self-reported delinquency measures, victimization items, and attitudinal measures. Surveys were completed by 342 male and 324 female students in grades 10 through 12.

Measures and Constructs

The survey items included explanatory and behavioral measures corresponding to the inte-

grated theory. The self-reported delinquency items (SRD) were derived from the National Youth Survey items and included questions on delinquent behavior, alcohol and drug use, and other "problem" behaviors. The original 47-item instrument was modified in two ways. First, since the surveys were designed for students in high-crime, inner-city neighborhoods, adjustments to eliminate trivial offenses were necessary. These types of adjustments resulted in the refinement and specification of questions regarding weapons use, specification of victims (i.e., teacher, student, other adult), and elimination of items such as "ran away from home" or "made obscene phone calls." The items modified and retained were those that are serious, actionable crimes which harm, injure, or do damage. Second, at the request of school officials, certain items in the original scales were eliminated, modified, or collapsed. For example, items on family violence were deemed by school administrators to be too sensitive or intrusive and were eliminated.

The prevalence of SRD items within the past 12 months was measured dichotomously, and incidence was measured simply by asking those who reported "yes" how many times they had committed that act. Offense-specific scales, such as ROBBERY or FELONY THEFT, were constructed for homogeneous crime types parallel to UCR categories. The scale scores were derived by summing across nonoverlapping items within the scale. Also, offense-summary scales were constructed to measure broader categories of behavior. These scales increased the range of seriousness of each domain while preserving homogeneity of behavior. These general scales, such as VIOLENCE or PROPERTY, capture broader behavioral characteristics while retaining validity with respect to type of behavior. Finally, GENERAL scales were constructed as summary scales for all types of behavior.

Drug and alcohol use items measured the number of occasions of smoking marijuana, drinking "hard" liquor (excluding beer or wine), and using cocaine, opiates, PCP, or "pills." Other items tapped drug sales (marijuana, cocaine, opiates, or PCP) and attending school "drunk or high."

Drug and alcohol "problem" scales each included six items, reflecting negative social and personal consequences of alcohol or drug use. Each scale asked if the respondent "ever felt you had a drug [or alcohol] problem?" Also, separate items asked whether in the past year, "you have had problems with your family, friends, girlfriend or boyfriend, in school, with the police because of your drinking [or drug use]." Additional items asked the respondent if he or she had gotten into fights or been arrested "because of drinking [or drug use]." Finally, an item asked the respondent if he or she had sought treatment, been in treatment, or been told to seek treatment for drinking or drug use in the past year.

VICTIMIZATION was a bivariate measure of self-reported victimization experiences within the past year. Respondents were asked whether they had been victims of each of four property crimes and three violent acts.

Scales measuring internal (personal) bonds and external (social) bonds within each salient domain (i.e., school, family, peers, and community) were constructed. In general, these variables tap the strength and extent of the youth's interactions with, attachments to, and involvement with the contemporary social institutions presumed to be influential in anchoring adolescents to mainstream social life. SCHOOL INTEGRATION measures participation in school activities, achievement and performance, and relationships with teachers and other students. PEER INTEGRATION and MOTHER ATTACHMENT measured interactions in these domains. ATTITUDE TOWARD THE LAW and ATTITUDE TOWARD VIOLENCE measure approving attitudes in each area: Both law-violating and law-supporting attitudes are assessed, as are attitudes supporting the use of violence for instrumental gain or to exert personal power. Additional variables were included to measure psychosocial domains such as LOCUS OF CONTROL (i.e., internal-external impulse control), and SOCIAL COMPETENCE assesses the respondents' basic functional and

social skills such as filling out a job application or balancing a checkbook.

Measures of the ecological context and social environment were also constructed for the same domains, representing the perceived learning contingencies of the respondent's social world. In this model, social learning variables which may weaken prosocial bonds include criminal behavior, antisocial values, and other deviant behavior perceived in the family, school, and in the neighborhood. The scales for these variables include violence among neighborhood families (in the same block or building) (NEIGHBORHOOD FAMILY VIOLENCE), in school by other students (STUDENTS DELINQUENCY), and in the neighborhood by peers (PEER DELINQUENCY) and neighbors (NEIGHBORHOOD CRIME). Parental supervision practices (MATERNAL SUPERVISION) measure the disciplinary and rule-setting practices in the home.

Those measures have strong explanatory power in both cross-sectional and longitudinal studies of serious delinquency. However, the measures have yet to be thoroughly tested under conditions with oversampling at the extremes of the distribution of SRD behaviors, or in social contexts where the correlates of serious delinquency seem to be concentrated.

RESULTS

Delinquency and Drug Use Typologies

A typology of delinquent involvement was developed to examine the patterns of substance use and delinquency. The typology is hierarchical in that less serious behaviors have been committed by those in successively more serious categories of offenders. Table 1 shows the prevalence and incidence of offense-specific behaviors for each type. Specific alcohol use, drug use, or drug-selling behaviors and incidents of intoxication (i.e., at school or while driving) are not considered in the typology. The categories range from petty acts (e.g., going to school "high" or drunk) to multiple-index felonies.

The categories and distribution of subjects include:

- Multiple-index offenders—those reporting at least three index offenses (felony assault, robbery, or felony theft) within the past year (5.6%).
- Serious delinquents—those reporting one or two index offenses (felony assault, robbery, or felony theft) in the past year, or three or more incidents in the past year of extortion or weapons offenses (12.9%).
- Minor delinquents—those reporting no index offenses and one or two incidents in the past year of extortion or weapons offenses, or four or more incidents in the past year of minor theft, minor assault, vandalism, or illegal services (buying or selling stolen goods, selling drugs) (19.8%).
- Petty delinquents—those reporting no index offenses and three or fewer incidents in the past year of minor assault, minor theft, vandalism, or illegal services (buying or selling stolen goods, selling drugs) (61.9%).

Table 1 shows the distribution of self-reported incidence and prevalence for each delinquent group, using the offense-specific and offense-summary scales of self-reported delinquency. The differences among groups are significant and in the expected directions. "Petty" delinquents are involved only in school-based offenses, generally coming to school high or rarely selling drugs. It appears that the distribution of serious delinquency among inner-city youths is consistent with its distribution in general population studies.

The typology of substance use developed here classifies respondents according to the most serious drug they had consumed in the past year. The seriousness of adolescent substance use has been associated with serious delinquency, and the frequency of *serious* drug use suggests habituation and mirrors the drug-crime patterns observed among adult populations. Accordingly, substances were ranked according to the intensity of the high they create, with a minimum of three annual occurrences to avoid false categorization of experimental use. Alcohol is considered the least serious drug, followed by marijuana, a composite item for other drugs (cocaine, opiates, PCP, barbiturates, and amphetamines), and heroin or other opiates. Four categories comprise the drug use typology: nonusers, and users of alcohol, marijuana, and "hard" drugs (heroin, cocaine, PCP, amphetamines). Nonusers include respondents who have used any drug only once, as well as those who abstain completely. For over 90% of the sample, the typology is hierarchical—users of the more serious drugs had in all cases used the less serious drugs and typically at higher rates than youths in the less serious categories.

*The Relationship Between
Drug Use and Delinquency*

The joint distribution of drug use and delinquency for inner-city high school students is shown in Table 2, which shows the incidence of drug use for each substance by delinquent type.

Some drug and alcohol use is reported among each of the four delinquent types, but use is more frequent among more serious juvenile offenders. Marijuana use was the drug used most frequently for males in all delinquent types, but for females only, among petty and minor offenders. Alcohol was the most frequently used substance for females in the two most serious delinquent types. Analysis of variance for substance use by sex and delinquent type showed that the frequency of smoking marijuana was associated with delinquent type for both males ($p < .001$) and females ($p < .05$)—marijuana use increased sharply for the serious and multiple-index delinquents.

Alcohol use followed similar patterns, though the incidence for multiple-index offenders was less than for marijuana use. Though alcohol use by delinquent type was significantly different, significant gender differences were not detected. Among males, the frequency of marijuana use was greater than alcohol use in

TABLE 1

Mean SRD offense-specific scale scores by delinquent type and sex.

Offense-Specific Scales	Delinquent Type				
	Petty (N = 412)	Minor (N = 131)	Serious (N = 86)	Multiple Index (N = 36)	Pearson R With Typology
Felony assault (a)					
Male	0	0	0.69	5.78	a
Female	0	0	0.64	2.50	.26
Minor assault (a, i)					
Male	0	0.16	0.56	5.14	a
Female	0	0.29	0.28	0.48	.16
Robbery (a, g)					
Male	0	0	0.23	6.76	a
Female	0	0	0.11	1.40	.24
Felony theft (a, g)					
Male	0	0	0.20	4.68	a
Female	0	0	0.15	0.67	.22
Minor theft (a, i)					
Male	0	2.09	9.80	2.55	a
Female	0	1.09	1.50	3.47	.15
Extortion (a, h)					
Male	0	0.14	0.89	11.58	a
Female	0	0.08	1.21	2.00	.25
Property damage (a, i)					
Male	0	3.10	3.56	7.77	a
Female	0	0.25	0.26	11.00	.22
Drug sales (a)					
Male	0.05	0.01	0.28	3.85	a
Female	0.11	0.00	0.00	9.90	.14
Weapons (a)					
Male	0	0.53	6.34	6.83	a
Female	0	0.72	2.78	8.89	.25
School crime (a, g)					
Male (f)	1.12	2.64	12.58	13.65	a
Female	0.81	3.09	0.41	0.89	.20
Offense-summary scales					
Violence (a, g)					
Male	0	0.16	1.48	17.48	a
Female	0	0.29	1.03	4.38	.30
Property (a, i)					
Male	0	5.19	13.49	14.91	a
Female	0	1.34	1.91	15.15	.26
General (a, h)					
Male	2.78	14.18	34.97	84.85	a
Female	2.32	7.87	11.57	40.63	.36

a. Type = $p < .001$.
b. Type = $p < .01$.
c. Type = $p < .05$.
d. Sex = $p < .001$.
e. Sex = $p < .01$.
f. Sex = $p < .05$.
g. Interaction = $p < .001$.
h. Interaction = $p < .01$.
i. Interaction = $p < .05$.

TABLE 2

Mean drug and alcohol use and drug sales in past year by delinquent type and sex.

	Delinquent Type			
"How many times in the past year did you . . ."	Petty (N = 412)	Minor (N = 131)	Serious (N = 86)	Multiple Index (N = 36)
Smoke marijuana (a, f)				
Male	2.88	4.60	12.83	15.59
Female	1.36	3.04	2.88	10.80
Use heroin, cocaine, PCP, speed, or pills (a, c)				
Male	0.01	0.81	0.28	4.03
Female	0.23	0.02	0.03	0.10
Drink whiskey, gin, vodka, or other liquor (c)				
Male	1.63	4.03	4.43	6.64
Female	0.79	2.49	4.34	9.90
Sell marijuana, heroin, cocaine, PCP, speed, or pills (a, i)				
Male	0.05	0.01	0.28	3.85
Female	0.11	0.00	0.00	9.90

a. Type = $p < .001$.   d. Sex = $p < .001$.   g. Interaction = $p < .001$.
b. Type = $p < .01$.   e. Sex = $p < .01$.   h. Interaction = $p < .01$.
c. Type = $p < .05$.   f. Sex = $p < .05$.   i. Interaction = $p < .05$.

all delinquent types, except for less serious female delinquents. In fact, the mean frequency of alcohol use and marijuana use for females was similar, controlling for delinquent type. It seems that among females, the frequencies of marijuana and alcohol use appear to be about the same, and are significantly associated with delinquent type.

Heroin/cocaine/PCP use patterns differed by gender, and they predictably were less frequently used than other substances. For females, most frequent use occurred among the least serious offenders, while for males, use was most frequent for multiple-index offenders. Also, minor offenders were the second most frequent users among males, but for females it was for multiple-index offenders. There was a significant difference by delinquent type ($p < .05$) and gender ($p < .01$).

Finally, drug sales are generally rare events, occurring at high rates only for the few multiple-index offenders. Rates were highest for multiple-index offenders ($p < .01$) for both males and females, and in fact were highest for females. Drug sales rates were higher for females among petty offenders and multiple-index offenders, indicated by a significant interaction effect ($p < .05$). The distribution of drug sales activity mirrors the use patterns, and suggests that selling occurs most often among more serious delinquents. But drug selling and drug use may occur independently, even among the most serious delinquents. It is also noteworthy that among generally poor inner-city youths, drug selling also occurs among some less serious juvenile offenders.

For all delinquent types, serious drug use was the least frequent. Nonusers were most prevalent, ranging from nearly 8 in 10 petty delinquents to about half the serious delinquents. Among petty delinquents, marijuana is the most typical drug used, while a very small number (about 1%) did more serious drugs. At the other extreme of delinquent behavior, nearly half of the most serious delinquents did not use drugs, but about 12% were involved in cocaine or heroin use. Thus, while the association is significant between drug use and delinquent type ($p < .001$), the percent of respondents who are concurrently in the most serious delinquent and drug use categories is about the same as those who use serious drugs but avoid delinquent behavior.

Among inner-city youths, the prevalence of those with serious delinquent and drug abuse problems is small, and there is little evidence that drug or alcohol use is disproportionately concentrated even among the most serious delinquents. Moreover, the data further illustrate the occurrence of substance use and other crimes as part of a more general pattern of deviant behavior, rather than of specialization in substance use or delinquency. There is some evidence that drug and alcohol use generally occur as part of an overall pattern of illicit use of multiple drugs, and that it is the frequency and intensity of highs that influence drug-related delinquency rather than specific drug types. The prevalence and frequency of drug use are highest for both male and female multiple-index offenders, and decrease with the severity of delinquent involvement.

Thus, there is evidence to suggest that the prevalence of serious substance users is higher among more serious delinquent categories. Yet the frequency of getting high across delinquent types does not necessarily increase with the severity of delinquent involvement, for either males or females. That is, while high rate substance users are more prevalent among the most serious delinquent types, the mean substance use does not vary significantly across types. For males, the mean frequency of substance use is actually greater for minor delinquents than for multiple-index types; for females, there is no

significant difference between minor, serious, and multiple-index offenders.

Explanatory Factors in Delinquency and Drug Use

Peer associations, drug and alcohol problem behaviors, and several school and family factors are consistent contributors to delinquency and drug use in general adolescent samples. A central question in this study is whether these relationships persist for inner-city adolescents. Based on the evidence from earlier studies with general adolescent populations, we sought in particular to examine the unique contributions of *problem* use of drugs and alcohol to each behavioral measure.

Stepwise regression analyses were conducted to determine the contributors to delinquency and drug use. Separate models were constructed for the entire sample and for males only. Models were constructed using severity (drug type, delinquent type) and frequency (total SRD, total drug use) measures of each behavior as dependent variables. Independent variables include both measures from control theory (social and attitudinal bonds) and social learning theory (social environment variables). The analyses controlled for the additional contributions of drug and alcohol problems to explained variance by introducing them in the last steps in each model.

All of the models were significant both before and after controlling for drug and alcohol problems (Table 3). However, the explained variance was relatively small, with none of the regression models explaining more than 23% of the variance. The models for the frequency and severity of delinquent involvement differ extensively in their explanatory power, but not in the relative contributions of the predictor variables. The models were consistent for males only and the total sample. PEER DELINQUENCY is the strongest contributor for each measure of delinquency. ATTITUDES TOWARD LAW contributed to both delinquency models, while SCHOOL INTEGRATION and MATERNAL

TABLE 3

Standardized regression coefficients for substance use and delinquency, controlling for problem substance use.

Social Development Variable	Delinquency Type		Frequency of Substance Use		SRD General		Drug Use Type	
		(Total Sample and Males Only)[a, b, c]						
Peer delinquency	.29	(.33)	.14	—	.19	(.19)	.16	(.14)
Victimization	.20	(.21)			.11	—		
Attitude toward law	−.16	(−.20)			−.09	(−.11)	—	(−.14)
School integration	−.13	(−.10)	−.14	(−.14)			−.07	—
Peer integration	.09	(.17)						
Father authority			−.07	(.17)			−.12	(−.10)
Students delinquency	.11	—	.14	—				
Maternal supervision					−.09	—	−.08	—
Social competence							.10	(.10)
Conventional values							−.09	—
R-squared	.229	(.246)	.079	(.049)	.069	(.059)	.118	(.087)
F value	32.6	(21.8)	14.2	(8.7)	16.4	(10.5)	12.4	(8.0)
Probability	.000	(.000)	.000	(.000)	.000	(.000)	.000	(.000)
Drinking problems	.04	(.06)	.20	(.19)	.10	(.08)	.04	(.08)
Drug problems	.02	(.07)	.27	(.36)	.06	(.05)	.25	(.30)
R-squared	.232	(.256)	.230	(.253)	.089	(.071)	.186	(.200)
F value	24.7	(16.4)	32.7	(28.5)	12.8	(6.4)	16.4	(13.8)
Probability	.000	(.000)	.000	(.000)	.000	(.001)	.000	(.000)

a. $N = 665$ total; $n = 323$ males.
b. Total SRD excludes Substance Use.
c. Coefficients for males in parentheses.

SUPERVISION contributed only to SRD frequency. Victimization also contributes to delinquent type but not to the incidence of delinquent acts.

Overall, Table 3 shows that the results for inner-city youths confirm the explanations of delinquency found in longitudinal studies with general adolescent populations. The oft-cited correlates of peer associations, school attachments, and other sources of social "bonding" seem to apply equally well to inner-city youths as more heterogeneous adolescent groups.

DRINKING PROBLEMS and DRUG PROBLEMS added little to the explanatory power of the regression models for delinquency. The explained variance increases about 1% for delinquent acts. The regression coefficients for the two problem variables did not exceed .10 in these models, less than other predictors, and overall were relatively weak contributors to explanations of delinquency. The models suggest that, contrary to Jessor and Jessor and to Elliott and Huizinga, the problem use of drugs or alcohol adds little to explanations of the seriousness or frequency of delinquent involvement.

The marginal contributions of the frequency and seriousness of drug and alcohol problems were analyzed in the same way. Table 3 shows that, before adding problem substance use to the model, variables from control and learning theories yielded weak explanatory power: 7.9% explained variance for frequency of substance use and 11.8% for severity of substance use, prior to considering the contributions of drug or alcohol problem behaviors. Influences from peers, school, and family were strong predictors in both models. For frequency of substance use, school factors were influential at both individual (SCHOOL INTEGRATION) and environmental (STUDENTS DELINQUENCY) levels. The explained variance for males was slightly less than for the total sample. For males, peer influences dropped out of the model for frequency of use, while FATHER AUTHORITY became the strongest contributor in an overall weak model. For type (severity) of drug used, peer influences were the strongest predictors, for both the male and total samples, with VICTIMIZATION and FATHER AUTHORITY making smaller contributions. For males only, ATTITUDE TOWARD LAW entered the model as the strongest contributor.

When DRUG PROBLEMS and DRINKING PROBLEMS are added to the models for severity and frequency of substance use, their explanatory power increases dramatically. The explained variance for frequency of substance use increases from 7.9% to 23.0% overall and from 4.9% to 25.3% for males. For drug type, explained variance increases from 11.8% to 18.6% for the total sample, and from 8.7% to 20.0% for males only. Moreover, the standardized regression coefficients for the problem use variables were the strongest contributors in each model. For frequency of substance use, DRUG PROBLEMS had the highest coefficients for both the total and male samples, and DRINKING PROBLEMS also was a strong contributor. For drug type, only DRUG PROBLEMS was a strong predictor. This suggests that alcohol and drug use may create unique types of "problems" that, in turn, contribute in different ways to the frequency of getting high and the severity of the drug used. That is, problematic use of alcohol may contribute to the frequency of intoxication irrespective of the type of substance used, while problematic use of drugs appears specifically fitted to the use of serious drugs.

This is not surprising, however, given the correlation between frequency of use and the construction of the drug type variable. Apparently, more frequent drug use results in more related social and functional problems. Also, these problems are more likely to occur when the drug used produces a more intense high. The observed patterns suggest that frequent or serious substance use may have disinhibiting effects or simply erode youths' social judgments while intoxicated. However, the moderate explained variances for frequency and type of drug used also suggest that many frequent or serious substance users are not affected by such "problems" and that other factors need to be included to explain their behavior.

The data suggest that explanatory variables from social control and learning theories are significantly related to substance use only for youths with least serious delinquent involvement. For more serious delinquent involvement, there are few differences in theoretical variables by involvement in substance use. Drug use and delinquency are unrelated only for those already involved in more serious delinquent acts. That is, knowledge of school, peer, or other social bonds can differentiate high- and low-severity (or rate) substance abuse only among petty delinquents. Substance use and delinquency seem to be explained by different processes, and it is "problem" use which determines high-rate drug use but not delinquent involvement. Serious substance use and other crime may be independent manifestations of a general and shared pattern of deviant behavior.

CONCLUSIONS

Based on self-reports of high school students in four inner-city neighborhoods, the percent of youths who report serious delinquent involvement in the past year is comparable to that found in general adolescent samples using similar methods and measures. Most students avoid the predictable consequences of relative deprivation in inner cities and are only involved in minor delinquent activities. Moreover, the social correlates of serious crime and substance use are similar for inner-city students and adolescents elsewhere.

The results also reaffirm for inner-city youths the association between substance use and delinquency, but provide new evidence on specific patterns and interactions between the severity and frequency of each type of behavior. The frequency and seriousness of specific types of substance use increase with the severity of delinquent involvement, but the total frequency of use of all substances varies little with the severity or frequency of delinquency.

The data suggest three important relationships. First, the association between substance use and delinquency depends on the severity of delinquency and the type(s) of substance used. Alcohol and illicit drugs have different associations with delinquent involvement, and, consequently, their etiological effects on delinquency also may differ. Moreover, the separate contributions of alcohol and drug "problems" provide further evidence that these substances may be independent contributors to developmental processes.

Second, there appears to be a skewed relationship between substance use and delinquency. Explaining drug use from knowledge of the severity of delinquent involvement is more valid than vice versa; knowing the frequency of drug use by adolescents adds little to explaining the severity of their delinquency. The frequency of delinquent acts is only weakly associated with the frequency of getting high, but the severity of delinquent involvement is more strongly related. Thus, it appears that drug use is associated selectively with serious delinquent involvement: The type of drug used, as well as its frequency, may influence the severity of delinquent involvement.

Third, the intensity of the high produced by specific drugs, rather than simply the frequency of getting high, is associated with the seriousness of delinquent involvement. Sustained use of less serious drugs may be associated differently with delinquency than less frequent but more patterned use of other substances. For example, persistent marijuana use is not associated with serious delinquency, while less frequent cocaine or opiate use is associated with serious delinquency.

Specific findings regarding patterns of substance use also portray inner-city youths as unique from their counterparts in other ecological contexts. First, although females are rarely involved in serious drug use, they frequently are involved in drug sales. Surprisingly, within the multiple-index type of offender, the rate of drug selling by females is more than twice the rate for males. This suggests an important difference between inner-city females and female adolescents in other social contexts. Second, for both males and females in all delinquent types, marijuana is the most frequently used substance. The prevalence and frequency of marijuana use is higher than for either alcohol or cocaine use. This departs from nationwide trends based on surveys of high school seniors and general youth populations.

QUESTIONS FOR DISCUSSION AND WRITING

1. What four categories did the authors use in their delinquency typology, and what percentage of youths were classified into each?

2. What was true about the relationship between drug use and delinquency? What drug was most used by males in all delinquency types? By females?
3. What is true for all delinquent types regarding drug use?
4. What three important relationships do the data suggest?

Data Analysis Exercise

An Exploration of the Correlates of Juvenile Delinquency

In this data analysis exercise, we will again use the Wave I data from the National Youth Survey (NYS) to examine the distribution and correlates of delinquency that are discussed in Part III.

DESCRIPTION OF THE DATA SET

See the exercise for Part II for a description of our data set. Before we start our analyses, we will need to load up our data set, "JDPREV1."

EXPLORING THE CORRELATES OF DELINQUENCY: GETTING A HANDLE ON THE DATA

Now, let's take a quick look at some demographic factors to get a handle on the data. To do this, run frequencies on WHITE,[1] AGE, BROKEN_H, and INCOME.[2] We briefly examined gender in the exercise for Part II, so we do not need to rerun those frequencies again. If you need to refresh your memory regarding how to run frequencies, see Box 1 in the Part II exercise. The frequencies appear in Tables 1 through 4.

Table 1 is the table for WHITE. Remember that other races have been excluded from this data set.

Table 2 is the table for AGE. Notice the range of ages; although it is a small range, it involves some important changes. Although it is difficult to argue

TABLE 1

Frequency for WHITE.

Y1-2: ETHNICITY (v168)

		Frequency	Percent	Valid Percent	Cumulative Percent
Valid	Anglo	1285	85.7	85.7	85.7
	Black	215	14.3	14.3	100.0
	Total	1500	100.0	100.0	

TABLE 2

Frequency for AGE.

Y1-3: AGE (v169)

		Frequency	Percent	Valid Percent	Cumulative Percent
Valid	11	214	14.3	14.3	14.3
	12	229	15.3	15.3	29.5
	13	233	15.5	15.5	45.1
	14	220	14.7	14.7	59.7
	15	225	15.0	15.0	74.7
	16	207	13.8	13.8	88.5
	17	172	11.5	11.5	100.0
	Total	1500	100.0	100.0	

that 31-year-olds are much different from 37-year-olds, it is easy to say that 11-year-olds differ in many important ways from 17-year-olds (especially because the legal system treats them very differently).

Table 3 is the table for BROKEN_H.

TABLE 3

Frequency for BROKEN_H.

Youth from broken home

		Frequency	Percent	Valid Percent	Cumulative Percent
Valid	Intact home	1081	72.1	72.1	72.1
	Broken home	419	27.9	27.9	100.0
	Total	1500	100.0	100.0	

Table 4 is the table for INCOME. Notice the higher numbers of youths at the low end of the income spectrum when compared with the high end of the spectrum. Also notice the 57 missing cases; missing cases are those for which no data are included for a variable for a particular individual (e.g., because the individual did not answer a question on a survey).

TABLE 4

Frequency for INCOME.

Recoded family income

		Frequency	Percent	Valid Percent	Cumulative Percent
Valid	$10,000 or less	342	22.8	23.7	23.7
	$10,001–18,000	487	32.5	33.7	57.4
	$18,001–26,000	378	25.2	26.2	83.6
	$26,001–34,000	139	9.3	9.6	93.3
	$34,001 or more	97	6.5	6.7	100.0
	Total	1443	96.2	100.0	
Missing	System	57	3.8		
Total		1500	100.0		

From the frequencies, we can see that our data contain responses from a large percentage (85.7%) of Anglos and smaller numbers of blacks (14.3%). More than one fourth (27.9%) of the youths come from broken homes.[3] We can also see that our sample contains responses from individuals aged 11 to 17. Some people believe that age can effectively be broken down into high schoolers and younger students, so I created an age-related variable (HS_AGE) that divided the youths into two groups: (1) high school-aged youths, aged 15 to 17 years, and (0) younger students. Run a frequency for HS_AGE to see what it looks like.

With respect to income, we can see that our sample contains more individuals from the lower-income groups when compared with the two highest income groups; in fact, more than half (55.3%, valid percent = 57.4%) of the youths live in families in the lowest two income categories, whereas only one sixth (15.8%, valid percent = 16.3%) have incomes in the highest two brackets. Look again at the INCOME frequency table; this is the first time we have seen "missing" cases. For some reason or other, 57 people did not provide a response to this question. Either the respondents did not know or did not wish to disclose their income to the researchers. For our analysis, this means that these 57 cases will be excluded from any analysis that includes the variable INCOME. You might also have noticed that the Percent and Valid Percent columns contain different percentages. This is due to the recalculation, by SPSS, of the percentages with and without the missing cases factored in. The first column contains the raw percent, which is calculated with the missing cases included; the valid percent, however, is recalculated after excluding the missing cases. Whenever there are missing cases, the valid percent will be higher than the raw percent. Whenever the two percentages differ, I will report them thusly: "(22.8%, valid = 23.7%)." When the raw and valid percents differ in these exercises, you should report the raw percent. Some professors believe you should report the valid percents, but we will use the raw percents here because the valid percents are sometimes misleading (e.g., when few cases are considered valid, the "valid percents" may be inflated a great deal).

EXPLORING THE CORRELATES OF DELINQUENCY WITH CROSS-TABULATION TABLES

Now, let's discuss some replication and exploration. *Replication* means that we will reproduce the research of other scholars; in our case, we will run some of the analyses performed by the authors whose writings are in Part III. We will also run some exploratory analyses of our own.

For our first exploratory activity, let's examine the correlates of delinquency that are mentioned in the reading. We will examine the same eight combined delinquency measures we used in the exercise for Part II. In this section, we will examine only DIDANY; the others are left for you to examine for the Further Exploration questions or on your own. Because we ran the frequencies for these variables in our last exercise, we will skip that formality and get right into determining if any of the correlates of delinquency in Part III play a role in general delinquency, violence, or status offenses. To explore this possibility, we will use our old friend, the cross-tabulation table.

Using the directions in Box 5 if necessary, run cross-tabulation tables with DIDANY as the dependent (row) variable and WHITE, AGE, HS_AGE, BROKEN_H, and INCOME as independent (column) variables. Make sure to choose "Phi and Cramer's *V*" under **Statistics,** and check off "Column percentages" under **Cells.** The cross-tabulation tables are shown in Tables 5 through 8, followed by descriptions for each.

Now, let's examine the effects of WHITE (Table 5). Huizinga and Elliott found that black youths are not always more likely to commit delinquent acts; instead, the pattern is less predictable, with a higher percentage of blacks committing index offenses (and, to a lesser extent, general delinquency and felony theft) but slightly fewer committing felony assaults. Although we could try to replicate and verify those same statistics using our data, it would not be an important exercise because Huizinga and Elliott used the same data we are using;[4] thus, we could not extend their findings in any way. We can, however,

TABLE 5

WHITE → DIDANY.

Crosstab

			Y1-2: ETHNICITY (v168)		Total
			Anglo	Black	
DIDANY	0	Count	146	35	181
		% within Y1-2: ETHNICITY (v168)	11.4%	16.3%	12.1%
	1	Count	1139	180	1319
		% within Y1-2: ETHNICITY (v168)	88.6%	83.7%	87.9%
Total		Count	1285	215	1500
		% within Y1-2: ETHNICITY (v168)	100.0%	100.0%	100.0%

Symmetric Measures

		Value	Approx. Sig.
Nominal by	Phi	−.053	.040
Nominal	Cramer's V	.053	.040
N of valid cases		1500	

a. Not assuming the null hypothesis.
b. Using the asymptotic standard error assuming the null hypothesis.

examine our combined measures because they differ from the measures used by Huizinga and Elliott.

Therefore, look at the table for WHITE. Were blacks more likely than whites to have committed delinquent acts during the past year? In actuality, our WHITE → DIDANY shows that whites were slightly more likely to commit delinquent acts than blacks. Although the difference is not huge (4.90% is not enough of a difference to convince many to enact major policy changes), the finding is significant. Notice the strength of the association, however, before you decide to print this one up as a major finding.

POINTS TO PONDER: Because we used the same data, how could our findings differ from those of Huizinga and Elliott? Could the slight differences in our samples account for the switch? Consider the different ways we created our measures (What factors did Huizinga and Elliott include in their "general delinquency" measure? Which factors did we include in our DIDANY measure?).

TABLE 6

AGE → DIDANY.

Crosstab

			Y1-3: AGE (v169)							Total
			11	12	13	14	15	16	17	
DIDANY	0	Count	45	47	34	14	18	17	6	181
		% within Y1-3: AGE	21.0%	20.5%	14.6%	6.4%	8.0%	8.2%	3.5%	12.1%
	1	Count	169	182	199	206	207	190	166	1319
		% within Y1-3: AGE	79.0%	79.5%	85.4%	93.6%	92.0%	91.8%	96.5%	87.9%
Total		Count	214	229	233	220	225	207	172	1500
		% within Y1-3: AGE	100.0%	100.0%	100.0%	100.0%	100.0%	100.0%	100.0%	100.0%

Symmetric Measures

		Value	Approx. Sig.
Nominal by	Phi	.197	.000
Nominal	Cramer's V	.197	.000
N of valid cases		1500	

a. Not assuming the null hypothesis.
b. Using the asymptotic standard error assuming the null hypothesis.

As you probably noted, the age table (Table 6) is much larger than our previous tables. You can still compare the percentages along the bottom row, however. What do you notice as the youth ages increase? Are the changes significant? What is the Cramer's V value? (Note: We use Cramer's V for this table because there are three columns, which makes it larger than a 2×2 table.) What is the strength of this relationship? If you look at the table for HS_AGE → DIDANY, the findings are similar.

Now look at Table 7. What did Wells and Rankin find with respect to family structure? Are our findings, reported in Table 7, consistent with those of Wells and Rankin?

Now turn your attention to Table 8. In his article, Joe Weis noted that researchers had found a "moderate inverse" (i.e., higher-socioeconomic status individuals are less likely to commit the acts) relationship for intrapersonal and "serious property" crimes in other analyses of the NYS (Table 8). This means we probably will not find any differences for our DIDANY measure, but let's examine it anyway because it is a good exercise for us to flex our table interpretation muscles. Sure enough, the percentages increase, but not quite enough to make the finding significant.

TABLE 7

BROKEN_H → DIDANY.

Crosstab

			Youth from broken home		Total
			Intact home	Broken home	
DIDANY	0	Count	143	38	181
		% within youth from broken home	13.2%	9.1%	12.1%
	1	Count	938	381	1319
		% within youth from broken home	86.8%	90.9%	87.9%
Total		Count	1081	419	1500
		% within youth from broken home	100.0%	100.0%	100.0%

Symmetric Measures

		Value	Approx. Sig.
Nominal by	Phi	.057	.026
Nominal	Cramer's V	.057	.026
N of valid cases		1500	

a. Not assuming the null hypothesis.
b. Using the asymptotic standard error assuming the null hypothesis.

Related to income is whether or not the youths' families were on public assistance during the previous year. Some people argue that kids on welfare are more likely to commit delinquent acts, so let's see if our data support this belief. Look at the WELFARE → DIDANY table. Wow, talk about a lack of a difference! Also, that is the highest significance value I have seen in a long time. It appears that welfare recipients are identical to others with respect to their likelihood of committing a delinquent act: 88% of either group dabbled in delinquency during the past year.

The process we just completed is one part of replication—when researchers determine if the findings reported by other researchers are true for their own data. Replication is a very important part of research because it shows the consistency of findings and allows for sound theories to be developed. Granted, our findings are more reproduction than replication because we used the very same data that others have used, but the process is identical. If you wish, you may find some other data and replicate the findings reported in the text.

TABLE 8

INCOME → DIDANY.

Crosstab

			Recoded family income					
			$10,000 or less	$10,001 - 18,000	$18,000 - 26,000	$26,001 - 34,000	$34,001 or more	Total
DIDANY	0	Count	40	73	42	11	7	173
		% within recoded family income	11.7%	15.0%	11.1%	7.9%	7.2%	12.0%
	1	Count	302	414	336	128	90	1270
		% within recoded family income	88.3%	85.0%	88.9%	92.1%	92.8%	88.0%
Total		Count	342	487	378	139	97	1443
		% within recoded Family Income	100.0%	100.0%	100.0%	100.0%	100.0%	100.0%

Symmetric Measures

		Value	Approx. Sig.
Nominal by	Phi	.078	.068
Nominal	Cramer's V	.078	.068
N of valid cases		1443	

a. Not assuming the null hypothesis.
b. Using the asymptotic standard error assuming the null hypothesis.

ADDITIONAL EXPLORATION OF THE CORRELATES OF DELINQUENCY

Are specific types of delinquent acts affected by the correlates we examined previously? For the Further Exploration questions, you will run the analyses we ran previously for two of the combined measures, violence (DIDVIO) and status offenses (DIDSTAT). This is an important part of research; we need to know if our findings generalize to other offenses or whether they are limited to a few select offenses or measures.

THE CORRELATES OF DELINQUENCY ON YOUR OWN

What else might influence the commission of delinquent acts? Now that we have explored some correlates of delinquency, you could expand your list of independent variables. Try running the analyses we ran for some other potential correlates of delinquency, and try adding some independent variables of your own. Perhaps you believe that the level of urban development where the respondents live (RURAL) or their grade point averages (GPA) in school have effects on delinquency. Explore the variables, and find out for yourself. You can "control" for the effects of a variable (i.e., statistically remove the effects of a variable) by listing it in the third box (labeled "Layer 1 of 1") when you run your cross-tabulations. While you are exploring the correlates of delinquency, reflect on the readings and how they help us understand delinquency.

NOTES

1. To make the analyses easier, I recoded race into a new variable with two categories: (1) white and (0) black.
2. To make the analyses easier, I recoded INCOME into 5 (rather than 10) categories. To preserve the original coding schema, I simply combined the two lowest categories into one, the next two into another, and so on. Reducing the categories makes it easier to understand cross-tabulation tables but is less appropriate when you are doing multivariate analyses such as regressions, for which you want as much detail in a variable as possible. I was also careful not to recode the variables into categories that I believed were applicable by current standards, such as recoding them based on current wage earning capability, because it is important to recognize that these data were collected for 1976. Incomes were lower then.
3. This variable was derived from a question that asked what adults lived with the youth. Regardless of marital status, I coded a home as intact if both parents shared a home with the youth and broken if either parent was absent from the home.
4. In actuality, Huizinga and Elliott examined the first five waves of NYS data, and their first-wave data contained all 1,725 cases (compared to our reduced sample of 1,500).

Homework for Part III: General Questions
Correlates of Juvenile Delinquency

Name: _____   Date: _____

Directions: Answer the following questions by filling in the blanks or circling the appropriate responses. A couple of answers have been filled in for you to make sure you are on the right track.

EXPLORING THE CORRELATES OF DELINQUENCY: GETTING A HANDLE ON THE DATA

1. In the 1976 NYS sample, _____ (_____%) of the sample was white/Anglo; _____ (_____%) were black. This division *is/is not* roughly equal.

2. In the 1976 NYS sample, the age breakdown was as follows:

   _____ 11-year-olds, comprising _____% of the sample

   _____ 12-year-olds, comprising _____% of the sample

   _____ 13-year-olds, comprising _____% of the sample

   _____ 14-year-olds, comprising _____% of the sample

   _____ 15-year-olds, comprising _____% of the sample

   _____ 16-year-olds, comprising _____% of the sample

   _____ 17-year-olds, comprising _____% of the sample

   This division *is/is not* roughly equal.

3. In the 1976 NYS sample, _____ (_____%) youths were high school aged; the _____ (_____%) were younger youths. This division *is/is not* roughly equal.

4. In the 1976 NYS sample, _____ (_____%) of the youths were from intact homes; the remaining _____ (_____%) were from homes that can be described as "broken homes" in which one or more parents were absent from the home. This division *is/is not* roughly equal.

5. In the 1976 NYS sample, there were _____ lowest income youths ($10,000 or less), and they comprise _____% of the sample. _____ (_____%) youths were in the second income category ($10,001-$18,000); _____ (_____%) were in the middle income category ($18,001-$26,000); _____ (_____%) were in the fourth income category ($26,001-$34,000); and _____ (_____%) were in the highest income category. This division *is/is not* roughly equal.

EXPLORING THE CORRELATES OF DELINQUENCY
WITH CROSS-TABULATION TABLES

1. In the WHITE → DIDANY cross-tabulation, 1,139 (_____%) of the Anglo respondents said they had engaged in any delinquent acts during the previous year, compared to _____ (_____%) of the black respondents. The difference between the two percentages is _____%, which appears to be *negligible/potentially interesting*. The *phi/Cramer's V* value is _____, which means that we can do _____% better predicting general delinquency when we know a respondent's race. This relationship is *weak/moderate/strong*. The approximate significance is _____, which means there is a _____% chance that the relationship between WHITE and DIDANY is due to chance. This relationship *is/is not* statistically significant.

   In their article, Huizinga and Elliott report that blacks *are always/are not always* more likely to engage in delinquency. Because we used the same data Huizinga and Elliott used, the relationship between race and general delinquency we found should be similar to that reported by Huizinga and Elliott.

2. In the AGE → DIDANY cross-tabulation, it appears that as age increases, the likelihood of youths engaging in delinquency goes *up/down*. This relationship is *weak/moderate/strong*, and it *is/is not* statistically significant. In the HS_AGE → DIDANY cross-tabulation, _____ (_____%) of the high school-aged respondents said they had engaged in any delinquent acts during the previous year, compared to _____ (_____%) of the younger respondents. The difference between the two percentages is _____%, which appears to be *negligible/ potentially interesting*. The *phi/Cramer's V* value is _____, which means that we can do _____% better predicting general delinquency when we know a respondent's age. This relationship is *weak/moderate/strong*. The approximate significance is _____, which means there is a _____% chance that the relationship between HS_AGE and DIDANY is due to chance. This relationship *is/is not* statistically significant.

   Other researchers have found that older adolescents engage in more delinquency when compared with their younger counterparts. The relationship between age and delinquency found using the 1976 NYS data *is similar to/differs from* those findings.

3. In the BROKEN_H → DIDANY cross-tabulation, 381 (_____%) of the youths from broken homes said they had engaged in any delinquent acts during the previous year, compared to _____ (_____%) of the youths from intact homes. The difference between the two percentages is _____%, which appears to be *negligible/potentially interesting*. The *phi/Cramer's V* value is _____, which means that we can do _____% better predicting general delinquency

use when we know a respondent's family structure. This relationship is *weak/moderate/strong*. The approximate significance is _____, which means there is a _____% chance that the relationship between BROKEN_H and DIDANY is due to chance. This relationship *is/is not* statistically significant.

In their article, Wells and Rankin found that youths from broken homes were *more/less* likely to engage in delinquency. The relationship between family structure and delinquency found using the 1976 NYS data *is similar to/differs from* those findings.

4. In the INCOME → DIDANY cross-tabulation, _____ (_____%) of the lowest income respondents said they had engaged in delinquency during the previous year, compared to _____ (_____%) of the second income category, _____ (_____%) of the middle income category, _____ (_____%) of the fourth income group, and _____ (_____%) of the highest income respondents. The largest difference between the five percentages is _____%, which appears to be *negligible/potentially interesting*. The *phi/Cramer's V* value is _____, which means that we can do _____% better predicting general delinquency when we know a respondent's income category. This relationship is *weak/moderate/strong*. The approximate significance is _____, which means there is a _____% chance that the relationship between INCOME and DIDANY is due to chance. This relationship *is/is not* statistically significant.

In the WELFARE → DIDANY cross-tabulation, _____ (_____%) of the youths supported by public assistance said they had engaged in delinquency during the previous year, compared to _____ (_____%) of other youths. The difference between the two percentages is _____%, which appears to be *negligible/potentially interesting*. The *phi/Cramer's V* value is _____, which means that we can do _____% better predicting general delinquency when we know whether a youth receives public assistance. This relationship is *weak/moderate/strong*. The approximate significance is _____, which means there is a _____% chance that the relationship between WELFARE and DIDANY is due to chance. This relationship *is/is not* statistically significant.

In his article, Joe Weis stated that social class *has/has not* been linked to general delinquency (as opposed to intrapersonal and "serious property" offenses). The relationship between income and delinquency found using the 1976 NYS data *is similar to/differs from* the statements by Weis.

5. Overall, we can say our findings regarding correlates for DIDANY *are/are not* consistent with prior research.

Homework for Part III: Further Exploration Questions
Correlates of Juvenile Delinquency

Name: _____ Date: _____

TASK: Run the cross-tabulation analyses we ran previously for the eight other combined measures.

Directions: Answer the following questions by filling in the blanks or circling the appropriate responses. Some answers have been filled in for you to make sure you are on the right track.

FURTHER EXPLORATION OF THE CORRELATES OF DELINQUENCY

1. Complete the table on the following page using percentages of respondents who engaged in various forms of delinquency during the past year and statistics from the cross-tabulation tables for the effects of race and HS_AGE on the eight combined measures:

	% of Youths Who Engaged in Delinquency During the Past Year by Category				
	Race			High School-Aged	
	White	Black		High School-Aged	Younger
DIDDAMP Cramer's V/phi = .02 Sig. = .458	36.1%	33.5%	DIDDAMP Cramer's V/phi = _____ Sig. = .103	33.3%	
DIDTHFT Cramer's V/phi = _____ Sig. = _____			DIDTHFT Cramer's V/phi = _____ Sig. = _____		
DIDVIO Cramer's V/phi = _____ Sig. = _____			DIDVIO Cramer's V/phi = _____ Sig. = _____		
DIDSTAT Cramer's V/phi = _____ Sig. = _____			DIDSTAT Cramer's V/phi = _____ Sig. = _____		
DIDOTH Cramer's V/phi = _____ Sig. = _____			DIDOTH Cramer's V/phi = _____ Sig. = _____		
DIDDRUG Cramer's V/phi = _____ Sig. = _____			DIDDRUG Cramer's V/phi = _____ Sig. = _____		
DIDDRGS Cramer's V/phi = _____ Sig. = _____			DIDDRGS Cramer's V/phi = _____ Sig. = _____		
DIDSKL Cramer's V/phi = _____ Sig. = _____			DIDSKL Cramer's V/phi = _____ Sig. = _____		

2. From the previous table, we can see that race has *consistent/inconsistent* effects on the eight measures. From the previous table, we can see that HS_AGE has *consistent/inconsistent* effects on the eight measures. High school-aged youths are *more/less* likely to engage in delinquency.

3. Complete the following table using percentages of respondents who engaged in various forms of delinquency during the past year and statistics from the cross-tabulation tables for the effects of family structure and WELFARE on the eight combined measures:

	% of Youths Who Engaged in Delinquency During the Past Year by Category				
	Youth's Family Structure		Youth Receiving Public Assistance		
	Intact Home	Broken Home		No	Yes
DIDDAMP Cramer's *V*/phi = _____ Sig. = _____		41.1%	DIDDAMP Cramer's *V*/phi = _____ Sig. = _____		
DIDTHFT Cramer's *V*/phi = _____ Sig. = _____			DIDTHFT Cramer's *V*/phi = _____ Sig. = _____		
DIDVIO Cramer's *V*/phi = _____ Sig. = _____			DIDVIO Cramer's *V*/phi = _____ Sig. = _____		
DIDSTAT Cramer's *V*/phi = _____ Sig. = _____			DIDSTAT Cramer's *V*/phi = _____ Sig. = _____		
DIDOTH Cramer's *V*/phi = _____ Sig. = _____			DIDOTH Cramer's *V*/phi = _____ Sig. = _____		
DIDDRUG Cramer's *V*/phi = _____ Sig. = _____			DIDDRUG Cramer's *V*/phi = _____ Sig. = _____		
DIDDRGS Cramer's *V*/phi = _____ Sig. = _____			DIDDRGS Cramer's *V*/phi = _____ Sig. = _____		
DIDSKL Cramer's *V*/phi = _____ Sig. = _____			DIDSKL Cramer's *V*/phi = _____ Sig. = _____		

4. From the previous table, we can see that WELFARE has *consistent/inconsistent* effects on the eight measures. From the previous table, we can see that youths from broken homes are typically *more/less* likely to engage in delinquency.

5. Complete the following table using percentages of respondents who engaged in various forms of delinquency during the past year and statistics from the cross-tabulation tables for the effects of INCOME on the eight combined measures:

	% of Youths Who Engaged in Delinquency During the Past Year by Income				
	$10,000 or less	$10,001–18,000	$18,001–26,000	$26,001–34,000	$34,001 or more
DIDDAMP Cramer's V/phi = .115 Sig. = .001		29.0%			
DIDTHFT Cramer's V = _____ Sig. = _____					
DIDVIO Cramer's V = _____ Sig. = _____					
DIDSTAT Cramer's V = _____ Sig. = _____					
DIDOTH Cramer's V = _____ Sig. = _____					
DIDDRUG Cramer's V = _____ Sig. = _____					
DIDDRGS Cramer's V = _____ Sig. = _____					
DIDSKL Cramer's V = _____ Sig. = _____					

6. From the previous table, we can see that income has *consistent/inconsistent* effects on the eight measures.

7. Overall, we can say that our findings for the combined measures *are/are not* consistent with prior research.

Homework for Part III: On Your Own
Correlates of Juvenile Delinquency

Name: _____ Date: _____

TASK: Expand your list of independent variables to include at least two other potential correlates of delinquency (e.g., RURAL and GPA). You may choose any variables you believe make sense. You may use any dependent variable you believe is appropriate (e.g., DIDANY, DIDTHFT, STATSEX, or any other suitable variable).

Directions: Answer the following questions.

NOTE: Please print out and include your tables with these questions so your work can be graded.

THE CORRELATES OF DELINQUENCY ON YOUR OWN

1. Which variables did you choose as your independent variables?

2. Why did you select these variables?

3. Which variables did you choose as your dependent variables?

4. Why did you select these variables?

5. How did your first independent variable affect your dependent variable? Make sure to provide a description that includes the percentages, phi or Cramer's V value, the strength of the relationship, and the significance value.

6. How did your second independent variable affect your dependent variable? Make sure to provide a description that includes the percentages, phi or Cramer's V value, the strength of the relationship, and the significance value.

If you included more than two independent variables, you may summarize the findings here for future reference.

IV

WHAT CAUSES DELINQUENCY? HOW IS IT CONTROLLED?
The Interdependence of Theory and Practice

A theory of juvenile delinquency is simply a "best guess," although usually a systematically informed one made by a professional criminologist, about the causes of delinquent behavior. It attempts to make sense of the distribution, or correlates, of delinquency. For example, why is crime more likely to be committed by juveniles who have delinquent friends? By boys? By school failures? By older juveniles? By certain minority groups? By juveniles from dysfunctional families? There are as many competing theories as there are criminologists willing and courageous enough to hazard a guess about the causes and to propose an explanation of delinquent behavior.

A theory is not "true" by definition. It is never completely accurate or "valid." The extent to which it is true, valid, or makes sense of juvenile delinquency is determined by testing the theory: How close does the theory fit the empirical evidence regarding the "facts" of juvenile delinquency? On the basis of this process of scientific verification, some theories are shown to be more valid than others; different theories "explain" different amounts of variation in delinquency (i.e., they explain more of the facts than others); a theory may account for some kinds of variation in delinquency better than others (i.e., it may be more valid as an explanation of less serious than more serious offenses); and, finally, those theories that receive some empirical support have more useful implications for "practice," or the control and prevention of juvenile delinquency.

We believe there is a vital interdependence between theories and practice. Theories, even if not directly, suggest what should be done to keep delinquency from happening. In 1977, Weis reviewed the major sociological theories of juvenile delinquency and elaborated each of their implications for delinquency control. As one example, one of the major theoretical perspectives included here—"opportunity" or "strain" theory—has practice implications for intervention strategies that revolve around "equalizing opportunity" for youths at the bottom of the social class structure: (a) The motivation to engage in delinquent behavior can be neutralized by establishing a balance between aspirations and opportunities for achievement;

(b) aspirations, especially for economic and social success, should be socially regulated; (c) the key to delinquency prevention is the expansion and equalization of access to legitimate opportunities to achieve; (d) access to illegitimate opportunities should be restricted; and (e) the alienation of frustrated youths should be directed into legitimate expressions of discontent.

After all, if a theory identifies the "causes" of delinquent behavior, logic suggests that changing the causes should change the behavior. For example, Hawkins, Pastor, Bell, and Morrison (1979) identified 12 major causes of delinquency, derived from a thorough review of existing theories, and 12 corresponding intervention strategies aimed at modifying or eliminating each cause (Table 1).

This means that the propositions and hypotheses of theories, as well as the more specific causes they identify, can serve as blueprints for practice and, in turn, that attempts to control and prevent delinquency can also serve as tests of the theories. We believe that a good theory will have both demonstrated validity and utility. Consequently, the essays in this section are organized into eight subsections, corresponding to major theoretical perspectives in the field. Within each subsection, one or more examples of the theory will be presented, coupled with one or more examples of the theoretical perspective put into practice as policy implications, related initiatives or programs, or, in some cases, a project based specifically on a theory.

TABLE 1

Causes of delinquency and associated strategies of delinquency prevention.

Cause	Strategy	Goal
Physical abnormality/ illness	Biological-physiological Health promotion Nutrition Neurological Genetic	Remove, diminish, control under-lying physiological, biological, or biopsychiatric conditions.
Psychological disturbance disorder	Psychological/mental health Epidemiological/early intervention Psychotherapeutic Behavioral	Alter internal psychological states or conditions generating them.

Cause	Strategy	Goal

Weak attachments to others	Social network development
	    Linkage
	    Influence
		Increase interaction/involvement between youths and nondeviant others; increase influence of nondeviant others on potentially delinquent youths.

Criminal influence	Criminal influence reduction
	    Disengagement from
	        criminal influence
	    Redirection away from
	        criminal norms
		Reduce the influence of delinquent norms and persons who directly or indirectly encourage youths to commit delinquent acts.

Powerless	Power-enhancement
	    Informal influence
	    Formal power
		Increase ability or power of youths to influence or control their environments, directly or indirectly.

Lack of useful worthwhile roles	Role development/role enhancement
	    Service roles
	    Production roles
	    Student roles
		Create opportunities for youths to be involved in legitimate roles or activities that youths perceive as useful, successful, and competent.

Unoccupied time	Activities/recreation	Involve youths in nondelinquent activities.

Inadequate skills	Education/skill development
	    Cognitive
	    Affective
	    Moral
	    Informational
		Provide individuals with personal skills that prepare them to find patterns of behavior free from delinquent activities.

Conflicting environmental demands	Clear and consistent social expectations	Increase consistency of expectations/messages from institutions, organizations, and groups that affect youths.

Economic necessity	Economic resources
	    Resource maintenance
	    Resource attainment
		Provide basic resources to preclude the need for delinquency.

Low degree of risk/difficulty	Deterrence
	    Target hardening/removal
	    Anticipatory intervention
		Increase cost and decrease benefits of criminal acts.

Exclusionary social responses	Abandonment of legal control/social tolerance
	    Explicit jurisdictional
	        abandonment
	    Implicit jurisdictional
	        abandonment
	    Covert jurisdictional
	        abandonment
	    Environmental tolerance
		Remove certain behaviors from control of the juvenile justice system; decrease the degree to which youths' behaviors are perceived, labeled, and treated as delinquent.

PSYCHOLOGICAL CONTROL, EARLY IDENTIFICATION, AND INTERVENTION

Psychodynamic control theory, anchored in the ideas of Freudian psychology, was the dominant theoretical perspective on juvenile delinquency for many years, in good part because it supported the "rehabilitative ideal" and treatment model of the juvenile court and juvenile justice system. As Empey and Stafford pointed out in *American Delinquency* in 1991, the theoretical emphasis on the importance of early child-rearing practices in personality development and delinquent behavior "has probably been the most influential of all theoretical doctrines," and the implied treatment model, based on the early identification of delinquents and predelinquents and intensive treatment, "has remained the standard to which most courts and correctional agencies have aspired until very recently."

The extensive research of the Gluecks, as represented in "Unraveling Juvenile Delinquency," served as the foundation for a more social psychological version of psychodynamic theory. Laub and Sampson, in "Unraveling Families and Delinquency: A Reanalysis of the Gluecks' Data," have applied the latest statistical techniques to the Gluecks' original data, collected about 50 years ago, and arrive at the same general conclusions about the importance of early family socialization experiences on delinquent behavior. The Gluecks' theoretical ideas were the rationale for one of the first true "experiments" on the prevention of delinquency among an identified group of young predelinquents, the Cambridge-Somerville Youth Study, as described by Powers and Witmer and later reevaluated by McCord in a "Thirty-Year Follow-Up of Treatment Effects."

Unraveling Juvenile Delinquency

SHELDON GLUECK
ELEANOR GLUECK

IN order to arrive at the clearest differentiation of disease and health, comparison must be made between the unquestionably pathologic and the normal. (This metaphor does not carry with it any implication that we view delinquency as a disease.) Therefore, nondelinquents as well as delinquents become the subjects of our inquiry. Comparison is a fundamental method of science, and the true value of any phenomenon disclosed by exploration of human behavior cannot be reliably determined without comparing its incidence in an experimental group with that in a control group. This method in the present research should result not only in isolating the factors which most markedly differentiate delinquents from nondelinquents but in casting light on the causal efficacy of a number of factors generally accepted as criminogenic.

We therefore decided to match 500 delinquent boys with 500 nondelinquent boys in four respects:

1. *Age,* because it is often asserted that tendencies to maladjustment and misbehavior vary with age (especially puberty and adolescence); also because morphologic and psychologic factors are more or less affected by age.
2. *General intelligence,* because there is considerable claim that intelligence, as measured by standard tests, bears an intimate relationship to varieties of behavior-tendency.

3. *National (ethnico-racial) origin,* because there is a school of thought which stresses ethnic derivation and associated culture patterns in accounting for variations in behavior tendencies.
4. *Residence in underprivileged neighborhoods,* because the conception is widespread that delinquency is largely bred by the conditions in such areas. In selecting both delinquents and nondelinquents from unwholesome neighborhoods, we were attempting to control a complex of socioeconomic and cultural factors whose similarity would permit us to find out why it is that even in regions of most adverse social conditions, most children do not commit legally prohibited acts of theft, burglary, assault, sexual aggression, and the like.

LEVELS OF THE INQUIRY

Although we look at the problem of delinquency from the point of view of the integration of the total personality, it is revealing to study discord or conflict and accord or harmony at various levels: (a) the sociocultural level, where conflict is shown by delinquency, crime, or other forms of maladjustment of the individual to the taboos, demands, conventions, and laws of society; (b) the somatic level, where disharmony is indicated by dysplasias or disproportions between the structure of two or more segments of the physique and by ill health; (c) the intellectual level, where discord may be revealed by contrasts between capacities of abstract intelligence and those of concrete intelligence, or between special abilities and special disabilities, or by excessive variability in types of intellectual capacity; and (d) the emotional-temperamental level, where disharmony is shown by mental conflict and by the tensions between repressed and forgotten emotional experiences and more recent experiences or between divergent instinctual energy propulsions typically reflected in the phenomenon of ambivalence.

It should be added that an adequate investigation of personality-in-action requires study not only of the interrelationship of soma and psyche within the person but also of the interplay between the person and the environment.

If we are to isolate the probable causal factors, we must focus attention on the ones that differentiate the delinquents and nondelinquents and that were operative before delinquency became evident.

Three points ought to be borne in mind:

1. The selection and matching of the two groups of boys with respect to ethnic-racial derivation, age, intelligence quotient, and residence in underprivileged areas has, of course, meant the exclusion of these controlled variables from the comparison.
2. In planning the research, we took into account the fact that statistical correlation in itself may not necessarily mean actual functional relationship. Therefore, in choosing factors for comparison, we selected only those which, from our own experience and from the writings of those who have made inquiries into various branches of the behavior disciplines, seemed to us to have a possible functional connection with delinquent or nondelinquent behavior tendencies.
3. Although we included a great many factors, further investigations may well disclose still other causal factors.

FACTORS WITH PROBABLE CAUSAL SIGNIFICANCE

We are now ready to focus attention on those factors that may have causal significance. It should be emphasized that in examining the tapestry of delinquency it is difficult to differentiate the warp of hereditary (genetic) factors from the woof of conditioned (environmental, cultural) factors.

Nevertheless, our data do permit a rough division. There are, on the one hand, factors that are closer to the genetic than to the environmental end of the biosocial scale, and, on the other, those that are closer to the "conditioned," cultural end of the scale.

Physique

Thus, the delinquents, as a group, tend toward the outline of a solid, closely knit, muscular type, one in which there is a relative predominance of muscle, bone, and connective tissue.

Temperamental Traits and Emotional Dynamics

On the whole, the delinquents are more extroverted, vivacious, impulsive, and less self-controlled than the nondelinquents. They are more hostile, resentful, defiant, suspicious, and destructive. They are less fearful of failure or defeat than the nondelinquents. They are less concerned about meeting conventional expectations and are more ambivalent toward or far less submissive to authority. They are, as a group, more socially assertive. To a greater extent than the control group, they express feelings of not being recognized or appreciated.

Intellectual Traits

The delinquents tend to express themselves intellectually in a direct, immediate, and concrete manner rather than through the use of intermediate symbols or abstractions. There seems also to be a somewhat greater emotional disharmony connected with their performance of intellectual tasks.

BEHAVIOR REFLECTING SIGNIFICANT TRAITS

Certain forms of behavior, in and out of school, are in a sense not fundamentally etiologic. But since they reflect, at least partially, temperamental tendencies and character traits that have their roots in early childhood, they may be included in the general pattern. These forms of behavior are school attainment, school misbehavior, general misbehavior tendencies, use of leisure, and type of companions.

School Attainment

Here again, we have strands of the delinquent pattern, namely, evidences of restless energy with accompanying difficulties in social adaptation and conformity to a regime of rules and discipline involving distasteful intellectual tasks.

School Misbehavior

Some manifestations of school misconduct may, of course, be essentially reactive; others seem to reflect root traits and fundamental drives. They all fit consistently, however, into the temperamental segment of the general pattern that has been inductively achieved.

General Misbehavior Tendencies

In their general misbehavior tendencies, there is further evidence of a driving, uninhibited energy and thirst for adventure on the part of the delinquents.

Leisure Time and Companions

In their recreational activities and companionships, the delinquents further evidence a craving for adventure and for opportunities to express aggressive energy-output, with the added need of supportive companionship in such activities.

Thus far it seems clear that the physical, temperamental, intellectual, and behavioral segments of the inquiry tend to interweave into a meaningful pattern: The delinquents, far more than the nondelinquents, are of the essentially mesomorphic, energetic type, with tendencies to restless and uninhibited expression of instinctual-affective energy and to direct and concrete, rather than symbolic and abstract, intellectual expression. It is evidently difficult for them to develop the high degree of flexibility of adaptation, self-management, self-control, and sublimation of primitive tendencies and self-centered desires demanded by the complex and confused culture of the times. Nevertheless, there are some delinquents who do not fit into this pattern, either on a somatic or a temperamental level, and there are some nondelinquents who do.

Sociocultural Factors

An examination of sociocultural factors should shed some light on the reasons for these difficulties of adaptation. Character is the result of training as well as of natural equipment. Mechanisms of sublimation and of constructive or harmless energy-canalization, as well as "knowledge of right and wrong," are part of the apparatus of character expression. However, a boy does not express himself in a vacuum, but in a cultural milieu ranging from the intimate, emotion-laden atmosphere of the home to that of the school, the neighborhood, and general society. Primitive tendencies are morally and legally neutral. It is the existence of laws and taboos that qualifies their expression in certain ways as delinquent, or criminal, or otherwise dissocial or antisocial from the point of view of the particular society and culture in question. Adaptation to the demands and prohibitions of any specific social organization requires certain physical, temperamental, and intellectual capacities dependent on the values protected by that society through law and custom and the characteristics of the cultural matrix.

Modern culture, especially in crowded urban centers, is highly complex, and it is ill defined because of conflicting values. The demands on the growing human organism by every vehicle of today's culture are numerous, often subtle, and sometimes inconsistent. This is true of the home, the school, the neighborhood, and the general, all-pervasive culture of the times. Against insistence that he be honest, nonaggressive, self-controlled, and the like, the child soon finds vivid contradicting attitudes, values, and behavior all about him in an environment that in large measure rewards selfishness, aggression, a predatory attitude, and success by any means. Thus, the demands made upon the growing child at every level at which he is called upon to adapt his natural inclinations to the taboos, laws, and other prohibitions are neither simple nor well defined. They require a great deal of adaptive power, self-control, and self-management, the ability to choose among alternative values and to postpone immediate satisfactions for future ones—all this in a cultural milieu in which fixed points are increasingly difficult to discern and to hold to. This means that during the earliest years, when the difficult task of internalization of ideals and symbols of authority is in process, desirable attitudes and behavior standards are not clearly enough defined, or are inconsistent, leaving a confused residue in the delicate structure of personality and character.

How did the home conditions of the delinquents and nondelinquents in this study tend to facilitate or hamper the process of internalization of authority, the taming and sublimation of primitive impulses, and the definition of standards of good and bad?

We found that while the divergencies between the delinquents and nondelinquents were sometimes not as marked as those found in other aspects of the research, *the biosocial legacy of the parents of the delinquents was consistently poorer than that of the nondelinquents.* There was a greater incidence of emotional disturbances, mental retardation, alcoholism, and criminal-ism among the families of the mothers of the delinquents. These differences existed despite the fact that the economic condition of the homes in which the mothers of the delinquent boys had been reared was not very different from that of the homes in which the mothers of the nondelinquents grew up. In the families of the fathers of the delinquents, also, there was more emotional disturbance and criminalism than among the families of the fathers of the nondelinquents.

Thus, to the extent that the parents of the boys communicated the standards and ideals of their own rearing to that of their children, it is evident that the social—and perhaps, partially also, biologic—legacy of the delinquents was worse than that of the nondelinquents.

As for the parents themselves, their biosocial handicaps should be considered as at least partly influencing their capacity to rear their children properly. A higher proportion of the parents of the delinquents suffered from serious physical ailments, were mentally retarded, emotionally disturbed, alcoholic, and—most significant—many more of them had a history of delinquency.

The generally poorer hygienic and moral climate in which the delinquents were reared is further emphasized in the greater burden among their brothers and sisters of serious physical ailments, mental retardation, emotional disturbances, excessive drinking, and delinquency.

These are not the only ways in which the familial background of the delinquents was less adequate than that of the nondelinquents. There are other aspects of family life in which the delinquents were more deprived, often markedly so. For example, a somewhat higher proportion of their parents than of the parents of the nondelinquents came to the responsibilities of marriage with no more than grade-school education. A far higher proportion of the marriages proved to be unhappy. More of the homes of the delinquents were broken by desertion, separation, divorce, or death of one or both parents, many of the breaches occurring during the early childhood of the boys. Because of this, many more delinquents than nondelinquents have had substitute parents, and more of them were shifted about from one household to another during their formative years. Further, there has been less of an effort among the families of the delinquent group to set up decent standards of conduct—less ambition, less self-respect, and less planning for the future.

As for the economic status of the two groups of families, a finding has emerged which is particularly significant in view of the fact that the boys were matched at the outset on the basis of residence in underprivileged areas, namely, that sporadic or chronic dependency has been markedly more prevalent among the families of the delinquents. This is attributable, at least in part, to the far poorer work habits of the fathers, and in part also to less planful management of the family income.

These differences between the families of the delinquents and the families of the nondelinquents do not so much pertain to the obvious issue of the relationship of dependency or poverty to crime (the vast majority of both groups of families are of the underprivileged class); they are important, rather, as reflecting the differences in the quality of the adults in the families and therefore the variance in influence on the children.

The greater inadequacy of the parents of the delinquents is also reflected in the extremes of laxity and harshness with which they attempted to meet the disciplinary problems of their children and in the greater carelessness of their supervision of the children, amounting often to outright neglect.

It is, however, within the family emotional setting—the family drama—that the most deep-rooted and persistent character and personality traits and distortions of the growing child are developed.

We may at once dispose of the claim often made that being the only, or the first-born, or the youngest child has special implications for delinquency. The fact is that, in our study, a *lower* proportion of the delinquents than of the nondelinquents were so placed in order of birth.

In interpersonal family relationships, however, we found an exceedingly marked difference between the two groups under comparison. A much higher proportion of the families of the delinquents were disorganized (not cohesive). Family disorganization, with its attendant lack of warmth and of respect for the integrity of each member, can have serious consequences for the growing child. It may prevent the development of both an adequate sense of responsibility and an effective mechanism for the inhibition of conduct that might disgrace the family name. Since the family is the first and foremost vehicle for the transmission of the values of a culture to the young child, noncohesiveness of the family may leave him without ethical moorings or convey to him a confused and inconsistent cultural pattern.

Apart from the lesser cohesiveness of the families in which the delinquents grew up, many more of their fathers, mothers, brothers, and sisters have been indifferent or frankly hostile to the boys. A far *lower* proportion of the delinquents than of the nondelinquents have been affectionately attached to their parents, and considerably more of them have felt that their parents have not been concerned about their welfare. Finally, twice as many of the delinquents do not look upon their fathers as acceptable symbols for emulation.

In the light of the obvious inferiority of the families of the delinquents as sources of sound personality development and character formation, it is not surprising that these boys were never adequately socialized, and that they developed persistent antisocial tendencies, even apart from the fundamental somatic and temperamental differentiations between them and the nondelinquents.

Without attempting a psychoanalytic discussion of interpersonal emotional dynamics, we may point out that the development of a mentally hygienic and properly oriented superego (conscience) must have been greatly hampered by the kind of parental ideals, attitudes, temperaments, and behavior found to play such a major role on the family stage of the delinquents.

THE CAUSAL COMPLEX

It will be observed that in drawing together the more significant threads of each area explored, we have not resorted to a theoretical explanation from the standpoint, exclusively, of any one discipline. On the contrary, the evidence seems to point to the participation of forces from several areas and levels in channeling the persistent tendency to socially unacceptable behavior. The foregoing summation of the major resemblances and dissimilarities between the two groups included in the present inquiry indicates that the separate findings, independently gathered, integrate into a dynamic pattern which is neither exclusively biologic nor exclusively sociocultural, but which derives from an interplay of somatic, temperamental, intellectual, and sociocultural forces.

If we take into account the dynamic interplay of these various levels and channels of influence, a tentative causal formula or law emerges, which tends to accommodate these puzzling divergencies so far as the great mass of delinquents is concerned:

The delinquents as a group are distinguishable from the nondelinquents: (a) physically, in being essentially mesomorphic in constitution (solid, closely knit, muscular); (b) temperamentally, in being restlessly energetic, impulsive, extroverted, aggressive, destructive (often sadistic)—traits which may be related more or less to the erratic growth pattern and its physiologic correlates or consequences; (c) in attitude, by being hostile, defiant, resentful, suspicious, stubborn, socially assertive, adventurous, unconventional, nonsubmissive to authority; (d) psychologically, in tending to direct and concrete, rather than symbolic, intellectual expression, and in being less methodical in their approach to problems; and (e) socioculturally, in having been reared to a far greater extent than the control group in homes of little understanding, affection, stability, or moral fiber by parents usually unfit to be effective guides and protectors or, according to psychoanalytic theory, desirable sources for emulation and the construction of a consistent, well-balanced, and socially normal superego during the early stages of character development. While in individual cases the stresses contributed by any one of the above pressure-areas of dissocial behavior tendency may adequately account for persistence in delinquency, in general the high probability of delinquency is dependent on the interplay of the conditions and forces from all these areas.

In the exciting, stimulating, but little-controlled and culturally inconsistent environment of the underprivileged area, such boys readily give expression to their untamed impulses and their self-centered desires by means of various forms of delinquent behavior. Their tendencies toward uninhibited energy-expression are deeply anchored in soma and psyche and in the malformations of character during the first few years of life.

QUESTIONS FOR DISCUSSION AND WRITING

1. What three factors with probable causal significance did the Gluecks find?

2. What five forms of behavior did the authors find that reflect, at least partially, temperamental tendencies and character traits that have their roots in early childhood?

3. How did the home conditions of the delinquents and nondelinquents in this study tend to facilitate or hamper the process of internalization of authority, the taming and sublimation of primitive impulses, and the definition of standards of good and bad?

Unraveling Families and Delinquency: A Reanalysis of the Gluecks' Data

JOHN H. LAUB

ROBERT J. SAMPSON

For more than 40 years, Sheldon and Eleanor Glueck performed fundamental research in the area of crime and delinquency at Harvard University. Their primary interests were in discovering the causes of juvenile delinquency and adult criminality and in assessing the overall effectiveness of correctional treatment in restraining criminal careers.

Undoubtedly, the work that the Gluecks are best known for is *Unraveling Juvenile Delinquency* (hereafter *UJD*). This study of the etiology of juvenile delinquency was undertaken during the 1940s and involved a matched sample of 500 official delinquents and 500 officially defined nondelinquents.

The most unique and compelling feature of their research design is that all male subjects were matched as to age, race/ethnicity, general intelligence, and low-income residence—all classic criminological variables thought to influence both delinquency and official reaction. Hence, all boys grew up in similar high-risk environments with respect to poverty and exposure to delinquency and antisocial conduct.

A large amount of information on social, psychological, and biological characteristics, family life, school performance, work experiences, and other life events was collected on the delinquents and controls in the period 1939–1948.

These data were collected through detailed investigations by the Gluecks' research team, including interviews with the subjects themselves and their families, employers, schoolteachers, neighbors, and criminal justice and social welfare officials.

THE CRITICS OF THE GLUECKS

Despite their collection of a wealth of delinquency data, the Gluecks' substantive research contributions have been largely rejected in contemporary sociological theories of crime. There are several reasons for this. Perhaps most important has been the severe methodological critiques of their work. The ideological critiques have been equally powerful.

The Gluecks' research was also rejected by contemporary sociological theories due to the Gluecks' focus on the family as a major source of delinquency. Hirschi has argued that modern theories of crime ignore the importance of the family as a socializing institution in discussions of crime causation.

Wilkinson has contended that ideological bias in sociology has played a role in accepting and rejecting the research on broken homes and delinquency throughout this century. Given the Gluecks' emphasis on family variables in the *UJD* study, it is not surprising that their research findings were rejected by sociological criminologists.

In addition to the ideological criticisms noted above, the Gluecks' methodology was also criticized. We argue, however, that the criticisms have been overblown and often confuse concerns relating to the quality of the data analysis used by the Gluecks with the overall quality of the data they collected. In other words, the conclusion that the Gluecks' data analysis was ill conceived ought not lead to the conclusion that their data were of equally poor quality. The latter is an empirical and logical issue.

We believe that the criticisms can be addressed through a reanalysis of the basic Glueck data. We now turn to our attempt to replicate the major results of the Gluecks' research. Given the Gluecks' research design in the *UJD* study, we devote special attention to identifying family variables within a social control framework that distinguishes serious, persistent delinquents from nondelinquents.

THE PRESENT ANALYSIS

Recently, we obtained a subset of the original *UJD* data. These data comprise 110 variables for both delinquents and nondelinquents between the ages of 11 and 17. The variables include social, psychological, and biological measures for the total sample of 1,000 delinquents and nondelinquents. The data have been carefully checked for errors, and our preliminary analyses have successfully matched the Gluecks' published tables.

Research Design

Over the past two decades, theorists, researchers, and policymakers have refocused attention on the role of the family in explaining delinquency. This renewed interest in the relationship between family life and delinquency led us to focus on the extensive family variables available in the Glueck subfile.

Drawing on the family process literature, we identified a set of structural background factors that are relevant to understanding both family functioning and delinquency. Recall that age, race/ethnicity, neighborhood socioeconomic status (SES), and IQ are controlled via the matching design. Independent of these factors, the *UJD* data enable us to assess directly the relevance of the following structural variables: household crowding, family disruption, economic dependence, nativity (foreign born), residential mobility, and mother's irregular employment.

The remaining two structural background factors combine dichotomous indicators of the criminality and drunkenness of mother and father.

The five intervening family process variables are father and mother's style of discipline, parent-child and child-parent attachments, and mother's supervision.

The two measures labeled "Ferratic" and "Merratic" were constructed by summing three variables tapping the discipline and punishment practices of the mother and father. The first constituent variable concerns use of physical punishment by the parent and refers to rough handling, strappings, and beatings eliciting fear and resentment in the boy—not to casual or occasional slapping that was unaccompanied by rage or hostility. The second constituent variable measures threatening and/or scolding behavior by mother/father that elicited fear in the boy. The third component taps erratic and harsh discipline; that is, if the parent was harsh and unreasoning, if the parent vacillated between strictness and laxity and was not consistent in control, or if the parent was negligent or indifferent with regard to disciplining the boy. Thus, the Ferratic and Merratic scales range from 0 to 3 and measure the degree to which parents used inconsistent disciplinary methods in conjunction with harsh, physical punishment and/or threatening or scolding behavior.

Mother's supervision is coded 1 if the mother provided suitable or fair supervision over the boy's activities at home or in the neighborhood. The complete list of variables, labels, and descriptive statistics is displayed in Table 1.

TABLE 1

Variable labels, definitions, and descriptive statistics, reanalysis of *UJD*[a] coded data.

Variable Label	Variable Definition and Descriptive Statistics
Hcrowd	Household crowding of more than 2 per bedroom (mean = .32; range = 0-1)
Fcrdrunk	Criminal record and alcoholism/drunkenness of father (mean = .99; range = 0-2)
Mcrdrunk	Criminal record and alcoholism/drunkenness of mother (mean = .41; range = 0-2)
Famdis	One or both parents absent during childhood (mean = .39; range = 0-1)
Ecdep	Economic dependence of family (e.g., welfare) (mean = .21; range = 0-1)
Memploy	Mother's irregular employment outside the home (mean = .20; range = 0-1)
Foreignb	One or both parents foreign-born (mean = .61; range = 0-1)
Mobility	Number of moves by family (mean = .34; range = 0-1)
Ferratic	Father's inconsistent use of threatening control and physical punishment (mean = 1.52; range = 0-3)
Merratic	Mother's inconsistent use of threatening control and physical punishment (mean = 1.50; range = 0-3)
Msuperv	Supervision of boy by mother (mean = .63; range = 0-1)
Preject	Indifferent attention or open hostile rejection of the boy by mother and/or father (mean = .50; range = 0-2)
Attachp	Warm emotional ties of boy to mother and/or father (mean = 1.34; range = 0-2)

a. *UJD* = *Unraveling Juvenile Delinquency*, by Sheldon Glueck and Eleanor Glueck, 1950.

Causal Model and Hypotheses

The causal model to be examined empirically is shown in Figure 1. The mediating constructs of family processes are hypothesized to have the strongest effects on delinquency. Specifically, we expect that erratic and harsh discipline by mothers *and* fathers, weak parental supervision, parental rejection of the child, and weak emotional attachment of the boy to his parents will increase delinquency. This conceptualization is derived in part from the work of Travis Hirschi. Hirschi focuses on child-rearing practices and presents a model of effective parenting that

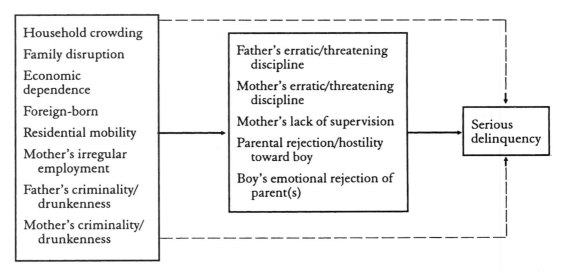

FIGURE 1 *Causal model of structural background factors, family process, and delinquency in the UJD data.* Note: Because of the *UJD* matching design, age, race/ethnicity, neighborhood SES, and IQ are controlled. Also, gender is controlled in that the study involved only males. Broken line indicates hypothesized weak or insignificant relationship. Solid line indicates hypothesized strong effect.

entails monitoring the behavior of children, recognizing their misdeeds, and punishing those misdeeds accordingly. In addition, Hirschi argues that parental affection and/or a willingness to invest in children is an essential underlying condition of good parenting and, ultimately, the prevention of misbehavior. These dimensions of family social control—discipline, supervision, and attachment—have rarely been examined simultaneously in previous research. Thus, our model will enable us to assess the relative contributions of family process variables to the explanation of delinquency.

The model also posits that structural background factors influence delinquency largely through their effects on family process. Previous research on families and delinquency often fails to account for social structural context and how it influences family life. According to the logic of causal inference, we *expect* structural context to have weak direct effects on delinquency. In other words, the effects of family process are hypothesized to mediate structural background. Note that this specification may shed light on the controversial link between

criminality of parents and delinquency of their children. Parental deviance is hypothesized to influence son's delinquency through the disruption of family social control. More precisely, we argue that parents who commit crimes and/or drink excessively often use harsh discipline in an inconsistent manner or are lax in disciplining their children; their supervision is weak or nonexistent; and the parent-child/child-parent attachments are tenuous.

Our model and data further enable us to ascertain the direct and indirect effects of such key factors as family disruption, economic dependence, household crowding, residential mobility, mother's irregular employment, and nativity of parents. It is our contention that these structural factors will also affect family social control mechanisms. For instance, it is likely that residential mobility and irregular employment by mothers are related to difficulties in supervising and monitoring children. Similarly, family disruption not only affects supervisory capacity but also attachment and disciplinary practices.

Finally, although various indicators of poverty and poor living conditions (e.g., economic dependence, household crowding, and foreign-born status) have been linked to delinquency, these same variables are posited to have an effect on family social control mechanisms. Thus, we expect economic dependence, household crowding, and nativity of parents to be related to delinquency largely through their effects on family process variables as defined here.

Our causal model (Figure 1) in conjunction with the unique nature of the Gluecks' data also contributes to the literature on families and delinquency in other specific ways. First, the attachment variables used in this study contain measures of attachment in both directions, namely, parent to the child and child to the parent. Thus, we are able to construct two measures of attachment, parent-child and child-parent, which allows fuller specification of the attachment dimension.

Second, in this study we are able to assess the different effects of mothers and fathers separately with regard to such key variables as criminality/drunkenness and style of discipline. It seems important to begin to explore whether the behavior of mothers and fathers has similar or different effects on the children.

Third, on the basis of the information available, we combined alcoholism of the parent with criminality of the parent in order to determine more fully the effect of parental deviance on intervening variables, like attachment, discipline practices, and supervision. Although few studies consider parental alcoholism as an important variable it seems to be potentially as important as parental criminality in an examination of family functioning.

RESULTS

The full structural equation results are presented in Table 2. In columns 1 and 2, the OLS regression estimates paint a strikingly clear picture that almost fully supports the causal model. Note, first, that of all the structural background factors, only one (mobility) has a direct effect on delinquency. On the other hand, all of the family process variables have significant effects on delinquency in the predicted theoreti-

cal direction. Moreover, several of these effects are quite substantial. Mother's supervision has the largest effect (−.25) and sharply differentiates delinquents from nondelinquents. Perhaps more interesting, both mother's and father's erratic discipline have independent positive effects on delinquency of virtually the same magnitude.

While the family process variables relating to discipline and supervision have the largest effect, the data also reveal that the affective dimension of family process is important too. In this regard, parental rejection of the child has a direct positive effect on delinquency (.14), and boy's attachment to parent seems to suppress delinquency (−.11). Hence, independent of both background factors and family discipline factors, emotional ties of child to parent and parent to child appear to distinguish serious, persistent delinquents from nondelinquents.

Overall, the results clearly support the theoretical model in Figure 1. Indeed, examination of the results verifies that, except for mother's irregular employment, all structural background factors have significant effects on delinquency in the expected manner. But as seen in Table 2, only mobility retains a significant (albeit considerably reduced) effect on delinquency when the family dimensions of discipline, supervision, and attachment are controlled. Not surprisingly, then, calculation of indirect effects reveals that of the total effect of the structural background factors on delinquency, a substantial portion is mediated by family process (79%).

CONCLUSIONS

A major finding of our research is that family process variables are directly related to serious and persistent delinquency in the predicted theoretical direction. These results support our version of social control theory. Moreover, these family process variables—supervision, attachment, and discipline—were identified by the Gluecks as the most important family correlates of serious, persistent delinquency. Thus, our study using multivariate analysis essentially

TABLE 2

OLS linear and ML logistic regression of delinquency status on structural background factors and family process variables, reanalysis of *UJD* coded data.

	Delinquency			
	OLS Linear Regression		ML Logistic Regression	
Full model	B	t ratio	Coefficient	C/SE
Hcrowd	−.00	−.07	.02	.11
Fcrdrunk	.02	.72	.04	.28
Mcrdrunk	.02	.64	.20	1.18
Famdis	.03	1.05	.27	1.18
Ecdep	.02	.88	.12	.49
Memploy	.01	.47	.07	.28
Foreignb	.01	.49	.14	.65
Mobility	.07**	2.22	.46	2.03
Ferratic	.16**	4.92	.55**	4.30
Merratic	.17**	5.35	.60**	4.78
Msuperv	−.25**	−7.71	−1.41**	−6.38
Preject	.14**	4.16	.68**	3.92
Attachp	−.11**	−3.76	−.47**	−3.46
	$R^2 = .44, p < .01$		Model $\chi^2 = 433.9$ (13 *df*)	

**$p < .05$.

confirms the findings generated by the Gluecks over 30 years ago.

Another major finding is that, with the exception of residential mobility, none of the structural background factors had a significant, direct effect on delinquency. Instead, family process mediated some 80% of the effect of structural background on delinquency. We believe this model has considerable significance for future research in that it explains *how* key background factors influence delinquency. Moreover, our model points to the importance of previously neglected variables in criminology—especially the alcoholism and criminality of parents. Parental deviance of both mother and father strongly disrupts family processes of social control, which in turn increases delinquency.

Of perhaps greatest importance is that our analysis reveals the potential of the Glueck data for basic criminological research. Clearly, our study is a modest beginning and more research should be devoted to reanalyses of the available coded data from the *UJD* study. Indeed, the Gluecks' data in all likelihood are superior to many of the current longitudinal data sets in criminology. The raw records in the Gluecks' data, for example, contain richer information on social factors than most sociological studies, and more extensive criminal history information than most criminal career databases. And perhaps most intriguing (and unknown to most criminologists), the unpublished data contain a rich array of self-reported, parental-reported, and teacher-reported indicators of delinquent and antisocial behavior.

QUESTIONS FOR DISCUSSION AND WRITING

1. Why did the authors reanalyze the Gluecks' data?
2. How do the OLS regression estimates paint a strikingly clear picture that almost fully supports the authors' causal model?
3. Why do the authors believe this model has considerable significance for future research?

The Cambridge-Somerville Youth Study

EDWIN POWERS
SHIRLEY WITMER

THE experimental design is simple and scientifically correct. Two groups of 325 boys each, carefully matched, were formed out of a much larger number of referrals. Each group had the same number of "problem boys" judged by teachers and by a team of experts to be "predelinquents." One group was to be let alone, thus serving as a "control" to the other, experimental or "treated" group. This latter group was to receive all the aid that a resourceful counselor, backed by the study, the school, and community agencies, could possibly give.

The original plan called for a 10-year period of work with the treatment (T) boys, starting at as early an age as possible. (Actually, the median age at the start of treatment was 10½ years.) Ideally, each boy should have one and only one counselor throughout this entire period. At the conclusion of the 10-year treatment, an evaluation of the conduct (and character) of the T-boys should be made in comparison with the conduct (and character) of their "twins," the control (C) boys.

The turnover in personnel made it difficult indeed to test the essential hypothesis, namely, that the influence of skilled and directed friendship on the part of a continuously available counselor may succeed in preventing delinquency in boys. Furthermore, many of the boys reached the age of 17 after only 5 or 6 years of treatment. Thus, the study was forced to restrict its period of operation and to reduce the number of boys in the treatment group. No boy received more than 8 years of treatment, the median period being about 5 years.

Although the results are not as definitive and conclusive as we should like, still the trends and indications that emerge are probably "in the right direction."

THE TREATMENT METHOD

"To these boys," said Dr. Cabot, "we plan to give personal advice and guidance through the services of paid visitors, both men and women, who will come to know the boys intimately, to see them frequently, and to influence their conduct." The counselor's behavior constitutes the independent variable in the research.

Is this conception of treatment to be equated with the practice and policy of modern social work? Directed friendship, as conceived by Dr. Cabot, differs in two essential respects from the accepted practice of social work. In the first place, it took the initiative in seeking out "clients." Neither the boy nor his parents asked for help. They were wooed and won to the study, led into accepting its services. In the second place, the relationship was sustained whether or not there was an acute problem to be met or a specific service to render. No case was closed simply because its presenting problem, if indeed it had one, was "solved."

The research design hoped to find out the answer. Presumably, the C-boys had the benefits of much ordinary social service, while the T-boys had the extra benefit of sustained and directed friendship. All counselors did to some degree employ approved techniques of casework—meeting specific needs, cooperating with other agencies. Furthermore, the majority of counselors did in fact have social work training, and for the greater part of the treatment period, casework supervision was available to all the counselors, a supervision with a definitely psychiatric slant. Much emphasis was placed on health, tutoring, camping—common practices in any child welfare agency.

The next section deals with the evaluation of the study as a delinquency-prevention program. Our experimental hypothesis was simple. If the counselors' work had been reasonably successful, then the C-boys, who had been denied the services of experienced and talented personal counselors, should show a proportionately higher frequency of delinquent behavior. The question we are seeking to answer is, Did this enduring, personal relationship of counselor and boy actually prevent the predelinquent child from becoming a delinquent youth?

USEFULNESS OF THE CONTROL GROUP

The usefulness of the control group is apparent, for if there had been none we could not interpret the following outcomes:

1. Not more than one third of the older boys in the treatment group whose careers were closely followed and who appeared to be predelinquent boys when under 12 actually became delinquents in any serious sense.
2. Surprisingly few (less than one sixth) of the boys who were rated on the minus side by the predictors were actually committed to correctional institutions.
3. The counselors believed that the study's program had "substantially benefited" about two thirds of the boys whom it served.
4. Considerably more than half of the boys acknowledged that they had been helped by their association with the study.

Obviously, these facts alone do not prove that the outcome would have been any different without the intervention of the counselors. The control group was therefore indispensable in measuring the effectiveness of the counselors' work.

The C-boys, of course, did not live in a social vacuum. Although receiving no help from the counselors, we cannot assume that they received no help at all. On the contrary, we know that many, if not all, of the C-boys in the usual course of events received guidance from their families, the school, and the church, and a few were aided by the social agencies in the two cities. It is impossible for us to measure the extent of this help. All the study could hope to show, therefore, was what its treatment amounted to *over and above* the influences ordinarily brought to bear upon a child in these communities; or, to state it another way, whether coordinated and sustained counseling or personal case work was better than a more sporadic variety. By and large, however, we believe that a comparison between the T-boys and C-boys can be based on the fact that the T-boys received a *special* kind of service, not available to the controls, having the unique features of a continuous, friendly relationship of an older counselor. Did this special service keep them out of trouble?

How Long Did the Period of Treatment Continue?

Under the original plan, each boy was to have received 10 years of continuous counseling. For certain reasons the program fell short of realization by a number of years. For more than three fourths of the group, the counselors' visits ceased before the official close. The boys who were retired from the treatment program early in its operation received on the average only about 2½ years of attention from the counselors; those who were dropped were seen for only 4 years and 2 months on the average, while those boys who were terminated (after reaching their 17th birthdays) were, on the average, in touch with their counselors for a period of 5 years and

TABLE 1

Number of boys appearing before the Crime Prevention Bureau from 1938 to 1946, inclusive.

Number of Appearances	Number of Boys	
	T	C
One	49	49
Two or more	65	52
Total	114	101

11 months. There were, in fact, only 75 boys who were carried from the very beginning of the treatment program to its official termination. For them, treatment extended for an average period of 6 years and 9 months (with a range from 8 years and 1 month to 6 years and 7 months). For the entire group of 325 boys who were originally nominated for treatment, the average length of the treatment period was no more than 4 years and 10 months.

Our comparison of the treatment and control groups in respect to delinquent behavior is confined to official records, because of insufficient data relating to the offenses of C-boys unknown to the police and courts. We shall consider offenses known to the police in Cambridge, court appearances (frequency and seriousness), and commitments to juvenile or correctional institutions.

COMPARISON OF THE T- AND C-BOYS IN RESPECT TO POLICE STATISTICS IN CAMBRIDGE

This comparison is based on the records of the Crime Prevention Bureau of the Police Department in the City of Cambridge. Through the courtesy of its officials, an examination was made of the records on file from its inception in 1938 through 1946, the year following the termination of the treatment program. Most of the cases appearing before this bureau were handled in an informal manner after an investigation and interview with the boy and his parents.

Relatively few cases were referred to the district court for disposition, for most of the offenses were of a minor nature. Nevertheless, they represented behavior that was sufficiently harmful or annoying to come to the attention of the police.

Table 1 shows the total number of T- and C-boys who appeared before the bureau in a given period.

FINDINGS

1. The number of T-boys who made only one appearance before the bureau equals the number of C-boys making only one appearance.
2. The number of T-boys who appeared two or more times exceeds the number of C-boys who were repeaters.
3. The number of T-boys who appeared before the bureau exceeded the number of C-boys (53% of the total were T-boys).
4. From 1938 to 1946 inclusive, 282 T-boys and 256 C-boys appeared before the bureau. The average number of appearances per boy was similar in the two groups, 2.45 for T-boys compared to 2.53 for C-boys.
5. The number of T-boys appearing two or more times, three or more times, and four or more times exceeded the number of C-boys who appeared a like number of times, but the C-boys exceeded the T-boys in making five or more, six or more, or eight or more appearances. The number of T- and C-boys making at least seven appearances was equal.

CONCLUSIONS

Throughout the treatment period, the counselors were evidently not successful in preventing boys from committing offenses that brought them to the attention of the police in Cambridge (where two thirds of them resided). Indeed, the counselors seem to have had no positive effect whatever in this respect, as measured by the number of T-boys appearing before the bureau in comparison with a matched group equal in number who did not receive this special counseling service. The number of boys who appeared, as well as the total number of appearances, was greater for the treatment group than for the control groups. It can be said, nevertheless, that there was *a slight* preponderance of C-boys among the most active recidivists.

Comparison of the T- and C-Boys in Respect to Frequency of Court Appearances

Through the courtesy of the Massachusetts Commissioner of Probation, all cases were cleared through the state probation files. In the central files, the names of all boys who had been brought into court on a delinquent or criminal charge were noted. Offenses committed outside the state were disregarded in these comparisons. From these data, the following tabulations are derived:

1. We first compare the frequency of offenses and of court appearances of the 325 T-boys and the 325 C-boys, regardless of age at that time or the length of time the T-boys had remained in the treatment group.

Court Appearances	T	C
Number of boys	96	92
Number of offenses	264	218

2. We now compare the T-boys who had reached the age of 17 with the C-boys matched with them in respect to the frequency of court appearances. This comparison concerns only 89.8% of the total group of 650 boys, for 10.2% were at that time still under 17. As the treatment and control groups were matched closely for age the number in each group who were under 17 on that date is approximately the same.

Court Appearances	T	C
Number of boys	68	63
Number of offenses	141	132

3. Compared to C-boys, how many T-boys committed offenses for which they were brought into court after their 17th birthdays? We find here that the number of T-boys who made court appearances in their 18th, 19th, 20th, or 21st years exceeded the number of C-boys, and also that the number of offenses committed by them was larger.

4. Were the boys who remained with the study for a longer consecutive period and who presumably were the recipients of more intensive efforts of the counselors less delinquent or more delinquent than their matched controls? To answer this question, we now compare the official delinquent records of the 74 boys who were in the treatment program from the beginning to the end, together with the 68 boys whose cases were not terminated until they had reached their 17th birthdays, with 142 C-boys who were originally matched with these T-boys.

Comparing the 142 boys in the T-group who received the most extensive treatment with the 142 boys matched with them in the C-group during a 6-year period commencing 8 months (on the average) after treatment began we find an excess of T-offenders. In this analysis a higher proportion of T-boys than was evident in the previous analyses might be due to selective factors appearing subsequent to the matching. Boys retained for treatment were, as a rule, those whose problems persisted. Presumably, these two original groups (325 T-boys and 325 C-boys) were well matched at the outset, but it does not follow that a subgroup of 142 T-boys selected on the basis of factors arising after the original matching would still be as well matched with their 142 C-twins.

Comparison of T- and C-Boys in Respect to Seriousness of Offenses

Did either group commit more serious offenses than the other? Although the total number of offenses committed by the T-boys (264) considerably exceeded the number of offenses by C-boys (218), nevertheless the distribution into categories of seriousness differed considerably. Of the offenses committed by the C-boys, 59.6% were placed in the two more serious categories as compared to 51.5% committed by the T-boys. In the category of "most serious" offenses, the C-boys exceeded the T-boys in number of offenses committed (58 compared to 48). Also, more C-boys (35) than T-boys (30) committed such offenses. In comparing the proportion of such offenses to the total in the series, we also find that a larger proportion of "most serious" offenses were committed by C-boys (26.6%) than by T-boys (18.2%). Taken as a whole, the average index of offenses was slightly less serious for T-boys (2.41) than for C-boys (2.56). Although the T-boys have committed, on the whole, more offenses in the aggregate and more T-boys than C-boys have committed the "serious" offenses, there is some evidence, though slight, that the most serious offenders are in the control group.

Comparison of the T- and C-Boys in Respect to Commitments to Correctional Institutions

Another way to measure "seriousness" may be by noting the incidence of commitments in the two groups, for the more serious delinquent presumably is the boy who was committed to a correctional institution on the theory that he could not be expected to make a satisfactory adjustment to society while living in his own home. We have maintained that this presumption is not necessarily true in the individual case but, by and large, in considering delinquents in

groups rather than individually, commitment to an institution is a reasonable indication that the delinquent behavior of the group has been serious and/or persistent as judged by the court. We now compare the 325 T-boys and the 325 C-boys in respect to commitments.

Findings

1. An almost identical number of T- and C-boys were committed to institutions for juvenile offenders: 23 T-boys and 22 C-boys.
2. More C-boys than T-boys were committed to institutions for older offenders: 8 T-boys compared to 15 C-boys. Although the total numbers were small, the control group is almost double the treatment group in this respect.
3. C-boys were more frequently committed to more than one institution: 4 T-boys compared to 9 C-boys.

GENERAL CONCLUSIONS

From our comparison of the delinquent behavior of the T- and C-boys, two main conclusions can be drawn:

1. The special work of the counselors was no more effective than the usual forces in the community in preventing boys from committing delinquent acts. Evidence for this conclusion was found in our analysis of official records. We found in the records of the Cambridge Crime Prevention Bureau that more T-boys appeared before this bureau than C-boys. From a study of court records, it appeared that slightly more T-boys were in court than C-boys, regardless of age or the number of years in the study, and again a preponderance of T-boys appeared when analyzed by age into two groups—under and over 17. In considering only the boys who presumably were the recipients of more intensive and extensive efforts of the counselors, we found again that the T-boys had more official records than the C-boys matched with them. In appraising the seriousness of the offenses of the

two groups, we found a striking similarity in degree, although the control group showed a slight trend toward more serious offenses, and finally, from the records of commitments to institutions we found close correspondence between the T- and C-boys, with a slight preponderance of C-boys.

2. Our second conclusion is that, although the counselors were unable to stop the advance of young boys into delinquency with any greater success than the usual deterrent forces in the community, some of the boys were evidently deflected from delinquent careers which, without the counselors' help, might have resulted in continued or more serious violations. Thus, the evidence seems to point to the fact that, although the first stages of delinquency are not wholly averted when starting treatment at the 8- to 10-year level, the later and more serious stages may to some degree be curtailed. Evidence for this conclusion was found in the analysis of official records which showed that the more frequent repeaters (Police Bureau statistics) and the more serious offenders (court statistics) were more often in the control group, although the differences were not large. We found a considerable preponderance of C-boys committed to institutions for older offenders.

QUESTIONS FOR DISCUSSION AND WRITING

1. How did the T-boys and C-boys compare regarding making one appearance before the criminal prevention bureau? Two or more appearances? Which group made more appearances on average?
2. Which group made more court appearances? What about when the authors compared the T-boys who had reached the age of 17 with the C-boys matched with them in respect to the frequency of court appearances? When the authors looked at those boys who were brought into court after their 17th birthdays? Those who received the most extensive treatment?
3. Did either group commit more serious offenses than the other? What about commitments to correctional institutions?

A Thirty-Year Follow-Up of Treatment Effects

JOAN McCORD

IN 1935, Richard Clark Cabot instigated one of the most imaginative and exciting programs ever designed in hopes of preventing delinquency. Several hundred boys from densely populated, factory-dominated areas of eastern Massachusetts were included in the project, known as the Cambridge-Somerville Youth Study. Schools, welfare agencies, churches, and the police recommended both "difficult" and "average" youngsters to the program. These boys and their families were given physical examinations and were interviewed by social workers who then rated each boy in such a way as to allow a selection committee to designate delinquency-prediction scores. In addition to giving delinquency-prediction scores, the selection committee studied each boy's records in order to identify pairs who were similar in age, delinquency-prone histories, family background, and home environments. By the toss of a coin, one member of each pair was assigned to the group that would receive treatment.

The treatment program began in 1939, when the boys were between 5 and 13 years old. Their median age was 10½. Counselors assigned to each family visited, on the average, twice a month. They encouraged families to call on the program for assistance. Family problems became the focus of attention for approximately one third of the treatment group. Over half of the boys were tutored in academic subjects; over 100 received medical or psychiatric attention; one fourth were sent to summer camps; and most were brought into contact with the Boy Scouts, the YMCA, and other community programs. The control group, meanwhile, participated only through providing information about themselves. Both groups, it should be remembered, contained boys referred as "average" and boys considered "difficult."

The present study compares the 253 men who had been in the treatment program with the 253 "matched mates" assigned to the control group.

METHOD

Official records and personal contacts were used to obtain information about the long-term effects of the Cambridge-Somerville Youth Study. In 1975 and 1976, the 506 former members of the program were traced through court records, mental hospital records, records from alcoholic treatment centers, and vital statistics in Massachusetts. Telephone calls, city directories, motor-vehicle registrations, marriage and death records, and lucky hunches were used to find the men themselves.

Four hundred and eighty men (95%) were located; among these, 48 (9%) had died and 340 (79%) were living in Massachusetts. Questionnaires were mailed to 208 men from the treatment group and 202 men from the control group.

The questionnaire elicited information about marriage, children, occupations, drinking, health, and attitudes. Former members of the treatment group were asked how (if at all) the treatment program had been helpful to them.

COMPARISON OF CRIMINAL BEHAVIOR

The treatment and control groups were compared on a variety of measures for criminal behavior. With the exception of Crime Prevention Bureau records for unofficial crimes committed by juveniles, court convictions serve as the standard by which criminal behavior was assessed. Almost equal numbers in the treatment and control groups had committed crimes as juveniles, whether measured by official or by unofficial records. It seemed possible that the program might have benefited those referred as "difficult" while damaging those referred as "average." The evidence, however, failed to support this hypothesis. Among those referred as difficult, 34% from the treatment group and 30% from the control group had official juvenile records; an additional 20% from the treatment group and 21% from the control group had unofficial records. Nor were there differences between the groups for those who had been referred as average.

As adults, equal numbers (168) had been convicted for some crime. Among men who had been in the treatment group, 119 committed only relatively minor crimes (against ordinances or order), but 49 had committed serious crimes against property (including burglary, larceny, and auto theft), or against persons (including assault, rape, and attempted homicide). Among men from the control group, 126 had committed only relatively minor crimes; 42 had committed serious property crimes or crimes against persons. Twenty-nine men from the treatment group and 25 men from the control group committed serious crimes after the age of 25.

The treatment and control groups were compared to see whether there were differences (a) in the number of serious crimes committed, (b) in age when a first crime was committed, (c) in age when committing a first serious crime, and (d) in age after which no serious crime was committed. None of these measures showed reliable differences.

Benefits from the treatment program did not appear when delinquency-prediction scores were controlled or when seriousness of juvenile record and juvenile incarceration were controlled. Unexpectedly, however, a higher proportion of criminals from the treatment group than of criminals from the control group committed more than one crime. Among the 182 men with criminal records from the treatment group, 78% committed at least two crimes; among the 183 men with criminal records from the control group, 67% committed at least two crimes.

SUBJECTIVE EVALUATION OF THE PROGRAM

Former members of the treatment group were asked, "In what ways (if any) was the Cambridge-Somerville project helpful to you?" Two thirds of the men stated that the program had been helpful to them. Some wrote that, by providing interesting activities, the project kept them off the streets and out of trouble. Many believed that the project improved their lives through providing guidance or teaching them how to get along with others. The questionnaires were sprinkled with such comments as "helped me to have faith and trust in other people"; "I was put on the right road"; "helped prepare me for manhood"; "to overcome my prejudices"; "provided an initial grasp of our complex society outside of the ghetto"; and "better insight on life in general."

A few men believed that the project was responsible for their becoming law-abiding citizens. Such men wrote that, had it not been for their particular counselors, "I probably would be in jail"; "My life would have gone the other way"; or "I think I would have ended up in a life of crime."

SUMMARY AND DISCUSSION

Thirty years after termination of the program, many of the men remembered their counselorship, sometimes recalling particular acts of kindness and sometimes noting the general support they felt in having someone available with whom to discuss their problems. There seems to be little doubt that many of the men developed emotional ties to their counselors.

Were the Youth Study program to be assessed by the subjective judgment of its value as perceived by those who received its services, it would rate high marks. To the enormous credit of those who dedicated years of work to the project, it is possible to use objective criteria to evaluate long-term impact of this program, which seems to have been successful in achieving the short-term goals of establishing rapport between social worker and teenage clients.

Despite the large number of comparisons between treatment and control groups, none of the objective measures confirmed hopes that treatment had improved the lives of those in the treatment group. The objective evidence presents a disturbing picture. The program seems not only to have failed to prevent its clients from committing crimes—thus corroborating studies of other projects—but also to have produced negative side effects. As compared with the control group:

1. Men who had been in the treatment program were more likely to commit (at least) a second crime.

2. Men who had been in the treatment program were more likely to evidence signs of alcoholism.
3. Men from the treatment group more commonly manifested signs of serious mental illness.
4. Among men who had died, those from the treatment group died younger.
5. Men from the treatment group were more likely to report having had at least one stress-related disease; in particular, they were more likely to have experienced high blood pressure or heart trouble.
6. Men from the treatment group tended to have occupations with lower prestige.
7. Men from the treatment group tended more often to report their work as not satisfying.

It should be noted that the side effects that seem to have resulted from treatment were subtle. There is no reason to believe that treatment increased the probability of committing a first crime, although treatment may have increased the likelihood that those who committed a first crime would commit additional crimes.

At this juncture, it seems appropriate to suggest several possible interpretations of the subtle effects of treatment. Interaction with adults whose values are different from those of the family milieu may produce later internal conflicts that manifest themselves in disease and/or dissatisfaction. Agency intervention may create dependency on outside assistance. When this assistance is no longer available, the individual may experience symptoms of dependency and resentment. The treatment program may have generated such high expectations that subsequent experiences tended to produce symptoms of deprivation. Or finally, through receiving the services of a "welfare project," those in the treatment program may have justified the help they received by perceiving themselves as requiring help.

QUESTIONS FOR DISCUSSION AND WRITING

1. As adults, how many of the T-boys and C-boys had been convicted for some crime?
2. What did former members of the treatment group say about the Cambridge-Somerville project?
3. What negative side effects were associated with the treatment group? What does the author suggest may be responsible for those negative side effects?

RISK FACTORS AND PREVENTION

A more contemporary version of the early identification and intervention approach to preventing delinquency is based in the growing field of identifying "at-risk" youths, based on a variety of biological, psychological, and social characteristics that are predictive of delinquency. This is also primarily a psychological perspective, but one that is typically more atheoretical than the Gluecks'. In fact, it has been suggested by critics that it only identifies correlates, rather than causes, of delinquency and is more a model of strategic intervention than a causal model. Rather than attempting to modify the causes of delinquency as proposed in a theory, the focus is on those "factors" that are associated, directly or indirectly, with delinquent behavior. Jessor provides one of the better examples of the approach in "Risk Behavior in Adolescence," and Zigler, Taussig, and Black describe a number of applications of risk factor analysis in programs designed for high-risk children.

Risk Behavior in Adolescence: A Psychosocial Framework for Understanding and Action

RICHARD JESSOR

IN this chapter, a general social-psychological framework is developed that makes clear the complexity required of any explanation of adolescent risk behavior and, it is hoped, the advantage that derives from incorporating attention to both person and context. The exploration begins with some considerations about the basic notion of *risk* itself; it then turns to an examination of the organization of adolescent risk behavior and the utility of the concept of *lifestyle*; that leads into a general conceptual framework for understanding risk behavior and an explication of its content; finally, some implications of the conceptual framework for action, that is, for prevention/intervention, will be noted.

A PSYCHOSOCIAL CONCEPT OF RISK

Insofar as behaviors constitute risk factors for morbidity and mortality, the challenge for epidemiology is to move beyond its usual biomedical focus and address a new task—the understanding of behavior and its antecedents and consequences. It is in undertaking this enterprise that epidemiology has begun to find a confluence with social/developmental psychology.

From *Adolescents at Risk: Medical and Social Perspectives* (pp. 374-389) D. Rogers and E. Ginzburg, editors, 1992, Boulder, CO: Westview Press. Copyright 1992 by E. Ginzburg. Reprinted by permission.

For the latter, of course, the understanding of social behavior has been a traditional and important raison d'être.

The incorporation of behaviors into the rubric of risk factors entails a reformulation of thinking about the very concept of risk and about what it is that is at risk. First, it requires that the traditional restriction of the concept of risk to biomedical outcomes alone be loosened. Although behaviors do indeed have biomedical consequences, they also eventuate in social and personal or psychological outcomes. The behavior of, say, marijuana smoking by an adolescent may well involve a higher probability of pulmonary disease, but it also may involve a higher probability of legal sanctions or conflict with parents or loss of interest in school or a sense of personal guilt and anxiety. These latter are psychosocial outcomes or consequences that are linked, simultaneously, to the very same risk behavior. A *psychosocial* understanding of risk, when behaviors are risk factors, requires attention to all of their potential outcomes or consequences, not just to those that are biomedical.

Second, the reformulation requires that the restriction of the concept of risk to adverse, negative, or undesirable outcomes be loosened. Returning to the preceding example, it is clear that some of the outcomes or consequences of the behavioral risk factor of marijuana smoking can be positive, desirable, and sought after by adolescents. Smoking marijuana can lead, for example, to social acceptance by peers and to a subjective sense of autonomy and maturity. When behaviors are risk factors, the notion of risk needs to be expanded to encompass positive or desired outcomes as well as those that are adverse or negative. A psychosocial reformulation of risk calls for a thoroughgoing cost-*and*-benefit analysis of risk factors rather than the traditional preoccupation with only their potential costs. Behavior, including risk behavior, is clearly influenced by both.

Thus, *what* is at risk from engaging in risk behavior includes but far transcends physical health and physical growth. Risk behaviors can jeopardize the accomplishment of normal developmental tasks, the fulfillment of expected social roles, the acquisition of essential skills, the achievement of a sense of adequacy and competence, and the appropriate preparation for transition to the next stage in the life trajectory—young adulthood. The term *risk behavior* refers, then, to any behaviors that can compromise these psychosocial aspects of successful adolescent development. Substance abuse, withdrawal from school involvement, unprotected sexual intercourse, driving after drinking, or engaging in violence are some obvious examples.

THE ORGANIZATION OF ADOLESCENT RISK BEHAVIOR AND THE CONCEPT OF LIFESTYLE

Another issue requires attention as we explore the way toward a general conceptual framework for adolescent risk behavior. This issue has to do with the degree to which there is structure and organization among the different risk behaviors in adolescence. Stated in other terms, the issue is whether there is intraindividual covariation among risk behaviors so that they cluster or form what might be called a risk behavior syndrome. It makes an enormous difference, for both understanding and intervention, to be dealing with separate, independent, and isolated risk behaviors or, instead, with an orga-

nized constellation of risk behaviors that are interrelated and covary.

By now, a fair amount of evidence has been accumulated on this question, and there is considerable support for the covariation perspective. The evidence for covariation is strongest for those risk behaviors that are also problem behaviors, for example, drug use, delinquency, alcohol abuse, and sexual precocity. In one of our early longitudinal studies of high school youths, for example, we found that 61% of marijuana users were sexually experienced, whereas only 18% of the nonusers were. In our later research, we provided additional support for the interrelatedness of adolescent problem behaviors by showing that a single common factor accounts for their positive intercorrelations.

Overall, the empirical evidence supports the existence of organized patterns of adolescent risk behaviors. These structures of behaviors, taken together, reflect an adolescent's way of being in the world. Their structure or organization raises interesting questions about the origin or source of the covariation and patterning.

The key import of the evidence about covariation among risk behaviors is the support it provides for the organizing concept of *lifestyle*. The lifestyle notion has a core meaning denoting an organized pattern of interrelated behaviors. The utility of the concept of lifestyle, referring as it does to the constellation or syndrome of risk behavior, is that it directs our attention to the adolescent as a whole actor rather than to each of the risk behaviors, one after another. Equally important, it raises a serious question about whether intervention efforts should remain focused, as they have been, on specific behaviors, for example, illicit drug use, or whether they should be oriented, instead, toward influencing an adolescent's lifestyle as a whole.

A GENERAL CONCEPTUAL FRAMEWORK FOR ADOLESCENT RISK BEHAVIOR

The focus, thus far, has been on the psychosocial *outcomes and consequences* of risk factors when they are behaviors. It is now possible to explore behavioral risk factors in the other direction, that is, in terms of their psychosocial *antecedents and determinants*. Such exploration will lead us to a general conceptual framework for adolescent risk behavior and will illuminate, at the same time, the merging of the epidemiological perspective with that of social-developmental psychology.

Now the key question becomes: "What are the risk factors for the (behavioral) risk factors?" Or, in the present case, "What are the risk factors for the risk behaviors?" That epidemiological concern turns out to be identical to the standard concern of social-psychological inquiry, namely, how to provide an explanatory account of complex social behavior.

A comprehensive social-psychological framework for explaining behavior generally includes four major explanatory domains or sources of variance: the social environment, the perceived environment, personality, and (other) behavior. Although not traditional, more recent explanatory efforts have increasingly sought to engage a fifth domain, namely, biology/genetics. Taken together and fully articulated, these five domains would constitute the "web of causation" or the general explanatory framework for adolescent risk behavior. The schema presented in Figure 1 represents the five domains, illustrates their content, and specifies their relationships to each other, to risk behavior, and to the potential outcomes of risk.

The particular risk factors that have been listed in each of the different risk domains are, for the most part, drawn from the research literature or implicated in various conceptual analyses of adolescent risk behavior. Measures of many of the variables, especially those in the perceived environment, the personality, and the behavior domains, have been employed repeatedly in our own work on problem-behavior theory, which is a specific variant of the general framework in Figure 1. Multiple regression analyses, employing about a dozen or so of the measures, generally yield multiple correlations (*R*s) of about .70 when accounting for an index of multiple problem behavior among adolescents, and the *R*s range between .50 and .80

when various specific risk behaviors such as problem drinking or illicit drug use are being predicted. Thus, between 25% and 65% of the variance in adolescent risk behavior is explained, with close to 50% being modal. The measures that tend to be invariantly important across our different studies include low expectations for school achievement and low attitudinal intolerance of deviance in the personality domain; models for problem behavior among friends in the perceived environment domain; and marijuana use and poor school work in the behavior domain.

These results, ours and those of many other workers in the field, provide encouraging empirical support for the web of causation shown in Figure 1. At the same time, however, they reveal that a large segment of the variance is left unexplained. I believe this is due at least in part to a less than satisfactory grasp on the properties of the social environment. The distribution of a variety of adolescent risk behaviors reflects the circumstances of poverty, racial/ethnic marginality, and limited life-chances, as well as the presence of an underground structure of illegitimate opportunity.

THE ROLE OF PROTECTIVE FACTORS IN ADOLESCENT RISK BEHAVIOR

There is a final aspect of the framework shown in Figure 1 that remains to be addressed, namely, the *protective factors* that are listed in each of the risk domains. The conceptual role of protective factors is to help explain a fact that is part of common awareness, namely, that many adolescents who seem to be at high risk nevertheless do not succumb to risk behavior, or get less involved in it than their peers, or, if involved, seem to abandon it more rapidly than others do. Stated otherwise, many adolescents growing up under conditions of pervasive adversity, limited resources, and intense pressures toward the transgression of conventional norms manage to overcome such circumstances and to "make it." What enables them to avoid entanglements with the criminal justice system, to

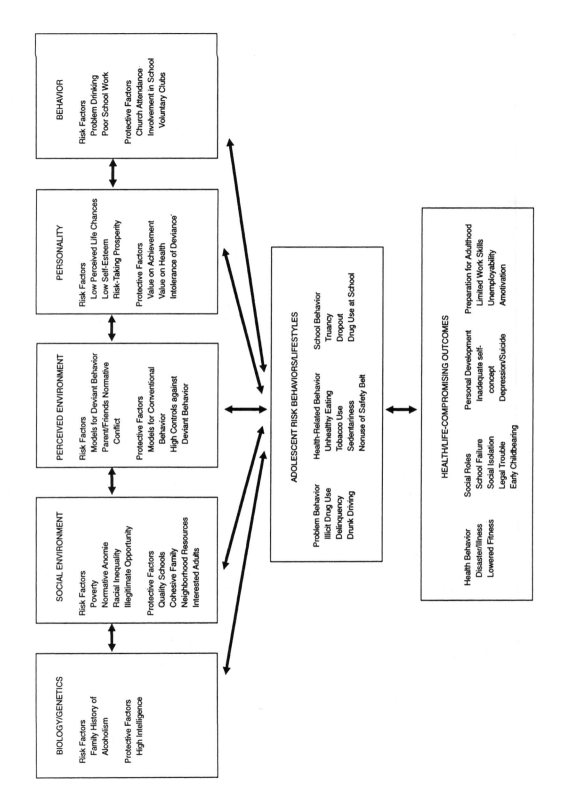

FIGURE 1 *A conceptual framework for adolescent risk behavior: Risk and protective factors, risk behaviors, and risk outcomes.*

remain aloof from antisocial peer groups, to avoid getting pregnant, to do well in school, to acquire the necessary skills for the transition to work and other adult roles, and to develop a sense of personal adequacy and competence?

A likely answer is that there was exposure to and experience of risk, *but that it was countered by exposure to and experience of protection.* Protective factors are considered by both Garmezy and Rutter to moderate, buffer, insulate against and, thereby, to mitigate the impact of risk on adolescent behavior and development.

It is useful to think of protective factors as operating within each of the conceptual domains: in the social environment, a cohesive family, a neighborhood with informal resources, a caring adult; in the perceived environment, peer models for conventional behavior and strict social controls; in the personality domain, high value on academic achievement and on health and high intolerance of deviance; and, in the behavior domain, involvement in conventional behavior, such as church attendance and school clubs. To the extent that protective factors such as these are present and operative, they should serve to attenuate, counter, or balance the impact and effects of risk factors.

ADOLESCENTS AT RISK: WHAT DOES "AT RISK" REALLY MEAN?

What is immediately apparent from the conceptual framework is that being "at risk" can have two quite different meanings. *For adolescents already involved in risk behavior*—usually those who are older—at risk can mean being at risk for health- and life-compromising *outcomes*: early pregnancy, school failure, trouble with the law, unemployability, and inadequate self-concept. The focus here is on the degree of risk associated with the engagement in risk behaviors—illicit drug use, problem drinking, cigarette smoking, precocious sex, or truancy. What is the risk that such engagement will compromise adolescent health, adolescent life, or successful adolescent

development? This meaning of being at risk represents a later developmental stage in the ontogeny of risk, a stage wherein risk behaviors are already practiced and at which the concept of intervention rather than of prevention seems more appropriate.

For this stage, the assessment of the magnitude of risk would certainly include (a) the intensity of involvement in any particular risk behavior, from a level of exploration to a level of commitment; (b) the number of different risk behaviors an adolescent is involved in, and the degree to which they constitute an organized pattern or lifestyle; (c) the earliness of age of onset of the risk behaviors (since there is evidence linking early onset to chronicity and intensity); and (d) the degree of involvement simultaneously in protective behaviors. To be at high risk, at this stage, would imply serious and long-term involvement in an organized pattern of risk behaviors, with little involvement in protective behaviors.

For adolescents not yet involved in risk behavior—usually those who are younger—being at risk means something else, namely, the risk for *initiating, onsetting, or becoming involved in risk behaviors:* for beginning sexual intercourse, for onsetting the use of alcohol and illicit drugs, for starting to cut school, and for engaging in delinquent acts. The "at risk" focus here is the degree of risk and the likelihood that that risk will generate involvement in risk behaviors. This meaning of being at risk represents an earlier stage in the ontogeny of risk, a stage before risk behaviors have been engaged in and in which the term prevention, or primary prevention, seems more appropriate. For this stage, the assessment of the magnitude of risk would require consideration of the following: (a) the number and intensity of risk factors in a particular risk domain; (b) the number and intensity of protective factors in that same domain; (c) the pervasiveness of risk factors across the multiple risk domains; and (d) the pervasiveness of protective factors across the multiple domains. To be at high risk at this stage would mean that there are multiple and serious risk factors in multiple domains and little in the way of protective factors in those same domains.

A final point needs to be made in considering the appraisal of variation in magnitude of risk, one that has been assumed in the discussion but not stated explicitly. Degree of risk needs to be treated conceptually as a *resultant*, an outcome of the balance of risk and protection. Two adolescents characterized by the same pattern of risk factors may be very differently at risk depending on the protective factors that affect their lives. *The logic of the conceptual framework requires arriving at a resultant that reflects the balance of risk and protection.*

IMPLICATIONS FOR PREVENTION/ INTERVENTION

A few comments about the implications of these considerations for prevention/intervention, beyond those already mentioned, may be useful. First, and perhaps of overriding importance, is the import of the complexity of the web of causation that has been proposed. What that complexity suggests is that prevention/intervention efforts that are comprehensive promise to yield greater success than those that are more limited in scope. Programs that fail to engage multiple risk domains are unlikely to be successful or to generate lasting effects. Second, programs need to design efforts that can simultaneously reduce risk and promote protection; neither strategy alone would seem optimal for effecting change. Third, programs directed at the organization and patterning of multiple risk behaviors may be more appropriate than programs focused on specific behaviors alone. Lifestyle change, while obviously a challenge, has the promise of more pervasive and more enduring impact on the repertoire of risk behaviors. Fourth, programs that acknowledge the salience of the social environment would seem especially critical. Young people growing up in adverse social environments are in double jeopardy. Not only are risk factors more intense and more prevalent in such contexts, but protective factors are less available if not, indeed, absent for many. Finally, the emphasis on risk behavior and on lifestyle should not be translated into making individuals alone responsible for removing the risk in their lives; such an approach would tend to "blame the victim." The present conceptual framework makes it patently clear that risk is embedded in the larger social context of adolescent life and that reduction in risk requires social change as well.

QUESTIONS FOR DISCUSSION AND WRITING

1. What does evidence about covariation among risk behaviors support, and what is the utility of this concept? What serious question does it raise?
2. What do multiple regression analyses, employing approximately a dozen of the measures, yield? How much of the variance in adolescent risk behavior is explained?
3. What are protective factors, and how do they prevent risk behaviors?

Early Childhood Intervention

EDWARD ZIGLER
CARA TAUSSIG
KATHRYN BLACK

LONGITUDINAL studies of some early childhood intervention programs are beginning to suggest that they may have an impact on future delinquency and criminality rates. These programs, although by no means standard in purpose and methodology, were never initiated to reduce delinquency but rather to prevent school failure among at-risk populations. Some of the most effective early intervention projects have taken a multipronged approach to this goal by including noneducational supports, such as providing health care, involving parents in the program, and offering specific services to the families of children enrolled.

These programs embrace an ecological view of child development by treating children through their broad environment rather than through an isolated intervention. The success of this approach is documented by solid evidence that graduates of several preschool programs demonstrate lasting improvements in social competence. Because not engaging in delinquent behavior is one sign of social competence (as is success in school), it does seem conceivable that comprehensive early childhood programs could alleviate some of the risk factors that make a child prone to delinquency.

EARLY INTERVENTION PROGRAMS

Major reports over the past decade have consistently shown that some early childhood intervention programs have lasting effects on socially competent behavior. Several of these programs have been subjected to years of outcome evaluation, which most delinquency prevention programs have not. Because early childhood interventions, however, were designed to address goals other than delinquency, few researchers collected data on this behavior. Several studies that included outcomes on delinquency or related factors are discussed below.

Perry Preschool Project

Investigators at the High/Scope Education Research Foundation designed this program for preschoolers deemed at risk for retarded intellectual functioning and eventual school failure. Low-income, black 3- and 4-year-olds were randomly assigned to preschool and control conditions. Those who attended preschool received high-quality, cognitively oriented, early childhood education for 1 to 2 academic years. Teachers conducted frequent home visits to keep parents apprised of their child's activities and to encourage participation in the education process. Monthly small group meetings provided opportunities for parents to exchange views and to support one another's changing perceptions of child rearing. Some mothers became very active in these meetings, eventually becoming part of a planning committee.

Longitudinal data on children up to age 19 show a number of positive outcomes indicative of good social competence in program graduates. Compared with control group children, those who attended the preschool showed better attitudes toward school, had lower rates of grade retention and placement in special education, and performed better on measures of achievement, including school grades and standardized test scores. They also had better high school graduation rates (67% vs. 49%) and postsecondary enrollments. At age 19, higher scores on measures of literacy and competence in skills of everyday life, higher employment, and lower use of welfare assistance seem to corroborate indications from school achievement that preschool graduates were more socially competent than those in the control group.

Finally, attendance at the Perry Preschool was associated with fewer arrests or charges, generally for less serious crimes. Record searches indicated that 31% of the preschool group had been arrested or charged at least one time, compared with 51% of the control group. The total number of arrests was twice as high in the control group, although there was no difference in the number of persons sentenced. The preschool program was credited with reducing the cost of delinquency and crime by approximately $2,400 per child.

Syracuse University Family Development Research Program

This program attempted to bolster family and child functioning in an economically disadvantaged sample through extensive parent contact and supplementary child care. Low-SES women were recruited during their last trimester of pregnancy, and a matched control group was later established. They were mostly young, single parents who had less than a high school education and poor work records. Many had histories of arrest or appearance in court.

Paraprofessionals worked with target families once a week to encourage sound mother-child relationships. They provided nutrition information, taught and modeled processes of parent interaction with the child, were supportive of the mother, and helped her develop contacts with service agencies and later with elementary school personnel. For the children, the program provided 4½ continuous years of quality child care at Syracuse University Children's Center, beginning with half-day care from 6 to 15 months, followed by full-day care until school age. Through the combination of attention to parent and child, the intervention planners hoped to change the permanent environment of the home and to teach parents how to support their child's course of development.

Longitudinal follow-ups showed a number of positive outcomes, including a reduction in delinquent behavior. Ten years after completion of the program, when children were between the ages of 13 and 16 years, only 6% of the program graduates in the follow-up sample (4 out of 65), compared with 22% of the control group (12 out of 54), had been processed as probation cases by the County Probation Department. In addition, the severity of the offenses and the degree of chronicity were much higher in the control group. Averaging across the entire sample, the costs for court and penal procedures were $186 for each child in the program group and $1,985 for each of the control children.

Yale Child Welfare Research Program

The efficacy of parent education and support as a means to better developmental outcomes of children is further evidenced by the Yale Child Welfare Research Program. This program focused intervention efforts primarily on mothers raising young children in high-risk environments. The goal was to alleviate some of the stresses of poverty and provide supports so the mothers could devote more of their energies to parenting. Services were provided to 17 impoverished women who were expecting a first-born child until 30 months postpartum. These included home visits by clinical and health professions who counseled the mothers in solving practical problems, such as how to secure adequate food and housing, and in making decisions about future education, career, and family goals. Program workers also acted as liaisons with other local services that could benefit the families. For the children, pediatric services were provided. Child care was offered, and all but one child attended for periods ranging from 2 to 28 months. Parents were free to discuss daily problems with the child care staff. They also learned about their child's development during periodic well-baby exams and developmental assessments. After the program ended, a matched control group was recruited.

At the 10-year follow-up, intervention mothers had obtained significantly more education than had control group mothers. Almost all intervention families had become self-supporting by the time their firstborns were 12½ years old. Intervention mothers also had fewer children and spaced their births more widely. They were more likely to report that they enjoyed their children and that their children were affectionate toward them. Finally, intervention mothers appeared to be more involved in their children's education. They were more likely to seek out information from teachers, and they maintained closer surveillance of their children's school performance. As a result, intervention group children had better school attendance and adjustment than did those in the control group.

Although the Yale intervention did not target or assess the reduction of predelinquent or delinquent behavior, teacher ratings made it clear that control boys were likely to show aggressive, acting-out, predelinquent behavior serious enough to require such actions as placement in classrooms for emotionally disturbed children or suspension from school. Mothers of control boys also reported such problems as the child's staying out all night without the mother's knowledge of his whereabouts, stealing, cruelty to animals, and behaving aggressively toward parents and siblings.

Because these children were just approaching the ages when delinquency rates increase, these behaviors suggested that boys in the control group might be more likely to become involved in delinquent acts. Children of mothers who received the intervention appeared to be more socially competent and to have overcome some of the risks associated with problem behavior.

Houston Parent-Child Development Center

Like the Yale program, the Houston Parent-Child Development Center (PCDC) offered a parent-oriented intervention. The program sought to enhance school performance, to reduce the incidence of behavioral problems in school-age children, and to promote the mental health of participating families. Each year between 1970 and 1977, approximately 100 low-income Mexican American families with a healthy 1-year-old child were randomly assigned to experimental or control groups for a 2-year intervention.

The major program focus was on the mother-child interaction in the family setting. During the first year of the intervention, paraprofessionals conducted home visits to provide the mothers with information on baby care and child development and to give advice on coping with stress and creating a stimulating home environment. Entire families attended many weekend workshop sessions designed to involve fathers and siblings in the program. In the second year, children attended morning nursery school while mothers participated in child management and homemaker classes at the center. Approximately 550 hours of family involvement were required over the 2-year period.

The first longitudinal follow-up showed that at ages 4 to 7, boys in the control group were more destructive, overactive, and negative-attention seeking and were less emotionally sensitive than children in the intervention group. At 5 to 8 years postprogram (Grades 2 to 5), intervention children showed fewer aggressive, acting-out behaviors and were less hostile and more considerate than control children.

Less impressive outcome data were found in the most recent follow-up when the children were in Grades 4 through 11 (7 to 15 years after program completion). Although some positive, significant outcomes were found for the oldest group of cohorts, the earlier differences in aggressive behavior were not apparent.

Other Programs

The University of Rochester Nurse Home-Visitation Program was conducted with 400 women randomly assigned to four intervention groups. Women were eligible if they were pregnant with their first child and met one or more of the following requirements: low SES, age of less than 19 years, or single-parent status. The most intensively treated group of mothers received regular prenatal and well-child physicians' visits and nurse home visits from pregnancy through 2 years postpartum. Home visits emphasized the mother's health during pregnancy, the child's health and postpartum development, and enhancement of the family's formal and informal support systems within the community.

The most striking result of this intervention was the reduction of verifiable child abuse and neglect among mothers considered to be at especially high risk, that is, poor, unmarried teenagers (45% for those visited postnatally vs. 19% for other poor, unmarried teenagers). A link between child abuse/neglect and later delinquency has been suggested, and there is convincing evidence that a high percentage of violent adult criminals had been severely abused as children. Parke and Collmer have hypothesized that children exposed to aggressive models imitate this type of behavior; aggressive patterns of reaction are one of the risk factors for delinquency. The home-visitation strategy of the Rochester program may have had some effect in reducing this risk by improving caregiving methods and helping mothers to become more positive behavior models.

The Gutelius Child Health Supervision Study also produced a number of beneficial results for both mother and child. The program provided long-term, intensive family support services to low-income, black teenage mothers in Washington, D.C. By the age of 5 or 6 years, significantly fewer intervention group children exhibited behavior problems, an early precursor of chronic delinquency. Their mothers evidenced more appropriate interaction with and discipline of their children than did control group mothers. Evidence seems to link ineffective disciplinary methods with later delinquency. Again, intensive parental education about child rearing, coupled with other family supports, seems to have lowered the risks in these children's environments.

DISCUSSION

Longitudinal evidence from the Perry Preschool Project, the Syracuse University Family Development Research Project, and the Yale Child Welfare Research Program give some indication that early childhood intervention programs may reduce juvenile delinquency and predelinquent behavior. On balance, evaluations of the other interventions reviewed in this chapter suggest that such programs may alleviate some of the risk factors associated with delinquency and antisocial behavior. The specific factors that mediate such improvements have yet to be addressed empirically, but a number of viable hypotheses have been proposed. Among them, the effects of successful experiences early in childhood snowballed to generate further success in school and other social contexts; the programs enhanced physical health and aspects of personality such as motivation and sociability, helping the child to adapt better to later social expectations; and family support, education, and involvement in intervention improved parents' child-rearing skills and thus altered the environment where children were raised.

As discussed earlier, the snowball hypothesis presumes that children who attend quality intervention programs are better prepared socially and academically when they begin school. Children who make an initial impression that they are capable students will avoid the failure chain and the delinquency it sometimes breeds.

Of course, not all of the intervention programs reviewed here resulted in lasting improvements in school performance, but they did appear to reduce antisocial behavior. A reasonable explanation is that they enhanced socioemotional development so that children were more willing and capable of meeting behavioral standards set by teachers, parents, and other adults. Personality factors such as motivation, aspiration level, and self-confidence can undoubtedly be affected by positive experiences and appropriate rewards, just as traits such as aggression, temper, and poor conduct may be lessened by lack of same. This is not the behavioral modification approach of some delinquency prevention programs but instead derives from opportunities for successful involvement provided by comprehensive intervention efforts. This suggests that parental participation in the intervention process may enable them to adopt and support the same behavioral goals, promoting sound social and emotional development and reducing the risk of delinquent or antisocial behavior in later years.

Several of the intervention programs reviewed above sought to improve the child-rearing skills of parents and offered children little more than health or child care services. When lasting benefits in child behavior resulted, they could be attributed only to improved parenting. A similar conclusion can be drawn from some delinquency prevention efforts, where "parent-training programs have been one of the few success stories in the treatment of conduct-problem children." Of course, the early intervention efforts did much more for parents than teach them about effective child-rearing methods. They offered comprehensive family support by providing health services and child care, by establishing linkages with community sources of assistance, and often by creating social networks through formal or informal group meetings. Parental involvement and education are parts of an overall support system offered by the early intervention programs that worked to improve family functioning and, in turn, child functioning.

Because it is not yet definitely known why early childhood programs appear to have lasting effects on behavior, another track might be to look for threads common to successful intervention projects to see what elements are necessary. Certainly one is parental involvement. Another is that they begin early in a child's life—typically before school entry but some before birth. The need to begin training at young ages also makes sense for delinquency prevention efforts. Data on the predelinquency programs reviewed here show that, for the short term, at least, they appear to be more effective than those initiated after delinquent habits have emerged. There is also growing evidence that problem behavior in small children predicts with some confidence later delinquency.

A valuable lesson for both delinquency prevention and early childhood programs concerns continuity of intervention. Although it is impressive that intervention programs of limited duration have produced many lasting benefits, the fade-out of some program effects over time raises a caution not to oversell the value of these efforts.

If there are to be more robust long-term effects, the conventional short-term inoculation models must be dropped in favor of dovetailed interventions that support the child through each stage of development. The message for delinquency prevention efforts is that no behavioral training program offered to elementary grade children for a few weeks or a single academic year should promise to make a difference in delinquency at later ages. During the adolescent years, the importance of the peer group, the appearance of contrary attitudes and desires for independence, and the sudden disappearance of age-appropriate child care during nonschool hours are factors that simply cannot be dealt with at earlier stages of development. Thus, children need support and guidance on different levels as they progress from the early years to the preteen and teenage periods.

Another thread that links early intervention efforts is the comprehensiveness of their approaches and goals. Successful intervention programs include many systems that influence the child, as opposed to delinquency programs that target one or another setting or behavior. Because the risk factors associated with delinquency are based in various systems, comprehensive prevention approaches are bound to be more effective than those of more narrow range. Furthermore, by enhancing the child's interactions with multiple systems, broad-based interventions can positively affect behavior in many domains. There is no doubt that a child who relates well to family and peers, who is successful in school, and who has access to community supports will have little reason or need to engage in delinquent activities. Thus, programs that work toward improving overall social competence will be more likely to reduce delinquency than those that focus on circumscribed behaviors such as self-control or peer group interactions.

The lack of a definition for competence is only one reason why the link between early intervention programs and delinquency reduction cannot be drawn with certainty. The impact of such programs on delinquency is a totally unanticipated benefit uncovered in a few longitudinal studies designed years after the interventions were planned. As program graduates became older and stated goals of the intervention less meaningful (e.g., school readiness), evaluators committed to long-term study individually chose other possible outcomes to assess. Some results were uncovered by chance, such as the lower birth rates among mothers in the Yale project. The wide range of findings from various evaluations suggest the potential of early intervention to reduce teenage pregnancy, welfare dependency, and juvenile delinquency. The inclusion of these variables in more longitudinal research will be required to form a convincing body of evidence.

Early childhood intervention programs are a form of primary prevention in that most attempt to prevent school failure by serving children before they enter school. Yet this chapter illustrates that it is a mistake to take a categorical approach to evaluating these programs in terms of school success alone. When broad prevention efforts that build on the strengths of families as well as children are engaged, much more than poor report cards are prevented. These programs have demonstrated their value in preventing poor social competence, gauged by various indicators that graduates are better able to meet societal expectations. Not engaging in delinquent acts is certainly one expectation with worthwhile consequences for both the individual and the society. Should the impact of early intervention programs on delinquency reduction be supported in future studies, gratifying evidence will be presented that the benefits of these efforts are much greater and more cost-effective than their planners could have possibly imagined.

QUESTIONS FOR DISCUSSION AND WRITING

1. What have major reports during the past decade consistently shown, and are we certain that these effects are sound?
2. What four early intervention programs are discussed, and what were their effects on delinquency?
3. What thread links early intervention efforts, and what is true about successful intervention programs?

ECOLOGY, ENCULTURATION, AND COMMUNITY ORGANIZATION

A mong the first sociological theories of juvenile delinquency was the "cultural transmission" or "learning" theory developed by the social ecologists (e.g., Shaw and McKay) and social psychologists (e.g., Sutherland) at the University of Chicago during the 1920s through the 1940s. They observed a patterned ecological distribution of juvenile and adult crime, with some communities in the city having consistently higher rates of criminality than others. They wanted to understand and explain those spatial variations in delinquency rates. They also observed that the high rate areas were toward the center of the city, in low-rent neighborhoods characterized by high population density, residential mobility, deterioration of the buildings, and a host of other social problems. They were communities, they proposed, with substantial "social disorganization"—the usual social controls that keep crime in check were rendered less effective because the community was not organized to counteract the criminogenic influences that became part of the culture of the community. Kids growing up in those high-rate, disorganized communities were simply "learning" a community-based culture that made it easier to get into trouble.

An excellent review of this theoretical perspective is provided by Bursik in "Social Disorganization and Theories of Crime and Delinquency," and Stark specifies the ecological and enculturation model in "Deviant Places: A Theory of the Ecology of Crime" by deducing 30 propositions from the general principles of the perspective, each of them ready to be tested, perhaps by an ambitious student.

 The theoretical ideas of Shaw and McKay were applied directly in one of the most famous and long-standing efforts to prevent and control delinquency in history—the Chicago Area Project (CAP). In fact, Shaw played a critical role in getting the project off the ground and overseeing its implementation. The CAP still exists today in communities in Chicago. It was designed to organize communities, particularly those with high delinquency rates, against those forces that were attracting young people to crime. The specific features of the project in any particular community were decided by residents and indigenous leaders, who were also responsible for its implementation, based on the conviction that it was the informal organization and culture of the community that would be most effective in impacting delinquency. Kobrin evaluates the effectiveness of "The Chicago Area Project" 25 years after it began, and Schlossman and Sedlak also engage in a retrospective analysis, in "The Chicago Area Project Revisited," by focusing on the beginnings and internal workings and politics of the very first of the community projects, in the Russell Square neighborhood of Chicago.

Deviant Places:
A Theory of the Ecology of Crime

RODNEY STARK

NORMAN Hayner, a stalwart of the old Chicago school of human ecology, noted that in the area of Seattle having by far the highest delinquency rate in 1934, "half the children are Italian." In vivid language, Hayner described the social and cultural shortcomings of these residents: "largely illiterate, unskilled workers of Sicilian origin. Fiestas, wine-drinking, raising of goats and gardens . . . are characteristic traits." He also noted that the businesses in this neighborhood were run down and on the wane and that "a number of dilapidated vacant business buildings and frame apartment houses dot the main street," while the area has "the smallest percentage of homeowners and the greatest aggregation of dilapidated dwellings and run-down tenements in the city." Today, this district remains the prime delinquency area. But there are virtually no Italians living there. Instead, this neighborhood is the heart of the Seattle black community.

Thus, we come to the point. How is it that neighborhoods can remain the site of high crime and deviance rates *despite a complete turnover in their populations?* If this district was tough *because* Italians lived there, why did it stay tough after they left? Indeed, why didn't the neighborhoods the Italians departed to become tough? Questions such as these force the perception that the composition of neighborhoods, in terms of characteristics of their populations, cannot provide an adequate explanation of variations in deviance rates. Instead, *there must be something about places as such* that sustains crime.

This chapter attempts to fashion an integrated set of propositions to summarize and extend our understanding of ecological sources of deviant behavior. In so doing, the aim is to revive a *sociology* of deviance as an alternative to the social psychological approaches that have dominated for 30 years. That is, the focus is on traits of places and groups rather than on traits of individuals. Indeed, I shall attempt to show that by adopting survey research as the *preferred* method of research, social scientists lost touch with significant aspects of crime and delinquency. Poor neighborhoods disappeared to be replaced by individual kids with various levels of family income, but no detectable environment at all. Moreover, the phenomena themselves became bloodless, sterile, and almost harmless, for questionnaire studies cannot tap homicide, rape, assault, armed robbery, or even significant burglary and fraud—too few people are involved in these activities to turn up in significant numbers in feasible samples, assuming that such people turn up in samples at all. So delinquency, for example, which once had meant offenses serious enough for court referrals, soon meant taking $2 out of mom's purse, having "banged up something that did not belong to you," and having a fistfight. This transformation soon led repeatedly to the "discovery" that poverty is unrelated to delinquency.

Yet, through it all, social scientists somehow still knew better than to stroll the streets at night in certain parts of town or even to park there. And despite the fact that countless surveys showed that kids from upper- and lower-income families scored the same on delinquency batteries, even social scientists knew that the parts of town that scared them were not upper-income neighborhoods. In fact, when the literature was examined with sufficient finesse, it was clear that class *does* matter—that serious offenses are very disproportionately committed by a virtual underclass.

So, against this backdrop, let us reconsider the human ecology approach to deviance. To begin, there are five aspects of urban neighborhoods which characterize high-deviance areas of cities. To my knowledge, no member of the Chicago school ever listed this particular set, but these concepts permeate their whole literature starting with Park, Burgess, and McKenzie's classic, *The City* (1925). And they are especially prominent in the empirical work of the Chicago school. Indeed, most of these factors were prominent in the work of nineteenth-century moral statisticians such as the Englishmen Mayhew and Buchanan, who were doing ecological sociology decades before any member of the Chicago school was born. These essential factors are (a) density, (b) poverty, (c) mixed use, (d) transience, and (e) dilapidation.

Each of the five will be used in specific propositions. However, in addition to these characteristics of places, the theory also will incorporate some specific impacts of the five on the moral order as people respond to them. Four responses will be assessed: (a) moral cynicism among residents, (b) increased opportunities for crime and deviance, (c) increased motivation to deviate, and (d) diminished social control.

Finally, the theory will sketch how these responses further *amplify* the volume of deviance through the following consequences: (a) by attracting deviant and crime-prone people and deviant and criminal activities to a neighborhood, (b) by driving out the least deviant, and (c) by further reductions in social control.

The remainder of the chapter weaves these elements into a set of integrated propositions, clarifying and documenting each as it proceeds. Citations will not be limited to recent work, or even to that of the old Chicago school, but will include samples of the massive nineteenth-century literature produced by the moral statisticians. The aim is to help contemporary students of crime and deviance rediscover the past and to note the power and realism of its methods, data, and analysis. In Mayhew's (1851) immense volumes, for example, he combines lengthy, first-person narratives of professional criminals with a blizzard of superb statistics on crime and deviance.

> *Proposition 1.* The greater the density of a neighborhood, the more association between those most and least predisposed to deviance.

At issue here is not simply that there will be a higher proportion of deviance-prone persons in dense neighborhoods (although, as will be shown, that is true too); rather, it is proposed that there is a higher average level of interpersonal interactions in such neighborhoods and that individual traits will have less influence on patterns of contact. Consider kids. In low-density neighborhoods—wealthy suburbs, for example—some active effort is required for one 12-year-old to see another (a ride from a parent often is required). In these settings, kids and their parents can easily limit contact with bullies and those in disrepute. Not so in dense urban neighborhoods—the "bad" kids often live in the same building as the "good" ones, hang out close by, dominate the nearby playground, and are nearly unavoidable. Hence, peer groups in dense neighborhoods will tend to be inclusive, and all young people living there will face maximum peer pressure to deviate—as differential association theorists have stressed for so long.

> *Proposition 2.* The greater the density of a neighborhood, the higher the level of moral cynicism.

Moral cynicism is the belief that people are much worse than they pretend to be. Survey data suggest that upper-income couples may be about as likely as lower-income couples to have physical fights. Whether that is true, it surely is the case that upper-income couples are much less likely to be *overheard* by the neighbors when they have such a fight. In dense neighborhoods, where people live in crowded, thin-walled apartments, the neighbors do hear. In these areas, teenage peers, for example, will be much more likely to know embarrassing things about one another's parents. This will color their perceptions about what is normal, and their respect for the conventional moral standards will be reduced. Put another way, people in dense neighborhoods will serve as inferior role models for one another; the same people would *appear* to be more respectable in less dense neighborhoods.

Proposition 3. To the extent that neighborhoods are dense and poor, homes will be crowded.

The proposition is obvious, but serves as a necessary step to the next propositions on the effects of crowding.

Proposition 4. Where homes are more crowded, there will be a greater tendency to congregate outside the home in places and circumstances that raise levels of temptation and opportunity to deviate.

Gove and his associates reported that crowded homes caused family members, especially teenagers, to stay away. Since crowded homes will also tend to be located in mixed-use neighborhoods (see Proposition 9), when people stay away from home they will tend to congregate in places conducive to deviance (stores, pool halls, street corners, cafes, taverns, and the like).

Proposition 5. Where homes are more crowded, there will be lower levels of supervision of children.

This follows from the fact that children from crowded homes tend to stay out of the home

and that their parents are glad to let them. Moreover, Gove and his associates found strong empirical support for the link between crowding and less supervision of children.

Proposition 6. Reduced levels of child supervision will result in poor school achievement, with a consequent reduction in stakes in conformity and an increase in deviant behavior.

This is one of the most cited and strongly verified causal chains in the literature on delinquency. Indeed, Hirschi and Hindelang claim that the "school variables" are among the most powerful predictors of delinquency to be found in survey studies.

Here Toby's vital concept of "stakes in conformity" enters the propositions. Stakes in conformity are those things that people risk losing by being detected in deviant actions. These may be things we already possess as well as things we can reasonably count on gaining in the future. An important aspect of the school variables is their potential for future rewards, rewards that may be sacrificed by deviance, but only for those whose school performance is promising.

Proposition 7. Where homes are more crowded, there will be higher levels of conflict within families—weakening attachments and thereby stakes in conformity.

Gove and his associates found a strong link between crowding and family conflict. Here we also recognize that stakes in conformity are not merely material. Indeed, given the effort humans will expend to protect them, our attachments to others are among the most potent stakes in conformity. We risk our closest and most intimate relationships by behavior that violates what others expect of us. People lacking such relationships, of course, do not risk their loss.

Proposition 8. Where homes are crowded, members will be much less able to shield discreditable acts and information from one another, further increasing moral cynicism.

As neighborhood density causes people to be less satisfactory role models for the neighbors, density in the home causes moral cynicism. Crowding makes privacy more difficult. Kids will observe or overhear parental fights, sexual relations, and the like. This is precisely what Buchanan noted about the dense and crowded London slums in 1846. Granted that conditions have changed since then and that dense, poor, crowded areas in the center cities of North America are not nearly so wretched. But the essential point linking "decency" and "shame" to lack of privacy retains its force.

Proposition 9. Poor, dense neighborhoods tend to be mixed-use neighborhoods.

Mixed use refers to urban areas where residential and commercial land use coexist, where homes, apartments, retail shops, and even light industry are mixed together. Since much of the residential property in such areas is rental, typically there is much less resistance to commercial use (landlords often welcome it because of the prospects of increased land values). Moreover, the poorest, most dense urban neighborhoods often are adjacent to the commercial sections of cities, forming what the Chicago school called the "zone of transition" to note the progressive encroachments of commercial uses into a previously residential area.

Proposition 10. Mixed use increases familiarity with and easy access to places offering the opportunity for deviance.

A colleague told me he first shoplifted at age 8, but that he had been "casing the joint for 4 years." This particular "joint" was the small grocery store at the corner of the block where he lived, so he didn't even have to cross a street to get there. In purely residential neighborhoods, there simply are far fewer conventional opportunities (such as shops) for deviant behavior.

Proposition 11. Mixed-use neighborhoods offer increased opportunity for congregating outside the home in places conducive to deviance.

It is not just stores to steal from that the suburbs lack, they also do not abound in places of potential moral marginality where people can congregate. But in dense, poor, mixed-use neighborhoods, when people leave the house they have all sorts of places to go, including the street corner. A frequent activity in such neighborhoods is leaning. A bunch of guys will lean against the front of the corner store, the side of the pool hall, or up against the barber shop. In contrast, out in the suburbs young guys do not gather to lean against one another's houses, and since there is nowhere else for them to lean, whatever deviant leanings they might have go unexpressed.

Proposition 12. Poor, dense, mixed-use neighborhoods have high transience rates.

This aspect of the urban scene has long attracted sociological attention. Thus, McKenzie wrote in 1926: "Slums are the most mobile . . . sections of a city. Their inhabitants come and go in continuous succession."

Proposition 13. Transience weakens extrafamilial attachments.

This is self-evident. The greater the amount of local population turnover, the more difficult it will be for individuals or families to form and retain attachments.

Proposition 14. Transience weakens voluntary organizations, thereby directly reducing both informal and formal sources of social control (see Proposition 25).

Recent studies of population turnover and church membership rates strongly sustain the conclusion that such membership is dependent on attachments and hence suffers where transience rates reduce attachments. In similar fashion, organizations such as PTA or even fraternal organizations must suffer where transience is high. Where these organizations are weak, there will be reduced community resources to launch local, self-help efforts to confront problems such as truancy or burglary. Moreover, neighborhoods deficient in voluntary organizations also will be less able to influence how external forces such as police, zoning boards, and the like act vis-à-vis the community.

Proposition 15. Transience reduces levels of community surveillance.

In areas abounding in newcomers, it will be difficult to know when someone does not live in a building he or she is entering. In stable neighborhoods, on the other hand, strangers are easily noticed and remembered.

Proposition 16. Dense, poor, mixed-use, transient neighborhoods will also tend to be dilapidated.

This is evident to anyone who visits these parts of cities. Housing is old and not maintained. Often these neighborhoods are very dirty and littered as a result of density, the predominance of renters, inferior public service, and a demoralized population (see Proposition 22).

Proposition 17. Dilapidation is a social stigma for residents.

It hardly takes a real estate tour of a city to recognize that neighborhoods not only reflect the status or their residents, but confer status upon them. In Chicago, for example, strangers draw favorable inferences about someone who claims to reside in Forest Glen, Beverly, or Norwood Park. But they will be leery of those who admit to living on the Near South Side. During my days as a newspaper reporter, I discovered that to move just a block north, from West Oakland to Berkeley, greatly increased social assessments of individuals. This was underscored by the frequent number of times people told me they lived in Berkeley although the phone book showed them with an Oakland address. As Goffman discussed at length, stigmatized people will try to "pass" when they can.

Proposition 18. High rates of neighborhood deviance are a social stigma for residents.

Beyond dilapidation, neighborhoods abounding in crime and deviance stigmatize the moral standing of all residents. To discover that you are interacting with a person through whose neighborhood you would not drive is apt to influence the subsequent interaction in noticeable ways. Here is a person who lives where homicide, rape, and assault are common, where drug dealers are easy to find, where prostitutes stroll the sidewalks waving to passing cars, where people sell TVs, VCRs, cameras, and other such items out of the trunks of their cars. In this sense, place of residence can be a dirty, discreditable secret.

Proposition 19. Living in stigmatized neighborhoods causes a reduction in an individual's stake in conformity.

People living in slums will see themselves as having less to risk by being detected in acts of deviance. Moreover, as suggested below in Propositions 25-28, the risks of being detected also are lower in stigmatized neighborhoods.

Proposition 20. The more successful and potentially best role models will flee stigmatized neighborhoods whenever possible.

Presumably, it is easier for persons to correct a stigma attached to their neighborhood than one attached to their bodies. Since moving is widely perceived as easy, the stigma of living in particular neighborhoods is magnified. Indeed, as we see below, some people do live in such places because of their involvement in crime and deviance. But, even in the most disorderly neighborhoods, most residents observe the laws and norms. Usually, they continue to live there simply because they cannot afford better. Hence, as people become able to afford to escape, they do. The result is a process of selection whereby the worst role models predominate.

> *Proposition 21.* More successful and conventional people will resist moving into a stigmatized neighborhood.

The same factors that *pull* the more successful and conventional out of stigmatized neighborhoods push against the probability that conventional people will move into these neighborhoods. This means that only less successful and less conventional people will move there.

> *Proposition 22.* Stigmatized neighborhoods will tend to be overpopulated by the most demoralized kinds of people.

This does not mean the poor or even those engaged in crime or delinquency. The concern is with persons unable to function in reasonably adequate ways. For here will congregate the mentally ill (especially since the closure of mental hospitals), the chronic alcoholics, the retarded, and others with limited capacities to cope.

> *Proposition 23.* The larger the relative number of demoralized residents, the greater the number of available "victims."

As mixed use provides targets of opportunity by placing commercial firms within easy reach of neighborhood residents, the demoralized serve as human targets of opportunity. Many muggers begin simply by searching the pockets of drunks passed out in doorways and alleys near their residence.

> *Proposition 24.* The larger the relative number of demoralized residents, the lower will be residents' perception of chances for

success, and hence they will have lower perceived stakes in conformity.

Bag ladies on the corner, drunks sitting on the curbs, and schizophrenics muttering in the doorways are not advertisements for the American Dream. Rather, they testify that people in this part of town are losers, going nowhere in the system.

> *Proposition 25.* Stigmatized neighborhoods will suffer from more lenient law enforcement.

This is one of those things that "everyone knows," but for which there is no firm evidence. The police tend to be reactive, to act on complaints rather than seek out violations. People in stigmatized neighborhoods complain less often. Moreover, people in these neighborhoods frequently are much less willing to testify when the police do act—and the police soon lose interest in futile efforts to find evidence. In addition, it is primarily vice that the police tolerate in these neighborhoods, and the police tend to accept the premise that vice will exist somewhere. Finally, the police frequently come to share the outside community's view of stigmatized neighborhoods—as filled with morally disreputable people who deserve what they get.

> *Proposition 26.* More lenient law enforcement increases moral cynicism.

Where people see the laws being violated with apparent impunity, they will tend to lose their respect for conventional moral standards.

> *Proposition 27.* More lenient law enforcement increases the incidence of crime and deviance.

This is a simple application of deterrence theory. Where the probabilities of being arrested and prosecuted for a crime are lower, the incidence of such crimes will be higher.

Proposition 28. More lenient law enforcement draws people to a neighborhood on the basis of their involvement in crime and deviance.

Reckless noted that areas of the city with "wholesome family and neighborhood life" will not tolerate "vice," but that "the decaying neighborhoods have very little resistance to the invasions of vice." Thus, stigmatized neighborhoods become the "soft spot" for drugs, prostitution, gambling, and the like.

Proposition 29. When people are drawn to a neighborhood on the basis of their participation in crime and deviance, the visibility of such activities and the opportunity to engage in them increases.

It has already been noted that vice must be relatively visible to outsiders in order to exist. Hence, to residents, it will be obvious. Even children not only will know *about* whores, pimps, drug dealers, and the like, they will *recognize* them.

Proposition 30. The higher the visibility of crime and deviance, the more it will appear to others that these activities are safe and rewarding.

There is nothing like having a bunch of pimps and bookies flashing big wads of money and driving expensive cars to convince people in a neighborhood that crime pays. Hence, in some neighborhoods, deviants serve as role models that encourage residents to become "street wise."

CONCLUSION

A common criticism of the ecological approach to deviance has been that although many people live in bad slums, most do not become delinquents, criminals, alcoholics, or addicts. Of course not. For one thing, as Gans, Suttles, and others have recognized, bonds among human beings can endure amazing levels of stress and thus continue to sustain commitment to the moral order even in the slums. Indeed, the larger culture seems able to instill high levels of aspiration in people even in the worst ecological settings. However, the fact that most slum residents are not criminals is beside the point to claims by human ecologists that aspects of neighborhood structure can sustain high rates of crime and deviance. Such propositions do not imply that residence in such a neighborhood is either a necessary or a sufficient condition for deviant behavior. There is conformity in the slums and deviance in affluent suburbs. All the ecological propositions imply is a substantial correlation between variations in neighborhood character and variations in crime and deviance rates. What an ecological theory of crime is meant to achieve is an explanation of why crime and deviance are so heavily concentrated in certain areas, and to pose this explanation in terms that do not depend entirely (or even primarily) on *compositional* effects—that is, on answers in terms of "kinds of people."

To say that neighborhoods are high in crime because their residents are poor suggests that controls for poverty would expose the spuriousness of the ecological effects. In contrast, the ecological theory would predict that the deviant behavior of the poor would vary as their ecology varied. For example, the theory would predict less deviance in poor families in situations where their neighborhood is less dense and more heterogeneous in terms of income, where their homes are less crowded and dilapidated, where the neighborhood is more fully residential, where the police are not permissive of vice, and where there is no undue concentration of the demoralized.

As reaffirmed in the last paragraphs of this essay, the aim here is not to dismiss "kinds of people" or compositional factors, but to restore the theoretical power that was lost when the field abandoned human ecology. As a demonstration of what can be regained, let us examine briefly the most serious and painful issue confronting contemporary American criminology—black crime.

Social scientists have been almost unwilling to discuss the question of why black crime rates are so high. Nearly everybody knows that in and of itself, poverty offers only a modest part of the answer. So, what else can safely be said about blacks that can add to the explanation? Not much, if one's taste is for answers based on characteristics of persons. A lot, if one turns to ecology.

Briefly, my answer is that high black crime rates are, in large measure, the result of *where* they live. For several years, there has been comment on the strange fact that racial patterns in arrest and imprisonment seem far more equitable in the South than in the North and West. It would be absurd to attribute these variations to racism. Although the South has changed immensely, it is not credible that cops and courts in Minnesota are far more prejudiced than those in South Carolina.

But what is true about the circumstance of southern blacks is that they have a much more normal ecological distribution than do blacks outside the South. For example, only 9% of blacks in South Carolina and 14% in Mississippi live in the central core of cities larger than 100,000, but 80% of blacks in Minnesota live in large center cities and 85% of blacks in Nebraska live in the heart of Omaha. What this means is that large proportions of southern blacks live in suburbs, small towns, and rural areas where they benefit from factors conducive to low crime rates. Conversely, blacks outside the South are heavily concentrated in precisely the kinds of places explored in this essay—areas where the probabilities of *anyone* committing a crime are high. Indeed, a measure of black center-city concentration is correlated .49 with the black/white arrest ratio and accounts for much of the variation between the South and the rest of the nation.

"Kinds of people" explanations could not easily have led to this finding. Is there any reason why social scientists must cling to individual traits as *the only* variables that count? It is not being suggested that we stop seeking and formulating "kinds of people" explanations. Age and sex, for example, have powerful effects on deviant behavior that are not rooted in ecology. What is suggested is that, although males will exceed females in terms of rates of crime and delinquency in all neighborhoods, males in certain neighborhoods will have much higher rates than will males in some other neighborhoods, and female behavior will fluctuate by neighborhood too. Or, to return to the insights on which sociology was founded, social structures are real and cannot be reduced to purely psychological phenomena.

QUESTIONS FOR DISCUSSION AND WRITING

1. What are five essential factors that characterize high-deviance areas of cities, and what four responses to the impacts of the five on the moral order did the author include in his theory? How do the four responses amplify the volume of deviance?
2. What do the author's propositions imply? What is an ecological theory of crime meant to achieve?
3. What is the author's answer for why black crime rates are so high?

Social Disorganization and Theories of Crime and Delinquency

ROBERT J. BURSIK, JR.

AFTER a relatively brief period of promi-nence during the 1950s and 1960s, many criminologists came to view the concept of so-cial disorganization developed by Shaw and McKay as largely marginal to modern crimino-logical thought. The past few years, however, have seen the publication of three major works and many related papers that clearly indi-cate that the perspective continues to have im-portant ramifications for modern criminology. This chapter examines two basic aspects of the revitalization of the social disorganization approach.

First, five central criticisms that led to the temporary dormancy of the social disorganiza-tion tradition are discussed, and the attempts of recent formulations to address the problematic theoretical and empirical aspects of the earlier work are examined. Second, some successful extensions of the framework into substantive areas not traditionally associated with social disorganization are reviewed.

THE SOCIAL DISORGANIZATION APPROACH OF SHAW AND MCKAY

Although the work of Shaw and McKay is still widely cited, it is primarily in respect to the finding that the economic composition of local communities is negatively related to rates of delinquency. It is important, however, to stress

---

the central difference between their docu-mentation of that negative association and their theoretical interpretation of the relationship, for it has led to some very basic misunderstandings of the social disorganization perspective. Shaw and McKay did *not* posit a direct relationship between economic status and rates of delin-quency. Rather, areas characterized by eco-nomic deprivation tended to have high rates of population turnover (they were abandoned as soon as it was economically feasible) and population heterogeneity (the rapid changes in composition made it very difficult for those communities to mount concerted resistance against the influx of new groups). These two processes, in turn, were assumed to increase the likelihood of social disorganization, a concept that is very similar to Park and Burgess's 1924 formulation of social control as the ability of a group to engage in self-regulation.

In its purest formulation, social disorganiza-tion refers to the inability of local communities to realize the common values of their residents or solve commonly experienced problems. Pop-ulation turnover and heterogeneity are as-sumed to increase the likelihood of disorgani-zation for the following reasons:

1. Institutions pertaining to internal control are difficult to establish when many residents are "uninterested in communities they hope to leave at the first opportunity."
2. The development of primary relationships that result in informal structures of social control is less likely when local networks are in a contin-ual state of flux.

3. Heterogeneity impedes communication and thus obstructs the quest to solve common problems and reach common goals.

The causal linkage between social disorganization and neighborhood delinquency rates was not clearly explicated by Shaw and McKay. Given the intimate theoretical connection between processes of rapid ecological change and the social disorganization framework, a control-theoretic approach offers perhaps the best general basis for understanding the process. That is, the dynamics of social disorganization lead to variations across neighborhoods in the strength of the commitment of the residents to group standards. Thus, weak structures of formal and informal control decrease the costs associated with deviation within the group, making high rates of crime and delinquency more likely. Framed in this manner, the Shaw and McKay model of social disorganization is basically a group-level analog of control theory and is grounded in very similar processes of internal and external sources of control.

CRITICISM I: THE DISCIPLINARY SHIFT IN EMPHASIS

Short has presented an excellent summary of the dangers involved in confusing the levels of analysis implied by various theoretical models. Macrosociological models, such as social disorganization, refer to properties *of groups;* that is, they assume that there are important community-level dynamics related to crime that are not simple reifications of individual motivational processes. Some, however, dismiss the social disorganization perspective simply because its findings do not (and usually cannot) lead to predictions concerning individual behavior. Although such criticisms are based on an inappropriate standard of evaluation, they are understandable given an important historical trend in the orientation of criminological research.

Many of the early sociological theories of crime and delinquency assumed that a full understanding of the etiology of illegal behavior was only possible through an examination of the social structure, the individual, and proximate social contexts (such as primary groups) that mediated between the individual and that structure. Given the macrosocial thrust of the broader frameworks upon which these approaches were based, however, the individual-level aspects of these theories were only roughly developed.

In recent years, however, the traditional emphasis on group dynamics and organization has given way to a concern with the sources of individual motivation. This is perhaps most apparent in the resurgence of deterrence research in the discipline and its relatively recent concern with individual perceptions of the certainty and severity of punishment. Yet it is also true of other theoretical perspectives that at one time strongly emphasized group dynamics. The influential reformulation of control theory by Hirschi in 1969, for example, is basically an individual decision-making model of delinquency, in which one weighs the benefits of an illegal activity against the potential costs of losing investments one has made in conventional behaviors, institutions, and persons.

This disciplinary trend had a particularly devastating effect on the development of the social disorganization approach with the publication of Robinson's classic article on ecological correlation. The basic thrust of Robinson's argument concerned the problematic nature of making individual-level inferences on the basis of aggregate data; nowhere in the paper does he suggest that an aggregate level of measurement is inappropriate for the investigation of all theoretical issues.

As noted by Brantingham and Brantingham, many researchers (especially those who were interested in finding the causes of criminal motivation) used Robinson's findings to conclude that ecological models of crime were fairly meaningless. This sentiment resulted in an important shift in the orientation of spatial research from models that emphasized social disorganization to "opportunity models" of crime, which focus on the geographic distribution of targets of crime and the means of crime commission, the routine activities of people that may lead to an increased likelihood of crime and victimization, and the situations in which crime takes place. Even though such models often used aggregate data in their analyses, the ensuing inferences had a very individualistic flavor until relatively recently.

The discipline has, however, in a sense overcompensated in that the group aspects of criminal behavior have almost ceased to be examined and at times are virtually ignored. As Stark laments, "Poor neighborhoods disappeared to be replaced by individual kids with various levels of family income." That is, most of our theories became more social-psychological than sociological.

Group- and individual-level dynamics, however, are actually complementary components of a comprehensive theory of crime. This is well illustrated in Stark's paper, in which several of the propositions concerning the volume of crime that he deduces on the basis of community characteristics converge in a very interesting manner with those developed by those opportunity theorists who have focused on individual motivational processes. In fact, Reiss argues that a full understanding of many criminological issues is only possible through the linkage of the two traditions.

In sum, the group orientation of the social disorganization perspective is not in itself a valid basis for criticism. Rather, it emphasizes certain social processes that have tended to become somewhat marginal to "mainstream" criminology over the years. Unfortunately, other, very serious criticisms of social disorganization have hindered its general reacceptance as a theoretical model.

CRITICISM II: THE ASSUMPTION OF STABLE ECOLOGICAL STRUCTURES

The concept of social disorganization is grounded in the human ecology theory of urban dynamics, in which the notions of change and adaptation are central. Thus, the full set of dynamics that may lead to such disorganization can only be discerned when long-term processes of urban development are considered. Luckily, Shaw and McKay had access to a unique set of data that enabled them to analyze the relationship between ecological change and delinquency over a period of several decades. Without such a research strategy, it would have been impossible for them to document their central finding that local communities tend to retain their relative delinquency character despite changing racial and ethnic compositions.

The reappearance of the social disorganization perspective has been accompanied by a renewed emphasis on the dynamics of urban change and their reflection in changing spatial distributions of crime and delinquency. Bursik, for example, has shown that the ecological structure of Chicago was relatively stable between 1930 and 1940, but dramatic changes in that structure began to appear after 1940. The redefinition of the ecological position of Chicago's local neighborhoods was accompanied by significant changes in the relative levels of delinquency found in those areas. Bursik and Webb attribute this pattern to changes in the dominant forms of population invasion and succession that characterized northern urban centers after World War II.

The number of available longitudinal ecological data sets for the testing of social disorganization models within various urban areas has been increasing in recent years. In addition to the Chicago, Los Angeles, and Racine material, for example, research is beginning to appear that examines the relationship between ecological change and crime and delinquency rates in

Cleveland and San Diego and Baltimore. As the number of cities for which such data are available increases, much more confidence can be placed in the inferences that can be made concerning the general dynamics of social disorganization.

CRITICISM III: THE MEASUREMENT OF SOCIAL DISORGANIZATION

Operationalizing Social Disorganization

Two specific sources of confusion concerning social disorganization have been especially recurrent. First, and most basically, Shaw and McKay sometimes did not clearly differentiate the presumed outcome of social disorganization (i.e., increased rates of delinquency) from disorganization itself. This tendency led some to equate social disorganization with the phenomena it was intended to explain, an interpretation clearly not intended by Shaw and McKay and their associates.

The common confounding of cause and effect added a great deal of confusion to the evaluation of the Shaw and McKay model. Yet, as Berry and Kasarda note, the ecological model of Park and Burgess, which provided the intellectual context for the work of Shaw and McKay, was an early version of the systemic approach to local community structure, which considers a neighborhood to be a complex system of friendship and kinship networks and associational ties. Drawing from this orientation, a recent body of work has attempted to clarify the unique conceptual status of social disorganization by defining it in terms of the capacity of a neighborhood to regulate itself through formal and informal processes of social control. Such an operational definition has made it much easier to differentiate social disorganization conceptually from the ecological processes that make internal self-regulation problematic and from the rates of crime and delinquency that may be a result.

This current formulation of social disorganization assumes that the breadth and strength of local networks directly affect the effectiveness of two forms of community self-regulation. The first reflects the ability of local neighborhoods to supervise the behavior of their residents. The dynamics of this dimension of local community social control have been most fully developed in the work of Greenberg and her colleagues, who identify three primary forms:

1. Informal surveillance: the casual but active observation of neighborhood streets that is engaged in by individuals during daily activities.
2. Movement-governing rules: avoidance of areas in or near the neighborhood or in the city as a whole that are viewed as unsafe.
3. Direct intervention: questioning strangers and residents of the neighborhood about suspicious activities. It may also include chastening adults and admonishing children for behavior defined as unacceptable.

The systemic formulation of social disorganization does not assume that networks of affiliation and association have solely a supervisory effect on local rates of crime and delinquency. In fact, to concentrate exclusively on this form of self-regulation would seriously distort the original argument of Shaw and McKay, for as Kornhauser has argued, they were centrally concerned with the "effectiveness of socialization in preventing deviance." Shaw and McKay argued, for example, that children living in areas of low economic status "are exposed to a variety of contradictory standards and forms of behavior rather than to a relatively consistent and conventional pattern." Such a statement obviously indicates that there are subcultural aspects to the general Shaw and McKay model. In fact, they eventually conclude that certain neighborhoods were characterized by a "coherent system of values supporting delinquent acts." Current models of social disorganization have also downplayed the notion of subcultural variability and have emphasized the viability of the institutions of socialization embedded in the local networks of association and affiliation. Thus, the second form of community self-regulation implicit in the notion of social disorganization reflects the socializing, rather than supervisory, capabilities of a neighborhood.

Few criminologists would dispute the contention that the family represents one of the key socializing agencies in our society, and many studies have examined the relationship between the distribution of family structures and crime/delinquency rates within local communities. Social disorganization models, however, have generally failed to consider the degree to which the socializing capabilities of local schools are a source of neighborhood self-regulation, although it has been shown that rates of high school suspension are related to the neighborhood contexts in which the schools are embedded.

Given the central role of educational systems in our society, social disorganization models will not be fully specified until the role of such institutions is integrated into the larger conceptualization of community self-regulation. However, this will be a very complicated task for several reasons. First, neighborhoods are rarely served by a single school; rather, the children of local residents attend a varying mixture of public and private schools. Second, due to busing, the existence of "magnet" schools, and so forth, many of the schools attended by these youths are outside the local community. Third, school districts (both public and private) rarely correspond to the boundaries of local communities. Nevertheless, future research within the social disorganization framework must begin to pay greater attention to the role of educational institutions.

The Traditional Study Design

In addition to the confusion that has surrounded the conceptualization of social disorganization, the perspective has been characterized by a second major problem pertaining to the empirical deficiencies of the study designs typically used in such research. Most studies have used the population of local community areas within a given urban context as the unit of analysis. Shaw and McKay, for example, analyzed the distribution of delinquency in 140 square-mile areas of Chicago. More often, census boundaries (or some rearrangement of those boundaries) are used to demarcate the local community areas. Arrest and/or court referral records are then geographically aggregated and the corresponding rates are computed. The compilation of such records in itself is a formidable task, but the information is usually housed in a central location and the costs of data collection (especially if the records are in a computerized form) are not especially high.

It is fairly easy to derive measures of the ecological dynamics pertinent to the social disorganization model (i.e., socioeconomic composition, population turnover, and population heterogeneity) from published census materials. This is not the case for the concept of social disorganization itself, however, except to the extent that it is reflected in the distribution of family structures in a community. The collection of relevant data would entail a very intensive series of interviews, surveys, and/or fieldwork within each of the local neighborhoods in the urban system. The logistic and economic problems of such an approach are obvious in large metropolitan areas, which may have over 100 locally recognized communities. Thus, even the most recent studies of entire urban systems have been forced either to rely on very crude indicators of social disorganization or to concentrate on the relationship between ecological processes and crime/delinquency, assuming that this central unmeasured process intervened between the two.

As might be expected, such a state of affairs has compounded the confusion that already existed concerning the measurement and conceptualization of social disorganization. It becomes hard to distinguish the various components of the Shaw and McKay model, and because only the ecological indicators appear in most models, the social disorganization framework may therefore appear to many to implicitly assume that lower-class neighborhoods with a large proportion of black or foreign-born residents are disorganized. Yet it is important to emphasize that this is definitely *not* an inherent assumption of the theory. Rather, the degree to which these ecological processes are associated with the ability of a community to regulate itself is an empirical question. This is especially clear in McKay's later work, in which he interpreted the decline in the delinquency rates of several black communities in Chicago as representing a movement toward institutional stability in those areas.

To date, the only feasible way to obtain relatively direct indicators of social disorganization in order to analyze the full Shaw and McKay framework has been to concentrate on a relatively few communities. Kapsis, for example, conducted an extensive series of interviews with adults, adolescents, and community leaders who resided in three neighborhoods in the Richmond-Oakland area. His results suggest that communities with broad networks of acquaintanceship and organizational activity have lower rates of delinquency, even when the racial and economic composition of the area would predict otherwise. The effects of such controlling networks are most striking in his discussion of each neighborhood's response to a local racial disturbance that occurred in 1969. There were significant increases in law-violating behavior in the less organized neighborhoods, but the crime rate actually decreased in the most organized one as an indigenous citizen patrol committee emerged. These studies indicate that the level of social disorganization may have an important mediating effect between the ecological composition of a community and its delinquency rate.

Overall, it has not been possible to collect appropriate data concerning social disorganization for all of the neighborhoods in an ecological system due to some very practical limitations. Unfortunately, a full test of the model on the scale of the traditional studies will be impossible without an enormous outlay of funds for data collection by an interested funding agency. Nevertheless, the results of these smaller-scale analyses are very supportive of the predictions made by the Shaw and McKay model.

CRITICISM IV: THE MEASUREMENT OF CRIME AND DELINQUENCY

This section and the one following address two criticisms particularly associated with the social disorganization model that seriously question the findings of such studies even when the model has been completely and correctly specified.

The first criticism focuses on the official nature of the data that have been typically used to compute the rates of crime and delinquency for the local community areas. As early as 1936, Robison criticized the use of official records in the Shaw and McKay research, arguing that systematic biases existed in the juvenile justice system that gave rise to the differences among local community areas and that the "actual" distribution of delinquency would be more evenly dispersed throughout the city. Shaw and McKay were very aware of the less-than-ideal nature of their official data sources. They noted, for example, the possibility that areal variations in delinquency may only reflect variations in the number of offenders that are apprehended.

It is interesting that Shaw and McKay foresaw one aspect of the individual-level resolution of the official record versus self-report debate—the ability of each approach to measure behaviors of varying seriousness—by stating "there is not evidence to show that the children living in areas of low rates are involved in such serious behavior . . . if they were involved in such offenses, it is certain that their names would appear in the records of juvenile probation officers." Studies that have examined the relative validity and reliability of these data sources, however, have primarily concentrated on characteristics of individuals or changes in police organizational priorities that may lead to differential handling by the justice system.

The limited work that has been done indicates that, despite the possibility that systematic bias in police records may distort the actual spatial distribution of crime and delinquency, social disorganization is still an important determinant of this distribution. The Kapsis research discussed earlier in this section analyzed both official records and self-reported data and found patterns in accordance with those predicted by social disorganization. Thus, although only a few studies have examined alternative indicators, evidence has been consistently presented that officially based distributions of neighborhood crime and delinquency rates are not primarily an artifact of police decision-making biases.

CRITICISM V: THE NORMATIVE ASSUMPTIONS OF SOCIAL DISORGANIZATION

The definition of social disorganization as the inability of a local community to regulate itself in order to attain goals that are agreed to by the residents of that community implies that the notion of consensus is a central component of the model. With the increasing emphasis in the criminological literature on the dynamics of power, the political ramifications of crime control, and the relativistic nature of definitions of behavior as crime, the normative assumptions of the social disorganization framework appear to many to be insensitive to the realities of political and social life.

In one respect, this aspect of social disorganization is not nearly as restrictive an assumption as it may appear. As Janowitz argues, a normative approach to social control (i.e., community self-regulation) does not necessarily mean rigid control and social repression. Rather, nonconformity in an area can be tolerated as long as it does not interfere with the attainment of a commonly accepted goal. In this regard, all that has to be demonstrated is that the residents of an area value an existence relatively free of crime; it is not necessary to accept the assumptions of the other "universal human needs" that Kornhauser detects in the work of Shaw and McKay, such as economic sufficiency, education, and family stability.

Nevertheless, the social disorganization framework does not seem suitable for the study of all behaviors that have been designated as criminal. This inability arises from two sources. First, the findings of the research on the perceived seriousness of crime show that for many less serious offenses a strong degree of consensus does not exist. It would be inappropriate to examine a community's ability to attain a mutual goal of minimizing the incidence of such crimes within its boundaries when such general agreement cannot be demonstrated.

In addition, for certain extremely serious crimes the social disorganization model may not provide an especially powerful explanation. Schrager and Short, for example, compare the perceptions of seriousness for organizational crimes (such as manufacturing and selling drugs known to be harmful, selling contaminated food, overcharging for credit, selling unsafe cars, and price-fixing) and crimes more commonly analyzed in social disorganization models (such as homicide, burglary, robbery, and theft). They present strong evidence that organizational and common crimes with the same type of social impact (either physical or economic) are rated very similarly. Thus, since organizational offenses are considered to be as serious as the types of "street crime" discussed by Shaw and McKay, it might be reasonable to expect the social disorganization approach to provide a viable explanation of their distribution in neighborhoods.

In addition to the obvious considerations concerning the feasibility of assuming that a consensus exists concerning the control of crime within a neighborhood, a much more subtle normative assumption is embedded in the Shaw and McKay model that is even more problematic. Shaw and McKay at least implicitly assume that the ecological distribution and movement of populations within an urban area reflect the "natural" market of housing demand; they did not discuss in any detail the degree to which population turnover, population heterogeneity, and social disorganization could in fact be manipulated by nonmarket mechanisms. Suttles, for example, has noted that modern neighborhoods not only reflect the economic processes considered by Shaw and McKay but also "politics and some cultural image of what the city ought to be like."

Skogan, for example, has highlighted four key factors with sources outside the local community that can affect neighborhood stability:

disinvestment, demolition and construction, demagoguery (i.e., real estate panic peddlers and politicians), and deindustrialization. The effects of such processes on the distribution of populations within Chicago have been strongly documented by Hirsch, who presents evidence suggesting that the activities of slumlords in Chicago's traditional Black Belt may have accelerated movement out of that area over what might have been expected given the economic status of the residents.

Such developments external to the local community can have three kinds of effects on the relative distribution of crime and delinquency rates. First, they may directly affect those rates by providing inducements to high-risk populations to move into a specific neighborhood. Second, these developments may indirectly affect the rates of crime and delinquency by accelerating (or decelerating) the degree of residential stability in a neighborhood. A third, and somewhat surprising, effect is also possible. Suttles has given the label of "defended community" to areas in which residents attempt to maintain a stable neighborhood identity in the context of changes that appear to be imposed on them by city planners, realtors, politicians, and industry. In such neighborhoods, gang activities are often seen as a protection of local residents from a perceived threat of invasion from "undesirable" residents of nearby communities. Thus, the increased level of internal organization of the community may in fact result in *higher* rates of crime and delinquency.

Thus, in an important sense, the social disorganization model that has traditionally appeared in the literature is conceptually incomplete. A full specification will require a broadening of the perspective to include the broader economic, historical, and political dynamics in which the development of local communities is embedded. This will be much more feasible than it has been in the past in that the reappearance of longitudinal data sets will make it possible to examine these processes in detail.

Such a development reflects the recent broad efforts in criminology to integrate apparently disparate theoretical orientations in an attempt to obtain a more complete understanding of a phenomenon. There is nothing wrong with the social disorganization framework in particular for failing to have successfully completed such an integration. Thus, the preceding arguments do not imply that the model as it has generally been used in the past should be rejected in any way; rather, its focus should simply be expanded.

NEW EXTENSIONS OF SOCIAL DISORGANIZATION

As the preceding sections have indicated, a great deal of effort has been expended in recent work to deal with the important criticisms that have been made of the social disorganization perspective. Those attempts, however, have also opened up new avenues of investigation that were not traditionally considered by disorganization theorists. Three in particular are especially worth noting.

The Neighborhood as a Context for Individual Behavior

It was noted earlier in this chapter that the classic criminological theorists recognized the necessity of linking individual- and group-level dynamics into a single "grand" theory. Yet historically, as also noted, research has been characterized by a shifting emphasis on only one of these dynamics. One of the most exciting developments in social disorganization research has been the appearance of efforts to achieve the linkage of these two traditions. Stark, for example, has presented a series of theoretically derived propositions that can easily form the basis of a research agenda aimed at understanding the effects of neighborhood contexts on motivational processes that may lead to the commission of a delinquent or criminal act. Unfortunately, since such study designs require extensive data at both the individual and community level, they are not yet common. Two basic approaches to the contextual-effects issue have emerged, however.

The first approach integrates individual-level official records with aggregate statistics pertaining to the community or residence. Bursik, for example, examines variations in the effectiveness of juvenile court sanctions that are associated with the crime-related characteristics of a youth's community. He finds that the effect of these sanctions on recidivism is not consistent across communities: It differs according to the rate of crime in the area and the likelihood that illegal behavior in that community receives official handling by the police and courts.

Gottfredson and Taylor have examined the effects of more general aspects of the community on the likelihood of arrest after release from prison. They present evidence that the neighborhood context not only has a significant effect on the likelihood of recidivism, but it also has an additional effect through an interaction with individual characteristics. Those offenders with an extensive past history of criminal involvement, for example, were more likely to be rearrested if released from prison into socially disorganized neighborhoods.

The second solution to the design of such contextual analyses does not restrict itself to the use of official records in its characterization of the individual; although such information may be used, it is supplemented by other data collected through self-reported techniques. This added source of information significantly increases the power of such studies. Not only does it broaden the types of problematic behavior that can be examined, but it also increases the types of social data that can be collected pertaining to individual processes.

Although the costs of such an approach are generally large, several important studies have appeared. Johnstone has examined the degree to which the economic structure of a youth's community affects the relationship between family socioeconomic status and delinquency; he found that low-status youths tend to be more delinquent if their families live in relatively affluent communities rather than poor ones.

To date, such contextual research has appeared rarely in the literature, and much of it has an admittedly exploratory quality. Such studies, however, provide a clear indication of the role that social disorganization can play in the development of a "full" criminology. The continuation of such research is essential to the vitality of the ecological approach.

Social Disorganization and Victimization

Reiss has argued that one of the clearest areas in which the individual and community traditions in criminology can be linked is in the area of victimology. At first glance, this may seem to be an unusual extension of social disorganization, which has almost without exception focused on the group regulation of offending behavior. The formal and informal dynamics of social control that have been discussed throughout this chapter, however, are very similar to the notion of guardianship developed by Felson and Cohen within their "routine activities" approach. If, as they argue, the spatial structure of a city partially determines the rate at which motivated offenders meet criminal opportunities, then the degree to which a local community is disorganized should be reflected in its ability to supervise the interaction of potential offenders and opportunities and, therefore, affect the rate of victimization. This is the approach to victimization taken by Sampson in a recent pair of papers, where he argues that areas with high levels of organization are able to take note of or question strangers, watch over property, supervise youth activities, and intervene in local disturbances.

An important exception to the general lack of suitable alternatives to the National Crime Survey (NCS) data can be found in the recent work of Smith and Jarjoura. The data set used in that analysis, reflecting the patterns of victimization in 57 neighborhoods, has two great advantages over the traditional NCS victimization data. First, the sampling design enables robust estimates of neighborhood-level effects. Second, Smith and Jarjoura are able to distinguish between all acts of victimization and those that occur within the boundaries of the local community. This second group of victimizations is the one most pertinent to the notion of community guardianship and social control.

Smith and Jarjoura use these data to examine the main and conditional effects of poverty, residential mobility, and heterogeneity (as well as several other structural variables) on rates of victimization in the 57 neighborhoods. Their findings are very consistent with the predictions of social disorganization for burglary victimizations, but for violent crimes they find that the effect of residential mobility depends on the level of poverty in a neighborhood. This leads them to conclude that a community's capacity for social control "must be viewed in relation to other community characteristics that can facilitate criminal activity." Such work has the exciting potential to integrate fully two perspectives (social disorganization and opportunity theories) that have been traditionally seen as competing, alternative explanations of the spatial distribution of crime and delinquency. The continuation of this work in the area of victimology will be an important component of future research in the area of social disorganization.

The Reciprocal Aspects of the Social Disorganization Model

The research discussed in this chapter has generally focused on the extent to which rates of crime and delinquency depend on the ability of local communities to regulate themselves. It may be, however, that most models of social disorganization are substantively incomplete by failing to consider the degree to which rates of crime and delinquency may also affect a community's capacity for social control.

The rationale for the consideration of a reciprocal relationship between crime and social disorganization has been most thoroughly developed by Skogan in his discussion of neighborhood feedback loops. As Skogan argues, the level of crime in a neighborhood has a

marked (although imperfect) effect on the fear of crime experienced by the residents of that area. High levels of fear, in turn, may result in the following:

1. Physical and psychological withdrawal from community life
2. A weakening of the informal social control processes that inhibit crime and disorder
3. A decline in the organizational life and mobilization capacity of the neighborhood
4. Deteriorating business conditions
5. The importation and domestic production of delinquency and deviance
6. Further dramatic changes in the composition of the population

In turn, these conditions can increase the existing level of crime. For example, Bursik found that the rate of increase in the nonwhite population in Chicago's local communities between 1960 and 1970 was significantly related to simultaneous increases in the delinquency rate. The magnitude of the effect of racial change on delinquency change, however, was not nearly so great as that for the effect of changes in delinquency rates on concurrent changes in the racial composition of an area. Such findings suggest that a large part of the traditionally high association between race and crime may reflect processes of minority groups being stranded in high-crime communities from which they cannot afford to leave.

CONCLUSION

This paper has addressed some serious criticisms that have been leveled at social disorganization models of crime and delinquency. The framework is currently undergoing a significant reformulation from that presented by Shaw and McKay, and many problems remain to be resolved. Yet the findings that are emerging from this work are sufficiently relevant to the current issues facing criminology to ensure a revived appreciation of the model within the discipline.

QUESTIONS FOR DISCUSSION AND WRITING

1. For what three reasons are population turnover and heterogeneity assumed to increase the likelihood of disorganization?
2. What five criticisms have been levied against social disorganization theory?
3. What three new avenues of investigation were not traditionally considered by disorganization theorists?

The Chicago Area Project

SOLOMON KOBRIN

THE Chicago Area Project shares with other delinquency prevention programs the difficulty of measuring its success in a simple and direct manner. At bottom this difficulty rests on the fact that such programs, as efforts to intervene in the life of a person, a group, or a community, cannot by their very nature constitute more than a subsidiary element in changing the fundamental and sweeping forces which create the problems of groups and of persons or which shape human personality. Declines in rates of delinquents—the only conclusive way to evaluate delinquency prevention—may reflect influences unconnected with those of organized programs and are difficult to define and measure.

The present assessment of the Chicago Area Project will have to rest, therefore, on an appraisal of its experience in carrying out procedures assumed by its founders and supporters to be relevant to the reduction of delinquency. To this end, the theory of delinquency causation underlying the Area Project program will be presented. This will be followed by a description of the procedures regarded as essential to the modification of conditions which produce delinquency. Finally, the adaptations and modifications of these procedures will be described and evaluated.

CONCEPTION OF THE DELINQUENCY PROBLEM

A distinctive feature of the Area Project program is that at its inception it attempted explic-

itly to relate its procedures in a logical manner to sociological postulates and to the findings of sociological research in delinquency. Under the leadership of the late Clifford R. Shaw, founder of the Area Project and its director during virtually all of its existence, a series of studies completed between 1929 and 1933 brought to the investigation of this problem two heretofore neglected viewpoints: the ecological and the sociopsychological. The first was concerned with the epidemiology of delinquency in the large city; the second with the social experience of the delinquent boy in the setting of his family, his play group, and his neighborhoods.

With respect to the first problem, it was found that certain areas of the large city produced a disproportionately large number of the delinquents. The high-rate areas were characterized as "delinquency areas," and subsequently an effort was made to define their major social features. In the American city of the period, the populations of these communities were made up of predominantly recent migrants from the rural areas of the Old World. As a group, they occupied the least desirable status in the economic, political, and social hierarchies of the metropolitan society, and in many ways showed an acute awareness of their position. Their efforts to adapt their social institutions to the urban industrial order were at the most only partly successful.

However, the immigrant generation was notably unable to preserve the authority of the old institutions, including the family, in the eyes of the rising generation and was quickly confronted with a problem of conflict with their children. Disruption of cross-generational control produced the conditions for the emergence of a variant species of youth subculture in these communities marked by a tradition of sophisticated delinquency. At the same time, this tradition was sustained and fostered by the anonymity of much of the population of slum areas, by the presence of a young adult element which engaged in crime both as an occupation and a way of life, and by the extraordinary harshness of the competitive struggle which arises when the controls of social usage decay. The distribution of official delinquents pointed firmly to the conclusion that the high-rate areas constituted the locus of the city's delinquency problem, both as to number of delinquents and seriousness of offenses.

With respect to the second problem, these investigations suggested that delinquency in most cases was the product of the simple and direct processes of social learning. Where growing boys are alienated from the institutions of their parents and are confronted with a vital tradition of delinquency among their peers, they engage in delinquent activity as part of their groping for a place in the only social groups available to them.

Thus, the theory on which the Area Project program is based is that, taken in its most general aspect, delinquency as a problem in the modern metropolis is principally a product of the breakdown of the machinery of spontaneous social control. The breakdown is precipitated by the cataclysmic pace of social change to which migrants from a peasant or rural background are subjected when they enter the city. In its more specific aspects, delinquency was seen as adaptive behavior on the part of the male children of rural migrants acting as members of adolescent peer groups in their efforts to find their way to meaningful and respected adult roles essentially unaided by the older generation and under the influence of criminal models for whom the inner-city areas furnish a haven.

SOCIALIZATION AND COMMUNITY ACTION

It is a commonplace of sociological observation that the source of control of conduct for the person lies in his natural social world. The rules and values having validity for the person are those which affect his daily nurturance, his place in primary groups, and his self-development. He is responsive as a person within the web of relationships in which his daily existence as a human being is embedded.

The inference seemed unavoidable, therefore, that to succeed delinquency prevention activities must somehow first become activities of the adults constituting the natural social world of the youngster. Or, put another way, a delinquency prevention program could hardly hope to be effective unless and until the aims of such a program became the aims of the local populations. Thus, an indispensable preliminary task of delinquency prevention is to discover effective methods of inducing residents of the disadvantaged city areas to take up the cause of prevention in a serious manner. The disposition of the founders of the Area Project was to regard this element of the program as so indispensable that if these populations proved unable to act in relation to the problem, the prevention of delinquency was a lost cause.

A second postulation concerned the problem of developing collective action toward delinquency. Here another commonplace of sociological observation suggested that people support and participate only in those enterprises in which they have a meaningful role. The organized activity of people everywhere flows in the channels of institutions and organizations indigenous to their cultural traditions and to the system of social relationships which defines their social groups. Consequently, one could not expect people to devote their energies to enterprises which form part of the social system of groups in which they have no membership. The relevance of this observation is that there had always existed an expectation that people residing in the high-delinquency-rate areas could somehow be induced to support the welfare agencies established there. A basic assumption of the Area Project program was that under prevailing conditions it was illusory to expect this to happen.

Thus, in view of the primacy of the local social life in the socialization and control of the young person, all effort, it was felt, should be devoted to helping residents of high-delinquency-rate areas to take constructive action toward the problem. The interest of the wider society in winning the rising generation of these communities to orderliness and conformity had first to become a vital interest of the local society.

ORGANIZATION OF THE DELINQUENCY AREA

A final assumption necessary to the rationale of the Area Project program had to do with the social and institutional organization of the high-delinquency-rate neighborhood and with the related issue of the capacity of residents of these areas to organize and administer local welfare programs. It was observed that despite the real disorder and confusion of the delinquency area, there existed a core of organized communal life centering mainly in religious, economic, and political activity. Because the function of the slum area is to house the flow of impoverished newcomers and to furnish a haven of residence for the multitudes who, for various reasons, live at the edge of respectability, the nucleus of institutional order actually present is sometimes difficult to discern. There seemed further to be strong evidence that the residents most active in these local institutions were, in terms of interest, motivation, and capacity, on their way up the social class ladder. With respect to these elements of the population, it was assumed, therefore, that they represented forces of considerable strength for initiating delinquency prevention activities.

In summary it may be said, then, that the Area Project program regards as indispensable to the success of welfare activity in general and delinquency prevention in particular the participation of those who form a significant part of the social world of the recipients of help.

PROCEDURES IN NEIGHBORHOOD ORGANIZATION

It follows that the basic procedure in the program is the development of local welfare organization among residents of high-delinquency-rate neighborhoods. This undertaking called for skill in the organizer in identifying the residents holding key positions of influence and the ability to arouse their interest in youth welfare activities. The first phase requires a knowledge of the local society; the second a capacity for sympathetic identification with the local resident. Knowledge of the local society implies familiarity with its culture and history, in the case of ethnic groups; with the local institutions; with the structure of power through which decisions are made and executed; and with the conflicts and cleavages which orient and align the population.

Initial organization in several of Chicago's delinquency areas was undertaken by sociologists employed jointly by the Behavior Research Fund, now dissolved, the Chicago Area Project, and the Illinois Institute for Juvenile Research. The institute, an agency of state government, until recently has furnished a major share of the salaries of the staff engaged in this program.

It became quickly evident, however, that for cogent reasons, the employment of qualified local residents offered advantages in the establishment of such programs. In the first place, the indigenous worker usually possessed a natural knowledge of the local society. Second, he was hampered by none of the barriers to communications with residents for whom the nonresident, especially those identified with "welfare" enterprise, tended to be an object of suspicion and hostility. Third, his employment was a demonstration of sincere confidence in the capacity of the area resident for work of this sort. Fourth, he was more likely than the nonresident to have access to the neighborhood's delinquent boys and therefore to be more effective in redirecting their conduct. Fifth, his employment represented a prime means of initiating the education of the local population in the mysteries of conducting the welfare enterprise. Hence, virtually from the first, one of the most distinctive features of Area Project procedure was the employment, in appropriate categories and under the tutelage of staff sociologists of the institute, of local residents to aid in the organization of the approximately dozen community or civic "committees" which were established in Chicago over the course of two decades.

A second major procedural feature of the Area Project program is represented by efforts to preserve the independence of the neighborhood groups after they become established as functioning units. This turned out to be mainly an exercise in self-restraint, for the easier and in many ways more natural course would have been to maintain a close supervision and control of their activities. However, since it was the aim of the program to foster the development of knowledge and competence in the conduct of youth welfare activities and to encourage among residents of delinquency areas confidence in their own capacities to act with respect to their problems, the policy was followed of insisting on a formal, structural autonomy of the organization. The problem in this connection was to maintain full support and help without rendering the independence of the group an empty formality.

MAINTAINING AUTONOMY

Three devices were found to be useful in dealing with this problem. First, neighborhood groups either exercised the power of veto in the assignment of Area Project staff to function as their executives, or more frequently, nominated a qualified local resident as their executive who was then employed as an Area Project staff member. Second, staff members were required to function as representatives and spokesmen of the local groups rather than as representatives of the Area Project central office or of the Sociology Department of the Institute for Juvenile Research. This served to foster an identification of the worker with the point of view and the needs of the local group. Third, policy decisions of neighborhood groups which appeared to Area

Project staff to be unsound were nonetheless accepted and acted on by them. Since staff members exercised much informal influence with the groups to which they were assigned, this problem arose infrequently. However, when it did arise, the autonomy of the neighborhood group was scrupulously respected.

These, then, are the procedural principles of the Area Project program: development of youth welfare organizations among residents of delinquency areas; employment of so-called indigenous workers wherever possible; and the fostering and preservation of the independence of these groups.

TYPES OF NEIGHBORHOOD GROUPS

Before moving to an evaluation of the Area Project as a delinquency prevention program, some indication ought to be made of the specific activities and forms of organization found among these neighborhood groups. The founders of the Area Project were always mindful of variety in the forms of social life and of the necessity, therefore, of adapting the approach to problems of organization as well as the content of program to conditions existing in each work location. In consequence, each neighborhood organization within the Area Project differs somewhat from the others in both these respects.

Generally, these differences are related to the patterns of social organization existing in their areas of operation and to the degree of unity and coordination among local institutions. On this axis, delinquency areas may be classified as structured and stable, structured but unstable, and unstructured and unstable.

In the structured and stable communities, Area Project neighborhood organizations reflect a direct expansion in interests and functions of established neighborhood institutions. In some cases in this category, the dominant local church sponsors the organization, encouraging influential lay leaders to assume responsibility in the development of its program. However, there are few urban neighborhoods in which a single institution exercises complete dominance of the life of the residents. The more usual case in this class is represented by the local organization in which a number of important neighborhood institutions participate. These may include one or more churches, local political bodies, businessmen's groups, and lodges and fraternal groups. However, the representation is always informal, and membership belongs to participating persons as individuals. This informal mode of representation has come to be preferred, probably because it permits the inclusion of important groups which are not formally constituted. Such, for example, are extended kinship groups, friendship cliques, and aggregations of persons temporarily unified around specific problems or issues. In unstructured or unstable communities, the member usually represents only himself.

VARIETY IN PROGRAM CONTENT

Area Project neighborhood organizations all include, with varying emphasis on elaboration, three elements in their programs. The first is the sponsorship of a standard kind of recreation program for the children of the neighborhood, including in some instances programs of summer camping of considerable scope. Such recreation programs are likely to have two distinctive features: the use of residents, usually active members of the Area Project group, as volunteers assisting in carrying on the recreation program; and the improvisation of store-front locations or unused space in churches, police stations, and even basements of homes for recreational use.

The second element of the program is represented by campaigns for community improvement. These are usually concerned with such issues as school improvement, sanitation, traffic safety, physical conservation, and law enforcement.

The third element of the program is reflected in the activity directed to the delinquent child, gangs of boys involved in delinquency, and, in some cases, adult offenders returning to the neighborhood from penal institutions. The activity includes helping police and juvenile court personnel develop plans for the supervision of delinquent youngsters; visiting boys committed to training schools and reformatories; working with boys' gangs in the informal settings of the neighborhood; and assisting adult parolees in their problems of returning to the community.

Specific program content in each of the local groups varies in relation to a number of factors. Among these are the facilities available for recreation or camping; the character and intensity of problems of safety, physical maintenance, or law enforcement in the area; and the staff's ability to arouse enthusiasm and effort from the leaders of the local organization in carrying on direct work with delinquents. Some groups are committed to an extensive program of recreation, including the development and operation of summer camps. Others, located in neighborhoods well equipped with such facilities, carry on no recreation work at all. Some have labored strenuously in programs of neighborhood conservation; others have not concerned themselves with such issues. All have been continuously encouraged and helped by state-employed Area Project staff to maintain direct work with delinquent children and with street gangs, and with virtually no exception all local groups have done so.

ACHIEVEMENTS OF THE
AREA PROJECT

The achievements of the Area Project may best be assessed in relation to its theory of delinquency causation in the social setting of the high-rate neighborhoods. In this theory, delinquency is regarded as a product of a local milieu (a) in which adult residents do little or nothing in an organized public way to mobilize their resources in behalf of the welfare of the youth of the area; (b) in which the relative isolation of the adolescent male group, common throughout urban society, becomes at its extreme an absolute isolation with a consequent absolute loss of adult control; and (c) in which the formal agencies of correction and reformation fail to enlist the collaboration of persons and groups influential in the local society. Leaders of the Area Project assume that progress in the prevention of delinquency cannot be expected until these three problems are well on their way to solution. Since progress in the solution of these problems comes only slowly, permanent declines in delinquency are not expected even after years of effort.

First among the accomplishments claimed by the Area Project is its demonstration of the feasibility of creating youth welfare organizations among residents of delinquency areas. Even in the most unlikely localities capable persons of good will have responded to the challenge of responsibility and have, with help and guidance, operated neighborhood programs. On the whole, these organizations have exhibited vitality and stability and have come to represent centers of local opinion regarding issues which concern the welfare of the young. Above all, they have justified the assumption made by Clifford Shaw and his associates that persons residing in these localities have the capacity to take hold of such problems and contribute to their solution.

The Area Project has made an equally distinctive contribution respecting the problem of the isolation of the male adolescent in the delinquency area. From the beginning it called attention to the fact that the recreational and character-building agencies in these areas were unable, through their established programs, to modify the conduct of boys caught up in gang delinquency. In all probability, the Area Project was the first organized program in the United States to use workers to establish direct and personal contact with the "unreached" boys to help them find their way back to acceptable norms of conduct. The adoption of this pattern in many cities during recent years may be regarded as in part, at least, a contribution of the Area Project to the development of working methods in the delinquency prevention field. At the same time, it should be indicated that from the viewpoint of Area Project assumptions and procedures such work, to be effective, must be carried on as an integral part of a more general program sponsored by residents of the locality.

Finally, the Area Project has pioneered in exploring the problem of tempering the impersonality of the machinery which an urban society erects to control and correct the wayward child. Leaders of the Area Project have tended to regard the procedures of juvenile courts, school systems, police departments, probation and parole systems, training schools, and reformatories as inescapably bureaucratic. That is, the procedures of these organizations tend to become set ways of dealing with persons as members of categories. While it is both rational and efficient as a way of processing human problems, of doing something about and hence disposing of cases, this mode of operating results in serious loss of control of the conduct of the young person. The young person in particular is regarded as responsive mainly to the expectations of his primary groups. Thus, to enhance the effectiveness of the corrective agencies of society, it is necessary to enlist the disciplining power of such groups. This is a difficult and complex undertaking, since the customary primary groups for the child, namely, family and peers, are often, in the disorder of the delinquency area, unable or undisposed to exercise the needed discipline.

However, it has been found that in no area is the disorder so unmitigated as to be devoid of persons, whether residents or staff employees of the local organization or both, who staunchly represent the values of conformity, many of whom have or can gain the trust of the wayward. Such relationships capture the essential element of the primary group. The Area Project effort has been to discover an effective pattern through which the good offices of these persons may be used by teachers, police, social workers, and court officials to formulate and execute for the supervision of delinquent children jointly conceived plans designed to meet the specific problems and needs of the person. In this exploration the Area Project has found that there are natural primary relationships with delinquents which may be used effectively for delinquency prevention and that they are best used in collaboration with the agencies having formal responsibility for the welfare of the children and the protection of the community.

CONCLUDING OBSERVATIONS

In all probability, these achievements have reduced delinquency in the program areas, as any substantial improvement in the social climate of a community must. However, the extent of the reduction is not subject to precise measurement. The effects of improvement in the environment of children are diffuse, cumulative, and intertwine with trends and forces which have their origin outside of programs of this character. In the final analysis, therefore, the Area Project program must rest its case on logical and analytic grounds.

No assessment of this program can be complete without defining its historically unique character. The genius of its founder, Clifford Shaw, lay in his sharp perception of delinquency as human behavior and in his sense of the naturalness or inevitability of violative activity in the youngster who, whether singly or in groups, is neglected, despised, or ignored as a person. This is the spirit which has animated the Area Project program and which has made it distinctive among delinquency prevention programs. This image of the delinquent and this notion of the delinquency-making process have led to the program's insistence on centering the operation within the milieu directly productive of delinquency, upon drawing into the operation as many as possible of the persons involved in the basic socializing experiences of youngsters, and upon dealing with delinquents or incipient delinquents as persons worthy of consideration and respect.

Not uncommonly, programs of prevention, whatever their initial intention or resolve, understandably tend to move away from direct contact with the delinquent and his milieu. Distance is achieved by interposing institutional forms between workers and delinquents, as in programs of formal and official treatment, or by dealing with the delinquent as a person arbitrarily abstracted from his social environment, as in programs based on individual therapy. This kind of evolution is comprehensible in the former type of retreat because the delinquent arouses anger and resentment in the law-abiding person, who consequently is hard put to form a sympathetic identification with him. Retreat from the milieu of the delinquent is even more understandable, for nothing would seem more unrewarding than to attempt to put aright the social disorder of the delinquency area.

It may well be that in perspective the Area Project's distinctive contribution to delinquency prevention as a field of practice and technique will be seen in its development of a method designed to keep preventional work focused on its proper object, the delinquent as a person in his milieu. Central to this method is not only a view of the problem which stubbornly refuses to uncouple the delinquent from the social world which has created him, but a set of procedures which have demonstrated a capacity to draw into the preventional process itself the inhabitants of this world.

QUESTIONS FOR DISCUSSION AND WRITING

1. On what theory was the Area Project based?
2. What advantages in the establishment of such programs did the employment of qualified local residents offer?
3. What three accomplishments can be claimed by the Area Project?

The Chicago Area Project Revisited

STEVEN SCHLOSSMAN

MICHAEL SEDLAK

THE Chicago Area Project (CAP) has assumed legendary status in the annals of American sociology, criminology, and social work. This is hardly surprising. The CAP embodied the first systematic challenge by sociologists to the dominance of psychology and psychiatry in public and private programs for the prevention and treatment of juvenile delinquency in the early twentieth century. The CAP drew conspicuously on the theoretical premises derived directly from the work of the country's most famous sociologists, the so-called Chicago school: Robert Park, W. I. Thomas, George H. Mead, Ernest Burgess, Louis Wirth, Harvey Zorbaugh, Frederic Thrasher, and, of course, the principal spirits behind the Area Project—Clifford Shaw and Henry McKay. Sociologically speaking, the CAP was where the action was in the 1930s.

Despite the deference accorded to the CAP as a pioneer in delinquency prevention, we know remarkably little about it as an operational reality. To be sure, dozens of scholars and laymen have written about the early days of the CAP, often in heroic terms. By and large, however, they have examined the project primarily as an episode in the history of changing ideas about crime causation, and as an unimportant skirmish in ongoing ideological battles between sociologists and psychologists on the proper focus of correctional treatment. There has been virtually no empirical assessment of the CAP's particular operational schema and day-to-day activities in individual locations.

This chapter seeks to provide the first systematic study of the CAP in action in its early years. We focus on the very first and, it would appear, the most successful of the three pioneer "community committees" Clifford Shaw organized to launch his novel experiment in "social treatment," that in the Russell Square neighborhood of South Chicago.

THE BEGINNINGS OF THE PROJECT IN SOUTH CHICAGO

Using an elaborate plotting of the home addresses of over 100,000 juvenile delinquents processed by the Juvenile Court of Cook County between 1900 and 1927, Clifford Shaw and his colleagues at the Illinois Institute for Juvenile Research (IJR) determined that several Chicago neighborhoods produced vastly disproportionate numbers of criminals. Delinquency was concentrated in four areas: the predominantly Italian near west and near north sides, the black ghetto on the south side, and the overwhelmingly Polish sections of South Chicago that surrounded Russell Square Park and were known colloquially as the "Bush" (because of the plentiful wild shrubs in the neighborhood). Russell Square in 1930 was a working-class, Catholic neighborhood largely dependent on the adjacent steel mills for its economic life. Nearly 70% of the men worked in the mills as semiskilled and unskilled laborers.

Despite the self-evident failure of informal social controls to contain juvenile crime in the

Russell Square neighborhood, Clifford Shaw considered it an excellent locale for testing his innovative ideas on delinquency prevention and community organization. Russell Square possessed sufficient territorial identity and ethnic cohesiveness, he believed, to serve as a building block for communal self-renewal with only minimal guidance from the CAP. Shaw's first step was to determine which local institutions were most critical for the CAP to link up with in order to gain entree to the social life of the community and, most important, to gain direct access to juveniles via their play groups or gangs. Shaw, it would appear, expected initially to ally the CAP with the two social settlements in Russell Square: the nonsectarian Common Ground, founded in 1930, and, especially because of its long-established roots, the Baptist-controlled Neighborhood House, founded in 1911. Fairly soon, however, Shaw recognized that Neighborhood House was of only marginal significance to the Polish community in Russell Square. Few local youth attended its programs, and they derided its motivations by labeling it "Sunday school." Shaw eventually shifted his search for local sponsorship to the institution that evoked universal allegiance, St. Michael's Church. In the beginning, though, he channeled his efforts through the settlements, hoping to build upon their prior organizational experience in recreational activities to sponsor an athletic league of his own as the single best means to attract neighborhood male youth to the CAP.

RUSSELL SQUARE: A NEIGHBORHOOD AND ITS DELINQUENT YOUTH

Clifford Shaw chose Russell Square as the site of his initial CAP experiment in part because he felt he could build on and redirect the neighborhood's sense of place to help it function more effectively as a vehicle of social control. Juvenile delinquency was rampant in the Bush. Only the west- and north-side Italian neighborhoods, and perhaps the core of the spreading southside black ghetto, posted higher rates.

Approximately 15 well-established youth gangs were in operation in the Bush, and all were actively involved in crime. It is important, however, not to confuse gang-related crime in the 1920s and 1930s with the crimes of the more violent youth gangs that achieved notoriety in the 1950s. There was little gang violence in the Bush, nor did organized crime gain a foothold in South Chicago as it did on Chicago's west side. Armed robberies were rare. Gangs occasionally battled with one another, but not with weapons that usually led to serious injuries. The most common form of juvenile crime was theft. Petty thefts dominated: raiding fruitstands, snatching purses, siphoning gasoline, stripping cars, and raiding businesses for materials to "fence" or "junk." There was also occasional grand theft, especially auto stealing, and theft with potential for doing bodily harm, notably "jackrolling." The next most common form of deviant acts fell under the label of "incorrigibility." This included a hodgepodge of antisocial behavior: truancy, running away from home, lewdness, gambling, sneaking into movies and athletic events, hitching rides on streetcars, vandalism and "malicious mischief," harassing shopkeepers, drinking, smoking, fighting, and various kinds of sexual misconduct.

The characteristic patterns of delinquency in Russell Square should be kept in mind as we examine the methods by which the CAP attempted to contain gangs and enhance communal ability to exercise informal social control over youth. Gangs in Russell Square were persistent nuisances more than they were agents of serious crime or violence. True, youth in the Bush almost always committed crimes in groups; the gang structure moved adolescents to perform criminal acts that as individuals they would probably never commit. Even when gangs went on a rampage that lasted several weeks, however, their crimes consisted principally of petty larceny, vandalism, and lewdness. Gangs served adolescents in the Bush largely as block organizations or territorial entities that circumscribed their members' contacts with youth living across the alley or down the street. Their names reflected their geographic base:

Houston Herrings, Brandon Street Speedboys, Brandon Lions, and Burley Lions, for example. Gangs were the scourge of Russell Square and a danger to those who failed to defer to their territorial prerogatives, but they rarely posed a threat to life or limb. At least in the Bush, the Area Project was not trying to rehabilitate many "violent predators."

One of the signal contributions of the CAP was to give gang behavior a human face. CAP street workers intermingled with gang youth on a day-to-day basis, recorded their activities, and elicited their "oral histories" or "life stories." Selections from their voluminous accounts suggest something of the flavor of juvenile delinquency in the Bush, beyond what one can gather from official statistical data on the nature and incidence of crime.

The oral histories indicate clearly that petty theft was commonplace among Russell Square youth and that the crimes were generally committed by small groups of boys. The picture may be somewhat overdrawn, but one gets the impression that youth were a threat to everything that was not carefully guarded. Even at the annual handicrafts exhibit held at St. Michael's, "it was necessary to put wire netting over such exhibits as were not too heavy or bulky to move or as in the case of the leather products, to nail them to the tables on which they were exhibited. Otherwise everything of any value would have been stolen." It was customary for boys to steal from swimmers who naively thought that their clothes and possessions would be safe in a locker or on the beach.

Shoplifting from department and grocery stores was a regular pastime of youth in Russell Square. Against a larger chain store like Goldblatt's, they conducted "raids" during which several boys held the clerk's attention while their friends removed items from the counters. The boys then passed the goods off to colleagues so that if observed by a store detective, the young men actually responsible for the theft would not be in possession of the items when apprehended. The boys regularly stole from the local schools, most often from the staff, but occasionally from other students as well. One inves-

tigator from the CAP "observed on many occasions pupils returning from high school with shop tools under their belts," including "planes, chisels, hammers, and items from the machine shop," which they quickly sold to older acquaintances in Russell Square.

Vandalism and random property damage were also frequent. "It was not uncommon for the boys in the 'Bush' area to break into schools and desecrate them," one observer commented. Often they stole nothing but they delighted in recounting to Area Project workers "the amount of damage which they or their associates had succeeded in causing the property of the Board of Education." They threw ink on the walls and ceilings, smashed furniture, carved desk tops, broke windows, tore books apart, and emptied desks. If they were able to break into the school lunchroom and get at the food, "the boys would take a special delight in throwing the eggs, smearing the butter and urinating in the milk and on other food supplies. In some cases the desecration included even such acts as defecation on the teachers' desks."

EVALUATION

The Area Project experiment in South Chicago received sporadic criticism from a wide range of individuals, including some of its most ardent community supporters. There were times, for example, when Father Lange and other priests at St. Michael's concluded that the CAP's generous tolerance of youths' antisocial conduct and its readiness to mediate on behalf of delinquent youth before social control agents were undermining efforts by schools, churches, and upright parents to establish behavioral standards and wield disciplinary authority over children in the Bush.

A very different line of criticism emerged among CAP staff in South Chicago. The internal dispute that received the greatest publicity was that between Clifford Shaw and one of his most aggressive young street workers, Saul Alinsky. Alinsky's experiences with delinquent youth and their families in Russell Square were crucial in persuading him (as articulated most boldly in *Reveille for Radicals*) that community organizations like the RSCC were grossly inadequate to effect significant social change in lower-class, immigrant, industrial neighborhoods. Confrontational tactics, Alinsky insisted, were the only viable means of alleviating the "social disorganization" which Shaw and the Chicago school of sociology so eloquently described.

We doubt whether Alinsky's harsh opinion of Shaw was widespread among CAP staff who were less willing to speak out and jeopardize their employment and effectiveness as street workers and community organizers. Nonetheless, a somewhat similar disquiet appeared in a conversation in 1938 between Shaw's chief representative in Russell Square, James McDonald, and street worker John Brown. "You know in so far as achieving the fundamental aim of the Chicago Area Project we have completely failed," McDonald began. Asked to articulate that aim, he replied, "to get the people conscious of their existing conditions and have organizational action take place to better them." Brown countered that McDonald was too harsh and reminded him that the Area Project's method was experimental and would ultimately depend on the local residents' initiative in shaping the future of their community. If a problem surfaced or a "wrong method of approach is revealed," that did not mean the effort was entirely wasted. "That's what we did," McDonald responded, "we used a wrong method. We superimposed a Club upon them and they (people of the community) didn't know what it was all about, or why it was set up, etc. Why even today people don't know the reason why the Club exists." Brown disagreed. Several young adults who spoke Polish, he stated, were spreading the word about the CAP's ultimate purposes throughout the neighborhood. Public sentiment was, for the first time, beginning to organize against evil social conditions. "I feel that we are just beginning to move."

Of a different order still were the stringent criticisms leveled at the Area Project by professional social workers and/or representatives of traditional social agencies. We do not want to exaggerate the level of open conflict between the CAP and its competitors in the field of delinquency prevention. In Russell Square, the CAP worked amicably with other agencies to identify taverns that admitted adolescents, peddlers of pornography, unscrupulous pool-hall owners, fathers without jobs, families requiring medical assistance, and so forth. As noted earlier, the CAP developed a close relationship with the Juvenile Protective Association, which was very active in South Chicago. In addition, the Area Project was eventually integrated into the Community Fund, which after 1939 supplied one third of the RSCC's budget. Thus, the conflicts were often more a matter of concealed hurts than open antagonisms, although they clearly rankled professionals in social work who refused to defer to the Area Project as a unique repository of virtue and insight in the pursuit of solutions to juvenile delinquency and community disorganization.

Indeed, by the end of the decade, Area Project staff and volunteers had begun to have strained relations with most private, professional social agencies in Chicago. To try to defuse the tension, especially after the CAP had gained control of many appointments to the city's W.P.A. positions, Chicago's Council of Social Agencies called a meeting of social agency representatives. Area Project representatives were pointedly excluded from this confidential session, although Millard Collins and the head of another South Chicago settlement house were among the invited agency participants.

Nearly all in attendance shared the view that the Area Project was "becoming a Frankenstein on the scene." Few believed Shaw's prediction that the CAP community committees would eventually give up their service programs and serve primarily coordinating functions. In fact, the Area Project community committees in South Chicago, the near west side, and the near north side had shown no "evidence of a desire to cooperate for mutual planning." Furthermore, none of the agency professionals understood how Area Project workers conceived their mission. The CAP workers seemed to want to do anything and everything in the name of delinquency prevention and refused to recognize the superior expertise of other agencies in dealing with personal and social problems of individuals that had little to do with delinquency per se.

Communications between the private agencies and Clifford Shaw had been particularly frustrating. "In working with Dr. Shaw it has not been easy to get our point across," complained one of several individuals who had tried unsuccessfully to get Shaw to intervene in the affairs of local community committees whose programs conflicted with those of other organizations in the same neighborhood. The agency representatives suspected that Shaw could exert more direct influence if he wanted to do so. For him to continue to maintain that his sole object was to conduct research on delinquency and its control, they felt, was a dangerous ploy.

Conference participants also rejected Shaw's claim that CAP staff and volunteers were not intensely antiprofessional in their approach to community self-renewal. In actuality, they asserted, Area Project workers believed "that any leadership, if local, is better than any leadership if it is from the outside." This holier-than-thou attitude grated on the professionals. Regardless of the topic under discussion, workers for the Area Project "immediately go off into a tirade on agencies versus local groups." This attitude made it "difficult to discuss things with the workers as one professional worker would with another." CAP staff and volunteers considered themselves immune to criticism, charged one north-side settlement leader, who added sarcastically, "anyone who makes a remark about the Area Project is talking about 'we, the people.'" A YMCA spokesman extended this viewpoint by claiming that the Area Project had assumed "the role of agitators—stirring up the community against private agencies."

The private agencies readily agreed that it was a good idea to recruit indigenous leaders to foster communitywide delinquency prevention programs. But they also pointed out that the Area Project generated its own resources and used W.P.A. funds to pay many of its workers,

whereas private agencies were wholly dependent on volunteers beyond their paid professional staff. In a nastier vein, agency representatives strongly implied that the Area Project philosophy rewarded delinquent behavior by "buying off" young criminals and placing them in positions of responsibility. As Millard Collins added sarcastically, the RSCC takes "a person who has been refused recognition by us—a gang leader. He is placed on the payroll. Here is a person who is placed on the staff as a leader—when he is removed from jail."

The sponsors of the CAP would probably have had little difficulty in responding to the criticism the private social agencies leveled at them in this closed session. Indeed, a Shaw or a Burgess could easily have turned many of the agencies' gripes on their heads and could have demonstrated why various points were strengths rather than weaknesses of the CAP's philosophy and practice. Yet the critics did reinforce one fact that other evidence makes abundantly clear: The Area Project was a reign largely unto itself. Its philosophy and method were different; its sponsors and participants were enormously proud of that fact, and they demanded the opportunity to realize and demonstrate their potential for rebuilding community in Chicago's most dangerous urban neighborhoods. The populist ideology which suffused the Area Project was a source of enormous inspiration, but it also set sharp limits on the degree to which the CAP could cooperate with other devoted social reformers who refused to kneel before the philosophy of Clifford Shaw.

The numerous encomiums that Shaw received from distinguished visitors who observed the CAP in action more than neutralized the divergent criticisms of social radicals like Alinsky and professional social workers like those assembled by the Council of Social Agencies. For example, the famed criminologist and former chief of police in Berkeley, California, August Vollmer, told Shaw, "You are making history with your Area Project in Chicago, because, in my opinion, the principles you are using will be used in solving most of our social problems in the future."

For his part, Shaw never claimed more for the success of the Area Project in reducing crime and upbuilding community than "objective evidence" allowed. Indeed, he often had to temper the enthusiasm and extravagant claims of *community* spokespersons whose sense of accomplishment outpaced the accumulation of verifiable empirical data. Above all, Shaw insisted that the CAP be understood as a "social experiment" subject to the principles and procedures of scientific evaluation:

Its merits will be determined by the extent to which the leadership of the neighborhood can be constructively utilized in a welfare program and the volume of juvenile delinquency thus reduced. How far this objective can be achieved will be determined not by making claims but by an impartial measurement of results. . . . This means a critical and penetrating analysis of particular cases of crime and delinquency with a detailed account of treatment procedures, as well as timely statistical accounts of the relative amount of crime and delinquency which emanates from the particular problem situation. In this way it may be determined to what extent particular methods employed are of more or less value in the prevention and treatment of crime.

Two years later, Shaw specified more precisely the kinds of questions to which he felt the Area Project would provide scientifically verifiable answers:

(1) What has been the extent and character of the neighborhood's participation in the development and operation of the program? To what extent has there been actual assumption of responsibility on the part of the community for meeting its own needs?

(2) To what extent have community residents become increasingly aware of community problems? To what extent have they manifested a quickened interest in a fuller use of community resources to deal with these problems? What constructive changes have been demonstrated in attitudes of parents, community leaders, and others in the community toward the task of promoting the welfare of their children? To what extent have local leaders utilized their prestige and influence for constructive purposes? What evidence has there been of a new community morale for neighborhood improvement, reflected in a move toward better schools, playgrounds, parks, and a fuller use of churches, societies, athletic clubs, etc.?

(3) To what extent do case records show that changes have been effected in the attitudes and conduct of truant and delinquent children during their participation in the program?

(4) What has been the trend in the volume of truancy, delinquency, and crime in each area since the inauguration of the program as compared to (1) the trend during previous years, and (2) the trend in adjoining areas in which similar communitywide programs have not been carried out?

Shaw offered periodic answers to some or all of these questions throughout the course of the project. His most systematic appraisal came in 1944, to commemorate the tenth anniversary of the CAP's formal incorporation (although its program in South Chicago had been in operation for over 12 years). Shaw pointed up a variety of "conditions which complicate delinquency prevention in low-income communities." He also singled out a number of factors—notably the conservatism of professional social workers—which impeded the widespread application of "the self-help principle." Nonetheless, his overall assessment was decidedly optimistic. When given the chance, Shaw argued, residents in high-crime areas had demonstrated that they could "organize themselves into effective working units for the promotion of welfare programs," that they could uncover and effectively use previously untapped talent and leadership, that their organizations were stable and evidenced increasing solidarity over time, and that they were remarkably efficient in both raising and expending funds locally. Moreover, because of their greater knowledge of immigrant languages, cultural traditions, and neighborhood social processes, the community committees had been able to elicit interest and participation from individuals and institutions that were previously indifferent or hostile to the appeals of professional social workers. School-community relations had been vastly improved, the activities of junk dealers and tavern owners had been substantially curtailed, and a few communities had begun their own summer camp programs.

The two accomplishments that Shaw elaborated at length in his 1944 evaluation were both identified principally with the RSCC. First was the parole program, which had been "unusually successful" in Russell Square and which promised to "yield facts which may have far-reaching significance for probation and parole officers throughout the country." Second, and the point to which he devoted greatest attention, was the substantial decline in official rates of delinquency in two of the three pioneer CAP communities (South Chicago and the near west side). The decline in South Chicago was especially sharp. Between 1932 and 1942, police contacts of juveniles between the ages of 12 and 16 in Russell Square dropped from approximately 60 per 1,000 to 20 per 1,000, a decline of two thirds. On the near west side, police contacts dropped from approximately 39 per 1,000 to 23 per 1,000, a decline of less than two fifths. Equally telling was the fact that for Russell Square, Shaw could not employ an additional statistical measure which he used to assess delinquency rates on the near west and north sides—petitions filed in juvenile court—"because the number of cases was too small to provide an adequate sample." Thus, the RSCC stood out as a brilliant success on the two measures that lent themselves most easily (in Shaw's view) to statistical evaluation.

These downward trends first became evident to Shaw in the mid-1930s. He was then inclined to believe that they provided conclusive proof of the CAP's direct impact on crime. He was especially confident of the statistical results because, he asserted, in a comparable South Chicago neighborhood which the CAP did not serve, juvenile delinquency (as measured by police arrests) did not decline at all whereas in Russell Square the rate was more than halved between 1932 and 1937. Thus, Shaw concluded:

This trend has been so consistent and proportionately so great that it can be interpreted to represent a significant change in the community situation . . . it seems reasonable to suppose that the application of the same program of community organization and integration in other areas of the city might eventually result in a similar downward trend in the number of delinquents.

By 1944, Shaw had doubtless been made aware of some of the statistical inadequacies of his measures and of more general difficulties in empirical assessment of delinquency prevention programs. His comments remained upbeat, but his language was more guarded: "The reader is cautioned against ascribing the marked decrease in delinquency in Russell Square and the West Side to the activities of the Area Project," he cautioned. "Less marked decreases have been observed in some areas in which no special program has been carried on. We believe there is valid reason for saying that the Area Project activities have been one of the influences which have contributed to the decreases in Russell Square and the West Side." And again: "While it is impossible to ascertain accurately the extent to which this trend is due to the work of these committees, it is not improbable that the heightened activity of the citizenry and the downward trend of delinquency are related phenomena."

As time went on, Shaw became more and more reluctant to cite statistical data on delinquency rates to demonstrate the wisdom and effectiveness of the Area Project. He never even bothered to publish the statistics he collected on crime in individual project communities after 1942. In fact, as he wrote in 1953 to Helen Witmer (who was preparing a national evaluation of delinquency prevention programs), he doubted that it would ever be possible to demonstrate statistically a causal link between the Area Project and downward delinquency rates in Russell Square or elsewhere. Shaw was no longer much interested in statistical trends on delinquency, Witmer stated. He had now turned his attention to developing means to assess the results of the CAP's intervention with individual, seriously delinquent youth.

If Shaw was no longer willing to trumpet the RSCC's success in measurably reducing crime within its neighborhood domain, certainly no one else in the scholarly community would be willing to do so either. Nearly all commentators on the Area Project during the past 40 years have viewed the pioneer communities as a more or less indistinguishable group, none of which demonstrated statistically verifiable effects on local crime rates. Russell Square's early claim to special fame was casually forgotten.

The bulk of Clifford Shaw's public utterances on the Area Project further contributed to the tendency of scholars to view the several pioneer communities en masse rather than individually. Shaw stressed how all community committees subscribed to a common philosophy of delinquency prevention, rather than the particularities of practice. Promised case studies of individual communities (although apparently in preparation in the late 1930s) never materialized. Shaw seemed most interested in demonstrating the workability of general organizational principles—particularly the self-help principle in coping with urban social disorganization—and in emphasizing that the CAP was a genuine scientific experiment based on specific theories of crime causation. Like most commentators on the Area Project, Shaw usually interpreted the CAP's significance in highly ideological terms, as a battle of philosophies of social amelioration.

In our judgment, however, to portray the Area Project mainly in ideological terms is to create serious distortion. Most important, it encourages neglect of *the process of implementation*, obscures the CAP as an *operational reality*, and directs attention away from Shaw's own strong *pragmatic, adaptive strain* in his relations with individual community committees. All of these elements, as recent evaluation research indicates, are critical for understanding success or failure in a wide range of social innovations. By failing to examine these facets of his own "social experiment," Shaw may well have missed an opportunity to explain systematically why the CAP was more successful in some communities than in others.

Obviously, it is impossible today to analyze the genesis, programmatic structure, and evolution of the CAP's pioneer experiment in Russell Square at the level of fine detail and nuance that would have been possible in the 1930s and 1940s. Considerable oversimplification of the early history is inevitable. Yet, accepting these limitations, it seems to us that two broad features of the RSCC's early history stand out with considerable clarity. First, implementation conformed to several criteria that social scientists today consider essential to successful social innovation. Second, the RSCC managed to overcome many of the operational hurdles that continue to bedevil the vast majority of innovative programs in delinquency prevention today.

We have already reviewed the basic facts regarding implementation. Shaw's vision of the CAP did indeed include a grand reform strategy, but that strategy was not unchangeable and, most important, Shaw believed it could not be imposed on local residents without subverting the principle of communal self-help. Consequently, the CAP entered Russell Square slowly and cautiously, and by the timeworn path of least resistance to children and parents alike: organized recreation. But recreation was only a means to larger programmatic and organizational ends. In short order, Shaw expanded recreational contacts with juvenile gangs to include extensive curbstone counseling. Becoming fully rooted and accepted in the neighborhood, though, required more than CAP energies alone could provide. Thus, Shaw began his careful courting of the Catholic Church and influential Catholic laymen. This turned out to be a lengthy process, but one that Shaw would not force or rush. In the end, "inside" sponsorship proved crucial for galvanizing widespread community support and participation in all phases of the CAP's venture in Russell Square. To local residents, the CAP may have appeared mainly as an appendage to St. Michael's. To the pragmatist in Shaw, however, the church connection was essential to get his own experiment off the ground, even if it entailed risks, demanded compromises, and necessitated occasional smoothing of priestly feathers. The implementation of the Area Project in Russell Square was a classic example of mutual adaptation of ideology to local context.

Mutual adaptation continued throughout the early years. Shaw exercised his authority minimally and discreetly, but his presence remained unmistakable, an energizing force to inspire local "natural" leaders and CAP staff alike. Ideology may have dictated turning over control of local operations to indigenous residents without delay, but James McDonald, assigned from CAP headquarters, remained in charge for over 4 years until an especially talented local leader (Stephen Bubacz) could be found, trained, and set loose. Ideology may have dictated that indigenous street workers carry the burden of curbstone counseling because they shared the local youths' culture and worldview, but nonindigenous street workers from CAP headquarters remained the bulwark of curbstone counseling throughout the 1930s. At first glance, furthermore, camping seemed irrelevant to CAP ideology. Camping smacked of rural sentimentality and inappropriate genteel solutions to the problems of streetwise gang youth. Ideology notwithstanding, however, once it became clear that Russell Square youth wanted to go to camp, that their parents wanted it for them, and that the community considered camping an essential tool of delinquency prevention, Shaw became reconciled to camping as integral to the Area Project philosophy—an extension into the countryside of Russell Square's revitalized community spirit. In this as in other CAP endeavors in the Bush, Shaw both guided and followed as the occasion dictated. He was a pragmatic ideologue, ever ready to adapt general principles to local conditions and desires.

If implementation of the CAP's program in Russell Square combined authoritative direction, flexibility, and adaptation in a manner that appears (in retrospect) conducive to successful social innovation, so was its mode of daily operation consistent with its ultimate objective, namely, the reduction of crime. That this was no mean achievement is attested to by the inglorious history of federally sponsored innovations in delinquency prevention during the 1970s. These programs were ostensibly designed to upbuild the capacity of local youth-serving institutions to reduce rates of delinquency in relatively small areas (not unlike the CAP). In practice, however, these programs—in addition to floundering in purpose due to diffuse, often conflicting theoretical orientations—rarely dealt with and often assiduously avoided seriously delinquent youth; confined their treatments largely to recreation; fostered only superficial cooperation among youth-serving agencies and between agencies and schools; systematically avoided developing close working relationships with vital social control institutions, notably police and juvenile courts; ignored problems and characteristics distinctive to the particular communities; and failed to elicit sustained participation from local volunteers.

We have already seen how different the CAP's program was in practice. A clear but relatively unconfining theoretical orientation guided the enterprise from beginning to end. The RSCC reached out especially toward seriously delinquent youth, including highly antisocial gang members and ex-convicts, and dealt with them in every phase of its program. Recreation remained central to the program, but it served as a springboard for attaining broader goals: facilitating counseling with gang youth; providing employment for "natural" youth leaders; eliciting adult participation in structuring and monitoring social activities for youth, and introducing adults to one another; solidifying the Catholic Church's authority in the community; and so forth. There were obvious limits to the RSCC's willingness to cooperate with other youth-serving agencies—as witness its hostility toward Neighborhood House. But the RSCC did work closely with the Juvenile Protective Association and, perhaps, most important, it developed very close links with local police and parochial schools, serving children as advocates and prodding administrators and teachers to more conscientious performance and assessment of children's individual needs. Even more systematic were the RSCC's links with the police and juvenile court, for whom, in modern-day terms, the RSCC served essentially as a community-based diversion agency. Throughout its endeavors, the RSCC shaped programs and assigned personnel to take maximum advantage of its knowledge of local communal needs and sensibilities. Finally, the RSCC was built on volunteer, indigenous leadership and elicited sustained participation and financial support from a sizable portion of the local residents, men and women. The RSCC's program in the 1930s and 1940s, in short, appears in practice to have embodied the very features whose absence, in the opinion of recent scholars, foredoomed attempts in the 1970s to innovate in the field of delinquency prevention.

Dare we conclude, then, that the CAP actually "worked" and resulted in a two thirds reduction in rates of delinquency in Russell Square? Of course not. However, we do feel justified in concluding that until scholars and policy analysts develop more imaginative means to assess performance in the field, it is premature to generalize that "nothing works." History never provides incontrovertible "lessons" for current application, but it can suggest possibilities for social invention to which we might otherwise be indifferent or unaware. The CAP, we believe, embodies one such possibility. In light of our case study, it seems prudent not to dismiss out of hand the initial statistical picture that Shaw presented of unique achievement in Russell Square; that picture may well have captured social reality to some degree. In a field where a quest for perfect knowledge has proved so frustrating and where there is no consensus on appropriate designs for research or evaluation, the numerous distinctive features that separated the CAP from virtually all other experiments in delinquency prevention would appear to warrant serious study and reconsideration.

QUESTIONS FOR DISCUSSION AND WRITING

1. Why has the Chicago Area Project assumed legendary status in the annals of American sociology, criminology, and social work?
2. What two accomplishments did Shaw elaborate at length in his 1944 evaluation? Why was Shaw confident of the statistical results? But what happened in 1953?
3. Dare we conclude, then, that the Chicago Area Project actually "worked" and resulted in a two-thirds reduction in rates of delinquency in Russell Square? What do the authors feel justified in concluding?

CULTURAL DEVIANCE
AND GANG WORK

Beginning with the early work of Thrasher on delinquent gangs in Chicago in the 1920s, variations of the general "cultural deviance" perspective have been used to understand gang delinquency and to launch major efforts to control the gang problem. Miller, a cultural anthropologist, has probably invested more time and energy studying gangs, typically using ethnographic methods of field observation, than any other criminologist. He has proposed a theory of lower-class gang delinquency in which he sees the whole "Lower-Class Culture as a Generating Milieu of Gang Delinquency." The core values—or "focal concerns"—of the lower-class culture are likely to get a youth in trouble who undergoes a normal socialization within that criminogenic cultural context or learning environment. Chin describes a more recent gang phenomenon, the emergence of delinquent gangs in the Chinese community. In "Social Sources of Chinese Gang Delinquency," he proposes that there is a distinct "Chinese subculture" that, historically, has supported adult criminal organizations and, now—particularly among recent immigrants—juvenile gangs with ties to the more traditional adult criminal enterprises.

The fear of gangs has led to many efforts to control them, ranging from the proliferation of "gang units" in police departments to community-based gang projects. Miller was involved in one of the most notable "gang work" efforts to control gang delinquency in a community, the Midcity Project in Boston. His theory was used to design the project interventions—community organization, family crisis services, and detached workers assigned to work with the most notorious gangs in the community. Contrary to expectations, a variety of measures suggested that the project had "negligible impact" on gang delinquency in the community. These kinds of findings, repeated in evaluations of other gang control projects, as well as the apparent escalation of the gang problem in the United States, in terms of both the growing number of gang members and the greater utilization of guns, led Miller almost 30 years later in 1990 to consider "Why the United States Has Failed to Solve Its Youth Gang Problem."

Lower-Class Culture as a Generating Milieu of Gang Delinquency

WALTER B. MILLER

THIS chapter selects one particular kind of "delinquency"—law-violating acts committed by members of adolescent, street corner groups in lower-class communities—and attempts to show that the dominant component of motivation underlying these acts consists in a directed attempt by the actor to adhere to forms of behavior and to achieve standards of value as they are defined within the community. It takes as a premise that the motivation of behavior in this situation can be approached most productively by attempting to understand the nature of cultural forces impinging on the acting individual as they are perceived *by the actor himself*—although by no means only that segment of these forces of which the actor is consciously aware—rather than as they are perceived and evaluated from the reference position of another cultural system. In the case of "gang" delinquency, the cultural system which exerts the most direct influence on behavior is that of the lower-class community itself—a long-established, distinctively patterned tradition with an integrity of its own—rather than a so-called delinquent subculture which has arisen through conflict with middle-class culture and is oriented to the deliberate violation of middle-class norms.

The bulk of the substantive data on which the following material is based was collected in connection with a service-research project in the control of gang delinquency. During the service aspect of the project, which lasted for 3 years, seven trained social workers maintained contact with 21 corner group units in a "slum" district of a large eastern city for periods of time ranging from 10 to 30 months. Groups were Negro and white, male and female, and in early, middle, and late adolescence. Over 8,000 pages of direct observational data on behavior patterns of group members and other community residents were collected; almost daily contact was maintained for a total time period of about 13 worker years. Data include workers' contact reports, participant observation reports by the writer—a cultural anthropologist—and direct tape recordings of group activities and discussions.

FOCAL CONCERNS OF LOWER-CLASS CULTURE

There is a substantial segment of present-day American society whose way of life, values, and characteristic patterns of behavior are the product of a distinctive cultural system which may be termed "lower class." Evidence indicates that this cultural system is becoming increasingly distinctive, and that the size of the group which shares this tradition is increasing. The lower-class way of life, in common with that of all distinctive cultural groups, is characterized by a set of focal concerns—areas or issues which command widespread and persistent attention and a high degree of emotional involvement. The specific concerns cited here, while by no means confined to the American lower classes, constitute a distinctive patterning of concerns which differs significantly, both in rank order and weighing, from that of American middle-class culture. The following presents a simplified listing of six of the major concerns of lower-class culture. Each is conceived as a "dimension" within which a fairly wide and varied range of alternative behavior patterns may be followed by different individuals under different situations. They are listed roughly in order of the degree of *explicit* attention accorded each and, in this sense, represent a weighted ranking of concerns. The "perceived alternatives" represent polar positions which define certain parameters within each dimension. As will be explained in more detail, it is necessary in relating the influence of these concerns to the motivation of delinquent behavior to specify *which* of its aspects is oriented to, whether orientation is *overt or covert, positive* (conforming to or seeking the aspect), or *negative* (rejecting or seeking to avoid the aspect).

The concept "focal concern" is used here in preference to the concept "value" for several interrelated reasons: (a) It is more readily derivable from direct field observation; (b) it is descriptively neutral—permitting independent consideration of positive and negative valences as varying under different conditions, whereas value carries a built-in positive valence; and (c) it makes possible more refined analysis of subcultural differences, since it reflects actual behavior, whereas value tends to wash out intracultural differences, since it is colored by notions of the "official" ideal.

Trouble

Concern over "trouble" is a dominant feature of lower-class culture. The concept has various shades of meaning; trouble in one of its aspects represents a situation or a kind of behavior which results in unwelcome or complicating involvement with official authorities or agencies of middle-class society. "Getting into trouble" and "staying out of trouble" represent major issues for male and female, adults and children.

For men, trouble frequently involves fighting or sexual adventures while drinking; for women, sexual involvement with disadvantageous consequences. Expressed desire to avoid behavior which violates moral or legal norms is often based less on an explicit commitment to official moral or legal standards than on a desire to avoid getting into trouble, that is, the complicating consequences of the action.

The dominant concern over trouble involves a distinction of critical importance for the lower-class community—that between "law-abiding" and "non-law-abiding" behavior. There is a high degree of sensitivity as to where each person stands in relation to these two classes of activity. Whereas in the middle-class community a major dimension for evaluating a person's status is "achievement" and its external symbols, in the lower class, personal status is very frequently gauged along the law-abiding/non-law-abiding dimension. A mother will evaluate the suitability of her daughter's boyfriend less on the basis of his achievement potential than on the basis of his innate "trouble" potential. This sensitive awareness of the opposition of "trouble-producing" and "non-trouble-producing" behavior represents both a major basis for deriving status distinctions and an internalized conflict potential for the individual.

As in the case of other focal concerns, which of two perceived alternatives—law-abiding or non-law-abiding—is valued varies according to the individual and the circumstances; in many instances there is an overt commitment to the law-abiding alternative, but a covert commitment to the non-law-abiding. In certain situations, getting into trouble is overtly recognized as prestige-conferring; for example, membership in certain adult and adolescent primary groupings (gangs) is contingent on having demonstrated an explicit commitment to the law-violating alternative. It is most important to note that the choice between law-abiding and non-law-abiding behavior is still a choice within lower-class culture; the distinction between the policeman and the criminal, the outlaw and the sheriff, involves primarily this one dimension; in other respects they have a high community of interests.

Toughness

The concept of "toughness" in lower-class culture represents a compound combination of qualities or states. Among its most important components are physical prowess, evidenced both by demonstrated possession of strength and endurance and athletic skill; "masculinity," symbolized by a distinctive complex of acts and avoidances (body tattooing; absence of sentimentality; nonconcern with "art," "literature"; conceptualization of women as conquest objects; etc.); and bravery in the face of physical threat. The model for the "tough guy"—hard, fearless, undemonstrative, skilled in physical combat—is represented by the movie gangster of the thirties, the "private eye," and the movie cowboy.

The genesis of the intense concern over toughness in lower-class culture is probably related to the fact that a significant proportion of lower-class males are reared in a predominantly female household and lack a consistently present male figure with whom to identify and from whom to learn essential components of a "male" role. Since women serve as a primary object of identification during preadolescent years, the almost obsessive lower-class concern with masculinity probably resembles a type of compulsive reaction-formation. A concern over homosexuality runs like a persistent thread through lower-class culture. This is manifested by the institutionalized practice of baiting "queers," often accompanied by violent physical attacks, an expressed contempt for "softness" or frills, and the use of the local term for "homosexual" as a generalized pejorative epithet (e.g., higher-class individuals or upwardly mobile peers are frequently characterized as "fags" or "queers"). The distinction between "overt" and "covert" orientation to aspects of an area of concern is especially important in regard to toughness. The highly intimate circumstances of the street corner gang involve the recurrent expression of strongly affectionate feelings toward other men. Such expressions, however, are disguised as their opposite, taking the form of ostensibly aggressive verbal and physical interaction (kidding, "ranking," roughhousing, etc.).

Smartness

"Smartness," as conceptualized in lower-class culture, involves the capacity to outsmart, outfox, outwit, "dupe," "take," "con" another or others, and the concomitant capacity to avoid being outwitted, "taken," or duped oneself. In its essence, smartness involves the capacity through which to achieve a valued entity—material goods, personal status—through a maximum use of mental agility and a minimum use of physical effort. This capacity has an extremely long tradition in lower-class culture and is highly valued. Lower-class culture can be characterized as "nonintellectual" only if intellectualism is defined specifically in terms of control over a particular body of formally learned knowledge involving "culture" (art, literature, "good" music, etc.), a generalized perspective on the past and present conditions of our own and other societies, and other areas of knowledge imparted by formal educational institutions. This particular type of mental attainment is, in general, overtly disvalued and frequently associated with effeminacy; smartness in the lower-class sense, however, is highly valued.

The lower-class child learns and practices the use of this skill in the street corner situation. Individuals continually practice duping and outwitting one another through recurrent card games and other forms of gambling, mutual "conability." Those who demonstrate competence in this skill are accorded considerable prestige. Leadership roles in the corner group are frequently allocated according to demonstrated capacity in the two areas of smartness and toughness; the ideal leader combines both, but the "smart" leader is often accorded more prestige than the "tough" one—reflecting a general lower-class respect for "brains" in the "smartness" sense.

The model of the smart person is represented in popular media by the card shark, the professional gambler, the con artist, the promoter. A conceptual distinction is made between two kinds of people: "suckers," easy marks, "lushes," dupes, who work for their money and are legitimate targets of exploitation; and sharp operators, the "brainy" ones, who live by their wits and "getting" from the suckers by mental adroitness.

Excitement

For many lower-class individuals, the rhythm of life fluctuates between periods of relatively routine or repetitive activity and sought situations of great emotional stimulation. Many of the most characteristic features of lower-class life are related to the search for excitement or "thrill." Involved here are the highly prevalent use of alcohol by both sexes and the widespread use of gambling of all kinds—playing the numbers, betting on horse races, dice, cards. The quest for excitement finds what is perhaps its most vivid expression in the highly patterned practice of the recurrent "night on the town." This practice, designated by various terms in different areas ("honky-tonkin' "; "goin' out on the town"; "bar hoppin' "), involves a patterned set of activities in which alcohol, music, and sexual adventuring are major components. A group of individuals sets out to "make the rounds" of various bars or night clubs. Drinking continues progressively throughout the evening. Men seek to "pick up" women, and women play the risky game of entertaining sexual advances. Fights between men involving women, gambling, and claims of physical prowess, in various combinations, are frequent consequences of a night of making the rounds. The explosive potential of this type of adventuring with sex and sex and aggression, frequently leading to trouble, is semiexplicitly sought by the individual. Since there is always a good likelihood that being out on the town will eventuate in fights, and so on, the practice involves elements of sought risk and desired danger.

Fate

Related to the quest for excitement is the concern with fate, fortune, or luck. Here also a distinction is made between two states—being "lucky" or "in luck," and being unlucky or jinxed. Many lower-class individuals feel that their lives are subject to a set of forces over which they have relatively little control. These are not directly equated with the supernatural forces of formally organized religion, but relate more to a concept of "destiny," or man as a pawn of magical powers. Not infrequently, this often implicit worldview is associated with a conception of the ultimate futility of directed effort toward a goal: If the cards are right, or the dice good to you, or if your lucky number comes up, things will go your way; if luck is against you, it is not worth trying. The concept of performing semimagical rituals so that one's "luck will change" is prevalent; one hopes that as a result one will move from the state of being "unlucky" to that of being lucky. The element of fantasy plays an important part in this area. Related to and complementing the notion that "only suckers work" (smartness) is the idea that once things start going your way, relatively independent of your own effort, all good things will come to you. Achieving great material rewards (big cars, big houses, a roll of cash to flash in a fancy night club), valued in lower-class as well as in other parts of American culture, is a recurrent theme in lower-class fantasy and folklore; the cocaine dreams of Willie the Weeper or Minnie the Moocher present the components of this fantasy in vivid detail.

Autonomy

The extent and nature of control over the behavior of the individual—an important concern in most cultures—has a special significance and is distinctively patterned in lower-class culture. The discrepancy between what is overtly valued and what is covertly sought is particularly striking in this area. On the overt level, there is a strong and frequently expressed resentment of the idea of external controls, restrictions on behavior, and unjust or coercive authority. "No one's gonna push *me* around" or "I'm gonna tell him he can take the job and shove it" are commonly expressed sentiments. Similar explicit attitudes are maintained to systems of behavior-restricting rules, insofar as these are perceived as representing the injunctions, and bearing the sanctions of superordinate authority. In addition, in lower-class culture a close conceptual connection is made between "authority" and "nurturance." To be restrictively or firmly controlled is to be cared for. Thus, the overtly negative evaluation of superordinate authority frequently extends as well to nurturance, care, or protection. The desire for personal independence is often expressed in such terms as "I don't need *nobody* to take care of me. I can take care of myself!" Actual patterns of behavior, however, reveal a marked discrepancy between expressed sentiment and what is covertly valued. Many lower-class people appear to seek out highly restrictive social environments wherein stringent external controls are maintained over their behavior.

A similar discrepancy between what is overtly and covertly desired is found in the area of dependence-independence. The pose of tough, rebellious independence often assumed by the lower-class person frequently conceals powerful dependency cravings. These are manifested primarily by obliquely expressed resentment when "care" is not forthcoming rather than by expressed satisfaction when it is. The concern over autonomy-dependency is related both to trouble and fate. Insofar as the lower-class individual feels that his behavior is controlled by forces which often propel him into trouble in the face of an explicit determination to avoid them there is an implied appeal to "save me from myself." A solution appears to lie in arranging things so that his behavior will be coercively restricted by an externally imposed set of controls strong enough to forcibly restrain his inexplicable inclination to get in trouble.

FOCAL CONCERNS OF THE LOWER-CLASS ADOLESCENT STREET CORNER GROUP

The one-sex peer group is a highly prevalent and significant structure form in the lower-class community. There is a strong probability that the prevalence and stability of this type of unit is directly related to the prevalence of a stabilized type of lower-class child-rearing unit—the "female-based" household. This is a nuclear kin unit in which a male parent is either absent from the household, present only sporadically, or, when present, only minimally or inconsistently involved in the support and rearing of children. This unit usually consists of one or more females of child-bearing age and their offspring. The females are frequently related to one another by blood or marriage ties, and the unit often includes two or more generations of women, for example, the mother and/or aunt of the principal child-bearing female.

The nature of social groupings in the lower-class community may be clarified if we make the assumption that it is the *one-sex peer* unit rather than the two-parent family unit which represents the most significant relational unit for both sexes in lower-class communities. Lower-class society may be pictured as comprising a set of age-graded one-sex groups which constitute the major psychic focus and reference group for those over 12 or 13. Men and women of mating age leave these groups periodically to form temporary marital alliances, but these lack stability, and after varying periods of "trying out" the two-sex family arrangement, gravitate back to the more "comfortable" one-sex grouping, whose members exert strong pressure on the individual not to disrupt the group by adopting a two-sex household pattern of life. Membership in a stable and solidary peer unit is vital to the lower-class individual precisely to the extent to which a range of essential functions—psychological, educational, and others—are not provided by the "family" unit.

The adolescent street corner group represents the adolescent variant of this lower-class structural form. What has been called the "delinquent gang" is one subtype of this form, defined on the basis of frequency of participation in law-violating activity; this subtype should not be considered a legitimate unit of study per se, but rather as one particular variant of the adolescent street corner group. The "hanging" peer group is a unit of particular importance for the adolescent male. In many cases, it is the most stable and solidary primary group he has ever belonged to; for boys reared in female-based households the corner group provides the first real opportunity to learn essential aspects of the male role in the context of peers facing similar problems of sex-role identification.

The form and functions of the adolescent corner group operate as a selective mechanism in recruiting members. The activity patterns of the group require that a high level of individual members must possess a good capacity for subordinating individual desires to general group interests as well as the capacity for intimate and persisting interaction. Thus, highly "disturbed" individuals, or those who cannot tolerate consistently imposed sanctions on "deviant" behavior, cannot remain accepted members; the group itself will extrude those whose behavior exceeds limits defined as "normal." This selective process produces a type of group whose members possess to an unusually high degree both the *capacity* and *motivation* to conform to perceived cultural norms, so that the nature of the system of norms and values oriented to is a particularly influential component of motivation.

Focal concerns of the male adolescent corner group are those of the general cultural milieu in which it functions. The nature of this patterning centers around two additional "concerns" of particular importance to this group—concern with "belonging" and with "status." These may be conceptualized as being on a higher level of abstraction than concerns previously cited, since status and belonging are achieved via cited concern areas of toughness, and so on.

Belonging

Since the corner group fulfills essential functions for the individual being, a member in good standing of the group is of vital importance for its members. A continuing concern over who is "in" and who is not involves the citation and detailed discussion of highly refined criteria for "in-group" membership. The phrase "he hangs with us" means "he is accepted as a member in good standing by current consensus"; conversely, "he don't hang with us" means he is not so accepted. One achieves "belonging" primarily by demonstrating knowledge of and a determination to adhere to the system of standards and valued qualities defined by the group. One maintains membership by acting in conformity with valued aspects of toughness, smartness, autonomy, and so on. In those instances where conforming to norms of this reference group at the same time violates norms of other reference groups (e.g., middle-class adults, institutional "officials"), immediate reference group norms are much more compelling since violation risks invoking the group's most powerful sanction: exclusion.

Status

In common with most adolescents in American society, the lower-class corner group manifests a dominant concern with "status." What differentiates this type of group from others, however, is the particular set of criteria and weighing thereof by which status is defined. In general, status is achieved and maintained by demonstrated possession of the valued qualities of lower-class culture—toughness, smartness, expressed resistance to authority, daring, and so on. It is important to stress once more that the individual orients to these concerns *as they are defined* within lower-class society, for example, the status-conferring potential of smartness in the sense of scholastic achievement generally ranges from negligible to negative.

The concern with status is manifested in a variety of ways. Intragroup status is a continued concern and is derived and tested constantly by means of a set of status-ranking activities; the intragroup "pecking order" is constantly at issue. One gains status within the group by demonstrated superiority in toughness (physical prowess, bravery, skill in athletics and games such as pool and cards), smartness (skill in repartee, capacity to dupe fellow group members), and the like. The term *ranking*, used to refer to the pattern of intragroup aggressive repartee, indicates awareness of the fact that this is one device for establishing the intragroup status hierarchy.

The concern over status in the adolescent corner group involves in particular the component of "adultness," the intense desire to be seen as "grown up," and a corresponding aversion to "kid stuff." "Adult" status is defined less in terms of the assumption of adult responsibility than in terms of certain external symbols of adult status—a car, ready cash, and in particular, a perceived "freedom" to drink, smoke, and gamble as one wishes and to come and go without external restrictions. The desire to be seen as adult is often a more significant component of much involvement in illegal drinking, gambling, and automobile driving than the explicit enjoyment of these acts as such. The adolescent variant of lower-class culture represents a maximization or an intensified manifestation of many of its most characteristic features.

Concern over status is also manifested in reference to other street corner groups. The term "rep" used in this regard is especially significant and has broad connotations. In its most frequent and explicit connotation, rep refers to the toughness of the corner group as a whole relative to that of other groups; a pecking order also exists among the several corner groups in a given interactional area, and there is a common perception that the safety or security of the group and all its members depends on maintaining a solid rep for toughness vis-à-vis other groups. This motive is most frequently advanced as a reason for involvement in gang fights: "We can't chicken out on this fight; our rep would be shot!" This implies that the group would be relegated to the bottom of the status ladder and become a helpless and recurrent target of external attack.

On the other hand, there is implicit in the concept of rep the recognition that rep has or may have a dual basis—corresponding to the two aspects of the "trouble" dimension. It is recognized that group as well as individual status can be based on both law-abiding and law-violating behavior. The situational resolution of the persisting conflict between the law-abiding and law-violating bases of status comprises a vital set of dynamics in determining whether a delinquent mode of behavior will be adopted by a group, under what circumstances, and how persistently.

What remains constant is the critical importance of status—both for the members of the group as individuals and for the group as a whole insofar as members of the gang perceive their individual destinies as linked to the destiny of the group, and the fact that action geared to attain status is acutely oriented to the fact of status itself rather than to the legality or illegality, morality or immorality of the means used to achieve it.

LOWER-CLASS CULTURE AND THE MOTIVATION OF DELINQUENT BEHAVIOR

The customary set of activities of the adolescent street corner group includes activities which are in violation of laws and ordinances of the legal code. Most of these center around assault and theft of various types: the gang fight, auto theft, assault on an individual, petty pilfering and shoplifting, "mugging," and pocketbook theft. Members of street corner gangs are well aware of the law-violating nature of these acts; they are not psychopaths nor physically or mentally "defective"; in fact, since the corner group supports and enforces a rigorous set of standards which demand a high degree of fitness and personal competence, it tends to recruit from the most "able" members of the community.

Why, then, is the commission of crimes a customary feature of gang activity? The most general answer is that the commission of crimes by members of adolescent street corner groups is motivated primarily by the attempt to achieve ends, states, or conditions which are valued and to avoid those that are disvalued within their most meaningful cultural milieu, through those culturally available avenues which appear as the most feasible means of attaining those ends.

The operation of these influences is well illustrated by the gang fight—a prevalent and characteristic type of corner group delinquency. This type of activity comprises a highly stylized and culturally patterned set of sequences. Although details vary under different circumstances, the following events are generally included. A member or several members of Group A "trespass" on the claimed territory of Group B. While there they commit an act or acts which Group B defines as a violation of its rightful privileges, an affront to their honor, or a challenge to their rep. Frequently, this act involves advances to a girl associated with Group B; it may occur at a dance or party; sometimes the mere act of trespass is seen as deliberate provocation. Members of Group B then assault members of Group A, if they are caught while still in B's territory. Assaulted members of Group A return to their "home" territory and recount to members of their group details of the incident, stressing the insufficient nature of the provocation ("I just *looked* at her! Hardly even said anything!") and the unfair circumstances of the assault ("About 20 guys jumped just the *two* of us!"). The highly colored account is acutely inflammatory; Group A, perceiving its honor violated and its rep threatened, feels obligated to retaliate in force. Sessions of detailed planning now occur; allies are recruited if the size of Group A and its potential allies appears to necessitate larger numbers, strategy is plotted, and messengers dispatched. Since the prospect of a gang fight is frightening to even the "toughest" group members, a constant rehearsal of the provocative incident or incidents and the essentially evil nature of the opponents accompanies the planning process to bolster possibly weakening motivation to fight. The excursion into "enemy" territory sometimes results in a full-

scale fight; more often Group B cannot be found, or the police appear and stop the fight, "tipped off" by an anonymous informant. When this occurs, group members express disgust and disappointment; secretly there is much relief; their honor has been avenged without incurring injury; often the anonymous tipster is a member of one of the involved groups.

The basic elements of this type of delinquency are sufficiently stabilized and recurrent as to constitute an essentially ritualized pattern, resembling both in structure and expressed motives for action classic forms such as the European "duel," the American Indian tribal war, and the Celtic clan feud. Although the arousing and "acting out" of individual aggressive emotions are inevitably involved in the gang fight, neither its form nor motivational dynamics can be adequately handled within a predominantly personality-focused frame of reference.

It would be possible to develop in considerable detail the processes by which the commission of a range of illegal acts is either explicitly supported by, implicitly demanded by, or not materially inhibited by factors relating to the focal concerns of lower-class culture. In place of such a development, the following three statements condense in general terms the operation of these processes:

1. Following cultural practices which comprise essential elements of the total life pattern of lower-class culture automatically violates certain legal norms.
2. In instances where alternate avenues to similar objectives are available, the non-law-abiding avenue frequently provides a relatively greater and more immediate return for a relatively smaller investment of energy.
3. The "demanded" response to certain situations recurrently engendered within lower-class culture involves the commission of illegal acts.

The primary thesis of this chapter is that the dominant component of motivation of delinquent behavior engaged in by members of lower-class corner groups involves a positive effort to achieve states, conditions, or qualities valued within the actor's most significant cultural milieu. If "conformity to immediate reference group values" is the major component of motivation of delinquent behavior by gang members, why is such behavior frequently referred to as negativistic, malicious, or rebellious? Albert Cohen, for example, in *Delinquent Boys* describes behavior which violates school rules as comprising elements of "active spite and malice, contempt and ridicule, challenge and defiance." He ascribes to the gang "keen delight in terrorizing 'good' children, and in general making themselves obnoxious to the virtuous." Such characterizations are obviously the result of taking the middle-class community and its institutions as an implicit point of reference.

A large body of systematically interrelated attitudes, practices, behaviors, and values characteristic of lower-class culture is designed to support and maintain the basic features of the lower-class way of life. In areas where these differ from features of middle-class culture, action oriented to the achievement and maintenance of the lower-class system may violate norms of middle-class culture and be perceived as deliberately nonconforming or malicious by an observer strongly cathected to middle-class norms. This does not mean, however, that violation of the middle-class norm is the dominant component of motivation; it is a by-product of action primarily oriented to the lower-class system. The standards of lower-class culture cannot be seen merely as a reverse function of middle-class culture as middle-class standards "turned upside down"; lower-class culture is a distinctive tradition many centuries old with an integrity of its own.

From the viewpoint of the acting individual, functioning within a field of well-structured cultural forces, the relative impact of "conforming" and "rejective" elements in the motivation of gang delinquency is weighted preponderantly on the conforming side. Rejective or rebellious elements are inevitably involved, but their influence during the actual commission of delinquent acts is relatively small compared to the influence of pressures to achieve what is valued by the actor's most immediate reference groups. Expressed awareness by the actor of the element of rebellion often represents only that aspect of motivation of which he is explicitly conscious; the deepest and most compelling components of motivation—adherence to highly meaningful group standards of toughness, smartness, excitement, and so on—are often unconsciously patterned. No cultural pattern as well established as the practice of illegal acts by members of lower-class corner groups could persist if buttressed primarily by negative, hostile, or rejective motives; its principal motivational support, as in the case of any persisting cultural tradition, derives from a positive effort to achieve what is valued within that tradition and to conform to its explicit and implicit norms.

QUESTIONS FOR DISCUSSION AND WRITING

1. What does this chapter do? How does this relate to the case of "gang" delinquency?
2. What six major concerns of lower-class culture does the author present?
3. Why, then, is the commission of crimes a customary feature of gang activity?

Social Sources of Chinese Gang Delinquency

KO-LIN CHIN

SOCIAL factors pertinent to the rise of Chinese gang delinquency can be categorized as causative and intervening. The causative factors are school problems, family problems, and the lack of employment opportunities. These causative factors, together with the isolation and disorganization of the Chinese communities, alienate immigrant youths from their communities and the larger society. Freed from both internal and external control, adolescents can easily drift into delinquency. However, affiliation with and internalization of Triad norms and values are critical intervening factors. If a group of Chinese delinquents is not exposed to these subcultural norms and values, the group will not develop into the type of street gang that flourished in American Chinatowns.

Immigrant youths are called "transplanted children." They are uprooted from their childhood environments and transplanted to a completely different, perhaps antagonistic, society. Those who grow up in a secluded and fragmented Chinese community are likely to feel alienated from both the community and the society, and they thus have only school and family to count on for support. However, instead of functioning as bonding agencies, both school and family can be sources of frustration and disappointment for immigrant youths.

From *Chinese Subculture and Criminality: Non-Traditional Crime Groups in America* (pp. 93-101) by K. Chin, 1990, Westport, CT: Greenwood Press. Copyright 1990 by Greenwood Publishing Group, Inc. Reprinted by permission of Greenwood Publishing Group, Inc., Westport, CT.

SCHOOL

Asian American students have achieved enormous success in the American school system. Educators are amazed by the success stories of these students. What they overlook is that most of those Asian students who excel in school were born here or came to the United States before they were teenagers. Those who arrive here as teenagers are most likely to do poorly in school. Although the drop-out rate for Asian American high school students in New York City in the class of 1987 was 12.7%, the lowest of all ethnic groups, those Asian students who do drop out are predominantly foreign-born, poor newcomers.

The chance for their children to acquire a good education is one of the most important motives for parents to bring their families to the United States. School systems in Hong Kong, Taiwan, and China are very competitive, and no more than one in four high school graduates is accepted into a college or university. When they come here, however, parents are convinced that their children will be admitted to a college.

But first their children have to get over the hurdle of the language barrier. In order to learn the language, older students are forced to start in lower grades with much younger, native-born classmates. Such arrangements are demoralizing and humiliating for the newly arrived youths. When they need help with schoolwork, they cannot turn to their parents because the latter may not speak English at all.

Along with their language problem, young Chinese immigrants have problems socializing with other ethnic groups in schools. Their difficulties with English encourage other students to ridicule them. To make matters worse, American-born Chinese scorn the foreign born for their inability or unwillingness to become assimilated into the culture, while the foreign born, in turn, view the native born as neither Chinese nor American.

A close examination of the emergence of Chinese gangs in San Francisco, Los Angeles, and New York City in the mid-1960s indicates that the gangs were formed in schools where racial tensions were high. Only at a later stage did the Chinese gangs begin to come into contact with adult groups, move their hangouts to the communities, and change their patterns of activity.

In short, going to school can be a frustrating experience for Chinese immigrants who find themselves unable to compete with younger students, belittled by other ethnic groups, and held in contempt by native-born Chinese. As a result, they tend to congregate with others who share their problems.

FAMILY

For Chinese, the family is the most important social unit. It provides members with a sense of identity and security, and it functions as the most powerful informal source of social control. Chinese may sometimes show little concern for their community or society, but they always have great respect for senior members of their immediate or extended families. In Chinese societies, the father is the authoritative figure and the role model; the mother has a domestic, subordinate role with primary responsibility for the children and household duties. When a child lacks discipline, the parents are usually the first to be blamed.

However, in its adjustment to the new environment of the United States, the Chinese family changed dramatically. For one thing, some Chinese immigrant families are not intact. They generally consist of only the father and several of the older children; the mother and younger children remain in Hong Kong because travel is prohibitively expensive for the entire family.

Also, immigration visas for certain family members may take longer to be approved. The family may not be reunited for many years, and some families never are. According to a gang member, his family was dispersed after he, his father, and a brother immigrated to the United States.

Even when both parents are present, more often than not they both have to work. It is not uncommon for the father to work in a restaurant and the mother in a garment factory. Both may work 10 hours a day, 6 days a week. When the youngsters encounter problems, they are unable to get help from their harried parents. Sung found that 32% of the Chinese high school students she interviewed did not see their fathers from one day to the next, and 17% did not see their mothers from one week to the next. Some immigrant families are virtually led by their bilingual children because the parents are unable to communicate with people outside the community.

Not only are parents incapable of disciplining their children because they have to work hard and lack the language proficiency to help their children with schoolwork, but they are also uncertain how to raise their children in a new environment where child-rearing practices are vastly different from those of their homeland. Most immigrant parents tend to discipline their children harshly and expect them to be quiet and family oriented. Parents are normally shocked and dismayed over their children's demand for autonomy in making decisions as to how they should dress, behave, and socialize. As a result, the relationship between parent and child in the immigrant families is often filled with uneasiness and conflicts.

In Chinese societies, when a family is in need of emotional or financial help, it normally turns to extended family members. The Chinese are reluctant to talk about their personal or family problems to people who are not related by blood. Extended families form a network in which a family is well protected and supported. However, when a Chinese family immigrates to the United States, it is cut off from its extended families. When parents are unable to provide emotional or financial support to the children, the children have no other family members to turn to. When the children are in trouble, parents have no relatives from whom they can obtain help.

A final source of stress for Chinese families is the shortage of adequate housing. As we have mentioned, families are often crowded in one- or two-bedroom apartments that have no living rooms or kitchens. Congestion within the household may drive adolescents to the streets.

OPPORTUNITY STRUCTURE

Chinese teenagers who drop out of school have few opportunities for employment. Even if they are willing to do menial work, their language problem is a major block to finding jobs within the mainstream society. They must look for work in the Chinese community, where most jobs do not require any knowledge of English. However, the most likely positions for young Chinese without an education, technical skills, or work experience are unskilled ones as waiters, kitchen helpers, or cooks. These jobs not only pay poorly but also require long hours of work under appalling conditions. Chinese employers, knowing that newcomers are ill equipped to seek jobs outside the community, take advantage of them. Young immigrants nowadays are reluctant to work in Chinese-owned restaurants and thus have no legitimate career to pursue.

CRIMINAL ROLE MODELS

When young immigrants fall behind in school or suffer ridicule from native-born students, they drop out. And when they cannot bring their problems to their parents because the parents either are working long hours or are themselves poorly educated, young dropouts seek support and understanding from peers with similar problems. Finding comfort with them, they hang around coffee shops or arcade stores within the community. Or they may start hanging around the gambling clubs to run errands for the house and the gamblers. Their association with the adult groups is a crucial turning

point for them; they are transformed from detached and alienated delinquents to para-professional criminals. For a loosely knit group of street-smart youths to develop into a street gang, the association they are affiliated with has to be a Triad-influenced *tong* organization. Without the transmission of Triad norms and values to the youth group by core tong members, and a tong territory in which the youth group can flourish, the delinquents will remain simply a group of marginally connected criminals, as is the case with many youth groups that hang around the gambling establishments of family and district associations. Although there are many such youth groups in Chinatown, they have never developed into street gangs.

As we have noted previously, most adult organizations in the Chinese community have their own gambling parlors. To function properly, a gambling parlor needs young people to run errands, maintain order, and protect the club from outsiders. As a result, gambling dens have many wayward youths hanging around most of the time. Members of the traditional adult associations, especially core members of the tongs, can identify with the alienated youths because they themselves have a strong feeling of being victims of prejudice by their own community and society. Thus, the tong elders and street-corner youths have more in common: alienation from the progressive community organizations and American society, and a history of being feared by law-abiding Chinatown residents.

As far as tong elders are concerned, hiring the alienated youths to work in the gambling establishments is a way to prevent them from becoming involved in predatory crimes within the community. Not only are the youths being saved, but the community is being spared the youths' depredations.

In order to solidify the youth groups' connections to the tongs, leaders of the youth groups are recruited into the tongs through a Triad initiating ceremony. This way, tong officials can control the gang kids through the gang leaders who are also tong officials. As tong officials, gang leaders then initiate their followers into the tongs. As a result, the relationship between tongs and gangs becomes indistinguishable because of the gang leaders' and members' dual membership. Members of the tongs and the gangs become "brothers" of one big "Triad family." In other words, Chinese gangs are linked to the tongs in subtle ways. The gang leaders serve as middlemen between the tong elders and the street soldiers. For this service, they receive from the tong money that they distribute to their members. In addition, the leaders relay the elders' messages to other members.

Some tong leaders never make direct contact with the leaders of the gang. Instead, the tong's youth activity coordinator acts as middleman between them and the gang. Usually, the youth coordinator is also in charge of the tong's gambling activity. The tong may also have another youth coordinator to sponsor the organization's basketball and soccer programs for young tong members. Other tong leaders, however, flaunt their links with the gangs and are not secretive about their close affiliations with gang members.

Law enforcement authorities are convinced that the Chinese street gangs function as the enforcers of the adult Chinese organizations. A former detective suggests that the tongs use the gangs in specific ways. First, if the tong has a problem with someone, it uses its gang members to intimidate the other party. Second, the tong uses the gang members to collect debts. Third, tong members who are shareholders of the gambling dens hire the youths to protect the dens from outsiders.

From the gang members' perspective, tong elders are the only people in the community to turn to for jobs. In addition, the gambling dens are the only places for them to earn money. Gang leaders revealed the importance of the gambling establishments for their survival.

The following is a true story of a young immigrant who was hired by a gambling parlor and later initiated into a gang. The teenager arrived in the United States alone. He worked as a store clerk in his uncle's grocery store, and was upset with his job that paid very little but required long hours of hard work. He was also disappointed with the poor living conditions. One day, while he was sitting in a park thinking about his unfortunate circumstances, he met a friend who was a gang member. With his friend's recommendation, he found a job with a gambling club. All he had to do was to stand in front of the club and make sure that only regular gamblers were admitted. His new job paid three times better than his old one.

A few months later, he subdued a rowdy gambler who was creating a scene inside the gambling den. A few days after the incident, the friend who introduced him to the job accompanied him to meet a man in his mid-30s. Also present were several other gang members. The man, who appeared to be the mentor of the gang and the operator of the gambling place, praised him for his courage and martial arts skills. The man announced that he was promoted as a "Third Brother," a person who is in charge of the street kids. He will no longer need to guard the place. He then went on to become a core member of the gang and was involved in extortion and street violence.

However, the good intentions of the tong elders often backfire. With the moral and financial support of the tongs, the gangs grow into powerful criminal organizations, and once that happens, tong elders lose control of the gangs. Without the sanction or knowledge of the tong elders, gang members begin to extort money from businesses, rob business and gambling establishments, and become involved in street violence. Even some of the tong elders are brutalized by the gangs. Nevertheless, tong elders continue to initiate gang leaders into their organizations, associate themselves with gang members, let gang members guard their gambling establishments, and allow the gangs to hang around their organizations. Thus, the gangs exist because the tongs not only initiate the groups but also sanction their existence. It would be difficult, if not impossible, for the gangs to develop as cohesive units if the tongs decided to withhold their support.

According to Cloward and Ohlin, the development of a criminal subculture in a community needs two types of environmental supports. First, there needs to be an integration of offenders at various age levels. Second, there should be an integration of carriers of conventional and illegitimate values. From what we have discussed above, it is clear that within the Chinese communities where criminal gangs flourish, there is an integration of offenders at various age levels. Teenage gang members follow their gang leaders who are in their late 20s or early 30s, and the leaders in turn are closely associated with certain tong members whose ages could range from mid-40s to late 70s. Furthermore, a small number of Chinese community leaders are the carriers of conventional and illegitimate values. These high-profile leaders, viewed by community residents as representatives, speak for the community, symbolize the community's political orientation, and appear in the community media almost on a daily basis. However, these are the same people who act as mentors of the gang members, drug traffickers, and providers of illegal services such as gambling and alien smuggling.

A CAUSAL MODEL OF CHINESE GANG DELINQUENCY

Sociologists such as Sellin, Sutherland, Cohen, Miller, and Wolfgang and Ferracuti have stressed the importance of learning and internalizing subcultural norms and values in the process of becoming deviant. When a person is associated with and internalizes subcultural norms and values that are at odds with those of the dominant culture, that person will become a deviant.

Contact with Triad subcultural norms, however, is not the only reason for gang delinquency among the Chinese. Thrasher, and Shaw and McKay, proposed that the most important cause of gang delinquency is social or community disorganization. Hirschi further theorized that social disorganization leads to loss of control of the youths by family, school, and other social institutions. As a result, young adolescents without any social bonds and commitments are free to become involved in delinquency.

My contention is that although social disorganization plays an important role in delinquency among Chinese adolescents, becoming a gang member invariably involves learning and internalizing Triad norms and values, transmitted by the tongs. Thus, if a Chinese boy is freed from social bonds, he may become a delinquent. However, for him to become a gang member, he has to come into contact with the values and norms of the Triads. Thus, we can see that the structure of Chinese communities has contributed significantly to the development of street gangs.

QUESTIONS FOR DISCUSSION AND WRITING

1. What are some stressors for Chinese immigrant families?
2. What happens when young Chinese immigrants associate with the adult groups?
3. Why do tong elders hire alienated youths to work in the gambling establishments? How do the good intentions of the tong elders often backfire?

Why the United States Has Failed to Solve Its Youth Gang Problem

WALTER B. MILLER

YOUTH gangs of the 1980s and 1990s are more numerous, more prevalent, and more violent than in the 1950s, probably more so than at any time in the country's history. It is obvious that the United States not only has failed to solve the problem of youth gang crime but also has failed to keep it from getting worse—much worse. How can this failure be understood? The United States is one of the richest and most powerful nations in the world, with abundant resources in money and human talent. Why has its ability to secure a reasonable degree of safety and stability to millions of citizens in thousands of communities been frustrated for so long by a relatively small group of youthful males?

HISTORY OF
GANG CONTROL EFFORTS

The nation's failure to remedy its gang problems is not attributable to lack of effort. Scores of programs have been implemented and millions of dollars spent in efforts to cope with gang problems. A historical examination of approximately 60 such enterprises reported between 1920 and 1985 can be summarized by citing five of its conclusions. First, programs were based on a limited number of basic philosophies

and methods; most programs used one or some combination of five major approaches. Second, with the exception of a small number of innovations, the great majority of programs could be described as pedestrian and unimaginative. Third, procedures were used repeatedly during the 65-year period independent of evidence on their effectiveness. Nor did the fact that a number of the most popular methods had been evaluated as ineffective keep them from being used again. Prominent among approaches showing poor results were those based on the philosophy of attempting to change gangs by changing the overall character of their communities. Finally, since the 1920s, methods based on a set of popular rallying cries—including those of "prevention" and "coordination"—have been advocated repeatedly despite little evidence of their feasibility or potential effectiveness.

If one accepts the proposition that youth gang problems are less intransigent than many other persisting crime problems, one might have expected a better record of success than appears from the historical review. In fact, it is possible that some of the programs did have a more positive impact than can be demonstrated, but the poor quality of available evidence makes it very difficult to determine which of the methods used were better and which were worse. As a consequence, those who face today's serious gang problems do not have at their disposal reliable information on a set of methods with a proven capacity to produce positive results. This is one reason for the low rate of success in coping with gang problems.

From *Gangs in America* (pp. 22-35) R. Huff, editor. Newbury Park, CA: Sage Publications. Copyright 1990 by Sage Publications, Inc. Reprinted by permission.

THEORY

It would seem logical that the prospects for developing more effective methods for dealing with a difficult social problem like youth gang crime would be enhanced greatly by the availability of an acceptable explanation of what causes that problem. What factors and conditions are associated with the emergence and persistence of law-violating youth gangs? Which of these are most susceptible to change through planned strategies, policies, and programs? Current answers to these questions are poor. One might expect that as youth gang problems have become more serious and more prevalent during the past two decades that there would have been a commensurate increase in research on basic causes—as, for example, in the case of AIDS. But in fact, the opposite seems to have happened.

During the 1950s, a brief period of concern with theories of youth gangs, mostly by sociologists, produced a number of theoretical formulations based on the circumstances of that period. Some 30 years later, these formulations, along with the Chicago school explanations of the 1920s and 1930s, still constitute the major set of sociological explanations available for explaining youth gang behavior.

There have been hundreds of gang control operations and programs during the past several decades, but few of them have been based on explicitly developed theoretical formulations. Two positions have been particularly influential: an "individual responsibility" position favored by conservatives and a social injustice position favored by liberals. The first blames youth gang problems on personal failings of gang members, their families, and their communities, related to a general decline in public morality. The second blames gang problems on discriminatory and exploitative policies by the larger society that foster inequality, race discrimination, and blocked opportunities.

It is unrealistic to expect the development of general explanations that are free of political philosophies, but it does seem reasonable to advocate a renewed effort to develop explanations that present their basic premises openly and rationally and are derived as much as possible from conclusions based on careful research.

EVALUATION

Without systematic evaluation, it is impossible to present credible evidence on program impact. The execution of a sound evaluation design poses difficult problems, technical and political. In the 1960s, serious efforts were made to identify and overcome these problems. As a result, a number of successful evaluations of gang programs were completed. Wright and Dixon describe six gang program evaluations conducted between 1959 and 1971, along with 12 evaluations of Area and Youth Service projects, some of which included gang components.

In recent years, as gang problems have increased, the conduct of program evaluation has decreased. A bibliography of juvenile gangs prepared in 1983 by the U.S. Office of Juvenile Justice cites 115 documents; of these, only 2 are evaluation studies.

The virtual abandonment of sound evaluation of gang control efforts is a major reason for our failure to reduce gang problems. Evaluation research permits rational, systematic progress in developing more effective methods by making it possible to decrease the use of methods that are shown to be less effective and to refine and increase the use of more effective methods. In the absence of the kind of outcome evidence provided by sound evaluation, officials can and often do make exaggerated claims of success without credible supporting evidence. Without evaluation, the choice of gang control methods is speculative and inefficient. Any hope of developing more effective methods requires that evaluation research on gang programs be resumed.

RESOURCES

Those who have access to financial and human resources must be willing to direct those resources to the solution of particular social problems if effective remedial methods are to be developed and implemented. Despite the popular slogan that social problems are not solved by throwing money at them, progress in coping with difficult problems such as youth gang crime is next to impossible without adequate financing. Resources available to youth gang control in the 1990s are meager in both absolute and relative terms.

What limited information is available strongly suggests that if the importance of a social problem is measured by the amount of money allocated to it, youth gang problems rank very low in the nation's priorities. Some evidence on the importance of gang problems at the federal level is provided by the *Catalog of Federal Domestic Assistance Programs*. The 1989 edition lists 1,139 grant programs under approximately 535 major subject categories, including alcoholism, crime, and juvenile delinquency. Youth gangs are not listed as a major or minor category. Of the 1,139 listed programs, the term *gang* appears in descriptions of four programs, or about one third of 1% of all programs; of these, two involve gang control as such, another a conference on gangs, and a fourth a program of drug abuse prevention and education as it relates to youth gangs. By contrast, there are 23 grant programs for alcoholism, 37 for narcotics, 16 for recreation, and 19 for youth programs not involving gangs.

The 1990 federal budget allocates about $10 billion to drug programs administered by the Office of National Drug Control Policy. There is no Office of National Gang Control Policy, and a generous estimate of the amounts allocated at the federal level to all gang-related enterprises produces a figure that is less than 1% of this amount. This follows a year that recorded the highest number of gang-related homicides in history for a single county—at least 570 gang homicide victims in 1989 in Los Angeles County.

How can one explain why the federal government places such a low priority on youth gang problems? Some see it as one consequence of a general reluctance by recent conservative administrations to allocate needed funds to domestic social programs. This is particularly evident, the argument goes, during periods of severe budget constraints. But this factor alone is not enough to account for the low priority. As just shown, another domestic problem, drugs, is granted a very high priority at the federal level. In addition, low funding for gang control has prevailed during both conservative and liberal administrations.

The difference between the priorities accorded to gangs and to drugs raises the issue of what it is that determines the priority of social problems. This complex issue cannot be examined here, but one important element is the role of victimization. Groups such as the homeless, abused children, or battered women are readily perceived as pitiable victims and thus more easily command higher priorities. Victimization in connection with gang crime is more ambiguous. There are thousands of individual victims of gang violence each year, but most of these share the same social characteristics as their victimizers; the same people are often both victims and assailants. It is hard to enlist the degree of sympathy evoked by a homeless mother with three small children for an 18-year-old minority youth shot in a gang dispute.

It is in the nation's slums, ghettos, and barrios that one finds the principal victims of gang activity. In these communities are many residents whose dominant concern is the security and stability of community life—a security that gangs seriously jeopardize. Prominent among these residents are mothers whose children are at risk. These are the Americans who are most directly victimized by gangs, and it is these Americans for whom gang control is a major priority.

Here one finds a serious disparity between priorities and resources. In most cases, these communities have limited political power, and hence little access to potential resources. Gang control is a low national priority in large part because those with good access to resources put a low priority on gang problems and those who put a high priority on gang problems have poor access to resources.

IMPLEMENTATION

There is not a single organized agency in the United States, public or private, that takes specific responsibility for youth gangs as a national problem. The traditional position of federal authorities is that youth gangs are a local problem and should be handled at the local level. There is no doubt that there are essential gang control tasks that can be performed only at the local level, but it is also true that there are other important tasks that locals are not in a position to perform. These include the formulation of a comprehensive national strategy, basic research and theory development, evaluation research, and conducting operations in the context of a national arena.

What type of organization should assume primary responsibility for youth gang problems? Organizations that in the past have played a major role are private foundations, universities, and the federal government. All have conducted important gang control activities, often in conjunction with one another.

For a variety of reasons, including its organizational continuity and access to resources as well as its constitutional obligation to ensure domestic tranquility, the federal government appears as the most appropriate locus of responsibility. But throughout the years, federal agencies have shown little inclination to assume major responsibility for gang problems, and have even—in some instances—evinced antagonism to the idea.

Federal agencies have in the past and still do support programs relevant to gang control, but these have been sporadic, unrelated to any coherent strategy, and scattered among various agencies without effective coordination. There is nothing like a Federal Office of Gang Control, analogous to the Office of Drug Control Strategy, located in a cabinet-level department or in an office with the responsibility for coordinating programs in several departments. Without a center of responsibility at the federal level—an office with the authority and resources to develop a national strategy and monitor efforts at the national, state, and local levels—the enterprise of gang control is severely handicapped.

SOCIAL CONTEXT

A particularly vexing reason for the nation's failure to solve its gang problem lies in a pervasive reluctance to face squarely the issue of the social context of gang crime. The social context of gang life and the social characteristics of most gang members entail a set of extremely sensitive issues involving social class and ethnicity that are highly charged in U.S. society and evoke strong passions.

During the 1950s, most sociologists studying gangs were in essential agreement that there was an American lower class and that most youth gangs were in some way a product of the life circumstances of that class. In the succeeding years, the existence and special characteristics of the lower class have become more firmly established, and the link between gangs and the lower class has grown even stronger. But during this time, the willingness of most policymakers and planners to use this link as a central key to gang control strategy has diminished.

My own position in the 1950s was that this class, in common with others, has a subculture with distinctive characteristics as well as characteristics shared with other class subcultures. During the past 30 years, few public figures have agreed. The terms used to refer to this population reveal a deep reluctance to characterize it in social class terms, let alone perceive the class as having a distinctive subculture. Commonly used terms include *the disadvantaged, the underprivileged, inner-city residents,* and *the culturally deprived.* Even during the height of national concern with this population, in the War on Poverty in the 1960s, the primary term used to refer to the population was *the poor,* a term based on income rather than on class.

What had been a virtual taboo among public figures against characterizing low-status populations as a class finally came to an end in the 1980s, with the surprisingly rapid acceptance and spread of the term *underclass.* Most analysts in the 1980s who examined the links between youth gangs and the lower class used the underclass concept—a concept whose connotation in the 1980s derived largely from a seminal study of young black males in the Watts district of Los Angeles in the 1960s.

The gangs and underclass position is essentially a variant of Cloward and Ohlin's blocked opportunity theory of the 1960s. Underclass theory postulates a new social class created by a new set of demographic, technological, and economic conditions whereby the demand for low-skilled workers in an increasingly service-oriented high-tech economy has been reduced drastically, permanently locking them out of the labor market and cutting off upward mobility routes available to earlier generations. At the same time, the sense of community formerly found in lower-class neighborhoods has weakened, alienating inner-city minorities not only from the society at large but from higher-status members of their own ethnic groups. The formation of gangs is a response by alienated minority youth to the unavailability of legitimate employment and potential for fulfillment in their local communities.

Briefly, the underclass is a product of technological and economic changes coupled with persisting racism in U.S. society. In common with Cloward and Ohlin, underclass theorists see economic forces and their impact on the availability of jobs as the primary forces that generate and sustain the underclass.

The subcultural position views the contemporary lower class quite differently. It is not outside the system, it is not new, and it is sustained by important subcultural influences that arise from a variety of social forces in addition to economic circumstances. Unlike the underclass position—which depicts the underclass as not only outside of, but permanently excluded from, the existing social class system of the United States—the contemporary lower class is seen as an intrinsic part of that system, sharing countless cultural characteristics with members of other social classes as well as manifesting distinctive characteristics. Lower-class citizens are as much a part of American society as their fellow citizens in other classes.

Rather than representing a "new" social class that manifests a sharp break with the past—a difference in kind, not degree—the contemporary lower class represents a logical historical development of a traditional population category. Major features used in the past to characterize this class, such as prevalence of female-based households, limited involvement in formal education, reliance on public welfare, and prevalence of births out of wedlock, have not disappeared or diminished significantly. On the contrary, many have become more prevalent. The contemporary lower class is not a new class, but a further developed and more distinctive version of a traditional class.

One logical policy option can be stated simply, but raises very complicated issues. If youth gangs are a product of the circumstances of the lower class, eliminating or substantially changing these circumstances will eliminate or substantially reduce gang problems. This position is seldom stated this baldly, but the general notion has served on some level as a rationale for many programs, past and proposed. If characteristics such as female-headed households, limited educational background, intermittent employment and low-skilled jobs, poor housing, inferior health resources, and others contribute to the persistence of the lower class, then successful efforts to raise job skill levels, ensure steady employment, and improve education, housing, health, and other services will change its essential character and ameliorate its major social problems—including high crime rates and youth gang crime.

There are serious problems with this formulation. As noted in the historical review of gang programs, major programs based on this approach were not successful. An important reason is that the major premise, that gangs arise out of the circumstances of lower-class life, is inadequate. It is almost always true that where you find youth gangs you will find lower-class communities, but the obverse does not obtain. As noted earlier, there are numerous lower-class communities that do not have youth gangs. This suggests that there are certain critical features of lower-class life whose presence enhances the development of gangs and whose absence inhibits that development; what these are is not known.

Taking the position that it is the totality of lower-class life that produces gangs and that this totality must be changed to affect gangs is like trying to kill a gnat with a pile driver. However desirable such change might be, if gang control is in fact one's objective a policy of effecting major changes in the character of lower-class life and the complex set of societywide forces that sustain it is misdirected, inefficient, and uneconomical.

As suggested by Spergel and his colleagues, what is needed are carefully targeted programs focused on specific objectives and based on explicit explications of how achieving specific program objectives will affect gangs. How can we know which elements are most critically associated with the presence or absence of gangs? As suggested earlier, we can use the fact of the absence of gangs in many lower-class communities and their intermittent absence in others as a key to research aimed at detecting and identifying these critical elements—elements known to be changeable because they have changed—and use this knowledge as a basis for devising more focused programs and policies. As noted earlier, compared to such "core" characteristics of lower-class life as female-headed households and low-skilled labor, youth gangs are less intrinsic to the subculture and thus less resistant to change.

The social class status of contemporary youth gang members is close to that of their counterparts in the 1950s; the same cannot be said of their ethnic status. In the 1950s, a substantial proportion of gang members were Caucasian; in the 1990s, almost all gang members belong to a category designated as "minority." This has made the task of developing solutions to the gang problem more difficult, both conceptually and tactically.

Today, as in the past, one can divide these populations into two gross categories—newcomers (more recently arrived) and established

minorities (less recent). It is likely that youth gangs belonging to these two categories come into being and are sustained by different kinds of causal influences and would require significantly different remedial strategies. In the 1990s, the established minority category consists primarily of youth of Puerto Rican, Mexican, and African backgrounds; the newcomer category is much more heterogeneous, comprising a variety of Latin American groups (Panamanians, Nicaraguans, and others) and about 10 different Asian nationalities.

A major difference between the newcomers and the established minorities is their potential for upward social mobility. If history is any guide, gangs in most of the newcomer groups will cease being a problem after a few generations of normal acculturation and upward mobility. The underclass explanation for gangs, which postulates little or no mobility for its minorities, has limited relevance to the newcomer gang phenomenon.

It is the problem of gangs among the established minorities that raises the most complicated and painful policy issues, because it taps into one of the most divisive and intractable issues in the history of the republic—that of race relations. There is deep concern in minority communities over tendencies in the media and elsewhere to stereotype gangs as a minority phenomenon. Programs aimed at controlling gangs in minority communities may face opposition from one community faction for unfairly stigmatizing minorities or violating their civil liberties while being supported by another faction as a necessary measure for protecting the safety of law-abiding citizens. For some, the explanation that minority gang problems are a product of racism is so compelling and complete as to obviate the need for further research into causes.

Another issue is that of the ethnic status of personnel involved in gang programs. In the 1950s, there was a fair amount of cross-ethnic involvement in gang work. In some cases, black adults provided services and guidance for white gangs, and whites worked with black gangs. In the 1990s, this kind of relationship is rare. Many minority workers claim a special competence and a special right to work with youth of their own ethnic status and are inhospitable to the involvement of persons of different backgrounds. There are certainly good grounds for the claim of special competence, but there is also a danger that capable and dedicated people of other ethnic statuses will be discouraged from contributing to an enterprise that needs all the help it can get.

CONCLUSION

This chapter has explained the nation's failure to solve its youth gang problems as a consequence of major procedural and policy deficiencies. The following reasons for the failure have been presented. The nation has failed to develop a comprehensive gang control strategy. The problem is viewed in local and parochial terms instead of from a national perspective. Programs are implemented in the absence of demonstrably valid theoretical rationales. Efforts to systematically evaluate program effectiveness have been virtually abandoned. Resources allocated to the gang problem are incommensurate with the severity of the problem. There is no organizational center of responsibility for gang

problems anywhere in the United States. There is a deep-rooted reluctance to face up to the implications of the social context of gang life.

But such a catalogue of deficiencies becomes valuable only insofar as it provides the basis of proposals for more effective policies. A comprehensive national gang control strategy must be developed. Efforts in local communities should be informed by policies based on a national-level perspective. Gang control operations should be undergirded by sound theoretical rationales. The determination of which methods are most effective must be based on carefully conducted evaluation research. Serious efforts must be made to convince those who control resources that gang control should be granted a much higher priority. A federal office of youth gang control should be established. Accurate information on the social class and ethnic characteristics of gang communities should be used as a major element in the development of more effective gang control strategies.

This is admittedly a very ambitious set of recommendations, and there is little likelihood at present that even a few might be considered seriously. But they will have served some useful purpose if they can be seen as indicating general directions for developing a more effective national youth gang policy.

QUESTIONS FOR DISCUSSION AND WRITING

1. What is a major reason for our failure to reduce gang problems?
2. What evidence does the author provide that youth gang problems rank very low in the nation's priorities?
3. How has this chapter explained the nation's failure to solve its youth gang problems? What are some more effective policies?

SOCIAL LEARNING AND BEHAVIOR MODIFICATION

The "differential association theory" proposed by Sutherland as a learning theory of individual criminal behavior has been modified to address one of the problems noted by critics. Differential association theory did not specify the learning mechanisms by which criminal behavior is actually learned in associations with pro- and anticrime influences. Burgess and Akers, a behavioral social psychologist and a criminologist, respectively, in our department at the University of Washington at the time, proposed a variation of differential association theory that incorporates "operant conditioning" learning mechanisms into "A Differential Association-Reinforcement Theory of Criminal Behavior." In general, they propose that individuals become involved in criminal behavior because it is "reinforced," or rewarded, within social contexts and associations where this is more likely to happen than not.

Johnson, Marcos, and Bahr explore the social influence of peers in "The Role of Peers in the Complex Etiology of Adolescent Drug Use." They reiterate the powerful effects of one's friends and associates, particularly if they are involved in delinquent behavior themselves, on delinquent behavior. They also describe the social process of how, and the social situations within which, peers actually influence the involvement of each other in drug use. It is not necessarily "bad" youths imposing negative peer pressure on innocents but more likely the reciprocal social reinforcement of predispositions to participate in social situations that are ripe for fun, risk taking, danger, and, perhaps, drug use and other delinquent behavior.

This behavioral model—commonly referred to as "social learning theory" among criminologists—has been the theoretical foundation for many "behavior modification" programs aimed at the treatment and rehabilitation of juvenile offenders. Braukmann, Fixsen, Phillips, and Wolf, a group of behavioral psychologists who created and implemented one of the most famous delinquent behavior modification programs, the Achievement Place model, review a variety of "Behavioral Approaches to Treatment in the Crime and Delinquency Field," all based on some version of social learning theory.

Probably the most widespread and popular drug prevention program in the United States—the D.A.R.E. (Drug Abuse Resistance Education) program—is based on social learning theory. Drug use is conceptualized as a product of socially learned prodrug attitudes and behaviors. Therefore, the program is based on a social influence model of intervention, based on the dissemination within school/classroom contexts of anti-drug messages, information, attitudes, values, and behavioral models. Rosenbaum and Hanson conducted a rigorous evaluation of D.A.R.E. interventions using a longitudinal experimental design, "Assessing the Effects of School-Based Drug Education," and came to the conclusion that it did not have either a long-term or a short-term effect on subsequent student drug use nor on the social influence variables. They did discover a differential effect based on area of residence—urban and rural students showed some benefits, but suburban students experienced increases in drug use after exposure to D.A.R.E.

A Differential Association-Reinforcement Theory of Criminal Behavior

ROBERT L. BURGESS
RONALD L. AKERS

IN spite of the body of literature that has accumulated around the differential association theory of criminal behavior, it has yet to receive crucial empirical test or thorough restatement beyond Sutherland's own revision in 1947. The attempts to subject the theory to empirical test are marked by inconsistent findings both within the study and between studies, as well as by highly circumscribed and qualified findings and conclusions. Whether the particular researcher concludes that his findings do or do not seem to support the theory, nearly all have indicated difficulty in operationalizing the concepts and recommend that the theory be modified in such a way that it becomes more amenable to empirical testing.

Suggested theoretical modifications have not been lacking, but the difficulty with these restatements is that they are no more readily operationalized than Sutherland's.

Regardless of the particular criticisms, the exceptions taken, and the difficulties involved in testing and reformulating the theory that have been offered, few take exception to the central learning assumptions in differential association. If we accept the basic assumption that criminal behavior is learned by the same processes and involves the same mechanisms as conforming behavior, then we need to recognize and make use of the current knowledge about these processes and mechanisms. Neither the extant statement of the theory nor the reformulations of it make explicit the nature of the underlying learning process involved in differential association. In short, no major revisions have been made using established learning principles.

It now appears, however, that there is a body of verified theory which is adequate to the task of accurately specifying this process. Learning theory has progressed to the point where it seems likely that differential association can be restated in a more sophisticated and testable form in the language of modern learning theory. But that restatement must be attempted in a thorough fashion before we can expect others to accept it.

The amount of empirical research in the social psychology of learning clearly has shown that the concepts in learning theory are susceptible to operationalization. Therefore, applying an integrated set of learning principles to differential association theory should adequately provide the revision needed for empirical testing.

A restatement of the theory—not an alternative theory—will be presented, although of necessity, certain ideas not intrinsic to differential association will have to be introduced and additions will be made to the original propositions. The tasks are (a) making explicit the learning process, as it is now understood by modern behavioral science, from which the propositions of differential association can be derived; (b) fully reformulating the theory, statement by statement, in light of the current knowledge of this learning process; and (c) helping criminologists become aware of the advances in learning theory and research that are directly relevant to an explanation of criminal behavior.

DIFFERENTIAL ASSOCIATION AND MODERN BEHAVIOR THEORY

In this section, the nine formal propositions in which Sutherland expressed his theory will be analyzed in terms of behavior theory and research and will be reformulated as seven new propositions (Table 1).*

I. "Criminal behavior is learned."

VIII. "The process of learning criminal behavior by association with criminal and anti-criminal patterns involves all of the mechanisms that are involved in any other learning."

Since both the first and eighth sentences in the theory obviously form a unitary idea, it seems best to state them together. Sutherland was aware that these statements did not sufficiently describe the learning process, but these two items leave no doubt that differential association theory was meant to fit into a general explanation of human behavior and, as much is unambiguously stated in the prefatory remarks of the theory, an "explanation of criminal behavior should be a specific part of a general theory of behavior." Modern behavior theory as a general theory provides us with a good idea of what the mechanisms are that are involved in the process of acquiring behavior.

According to this theory, there are two major categories of behavior. On the one hand, there is reflexive or *respondent* behavior which is behavior that is governed by the stimuli that elicit it. Such behaviors are largely associated with the autonomic system. The work of Pavlov is of special significance here. On the other hand, there is *operant* behavior: behavior which involves the central nervous system. Examples of operant behavior include verbal behavior, playing ball, driving a car, and buying a new suit. It has been found that this class of behavior is a function of its past and present environmental consequences. Thus, when a particular operant is followed by certain kinds of stimuli, that behavior's frequency of occurrence will increase in the future. These stimuli are called reinforcing stimuli or reinforcers and include food, money, clothes, objects of various sorts, social attention, approval, affection, and social status. This entire process is called positive reinforcement. One distinguishing characteristic of operant behavior as opposed to respondent behavior, then, is that the latter is a function of its antecedent stimuli, whereas the former is a function of its antecedent environmental consequences.

In everyday life, different consequences are usually contingent upon different classes of behavior. This relationship between behavior and its consequences functions to alter the rate and form of behavior as well as its relationship to many features of the environment. The process of operant reinforcement is the most important process by which behavior is generated and maintained. There are, in fact, six possible environmental consequences relative to the law of operant behavior. (1) A behavior may produce certain stimulus events and thereby increase in frequency. As we have indicated above, such stimuli are called positive reinforcers and the process is called positive reinforcement. (2) A behavior may remove, avoid, or terminate certain stimulus events and thereby increase in frequency. Such stimuli are termed negative reinforcers and the process, negative reinforcement. (3) A behavior may produce certain stimulus events and thereby decrease in frequency. Such stimuli are called aversive stimuli or, more recently, punishers. The entire behavioral process is called positive punishment. (4) A behavior may remove or terminate certain stimulus events and thereby decrease in frequency. Such stimuli are positive reinforcers and the process is termed negative punishment. (5) A behavior may produce or remove certain stimulus events which do not change the behavior's frequency

TABLE 1

A differential association-reinforcement theory of criminal behavior.

Sutherland's Statement	Reformulated Statement
1. "Criminal behavior is learned."	1. Criminal behavior is learned according to the principles of operant conditioning.
8. "The process of learning criminal behavior by association with criminal and anti-criminal patterns involves all of the mechanisms that are involved in any other learning."	
2. "Criminal behavior is learned in interaction with other persons in a process of communication."	2. Criminal behavior is learned both in nonsocial situations that are reinforcing or discriminative and through that social interaction in which the behavior of other persons is reinforcing or discriminative for criminal behavior.
3. "The principal part of the learning of criminal behavior occurs within intimate personal groups."	3. The principal part of the learning of criminal behavior occurs in those groups which comprise the individual's source of reinforcements.
4. "When criminal behavior is learned, the learning includes (a) techniques of committing the crime, which are sometimes very complicated, sometimes very simple; (b) the specific direction of motives, drives, rationalizations, and attitudes."	4. The learning of criminal behavior, including specific techniques, attitudes, and avoidance procedures, is a function of the effective and available reinforcers, and the existing reinforcement contingencies.
5. "The specific direction of motives and drives is learned from definitions of the legal codes as favorable or unfavorable."	5. The specific class of behaviors which are learned and their frequency of occurrence are a function of the reinforcers which are effective and available, and the rules or norms by which these reinforcers are applied.
6. "A person becomes delinquent because of an excess of definitions favorable to violation of law over definitions unfavorable to violation of law."	6. Criminal behavior is a function of norms which are discriminative for criminal behavior, the learning of which takes place when such behavior is more highly reinforced than noncriminal behavior.
7. "Differential associations may vary in frequency, duration, priority, and intensity."	7. The strength of criminal behavior is a direct function of the amount, frequency, and probability of its reinforcement.
9. "While criminal behavior is an expression of general needs and values, it is not explained by those general needs and values since noncriminal behavior is an expression of the same needs and values."	9. (Omit from theory.)

at all. Such stimuli are called neutral stimuli. (6) A behavior may no longer produce customary stimulus events and thereby decrease in frequency. The stimuli which are produced are neutral stimuli, and the process, extinction. When a reinforcing stimulus no longer functions to increase the future probability of the behavior which produced it, we say the individual is satiated. To restore the reinforcing property of the stimulus we need only deprive the individual of it for a time.

The increase in the frequency of occurrence of a behavior that is reinforced is the very property of reinforcement that permits the fascinating variety and subtlety that occur in operant as opposed to respondent behavior. Another process producing the variety we see in behavior is that of *conditioning*. When a primary or unconditioned reinforcing stimulus such as food is repeatedly paired with a neutral stimulus, the latter will eventually function as a reinforcing stimulus as well. An illustration of this would be as follows. The milk a mother feeds to her infant is an unconditioned reinforcer. If the food is repeatedly paired with social attention, affection, and approval, these latter will eventually become reinforcing as will the mother herself as a stimulus object. Later, these *conditioned reinforcers* can be used to strengthen other behaviors by making these reinforcers contingent upon those new behaviors.

Differential reinforcement may also alter the form of a response. This process is called *shaping* or *response differentiation*. It can be exemplified by a child learning to speak. At first, the parent will reinforce any vocalization, but as time wears on, and as the child grows older, the parent will differentially reinforce only those responses which successfully approximate certain criteria. The child will be seen to proceed from mere grunts to "baby-talk" to articulate speech.

Differential reinforcement not only increases the probability of a response, it also makes that response more probable upon the recurrence of conditions the same as or similar to those that were present during previous reinforcements. Such a process is called *stimulus control* or *stimulus discrimination*. For example, a child when he is first taught to say "daddy" may repeat it when any male is present, or even, in the very beginning, when any adult is present. But through differential reinforcement, the child will eventually use the word daddy when present or in other appropriate conditions.

The most general behavioral principle is the law of operant behavior, which says that behavior is a function of its past and current environmental consequences. There have been numerous studies with children as well as adults which indicate that individual behavior conforms to this law.

Many forms of "normal" social behavior function according to the law of operant behavior. But what about "deviant" behavior? Can we be sure these same principles are operating here? Unfortunately, there have been no studies which attempt to test directly the relevance of these behavioral principles to criminal behavior. But there have been several experimental investigations of deviant behaviors emitted by mental patients. For example, in a study by Ayllon and Michael, it is shown that the bizarre behaviors of psychotics functioned according to these learning principles. In this particular study, various behavioral problems of psychotic patients were "cured" through the manipulation of reinforcement contingencies. Such principles as extinction, negative and positive reinforcement, and satiation were effectively used to eliminate the unwanted behaviors. This study was one of the first experimental tests of the contention that not only conforming but many unusual, inappropriate, or undesirable behaviors are shaped and maintained through social reinforcement. Many forms of deviant behavior are shaped and maintained by various contingencies of reinforcement. Given this experimental evidence, we would amend Sutherland's first and eighth propositions to read: I. *Criminal behavior is learned according to the principles of operant conditioning.*

II. "Criminal behavior is learned in interaction with other persons in the process of communication."

From the perspective of modern behavior theory, two aspects of socialization are usually considered to distinguish it from other processes of behavioral change: (a) Only those behavioral changes occurring through learning are considered relevant; (b) only the changes in behavior having their origins in interaction with other persons are considered products of socialization. Sutherland's theory may, then, be seen to be a theory of differential socialization since he, too, restricted himself to learning having its origin in interaction with other persons. While social learning is, indeed, important and even predominant, it certainly does not exhaust the learning process. In short, we may learn (and, thus, our behavior would be modified) without any direct contact with another person. Consequently, to be an adequate theory of deviant behavior, the theory must be amended further to include those forms of deviant behavior that are learned in the absence of social reinforcement. Other people are not the only source of reinforcement, although they are the most important. As Jeffrey has aptly noted, stealing is reinforcing in and by itself whether other people know about it and reinforce it socially or not. The same may be said to apply to many forms of aggressive behaviors.

Glaser has attempted to reformulate Sutherland's differential association theory in terms of social identification. It should be recognized, however, that identification as well as modeling and imitative behavior (which are usually associated with identification) comprise just one feature of the socialization process. Furthermore, such behavior may be analyzed quite parsimoniously with the principles of modern behavior theory. For example, in a study by Bandura and Ross, a child experienced the pairing of adult with positive reinforcers. Presumably, this adult would become a conditioned reinforcer. And indeed, later it was found that the child imitated this adult more than he did an adult who was not paired with positive reinforcers. That is, the adult, as he became a stronger reinforcer, had also become a stronger SD for imitating or following behavior. Thus, Bandura's and Ross's results demonstrate that imitating or following behavior is at least in part a function of the reinforcing value of people as social stimuli.

The relevance of these studies is that they have isolated some of the determining variables as well as the principles by which these variables operate. We have, of course, only scratched the surface. Many other variables are involved. For instance, not all people are equally effective in controlling or influencing the behavior of others. The person who can mediate the most reinforcers will exercise the most power. Thus, the parent, who controls more of his child's reinforcers, will exercise more power than an older sibling or the temporary babysitter. As the child becomes older and less dependent upon the parent for many of his reinforcers, other individuals or groups such as his peers may exercise more power. Carrying the analysis one step further, the person who has access to a large range of aversive stimuli will exert more power than one who has not. Thus, a peer group may come to exercise more power over a child's behavior than the parent even though the parent may still control a large share of the child's positive reinforcers.

In addition to the reinforcing function of an individual or group, there is the discriminative stimulus function of a group. For example, specific individuals as physical stimuli may acquire discriminative control over an individual's behavior. The child in our example above is reinforced for certain kinds of behaviors in the presence of his parent, thus the parent's presence may come to control this type of behavior. He is reinforced for different behaviors in the presence of his peers, who then come to set the occasion for this type of behavior. Consequently, this proposition must be amended to read: II. *Criminal behavior is learned both in nonsocial situations that are reinforcing or discriminative and through that social interaction in which the behavior of other persons is reinforcing or discriminative for criminal behavior.*

III. "The principal part of the learning of criminal behavior occurs within intimate personal groups."

In terms of our analysis, the primary group would be seen to be the major source of an individual's social reinforcements. The bulk of behavioral training which the child receives occurs at a time when the trainers, usually the parents, possess a very powerful system of reinforcers. In fact, we might characterize a primary group as a generalized reinforcer (one associated with many reinforcers, conditioned as well as unconditioned). And, as we suggested above, as the child grows older, groups other than the family may come to control a majority of an individual's reinforcers, for example, the adolescent peer group.

To say that the primary group is the principal molder of an individual's behavioral repertoire is not to ignore social learning which may occur in other contexts. As we noted above, learning from social models can be adequately explained in terms of these behavioral principles. The analysis we employed there can also be extended to learning from the mass media and from "reference" groups. In any case, we may alter this proposition to read: III. *The principal part of the learning of criminal behavior occurs in those groups which comprise the individual's major source of reinforcements.*

IV. "When criminal behavior is learned, the learning includes (a) techniques of committing the crime, which are sometimes very complicated, sometimes very simple; (b) the specific direction of motives, drives, rationalizations, and attitudes."

Studies indicate that reinforcement contingencies are of prime importance in learning various behavioral techniques. And, of course, many techniques, both simple and complicated, are specific to a particular deviant act such as jimmying, picking locks of buildings and cars, picking pockets, short- and big-con techniques, counterfeiting, and safe-cracking. Other techniques in criminal behavior may be learned in conforming or neutral contexts, for example, driving a car, signing checks, shooting a gun. In any event, we need not alter the first part of this proposition.

The second part of this proposition does, however, deserve some additional comments. Sutherland's major focus here seems to be motivation. The topic of motivation is as important as it is complex. This complexity is related to the fact that the same stimulus may have two functions: It may be both a reinforcing stimulus and a discriminative stimulus controlling the behavior which is followed by reinforcement. Thus, motivation may be seen to be a function of the processes by which stimuli acquire conditioned reinforcing value and become discriminative stimuli. Reinforcers and discriminative stimuli here would become the dependent variables; the independent variables would be the conditioning procedures previously mentioned and the level of deprivation. For example, when a prisoner is deprived of contact with members of the opposite sex, such sex reinforcers will become much more powerful. Thus, those sexual reinforcers that are available, such as homosexual contact, would come to exert a great deal of influence and would shape behaviors that would be unlikely to occur without such deprivation.

Much, therefore, can be learned about the distinctive characteristics of a group by knowing what the available and effective reinforcers are and the behaviors on which they are contingent. Basically, we are contending that the nature of the reinforcer system and the reinforcement contingencies are crucial determinants of individual and group behavior. Consequently, a description of an individual's or group's reinforcers and an understanding of the principles by which reinforcers affect behavior would be expected to yield a great deal of knowledge about individual and group deviant behavior.

Finally, the rationalizations which Cressey identifies with regard to trust violators and the peculiar extensions of "defenses to crimes" or "techniques of neutralization" by which deviant behavior is justified, as identified by Sykes and Matza, may be analyzed as operant behaviors of the escape or avoidance type which are maintained because they have the effect of avoiding or reducing the punishment that comes from social disapproval by oneself as well as by others. We may, therefore, rewrite this proposition to read: IV. *The learning of criminal behavior, including specific techniques, attitudes, and avoidance procedures, is a function of the effective and available reinforcers, and the existing reinforcement contingencies.*

V. "The specific direction of motives and drives is learned from definitions of the legal codes as favorable or unfavorable."

In this proposition, Sutherland appears to be referring, at least in part, to the concept *norm*, which may be defined as a statement made by a number of the members of a group, not necessarily all of them, prescribing or proscribing certain behaviors at certain times. We often infer what the norms of a group are by observing reaction to behavior, that is, the sanctions applied to, or reinforcement and punishment consequences of, such behavior. We may also learn what a group's norms are through verbal or written statements. The individual group member also learns what is and is not acceptable behavior on the basis of verbal statements made by others, as well as through the sanctions (i.e., the reinforcing or aversive stimuli) applied to his behavior (and other norm violators) by others.

Behavior theory specifies the place of normative statements and sanctions in the dynamics of acquiring to conforming or "normative" behavior. Such normative behavior would be developed and maintained by social reinforcement. As we observed in the Ayllon-Azrin study of instructions and reinforcement contingencies, such verbal behavior would not maintain any particular class of behaviors if it were not at least occasionally backed by reinforcement consequences. Extending their analysis, an individual would not "conform" to a norm if he did not have a past history of reinforcement for such conforming behavior. We may now say that we can learn a great deal about an individual's or a group's behavior when we are able to specify not only what the effective reinforcers are but also what the rules or norms are by which these reinforcers are applied. For these two types of

knowledge will tell us much about the types of behavior that the individual will develop or the types of behaviors that are dominant in a group.

For example, it has often been noted that most official criminal acts are committed by members of minority groups who live in slums. One distinguishing characteristic of a slum is the high level of deprivation of many important social reinforcers. Exacerbating this situation is the fact that these people, in contrast to other groups, lack the behavioral repertoires necessary to produce reinforcement in the prescribed ways. They have not been and are not now adequately reinforced for lawful or normative behavior. And as we know from the law of operant reinforcement, a reinforcer will increase the rate of occurrence of any operant which produces it. Furthermore, we would predict that given a large number of individuals under similar conditions, they are likely to behave in similar ways. Within such groups, many forms of social reinforcement may become contingent upon classes of behaviors which are outside the larger society's normative requirements. Norms and legal codes, as discriminative stimuli, will only control the behavior of those who have experienced the appropriate learning history. If an individual has been, and is, reinforced for such normative behavior, that behavior will be maintained in strength. If he has not been and is not now reinforced for such behaviors, they would be weak, if they existed in his repertoire at all. And, importantly, the reinforcement system may shape and maintain another class of behaviors which do result in reinforcement and such behaviors may be considered deviant or criminal by other members of the group. Thus, we may formulate this proposition to read: V. *The specific class of behaviors which are learned and their frequency of occurrence are a function of the reinforcers which are effective and available, and the rules or norms by which these reinforcers are applied.*

VI. "A person becomes delinquent because of an excess of definitions favorable to violation of law over definitions unfavorable to violation of law."

This proposition is generally considered the heart of Sutherland's theory; it is the principle of differential association. It follows directly from Proposition V, and we must now refer back to that proposition. In Proposition V, the use of the preposition *from* in the phrase, "learned from definitions of the legal codes as favorable or unfavorable," is somewhat misleading. The meaning here is not so much that learning results *from* these definitions as it is that they form part of the *content* of one's learning, determining which direction one's behavior will go in relation to the law, that is, abiding or lawbreaking.

These definitions of the law make lawbreaking seem either appropriate or inappropriate. Those definitions which place lawbreaking in a favorable light in a sense can be seen as essentially norms directly conflicting with conventional norms. They are, as Sykes and Matza and Cressey note, "techniques of neutralization," "rationalizations," or "verbalizations," which make criminal behavior seem "alright" or justified, or which provide defenses against self-reproach and disapproval from others. The principle of negative reinforcement would be of major significance in the acquisition and maintenance of such behaviors.

This analysis suggests that it may not be an "excess" of one kind of definition over another in the sense of a cumulative ratio, but rather in the sense of the relative amount of discriminative stimulus value of one set of verbalizations or normative statements over another.

In other terms, a person will become delinquent if the official norms or laws do not perform a discriminative function and thereby control normative or conforming behavior. We know from the law of differential reinforcement that that operant which produces the most reinforcement will become dominant if it results in reinforcement. Thus, if lawful behavior did not result in reinforcement, the strength of the behavior would be weakened, and a state of deprivation would result, which would, in turn, increase the probability that other behaviors would be emitted which are reinforced, and such behaviors would be strengthened. And, of course, these behaviors, although common to one or more groups, may be labeled deviant by the larger society. And such behavior patterns, themselves, may acquire conditioned reinforcing value and, subsequently, be enforced by the members of a group by making various forms of social reinforcement such as social approval, esteem, and status contingent upon that behavior.

The concept *excess* in the statement, "excess of definitions favorable to violation of law," has been particularly resistant to operationalization. A translation of this concept in terms of modern behavior theory would involve the "balance" of reinforcement consequences, positive and negative. The law of differential reinforcement is crucial here. That is, a person would engage in those behaviors for which he had been reinforced most highly in the past. Criminal behavior would, then, occur under those conditions where an individual has been most highly reinforced for such behavior, and the aversive consequences contingent upon the behavior have been of such a nature that they do not perform a "punishment function." Let us reformulate the sixth proposition to read: VI. *Criminal behavior is a function of norms which are discriminative for criminal behavior, the learning of which takes place when such behavior is more highly reinforced than noncriminal behavior.*

VII. "Differential associations may vary in frequency, duration, priority, and intensity."

In terms of our analysis, the concepts frequency, duration, and priority are straightforward enough. The concept *intensity* could be operationalized to designate the number of the individual's positive and negative reinforcers, another individual or group controls, as well as the reinforcement value of that individual or group. As previously suggested, the group which can mediate the most positive reinforcers and which has the most reinforcement value, as well as access to a larger range of aversive stimuli, will exert the most control over an individual's behavior.

There is a good reason to suspect, however, that Sutherland was not so much referring to differential associations with other persons, as differential associations with criminal patterns. If this supposition is correct, then this proposition can be clarified by relating to differential contingencies of reinforcement rather than differential social associations. From this perspective, the experimental evidence with regard to the various schedules of reinforcement are of major importance. There are three aspects of the schedules of reinforcement which are of particular importance here: (a) the amount of reinforcement—the greater the amount of reinforcement, the higher the response rate; (b) the frequency of reinforcement, which refers to the number of reinforcements per given time period—the shorter the time period between reinforcements, the higher the response rate; and (c) the probability of reinforcement, which is the reciprocal of responses per reinforcement—the lower the ratio of responses per reinforcement, the higher the rate of response.

Priority, frequency, and intensity of association with criminal persons and groups are important to the extent that they ensure that deviant behavior will receive greater amounts of reinforcement at more frequent intervals or with a higher probability than conforming behavior. But the frequency, probability, and amount of reinforcement are the crucial elements. This means that it is the coming under the control of contingencies of reinforcement that selectively produces the criminal definitions and behavior. Consequently, let us rewrite this proposition to read: VII. *The strength of criminal behavior is a direct function of the amount, frequency, and probability of its reinforcement.*

> IX. "While criminal behavior is an expression of general needs and values, it is not explained by those general needs and values since noncriminal behavior is an expression of the same needs and values."

In this proposition, Sutherland may have been reacting, at least in part, to the controversy regarding the concept *need*. This controversy is now essentially resolved. For we have finally come to the realization that "needs" are unobservable, hypothetical, fictional inner-causal agents which were usually invented on the spot to provide spurious explanations of some observable behavior. Furthermore, they were inferred from precisely the same behavior they were supposed to explain.

While we can ignore the reference to needs, we must discuss values. Values may be seen as reinforcers which have salience for a number of the members of a group or society. We agree with Sutherland to the extent that he means that the nature of these general reinforcers does not necessarily determine which behavior they will strengthen. Money or something else of general value in society will reinforce any behavior that produces it. This reinforcement may depend on noncriminal behavior, but it also may become contingent upon a set of behaviors that are labeled as criminal. Thus, if Sutherland can be interpreted as meaning that criminal and noncriminal behavior cannot be maintained by the same set of reinforcers, we must disagree. However, it may be that there are certain reinforcing consequences which only criminal behavior will produce, for the behavior finally shaped will depend on the reinforcer that is effective for the individual. Nevertheless, it is the reinforcement, not the specific nature of the reinforcer, which explains the rate and form of behavior. But since this issue revolves around contingencies of reinforcement which are handled elsewhere, we will eliminate this last proposition.

CONCLUDING REMARKS

The purpose of this chapter has been the application of the principles of modern behavior theory to Sutherland's differential association theory. While Sutherland's theory has had an enduring effect on the thinking of students of criminal behavior, it has, until now, undergone no major theoretical revision despite the fact that there has been a steady and cumulative growth in the experimental findings of the processes of learning.

There are three aspects of deviant behavior which we have attempted to deal with simultaneously, but which should be separated. First, how does an individual *become* delinquent, or how does he learn delinquent behavior? Second, what *sustains* this delinquent behavior? We have attempted to describe the ways in which the principles of modern behavior theory are relevant to the development and maintenance of criminal behavior. In the process, we have seen that the principle of differential reinforcement is of crucial importance. But we must also attend to a third question, namely, what sustains the pattern or *contingency* of reinforcement? We only have hinted at some of the possibly important variables. We have mentioned briefly, for example, structural factors such as the level of deprivation of a particular group with regard to important social reinforcers, and the lack of effective reinforcement of lawful behavior and the concomitant failure to develop the appropriate behavioral repertoires to produce reinforcement legally. We have also suggested that those behaviors which do result in reinforcement may, themselves, gain reinforcement value and be enforced by the members of the group through the manipulation of various forms of social reinforcement such as social approval and status, contingent upon such behaviors. In short, new norms may develop and these may be termed delinquent by the larger society.

QUESTIONS FOR DISCUSSION AND WRITING

1. What are six possible environmental consequences relative to the Law of Operant Behavior?
2. Look at Table 1. What changes did Burgess and Akers make to Sutherland's theory?
3. What do we know from the law of differential reinforcement?

The Role of Peers in the Complex Etiology of Adolescent Drug Use

RICHARD E. JOHNSON

ANASTASIOS C. MARCOS

STEPHEN J. BAHR

THE single best predictor of the presence or amount of an adolescent's drug use is the extent to which the individual associates with other adolescents who use drugs. More generally, the best predictor of the extent of an adolescent's involvement in delinquent behavior is likewise the number of the youth's delinquent associates. Such findings clearly call for closer examination of the role of peers in the etiology of all forms of adolescent deviance, and particularly in the processes leading to adolescent drug use. Unfortunately, many studies of adolescent drug use are descriptive and atheoretical. The high correlation between friends' drug use and the subject's drug use is often simply noted, unguided by theoretical propositions and untied to other probable causes of adolescent drug use. The present study is an attempt to go beyond the usual examination of the role of peers in drug use by embedding peer variables within a causal model consisting of an integration of notions from differential association, social bonding, and group pressure perspectives.

SAMPLE AND DATA

The data were collected in the spring of 1985 from a private high school in a metropolitan area in the western United States. A self-report questionnaire was administered to all students from Grades 9 through 12 who were present in school that day. The sample of 768 consists of 55% females and 45% males, with ages ranging from 14 to 19. Of the total, 85% are white, with the majority of the remainder being Hispanic. Although the sample is certainly not representative of the nation, the prevalence of drug use among the seniors in the sample parallels that obtained in a national sample of high school seniors. Correlations among key matching variables in this sample likewise mirror those found in much broader samples obtained by the authors for other purposes.

MEASUREMENT

In this research, drug use is measured by self-reports on the use of four different categories of drugs: (a) cigarettes, (b) alcohol, (c) marijuana, and (d) amphetamines and depressants. Students were asked how often they had ever used each drug and how often they used that particular drug during the past 12 months and the past month. Only the findings using the lifetime measures are reported below, as the past-12-months and the past-month yield very similar results. Scoring ranges from 0 for *no use* to 4 for *use of a drug 10 or more times*. The responses in each category were summed to obtain a global measure of combined drug use.

Proportion of Drug-Using Friends is measured separately for each category of drug use and then summed for analysis of combined drug use. Students were asked how many of their best friends drink alcohol, smoke cigarettes, use marijuana, or use amphetamines or depressants. To construct this measure, the number of best friends that were reported to have used the particular drug(s) was divided by the number of people the respondent listed as best friends. In line with differential association theory, it is not the absolute number of drug-using friends that counts as much as the ratio of users to nonusers.

Parent-Derived Drug Definitions and Friend-Derived Drug Definitions are parallel scales that are also drug specific, with a summed score for analysis of combined drug use. Respondents were asked to report the attitudes that they had received from their parents (and, in separate items, from their friends) toward use of that particular drug. Responses to prodrug items (that it is okay to use the drug and that occasional use is harmless fun) were summed and divided by the sum of antidrug items (that use of the drug is harmful to health, that it is wrong to use it, and that too many people use the drug). The resultant quotients represent ratios of prodrug to antidrug definitions toward the four drug categories, measured separately, as received from one's parents and one's best friends.

RESULTS

The correlations between each of the relevant independent variables and each of the drug-use measures show that the patterns of correlations are very similar for each of the specific types of adolescent drug use. Drug-using friends and friend-derived definitions are consistently most highly related to drug use, followed by conventional values. It is associations with drug-using peers and peer-derived drug definitions that matter most, while associations with drug-using parents and parent-derived drug definitions rank at the bottom (along with parental attachment) in predicting drug use. By the time a child reaches adolescence, all of the direct parental influences seem to play only minor roles in determining his or her drug use.

CONCLUSIONS AND DISCUSSION

In general, the results confirm the initial supposition that drug-using peers are the best predictor of adolescent drug use. Placed in theoretical context, the results support the position that social learning variables (including both normative and situational notions) are more important in causing adolescent drug use than are the nonbelief attachments derived from social bond theory. While association with drug-using friends is certainly the key to predicting adolescent drug use, the probability of that kind of association is in turn partly a product of one's attachments and general values. It is not so much that adolescents use drugs because the drug use of their friends makes drug use seem right or safe; rather, they apparently use drugs *simply because their friends do.*

Here the data stop and one must speculate about the processes underlying such a finding. The authors propose that to the extent that differential association is the key to understanding adolescent drug use, it appears to be more appropriate to conceive of the key process as association with situational pressure to go along with the crowd rather than association with people, behavior, or definitions that alter one's views of the behavior in question. This proposal is based on the assumption that adolescent drug use is primarily a social behavior committed in the presence of others.

Situational pressure to jointly participate seems to be the most important process leading to adolescent drug use. And, of course, such pressures generally come from friends and not parents. If parents who used drugs simultaneously tried to coax their children into joining them in drug taking to "show their stuff" or "have a good time," then parental drug use would probably rank with friends' drug use as a major cause of adolescent drug use. Conversely, having friends known to use drugs may not be much of a predictor of personal drug use if drug use were a rationally planned or solitary type of behavior which did not involve such coaxing or daring.

In short, it may not be that friends are more important than parents per se, but rather that emotion-laden situational pressure is a stronger force than is more rational contemplation of less immediately pressing values, attachments, and role models in determining the behavior of adolescents. For adolescent drug use, then, the crucial differential association may not be association with people or definitions or "behavior patterns," but rather association with *situations* in which there is immediate pressure to use drugs at the risk of social discomfort or rejection.

QUESTIONS FOR DISCUSSION AND WRITING

1. What is the best predictor of an adolescent's drug use? What is the best predictor of adolescents' involvement in delinquent behavior? What do these findings "call for"?
2. What do the correlations between each of the relevant independent variables and each of the drug-use measures show?
3. When "placed in theoretical context," what position do the results support? What "seems to be" the most important process leading to adolescent drug use? Why is "emotion-laden situational pressure" important?

Behavioral Approaches to Treatment in the Crime and Delinquency Field

CURTIS J. BRAUKMANN
DEAN L. FIXSEN
ELERY L. PHILLIPS
MONTROSE M. WOLF

THE often disappointing results of traditional treatment and prevention approaches with juvenile and adult offenders have prompted, in part, an increased emphasis during the past decade on approaches using procedures based on learning principles. The systematic and explicit application of learning principles in remedying human problems constitutes the original meaning of the term *behavior modification*. There are behavior modification techniques based on both *operant* and *respondent* learning principles. Respondent learning principles are based on research on the acquisition of reflex-like responses (i.e., responses that are elicited by specific preceding stimuli). Operant learning principles are based on research on the acquisition of behaviors that operate on the environment to produce consequences for the operator. While there has been some application of respondent learning principles in interventions with offenders, operant approaches are more common.

Underlying operant behavior modification treatment approaches is the social-learning

view that behavior, including deviant behavior, is learned. This "educational" model for deviant behavior is in contrast to the traditional "medical" model, which depicts deviant behavior as symptomatic of underlying pathology. Stated differently, the socially maladaptive behaviors of an individual are not viewed as indicative of "illness" in the usual psychiatric sense. Rather, the assumption is made that the individual lacks certain skills necessary to function in ways that are more socially adaptive and/or that the individual lacks adequate regulation of and discrimination with respect to his behavior, thereby engaging in behaviors that are judged to be inappropriate or deviant.

The maintenance of desired changes in the absence of the treatment procedures, that is, in the natural environment, is critical to any effective treatment program. Such generalization cannot be assumed, and procedures must explicitly be designed to increase the likelihood of generalization. The results of follow-up evaluations of treatment are likely to be disappointing when appropriate generalization efforts have not been undertaken. Suggested guidelines for facilitating generalization include (a) using a treatment environment that approximates natural environmental conditions as closely as possible, (b) establishing behaviors likely to be maintained by naturally existing consequences, (c) "fading out" the treatment environment in gradual steps, and (d) teaching members of the participant's natural environment to provide consequences for the maintenance of the behavior change.

Practitioners and researchers in the operant-behaviorist tradition attempt to provide effective, efficient, and humane treatment. Toward this end, they generally stress objective measurement, demonstration of treatment effects, and accountability. Almost all of them gather data on the effectiveness of their procedures, and they are increasingly collecting measures on the satisfaction of their participants and other consumers of the treatment program. Evaluations have been conducted that assess the effectiveness of, and consumer preference for, operant behavior modification *procedures* and *programs*. The measurement methodology used in, and the results obtained from, several of these evaluations will be discussed in the following pages.

PROCEDURE EVALUATION

While an overall evaluation of a program with regard to its long-term effects on the lives of participants is critical, there is a need for more immediate feedback on the effectiveness of, and participants' preference for, various treatment procedures. Evaluations of the effectiveness of behavioral treatment procedures have generally involved the measurement and design methodology of the field of "applied behavior analysis." The field uses "single subject experimental designs in which it is possible to see whether the behavioral change under study is a reliable effect of the variable applied or only a coincidental random change that is not reliably associated with that variable." If desired changes in the target behavior(s) *reliably* correspond to the introduction of the treatment procedure, evidence is generated that the treatment procedure produced the changes.

In the crime and delinquency treatment area, procedural research using applied behavior analysis measurement and design techniques has found both contingent consequences and systematic teaching procedures to be effective in eliminating some maladaptive behaviors and in establishing (i.e., constructing, maintaining, reinstating, or transferring to new situations) a variety of social, self-care, academic, and vocational behaviors.

The evaluations that have shown treatment involving contingent consequences and comprehensive teaching procedures to be effective in teaching skills to predelinquent and delinquent youths have dealt with a number of skills, including (a) homework skills resulting in increased grades; (b) the skills involved in the appropriate acceptance of negative feedback; (c) employment interview skills; (d) conversational-interaction skills with adults in general and with policemen in particular; (e) employment-related skills; and (f) negotiation skills in interactions with parents.

Taken together, the procedural evaluation research that has been conducted in operantly based behavior modification programs in the crime and delinquency area suggests that an adequate evaluation methodology exists for determining the effectiveness of, and participant preference for, various procedures and that some effective and preferred techniques currently exist. In none of the above-mentioned studies was the generalization of behavioral changes to the natural environment measured. However, the next part of this chapter will address the question of the effectiveness of entire programs on posttreatment functioning in the natural environment.

PROGRAM EVALUATION

There needs to be an increased emphasis on program evaluation, especially on sound evaluation meeting the criteria of scientific research. The criteria for scientific program evaluation include the use of sensitive and reliable measures of the participants' community behavior and the use of control group experimental designs, preferably with participation in the treatment and control groups determined randomly.

Many program evaluations use a measure of whether participants are institutionalized after treatment. Some use police- and court-contact measures, which are made more sensitive by assessment of the seriousness of the offense involved in each contact. Other more positive measures include school attendance and grades, evaluations of the participant's social functioning by members of his family and community, and measures of employment and vocational functioning. To ensure that data collected from records (e.g., police, court, and school) are accurate, periodic assessments of the agreement between independent data gatherers should be conducted. Program evaluations should follow up all clients initially accepted into the program, whether or not they graduate, and should follow them up on a long-term basis. Cost evaluations should also be conducted comparing the evaluated program with available alternative programs.

If participation in a treatment program has resulted in desired changes in the behavior of its participants and if such changes have generalized to the natural environment, then these improvements should be reflected in the above-described program evaluation measures. As noted earlier, specific treatment efforts are required to facilitate generalization of treatment effects to the open community setting. The absence of or difficulties and inadequacies in this critically important treatment component would be expected to disrupt or even to militate against the desired generalization.

The evaluation results and descriptions of several of the behavioral programs in the crime and delinquency area, at the institutional level as well as at community-based residential and nonresidential levels, will now be discussed. At all levels, greater use has been made of behavioral treatment procedures with juveniles than with adults.

Token systems are currently used in several juvenile *institutional* programs. In general, when program evaluation comparisons between these behaviorally oriented programs and comparison programs have been possible, little or no differences in outcome have been reported. Indeed, there are some tentative comparisons to suggest that youths who have participated in some behavioral institutional programs have higher reinstitutionalization rates than comparison youths.

Institutional programs with juvenile and adult offender populations have too often been focused on the contingency management of behaviors necessary for smooth institutional functioning rather than on teaching a variety of skills useful to posttreatment functioning in the community. This problem is compounded by the marked differences between institutional environments and the clients' natural environment and the lack of community support programs. In general, participation in such institutional programs has not been under circumstances likely to ensure that such participation is voluntary. In the absence of any convincing data that institutional contingency management programs are more effective than alternatives, the issue of voluntary participation becomes all the more critical.

There are a number of behavioral treatment and prevention programs at the *community-based* level. From a behavioral point of view, community-based treatment has a number of advantages. If a participant's problems can be solved in his own community, then the chances of his eventual success in the community may be enhanced. Typically, behaviorally oriented, community-based residential treatment programs occur in group home situations. These programs are often based on the teaching-family model group-home treatment program developed at Achievement Place, a community-based, community-controlled, family-style group home for 12- to 16-year-old court-adjudicated youths in Lawrence, Kansas.

At Achievement Place, and in its direct replications, a professionally trained couple, the "teaching-parents," use intensive teaching procedures, a flexible motivation system, and a self-governing system to educate predelinquent and delinquent youths in a variety of social, academic, and self-care skills. Another critical component of the teaching-family model is the attempt to develop reciprocally rewarding relationships between the youths and the teaching-parents. Such a relationship enhances the effectiveness of the teaching-parents' social behavior in maintaining appropriate behavior. This allows the teaching-parents to reduce the youths' dependence on the point system as soon as possible while still maintaining their effectiveness as teachers.

The small (six to eight youths) family-style program allows the youths to participate in the direction of the program through self-government mechanisms of the manager system and the family conference. In the manager system, the youths exercise self-government through the daily democratic election of a manager who oversees and teaches routine skills. In the daily family conference, youths participate in the establishment and enforcement of program guidelines.

The teaching-parents indirectly supervise the youths in their regular schools (which the youths continue to attend) and natural homes (to which they return on weekends). Because the program is community based, the teaching-parents can work with the youths' parents and teachers. Further, they can continue to work with the youths even after the youths have been gradually eased back into their natural homes on a full-time basis. Direct replications of the teaching-family model are accountable to a local board of directors made up of community representatives. A comprehensive education program designed to teach couples the teaching-parent skills has been developed.

Extending an earlier evaluation, Kirigen et al. conducted a recent evaluation involving the first 18 youths who had participated in the program and 19 youths who had been judged by a probation officer to be comparable to Achievement Place youths, but who had participated in the state boys' training school. Within 2 years of their release, 47% of the boys' school youths had been reinstitutionalized. By comparison, only 22% of the Achievement Place boys had been institutionalized. While both groups showed pre- to postdecreases in rates of police and court contacts, there were no significant differences between the groups either before or after treatment. At comparable ages (2 years after treatment for Achievement Place youths and 1 year following release for the training school youths), 56% of the Achievement Place youths who could have been in school were in school as compared to 33% of the corresponding comparison youths.

Currently, whenever possible, youths are being randomly selected into the Achievement Place program from a pool of eligible candidates. This will allow a more creditable evaluation of program effectiveness. Selection into the program has resulted in immediate decreases in police and court contacts and increases in school attendance for the 8 randomly selected youths. Thus far, 56% of the 18 randomly not-selected youths have been institutionalized within 2 years, thereby demonstrating that Achievement Place provides an alternative to institutionalization for many of the youths who participate. In addition to being a less restrictive treatment environment, the per youth costs involved in establishing and operating a group home have been reported to be about half the corresponding institutional costs.

There have been a number of *nonresidential treatment and prevention programs at the community level*. For example, R. K. Schwitzgebel conducted a behavioral street corner research project in the Boston area by recruiting twenty 15- to 21-year-old delinquents with multiple arrests to participate in taped interviews. These interviews took place several times per week for an average of 9 months, and wages and social consequences were used to reward cooperation, promptness, and talking about feelings. A 3-year follow-up indicated that the youths had significantly fewer arrests and months incarcerated than a matched control group. In addition, although not statistically significant, the experimental group also had a lower recidivism rate (35%) than the controls (45%).

Steketee and Thorne et al. have described the use of behavioral procedures with *youths on probation*. Alexander and Parsons described one such program in which the families of 46 youths referred to the court for status crimes such as truancy and running away were taught negotiation and contingency contracting skills by 18 psychology graduate students. Families were randomly assigned to this group as well as to three other groups. An examination of court records 6 to 18 months posttreatment for the various families indicated that youths in the behavioral group had significantly fewer "behavioral" referrals, as well as nonsignificantly fewer "criminal" referrals, than youths in a client-centered therapy group, in a psychodynamic family program, or in a no-treatment control. However, such positive effects were not reported in a similar study which involved negotiation training and contingency contracting within the families of 14- to 17-year-old probationers with multiple offenses. In that study, the introduction of treatment had no effect on curfew violations or school attendance. In addition, at a 3-month follow-up point there were no differences between 6 treated youths and 16 untreated youths in the number of antisocial incidents recorded by the probation department or in school grades.

A number of behavioral programs generally aimed at delinquency prevention have been reported, such as specially designed *token economy classrooms for school dropouts* and *special programs for school-referred youths*. One program for school-referred junior high students, the Family and School Consultation Project, used behavioral contracts between referred youths and their parents and teachers. The researchers measured the subsequent effects on youth performance in their schools (e.g., grades, absences), homes (e.g., parental ratings), and community (e.g., court contacts). In a 4-month follow-up of 60 youths randomly assigned either to a treatment or control group, the treated youths did better than the controls on each of 13 measures. However, these differences were significant in only four measures: teacher and counselor ratings of school performance and mother ratings of her relationships with the youths and her marital adjustment.

Another program for school-referred youths, the PREP project (Preparation Through Respon-

sible Educational Programs), which operated in a Maryland junior high school, used a token system in which students earned points for performance in regular and programmed instructional classes. Thirty participating students did significantly better than matched controls on measures of grades, achievement test scores, and disciplinary referrals.

A behavioral program at Oregon Research Institute provides training for the parents of 5- to 13-year-old boys with aggressive behavior problems. In a follow-up of 27 boys whose parents were trained in behavioral techniques, direct in-home observation measures found significant decreases in deviant behaviors (e.g., physical aggression against siblings) over preintervention levels for two thirds of the youths. These changes were maintained over a 1-year follow-up period. Control groups did not show such decreases. Classroom intervention was needed for 14 of the 27 youths. As a group, their postintervention appropriate behaviors, as measured by direct in-class measures, had significantly improved.

In general, the above review of the outcomes of some of the behavioral programs at both the institutional and community-based level suggests that a number of these programs provide promising alternatives to traditional treatment and prevention approaches. However, there is a definite need for more and continued evaluations of such programs, especially evaluations involving random assignment, larger groups, and longer follow-up periods.

ASSESSMENT OF
CONSUMER SATISFACTION

In contrast to typical program effectiveness data, which are usually not available until a year or two after a program begins, consumer evaluation measures can provide more immediate, practical, and economical feedback on whether a program is meeting its service goals according to its consumers and how it might need to be changed in order to better meet these goals. Consumer satisfaction measures also provide feedback on whether a program's treatment goals are mutually satisfactory to the participants and other consumers.

Consumer satisfaction with a program can be measured through rating-scale questionnaires in which consumers evaluate the program on dimensions such as effectiveness and pleasantness. The ongoing use of these procedures and the review of their results by an advisory board made up of representative citizens can provide for ongoing program accountability to its consumers. These procedures are currently used in a number of programs, most notably programs using the teaching-family model of group home treatment. Such consumer satisfaction evaluations should be used as a standard procedure in all behavior modification treatment programs to aid such treatment staff in their attempt to serve the participants, their relatives, and other members of their community in an effective, efficient, accountable, and humane fashion.

CONCLUSIONS

This chapter attempts to describe the current status (in the crime and delinquency area) of those behavior modification treatment and prevention approaches that are based on the operant learning principle tradition. The measurement methodologies used in both effectiveness and consumer satisfaction evaluations of various operant behavior modification procedures and programs were discussed. An overview of the results of such evaluations indicated that several of the behavioral approaches promise to provide effective, efficient, and humane alternatives to traditional treatment and prevention approaches.

There is a need for more systematic outcome evaluations that use multiple and varied measures, random selection or random assignment, larger groups, and longer follow-up periods. Such outcome evaluations will allow more definitive statements concerning the effectiveness of various programs. There is also a need for more widespread use of consumer satisfaction evaluation procedures to ensure that these approaches are conforming to the goals and needs of their consumers.

The importance of generalization of treated behaviors to the natural environment, the rights of participants to the least restrictive treatment environment necessary, as well as cost-efficiency considerations, all point to the need for increased emphasis on community-based behavioral approaches. Increased and continued emphasis at both community-based and institutional levels needs to be given to (a) teaching adaptive community skills, (b) the participation of participants in program decision-making processes, (c) voluntary and informed program participation, and (d) programming generalization of desired treatment effects to the natural environment. In this way, behavioral approaches can provide a valuable contribution to crime and delinquency treatment and prevention.

QUESTIONS FOR DISCUSSION AND WRITING

1. Why does the field of "applied behavior analysis" use "single subject experimental designs," and what is the role of reliability?
2. What did Kirigen et al. find in their evaluation of Achievement Place?
3. What are the benefits of consumer evaluation measures, and what can the ongoing use of these procedures provide?

Assessing the Effects of School-Based Drug Education: A 6-Year Multilevel Analysis of Project D.A.R.E.

DENNIS P. ROSENBAUM
GORDON S. HANSON

DRUG Abuse Resistance Education (D.A.R.E.) is the most popular school-based drug education program in the United States. It is administered in about 70% of the nation's school districts, reaching 25 million students in 1996, and has been adopted in 44 foreign countries. Its effectiveness in combating drug usage, however, has been a matter of bitter controversy, and this debate is taking place in the context of rising drug use among our nation's youths. After large declines in drug use in the 1980s, the national trend began to reverse in the early 1990s.

This growing drug problem has caused a flurry of media coverage and political finger-pointing, all leading to closer scrutiny of our nation's efforts to control and prevent drug abuse. The spotlight has been especially strong on America's most popular and visible program—D.A.R.E. Whether or not D.A.R.E. has been an effective preventive program has been the subject of considerable debate and research. The publication of a national study that questioned the effectiveness of D.A.R.E. in preventing drug use opened the door to an avalanche of criticism

in the popular press and canceled endorsements by some police executives. Of course, the problem of demonstrating effectiveness in drug prevention is not unique to D.A.R.E. Several literature reviews and meta-analyses of school-based drug prevention programs have concluded that most are ineffective in preventing drug use.

The latest pressure on school-based drug education programs comes from federal legislation. Congress enacted the Drug-Free Schools and Communities Act in 1987 (and many subsequent amendments) to beef up our nation's drug education and prevention programs. Effective July 1, 1998, local school districts will be expected, for the first time, to provide evidence of program effectiveness to receive federal Title IV funds. Funding will only be available for "research-based" strategies that are consistent with the new "Principles of Effectiveness." One of the core principles is that "grant recipients shall . . . select and implement programs that have demonstrated that they can be effective in preventing or reducing drug use, violence, or disruptive behavior."

The present article reports on a comprehensive longitudinal evaluation of D.A.R.E. that occurred between 1989 and 1996 in the state of Illinois. This article includes the final analyses of the full data set collected as part of the Illinois D.A.R.E. study, which tracked students from fifth and sixth grades through their junior and senior years of high school.

THE D.A.R.E. PROGRAM

D.A.R.E. is a series of school-based drug and violence prevention programs for kids in kindergarten through 12th grade. It is a cooperative venture between law enforcement agencies, schools, and the local community, and it involves the use of trained, uniformed police officers in the classroom to teach a carefully planned drug prevention curriculum. Created in 1983 as a collaborative venture between the Los Angeles Police Department and the Los Angeles Unified School District, D.A.R.E. has expanded to become the largest drug education initiative in the world. The core D.A.R.E. curriculum, which is the subject of this research, focuses on children in their last year of elementary school (fifth or sixth grade). It is based on the assumption that students at this age are the most receptive to antidrug messages as they approach the age of drug experimentation.

THEORETICAL FRAMEWORK

Evaluations of D.A.R.E.'s effectiveness as a public policy can also be viewed as a test of its theoretical underpinnings. The program is primarily rooted in the social skills and social influence model of drug education. As Botvin notes, a variety of strategies can be characterized as part of this "psychosocial" approach to drug prevention, but three general categories of programs can be identified: psychological inoculation, resistance skills training, and personal and social skills training. D.A.R.E. has elements of each approach in its curriculum.

Botvin compares psychological inoculation to "traditional preventive medicine" in that individuals are exposed to weak doses of "infection" so that "antibodies" may be developed. (D.A.R.E.'s "vaccine" takes the form of simulated temptations and pressures to use drugs.) The resistance skills training approach places emphasis on teaching specific skills for evading or resisting these "negative social influences," including subtle media influences (D.A.R.E. students engage in role-playing scenarios to resist peer offers of drug use). The personal and social skills training approach is not problem specific but more broadly oriented to the "acquisition of generic personal and social skills." These will have the incidental effect of preventing the development of socially learned behaviors and attitudes that are believed to be associated with substance use.

From the outline of the curriculum (see Table 1), it is apparent that D.A.R.E. also includes "information dissemination" and "affective education." The former is designed to provide students with enough knowledge to make informed cost-benefit decisions about drug use (e.g., D.A.R.E. includes information on drug use, misuse, and consequences; media influences; and drug use alternatives). The latter is similar to the personal-and-social-skills approach but is focused on a strategy of "social enrichment." D.A.R.E. attempts to do this by focusing the curriculum on self-esteem building, managing stress, decision making, role modeling, and forming support systems. The general hypothesis implicit in the D.A.R.E. model is that classroom instruction by trained police officers will result in enhanced self-esteem, self-understanding, and assertiveness; a clearer sense of values; and more responsible decision-making habits, which, in turn, should make students less vulnerable to the enticements and pressures to use drugs and alcohol.

PREVIOUS D.A.R.E. EVALUATIONS

There have been many outcome evaluations of the core D.A.R.E. curriculum, but the methodological rigor of these assessments varies considerably. Most of these studies are of limited scientific value because of their weak research designs, poor sampling and data collection procedures, inadequate measurement, and analysis problems. Indeed, the boldest claims of D.A.R.E.'s success are especially vulnerable to

TABLE 1

Original D.A.R.E. curriculum.

Session	Topic	Description
1	First visit/personal safety	Introduction of DARE and law enforcement officer safety practices; discussion of personal rights
2	Drug use and misuse	Harmful effects from misuse of drugs
3	Consequences	Consequences of using and choosing not to use alcohol, marijuana, and other drugs
4	Resisting pressures	Sources of pressure, types of pressure to use drugs
5	Resistance techniques	Refusal strategies for different types of peer pressure
6	Building self-esteem	Identifying positive qualities in oneself; giving/receiving compliments; importance of self-image
7	Assertiveness	Personal rights/responsibilities discussion; situations calling for assertiveness skills
8	Managing stress without drugs	Identification of sources of stress; when stress can be helpful or harmful; ways to manage stress; deep-breathing exercise
9	Media influences	Media influences on behavior; advertising techniques
10	Decision making and risk taking	Risk-taking behaviors; reasonable and harmful risks; consequences of various choices; influences on decisions
11	Drug use alternatives	Reasons for using drugs; alternative activities
12	Role modeling	Meet older student leaders/role models who do not use drugs
13	Forming support system	Types of support groups; barriers to friendships; suggestions to overcoming barriers to forming friendships
14	Ways to deal with gang pressures	Types of gang pressure; how gangs differ from groups; consequences of gang activity
15	D.A.R.E. summary	D.A.R.E. review
16	Taking a stand	Taking appropriate stand when pressured to use drugs
17	D.A.R.E. culmination	Award assembly: recognition of participants

Note: D.A.R.E. = Drug Abuse Resistance Education.

such criticism given rampant problems with internal validity. Most evaluations have been posttest-only designs; that is, the survey instrument is administered for the first time after students have participated in the program. Some of these ex post facto evaluations did not include any type of control group. Many of these evaluations reached conclusions that were favorable to D.A.R.E., some on the basis of responses to as few as five survey items. The limitations of these

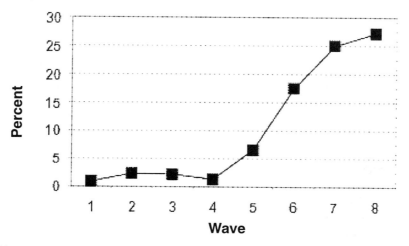

FIGURE 1 *Marijuana use: Past 30 days.*

studies are too numerous to be listed here, but clearly, the observed differences may be the result of self-selection processes (or other pre-existing differences) rather than the D.A.R.E. program.

There have been several D.A.R.E. evaluations that could be classified as "quasi-experimental." Three used pretest-posttest designs without a control group, and two of those were also flawed by survey instruments of the type used in the weakest of the ex post facto evaluations. A larger number of quasi-experimental evaluations have sufficient scientific integrity to allow estimates of causal effects. These quasi-experimental studies produced more modest assessments of D.A.R.E. than the weaker evaluations. They uncovered fairly consistent short-term effects of D.A.R.E. on mediating variables such as knowledge, attitudes, and social skills but provided little evidence of D.A.R.E.'s impact on drug use behaviors.

The strongest design used to assess D.A.R.E. (with the fewest threats to validity) is the randomized experiment. Only a few evaluations have used experimental designs with sufficiently large sample sizes and repeated measurement over 1 or more years. These studies clearly indicate that D.A.R.E.'s positive effects on students tend to dissipate over time. D.A.R.E. has its largest short-term benefits on

students' knowledge about drugs, but statistically significant positive effects have also been observed for social skills, drug-related attitudes, attitudes toward the police, and, less frequently, self-esteem. The effects on drug use behaviors are often small and nonsignificant, although significant short-term reductions in tobacco use have been noted on more than one occasion. The literature of D.A.R.E.'s effectiveness as a drug prevention strategy can be summarized in this way: The stronger the research design, the less impact researchers have reported on drug use measures.

One of the major limitations of even the best D.A.R.E. evaluations is the short lag between pretest and posttest. Despite the growth in the number of D.A.R.E. studies, surprisingly few are longitudinal in nature. Most of the stronger studies have examined program effects immediately after students participated in D.A.R.E.; a few have looked at 1-year and 2-year outcomes. Given the relatively low base rates for drug use at the ages of 11 or 12 (when D.A.R.E. is introduced), short time lags between pretest and posttest measurement can severely restrict the opportunity to detect preventive effects.

Figure 1 captures the essence of this problem: Most of the students in the present study entered high school at Wave 5 of the survey. This is the point at which marijuana use within the past

30 days, for example, begins to rise dramatically, from 2.5% of those surveyed at Wave 4 to more than 25% at Wave 8. D.A.R.E. is typically administered in sixth grade, well in advance of the steep rise in usage patterns common to most substances. Thus, a real test of program effectiveness must extend to the age group where opportunities for drug use are substantial; otherwise, there will be a ceiling or upper limit on the dependent variable.

Prior D.A.R.E. research has virtually ignored the possible effects of supplemental (i.e., post-D.A.R.E.) drug education during the middle school and high school years. School-based drug prevention is now mandatory in many states, including Illinois, where this study was conducted. This post-D.A.R.E. instruction could have the effect of contaminating the control group and confounding the effects of the treatment.

METHODOLOGY

The Illinois D.A.R.E. evaluation was conducted as a randomized field experiment with one pretest and multiple planned posttests. The researchers identified 18 pairs of elementary schools representing urban, suburban, and rural areas in Illinois. Schools were matched in each pair by type, ethnic composition, number of students with limited English proficiency, and the percentage of students from low-income families. None of these schools had previously received D.A.R.E. For the 12 pairs of schools located in urban and suburban areas, one school in each pair was randomly assigned to receive D.A.R.E. in the spring of 1990; the remaining schools were placed in the control group. For each of the remaining 6 pairs, all in rural communities, a nonrandom assignment process was necessary due to logistic considerations that affect the availability of D.A.R.E. officers. The remaining six "treatment" schools were selected from rural areas in which D.A.R.E. officers were already assigned, and six more control schools were then selected from nearby counties or in the same county. The same

matching variables were used for all schools in the study.

Two types of surveys were administered each year over the 6 years of data collection: one for students and one for specific teachers. The purpose of the student survey was to determine D.A.R.E.'s overall effects on students' beliefs, attitudes, and behaviors related to drug use. The student survey data are the primary focus of this longitudinal evaluation. The teacher survey provided additional information to assess the extent of students' exposure to post-D.A.R.E. drug prevention programs during each current academic year.

Recruitment of Schools and Students

Two waves of data (pre-post) were collected from the 36 schools in the first year (1989–1990). In the second year (Wave 3, 1991), when students left these elementary schools and entered middle school, the recruitment process was repeated with about 150 schools. In the third year and beyond, as students continued to move, transfer, and graduate, the number of schools in the sample fluctuated between 150 and 300. For the 1992–1993 academic year, most students of the evaluation sample entered high school for the first time, which required the research team to develop relationships with an entirely new group of school officials.

Similar to the initial procedure, letters were mailed to all high school superintendents and principals from the existing sample of schools, informing them of students' prior participation in the study, seeking their cooperation, requesting verification of enrollment, and explaining the research procedures. With all the transience in the sample, the research staff was continually making contacts with representatives from new schools. A financial inducement to participate in the study was offered to major schools, depending on the number of students participating from their school and the level of cooperation obtained. In each school, eligible students were those who had participated in the Wave 1 survey in 1989.

Changes in the Evaluation

Two issues emerged in the drug education literature during the course of this evaluation. First, there was the possible "contaminating" influence of students being exposed to additional drug education programs in the years following their participation in D.A.R.E. Evaluators inevitably face "multiple treatment interference" as they attempt to estimate the effects of D.A.R.E. in the context of subjects' exposure to other types of drug education. With the rapid growth of drug education in recent years (including the enactment of legislation requiring that schools teach drug education), students in both the experimental (D.A.R.E.) group and the control group were frequently given some additional drug prevention education in subsequent years. To the extent that these supplemental programs had some favorable impact on students, they may have equalized the two groups on drug-related outcomes and therefore biased the evaluation findings in favor of the null hypothesis (i.e., increase the likelihood of finding no difference between the experimental and control groups). The reverse outcome is also possible. With additional survey work, we were able to develop a cumulative index of a student's exposure to supplemental drug education programs over several years. This measure also allowed us to test the "booster" hypothesis, namely, that additional drug education programs at the middle school and high school levels will boost or reinforce the antidrug messages and skills received in the D.A.R.E. program, and that this consistent reinforcement will make a difference in drug use behaviors during the years of greatest opportunity and pressure.

A second issue concerns the proper approach to data analysis. As noted earlier, statisticians now recommend that school-level effects be assessed when analyzing data collected from students representing multiple school settings. There is now considerable support for this argument among statisticians and other methodologists, who have developed new statistical programs for conducting multilevel analysis. Furthermore, a time frame that carries well beyond the "nesting" of students in their original elementary schools, and involves a multiwave posttest analysis, is more likely to need some means of controlling for the difference between students who have been surveyed at all waves and those who dropped out or were absent at one or more waves.

RESULTS

Characteristics of the Student Sample

The results reported here are based on the combined sample of students surveyed at all waves. About two thirds of the students were in sixth grade at the time of Wave 1 data collection (with the remainder in fifth grade). Approximately 6 of 10 students indicated that they were living with both parents in the same household at all waves. Slightly more than half (52%) were exposed to D.A.R.E. in the spring of 1990, whereas the remaining students were assigned to the control group. Attrition over the 6 years was most noticeable among the urban and African American samples.

MERGING WAVES

Data from the seven posttest surveys were merged. The analysis strategy involved a level and trend comparison of the D.A.R.E. and control groups across all posttest waves. Cases were sorted by student identification number so that there would be up to seven observations per student, with each observation representing a different wave of posttest data.

Before adding each wave to the composite data set, a "time" variable was created, with all the observations for a particular wave receiving the same time value. After merging the seven posttest waves, the time variable was recoded so that Wave 2 was Time 0, Wave 3 was Time 1, and so on up to Wave 8 or Time 6. The time variable was the basis for determining the existence of significant changes in attitudes or drug usage over time and of controlling for this trend in the comparison of D.A.R.E. group and control group responses.

Effects on Hypothesized Mediating Variables

We tested the hypothesis that D.A.R.E. would have a sustained effect on the variables that are assumed to mediate the relationship between drug education and drug use, namely, students' attitudes, beliefs, and social skills pertaining to drug use. On the whole, the results did not support this hypothesis. When controlling for changes in these variables over time and for changes in cumulative exposure to supplemental drug education, only one significant D.A.R.E. effect remained. Specifically, students who participated in D.A.R.E. were more likely than students in the control group to report awareness of media efforts to make beer appear attractive.

Although not posited as a mediating variable, we also examined the impact of D.A.R.E. on violence and delinquency prevention. Our Delinquency Index, which measures incidents of theft, vandalism, and/or participation in group violence, showed change over time in the desired direction but not as a result of D.A.R.E. Also, a separate analysis of individual and group violence revealed no D.A.R.E. effects. Previous evidence that African American students reported less group violence after D.A.R.E. was no longer statistically significant.

In addition, we examined the hypothesis that D.A.R.E. would be able to improve academic performance. Self-reported grades, on a scale of 1 (below D) to 8 (mostly A's), were used to measure academic performance. Although the trend was favorable, the overall results did not support this hypothesis.

D.A.R.E. also appears to have differential subgroup effects. Curiously, D.A.R.E. has been less effective in communicating the costs associated with alcohol and cigarette use to African American participants but more effective in helping this group recognize media attempts to promote beer and cigarettes. Hispanic D.A.R.E. graduates had a significantly lower delinquency score than the reference group. D.A.R.E. appears to have had the desired effect of enhancing self-esteem and one's perceived ability to resist peer pressure in urban and rural areas but appears to have had negligible or counterproductive effects in suburban areas. Suburban D.A.R.E. graduates also had a significantly higher delinquency score than non-D.A.R.E. suburban students.

Effects on Drug Use

We tested the hypothesis that D.A.R.E. would have a sustained preventive effect on drug use behaviors. All analyses of drug use activity had to control for the reality of increased usage over time, as well as for dramatic shifts in level and rate of increase during the high school years (Grades 9-12). Students moving into and through the high school years provided the most powerful explanation for the increases in drug use beginning at Wave 5, Grade 9 for most students.

The results provide no support for the drug prevention hypothesis. After controlling for the effect of the high school years (Grades 9-12) and supplemental drug education, we found that D.A.R.E. had no significant impact on any of the four primary drug use scales. That is, students who participated in D.A.R.E. were no different from students in the control group with regard to their recent and lifetime use of drugs and alcohol.

There were few differences in D.A.R.E.'s impact on drug use across different communities. The only significant subgroup effect occurred with suburban D.A.R.E. students. Suburban students who participated in D.A.R.E. reported significantly higher rates of drug use on all four composite indexes than suburban students who did not participate in the program. Controlling for cumulative exposure to supplemental drug education reduced the probability value to marginally significant ($p < .10$) for three of the four measures, leaving untouched the apparent adverse effect on the Lifetime Total Drug Use index. We emphasize that the effect sizes are small. Suburban participation in D.A.R.E. is associated with an increased level of drug use of 3 to 5 percentage points on average, depending on the type of drug.

To rule out the possibility that D.A.R.E. might be having beneficial effects on specific types of drugs or alcohol (e.g., cigarette smoking) but not on composite indicators, we conducted a series of statistical tests on individual drug use items. The results are consistent with the previous analyses and provide no support for the hypothesis that D.A.R.E. would have a sustained preventive impact on specific types of drug use.

Finally, we tested the hypothesis that D.A.R.E. could delay the onset of drinking alcohol—measures believed to be important as students reached high school. The study measured the age at which students first "got drunk" and started having "at least one drink at least once a month." Students in the control group first got drunk and started drinking regularly between the ages of 14 and 15. The effect of D.A.R.E. on these two measures was not statistically significant. These small changes were in the positive direction for delaying the onset of getting drunk and in the negative direction for delaying regular drinking.

SUMMARY AND CONCLUSIONS

We believe the findings from this study are especially important given the centrality of D.A.R.E. to the national drug control policies of the United States and dozens of other countries. These results are also noteworthy because of the paucity of controlled longitudinal studies that can answer the most fundamental question: Can this popular school-based program prevent drug use at the stage in adolescent development when drugs become available and are widely used, namely, during the high school years? Unfortunately, the answer to this question is "No." Specifically, the main finding is that levels of drug use (using a variety of measures and analyses) did not differ as a function of whether students participated in D.A.R.E. This outcome confirms the results of previous controlled evaluations and goes further to provide an extended test of the D.A.R.E. hypothesis. Across many settings and research projects, D.A.R.E. has

been unable to show consistent preventive effects on drug use, and the observed effects have been small in size and short lived.

D.A.R.E. advocates argue that the null findings from this research provide evidence that more D.A.R.E. programming (not less) is needed at the junior high and high school levels to reinforce the lessons of the not-so-effective core program. Whether police officers can be effective with older students, who show considerably less respect for authority, is uncertain. Hence, there is a compelling need to evaluate these D.A.R.E. and other booster programs before widespread implementation. Unfortunately, the practice of school-based drug education at these higher grade levels is dismal (despite the availability of promising prototype programs), which may partially account for the observed positive correlation between supplemental drug education and drug use. However, self-selection is a simpler and more plausible explanation for this finding, suggesting that schools experiencing larger drug problems are more likely to initiate drug education programs. In any event, our data suggest that these cumulative prevention efforts are, at best, ineffective at combating the dramatic rise in drug use as youths become older.

The present study found that D.A.R.E. had the most beneficial effects on urban children and the fewest beneficial effects on suburban children. In fact, we found some evidence of a possible boomerang effect among suburban kids. That is, suburban students who were D.A.R.E. graduates scored higher than suburban students in the control group on all four major drug use measures. Because schools were carefully matched and then randomly assigned within the same suburban communities, we are doubtful that these effects can be explained by factors such as sampling or other design issues.

Collectively, these findings suggest that it may be time to reexamine our drug prevention policies and practices. Our society, searching for a silver bullet or a panacea to the drug problem, has expected far too much from a single program. Compounding the problem, parents, educators, and police officers have confused program popularity with program effectiveness. Drug prevention experts, both researchers and practitioners, have worked closely with the federal government to outline many of the key components of effective prevention strategies, and this dialogue is continuing. Whether these research-based prototypes can be implemented and sustained on a large scale, producing consistently favorable results under real-world conditions, remains an empirical question.

QUESTIONS FOR DISCUSSION AND WRITING

1. Why are most of the outcome evaluations of the core D.A.R.E. curriculum of limited scientific value? How can the literature of D.A.R.E.'s effectiveness as a drug prevention strategy be summarized?
2. What variables are assumed to mediate the relationship between drug education and drug use, and what happened when the authors tested the hypothesis that D.A.R.E. would have a sustained effect on those variables? What happened when the authors examined the impact of D.A.R.E. on violence and delinquency prevention?
3. What happened when the authors tested the hypothesis that D.A.R.E. would have a sustained preventative effect on drug use behaviors?

OPPORTUNITY, STRAIN, AND REHABILITATION/ REINTEGRATION

One of the most popular and influential theories of juvenile delinquency, commonly referred to as "opportunity" or "strain" theory, was derived from Merton's monumental "anomie" theory of deviance, including crime. This is a "structural" perspective, which proposes that the social class structure is responsible for producing the motivation to engage in delinquency, particularly among lower-class youths. It is based on the commonsense notion that "the end justifies the means." If you want something bad enough, you may do something bad to get it—that is, if you cannot get it by using appropriate, legitimate, or legal means, you will get it by using whatever means are necessary, including inappropriate, illegitimate, or illegal means. In Merton's original expression of the theory, the "end" is the paramount goal of "pecuniary success" as achieved in the occupational and economic marketplace.

The "differential opportunity" theory of Cloward and Ohlin, as described by Cloward in "Illegitimate Means, Anomie, and Deviant Behavior," is one of the first integrated theories of juvenile delinquency. Because Cloward was a student of Merton at Columbia University, and Ohlin had similar ties to criminologists at the University of Chicago, their collaboration led to the merger—or integration—of two major theoretical perspectives: first, the structural emphasis of "anomie" theory and, second, the social ecological emphasis on the influences of community organization and culture on delinquent behavior. They propose that lower-class youths are more likely to experience blocked opportunities, become frustrated, and look for other ways to get what they want. However, they propose that there is also an "illegitimate" opportunity structure that may be differentially available to youths who are motivated to get involved in delinquency.

Depending on the type of community organization that exists in the neighborhood, there are different types of illegal opportunities available to potential juvenile delinquents. Not only that, but the type of community organization determines in good part what kinds of gangs and delinquent subcultures are typical. In "organized" communities, where there is an integration of age-levels of offenders and of conventional and criminal values (i.e., there is an illegitimate opportunity structure), "criminal" gangs engaged in rational, money-making criminal enterprise, supported by a criminal delinquent subculture, are typical. In "disorganized" communities (i.e., there is not an illegitimate opportunity structure), "conflict" gangs that are more oriented toward irrational violence, supported by a conflict-oriented delinquent subculture, are typical. Last, in either organized or disorganized communities, there may be some youngsters who cannot make it in either the legitimate or illegitimate opportunity structures, and these "double failures" may withdraw, escape, or "retreat" into substance abuse.

Agnew has more recently proposed a social psychological version, "A Revised Strain Theory of Delinquency." The revised theory focuses on yet another source of frustration, blocked opportunities to avoid painful or aversive environments or contexts, for example, a dysfunctional family or negative school experiences. The blockage of legitimate "pain-avoidance" behavior produces the frustration that motivates a youth to engage in illegal acts to escape or attack the sources of the pain. The analysis of data collected from a national sample lends some support to the theory. These findings may be important to this theoretical tradition because, as Agnew points out, there is generally weak support for more traditional opportunity and strain theories.

Even though the empirical evidence may call into question the validity of opportunity theory, it has had a profound impact on policy and practice in the area of delinquency prevention and control. In fact, as Short points out in "The Natural History of an Applied Theory: Differential Opportunity and 'Mobilization for Youth,'" the differential opportunity theory of Cloward and Ohlin was developed hand-in-hand with a massive delinquency prevention program in New York designed to, as one would infer from the theory, open opportunities for disadvantaged youth, especially in the areas of employment and education. This is an example of theory and practice influencing each other simultaneously. The links between the ideas and policy were so tight that Ohlin was appointed to an important position in the federal government to expand "equal opportunity" programs throughout the United States.

"The Provo Experiment in Delinquency Rehabilitation," as described by Empey and Rabow, attempted to rehabilitate persistent juvenile offenders based on two of the main ideas of opportunity theory: First, delinquency is group behavior, anchored in a delinquent subculture, and second, because of their lower-class origins, delinquents have limited access to success goals. Therefore, rehabilitation should focus on guiding group processes toward "legal" collective solutions to problems of adjustment and on providing employment opportunities and the social and behavioral skills to succeed in making the best of them. In addition, for juveniles to stay out of trouble after they complete a "program," organized efforts to facilitate positive reintegration back into the community, family, school, and peer groups must be made. In the Provo Experiment, ties between the juvenile and the treatment program were maintained after release by periodic return visits to the guided group sessions. This kind of aftercare, maintenance, or follow-up was considered an essential component of the project. In fact, most delinquency projects do not attend to the problems of reintegration, and as a consequence kids return to their old haunts, street partners, dysfunctional families, and negative school experiences—all of the things that got them into trouble in the first place and will likely get them into trouble again.

Illegitimate Means, Anomie, and Deviant Behavior

RICHARD A. CLOWARD

THIS paper represents an attempt to consolidate two major sociological traditions of thought about the problem of deviant behavior. The first, exemplified by the work of Emile Durkheim and Robert K. Merton, may be called the anomie tradition. The second, illustrated principally by the studies of Clifford R. Shaw, Henry D. McKay, and Edwin H. Sutherland, may be called the "cultural transmission" and "differential association" tradition. Despite some reciprocal borrowing of ideas, these intellectual traditions developed more or less independently. By seeking to consolidate them, a more adequate theory of deviant behavior may be constructed.

DIFFERENTIALS IN AVAILABILITY OF LEGITIMATE MEANS: THE THEORY OF ANOMIE

The theory of anomie has undergone two major phases of development. Durkheim first used the concept to explain deviant behavior. He focussed on the way in which various social conditions lead to "overweening ambition," and how, in turn, unlimited aspirations ultimately produce a breakdown in regulatory norms. Merton has systematized and extended the theory, directing attention to patterns of disjunction between culturally prescribed goals

From "Illegitimate Means, Anomie, and Deviant Behavior" by R. A. Cloward, 1959, *American Sociological Review*, 24, p. 164. Reprinted by permission.

and socially organized access to them by *legitimate* means. In this paper, a third phase is outlined. An additional variable is incorporated in the developing scheme of anomie, namely, the concept of *differentials in access to success-goals by illegitimate means.*

Disjunction Between Cultural Goals and Socially Structured Opportunity

Durkheim's description of the emergence of "overweening ambition" and the subsequent breakdown of regulatory norms constitutes one of the links between his work and the later development of the theory by Merton. In his classic essay, "Social Structure and Anomie," Merton suggests that goals and norms may vary independently of each other, and that this sometimes leads to malintegrated states. In his view, two polar types of disjunction may occur.

Of the two kinds of malintegrated societies, Merton is primarily interested in the one in which "there is an exceptionally strong emphasis upon specific goals without a corresponding emphasis upon institutional procedures." He states that attenuation between goals and norms, leading to anomie or "normlessness," comes about because men in such societies internalize an emphasis on common success-goals under conditions of varying access to them. The essence of this hypothesis is captured in the following excerpt:

It is only when a system of cultural values extols, virtually above all else, certain *common* success-goals for the population at large while the social structure rigorously restricts or completely closes access to approved modes of reaching these goals *for a considerable part of the same population,* that deviant behavior ensues on a large scale.

The focus, in short, is on the way in which the social structure puts a strain upon the cultural structure. Here one may point to diverse structural differentials in access to culturally approved goals by legitimate means, for example, differentials of age, sex, ethnic status, and social class. Pressures for anomie or normlessness vary from one social position to another, depending on the nature of these differentials.

In summary, Merton extends the theory of anomie in two principal ways. He explicitly identifies types of anomic or malintegrated societies by focusing on the relationship between cultural goals and norms. Also, by directing attention to patterned differentials in the access to success-goals by legitimate means, he shows how the social structure exerts a strain upon the cultural structure, leading in turn to anomie or normlessness.

The Concept of Illegitimate Means

Once processes generating differentials in pressures are identified, there is then the question of how these pressures are resolved, or how men respond to them. In this connection, Merton enumerates five basic categories of behavior or role adaptations which are likely to emerge: conformity, innovation, ritualism, retreatism, and rebellion. These adaptations differ depending on the individual's acceptance or rejection of cultural goals, and depending on his adherence to or violation of institutional norms. Furthermore, Merton sees the distribution of these adaptations principally as the consequence of two variables: the relative extent of pressure, and values, particularly "internalized prohibitions," governing the use of various illegitimate means.

It is a familiar sociological idea that values serve to order the choices of deviant (as well as conforming) adaptations which develop under conditions of stress. Comparative studies of ethnic groups, for example, have shown that some tend to engage in distinctive forms of deviance; thus, Jews exhibit low rates of alcoholism and alcoholic psychoses. Various investigators have suggested that the emphasis on rationality, fear of expressing aggression, and other alleged components of the "Jewish" value system constrain modes of deviance which involve "loss of control" over behavior. In contrast, the Irish show a much higher rate of alcoholic deviance because, it has been argued, their cultural emphasis on masculinity encourages the excessive use of alcohol under conditions of strain.

Merton suggests that differing rates of ritualistic and innovating behavior in the middle and lower classes result from differential emphases in socialization. The "rule-oriented" accent in middle-class socialization presumably disposes persons to handle stress by engaging in ritualistic rather than innovating behavior. The lower-class person, contrastingly, having internalized less stringent norms, can violate conventions with less guilt and anxiety. Values, in other words, exercise a canalizing influence, limiting the choice of deviant adaptations for persons variously distributed throughout the social system.

Apart from both socially patterned pressures, which give rise to deviance, and from values, which determine choices of adaptations, a further variable should be taken into account: namely, *differentials in availability of illegitimate means.* For example, the notion that innovating behavior may result from unfulfilled aspirations and imperfect socialization with respect to conventional norms implies that illegitimate means are freely available—as if the individual, having decided that "you can't make it legitimately," then simply turns to illegitimate means which are readily at hand whatever his position in the social structure. However, these means may not be available. As noted above, the anomie theory assumes that conventional means are differentially distributed, that some individuals, because of their social position, enjoy certain advantages which are denied to others. Note, for example, variations in the degree to which members of various classes are fully exposed to and thus acquire the values, education, and skills which facilitate upward mobility. It should not be startling, therefore, to find similar variations in the availability of illegitimate means.

Several sociologists have alluded to such variations without explicitly incorporating this variable in a theory of deviant behavior. Sutherland, for example, writes that "an inclination to steal is not a sufficient explanation of the genesis of the professional thief." Moreover, "the person must be appreciated by the professional thieves. He must be appraised as having an adequate equipment of wits, front, talking-ability, honesty, reliability, nerve, and determination." In short, "a person can be a professional thief only if he is recognized and received as such by other professional thieves." But recognition is not freely accorded:

Selection and tutelage are the two necessary elements in the process of acquiring recognition as a professional thief. . . . A person cannot acquire recognition as a professional thief until he has had tutelage in professional theft, *and tutelage is given only to a few persons selected from the total population.*

Furthermore, the aspirant is judged by high standards of performance, for only "a very small percentage of those who start on this process ever reach the stage of professional theft." The burden of these remarks—dealing with the processes of selection, induction, and assumption of full status in the criminal group—is that motivations or pressures toward deviance do not fully account for deviant behavior. The "self-made" thief—lacking knowledge of the ways of securing immunity from prosecution and similar techniques of defense—"would quickly land in prison." Sutherland is in effect pointing to differentials in access to the role of professional thief. Although the criteria of selection are not altogether clear from his analysis, definite evaluative standards do appear to exist; depending on their content, certain categories of individuals would be placed at a disadvantage and others would be favored.

The availability of illegitimate means, then, is controlled by various criteria in the same manner that has long been ascribed to conventional means. Both systems of opportunity are (a) limited, rather than infinitely available, and (b) differentially available depending on the location of persons in the social structure.

When we employ the term *means*, whether legitimate or illegitimate, at least two things are implied: First, that there are appropriate learning environments for the acquisition of the values and skills associated with the performance of a particular role; and second, that the individual has opportunities to discharge the role once he has been prepared. The term subsumes, therefore, both *learning structures* and *opportunity structures.*

A case in point is recruitment and preparation for careers in the rackets. There are fertile criminal learning environments for the young in neighborhoods where the rackets flourish as stable, indigenous institutions. Because these environments afford integration of offenders of different ages, the young are exposed to "differential associations" which facilitate the acquisition of criminal values and skills. Yet preparation for the role may not ensure that the individual will ever discharge it. For one thing, more youngsters may be recruited into these patterns of differential association than can possibly be absorbed, following their "training," by the adult criminal structure. There may be a surplus of contenders for these elite positions, leading in turn to the necessity for criteria and mechanisms of selection. Hence a certain proportion of those who aspire may not be permitted to engage in the behavior for which they have been prepared.

This distinction between learning structures and opportunity structures was suggested some years ago by Sutherland. In 1944, he circulated an unpublished paper which briefly discusses the proposition that "criminal behavior is partially a function of opportunities to commit specific classes of crimes, such as embezzlement, bank burglary, or illicit heterosexual intercourse." He did not, however, take up the problem of differentials in opportunity as a concept to be systematically incorporated in a theory of deviant behavior. Instead, he held that "opportunity" is a necessary but not sufficient explanation of the commission of criminal acts, "since some persons who have opportunities to embezzle, become intoxicated, engage in illicit heterosexual intercourse or to commit other crimes do not do so." He also noted that the differential association theory did not constitute a full explanation of criminal activity, for, notwithstanding differential association, "it is axiomatic that persons who commit a specific crime must have the opportunity to commit that crime." He therefore concluded that "while opportunity may be partially a function of association with criminal patterns and of the specialized techniques thus acquired, *it is not determined entirely in that manner* [italics added], and consequently differential association is not the sufficient cause of criminal behavior."

In Sutherland's statements, two meanings are attributed to the term *opportunity*. As suggested above, it may be useful to separate these for analytical purposes. In the first sense, Sutherland appears to be saying that opportunity consists in part of learning structures. The principal components of his theory of differential association are that "criminal behavior is learned," and, furthermore, that "criminal behavior is learned in interaction with other persons in a process of communication." But he also uses the term to describe situations conducive to carrying out criminal roles. Thus, for Sutherland, the commission of a criminal act would seem to depend on the existence of two conditions: differential associations favoring the acquisition of criminal values and skills, and conditions encouraging participation in criminal activity.

This distinction heightens the importance of identifying and questioning the common assumption that illegitimate means are freely available. We can now ask (a) whether there are socially structured differentials in access to illegitimate learning environments, and (b) whether there are differentials limiting the fulfillment of illegitimate roles. If differentials exist and can be identified, we may then inquire about their consequences for the behavior of persons in different parts of the social structure. Before pursuing this question, however, we turn to a fuller discussion of the theoretical tradition established by Shaw, McKay, and Sutherland.

DIFFERENTIALS IN AVAILABILITY OF ILLEGITIMATE MEANS: THE SUBCULTURE TRADITION

The concept of differentials in availability of illegitimate means is implicit in one of the major streams of American criminological theory. In this tradition, attention is focused on the processes by which persons are recruited into criminal learning environments and ultimately inducted into criminal roles. The problems here are to account for the acquisition of criminal roles and to describe the social organization of criminal activities. When the theoretical propositions contained in this tradition are reanalyzed, it becomes clear that one underlying conception is that of variations in access to success-goals by illegitimate means. Furthermore, this implicit concept may be shown to be one of the bases on which the tradition was constructed.

In their studies of the ecology of deviant behavior in the urban environment, Shaw and McKay found that delinquency and crime tended to be confined to delimited areas and, furthermore, that such behavior persisted despite demographic changes in these areas. Hence they came to speak of "criminal tradition," of the "cultural transmission" of criminal values. As a result of their observations of slum life, they concluded that *particular importance must be assigned to the integration of different age-levels of offenders*. Thus,

Stealing in the neighborhood was a common practice among the children and approved by the parents. Whenever the boys got together they talked about robbing and made more plans for stealing. I hardly knew any boys who did not go robbing. The little fellows went in for petty stealing, breaking into freight cars, and stealing junk. The older guys did big jobs like stick-up, burglary, and stealing autos. The little fellows admired the "big shots" and longed for the day when they could get into the big racket. Fellows who had "done time" were the big shots and looked up to and gave the little fellow tips on how to get by and pull off big jobs.

In other words, access to criminal roles depends on stable associations with others from whom the necessary values and skills may be learned. Shaw and McKay were describing deviant learning structures—that is, alternative routes by which people seek access to the goals which society holds to be worthwhile. They might also have pointed out that, in areas where such learning structures are unavailable, it is probably difficult for many individuals to secure access to stable criminal careers, even though motivated to do so.

The concept of illegitimate means and the socially structured conditions of access to them were not explicitly recognized in the work of Shaw and McKay because, probably, they were disposed to view slum areas as "disorganized." Although they consistently referred to illegitimate activities as being organized, they nevertheless often depicted high-rate delinquency areas as disorganized because the values transmitted were criminal rather than conventional. Hence their work includes statements which we now perceive to be internally inconsistent, such as the following:

This community situation [in which Sidney was reared] was not only disorganized and thus ineffective as a unit of control, but it was characterized by a high rate of juvenile delinquency and adult crime, not to mention the widespread political corruption which had

long existed in the area. Various forms of stealing and many organized delinquent and criminal gangs were prevalent in the area. These groups exercised a powerful influence and tended to create a community spirit which not only tolerated but actually fostered delinquent and criminal practices.

Sutherland was among the first to perceive that the concept of social disorganization tended to obscure the stable patterns of interaction among carriers of criminal values. Like Shaw and McKay, he had been influenced by the observation that lower-class areas were organized in terms of both conventional and criminal values, but he was also impressed that these alternative value systems were supported by patterned systems of social relations. He expressly recognized that crime, far from being a random, unorganized activity, was typically an intricate and stable system of human arrangements. He therefore rejected the concept of "social disorganization" and substituted the concept of "differential group organization."

Having freed observation of the urban slum from conventional evaluations, Sutherland was able to focus more clearly on the way in which its social structure constitutes a "learning environment" for the acquisition of deviant values and skills. In the development of the theory of "differential association" and "differential group organization," he came close to stating explicitly the concept of differentials in access to illegitimate means. But Sutherland was essentially interested in learning processes, and thus he did not ask how such access varies in different parts of the social structure, nor did he inquire about the consequences for behavior of variations in the accessibility of these means.

The description of the organization of illegitimate means in slums is further developed by Solomon Kobrin in his article, "The Conflict of Values in Delinquency Areas." Kobrin suggests that urban slum areas vary in the degree to which the carriers of deviant and conventional values are integrated with one another. Hence he points the way to the development of a "typology of delinquency areas based on variations in the relationship between these two systems," depicting the "polar types" on such a continuum. The first type resembles the integrated areas described in preceding paragraphs. Here, claims Kobrin, there is not merely structural integration between carriers of the two value systems, but reciprocal participation by each in the value system of the other. Thus,

Leaders of [illegal] enterprises frequently maintain membership in such conventional institutions of their local communities as churches, fraternal and mutual benefit societies, and political parties. . . . Within this framework the influence of each of the two value systems is reciprocal, the leaders of illegal enterprise participating in the primary orientation of the conventional elements in the population, and the latter, through their participation in a local power structure sustained in large part by illicit activity, participating perforce in the alternate, criminal value system.

Kobrin also notes that in some urban slums there is a tendency for the relationships between carriers of deviant and conventional values to break down. Such areas constitute the second polar type. Because of disorganizing forces such as "drastic change in the class, ethnic, or racial characteristics of its population," Kobrin suggests that "the bearers of the conventional culture and its value system are without the customary institutional machinery and therefore in effect partially demobilized with reference to the diffusion of their value system." At the same time, the criminal "value system remains implicit" since this type of area is "characterized principally by the absence of systematic and organized adult activity in violation of the law, despite the fact that many adults in these areas commit violations." Since both value systems remain implicit, the possibilities for effective integration are precluded.

The importance of these observations may be seen if we ask how accessibility of illegal means varies with the relative integration of conventional and criminal values from one type of area to another. In this connection, Kobrin points out that the "integrated" area apparently constitutes a "training ground" for the acquisition of criminal values and skills.

The stable position of illicit enterprise in the adult society of the community is reflected in the character of delinquent conduct on the part of children. While delinquency in all high rate areas is intrinsically disorderly in that it is unrelated to official programs for the education of the young, in the [integrated community] boys may more or less realistically recognize the potentialities for personal progress in local society through access to delinquency. In a general way, therefore, delinquent activity in these areas constitutes a training ground for the acquisition of skill in the use of violence, concealment of offense, evasion of detection and arrest, and the purchase of immunity from punishment. Those who come to excel in these respects are frequently noted and valued by adult leaders in the rackets who are confronted, as are the leaders of all income-producing enterprises, with problems of the recruitment of competent personnel.

With respect to the contrasting or "unintegrated area," Kobrin makes no mention of the extent to which learning structures and opportunities for criminal careers are available. Yet his portrayal of such areas as lacking in the articulation of either conventional or criminal values suggests that the appropriate learning structures—principally the integration of offenders of different age levels—are not available. Furthermore, his depiction of adult violative activity as "unorganized" suggests that the illegal opportunity structure is severely limited. Even if youngsters were able to secure adequate preparation for criminal roles, the problem would appear to be that the social structure of such neighborhoods provides few opportunities for stable, criminal careers. For Kobrin's analysis—as well as those of Whyte and others before him—leads to the conclusion that illegal opportunity structures tend to emerge in lower-class areas only when stable patterns of accommodation and integration arise between the carriers of conventional and deviant values. Where these values remain unorganized and implicit, or where their carriers are in open conflict, opportunities for stable criminal role performance are more or less limited.

Other factors may be cited which affect access to criminal roles. For example, there is a good deal of anecdotal evidence which reveals that access to the upper echelons of organized racketeering is controlled, at least in part, by ethnicity. It has also been noted that kinship criteria sometimes govern access to stable criminal roles, as in the case of the pickpocket. And there are, of course, deep-rooted sex differentials in access to illegal means. Although women are often employed in criminal vocations—for example, thievery, confidence games, and extortion—and must be employed in others—such as prostitution—nevertheless females are excluded from many criminal activities.

Of the various criteria governing access to illegitimate means, class differentials may be among the most important. The differentials noted in the preceding paragraph—age, sex ethnicity, kinship, and the like—all pertain to criminal activity historically associated with the lower class. Most middle- or upper-class persons—even when interested in following "lower-class" criminal careers—would no doubt have difficulty in fulfilling this ambition because of inappropriate preparation. The prerequisite attitudes and skills are more easily acquired if the individual is a member of the lower class; most middle- and upper-class persons could not easily unlearn their own class culture in order to learn a new one. By the same token, access to many "white-collar" criminal roles is closed to lower-class persons. Some occupations afford abundant opportunities to engage in illegitimate activity; others offer virtually none. The businessman, for example, not only has at his disposal the means to do so, but, as some studies have shown, he is under persistent pressure to employ illegitimate means, if only to maintain a competitive advantage in the marketplace. But for those in many other occupa-

tions, white-collar modes of criminal activity are simply not an alternative.

SOME IMPLICATIONS OF A CONSOLIDATED APPROACH TO DEVIANT BEHAVIOR

It is now possible to consolidate the two sociological traditions described above. Our analysis makes it clear that these traditions are oriented to different aspects of the same problem: differentials in access to opportunity. One tradition focuses on legitimate opportunity, the other on illegitimate. By incorporating the concept of differentials in access to *illegitimate* means, the theory of anomie may be extended to include seemingly unrelated studies and theories of deviant behavior which form a part of the literature of American criminology. In this final section, we try to show how a consolidated approach might advance the understanding of both rates and types of deviant conduct. The discussion centers on the conditions of access to *both* systems of means, legitimate and illegitimate.

Modes of Adaptation: The Case of Retreatism

By taking into account the conditions of access to legitimate *and* illegitimate means, we can further specify the circumstances under which various modes of deviant behavior arise. This may be illustrated by the case of retreatism.

As defined by Merton, retreatist adaptations include such categories of behavior as alcoholism, drug addiction, and psychotic withdrawal. These adaptations entail "escape" from the frustrations of unfulfilled aspirations by withdrawal from conventional social relationships. The processes leading to retreatism are described by Merton as follows:

[Retreatism] arises from continued failure to near the goal by legitimate measures and from an inability to use the illegitimate route because of internalized prohibitions, *this process occurring while the supreme value of the success-*

goal has not yet been renounced. The conflict is resolved by abandoning *both* precipitating elements, the goals and means. The escape is complete, the conflict is eliminated, and the individual is asocialized.

In this view, a crucial element encouraging retreatism is internalized constraint concerning the use of illegitimate means. But this element need not be present. Merton apparently assumed that such prohibitions are essential because, in their absence, the logic of his scheme would compel him to predict that innovating behavior would result. But the assumption that the individual uninhibited in the use of illegitimate means becomes an innovator presupposes that successful innovation is only a matter of motivation. Once the concept of differentials in access to illegitimate means is introduced, however, it becomes clear that retreatism is possible even in the absence of internalized prohibitions. For we may now ask how individuals respond when they fail in the use of both legitimate and illegitimate means. If illegitimate means are unavailable, if efforts at innovation fail, then retreatist adaptations may still be the consequence, and the "escape" mechanisms chosen by the defeated individual may perhaps be all the more deviant because of his "double failure."

SUMMARY

This paper attempts to identify and to define the concept of differential opportunity structures. It has been suggested that this concept helps to extend the developing theory of social structure and anomie. Furthermore, by linking propositions regarding the accessibility of both legitimate and illegitimate opportunity structures, a basis is provided for consolidating various major traditions of sociological thought on nonconformity. The concept of differential systems of opportunity and of variations in access to them, it is hoped, will suggest new possibilities for research on the relationship between social structure and deviant behavior.

QUESTIONS FOR DISCUSSION AND WRITING

1. What further variable should be taken into account, and what does this mean?
2. What controls the availability of illegitimate means, and what two issues are true regarding both systems of opportunity?
3. How does the author use white-collar crime to illustrate his theory?

A Revised Strain Theory of Delinquency

ROBERT AGNEW

STRAIN theory is based on the idea that delinquency results when individuals are unable to achieve their goals through legitimate channels. In such cases, individuals may turn to illegitimate channels of goal achievement or strike out at the source of their frustration in anger. This is an appealing idea and it is not surprising that strain theory has had a major impact on delinquency research and public policy. Recent research, however, has been critical of strain theory or, at best, has provided only mixed support for the theory. This has led a number of researchers to call for either the abandonment or revision of strain theory. This chapter reviews the criticisms of current strain theories, examines some recent efforts to revise these theories, and then presents a new revision of strain theory based on the idea that delinquency results from the blockage of pain-avoidance behavior. This new revision is tested using data from a national sample of adolescent boys.

CRITIQUE OF CURRENT STRAIN THEORIES

Current strain theories are dominated by Merton, Cohen, and Cloward and Ohlin. While these theories differ from one another in many important ways, they all attribute delinquency to the inability of adolescents to achieve conventional goals through legitimate channels. Merton and Cloward and Ohlin focus on the inability of adolescents to achieve the goal of

economic success, while Cohen focuses on the somewhat broader goal of middle-class status. In Merton, the inability to achieve one's goals may lead directly to delinquent behavior as the adolescent searches for alternative means of goal achievement. According to Cohen and Cloward and Ohlin, goal blockage is unlikely to lead to delinquency unless adolescents first form or join delinquent subcultures.

These theories have been criticized on a number of points, with perhaps the most damaging criticism having to do with the research on the disjunction between aspirations and expectations. If strain theory were correct, we would expect delinquency to be greatest when aspirations were high and expectations were low. We would, for example, predict that delinquency would be greatest when there was a strong desire for monetary success and a low expectation of fulfilling that desire. Many studies have attempted to test this idea, focusing for the most part on educational and occupational goals. Most of these studies, however, have failed to support strain theory. Generally, these studies have found that delinquency is highest when both aspirations and expectations are low, and delinquency is lowest when both aspirations and expectations are high. This finding has been interpreted in terms of social control theory: High aspirations and expectations are said to be indicative of a strong commitment to the conventional order. Not wishing to jeopardize that commitment, the individual conforms.

A second major criticism of current strain theories deals with the relationship between social class and delinquency. The above strain theories predict that delinquency is concentrated in the lower class, since low-class individuals most often lack the means to achieve economic success or middle-class status. Recent data, however, have seriously challenged this prediction. While the relationship between social class and delinquency is still a matter of debate, data indicate that delinquency is quite common in the middle class and that the relationship between class and at least certain types of delinquency is negligible.

These theories have also been criticized because they cannot explain the fact that most delinquents abandon crime in late adolescence; they cannot explain why delinquents will often go for long periods of time without committing delinquent acts; and they neglect many variables that are strongly related to delinquency such as the quality of family relationships. While the validity of certain of these criticisms may be debated, it is clear that there are at least some facts about delinquency that strain theory has trouble explaining. As a result, a number of revisions in the above strain theories have been made.

REVISIONS IN STRAIN THEORY

Most of the revisions challenge the assumption that monetary success or middle-class status is the primary goal of adolescents. The general theme of most revisions is that adolescents may pursue a variety of goals and that goal commitment should be considered a variable rather than a given. Such an approach allows these theories to explain middle-class delinquency. If goal commitment is a variable, one can argue that the middle class has higher aspirations and this offsets whatever advantage they might have in achieving goals.

While most revisions state or imply that goal commitment is a variable, they also suggest that adolescents will be more interested in the achievement of immediate goals rather than long-range goals like monetary success. The immediate goals of adolescents may include such things as popularity with peers, good grades, doing well in athletics, and getting along with parents. (This focus on immediate goals has

been explained in terms of the special structural position of adolescents in our society.) Focusing on immediate goals also allows strain theory to explain middle-class delinquency, since the achievement of many immediate goals may be independent of social class. In addition, the focus on immediate goals allows strain theory to explain away those findings dealing with the disjunction between aspirations and expectations. Studies in this area focus on future goals like occupational status. If such goals are unimportant to the adolescent, then we would not expect the disjunction between aspirations and expectations to be related to delinquency. A disjunction between *immediate* goals and the achievement of these goals, however, might result in much delinquency.

Preliminary tests of this revision, unfortunately, have not been encouraging. While these tests are not definitive (see Agnew), it would nevertheless seem useful to explore other revisions in strain theory. This chapter presents a revised version of strain theory that differs from current strain theories and the revised versions of these theories discussed above. This new theory seeks to explain why individuals engage in delinquency, although it also has the potential to explain variations in delinquency rates over time and between groups.

STRAIN AS THE BLOCKAGE OF
PAIN-AVOIDANCE BEHAVIOR

The current and revised strain theories discussed above assume that frustration is due to the blockage of goal-seeking behavior. Individuals, however, not only seek certain goals, they also try to avoid painful or aversive situations. According to Zillan, individuals engage in both reward-seeking and punishment-escaping behaviors. Like goal-seeking efforts, efforts to avoid painful situations may be blocked. Adolescents who find school aversive, for example, may be prevented from quitting school. This blockage of pain-avoidance behavior is likely to be frustrating to the adolescent, irrespective of the goals the adolescent is pursuing.

The blockage of path-avoidance behavior, then, constitutes another major source of strain and it forms the basis for the revised strain theory in this chapter. In particular, it is argued that adolescents are often placed in aversive situations from which they cannot legally escape. This blockage of pain-avoidance behavior frustrates the adolescent and may lead to illegal escape attempts or anger-based delinquency.

One way to keep the distinction between the two sources of strain clear is as follows. In the blockage of goal-seeking behavior, the individual is walking toward *a valued goal* and his or her path is blocked. In the blockage of pain-avoidance behavior, the individual is walking away from *an aversive situation* and his or her path is blocked. The two sources of strain are not incompatible and the same situation may be related to both types of strain. For example, an adolescent picked on by teachers may be frustrated because there is no escape from this harassment or because the harassment interferes with the achievement of valued goals. Other situations, however, may only be relevant to the blockage of pain-avoidance behavior. Adolescents may find certain situations aversive even though these situations do not interfere with the achievement of valued goals. Certain situations may be intrinsically aversive (e.g., the infliction of physical pain, the deprivation of sensory stimuli); they may be conditioned aversive stimuli (e.g., verbal insults); or the adolescent may simply be taught to experience these situations as aversive. The inability to escape from these aversive situations will be frustrating, even though the achievement of valued goals is not threatened.

The idea that the blockage of pain-avoidance behavior may lead to frustration and aggression is common in the physiological literature, and psychological research indicates that exposure to various types of aversive stimuli may lead to aggression, especially when the individual believes that the exposure is undeserved. These findings are paralleled in the sociological literature, where data indicate that delinquency is related to such aversive stimuli as parental rejection, unfair or inconsistent discipline, paren-

tal conflict, adverse or negative school experiences, and unsatisfactory relations with peers. The sociological data, however, have not been interpreted in terms of the blockage of pain-avoidance behavior.

Occasionally, the effect of aversive environments is explained in terms of strain theory. For example, Cohen argues that aversive school experiences lead to delinquency because they interfere with the attainment of middle-class status. Morris argues that family conflict interferes with the ability of females to satisfy their relational goals. In each case, the aversive situation leads to delinquency because it interferes with the achievement of valued goals. As indicated earlier, however, limited tests of this idea have not produced promising results. The revised strain theory makes no assumptions about the valued goals of adolescents or how particular situations might interfere with the achievement of these goals. The revised strain theory only assumes that it is frustrating to be unable to escape from an aversive situation. This makes the revised strain theory somewhat more parsimonious than the above strain theories, and it allows the theory to explain the fact that aversive situations affect delinquency even when these situations do not seem to interfere with the achievement of valued goals.

So while the idea that frustration may result from the blockage of pain-avoidance behavior is not new, this idea has not been used by criminologists to explain delinquency among adolescents. The theory, however, would seem particularly well-suited to this task. One of the distinguishing features of adolescents is that they lack power and are often compelled to remain in situations which they find aversive. They are compelled to live with their family in a certain neighborhood, to go to a certain school, and within limits, to interact with the same group of peers and neighbors. If any of these contexts is aversive, there is little the adolescent can do legally to escape. Most adults, by contrast, have many legal avenues of escape available, such as divorce, quitting one's job, or moving to another neighborhood.

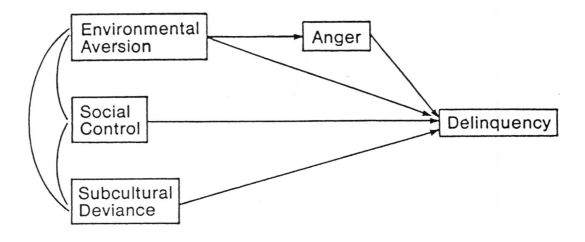

FIGURE 1 *A path model of the revised strain theory.*

Adolescents located in aversive environments may turn to delinquency for one of two reasons. First, delinquency may be a means to escape from the aversive environment or remove the source of aversion. Adolescents, for example, may escape from an aversive home environment by running away or by stealing to reduce their financial dependency on parents. Or adolescents may fight to end harassment from peers. When escape or removal of the aversive source is not possible, the adolescent may become angry and strike out in rage at the source of aversion or a related target. This second link is less instrumental and more emotional in nature.

Whether the blockage of pain-avoidance behavior actually results in delinquency is undoubtedly influenced by a number of factors. One crucial factor that will be considered in this chapter is whether the adolescent believes the aversion being experienced is undeserved. Other factors mentioned in the literature include the beliefs of the adolescent regarding delinquency, the presence of delinquent peers, whether aggression-provoking cues are present, the likelihood that the delinquent act will be punished, and the adolescent's level of social control. This study will not examine the extent

to which these additional factors condition the effect of aversion on delinquency.

If the revised strain theory is correct, we would expect location in an aversive environment to have a direct effect on delinquency since adolescents in such environments would be more likely to engage in illegal escape attempts. We would also expect an indirect effect on delinquency through anger. In examining the effect of aversion on delinquency, however, it is necessary to control for social control and subcultural deviance variables. This is because part of the direct effect of aversion on delinquency may be due to the fact that aversion causes or is correlated with low social control and deviant beliefs. These connections are summarized in the causal model in Figure 1. This model will be estimated using path analysis.

DATA

Data are from the Youth in Transition survey, a national survey of adolescent boys conducted by the Institute for Social Research, University of Michigan. A multistage sampling procedure was used to select 2,213 boys who, according to the researchers, constitute "an essentially unbiased representation of 10th grade boys in public high schools throughout the contiguous United States."

MEASURES

The survey contained numerous measures of the variables in Figure 1. Through the use of factor analysis, these measures were combined to create scales measuring environmental aversion, anger, parental and teacher attachment, commitment to school, and deviant beliefs. The survey already contained scales measuring delinquency.

Environmental Aversion

The adolescents in the survey were compelled to remain in at least two environments: family and school. Three scales were used to determine whether the adolescents believed these environments were undeservedly aversive.

PARENTAL PUNITIVENESS
High scorers on this 10-item scale report that their parents often scream, slap, threaten, nag, withdraw love, withdraw privileges, and ignore them. High scorers also state that their parents often disagree about whether punishment should be administered and that they "give out undeserved blame."

MEAN TEACHER
High scorers on this 3-item scale report that their teachers often lose their tempers, make negative comments, and talk down to students.

DISSATISFACTION WITH SCHOOL
High scorers on this 23-item scale report that they find school boring and a "waste of time," that they would rather be elsewhere, and that they can probably learn more outside of school.

While all adolescents were compelled to spend time with parents and teachers, there were undoubtedly differences in the amount of time spent with these agents. Future studies should attempt to measure both environmental aversion and the amount of time adolescents are compelled to spend in aversive environments.

Anger

High scorers on this 9-item scale state that they lose their temper easily, carry a chip on their shoulder, feel like a powder keg ready to explode, are irritated by small things, hold grudges, and "feel like" verbally and physically aggressing against parents and teachers. High scorers, in short, are angry, frustrated individuals. If the revised strain theory is correct, this scale should partly mediate the relationship between aversive environments and delinquency.

Social Control/Subcultural Deviance Measures

There are a total of 13 social control and subcultural deviance measures. Two scales measure attachment to parents, a 3-item scale called Father Attachment and a 2-item scale called Mother Attachment. High scorers report that they feel close to and want to be like their father or mother. One 3-item scale measures Teacher Attachment. High scorers report that teachers take a personal interest in them and that they talk privately with teachers about school and nonschool matters. Seven scales or single-item measures index commitment to school. These scales and items measure average school Grades, the Value Placed on Academic Achievement (4 items), the amount of Time Spent on Homework, the amount of Extra-curricular Reading, the adolescent's Self-Concept of School Ability (3 items), Occupational Aspirations, and the amount of Time Spent Dating (3 items). Finally, three scales measure the adolescent's values. A 13-item scale called Nonaggression measures the value placed on aggression. High scorers report that it is good to be kind and gentle, even if you are provoked or harmed by others. A 4-item scale called Deviant Beliefs measures the value placed on other types of deviance. High scorers report that it is good to engage in such deviant acts as charging bills without knowing how to pay for them, borrowing money without expecting to pay it back, and getting hold of a final exam copy. A 5-item scale called Guilt measures whether individuals feel guilty about their mistakes or wrongs. The presence of such guilt indicates that the individual possesses some degree of internalized control.

Delinquency

The blockage of pain-avoidance behavior may lead to any type of delinquency, since any delinquent act can be an escape attempt—however indirect—or an expression of anger. For this reason, a general measure called Seriousness of Delinquency is used. The 10 items measure the extent of the respondent's delinquent behavior during the prior 3 years. High scorers on this scale report that they have engaged in minor and serious theft, robbery, arson, and serious fighting. Response categories for each item range from 1 (*never committed the act*) to 5 (*committed the act five or more times*).

While the blockage of pain-avoidance behavior may lead to any type of delinquency, we would expect it to have an especially large effect on aggression and status offenses like truancy and cutting class. Compared to theft, aggression seems more suitable for the expression of anger and the removal of aversive sources. Status offenses like truancy and cutting class represent fairly direct ways of escaping from an aversive environment. An 8-item measure of Interpersonal Aggression is used. High scorers on this measure report that they have gotten into serious fights; have been in gang fights; and have hit their mother, father, and teacher. A 4-item scale measuring Escape Attempts From School is also used. High scorers on this scale report that they are often late for class and school and that they often skip class and school.

METHODS AND RESULTS

Path analytic methods are used to estimate the causal model in Figure 1. Through a series of regressions, the effects of the independent variables will be estimated.

All three measures of environmental aversion have a significant positive effect on anger. The combined effect of these variables on anger is .53. When aversion rises by one standard deviation unit, anger rises by .53 standard deviation units. Being in an aversive environment, then, clearly makes the individual angry. Anger, in turn, has a significant positive impact on all measures of delinquency. As we might expect, it has a somewhat larger effect on aggression. If we examine the direct and indirect effect of the aversion variables on delinquency, we find a direct effect of .12 on Seriousness of Delinquency and an indirect effect of .11, a direct effect of .21 on aggression and an indirect effect of .16, and a direct effect of .26 on Escape Attempts From School with an indirect effect of .10. As predicted, the total effect of the aversion variables on Interpersonal Aggression (.37) and Escape Attempts From School (.36) is larger than the total effect on Seriousness of Delinquency (.23).

To put the data in better perspective, it is useful to compare the effect of the aversion variables to the effect of the social control and subcultural deviance variables. Focusing on Interpersonal Aggression, we find that each of the aversion variables has a larger total effect than any other variable except dating. These variables have a larger effect than parental attachment, grades, aspirations, and values. Focusing on Escape Attempts From School, we find that Dissatisfaction With School has a larger total effect than all variables except dating, while the effect of Mean Teacher and Parental Punitiveness is only exceeded by dating and grades. The aversion variables also have a relatively large effect on Seriousness of Delinquency. Overall, these data attest to the importance of environmental aversion in the explanation of delinquency.

CONCLUSIONS

The data provide strong support for the idea that the blockage of pain-avoidance behavior is a major source of delinquency. Adolescents located in aversive environments from which they cannot escape are more likely to be delinquent. The relationship holds even after social control and subcultural deviance variables are controlled. These data are important because they suggest a new direction for the development of strain theory, and they supplement the explanations of delinquency provided by social control and subcultural deviance theory. Social control theory focuses on neutral relationships, in which the individual lacks ties to conventional people and institutions. Subcultural deviance theory focuses on *positive* relationships with deviant others. The revised strain theory supplements these theories by describing how *negative* relationships may lead to delinquency. While negative relationships may result in low social control and deviant beliefs in certain cases, the revised strain theory argues that a major effect of location in an aversive environment is frustration. This frustration may lead to illegal escape attempts or anger-based delinquency.

In addition to being supported by the data, the revised theory is able to overcome the major criticisms of current strain theories. First, the research on the disjunction between aspirations and expectations does not challenge the revised theory, since the revised theory is not based on the idea that delinquency results from the frustration of future goals. Second, the revised strain theory is able to explain the prevalence of middle-class delinquency, since middle-class adolescents may encounter aversive situations from which they cannot escape. In fact, a 5-item measure of SES was only weakly related to Parental Punitiveness ($r = -.09$, $p < .01$), Mean Teacher ($r = -.11$, $p < .01$), and Dissatisfaction With School ($r = -.17$, $p < .01$). Third, the revised theory is able to explain the decline in delinquency in late adolescence. We would expect such a decline since adolescents are leaving environments that they may have found aversive, such as family and school. Also, as adults, many legal avenues of escape become available to these individuals. Fourth, the revised theory is able to explain the sporadic nature of delinquency. We would expect environmental aversion to fluctuate, and delinquency should be most likely at those times that adolescents find family, school, or other environments most aversive. Finally, the revised strain theory assigns a central role to variables neglected by certain of the dominant strain theories, such as the quality of family relationships.

As indicated earlier, the revised strain theory seeks to explain individual variations in delinquency. The theory, however, could easily be extended to explain delinquency rates over time and between groups. Efforts to explain delinquency over time would argue that environmental aversion or the perception of such aversion changes with changes in such things as the nature of school, child-rearing practices, and cultural definitions of aversion. Also, one might argue that the legal avenues of escape available to adolescents change as the regulations regarding school attendance change or as norms regarding family obligations are altered. The explanation of group differences in delinquency would revolve around the fact that groups may vary in terms of environmental aversion and the ability to legally escape from such aversion. Aside from SES, however, the data did not allow us to explore group differences in these variables.

Overall, then, the theory has a demonstrated capacity to explain delinquency among individuals and the potential to explain delinquency rates over time and between groups. In addition to exploring the macro implications of the theory, future research should (a) focus on additional forms of environmental aversion, (b) examine the amount of time adolescents are compelled to remain in aversive environments, and (c) examine the factors that condition the link between aversion and delinquency.

QUESTIONS FOR DISCUSSION AND WRITING

1. What is one way to keep distinction between the two sources of strain (i.e., blockage of goal-seeking behavior and blockage of pain-avoidance behavior) clear?
2. What factors influence whether the blockage of pain-avoidance behavior actually results in delinquency?
3. According to the findings, what does being in an aversive environment do, and what does that do in turn?
4. In what five ways does the revised theory overcome the major criticisms of current strain theories?

The Natural History of an Applied Theory: Differential Opportunity and Mobilization for Youth

JAMES F. SHORT, JR.

THE LEGACY

Crime and juvenile delinquency are "naturals" for the analysis of sociological influence on social policy, so varied have been the research efforts and theoretical formulations of our colleagues in this area of human behavior and so "applied" the contexts within which most of these efforts have taken place. One need only reflect on a few classic examples: (a) Thrasher's work with Boys' Clubs of America delinquency prevention efforts in New York City; (b) the founding of the Chicago Area Project by Shaw and McKay and their colleagues, and their long-time association with the Illinois Institute for Juvenile Research; (c) Burgess's pioneer studies, "Factors Determining Success or Failure on Parole," undertaken at the request of the Illinois Parole Board and subsequently adopted for use by that board in determining parole policies and practices.

Three other sociological "events" of special importance for sociological involvement with respect to crime and delinquency policy occurred in the late 1930s and early 1940s: The first was Merton's "Social Structure and Anomie"; the second, *Street Corner Society* by Whyte; the third was Tannenbaum's *Crime and the Commu-*

nity. The first was important because it brought conforming and deviant behavior together into the same paradigm and provided an important basis for the theoretical flowering which occurred thereafter with respect to crime and delinquency. Merton's paradigm also had important implications for crime and delinquency control, for it challenged all programs predicated upon what has come to be known as the "evil causes evil fallacy." However, these implications were neither spelled out nor acted upon immediately. Two decades passed before the "action implications" of the paradigm and its embellishment by Cloward and Ohlin became the primary intellectual thrust behind the largest federally funded delinquency program in history.

OPPORTUNITY STRUCTURE THEORY

Prior to *Delinquency and Opportunity* by Cloward and Ohlin, Cloward had published in 1959 an article based on his PhD dissertation (written under Merton's direction) in which he modified Merton's paradigm. The nature of the modification is reflected in the article, titled "Illegitimate Means, Anomie, and Deviant Behavior." To Merton's basic independent variables, the culturally prescribed goals of success and the availability of legitimate means to attain these goals, Cloward added the intervening variable, availability of illegitimate means.

The Cloward modification of the Merton paradigm—together with its further development with Ohlin, hypothesizing two types of delinquent subcultures—is set forth in Table 1. A third delinquent subculture, the retreatist, is hypothesized to result from "double failure," that is, failure to achieve in both legitimate and illegitimate (conflict or criminal) terms.

Essentially, this paradigm became the basis for Mobilization for Youth (MFY), a large-scale delinquency prevention program on New York City's Lower Eastside. But this succinct formulation distorts the processes of theoretical development and of policy formation and neglects entirely the nature of the policies actually implemented. To begin at the beginning, "the idea which . . . developed into this proposal [MFY] originated at a meeting of the Board of Directors of the Henry Street Settlement in June of 1957." "The idea" was that a comprehensive program should be undertaken "commensurate in size and scope with the dimensions of the problem" (from "the alarming growth of delinquency on New York's Lower Eastside"). The effort to secure funds for a large-scale action program, the report continues, took 4½ years to complete, including a 2-year planning phase financed by the National Institute of Mental Health.

In the first stage of this process, a "many-faceted action program" was formulated by institutional representatives on the Lower Eastside, involving "settlement houses, other social agencies, religious institutions, and civil organizations," and a quite separate research design was developed by "faculty members of the Research Center of the New York School of Social Work of Columbia University." The National Institute for Mental Health's (NIMH) review found this proposal "to lack a sufficiently unifying principle . . . to make it the researchable laboratory experiment that its sponsors intended it to be," but in late 1959 NIMH funded a proposal for a planning grant which took "as the unifying principle the hypothesis developed by Cloward and Ohlin in their recent book, *Delinquency and Opportunity.*" Thus, the book, which figured only remotely in the original action proposal by the Henry Street Settle-

ment, became the "unifying principle" of the final MFY/action-research plan.

The MFY document, published at the end of the planning period, is explicit concerning the relationship between the theory and the action program even in its title: "A Proposal for the Prevention and Control of Delinquency by Expanding Opportunities."

The "Guidelines to Action" in the proposal explicitly relate to the Cloward and Ohlin theory:

In summary, it is our belief that much delinquent behavior is engendered because opportunities for conformity are limited. Delinquency therefore represents not lack of motivation to conform but quite the opposite: The desire to meet social expectations itself becomes the source of delinquent behavior if the possibility of doing so is limited or non-existent.

The importance of these assumptions in framing the large-scale program which is proposed here cannot be overemphasized. The essence of our approach to prevention, rehabilitation, and social control in the field of juvenile delinquency may be stated as follows: In order to reduce the incidence of delinquent behavior or to rehabilitate persons who are already enmeshed in delinquent patterns, we must provide the social and psychological resources that make conformity possible. . . . Our program is designed to enlarge opportunities for conformity and so to combat a major source of delinquent behavior among young people.

The task of developing "a general theory of action and a set of specific programs which are consistent with the theory of causation" was formidable, but the effort was made and a huge (by comparison with most such efforts) program was mounted, with a far clearer and closer relationship between the two sets of theory than is customary and with a much more ambitious research program built into the effort. Cloward, as Director of Research, was given "equal billing" with the Directors of Ac-

TABLE 1

Social context and modes of delinquent behavior: A paradigm.

Structural Features

		(Integrated areas)	(Unintegrated areas)
I.	*Independent variable*		
	A. Culturally prescribed success goals	Internalized	Internalized
	B. Availability of legitimate means to success goals	Limited; hence, intense pressures toward deviant behavior	Limited; hence, intense pressures toward deviant behavior
II.	*Intervening variables*		
	A. Institutional norms	Incomplete internalization	Incomplete internalization
	B. Availability of illegal means to success goals	Available	Unavailable
	1. Relations between adult carriers of conventional and criminal values	Accommodative; each participates in value system of other	Conflict; neither group well organized; value systems implicit and opposed to one another
	2. Criminal learning structure	Available; offenders at different age levels integrated	Unavailable; attenuated relations between offenders at different age levels
	3. Criminal opportunity structure	Stable sets of criminal roles graded for different ages and levels of competence; continuous income; protection from detection and prosecution	Unarticulated opportunity structure; individual rather than organized crime; sporadic income; little protection from detection and prosecution
	4. Social control	Strong controls originate in both legitimate and illegal structures	Diminished social control; "weak" relations between adults and adolescents
III.	*Dependent variables*		
	A. Expected type of collective response among delinquents	Pressures toward deviance originate in limited accessibility to success goals by legitimate means but are ameliorated by opportunities for access by illegal means. Hence, delinquent behavior is rational, disciplined, and crime oriented.	Pressures toward deviance originate in blocked opportunity by any institutionalized system of means. Hence, delinquent behavior displays expressive conflict patterns.

tion and Administration in the MFY Organization Chart.

Despite this effort, the connection between the theories of causation and action appears tenuous and uncertain in later developments. The emphasis of the "action theory" was solely on changing legitimate opportunities. Illegitimate opportunities, posited as an intervening variable by Cloward and Ohlin, were to be made less attractive by making legitimate opportunities more available and by better equipping youngsters to take advantage of such opportunities. And the focus of action programs was less on specific delinquent subcultures than on youth and community problems in general.

Cloward, in personal correspondence, defends the effort to manipulate legitimate opportunities rather than illegitimate means on grounds that they pertained, in theories of deviance, to the larger question of choices among alternative types of deviant adaptations. "Why delinquency rather than suicide, for example; or one type of delinquency rather than another?" Since MFY "was oriented toward preventing delinquency, not toward converting one form of delinquency into another . . . it focused on the legitimate opportunity variables, as it should have." He also notes that

the legitimate opportunity features of the theory directed attention to social structure as the main variable to be manipulated—as distinct from personality, which has been the emphasis in social work since World War II. We decried clinical approaches, and called for programs to open legitimate opportunities—that is, youth employment training, new educational programs, and so on. In this respect, opportunity theory was the overriding perspective, not alone in MFY but later in the poverty program.

Among those with whom I have corresponded in connection with this chapter, there appears to be consensus that MFY drew its intellectual support and legitimation from this broadly sociological perspective rather than from the more distinctive element in *Delinquency and Opportunity*, the role of illegitimate opportunities. It appears also to have been the case, however, that social structural variables proved extremely difficult to operationalize and to manipulate in the program effort, and that most MFY funding was directed toward changing individual characteristics, for example, job training and education.

The level of theoretical variables upon which the program was based is more than a mere quibble for academics. From the standpoint of the practitioners, the relationship of the theoretical orientation and social practice was even more important. Harold Weissman, official chronicler of the "Mobilization for Youth Experience," writes (personal correspondence):

The people at the top of MFY quickly lost interest in opportunity theory per se, in their desire to engage in a variety of social protest. Second, the issue should not be posed as social theory and social policy, but social theory and social practice. It is in the translation of theory into practice that tremendous gaps appear. Social workers need operable variables, and theory that is operationalized. This is what opportunity theory was not.

Returning to the relationship between theory and policy, a current student of MFY notes that MFY changed its primary emphasis from concern with juvenile delinquency to concern with poverty, as funds became available through the "War on Poverty." Cloward defends the shift as consistent with opportunity theory.

But this view begs important questions. What is the relationship of the "specific theory" to the "general perspective"? The lack of specificity of opportunity theory led mobilization "to attack pragmatically the problems of the neighborhood, leaning on the theory when it was helpful, ignoring it at other times, and expanding it on others." In this epilogue to the four-volume series describing the MFY "experience," Weissman chides the research department for not producing "a comprehensive critique of opportunity theory based on the Mobilization for Youth Experience."

This is not the place to analyze the success of these efforts either in "curbing delinquency" or "solving poverty," although considerable effort continues toward such assessment. It is sufficient at this point to note that MFY probably is the single most comprehensive delinquency control program ever undertaken. Opportunity structure theory, shortened simply to "opportunity theory," subsequently became the fundamental paradigm for this nation's largest-scale delinquency control effort. More than this, it became a sort of prototype for the Community Action Programs of the "War on Poverty." It was, as Piven and Cloward note, "the Great Society's first community action program"; indeed "the first Great Society agency." As MFY developed, that larger battle was joined by both the intellectual and the action leadership and their followers. In the process, delinquency prevention became a secondary, though still important, objective.

The relationship of opportunity theory to the national effort was even more complex than that between mobilization and the theory. MFY was the first and largest of several programs for delinquency control mounted by the federal government in major American cities. But the decisions to mount a large-scale effort to control delinquency and subsequently large-scale programs to provide mental health and other services to inner-city areas throughout the country were political decisions, "a response to new political imperatives." Once those decisions were made, opportunity theory became an important organizing principle, particularly after Ohlin was brought to Washington, D.C., to administer the new federal delinquency program.

SUMMARY AND APPRAISAL

The common, and perhaps the prevailing, view of sociologists, I suspect, is that "opportunity theory clearly suggests specific, relatively modest social policy innovations to control juvenile delinquency." That was my impression, too, prior to undertaking this project. Apparently, the persons responsible for policymaking and

implementation at MFY did not find it so. What did happen, it appears, is that sociologists were able to influence the course of juvenile delinquency research and action, and research and action related to poverty, welfare, and other problems. They did so and they continue to do so, most often by participating in review of funding proposals for both action and research programs, by carrying out research.

There is ample historical precedent for both of these modes. I have already referred to one of the better-known cases of sociological engineering, the Chicago Area Project, conceived and engineered during its early history by Clifford Shaw and other sociologists. It should be pointed out, however, that even in the early years Shaw and his colleagues functioned as much in the enlightenment mode as in direct involvement in the operations of Community Committees (consistent with Shaw's insistence upon indigenous leadership and community self-determination). More recently, the Highfields project, modeled after McCorkle's conception of "guided group interaction," has received much attention, as have "The Provo Experiment," and other experiments designed, directed, and evaluated by Empey and his associates.

Integration of theory, policy, and practice certainly has been closer in the latter of these projects than in most attempts to "apply" sociological theory. Yet problems similar to those alluded to in the MFY experience occur. In a particularly thoughtful response to this chapter, Empey reports on his own experience (personal correspondence):

I found staff members responding to emergent problems on ad hoc and individual bases, rather than turning to the theoretical guidelines of the project for solutions. There are always pressures to do this because . . . the problems of individuals often conflict with the problems of the organization and with what the theory says should be done. Therefore, faced with an ideological conflict, staff members reject the theory and do what they think is best for the individual. Consequently, I found myself continually having to say to staff that they should turn to the theoretical guidelines for answers as to what they should do when a problem emerged rather than responding on an ad hoc basis. Had I not been there, had I not been adamant in my stand, I believe our programs would have moved further and further away from their theoretical bases. It is often not the theory that is at fault, but emergent problems which cause people who run programs to discard the theory. The result is that the theory often does not get a test.

Thus, we return to the continuing tensions between theoretical specificity and problems of ongoing activity; between theoretical guidelines and ad hoc solutions pragmatically selected. Problems of this genre clearly need to be added to the agenda of applied sociological concern.

QUESTIONS FOR DISCUSSION AND WRITING

1. What did Cloward add to Merton's theory?
2. Why did the connection between the theories of causation and action appear tenuous and uncertain in later developments?
3. Although the persons responsible for policymaking and implementation at Mobilization for Youth did not find that opportunity theory clearly suggests specific, relatively modest social policy innovations to control juvenile delinquency, what did happen? How do sociologists continue to influence actions taken against juvenile delinquents?

The Provo Experiment in Delinquency Rehabilitation

LAMAR T. EMPEY
JEROME RABOW

DESPITE the importance of sociological contributions to the understanding of delinquent behavior, relatively few of these contributions have been systematically used for purposes of rehabilitation. This chapter presents the outlines of a program—the Provo Experiment in Delinquency Rehabilitation—which is derived from sociological theory and which seeks to apply sociological principles to rehabilitation. Because of its theoretical ties, the concern of the experiment is as much with a systematic evaluation and reformulation of treatment consistent with findings as with the administration of treatment itself. For that reason, research and evaluation are an integral part of the program. Its theoretical orientation, major assumptions, treatment system, and research design are outlined below.

THEORETICAL ORIENTATION

With regards to causation, the Provo Experiment turned to a growing body of evidence which suggests two important conclusions: (a) that the greater part of delinquent behavior is not that of individuals engaging in highly secretive deviations, but is a group phenomenon—shared deviation which is the product of differential group experience in a particular subculture, and (b) that because most delinquents tend to be concentrated in slums or to be the children of lower-class parents, their lives are characterized by learning situations which limit their access to success goals.

MAJOR ASSUMPTIONS FOR TREATMENT

In order to relate such theoretical premises to the specific needs of treatment, the Provo Experiment adopted a series of major assumptions. They are as follows:

1. Delinquent behavior is primarily a group product and demands an approach to treatment far different from that which sees it as characteristic of a "sick" or "well-meaning" but "misguided" person.

2. An effective program must recognize the intrinsic nature of a delinquent's membership in a delinquent system and, therefore, must direct treatment to him as a part of that system.

3. Most habitual delinquents are affectively and ideologically dedicated to the delinquent system. Before they can be made amenable to change, they must be made anxious about the ultimate utility of that system for them.

4. Delinquents must be forced to deal with the conflicts which the demands of conventional and delinquent systems place upon them. The resolution of such conflicts, either for or against further law violations, must ultimately involve a community decision. For that reason, a treatment program, in order to force realistic decision making, can be most effective if it per-

mits continued participation in the community as well as in the treatment process.

5. Delinquent ambivalence for purposes of rehabilitation can only be used in a setting conducive to the free expression of feelings—both delinquent and conventional. This means that the protection and rewards provided by the treatment system for *candor* must exceed those provided either by delinquents for adherence to delinquent roles or by officials for adherence to custodial demands for "good behavior." Only in this way can delinquent individuals become aware of the extent to which other delinquents share conventional as well as delinquent aspirations and, only in this way, can they be encouraged to examine the ultimate utility of each.

6. An effective program must develop a unified and cohesive social system in which delinquents and authorities alike are devoted to one task—overcoming lawbreaking. In order to accomplish this, the program must avoid two pitfalls:

(a) It must avoid establishing authorities as "rejectors" and making inevitable the creation of two social systems within the program, and

(b) It must avoid the institutionalization of means by which skilled offenders can evade norms and escape sanctions. The occasional imposition of negative sanctions is as necessary in this system as in any other system.

7. A treatment system will be most effective if the delinquent peer group is used as the means of perpetuating the norms and imposing the sanctions of the system. The peer group should be seen by delinquents as the primary source of help and support.

8. A program based on sociological theory will have to concentrate, instead, on matters of another variety: changing reference group and normative orientations, using ambivalent feelings resulting from the conflict of conventional and delinquent standards, and providing opportunities for recognition and achievement in conventional pursuits.

9. An effective treatment system must include rewards which are realistically meaning-

ful to delinquents. They would include such things as peer acceptance for law-abiding behavior or the opportunity for gainful employment rather than badges, movies, or furlough privileges which are designed primarily to facilitate institutional control. Rewards, therefore, must only be given for realistic and lasting changes, not for conformance to norms which concentrate upon effective custody as an end in itself.

10. Finally, in summary, a successful program must be viewed by delinquents as possessing four important characteristics: (a) a social climate in which delinquents are given the opportunity to examine and experience alternatives related to a realistic choice between delinquent or nondelinquent behavior; (b) the opportunity to declare publicly to peers and authorities a belief or disbelief that they can benefit from a change in values; (c) a type of social structure which will permit them to examine the role and legitimacy (for their purposes) of authorities in the treatment system; and (d) a type of treatment interaction which, because it places major responsibilities upon peer-group decision making, grants status and recognition to individuals, not only for their own successful participation in the treatment interaction but for their willingness to involve others.

THE TREATMENT SYSTEM

The Provo Program, consistent with these basic assumptions, resides in the community and does not involve permanent incarceration. Boys live at home and spend only a part of each day at Pinehills (the program center). Otherwise they are free in the community.

History and Locale. The Provo Program was begun in 1956 as an "in-between" program designed specifically to help those habitual delinquents whose persistence made them candidates, in most cases, for a reformatory. It was instigated by a volunteer group of professional and laypeople known as the Citizens'

Advisory Council to the Juvenile Court. It has never had formal ties to government except through the juvenile court. This lack of ties has permitted considerable experimentation. Techniques have been modified to such a degree that the present program bears little resemblance to the original one. Legally, program officials are deputy probation officers appointed by the juvenile judge.

The cost of treatment is financed by county funds budgeted through the juvenile court. So near as we can estimate, the cost per boy is approximately one tenth of what it would cost if he were incarcerated in a reformatory. Research operations are financed by the Ford Foundation. Concentrated evaluation of the program is now in its second year of a 6-year operation.

Relations with welfare agencies and the community, per se, are informal but extremely cooperative. This is due to three things: the extreme good will and guiding influence of the juvenile court judge, Monroe J. Paxman; the unceasing efforts of the Citizens' Advisory Council to involve the entire county as a community; and the willingness of city and county officials, not only to overcome traditional fears regarding habitual offenders in the community but to lend strong support to an experimental program of this type.

The treatment program is located in the city of Provo but draws boys from all major communities in the county—from a string of small cities, many of which border on each other, ranging in size from 4,000 to 40,000. The total population from which it draws its assignees is about 110,000.

Assignees. Only habitual offenders, 15-17 years, are assigned to the program. In the absence of public facilities, they are transported to and from home each day in automobiles driven by university students. Their offenses run the usual gamut: vandalism, trouble in school, shoplifting, car theft, burglary, forgery, and so forth. Highly disturbed and psychotic boys are not assigned.

Number in Attendance. No more than 20 boys are assigned to the program at any one time. A large number would make difficult any attempts to establish and maintain a unified, cohesive system. This group of 20 is broken into two smaller groups, each of which operates as a separate discussion unit. When an older boy is released from one of these units, a new boy is added. This is an important feature because it serves as the means by which the culture of the system is perpetuated.

Length of Attendance. No length of stay is specified. It is intimately tied to the group and its processes because a boy's release depends not only on his own behavior but on the maturation processes through which his group goes. Release usually comes somewhere between 4 and 7 months.

Nature of Program. The program does not use any testing, gathering of case histories, or clinical diagnosis. One of its key tools, peer group interaction, is believed to provide a considerably richer source of information about boys and delinquency than do clinical methods.

The program, per se, is divided into two phases. Phase I is an intensive group program, using work and the delinquent peer group as the principal instruments for change. During the winter, boys attend this phase 3 hours a day, 5 days a week, and all day on Saturdays. Activities include daily group discussions, hard work, and some unstructured activities in which boys are left entirely on their own. During the summer, they attend an all-day program which involves work and group discussions.

Phase II is designed to aid a boy after release from intensive treatment in Phase I. It involves two things: (a) an attempt to maintain some reference group support for a boy, and (b) community action to help him find employment.

Phase I: Intensive Treatment

Every attempt is made in Phase I to create a social system in which social structure, peer members, and authorities are oriented to the one task of instituting change. The more relevant to this task the system is, the greater will be its influence.

Social Structure. There is little formal structure in the Provo Program. Consequently, other than requiring boys to appear each day, and working hard on the job, there are no formal demands. The only other daily activities are the group discussions at which attendance is optional.

The absence of formal structure helps to do more than avoid artificial criteria for release. It has the positive effect of making boys more amenable to treatment. In the absence of formal structure, they are uneasy and they are not quite sure of themselves. Thus, the lack of clear-cut definitions for behavior helps to accomplish three important things: (a) It produces anxiety and turns boys toward the group as a method of resolving their anxiety; (b) it leaves boys free to define situations for themselves: Leaders begin to lead, followers begin to follow, and manipulators begin to manipulate—it is these types of behavior which must be seen and analyzed if change is to take place; and (c) it binds neither authorities nor the peer group to prescribed courses of action; each is free to do whatever is needed to suit the needs of particular boys, groups, or situations.

Perhaps the greatest difference lies in the fact that a considerable amount of power is vested in the delinquent peer group. It is the instrument by which norms are perpetuated and through which many important decisions are made. It is the primary source of pressure for change.

The Peer Group. Attempts to involve a boy with the peer group begin the moment he arrives. Instead of meeting with and receiving an orientation lecture from authorities, he receives no formal instructions. He is always full of such questions as, "What do I have to do to get out of this place?" or "How long do I have to stay?" but such questions as these are never answered. They are turned aside with, "I don't know," or "Why don't you find out?" Adults will not orient him in the ways that he has grown to expect,

nor will they answer any of his questions. He is forced to turn to his peers. Usually, he knows someone in the program, either personally or by reputation. As he begins to associate with other boys, he discovers that important informal norms do exist, the most important of which makes *inconsistency* rather than *consistency* the rule. That which is appropriate for one situation, boy, or group may not be appropriate for another. Each merits a decision as it arises.

Other norms center most heavily about the daily group discussion sessions. These sessions are patterned after the technique of Guided Group Interaction which was developed at Fort Knox during World War II and at Highfields. Guided Group Interaction emphasizes the idea that only through a group and its processes can a boy work out his problems. From a peer point of view, it has three main goals: (a) to question the utility of a life devoted to delinquency; (b) to suggest alternative ways for behavior; and (c) to provide recognition for a boy's personal reformation and his willingness to reform others.

Guided Group Interaction grants to the peer group a great deal of power, including that of helping to decide when each boy is ready to be released. This involves "retroflexive reformation." If a delinquent is serious in his attempts to reform others, he must automatically accept the common purpose of the reformation process, identify himself closely with others engaged in it, and grant prestige to those who succeed in it. In so doing, he becomes a genuine member of the reformation group and in the process may be alienated from his previous prodelinquent groups. Such is an ideal and long-term goal.

Before a group will help a boy "solve his problems," it demands that he review his total delinquent history. This produces anxiety because, while he is still relatively free, it is almost inevitable that he has much more to reveal than is already known by the police or the court. In an effort to avoid such involvement, he may try subterfuge. But any reluctance on his part to be honest will not be taken lightly. Norms dictate that no one in the group can be released until everyone is honest and until every boy helps to solve problems. A refusal to come clean shows a lack of trust in the group and slows down the problem-solving process. Therefore, any recalcitrant boy is faced with a real dilemma. He can either choose involvement or relentless attack by his peers. Once a boy does involve himself, however, he learns that some of his fears were unwarranted. What goes on in the group meeting is sacred and is not revealed elsewhere.

A second process for involvement lies in the use of the peer group to perpetuate the norms of the treatment system. One of the most important norms suggests that most boys in the program are candidates for a reformatory. This is shocking because even habitual delinquents do not ordinarily see themselves as serious offenders. Yet the tradition is clear; most failures at Pinehills are sent to the Utah State Industrial School. Therefore, each boy has a major decision to make: Either he makes serious attempts to change or he gets sent away.

The third process of involvement could only occur in a community program. Each boy has the tremendous problem of choosing between the demands of his delinquent peers outside the program and the demands of those within it. The usual reaction is to test the situation by continuing to identify with the former. Efforts to do this, however, and to keep out of serious trouble are usually unsuccessful. The group is a collective board on delinquency; it usually includes a member who knows the individual personally or by reputation, and it can rely on the meeting to discover many things. Thus, the group is able to use actual behavior in the community to judge the extent to which a boy is involved with the program and to judge his readiness for release. The crucial criterion for any treatment program is not what an individual does while in it, but what he does while he is *not* in it.

The fourth process involves a number of important sanctions which the group can impose if a boy refuses to become involved. It can employ familiar techniques such as ostracism or derision, or it can deny him the status and recognition which come with change. Furthermore, it can use sanctions arising out of the treatment system. For example, while authorities may impose restrictions on boys in the form of extra work or incarceration in jail, the group is often permitted, and encouraged, to explore reasons for the action and to help decide what future actions should be taken. For example, a boy may be placed in jail over the weekend and told that he will be returned there each weekend thereafter until his group decides to release him. It is not uncommon for the group, after thorough discussion, to return him one or more weekends despite his protestations.

The ultimate sanction possessed by the group is refusal to release a boy from the program. Such a sanction has great power because it is normative to expect that no individual will be tolerated in the program indefinitely. Pinehills is not a place where boys "do time."

Authorities. The third source of pressure toward change rests in the hands of authorities. The role of an authority in a treatment system of this type is a difficult one. On the one hand, he cannot be seen as a person whom skillful delinquents or groups can manipulate. But on the other hand, he cannot be perceived permanently as a "rejector." Everything possible, therefore, must be done by him to create an adult image which is new and different.

Initially, authorities are probably seen as "rejectors." Boys learn that authorities will strongly uphold the norm which says that Pinehills is not a place for boys to "do time." If, therefore, a boy does not become involved and the group is unwilling or unable to take action, authorities will.

There is no individual counseling since this would reflect heavily upon the integrity of the peer group. Consequently, he cannot resolve his problems by counseling with or pleasing adults. His only recourse is to the group. But since the group waits for him to bring up his troubles, he must involve himself with it or he cannot resolve them. Once he does, he must reveal why he is in trouble, what he has been doing to get into trouble, or how he has been abusing the program. If he refuses to become involved, he may be returned to court by authorities.

As a result of such experiences, boys are often confused and hostile. But where such feelings might be cause for alarm elsewhere, they are welcomed at Pinehills. But, in venting his confusion and hostility, it becomes possible for the group to analyze not only his own behavior but that of adults and to determine to what end the behavior of all is leading. Initial perceptions of adults which were confusing and provoking can now be seen in a new way. The treatment system places responsibility on a boy and his peers for changing delinquent behavior, not on adults.

Work and Other Activities

Any use of athletics, handicrafts, or remedial schooling involves a definition of rehabilitation goals. Are these activities actually important in changing delinquents? In the Provo Experiment, they are not viewed as having an inherent value in developing nondelinquent behavior. In fact, they are viewed as detrimental because participation in them often becomes criteria for release. On the other hand, work habits are viewed as vitally important. Previous research suggests that employment is one of the most important means of changing reference from delinquent to law-abiding groups. But such findings simply pose the important question: How can boys be best prepared to find and hold employment?

Sociologists have noted the lack of opportunity structure for delinquents, but attention to a modification of the structure (assuming that it can be modified) as the sole approach to rehabilitation overlooks the need to prepare delinquents to use employment possibilities. One alternative for doing this is an education program with all its complications. The other is an immediate attack on delinquent values and work habits. The Provo Experiment chose the latter alternative. It hypothesized that an immediate attack on delinquent values, previous careers, and nocturnal habits would be more

effective than an educational program. Sophisticated delinquents, who are otherwise very skillful in convincing peers and authorities of their good intentions, are often unable to work consistently. They have too long believed that only suckers work. Thus, concentration is upon work habits. Boys are employed by the city and county in parks, streets, and recreation areas. Their work habits are one focus of group discussion and an important criterion for change.

The Starter Mechanism: Putting the System in Motion

The Pinehills system, like many social systems, has some rigid prerequisites for continued membership. The broad structural outlines carefully define the limits beyond which members should not go. However, unlike most extreme authoritarian systems, there is an inner structure, associated with the meeting, which does not demand rigid conformity and which instead permits those deviations which are an honest expression of feelings.

The admission of deviations within the structural confines of the meeting helps lower the barriers which prevent a realistic examination of their implications for broader authoritarian structure, either at Pinehills or in society at large. Boys are able to make more realistic decisions as to which roles, conventional or delinquent, would seem to have the most utility for them.

This brief attempt to describe a complex system may have been misleading. The complexities involved are multivariate and profound. However, one important aspect of the experiment has to do with the theoretical development of, and research on, the nature of the treatment system. Each discussion is recorded, and efforts are made to determine means by which treatment techniques might be improved, and ways which group processes can be articulated. All would be very useful in testing theory which suggests that experience in a cohesive group is an important variable in directing or changing behavior.

Phase II:
Community Adjustment

Phase II involves an effort to maintain reference group support and employment for a boy after intensive treatment in Phase I. After his release from Phase I, he continues to meet periodically for discussions with his old group. The goal is to use this group in accomplishing three things: (a) acting as a check on a boy's current behavior; (b) serving as a law-abiding reference group; and (c) aiding in the solution of new problems. It seeks to continue treatment in a different and perhaps more intensive way than such traditional practices as probation or parole.

Efforts to find employment for boys are made by the Citizens' Advisory Council. If employment is found, a boy is simply informed that an employer needs someone. No efforts are taken by some well-meaning but pretentious adult to manipulate the boy's life.

These steps, along with the idea that delinquents should be permitted to make important decisions during the rehabilitative process, are consistent with structural-functional analysis, which suggests that in order to eliminate existing structure, or identification with it, one must provide the necessary functional alternatives.

APPROPRIATENESS OF TECHNIQUES

Many persons express disfavor with what they consider a harsh and punitive system at Pinehills. On the other hand, it should be remembered that in terms familiar to delinquents, every effort is made at Pinehills to include as many positive experiences as possible. The following are some which seem to function:

1. Peers examine problems which are common to all.

2. There is a recurring opportunity for each individual to be the focal point of attention among peers in which his behavior and problems become the most important concern of the moment.

3. Delinquent peers articulate in front of conventional adults without constraint with regard to topic, language, or feeling.

4. Delinquents have the opportunity, for the first time in an institutional setting, to make crucial decisions about their own lives. This in itself is a change in the opportunity structure and is a means of obligating them to the treatment system. In a reformatory, a boy cannot help but see the official system as doing things to him in which he has no say: locking him up, testing him, feeding him, making his decisions. Why should he feel obligated? But when some important decision making is turned over to him, he no longer has so many grounds for rejecting the system. Rejection in a reformatory might be functional in relating him to his peers, but in this system it is not so functional.

5. Delinquents participate in a treatment system that grants status in three ways: (a) For age and experience in the treatment process old boys have the responsibility of teaching new boys the norms of the system; (b) for the exhibition of law-abiding behavior, not only in a minimal sense, but for actual qualitative changes in specific role behavior at Pinehills, home or with friends; and (c) for the willingness to confront other boys, in a group setting, with their delinquent behavior. (In a reformatory where he has to contend with the inmate system, a boy can gain little and lose much for his willingness to be candid in front of adults about peers, but at Pinehills it is a primary source of prestige.) The ability to confront others often reflects more about the *confronter* than it does about the *confronted*. It is an indication of the extent to which he has accepted the reformation process and identified himself with it.

6. Boys can find encouragement in a program which poses the possibility of relatively short restriction and the avoidance of incarceration.

7. The peer group is a potential source of reference group support for law-abiding behavior.

Boys commonly refer to the fact that their group knows more about them than any other persons: parents or friends.

RESEARCH DESIGN

An integral part of the Provo Experiment is an evaluation of treatment extending over a 5-year period. It includes means by which offenders who receive treatment are compared to two control groups: (a) a similar group of offenders who at time of sentence are placed on probation and left in the community, and (b) a similar group who at time of sentence are incarcerated in the Utah State Industrial School. Since it is virtually impossible to match all three groups, random selection is used to minimize the effect of sample bias. All three groups are drawn from a population of habitual delinquents who reside in Utah County, Utah, and who come before the juvenile court. Actual selection is as follows.

The judge of the court has in his possession two series of numbered envelopes—one series for selecting individuals to be placed in the *probation* treatment and control groups and one series for selecting the *reformatory* treatment and control groups. These series of envelopes are supplied by the research team and contain randomly selected slips of paper on which are written either "Control Group" or "Treatment Group."

In making an assignment to one of these groups, the judge takes the following steps. First, after hearing a case, he decides whether he would ordinarily place the offender on probation or in the reformatory. He makes this decision as though Pinehills did not exist. Second, he brings the practice of random placement into play. He does so by opening an envelope from one of the two series supplied him. For example, if he decides initially that he would ordinarily send the boy to the reformatory, he would select an envelope from the *reformatory* series and depend on the designation therein as to whether the boy would actually go to the reformatory, and become a member of the control group, or

be sent to Pinehills as a member of the treatment group.

This technique does not interfere with the judicial decision regarding the alternatives previously available to the judge, but it does intercede, after the decision, by posing another alternative. The judge is willing to permit the use of this alternative on the premise that, in the long run, his contributions to research will enable judicial decisions to be based ultimately on a more realistic evaluation of treatment programs available.

SUMMARY AND IMPLICATIONS

This chapter describes an attempt to apply sociological theory to the treatment of delinquents. It concentrates not only on treatment techniques, per se, but the type of social system in which these techniques must operate. The overall treatment system it describes is like all other social systems in the sense that it specifies generalized requirements for continued membership in the system. At the same time, however, it also legitimizes the existence of a subsystem within it—the meeting—which permits the discussion and evaluation of happenings and feelings which *may or may not* support the overall normative structure of the larger system.

The purposeful creation of this subsystem simply recognized what seemed to be two obvious facts: (a) that the existence of contrary normative expectations among delinquent and official members of the overall system would ultimately result in the creation of such a subsystem anyway, and (b) that such a system, not officially recognized, would pose a greater threat, and would inhibit to a greater degree, the realization of the overall rehabilitative goals of the major system than would its use as a rehabilitative tool.

This subsystem receives not only official sanction but grants considerable power and freedom to delinquent members. By permitting open expressions of anger, frustration, and opposition, it removes social-psychological support for complete resistance to a realistic examination of the ultimate utility of delinquent versus conventional norms. At the same time, however, the freedom it grants is relative. So long as opposition to the demands of the larger system is contained in the meeting subsystem, such opposition is respected. But continued deviancy outside the meeting cannot be tolerated indefinitely.

At the same time, the overall treatment system includes elements designed to encourage and support the adoption of conventional roles. The roles it encourages and the rewards it grants, however, are peer-group oriented and concentrate mainly on the normative expectations of the social strata from which most delinquents come: working- rather than middle-class strata. This is done on the premise that a rehabilitation program is more realistic if it attempts to change normative orientations toward lawbreaking rather than attempting (or hoping) to change an individual's entire way of life. It suggests, for example, that a change in attitudes and values toward work per se is more important than attempting to create an interest in the educational, occupational, and recreational goals of the middle class.

The differences posed by this treatment system, as contrasted to many existing approaches to rehabilitation, are great. Means should be sought, therefore, in addition to this project by which its techniques and orientation can be treated as hypotheses and verified, modified, or rejected.

QUESTIONS FOR DISCUSSION AND WRITING

1. What two important conclusions did the growing body of evidence turned to by the Provo Experiment suggest?
2. What four important characteristics must delinquents see in a successful program?
3. Why is it important for the delinquents to make crucial decisions about their own lives?

SOCIAL CONTROL, SOCIAL DEVELOPMENT, AND PREVENTION

Contemporary social control theory is, we believe, the dominant theoretical perspective in criminology today. Its origins can be traced back to the sociological concept of "social integration" as it was developed by Durkheim about 100 years ago, the psychodynamic concept of "superego" described by Freud, and the psychological control theory of the Gluecks, with its emphasis on the importance of family socialization experiences in the development of personality, self-control, and delinquent behavior. The publication of Hirschi's *Causes of Delinquency* in 1969 put social control theory on the criminological map. "A Control Theory of Delinquency" is a chapter from that book which presents the theory that is subsequently tested with data collected in a large survey of juveniles in California. In essence, the theory proposes that delinquency is not caused but prevented: To the extent that a strong "social bond" (composed of conventional attachments, commitments, beliefs, and involvements) is developed through positive socialization experiences in the family, as well as in school and the wider community, delinquency is less likely to happen. Internalized self-control and external social constraints prevent the juvenile from getting into trouble.

Hirschi usually gets the credit for popularizing social control theory, and deservedly so, even though he carefully refers to and cites not only Durkheim, Freud, and the Gluecks but also other sociological contemporaries whose prior research played an important role in the refinement of this theoretical perspective, including Nye, Reckless, Toby, Sykes, Matza, and Reiss. For example, in 1951 Reiss wrote a paper that presaged many of the contemporary developments and issues in social control theory, particularly the distinction between internal (personal) controls produced through socialization and external (social) controls imposed by socially structured constraints.

The hundreds of empirical studies that have been conducted as tests or refinements of social control theory leave one with the impression that there is general support for most components of the theory. This may be so, but a careful analysis of many of those studies by Kempf, in "The Empirical Status of Hirschi's Control Theory," concludes that the voluminous research literature is uneven and disjointed, consisting of separate studies that do not build on each other to provide a coherent body of evidence regarding the general validity of social control theory. Therefore, Kempf concludes that many of the empirical tests have done as much to muddle as to clarify the overall viability of the theory.

Since social control theory is more a theory of prevention than causation, it is a natural foundation for delinquency prevention programming. In 1980 the Federal Office of Juvenile Justice and Delinquency Prevention (OJJDP) initiated a major research and development project on delinquency prevention in seven states, based on a modified version of social control theory, the Social Development Model. Weis and Hawkins, in "Preventing Delinquency: The Social Development Model," describe this theory—an integration of social control and social learning theories, although it is predominantly a dynamic version of Hirschi's control theory. They also describe the project design and the program elements, or interventions, that were derived from the theory and implemented in the prevention programs.

In an accompanying paper that was published simultaneously with the former, "The Prevention of Serious Delinquency: What to Do?" by Weis and Sederstrom, the social development approach to delinquency prevention is applied to social contexts within which there are high rates of serious and violent juvenile delinquency, including gang delinquency. Here, the suggested target of prevention activities is the high-rate neighborhood, and the prevention strategy is anchored in a philosophy of comprehensive community organization. These two papers served as the theoretical and program foundations for the national prevention R&D project and have been incorporated recently in OJJDP's current comprehensive strategy of delinquency prevention.

Hawkins, Von Cleve, and Catalano discuss some of the early results of this project in "Reducing Early Childhood Aggression: Results of a Primary Prevention Program." After 2 years of intervention, specifically focusing on parenting training and teacher training in classroom management skills, experimental first graders who were assessed at the end of second grade showed lower rates of aggressiveness among white boys and lower rates of self-destructive behavior among white girls. The project, however, seemed to have little impact on the behavior of the black children. The results offer qualified support for the social development approach to reducing antisocial behavior among young children, a predictor of more serious delinquent behavior at older ages.

A Control Theory of Delinquency

TRAVIS HIRSCHI

The more weakened the groups to which the individual belongs, the less he depends on them, the more he consequently depends on himself and recognizes no other rules of conduct than what are founded on his private interests.

Emile Durkheim

CONTROL theories assume that delinquent acts result when an individual's bond to society is weak or broken. Since these theories embrace two highly complex concepts, the *bond* of the individual to *society*, it is not surprising that they have at one time or another formed the basis of explanation of most forms of aberrant or unusual behavior. It is also not surprising that control theories have described the elements of the bond to society in many ways, and that they have focused on a variety of units as the point of control.

I begin with a classification and description of the elements of the bond to conventional society. I try to show how each of these elements is related to delinquent behavior and how they are related to each other. I then turn to the question of specifying the unit to which the person is presumably more or less tied, and to the question of the adequacy of the motivational force built into the explanation of delinquent behavior.

From *Causes of Delinquency* (pp. 83-109) by T. Hirschi, 1969, Berkeley: University of California Press. Copyright 1969 by Travis Hirschi. Reprinted by permission.

ELEMENTS OF THE BOND

Attachment

Durkheim said it many years ago: "We are moral beings to the extent that we are social beings." This may be interpreted to mean that we are moral beings to the extent that we have "internalized the norms" of society. But what does it mean to say that a person has internalized the norms of society? The norms of society are by definition shared by the members of society. To violate a norm is, therefore, to act contrary to the wishes and expectations of other people. If a person does not care about the wishes and expectations of other people—that is, if he is insensitive to the opinion of others—then he is to that extent not bound by the norms. He is free to deviate.

The essence of internalization of norms, conscience, or superego thus lies in the attachment of the individual to others. This view has several advantages over the concept of internalization. For one, explanations of deviant behavior based on attachment do not beg the question, since the extent to which a person is attached to others can be measured independently of his deviant behavior.

This dimension of the bond to conventional society is encountered in most social control-oriented research and theory. F. Ivan Nye's "internal control" and "indirect control" refer to the same element, although we avoid the problem of explaining changes over time by locating the "conscience" in the bond to others rather than making it part of the personality. Attachment to others is just one aspect of

Albert J. Reiss's "personal controls"; we avoid his problems of tautological empirical *observations* by making the relationship between attachment and delinquency problematic rather than definitional. Finally, Scott Briar and Irving Piliavin's "commitment" or "stake in conformity" subsumes attachment, as their discussion illustrates, although the terms they use are more closely associated with the next element to be discussed.

Commitment

"Of all passions, that which inclineth men least to break the laws, is fear. Nay, excepting some generous natures, it is the only thing, when there is the appearance of profit or pleasure by breaking the laws, that makes men keep them." Few would deny that men on occasion obey the rules simply from fear of the consequences. This rational component in conformity we label commitment. What does it mean to say that a person is committed to conformity?

The idea is that the person invests time, energy, himself, in a certain line of activity—say, getting an education, building up a business, acquiring a reputation for virtue. When or whenever he considers deviant behavior, he must consider the costs of his deviant behavior, the risk he runs of losing the investment he has made in conventional behavior.

If attachment to others is the sociological counterpart of the superego or conscience, commitment is the counterpart of the ego or common sense. To the person committed to conventional lines of action, risking 1 to 10 years in prison for a $10 holdup is stupidity, because to the committed person the costs and risks obviously exceed $10 in value. In the sociological control theory, it can be and is generally assumed that the decision to commit a criminal act may well be rationally determined—that the actor's decision was not irrational given the risks and costs he faces. Of course, as Becker points out, if the actor is capable of in some sense calculating the costs of a line of action, he

is also capable of calculational efforts: Ignorance and error return, in the control theory, as possible explanations of deviant behavior.

The concept of commitment assumes that the organization of society is such that the interests of most persons would be endangered if they were to engage in criminal acts. Most people, simply by the process of living in an organized society, acquire goods, reputations, prospects that they do not want to risk losing. These accumulations are society's insurance that they will abide by the rules. Many hypotheses about the antecedents of delinquent behavior are based on this premise. For example, Arthur L. Stinchcombe's hypothesis that "high school rebellion . . . occurs when future status is not clearly related to present performance" suggests that one is committed to conformity not only by what one has but also by what one hopes to obtain. Thus, "ambition" and/or "aspiration" play an important role in producing conformity. The person becomes committed to a conventional line of action, and he is therefore committed to conformity.

Most lines of action in a society are of course conventional. The clearest examples are educational and occupational careers. Actions thought to jeopardize one's chances in these areas are presumably avoided. Interestingly enough, even nonconventional commitments may operate to produce conventional conformity. We are told, at least, that boys aspiring to careers in the rackets or professional thievery are judged by their "honesty" and "reliability"—traits traditionally in demand among seekers of office boys.

Involvement

Many persons undoubtedly owe a life of virtue to a lack of opportunity to do otherwise. Time and energy are inherently limited. Involvement or engrossment in conventional activities is thus often part of a control theory. The assumption, widely shared, is that a person may be simply too busy doing conventional things to find time to engage in deviant behavior. The person involved in conventional activities is tied to appointments, deadlines, working hours, plans, and the like, so the opportunity to commit deviant acts rarely arises. To the extent that he is engrossed in conventional activities, he cannot even think about deviant acts, let alone act out his inclinations.

This line of reasoning is responsible for the stress placed on recreational facilities in many programs to reduce delinquency, for much of the concern with the high school dropout, and for the idea that boys should be drafted into the Army to keep them out of trouble.

The view that "idle hands are the devil's workshop" has received more sophisticated treatment in recent sociological writings on delinquency. David Matza and Gresham M. Sykes, for example, suggest that delinquents have the values of a leisure class, the same values ascribed by Veblen to the leisure class: a search for kicks, disdain of work, a desire for the big score, and acceptance of aggressive toughness as proof of masculinity. Matza and Sykes explain delinquency by reference to this system of values, but they note that adolescents at all class levels are "to some extent" members of a leisure class, that they "move in a limbo between earlier parental domination and future integration with the social structure through the bonds of work and marriage." In the end, then, the leisure of the adolescent produces a set of values, which, in turn, leads to delinquency.

Belief

Unlike the cultural deviance theory, the control theory assumes the existence of a common value system within the society or group whose norms are being violated. If the deviant is committed to a value system different from that of conventional society, there is, within the context of the theory, nothing to explain. The question is, "Why does a man violate the rules in which he believes?" It is not, "Why do men differ in their beliefs about what constitutes good and desirable conduct?" The person is assumed to have been socialized (perhaps imperfectly) into the group imposing its rules on the members of another group. In other words, we not only assume the deviant *has* believed the rules, we assume he believes the rules even as he violates them.

How can a person believe it is wrong to steal at the same time he is stealing? Given the control theory's assumptions about motivation, if both the deviant and the nondeviant believe the deviant act is wrong, how do we account for the fact that one commits it and the other does not?

Control theories have taken two approaches to this problem. In one approach, beliefs are treated as mere words that mean little or nothing if the other forms of control are missing. In short, beliefs, at least insofar as they are expressed in words, drop out of the picture since they do not differentiate between deviants and nondeviants; they are in the same class as "language" or any other characteristic common to members of the group. Since they represent no real obstacle to the commission of delinquent acts, nothing need be said about how they are handled by those committing such acts. The control theories that do not mention beliefs (or values), and many do not, may be assumed to take this approach to the problem.

The second approach argues that the deviant rationalizes his behavior so that he can at once violate the rule and maintain his belief in it. Donald R. Cressey has advanced this argument with respect to embezzlement, and Sykes and Matza have advanced it with respect to delinquency. In both Cressey's and Sykes and Matza's treatments, these rationalizations (Cressey calls them "verbalizations," Sykes and Matza term them "techniques of neutralization") occur prior to the commission of the deviant act. If the neutralization is successful, the person is free to commit the act(s) in question. Neutralization is difficult to handle within the context of a theory that adheres to control theory assumptions, because in the control there is no special motivational force to account for the neutralization. This difficulty is especially noticeable in Matza's later treatment of this topic, where the motivational component the "will to delinquency" appears after the moral vacuum has been created by the techniques of neutralization. The question thus becomes: Why neutralize?

The concept of neutralization assumes the existence of moral obstacles to the commission of deviant acts. In order to plausibly account for a deviant act, it is necessary to generate motivation to deviance that is at least equivalent in force to the resistance provided by these moral obstacles. However, if the moral obstacles are removed, neutralization and special motivation are no longer required. We therefore follow the implicit logic of control theory and remove these moral obstacles by hypothesis. Many persons do not have an attitude of respect toward the rules of society; many persons feel no moral obligation to conform regardless of personal advantage. Insofar as the values and beliefs of these persons are consistent with their feelings, and there should be a tendency toward consistency, neutralization is unnecessary; it has already occurred.

We do not assume, in other words, that the person constructs a system of rationalizations in order to justify commission of acts he *wants* to commit. We assume, in contrast, that the beliefs that free a man to commit deviant acts are unmotivated in the sense that he does not construct or adopt them in order to facilitate the attainment of illicit ends. In the second place, we do not assume, as does Matza, that "delinquents concur in the conventional assessment of delinquency." We assume, in contrast, that there is *variation* in the extent to which people believe they should obey the rules of society and, furthermore, that the less a person believes he should obey the rules, the more likely he is to violate them.

RELATIONS AMONG THE ELEMENTS

In general, the more closely a person is tied to conventional society in any of these ways, the more closely he is likely to be tied in the other ways. The person who is attached to conventional people is, for example, more likely to be involved in conventional activities and to accept conventional notions of desirable conduct.

THE BOND TO WHAT?

Control theorists sometimes suggest that attachment to any object outside one's self, whether it be the hometown, the starry heavens, or the family dog, promotes moral behavior. Although it seems obvious that some objects are more important than others and that the important objects must be identified if the elements of the bond are to produce the consequences suggested by the theory, a priori rankings of the objects of attachment have proved peculiarly unsatisfactory. Durkheim, for example, concludes that the three groups to whom attachment is most important in producing morality are the family, the nation, and humanity. Which is more important in the control of delinquency, the father or the mother, the family or the school?

Although delinquency theory in general has taken a stand on many questions about the relative importance of institutions (e.g., that the school is more important than the family), control theory has remained decidedly eclectic, partly because each element of the bond directs attention to different institutions. For these reasons, I shall treat specification of the units of attachment as a problem in the empirical interpretation of control theory, and not attempt at this point to say which should be more or less important.

WHERE IS THE MOTIVATION?

The most disconcerting question the control theorist faces goes something like this: "Yes, but *why* do they do it?" In the good old days, the control theorist could simply strip away the "veneer of civilization" and expose man's "animal impulses" for all to see. These impulses appeared to him (and apparently to his audience) to provide a plausible account of the motivation to crime and delinquency. His argument was *not* that delinquents and criminals alone are animals, but that we are all animals, and thus all naturally capable of committing criminal acts. It took no great study to reveal that children, chickens, and dogs occasionally assault and steal from their fellow creatures; that children, chickens, and dogs also behave for relatively long periods in a perfectly moral manner. So, too, no special motivation to crime within the human animal was required to explain his criminal acts.

Times changed. It was no longer fashionable (within sociology, at least) to refer to animal impulses. The control theorist tended more and more to deemphasize the motivational component of his theory. He might refer in the beginning to "universal human needs," or some such, but the driving force behind crime and delinquency was rarely alluded to. At the same time, his explanations of crime and delinquency increasingly left the reader uneasy. What, the reader asked, is the control theorist assuming? One reaction is simply to acknowledge the assumption, to grant that one is assuming what control theorists have always assumed about the motivation to crime—that it is constant across persons (at least within the system in question): "There is no reason to assume that only those who finally commit a deviant act usually have the impulse to do so. It is much more likely that most people experience deviant impulses frequently. At least in fantasy, people are much more deviant than they appear." There is certainly nothing wrong with *making* such an assumption. We are free to assume anything we wish to assume; the truth of our theory is presumably subject to empirical test.

A second reaction, involving perhaps something of a quibble, is to defend the logic of control theory and to deny the alleged assumption. We can say the fact that control theory suggests the absence of something causes delinquency is not a proper criticism, since negative relations have as much claim to scientific acceptability as do positive relations. We can also say that the present theory does not impute an inherent impulse *to delinquency* to anyone. That, on the contrary, it denies the necessity of such an imputation: "The desires, and other passions of man, are in themselves no sin. No more are the actions, that proceed from those passions, till they know a law that forbids them."

A third reaction is to accept the criticism as valid, to grant that a complete explanation of delinquency would provide the necessary impetus, and proceed to construct an explanation of motivation consistent with control theory. Matza agrees that delinquency cannot be explained simply by removal of controls:

Delinquency is only epiphenomenally action. . . . [It] is essentially infraction. It is rule-breaking behavior performed by juveniles aware that they are violating the law and of the nature of their deed, and made permissible by the neutralization of infractious [!] elements. Thus, Cohen and Short are fundamentally right when they insist that social control theory is incomplete unless it provides an impetus by which the potential for delinquency may be realized.

The impetus Matza provides is a "feeling of desperation," brought on by the "mood of fatalism," the "experience of seeing one's self as effect" rather than cause. In a situation in which manliness is stressed, being pushed around leads to the mood of fatalism, which in turn produces a sense of desperation. In order to relieve his desperation, in order to cast off the mood of fatalism, the boy "makes things happen"—he commits delinquent acts.

In the end, then, control theory remains what it has always been: a theory in which deviation is not problematic. The question "Why do they do it?" is simply not the question the theory is designed to answer. The question is, "Why don't we do it?" There is much evidence that we would if we dared.

QUESTIONS FOR DISCUSSION AND WRITING

1. What do control theories assume? What two highly complex concepts do control theories embrace?
2. What four elements of the bond does the author discuss?
3. Rather than "Why do they do it?," what question is control theory designed to answer?

The Empirical Status of Hirschi's Control Theory

KIMBERLY L. KEMPF

TRAVIS Hirschi introduced his theory of social control in 1969 in *Causes of Delinquency*, and it has been gaining popularity for nearly 25 years. There are several indications that social control theory is perhaps the most popular criminological theory, and yet to date there has been no systematic critique of control theory research.

The absence of an evaluation summarizing the research achievements of control theory has not, however, precluded the "wheel of science" from amassing results. Scholarly papers either cite the relevance of social control or purport to be formal tests of the theory with perhaps unrivaled frequency. This favored status of control theory has been explained by its testable nature, because the theory lends itself to self-report survey techniques, and because it has achieved support from empirical research. The likely acceptance of this theory for future policy development has been noted as well.

There are concerns, however, about the scope of social control theory. Just how generalizable are the elements of the social bond? Does the theory explain specific forms of delinquency (e.g., theft, damage, and violence), as well as general deviance. Is the theory equally applicable across age, race, and socioeconomic groups? Vold and Bernard argue that neither adult criminality nor truly offensive delinquency actually have been examined.

If social bonding theory is to be an "enduring contribution to criminology," then the basis should be the research results which support and lead to modification in the perspective. It is likely that Hirschi would agree to this standard because he has questioned the continued dominance of differential association theory based on its scientific adequacy. Hirschi also previously acknowledged the need for empirical tests to build on one another to achieve theoretical development. In doing so he stated, "it is easier to construct theories 'twenty years ahead of their time' than theories grounded on and consistent with data currently available." This paper attempts to determine the extent to which these objectives have been accomplished by the empirical tests of the theory of social control. Has causation been established and, if so, to what degree are the findings generalizable? Hirschi's theory will be outlined briefly and its connections to earlier theories highlighted. An overview of empirical tests of Hirschi's theory will be presented. The current state of the theory research will be identified for scholars interested in testing control theory today. Not only does the volume of published social control research merit an evaluation of this type, but it is important to determine the knowledge gained in 20 years.

THE THEORY OF SOCIAL CONTROL

The theory of social control offered by Hirschi evolved from many previous contributions. The ability to deviate from normative behavior is

From *New Directions in Criminological Theory* (pp. 143-173), F. Adler and W. S. Laufer, editors, New Brunswick, NJ: Transaction Publishers, 1993. Copyright Kimberly Kempf-Leonard. Adapted with permission.

considered universal by control theory. Most people do not indulge in deviant behavior because of their bond to society. The social bond was conceptualized by Hirschi through the following four elements:

1. Attachment of the individual to others (caring about others, their opinions, and expectations);
2. Commitment to conventional lines of action (the rational component including risk, energy, and self-investment in conventional behaviors);
3. Involvement (time engrossed in conventional activities); and
4. Belief in legitimate order (attribution of moral validity to social norms).

These components of the bond to society were viewed by Hirschi as independent and as having a generally negative association with the likelihood of engaging in delinquent behavior. Hirschi postulated that as the elements of the social bond become weakened, the probability of delinquency will increase.

Hirschi tested his theory through a survey administered in 1965 to a stratified random sample of 3,605 adolescent males drawn as part of the Richmond Youth Project in California. Based on a series of tabular analyses, Hirschi concluded support for his theoretical model. Hirschi conceded, however, that the theory underestimated the importance of peers, and the Richmond data failed to tap all domains of this concept. He also accepted that too much importance had been bestowed on the concept of involvement. He deferred revision of the theory until more is learned about the processes that affect the elements of the bond and whether delinquency itself motivates commitment.

The intent of this paper is to examine empirical investigations of the theory of social control since Hirschi's 1969 contribution. Among subsequent studies, attention will be given to the intent of the inquiry, the nature of the subjects tested, conceptualization technique of investigation, and relevance of findings. This quasi-meta-analysis will provide new information about the status of control theory and the contribution it has made to our understanding of crime and delinquency.

DESCRIPTIONS OF THE TESTS OF HIRSCHI'S THEORY

Empirical tests of control theory published between 1970 and 1991 were identified through a two-stage process. Studies initially were located through a search of the *Social Science Citation Indices, Criminal Justice Abstracts,* and *Psychological Literature Indices* using "control," "social control," "social bond," and "Hirschi" as key words.

Three criteria were adopted for screening the research. First, there must be an acknowledged test of control theory. Second, Hirschi must be cited, thereby increasing the likelihood that the test was of Hirschi's version of the theory. Third, the study must be published, utilizing the assumption that the publication process lends credibility to the scholarly contribution of the article. Although the selection process was rigorous, it was not presumed to be exhaustive, and undoubtedly some tests of Hirschi's theory are regrettably omitted. There is, however, no reason to believe the sample studies are not representative of control theory research so they should enable us to ascertain the general level of growth achieved since 1969.

Ultimately, 71 empirical tests of control theory were identified. These investigations included a variety of specific research objectives. There were 28 replication efforts, of which many attempted to extend the theory to demographic groups not examined by Hirschi, such as company executives, rural youth, females, and minority youths and other domains of deviance, including 16 studies of only drug or alcohol use, 4 studies of adult crime, 2 studies of sexual behavior, and 1 study of mental health disorders. There also were 16 studies in which social control was compared to another theory. Sixteen additional studies attempted to test theoretical models integrating social control with another theory. The integration efforts with social control most often included social learning or differential association, followed second by deterrence. In a few cases, elements of social control also were combined with strain, social disorganization, culture conflict, and conflict of interest theories. Eleven attempts to initiate contributions to theory development were reported. Potential improvements in these 11 studies included the application of new statistical procedures, analyses of unique data, and innovative sample groups.

With the exception of two studies that relied on official adult records and one study of aggregated data, control theory has been tested with survey data collected primarily through self-administered questionnaires. Tests of control theory have included as few as 72 subjects and as many as over 4,000. White adolescent students, a majority of whom are male, have been the usual target of the control theory research. In view of the overrepresentation of students, it is not surprising to discover that random selection of any type was not included in most studies.

The apparent lack of variation in design elements precludes this investigation from pursuing an empirically based meta-analysis, such as those used by Bridges and Weis to examine the accumulation of research on criminal violence or the structural covariates of homicide rates by Land. The similarity in research designs may serve as an advantage in this investigation of the empirical status of the theory, however, because differences among the empirical findings may be more readily attributed to operational definitions of the social bond.

Conceptual and Operational Definitions

Because these studies were self-acknowledged tests of control theory (rather than subjectively designated as such for our purpose), elements of the social bond were classified according to the original researchers' intent (e.g., if they used the label of attachment, so did I). In the rare event that the study did not mention the social bond specifically, an attempt was made to be inclusive and to categorize variables according to other studies with comparable indicators.

This classification revealed that all four elements of the social bond were included in only 17 studies. Attachment was the most frequently included element, but there was *no* single element that appeared in every study. The volume and variety of additional measures in these studies also is noteworthy. Many of the variables classified by some researchers as concepts from other theories or spurious factors were defined in other studies as elements of the social bond.

Not only were they omitted from study, but it is equally surprising that justification for the missing elements was rarely provided. Involvement is the least often measured element in the collection of studies. It is plausible that many investigators dismissed it based on Hirschi's interpretation of its lesser importance, or they may have adhered to Minor's argument that involvement is an ambiguous term. The absence of arguments defending the omission of the other three elements of the social bond remains perplexing.

A more parsimonious theoretical model of social control than that presented by Hirschi might have been achieved in the control theory research, and thereby explain the missing elements. In view of this possibility, this inquiry next examines the operational definitions of each element of the social bond adhered to in the sample of studies.

Attachment to Conventional Others (Parents, Peers, and School)

In Hirschi's own test, the number of measures of attachment exceeded those for the other elements of the social bond. He identified parents, the school, and peers as separate foci for attachment, and multiple dimensions were noted for each target.

Attachment to Parents

For attachment to parents, Hirschi was concerned about the direct and psychological holds the parent(s) had on the child, the intimacy of parent-child communication, and affection or respect. Virtual supervision was operationalized through a summated index of these questions: *Does your mother (father) know where you are when you are away from home? Does your mother (father) know whom you are with when you are away from home?* Two intimacy of communication indices were constructed. For the child to parent index, responses to the following items were summed: *Do you share your thoughts and feelings with your mother (father)? How often have you talked over your future plans with your mother (father)?* The parent to child index combined these items: *When you don't know why your mother (father) makes a rule, will she explain the reason? When you come across things you don't understand, does your mother (father) help you with them? Does your mother (father) ever explain why she feels the way she does?* Affection was noted as the crucial element by Hirschi. Affectional identification was measured by the item, *Would you like to be the kind of person your father (mother) is?* Equivalent importance was given to mothers and fathers for all dimensions.

Attachment to parents was the most frequent focus of attachment, as well as the most often examined element in the social bond among the studies reviewed. Fifty studies (70% of all studies) included attachment to parents, sometimes specified narrowly as only mother, or broadly as family.

Attachment to Peers

Hirschi measured attachment to peers according to the following items: *Would you like to be the kind of person your best friends are? A friend's reaction would be the worst thing about getting caught for stealing; Do you respect your best friend's opinions about the important things in life? The number of close friends who have been picked up by the police.*

There were 39 studies (55% of all reviewed) with indicators of attachment to peers (or friends, associates). Delinquent peer items were by far the most common. Delinquent peer items often differed from Hirschi's use of number of peers and usually specified the type of delinquency involvement or type of feelings for these friends. Interest in being like friends and respect for friend's opinions were equally represented among the studies.

Attachment to School

Affection for the school, measured by general like or dislike for school, was Hirschi's variable. There were other school-related variables, but they were mentioned in connection with "the causal chain." According to Hirschi, "the casual chain runs from academic incompetence to poor school performance to disliking of school to rejection of the school's authority to the commission of delinquent acts."

Twenty-nine studies (41% of the total) incorporated attachment to school as an element of the social bond, but none of them used Hirschi's measure to do so. Instead, 11 similar variables were substituted. Some of the other school variables Hirschi used, particularly those related to teachers, have since been considered within attachment. Attachment to school was measured by GPA and educational and occupational goals.

Involvement in Conventional Activities

Variables which identify activity type or length of time spent on certain activities account for most of the measures of involvement in conventional activities. Hirschi's items included the following: *currently working for pay; number of hours spent on homework per day; ever feel that "there's nothing to do"; number of hours spent talking with friends; number of hours spent riding around in a car.*

Involvement was adapted in only 25 (35%) subsequent investigations of control theory. Among these studies, hours spent on homework, followed by time working most often served to measure the concept. These two indicators also represented other concepts, however, and with nearly the same frequency. Time spent in school organizations, clubs, and community activities also were reported as involvement. Church attendance and religiosity were identified as involvement in three studies.

Commitment to Conventional Lines of Actions

Hirschi viewed achievement orientation, passage to "adult status," aspirations, and expectations as dimensions of commitment. His index of achievement orientation included the following items: *How important is getting good grades to you personally? Whatever I do, I try hard; I try hard in school.* A summated index with activities considered adult-like included *smoking, drinking, and dating.* Students were asked which of these they did and at what age they began. The importance of having a car and attitude about school intervention in smoking outside the classroom also were identified. Aspirations and expectations first were measured by Hirschi for education and employment. Individual items included the following: *How much schooling would you like to get eventually? How much schooling do you expect to get? Do your parents want you to go to college? The only reason to have a job is for money; You should not expect too much out of life; An easy life is a happy life; What type of job would you like to get eventually? What type of job do you expect to get? Do you think that either your competence or racial discrimination will*

keep you from getting the kind of job you want to have eventually?

The items specified as commitment appear in 41 studies (58% of all reviewed). Each of Hirschi's four concepts is represented, although there was less consensus among recent studies regarding the measurement of commitment than was shown for either the elements of attachment or involvement.

Belief

Hirschi identified values relative to law and the legal system, techniques of neutralization, and fatalistic statements as the dimensions of belief. He used items concerning *respect for the local police and concern for teacher's opinions* as indicative of respect for impersonal authority. Acceptance of the normative system was measured by the item *It is alright to get around the law if you can get away with it.* The techniques of neutralization were operationalized as follows: *Most criminals shouldn't really be blamed for the things they have done; I can't seem to stay out of trouble no matter how hard I try; Most things that people call "delinquency" don't really hurt anyone; The man who leaves the keys in his car is as much to blame for its theft as the man who steals it; Police try to give all kids an even break; Suckers deserve to be taken advantage of.* Three fatalistic statements also were tested: *What is going to happen to me will happen, no matter what I do; There is no sense looking ahead since no one knows what the future will be like; A person should live for today and let tomorrow take care of itself.*

In comparison to commitment, the more recent measurement of belief in the legitimate order in 37 studies (52%) offers a high level of consistency. The majority of the measures include value orientations toward the law and legal system, although 20 of them differed considerably from Hirschi's variables and 6 shared the focus of the perceived legitimacy, obedience, or likelihood of sanctions.

Explained Behavior

Finally, the outcome of the control model should be considered in reviewing the conceptual and operational definitions used in tests of the theory. Hirschi argued, however, that the findings of control theory research should not be dependent on the operational definition of delinquency.

There were several items on the Richmond questionnaire that dealt with delinquency, but Hirschi chose to test only six. Two of the items came from the Nye-Short scale of delinquency: *Have you ever taken little things (worth less than $2) that did not belong to you? Have you ever banged up something that did not belong to you on purpose?* The remaining four items were taken from the scale of theft developed by Dentler and Monroe: *Have you ever taken things of some value (between $2 and $50) that did not belong to you? Have you ever taken things of large value (worth over $50) that did not belong to you? Have you ever taken a car for a ride without the owner's permission? Not counting fights you may have had with a brother or sister, have you ever beaten up on anyone or hurt anyone on purpose?* Hirschi initially created three summated indices from the six items. The standard index measured the total number of acts ever committed. The persistence index took number and recency into account. The recency index tapped only the number of acts committed during the previous year. Despite its skewness and lower predictive capability, only the recency scale was analyzed because it "was considered most appropriate as an operationalization of delinquency in terms of the theory."

The theory of social control has been viewed by its researchers as capable of explaining delinquency, crime, adolescent sexual behavior, mental health disorders, and conformity. The domain of items cover a full range of deviant behavior, from skipping a school rally or theft of under $2 to armed robbery. Several studies adapted modified versions of the original Nye-Short scale of delinquency; others made a point of including dimensions of crime viewed as serious. A majority of the studies relied on summated scales of the number of infractions reported for each offense category.

Discussion of the Findings

This investigation will now turn to the empirical findings and conclusions of the reviewed studies to determine the current state of knowledge on control theory.

Although it achieved most significance in Hirschi's test, attachment was consistently identified as the weakest predictor of delinquency in the research by Krohn and Massey. But, perhaps the most consistent finding was the identified need for refinement in the sources of attachment.

Among the attachment foci, the most important indicators were affection for parents, mothers, regulation or pressure from parents and peers, and school. Although it remains controversial, attachment to delinquent friends contributed to the explanation of crime and delinquency in several studies.

Involvement in conventional activities was shown to be fairly unimportant unless it was concerned with commitment. Obviously, this sentiment was echoed by those researchers who omitted this element from their models and by Conger, who argued that "involvement can be dispensed with as a crucial element."

Commitment, also considered "stakes in conformity," was identified as the element with the strongest explanatory value in only the control model examined by Krohn and Massey. Their index and GPA were the most powerful commitment variables; gender differences in commitment also were shown.

Belief in the law had the greatest explanatory value in only one study, but the measure was consistently important in each of the five crime-specific models she examined. A moderate effect for belief was reported by Paternoster and Triplett. Weak or no effect for belief also was reported.

In sum, the empirical models of social control discussed above were tested for a variety of deviant behavior, and different, and sometimes contrary, results were found. When crime-specific models were examined, higher levels of explanation were found for the general crime model, minor delinquency, and school infractions.

THE MERITS OF CONTROL THEORY

There are three criteria by which a theory of crime may be judged. First, the degree to which people agree with the theory is a subjective standard. Control theory has succeeded by this gauge and become perhaps the most heralded theory of delinquency. Yet popularity based on intuitive appeal is not enough to distinguish sound theory from folk wisdom. Second, a theory also may be evaluated according to its relevance for policy and ability to effect program change. From this criteria, the potential importance of the theory of social control is clear. Interventions aimed at enhancing family, school, and peer attachments can easily be envisioned; many are in place now. The rise of curfew ordinances mandates virtual supervision by parents. Activities to occupy after-school and vacation leisure time receive great community support. Many such programs provide role models to help socialize youths to appropriate values and educate them about potential consequences of offending, thereby attempting to affect one or more elements of the bond. However, decisions on policy often reflect feasibility and ease of program administration as much as they consider theoretical merits. The scientific achievements of a theory is the third standard and the criteria by which criminology must evaluate its theories. To establish causation, the scientific method requires a correlation between theoretical elements and the phenomena being explained, clarification of temporal order, and the dismissal of potentially spurious factors.

Replication is then required to ensure generalizability across time, space, and subjects. By this important measure of scientific merit, social control theory has not fared well. Criminology has not yet determined the capacity of this theory.

Correlations

Hirschi provided the first test of his theory, and concluded support for it. Subsequently, as Vold and Bernard surmised, the majority of the reviewed studies also professed at least conditional support for control theory. These failures to refute control theory have been based primarily on associations observed between one or more elements of the social bond and delinquency.

Many correlations certainly have been reported among the tests of Hirschi's theory. The qualified conclusions of these studies, however, are misleading. As this review has shown, studies varied in their success with operationalizing elements of the social bond. Many investigations did not incorporate Hirschi's variables.

Attachment has been studied more often than any other element of the bond, but there remains a great deal about this concept to be explored. Aspects of affection and control need to be examined for attachment. The sources and targets of these attachments also need to be disentangled. Other potential sources of attachment surely exist as well. Neighborhood affiliation may hold prominence among some peers. Religion means more than church attendance to many people. Attitudes toward law and the legal system are either attachment or belief, but probably not both.

As an element of the social bond, rational behavior exists within the concept of commitment. In view of the popularity currently bestowed on deterrence, routine activity, and the intuitive appeal of rational choice theory, Hirschi's contention that these theories already are embodied within control theory must be considered. Therefore, many dimensions of commitment to conformity need to be better understood. It is important, for example, to disentangle the relationship between aspirations and expectations. Hirschi includes both as dimensions of commitment, but Elliott et al. treated three of Hirschi's expectation variables as measures of strain theory.

The time dimension of involvement also must be considered separately from the risk and rationality of commitment. The extent to which the relationship between involvement and delinquency is strong, conditional, or unimportant is far from resolved.

Belief, the moral validity of social norms, is the final element of the social bond. Despite general accord for the importance of the concept, diverse variables have measured belief. It is not surprising, as a consequence, that studies have reported different effects for this element. Tests of control theory must measure values toward the law and legal system, techniques of neutralization, and fatalistic orientations.

Temporal Order

With the focus on observation of associations, the second criteria for establishing causation has received even less attention. It is important to determine, first, whether the elements of the social bond precede delinquency, and, second, the temporal ordering among the elements.

The few tests of causal paths have not been replicated successfully. Many studies, however, have conceded the need to determine causal ordering of the elements of the social bond and their temporal priority to delinquency and crime.

The reliance on cross-sectional analysis may have precluded this advancement for control theory. Some researchers who retain this view also consider longitudinal data mandatory for establishing temporal order.

The Absence of Spurious Factors

With the other criteria for establishing causation unresolved, it is difficult to interpret the role of potentially spurious factors. Conditional relationships based on extraneous variables have been observed in many studies of control theory, including age, gender, race, urbanization of area, socioeconomic status, and offense type.

With original relationships between elements of the social bond and delinquency not even established, problems occur with the inclusion in some tests of variables that conflict with the tenet of control theory. The role of delinquent friends, whether guided correctly by social control or differential association theory, for example, must be interpreted cautiously. Reducing either of these theories to "number of delinquent peers" does an injustice to the rich conceptual frameworks they provide. Theoretical integration efforts definitely must await resolution of these and other unanswered queries about the effects of the social bond.

Generalizability Based on Time, Space, and Subjects

Questions about the extent to which control theory is generalizable to specific crime and across demographic groups remain unanswered as well. Better data, including more representative samples, are needed. Less than half of the studies included females, and race varied in even fewer. If control theory is expected to apply to adults as well as youths, the age range must be extended in tests of the theory. Offending must include variation in severity and type. The power of control theory for explaining mental health disorders, sexual behavior, and other forms of norm violation should be considered.

CONCLUSION

Many recommendations can be made for future research as criminology attempts to establish the scientific merits of control theory. Data appropriate for the task must be obtained. These data may require primary collection of surveys, but the potential of secondary data resources also has not been exhausted. These data must reflect attention to conceptualization of the social bond and criterion validity for the four elements. Multiple dimensions of each element also should be examined. The benefits accrued from multiple item indices should be determined. Causal order must be determined by all available techniques, until one preferred method is established. All other variables considered potentially spurious to the original relationship must be tested. Replication across time, space, and subjects must continue at least until dissimilar results are no longer common.

Hirschi offered suggestions for modifications and revisions both of the theory and of testing method, most of which subsequent efforts ignored. This review has shown that the control theory research comprises a large number of essentially separate studies which have little relation to each other and fail to build on experience. Thus, the research reveals little about the viability of social control as a scientific theory. Efforts to expand the theory with additional constructs and calls for the integration of control theory with differential association, deterrence, rational choice, or any other theory will continue to fail until the scientific groundwork for understanding control theory is done. Criminologists need a better understanding of the elements of the social bond as well as the conceptual scheme linking them and the conditions under which they prevail.

Although the large number of studies reviewed should have proved otherwise, it is disheartening to conclude that Cohen was correct in asserting that "Hirschi's theory of social control may be fertile but is not yet fecund." Criminology has done this theory a disservice. Hopefully, this assessment of control theory research will assist in motivating the growth and development of the theory of social control.

QUESTIONS FOR DISCUSSION AND WRITING

1. Of the 71 studies, how many included all four elements of the social bond? Did any single element appear in every study? How often was justification for the missing elements provided?
2. What is the third standard and the criteria by which criminology must evaluate its theories, and how has social control theory fared?
3. What has this review shown about control theory research?

Preventing Delinquency: The Social Development Model

JOSEPH G. WEIS

J. DAVID HAWKINS

THIS chapter describes the theoretical and programmatic foundation—the *social development model*—of a research and development project on delinquency prevention, funded by the Office of Juvenile Justice and Delinquency Prevention and implemented at school-based sites in seven states in the early 1980s.

WHAT IS DELINQUENCY PREVENTION?

Historically, what has been passed off as delinquency prevention within the juvenile justice system is basically delinquency "control," simply because it has been implemented after the illegal behavior and even after a juvenile justice system reaction has occurred. *Control* is a societal reaction to an infraction or a "measure taken after a criminal or delinquent act has been committed." Even the most recent and progressive juvenile justice reforms—for example, diversion and deinstitutionalization—are primarily control strategies, simply because they are aimed at previously identified juvenile offenders. *Prevention* is a societal action to preclude or correct illegal behavior. Prevention approaches can be differentiated into general categories: (a) corrective and (b) preclusive prevention.

From *Preventing Delinquency* by J. Weis and D. Hawkins, 1981, Washington, DC: Government Printing Office.

Corrective prevention has been the traditional approach to delinquency prevention. There are three types of corrective prevention: (a) tertiary corrective prevention within the juvenile justice system focused on "delinquents"; (b) secondary corrective prevention within the juvenile justice system focused on "predelinquents"; and (c) secondary corrective prevention outside the juvenile justice system focused on "high-risk youths."

All three types seek to identify and correct delinquents or potential delinquents. Tertiary corrective prevention within the juvenile justice system has been primarily attempts to "correct" identified individual delinquents in order to change their future behavior. The objective is to change delinquents into nondelinquents.

Secondary corrective prevention within the juvenile justice system is aimed at individuals who are identified as "predelinquent." These are youngsters whose behavior, environment, or other attributes are identified as predictive of more serious involvement in crime and, perhaps, a delinquent career. The object, then, is to prevent an identified predelinquent from becoming a delinquent. The clients of this early identification and corrective approach to prevention within the juvenile court have traditionally been status offenders or youths involved in noncriminal misbehavior.

Secondary corrective prevention outside of the juvenile justice system is aimed at high-risk youths who have not had any contact with the juvenile justice system or at least are not selected for a prevention program for this reason. This type of corrective prevention is based on the identification of behavior or attributes that place a population of juveniles at risk for delinquency. The corrective efforts may be directed at individuals, the classic example being the Cambridge-Somerville Study, or at groups, the classic example being the Chicago Area Project. The former served individual youths who were diagnosed as high risks while the latter served a social area with a high concentration of delinquents. However, neither project was directed at instant infractions or officially designated offenders.

Preclusive prevention is the purest type of prevention approach because it does not include efforts to "correct" individuals or groups who are identified as on the path to becoming delinquent. Rather, it attempts to "preclude" the initial occurrence of delinquency, primarily at the organizational, institutional, social structural, and cultural levels of intervention.

CORRELATES, CAUSES, AND THEORIES OF DELINQUENCY: THE CRITERIA FOR DELINQUENCY PREVENTION

Since the empirical evidence suggests that past efforts at delinquency prevention can be characterized as largely ineffective, one cannot propose that exemplary programs simply be replicated and generalized as the preferred approach to delinquency prevention. Rather, the apparently most valid correlates, causes, and theories of delinquent behavior, in conjunction with the best available evidence on prevention programs, should be used to establish criteria for the most promising techniques of prevention.

The research conducted by the authors and staff at the National Center for the Assessment of Delinquent Behavior and Its Prevention, including (a) comprehensive and systematic review of theories and research on delinquency, (b) secondary data analyses of 10 self-reported delinquency data sets, and (c) a national survey of prevention programs, has identified the strongest correlates of delinquent behavior, the apparently most important theoretically derived causal variables, and the theoretical model which holds the most promise for explaining and preventing delinquent behavior.

Correlates and Causes

Tabular, correlational, and multivariate regression analyses of a number of self-reported delinquency data sets have identified two sets of correlates of delinquent behavior which theory and, therefore, prevention should take into account. One set of correlates is primarily "causal," and consists of family, school, and peer variables, and the other set consists more properly of "sociodemographic" controls, including sex, age, and race. (As in most self-report research, socioeconomic status is not a strong correlate.) The strongest average zero-order correlation is between delinquency (both self-reported and official) and peer items (peer culture activities; delinquency of friends), followed by the sex of the respondent, and school variables (importance of grades; like school; grade point average). For self-reported delinquent behavior only, family variables (father and mother supervision; sharing thoughts and feelings with parents), employment (respondent works), and age are the next strongest correlates. Multivariate regression analyses, which allow the analyst to assess the simultaneous, interactive effects of a number of variables, show the same rank order of explanatory power among peer, school, and family variables. What is, perhaps, of most theoretical interest is that the ascending strengths of the correlates suggest a chain of causation which moves from family to school to peer variables.

Among the major theoretical perspectives of delinquency, *control theory* and *cultural deviance theory* seem to have the most to offer theoretically, as well as for the prevention of delinquency. There are a number of reasons for this conclusion. First, and most important, control theory has received the most empirical support of the major theoretical perspectives, with cultural deviance theory running a respectable second.

Second, and related, control theory and cultural deviance theory take into account and best explain the apparently strongest correlates of delinquency. The former is not class specific and focuses directly on the role of the family, school, and law in preventing delinquent behavior, while the latter is primarily a theory of peer influence on crime.

Third, the configuration of "causes" specified in these theories, particularly in control theory, is very similar to the public's perception of the causes of delinquency. It is also clear from our national survey of prevention program practitioners that those people who are involved directly in providing services to youth agree most with the propositions of control theory, followed by cultural deviance, and then psychological theoretical perspectives. Given that the general public and prevention practitioners should believe in and support the rationale of delinquency prevention, it suggests the prospect of easier acceptance, support, and implementation of prevention programs based on these particular theories of delinquent behavior.

Fourth, control theory is basically a theory of prevention rather than of causes of delinquency. Rather than attempt to explain why delinquency occurs, it attempts to explain why delinquency is not prevented. Consequently, as a theory, it seems to have direct and implementable implications for delinquency prevention.

Fifth, control theory has never been implemented systematically and comprehensively in a delinquency prevention program, whereas the other major theoretical perspectives have been implemented in both control and prevention efforts, and with little success. This is not a reflection of the validity or utility of control theory, but rather of its relative youth compared to other theories and, perhaps, of the simple and straightforward implications for prevention at the organizational and institutional levels of intervention.

Sixth, the implications for delinquency prevention of control and cultural deviance theories are for primary, preclusive prevention and secondary, corrective prevention—the theories primarily inform those aspects of prevention which are carried on outside of the juvenile justice system.

Seventh, control and cultural deviance theories are particularly suitable for theoretical integration.

The two theoretical perspectives can be complementary, and there have been a number of recent syntheses (e.g., Voss; Conger; Bahr; Johnson). This merger was hinted at by Hirschi, but as a way to "supplement rather than seriously modify the control theory," especially in the area of "companionship" and "group processes important in the causation of delinquency." Control theory does not take into account the role of peers, particularly within informal group processes, in delinquency causation; cultural deviance theory does, and it is here that the two theories have most to offer each other. A theoretical integration of control and cultural deviance theories offers the promise of a more complete, valid, and useful theory of delinquency and its prevention.

Integrating Control and Cultural Deviance Theories

Control and cultural deviance theories are a good combination because each makes up for the major deficiencies in the other, and together they offer the promise of a more complete and valid explanation of delinquent behavior. Both theories are primarily *socialization* theories of juvenile delinquency—control theory suggests that youngsters become delinquent because of inadequate socialization to conformity, while cultural deviance theory suggests that youngsters become delinquent because of socialization to delinquency. In the former, those who are not taught and do not learn to not engage in delinquent behavior will and do, and in the latter those who are taught and learn to engage in delinquent behavior will and do. Control theory specifies theoretically and empirically the important *units* (family, school, law) and *elements* (attachment, commitment, belief, involvement) of socialization that are necessary in the prevention of delinquency but does not offer an explanation of "how" the socialization process works. The theory specifies the units and elements of socialization that lead to the development of a generalized "bond" to the conventional order, but it does not pay much attention to the process of making an individual moral— for example, how are important affective attachments to parents developed or how is commitment to education within the context of the school achieved and maintained? If delinquent behavior is a by-product of incomplete socialization, an explanation of how people are socialized seems essential.

Cultural deviance theory focuses directly on the *process* of socialization to criminal behavior. It attempts to explain the social process of "learning" criminal values and behavior patterns and, in so doing, also suggests how one learns conventional values and behavior patterns. This is particularly the case with the "social learning" version of cultural deviance theory, which borrows from operant conditioning learning theory and develops a social behavioristic model of human conduct and learning. An integration of control and cultural deviance theories, specifically Hirschi's control theory and Akers's social learning theory, means that the *units, elements,* and *processes* of socialization are incorporated within one theoretical model which offers a major improvement in explanatory and predictive power.

Control and cultural deviance theories are also complementary in another important way. Even though cultural deviance theory does not specify the units within which learning occurs, except to propose that it takes place in interaction and association with others, it is basically a theory of peer influence, especially among juveniles. Given that (a) the influence of informal group processes, particularly among friends, companions, and acquaintances who are one's peers, was underestimated and falls outside the purview of control theory, (b) the empirical evidence shows that peer socialization and attachments are directly related to delinquent behavior, and (c) Hirschi suggests that the role of peer influence is probably a necessary supplement to control theory, the theoretical integration of the two perspectives is even more promising. Regarding the nature of the supplementary role of peer influence, it is suggested that "peers" be incorporated into the integrated theoretical model as another very important unit of socialization, and that the influence of peers be conceptualized as an intervening social process between an unattached, uncommitted, and disbelieving youngster and delinquent behavior. If the social process of making a youngster moral has been interrupted by uncaring parents, poor school performance, visions of occupational failure, and a questionably legitimate legal system, he or she is more free to engage in delinquent behavior and is more likely to come under the influence of peers who may be in the same situation and who provide each other the social and psychological support, rewards, and reinforcement that are not forthcoming in more conventional contexts. *Otherwise put, the more inadequate the socialization to conformity, the more likely the socialization to nonconformity.*

In Figure 1, the general model of delinquency which integrates control and cultural deviance theories—the social development model— shows the kinds of relationships among the units and elements of socialization as proposed in control and cultural deviance theories. Socialization within the family will be affected differentially by sociodemographic background variables, which for heuristic purposes are outside of the direct causal relationships but may influence the development of attachment to parents. For example, research has suggested that boys and girls are socialized differently within the family, and there may be cultural variation in family organization and concomitant socialization experiences, and that child-rearing practices vary across socioeconomic class. The development of attachment to parents will take place within the context of these types of sociodemographic "givens"—a child is born male or female and into a family unit with certain socioeconomic and cultural characteristics.

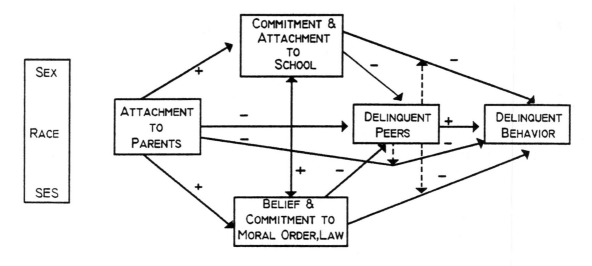

FIGURE 1 *A general model of delinquency: Integration of control and cultural deviance theories.*

Theoretically and empirically, the development of attachment to parents will lead to commitment to education and attachment to school, and to belief in and commitment to the conventional moral order and the law. These attachments, commitments, and beliefs to conformity, or what Toby refers to as "stakes in conformity," are intercorrelated and in turn directly prevent a youngster from engaging in delinquent behavior and indirectly prevent delinquent behavior by insulating a youngster against delinquent peer influence. Involvement with and attachment to nonconforming peers is directly related to delinquent behavior and also conditions the effects of family, school, and law on delinquent behavior by reinforcing the inclination to engage in crime among those youngsters who have low stakes in conformity.

Obviously, this simple model does not include all of the variables or relationships proposed by the two theories. Neither does the model depict the process by which the various components of the bond to conformity are developed (these process variables, derived from social learning theory, will be plugged into the model and discussed later). Nor does the model depict the interaction effects among some of the variables. Both the effects of the intervening "process" variables and the interactions among variables, particularly between the causal and sociodemographic control variables, have important consequences for delinquency theory and prevention.

A dynamic multivariate causal model of delinquency is desirable for theory and prevention. A dynamic causal model and its derivative implications for prevention should be responsive to the direct and interaction effects among variables over time. In the most general sense, the different "causes" of delinquency have different effects at different points in time in a youngster's life. More specifically, it is clear that the causal power of the important units of socialization varies by the age of a youngster. Children move through a number of significant "institutional passages" in their social development. These passages demarcate "stages" in the life of a youngster during which different units of socialization are most important. Those stages are mapped primarily by the education system: preschool, primary school, intermediate or junior high school, and high school. For preschool children, the family is the most significant unit of socialization; when a child begins

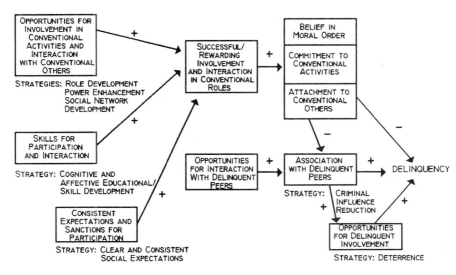

FIGURE 2 *The general prevention strategies which seek to facilitate the process of delinquency prevention.*

school in the primary grades, the school becomes an important socializing institution; beginning in junior high school, the role of peers in socialization emerges and becomes even more important as a youngster moves into high school.

These types of dynamic and complex relationships among variables suggest that delinquency prevention should not only be responsive to "causes" of delinquency but also to the manner in which the causes work within the social development process. If prevention efforts are to take into account and reflect the apparent complexity of causal relations, they should be directed at the causes of delinquency as they emerge and interact during the lives of youngsters. Different interventions are called for at different stages in the socialization of youths. A dynamic, multivariate theoretical model suggests an equally dynamic, multifaceted model of delinquency prevention.

The Process and Strategies of Delinquency Prevention

It is possible to specify in more detail the process by which the elements of the social devel-opment model prevent delinquent behavior. The process is repeated with minor modifications in each institutional setting encountered during social development (family, school, peer group, employment). In Figure 2, the process is illustrated without reference to specific institutions of socialization and social control.

Opportunities for involvement in conventional activities and for interaction with conventional others are necessary structural conditions for the development of commitment to conventional lines of action and attachment to conventional others. In order for these structural opportunities to produce social bonds which prevent delinquency, the individuals who participate in conventional activities and interactions must have certain requisite *skills*. The application of these skills makes participation *rewarding*. It should be emphasized that skills must be possessed by both youthful participants and by others (such as parents and teachers) with whom youths are involved. For example, for involvement in school to be rewarding, students must develop cognitive skills, but teachers must also be skilled in recognizing and reinforcing students' progress. Furthermore, different actors in youths' social environment must be consistent in their expectations for and responses to behavior if conforming behavior is to be continually reinforced and deviant behavior prevented or extinguished.

If youths do not find their participation in conventional activities and interactions with conventional others rewarding, they are likely to seek other associations and activities which promise alternative rewards. They are likely to associate with peers who are also disillusioned with their experiences. Together these alienated youths are likely to discover opportunities for delinquency and to influence one another toward delinquent acts. In contrast, those youths who are rewarded and successful develop commitments to conventional activities, attachment to conventional others, and beliefs in the moral order and are less likely to engage in delinquent behavior.

"Role development and power enhancement" strategies provide youths with opportunities for involvement in conventional activities which have the likelihood of being rewarding. Role development strategies assume that delinquency stems from a lack of opportunity to be involved in legitimate roles or activities which youths perceive as personally gratifying. Power enhancement strategies assume that delinquency stems from a lack of power or control over impinging environmental factors. They seek to increase the ability or power of youth to influence the institutions in which they participate.

"Social network development" strategies provide youths with opportunities for interactions with conventional others which are likely to be rewarding. Social network development strategies assume that delinquency results from weak attachments between youths and conforming members of society.

"Education/skill development" strategies seek to assist those involved in conventional activities and interactions to develop adequate cognitive and affective skills to ensure that youthful participants are successful in these involvements and interactions. Education/skill development strategies assume that delinquency stems from a lack of knowledge or skills necessary to live in society without violating its laws.

"Clear and consistent social expectations" strategies ensure that the institutions in which youths participate are clear and consistent in their expectations for and responses to behavior. These strategies assume that delinquency results from competing or conflicting demands and expectations placed on youths by institutions such as families, schools, communities, peer groups, and the law.

"Criminal influence reduction" strategies are applied to minimize the influence of delinquent norms and delinquent peers on behavior. These strategies assume that delinquency stems from the influence of others who directly or indirectly encourage youths to commit delinquent acts. They seek to reduce the influence of norms toward delinquency and of those who hold such norms.

Finally, "deterrence" strategies are applied to reduce the opportunities for delinquent behavior. Deterrence strategies assume that delinquency results because there is a low degree of risk or difficulty associated with committing delinquent acts. They seek to change the cost/benefit ratio of participation in crime by restructuring opportunities and minimizing incentives to engage in crime.

A Comprehensive Social Development Model of Delinquency Prevention

The process of delinquency prevention outlined in the preceding section can now be integrated with the general social development model of delinquency presented earlier. The resulting comprehensive model of delinquency prevention is shown in Figure 3.

Social development can be seen as a series of passages from one institution of socialization to another, during which the preceding institution gradually decreases in importance as a socializing force while the next institution becomes increasingly salient. Delinquency prevention processes should be present in each institutional

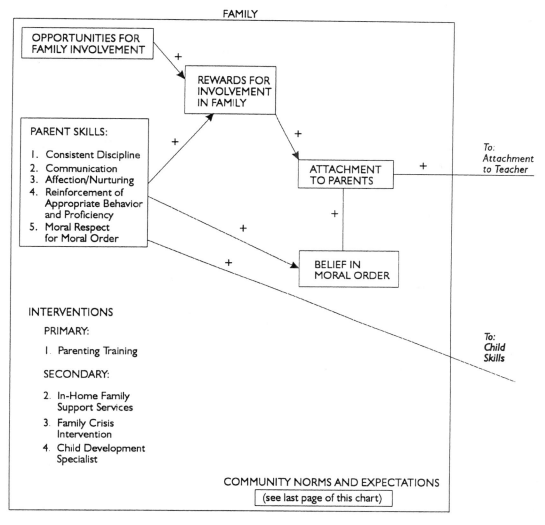

FIGURE 3 *Comprehensive model of delinquency prevention.*

setting if social development is to proceed without delinquency.

The first socializing institution in the sequence, the *family,* is of primary importance from birth until youths enter school. The process of delinquency prevention in the family is illustrated on the left side of Figure 3. Opportunities for involvement in certain roles in the family plus specific parent skills lead to rewarding family involvement for children. Rewarding involvement leads to attachment to parents. This attachment influences subsequent school experiences and belief in the moral order.

School becomes an important institution during the years from school entry until graduation or dropout. The process of delinquency prevention in schools is illustrated in the second box of Figure 3. Opportunities for involvement in certain school roles, consistency of expectations in the school environment, and teacher and child skills predict academic success experiences,

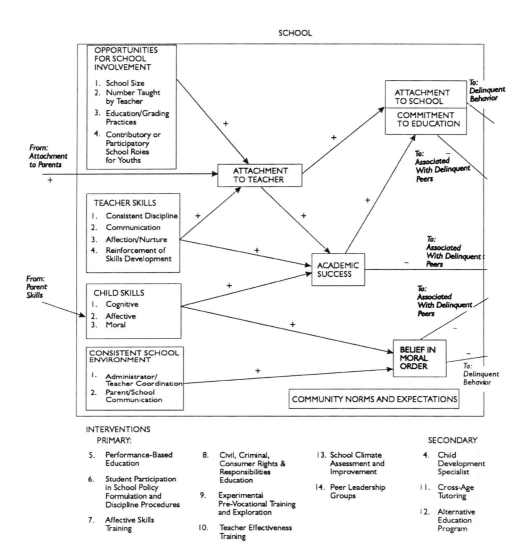

FIGURE 3 *(Continued)*

attachment to school, and commitment to education. These, in turn, enhance belief in the moral order, inhibit association with delinquency-prone peers, and prevent delinquency. School's influence may decrease differentially depending on academic and social experiences at school. For example, for students who do not experience academic success, school may decrease in importance and employment increase in importance earlier than for students who are successful and rewarded in school.

During adolescence, *peers* become increasingly important to the socialization process and continue to be important through high school. Their influence is shown in the third box in Figure 3.

For a portion of the youth population, especially those who do not experience rewarding involvement in school, *employment* may become an important socializing force from high-adolescence on as shown in the fourth box in Figure 3.

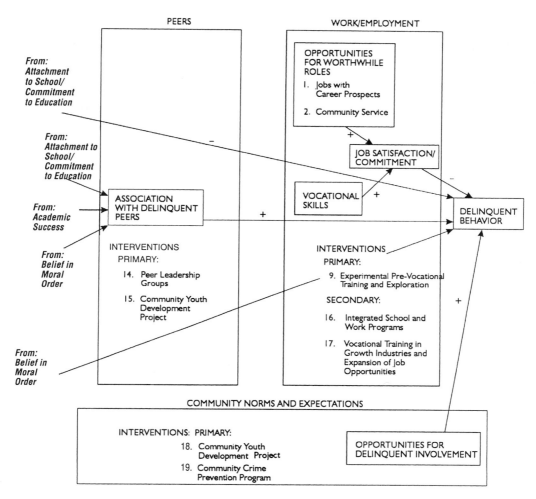

FIGURE 3 *(Continued)*

Finally, the *community* setting provides a context which may influence behavior throughout the process of social development as shown in the bottom portion of Figure 3.

AN EXPERIMENTAL TEST OF THE COMPREHENSIVE MODEL

A research and development project which studies the effects of both the combined elements of the social development model has been implemented at seven sites throughout the United States, with the support of the Office of Juvenile Justice and Delinquency Prevention. The project is designed to test the validity and utility of the proposed prevention model and provide a tested technology for delinquency prevention. The project is described below.

Project Overview

The project has two major components. One component is a *comprehensive* longitudinal research and development project in a single site

(Seattle, Washington), in which the theoretically derived and empirically supported causes of delinquency are addressed at the appropriate points in the process of social development. This project is designed to continue for 5 years with a possible 5-year extension. The second major component is a set of separate projects in *selected* sites (Bangor, Maine; Waterbury, Connecticut; Reading, Pennsylvania; Brooklyn, New York; Paterson, New Jersey; West Palm Beach, Florida) with a selected subset of program elements of the delinquency prevention model being tested at each site. The selected site projects are to continue for 3 years. Both components of the overall project have been designed and implemented with rigorous experimental and/or quasi-experimental research designs to assess program effects in preventing delinquency.

Intervention Components

Described below is the set of intervention components to be included in the comprehensive delinquency prevention research and development project only. These intervention components are ordered according to the institution targeted (i.e., family, school, peers, work, community). For each institution, the primary preclusive and secondary corrective interventions to be implemented and tested are described. In each section below, the major goals of the intervention, the setting where the intervention is implemented, and the content of the intervention are described. The lower half of Figure 3 provides a visual display of the intervention components as they are applied in the comprehensive project site, with component intervention numbers keyed to descriptions in the following section.

Family Interventions

The major goals of family-focused interventions are to increase attachment to parents and to increase belief in the moral order. Some research has suggested that family interactions have a direct relationship with delinquent behavior, while other evidence indicates that, at least for drug use, the influence of family is indirect. The prevention model assumes both direct and indirect influences of the family on delinquent behavior. The indirect links are mediated by school experiences, beliefs in the moral order, and peer group associations. Whether family influence is viewed as direct or indirect, there is sufficient evidence to conclude that attachment to parents is an important element of prevention which should be addressed in a comprehensive prevention project.

As with each of the units of socialization and social control in the prevention model, it is hypothesized that opportunities for involvement, the level of participant skills, and consistency of expectations and sanctions will determine the extent of attachment between children and parents. All three sets of variables can be addressed through parenting training. Therefore, in this project, parenting training is the primary prevention intervention focused on the family.

1. PARENTING TRAINING

Parenting training seeks to enhance the following characteristics of the family by teaching parents skills for more effective child rearing.

Opportunities for Involvement. Opportunities for family involvement are partially determined by background variables including socioeconomic status of the family, sex of the child, and age of the child which will not be directly addressed by the prevention intervention. These variables will be measured and their contribution to attachment and delinquency assessed. On the other hand, the child's role and responsibilities in the family represent opportunities for involvement which can be enhanced through training. It is hypothesized that when parents provide children with participatory roles in the family as contributors to family survival and functioning, attachment to the family will be enhanced and delinquency prevented, if performance of the roles is rewarded.

Consistency of Parental Discipline. Fairness and impartiality of discipline appear related to family attachment and family control. Sanctions used to punish should be moderate and inclusionary and imply no rejection or ostracism of the child. Consistent parental discipline also appears to increase the likelihood of belief in the conventional moral order. Parenting training can assist parents in establishing consistent discipline practices.

Communication Between Parents and Child. The more parents and children communicate with one another regarding thoughts, feelings, and values, the stronger the attachment between children and parents. Parents can be assisted through parenting training in opening and maintaining lines of communication to their children, in empathetic listening, and in basic interpersonal interaction skills.

Affection, Nurture, and Support. The greater the affection, nurture, and support shown children by parents, the greater the likelihood of attachment between parents and children and the less the likelihood of delinquency. Parenting training can provide parents skills in showing affection and support for their children.

Parental Reinforcement for Conforming Behavior and Skill Development. Parents should consistently reinforce desired behaviors and developing competence in their children. Parenting training can provide skills in positive reinforcement.

Modeling Belief and Respect for the Moral Order. Finally, parents should be consistent as models of law-abiding behavior for their children, if children are to develop belief in the conventional moral order. Parenting training can emphasize the importance of this modeling by parents.

The sampling and recruitment for parenting classes occurs through the schools. In the project, classrooms of first graders are the first sampling units. All parents with children in experimental classrooms will be recruited for participation in parenting classes. This will allow for a sample of parents from the general population and minimize possible perceived stigma associated with recruitment or selection for a parenting class, and allow intensive recruitment efforts with sampled parents. It is anticipated that by identifying parenting training as a school program and by recruiting intensively, broader cross sections of the parent population will be involved in the training than typically occurs in community-based parenting training programs. The parenting program will include approximately 12 to 16 two-hour sessions over a 2-month period and will focus on the development of parenting skills described earlier. We expect that a large proportion of parents who attend the first training session will be retained throughout the program.

Parenting classes will be offered again to parents of students in fourth- and seventh-grade experimental classrooms. The content of the class will be altered to suit the social development level of children whose parents are sampled. For example, for parents of fourth graders, emphasis will be on involving children in contributory roles in the family and rewarding or reinforcing satisfactory performance of these roles. Content for parents of seventh graders will emphasize negotiation of rights and responsibilities and training in dealing with adolescent issues including sexual development, drugs, and alcohol.

The general goals of parenting training are to improve parenting skills and therefore to increase attachment between children and parents and to improve the control effectiveness of the family as implied by control theory.

2. IN-HOME FAMILY SUPPORT SERVICES

In-home family support services are secondary prevention interventions which will be made available in the community to families of primary-grade children in experimental school catchment areas. The services will be offered through a not-for-profit, community-based service agency with links to school and social service agencies. Because this is a secondary prevention component, referrals of eligible individual families will be accepted from any source so long as the referral does not result from a delinquent act by the child. Referred families who voluntarily agree to use the family support services will be eligible, with preference given to those with the most severe presenting problems. Experimental and control families will be randomly selected from the pool of eligible families. Control families will be referred to existing social service programs in the community. Experimental families will receive in-home family support services.

The intent of in-home family support services is to provide services to families experiencing stress-producing physical or financial problems, as well as internal structural and interactional difficulties. Services will be provided by an in-home family support worker responsible for family assessment and collaborative execution of a family plan developed with the family. The plan may include homemaker services, training in family management and parenting skills, advocacy, respite care of children, and collaboration with other agencies to provide special services.

The hypothesis underlying this intervention is that providing parents with skills and resources to manage effectively their families when there is evidence that such skills and resources are seriously lacking will enable high-risk families to provide more effectively for physical needs, exercise more consistent discipline, and show affection to children. This should, in turn, increase attachment between parents and children, increase the control effectiveness of the family, and ultimately inhibit delinquency as suggested by control theory.

3. FAMILY CRISIS INTERVENTION SERVICES

Family crisis intervention services will be made available in the target community to families of children aged 12 to 16 in experimental school catchment areas and will be provided as a secondary prevention intervention through a community-based not-for-profit agency. Referrals of individual families experiencing severe conflict between children and parents will be accepted. An experimental sampling procedure will again be used to select referred families for participation and control conditions.

Family crisis intervention services will use a skill development approach to families as systems of communication and exchange. Both parents and children will be trained in communication, contingency contracting, and negotiation skills. Parents will also be taught consistent and explicit rule-setting behaviors. Experimental evidence indicated that this approach to secondary prevention as developed and tested by Alexander and Parsons is effective in reducing delinquency among "status offenders" and minor delinquents. It also appears to reduce the likelihood of delinquency among younger siblings in families who participate.

4. CHILD DEVELOPMENT SPECIALISTS

The child development specialist intervention is the final secondary prevention component directed at the family. The child development specialist is a school-based resource person and advocate whose tasks include ensuring adequate skill development among students in primary grades who are evidencing special difficulties in school. While the specialist's responsibilities are largely in the school setting, they also include working with parents to develop and implement plans for addressing learning and related problems which may inhibit academic success. Child development specialists will work with parents of students experiencing difficulties in experimental classes in the primary grades.

School-Based Interventions

A growing body of research results has linked immediate school experiences of academic failure, as measured by grades and achievement test scores, to delinquent behavior. At the individual level, academic achievement appears to be a predictor of delinquent behavior that transcends social class and ethnicity, suggesting that providing a greater proportion of students with opportunities to experience success in school should hold promise for preventing delinquency. A second school factor related to delinquency is commitment to academic or educational pursuits. When students are not committed to educational pursuits, they are more likely to engage in delinquent behavior.

Similarly, attachment to school is related to delinquency. Students who do not like school are more likely to engage in delinquent acts than those who do. These data suggest that educational innovations which encourage students to feel part of the school community and committed to educational goals hold promise for preventing delinquency.

The major goals of school-focused/education-focused prevention are (a) to increase attachment to teachers, (b) to increase student academic success experiences, (c) to increase attachment to school, (d) to increase commitment to education, and (e) to increase belief in the moral order.

To achieve these goals, three sets of variables categorized as (a) "providing opportunities for successful school involvement," (b) "enhancing participant (teacher and student) skills," and (c) "ensuring consistency of expectations and sanctions in the school environment" are addressed in the comprehensive prevention project.

Providing Opportunities for Successful School Involvement

The availability of opportunities for successful involvement in school is partially determined by funding and resource levels. For example, the size of the school itself and the number of students taught per teacher are usually determined by fiscal considerations. Yet these variables may help determine the availability of opportunities for successful school participation. In large schools where teachers see a number of different students each day, teachers are generally less able to establish interpersonal relationships with students and to use a broad range of rewards for student participation. In the absence of warm interpersonal relationships between students and teachers,

delinquency is more likely. Research has consistently shown correlations between both school size and average number of students taught by teachers and rates for school crime. Smaller schools are characterized by lower levels of student offenses when ability level, racial composition, and economic status of student are controlled. Similarly, where fewer students are seen each day by a teacher, rates of school crime are lower. The primary prevention interventions which seek to address these variables are discussed below.

5. PERFORMANCE-BASED EDUCATION

(Interventions are numbered as in Figure 3.) Traditional school curricula and grading practices do not provide success experiences for all students. A large number of students receive poor grades in most of their subjects for all of their school careers.

Performance-based education refers to a set of interrelated elements to be included in experimental schools to address this issue. These elements are (a) development and implementation of curricula tailored to students' learning needs and interests, (b) establishment of clear learning goals for each student, and (c) implementation of individually paced learning programs with clear rewards for individual improvement in academic competency.

Rather than intervene directly with students, teachers of experimental classes will be trained in skills necessary for performance-based education. Teachers will learn to select and develop high interest materials; to establish realistic attainable goals for each student; to tie clear rewards to different levels of demonstrated effort and proficiency based on students' original performance rather than on competition with classmates; and to broaden available rewards beyond traditional grades.

It is hypothesized that the use of performance-based education approaches with contingent reward systems will positively influence students' cognitive skills and performance levels, increase the proportion of students experiencing academic success rather than failure in school, increase student attachment to teachers, and increase student attachment to school and commitment to education. Instruction in performance-based education will be provided to primary and junior high teachers of experimental classrooms.

6. STUDENT INVOLVEMENT IN SCHOOL CLASSROOM POLICY FORMULATION AND DISCIPLINE PROCEDURES

A natural concomitant of entry into adolescence is a more critical questioning of adult authority. Until this time, the student role is largely a passive one. While adolescents in postindustrial society are not positioned to take on major production or work roles, commitments to conventional lines of action can be enhanced by providing them opportunities to find meaningful roles in shaping the institution in which they are most directly involved during this period of their social development—their school and classroom.

Student involvement in school policy formulation and discipline procedures consists of two elements. First is classroom-based skills training in participatory governance and shared decision making for seventh-grade students. The second element involves the development of opportunities for student involvement in school policymaking (such as participation in formulation of the school drug policy) and in review of student violations of school rules and expectations for sixth- to ninth-grade students.

Attention will be given to recruitment and involvement of a broad range of "natural peer group leaders" for participation in policymaking and disciplinary bodies to ensure that participatory roles in these activities are created for students not typically involved in traditional "student council" or other student leadership groups. As discussed later in this chapter, this intervention also targets peer influence.

It is hypothesized that simultaneously increasing opportunities for student involvement in school policy formulation and discipline procedures and increasing student skills for fulfilling these roles will increase student attachment to school, commitment to conventional lines of action, and belief in the moral order.

Enhancing Participant Skills

Developing youth cognitive and social skills is the major function of schools. Thus, many of the proposed school-based components of this project ultimately focus on student skill development. For example, the performance-based education discussed earlier is, in part, a method for ensuring successful development of students' cognitive skills. The components of the delinquency prevention project discussed in this section add specific elements to the school curriculum to achieve the major goals of increasing attachment to teachers and conventional others, attachment to school, and belief in the moral order. It should be noted that one such element (enhancing skills for democratic participation) has already been discussed in conjunction with student involvement approaches.

7. AFFECTIVE/SOCIAL SKILLS TRAINING

Programs which seek to increase students' interpersonal skills have been broadly implemented for drug abuse prevention in the past decade. The few available rigorous evaluations of drug abuse prevention efforts have shown these interpersonal skill development approaches to be among the most promising for drug abuse prevention. These approaches assume that young people need to learn basic communication, decision-making, negotiation, and conflict resolution skills in order to perform effectively in interpersonal situations with family members, teachers, or peers. The premise is that schools should teach these skills for interpersonal functioning just as they teach cognitive skills. If young people have these skills, they are more likely to find their interactions with conventional others rewarding and to develop attachments to these others. These skills may also contribute to academic success and to attachment and commitment to schools. On the other hand, when these skills are absent, young people may become frustrated in interaction with others, may be more susceptible to delinquent influences, and may turn to unacceptable behaviors to meet their needs.

To increase students' interpersonal skills, the project will train teachers of experimental classes in the use of social skills curricula appropriate for the age range of students in their classes. An integrated curriculum will be adapted from available curricula to provide a social skills development component with the greatest apparent applicability for interpersonal skills development for delinquency prevention.

8. CIVIL AND CRIMINAL LAW/ CONSUMER EDUCATION

A second primary prevention intervention focused on skills development seeks ultimately to increase belief in the moral order and the law by educating students about the functions of the law and their rights and responsibilities under it. In contrast to many law-related education (LRE) approaches, this intervention combines education with power enhancement strategy. By including attention to civil and consumer law as well as to criminal law, students learn how to use the law for their own protection and how to use legal means to achieve their goals. By exploring the use of the law to achieve personally desired ends rather than relying on a didactic approach emphasizing legal responsibilities, this intervention seeks to develop belief in the law.

This program element is introduced into experimental classes in ninth grade as part of the required course in civics or history. A program staff member trained in use of the curriculum will coordinate integration of the component with the regular classroom teacher.

9. EXPERIENTIAL PREVOCATIONAL EDUCATION AND EXPLORATION

The final curriculum addition focuses on preparing students for the world of work while still in school. Young people's expectations and aspirations are related to the development of commitments to conventional lines of action. School should provide young people with information and experiences which help them develop aspirations and expectations for attaining legitimate employment which they view as sufficiently re-

warding or worthwhile to justify commitment. If schools can help students make commitments to legitimate careers, delinquency should be reduced. One mechanism for achieving this goal is experiential prevocational training and exploration, in which students are exposed to a wide range of possible career options and informed of the skills and training required to attain these. Experiential exposure to career options can increase understanding of actual career opportunities while providing students with opportunities to contribute to their placement sites and thus enhance the likelihood that involvement will be perceived as immediately rewarding. This should, in turn, increase the likelihood of aspirations and commitments to conventional career roles.

Experiential prevocational training will begin in experimental classrooms in the eighth grade and continue through high school. During the first year, the program will be based largely in the classroom with field trips to work sites. In subsequent years, opportunities for work/internship experiences in the community will be included and articulated with traditional course work necessary for high school graduation.

10. TEACHER EFFECTIVENESS TRAINING

The final primary prevention intervention in this area targets teachers rather than students. Teacher effectiveness training will assist teachers to develop skills in consistent disciplining, in communicating with students, and in affective/nurturing behaviors. Research has shown that good relationships between teachers and students (attachments to teachers) can prevent school crime. This intervention seeks to assist teachers in becoming more skillful in their interactions with students in order to increase attachment between students and teachers. This component will be offered to teachers of experimental classes in primary grades and in intermediate or junior high schools.

11. CROSS-AGE TUTORING

Cross-age tutoring is a secondary prevention strategy aimed at ensuring satisfactory skill development for students in primary grades who are evidencing special difficulties in school. An additional function is to provide ninth- and 10th-grade students with opportunities to perform a productive role (as tutors) which may increase commitment to education and attachment to school. To maximize the preventive power of this intervention, secondary school students will be selected as tutors, based on teacher recommendations. Students whose cognitive skills are adequate for the tutoring role but whose commitments to school appear marginal will be included in the tutor pool along with students traditionally selected for leadership roles to accomplish retroflexive reformation.

12. ALTERNATIVE EDUCATION OPTIONS

A final secondary prevention approach aimed at ensuring academic success, attachment to school, and commitment to education through skill development is an alternative learning environment for junior and senior high school students who will not, or cannot, remain in traditional school environments because of disruptive behavior, disaffiliation, or disinterest. The project will work with the existing alternative education facility to ensure that the program contains the elements important for delinquency prevention.

Ensuring Consistency of Expectations and Sanctions in School

Consistent expectations and sanctions for behavior provide environmental conditions which make the existing social order appear fair and just to young people. Thus, consistent expectations are likely to facilitate belief in the conventional moral order. Students are probably more likely to develop attachments to school when their parents and the school staff are in agreement regarding expectations for behavior and performance. In contrast, parents' complaints about schools and teachers are not likely to inspire their children to believe in the school's authority or to like school. Collabora-

tive cooperation between parents and school personnel and among school personnel themselves is likely to enhance student commitment to education, attachment to school, and belief in the moral order and, thereby, to prevent delinquency.

13. SCHOOL CLIMATE ASSESSMENT
 AND IMPROVEMENT

An approach which has shown promise for enhancing administrator and teacher cooperation is school climate assessment and improvement. This is a process in which the administrator and staff commit themselves to realistic appraisal of program, process, and material determinants of the school's social and educational milieu. These determinants include 18 variables such as "opportunities for active learning," "varied reward systems," "continuous improvement of school goals," "effective communications," and "a supportive and efficient logistical system." Faculty and administration collaboratively identify school climate factors in need of improvement and implement activities to address these problems. The process involves both administration and faculty, as participants in the school community, in collaborative work to ameliorate conditions in the school. Thus, regardless of its specific focus, when properly implemented the process can enhance cooperation between administrator and teachers.

A second method for enhancing consistency of expectations and sanctions in the child's environment is to ensure ongoing communication between schools and parents. Child development specialists will ensure that parents are routinely contacted regarding special achievements of their children in the classroom and emerging needs for support or assistance from home to ensure skill development. They will also coordinate recruitment of parents for volunteer classroom involvement and participation in school decision making.

The major goal of the school/home communication and parent/school involvement activities will be to increase the likelihood that young people in experimental schools are receiving clear and consistent expectations from major actors in their social environment regarding performance and behavior. More specifically, it is hoped that success will be more consistently rewarded both at home and school and the problems will be recognized and collaboratively addressed by adults in both environments.

Peer-Oriented Interventions

As noted earlier, association with delinquent peers is one of the strongest correlates of delinquency. The theoretical model which is the basis of the prevention approach proposed here postulates that young people are likely to develop attachments to delinquent peers when their bonds to conforming others are weak or broken. Thus, to the extent that attachment to parents, attachment to school, commitment to education, and belief in the moral order can be generated by prior interventions in the prevention project, young people should be less susceptible to the influence of peers toward delinquency. Yet peer-oriented approaches remain important elements of a comprehensive prevention project because of the apparent strength of the effect of peers on youths' behaviors and because it is unlikely that all youths will be insulated from these effects by the foregoing program elements.

14. PEER LEADERSHIP GROUPS

Peer leadership groups will be organized in experimental intermediate or junior and senior high schools. Group members will be informal leaders of all major student cliques and groups, not just traditional student body leaders. Members will be nominated by teachers and students with the project's peer program coordinator responsible for final selection of members. Student members of the peer leadership groups will meet daily for an hour as part of their regular school activities. However, in contrast to many guided peer-group interaction programs, an explicit goal and task of the peer leadership groups will be to identify and address school

policy issues that are perceived as problems by students and to work with the school administration to develop reasonable and enforceable school policies regarding these problems. Peer leadership groups will also serve as recruitment pools for student judicial/disciplinary bodies which will handle student grievance and disciplinary referrals for violations of school policies. The peer leadership groups are an attempt to integrate implications of control and cultural deviance theories into a peer-oriented prevention strategy, while recognizing the failures of peer-oriented programs focused wholly on delinquent groups, such as the detached gang workers studied by Klein.

The peer leadership groups seek to encourage leaders of delinquency-prone groups to establish ties to more conventional peers. Rather than assuming that interaction per se will lead to development of these ties, the approach presumes that ties will be developed as peer leadership group members work together toward common goals of institutional change in the school and as they perform judicial functions. It is also assumed that attachment to school will be enhanced by performance of these functions. Finally, to the extent that informal peer group leaders are accurately identified and selected for participation, it is hypothesized that these leaders will, in turn, influence members of their own cliques toward more positive attitudes to school as school policies are altered in response to their participation. It is hoped that in this way delinquency-prone groups will be co-opted. As with most other interventions proposed here, this component is an adaptation of approaches currently in use.

15. COMMUNITY YOUTH DEVELOPMENT PROJECT

This component is a community-focused youth participation and advocacy project. Adult and youth community members will be recruited and organized into planning committees to assess and address community issues related to youth development. As in the peer leadership groups, a goal here will be to involve community youths who are not typically involved in leadership roles in schools and youths who are currently out of school. These youths will be involved with adults in planning and organizing activities and projects to improve opportunities for youth in the community. A range of projects may be initiated. The specific activities planned and implemented are viewed here as less important than the collaborative involvements of community youths and adults in attempting to make the community aware of, and more responsive to, youth. This intervention attempts to encourage youths to develop ties to this conventional group through their involvement. It can also provide a vehicle for co-opting delinquent groups into community development and enhancement activities.

Employment-Oriented Interventions

While positive correlations have been found between aggregate unemployment and crime rates, research also indicates a positive correlation at the individual level between having a job during high school and self-reported delinquency. For youths still in school, early employment may detract from commitments to school which can inhibit delinquency. Alternatively, it is possible that youths who have not developed attachments and commitments to school are more likely to become employed during middle-to-late adolescence. Either interpretation of the available data suggests that employment per se should not be implemented as a general strategy for primary prevention of delinquency.

However, research has also shown that delinquent youths who drop out of school become less delinquent after dropping out, especially if they secure employment. These data suggest that youth employment should be viewed as a secondary delinquent prevention approach for high-risk youth who have not, by the age of 16, developed attachments and commitments to other institutions which would preclude delinquency. All the following employment-oriented interventions are designed primarily for youth who are leaving school early.

16. SCHOOL AND WORK PROGRAMS

There are two elements of this portion of the project. One is a vocational placement service in the school. Students can use this service to assess both short-term and long-term job prospects in the community. This service will be provided in experimental high schools in coordination with the local employment assistance department. Its major function is to link students leaving school with jobs, to increase the likelihood that they develop commitments to conventional activities in the world of work and occupational expectations and aspirations which can inhibit delinquency.

The second element is a program for juniors and seniors in high school interested in vocational training. An extension of the experience-based career education program discussed in an earlier section, this element provides academic credit for certain work experiences using learning contract with specific individual learning goals and proficiency standards. Again, the goal is to increase attachment to legitimate school-related activities and commitment to conventional lines of action for students with marginal commitments to traditional school endeavors. This approach has been used extensively in alternative education programs.

17. VOCATIONAL TRAINING AND EXPANSION OF JOB OPPORTUNITIES

This component is an intensive integrated secondary prevention program for school dropouts which provides training in basic work habits, job skills, and vocational assessment to participants; recruits employers to provide job opportunities for participants; matches participants with appropriate placements; continually follows up with participants during the first 2 months of work adjustment; and advocates for job upgrading of youths who have performed successfully on the job for 3 to 6 months. Given difficulties experienced by existing programs of this type in finding jobs for youth which are viewed as either inherently worthwhile or which have long-term career potential, this component will focus on development of job opportunities and skill development in growth areas (such as energy-related occupations) and in community development projects.

Community Interventions

The community provides a context in which youths develop. While families, schools, and peers have more immediate effects on individual youths than do general community variables, community characteristics influence these socializing institutions. Furthermore, aggregate-level data show that crime rates are associated with characteristics of community areas. Community areas offer general norms and expectations for deviant or conforming behavior which may indirectly influence youths. Therefore, two general community-focused interventions will be included in the comprehensive project.

18. COMMUNITY YOUTH DEVELOPMENT
    PROJECT
This final component is a community-focused youth participation and advocacy project in which community members, including youths, are organized into planning committees to mobilize community resources to provide a community environment conducive to non-delinquent youth development. The major element here is the involvement of community youths who are not typically involved in planning and organizing activities and projects to improve opportunities for youth in the community. A range of projects from youth needs assessment surveys to police advisory committees may be initiated. Regardless of the specific activity, the major goal is to provide these youths who may not have established commitments to education or attachments to school with involvements in legitimate activities and ties to a legitimate group which can lead to conventional commitments and attachments outside the school.

19. COMMUNITY CRIME PREVENTION PROGRAM
This component is the community block-watch model which has been successful in reducing residential burglaries where implemented. This approach is included not only for its immediate and obvious deterrent potential but, more important, for its use of a social network strategy which engages neighborhood members in shared activities around a common goal of crime prevention. This involvement can generate a sense of shared concern and power in a community, which is manifested in a set of community norms against crime. It is hypothesized that these norms will contribute to a climate in which criminal actions are viewed by community youths as both risky and unacceptable rather than as a routine part of growing up.

QUESTIONS FOR DISCUSSION AND WRITING

1. Why are control and cultural deviance theories a good combination?
2. What five socializing institutions do the authors discuss in their comprehensive social development model of delinquency prevention?
3. The authors note that association with delinquent peers is one of the strongest correlates of delinquency. At what point in time does their model postulate that young people are likely to develop attachments to delinquent peers? Why aren't the other program results (i.e., attachment to parents, attachment to school, commitment to education, and belief in the moral order) sufficient to prevent delinquency? What two peer-oriented elements do the authors propose to address this concern?

The Prevention of Serious Delinquency: What to Do?

JOSEPH G. WEIS
JOHN SEDERSTROM

A large proportion of serious property and violent crime is committed by juveniles. It is also known that a small percentage of all juvenile offenders account for a majority of serious offenses. The arrest records of these individuals are indicative of only a small part of their total delinquent activity. While it is commonly believed that delinquents specialize in particular offenses—for example, violence—empirical evidence does not support this. The evidence suggests that the most useful distinction is between serious and less serious offenders. Coupled with this knowledge is the fact that techniques normally used to predict individual delinquent and other dangerous behaviors are not adequate to justify corrective interventions concentrating on "high-risk" individuals. Therefore, the prevention of serious juvenile crime must be placed within the context of what we know about prevention in general and the correlates and causes of delinquent behavior.

Historically, the favored societal reaction to juvenile delinquency has not been prevention but control or correction in an identified group of juvenile criminals or predelinquents within the juvenile justice system. Interventions with individual serious delinquents have limited

value for remediation, since serious offenders, including offending groups such as gangs, and serious offenses are concentrated in particular neighborhoods within cities and urban areas. These high-risk communities tend to exhibit weakened institutions of socialization; therefore, those social processes which can prevent delinquency are less effective. Intervention into serious delinquency, which includes but is not limited to violent crime, should focus on organizational change within the major socializing institutions, and given the importance of the high-risk neighborhood for serious delinquency, special emphasis must be placed on *community-based* strategies.

This approach to delinquency prevention was encapsulated by Ernest W. Burgess about 70 years ago:

If we wish to reduce delinquency, we must radically change our thinking about it. We must think of its causes more in terms of the community and less in terms of the individual. We must plan our programs with emphasis upon social rather than upon individual factors in delinquency. We must reaffirm our faith in prevention, which is so much easier, cheaper, and more effective than cure, and which begins with the home, the play group, the local school, the church, and the neighborhood.

These observations about juvenile delinquency were developed by sociologists at the Univer-

From *The Prevention of Serious Delinquency: What to Do?* by J. G. Weis and J. Sederstrom, 1981, Washington, D.C.: Government Printing Office.

sity of Chicago to understand and ameliorate the apparently growing and more serious problem of youth crime in Chicago in the 1920s and 1930s. As an approach to "doing something about delinquency," these ideas may be more valid and applicable today than ever before.

Juvenile delinquency is now a more pervasive and more serious national social problem, and past efforts of the juvenile justice system to control it have generally been ineffective. Regardless of whether or not there has been a recent significant growth in the problem of serious juvenile delinquency—because evidence suggests that the rates of being victimized by juveniles for both property and personal crimes have remained relatively stable—juvenile delinquency is still a problem, and serious and violent delinquency is an even greater problem. Clearly, the importance of reducing and preventing serious juvenile crimes is given higher priority as a goal than in the past. Unfortunately, recognizing a problem does not solve it—one is still left with the problem of "What to do?" This paper attempts to provide some answers regarding the prevention of juvenile delinquency in general, but more specifically of serious juvenile crime. It is informed by and reaffirms an approach to reducing delinquency which emphasizes the social causation of delinquent behavior and the potential efficacy of prevention strategies implemented in the community, particularly those which target the major socializing institutions of family, school, peers, law, and neighborhood, all based on the *social development model* of delinquency and its prevention proposed originally by Weis and Hawkins.

WHAT HAVE WE DONE?

There is scant evidence that the juvenile justice system has been effective in controlling or preventing delinquency. And because of its basically reactive and rehabilitative stance, there has been an emphasis on control—treatment and punishment after entrance to the juvenile justice system—to the neglect of prevention—

an action taken to preclude or correct illegal behavior before entrance to the system. Consequently, the number of bona fide prevention efforts, particularly those which are in the community, has been very small, of which even fewer target serious delinquency. Therefore, the knowledge and techniques of delinquency prevention have not been developed sufficiently.

A new "dual functions" philosophy of juvenile justice supports legal control—the juvenile court—for youths who engage in serious crime and more informal, social control—community services—for youths who engage in less serious crime and noncriminal misbehavior. The responsibility for control, primarily punishment and rehabilitation of identified juvenile criminals, has remained with the court, but the responsibility for prevention has been given back to the community. The primary responsibility for preventing youngsters from engaging in illegal behavior and getting into trouble with the law has been returned to those "frontline" community institutions—the family, school, clubs, church, neighborhood—which historically have been responsible for the social integration, socialization, and control of youth.

One can argue that the community should take primary responsibility for the illegal behavior of all its youth, even the more predatory among them, and rather than separate them from the community, should make every effort to integrate them into those community institutions which have the potential to help reduce delinquency. However, to do so would be on the basis of scant evidence—of the nature of the behavior, its correlates and causes, prevention strategies and interventions, specific program elements, and so on. This is not because it is a vacuous idea or an approach with no promise. To the contrary, community-based projects like the Chicago Area Project have clearly had some impact on delinquency—if nothing else its tenure supports this—but they are difficult to evaluate, and the most conscientious efforts to do so have not yielded results which will stand up under scientific scrutiny. This is primarily because it is very difficult to know whether the reductions in delinquency rates are caused by the project or by other factors.

WHAT IS PREVENTION?

Historically, what has passed as delinquency "prevention" within the juvenile justice system is basically delinquency "control," simply because it has been implemented after the illegal behavior and even after a juvenile justice system reaction has occurred. Control is a "measure taken after a criminal or delinquent act has been committed." Even the most recent and progressive juvenile justice reforms—for example, diversion and deinstitutionalization—are primarily control strategies, simply because they are aimed at previously identified juvenile offenders. These kinds of interventions are only indirectly preventive because, at best, they may inhibit further judicial processing, the reification of a delinquent career, or perhaps further involvement in crime, but they are not "pure" prevention.

Prevention is a societal action to preclude or correct illegal behavior. If societal action is motivated by an offense that has already taken place, we are dealing with control; if the offense is only anticipated, we are dealing with prevention. Prevention approaches can be differentiated into two general categories: (a) preclusive and (b) corrective prevention.

Each type of prevention has its own logic, limitations, and special relationship to prediction. Prediction is involved at both the beginning and end of any intervention effort: To justify intervention the decision is made that some kind of prevention is necessary to avert a predicted undesirable outcome; once intervention is completed, the actual outcome is observed to determine whether the intervention was successful—that is, is the observed outcome better than the outcome which was predicted on the basis of no intervention? Without clear definitions, and valid and reliable measurement of outcomes, there cannot be rigorous assessment of either prediction or prevention efforts.

Preclusive Prevention

Preclusive prevention is directed at social aggregates which may be defined in part by geographical, institutional, organizational, population, or group boundaries. There is no logical necessity that delinquency (or some subtype of delinquency) within the "target area" be high relative to surrounding areas or to some other comparison aggregate. The decision to intervene is based simply on the observation that the behavior to be prevented has been occurring at too high a rate. The relevant kind of prediction is thus an empirically derived baseline trend—the projected rate of the behavior. This baseline trend projection could be an increase, a steady rate, or conceivably a decreasing rate which decision makers consider too gradual. In a comprehensive delinquency prevention research and development project, another part of baseline measurement can and should consist of individual-level measures taken on area residents or a sample of residents, including potential delinquents. This would not be used to target individuals for special intervention but rather to allow detailed evaluation of the prevention project.

The primary aim of preclusive prevention is to reduce aggregate rates of delinquency (and victimization) by preventing the entry of persons into delinquent involvement and reducing the amount and seriousness of delinquency among those who do get involved. A necessary part of baseline measurement is therefore measurement and projection of entry rates in the target population, as well as incidence rates, and success or failure must be defined in terms of the trend which was predicted in the absence of intervention. Since individual predictions are not made, the only false predictions are inaccurate trend projections, which can only be determined (with a remaining degree of uncertainty) by comparison with a similar population or social area where similar preclusive prevention is not undertaken. How much improvement constitutes "success" cannot be precisely defined given the present state of the art. The reduction should probably be statistically significant, but further it should be nontrivial. In principle, after numerous research and development projects, it may be possible based on past observations to specify the results a certain kind of preclusive program should achieve, and hence to evaluate new programs relative to prior results. For now, any nontrivial reduction in entry rates and incidence rates which were attributable to a preclusive prevention program would have to be considered a success.

Preclusive prevention has several advantages which justify continuing efforts in research and development:

1. The entry of individuals into delinquency is prevented before it occurs, because the social-environmental processes which generate delinquency are altered in a positive direction. Thus, society is spared the large costs of victimization incurred from extended delinquent involvement of some of its members.
2. Most feasible preclusive prevention methods constitute changes, which are valuable in themselves, in institutions, organizations, social structures, and cultural systems. For example, a successful effort to improve youths' involvement and performance in school would result in a variety of gains both for recipients and the community at large, including reductions in delinquency.
3. Successful preclusive prevention measures are more likely to be maintained and institutionalized so that long-term benefits continue to accrue from initial costs. Promising preclusive interventions which might require substantial expenditures to initiate and evaluate could be maintained at little or no additional expense and indeed at a net saving considering the obvious costs of delinquency which would go unprevented.
4. Since individual-level prediction is not a part of preclusive prevention, the expense of such prediction is saved, intrusion into individuals' and families' privacy is avoided, and participating individuals are not labeled as "predelinquents" nor their families as "inadequate parents," avoiding the possible negative consequences of stigmatization.

There are, of course, limitations to preclusive prevention:

1. If the objective of delinquency prevention is overemphasized in programs which have additional broader objectives, their adoption may be perceived as jeopardizing the community's reputation, and participation may seem disreputable to individuals and groups within the community.
2. Resistance to some programs by established delinquent groups may be expected, as well as attempts by them to exploit programs. Established delinquent gangs which actively recruit young members may discourage participation by youths who are most in need of preclusive prevention.
3. The presumed causes of delinquency are not equally amenable to preclusive prevention. Dysfunctional family groups, for example, are more likely to insulate themselves from the effects of preclusive programs.
4. Some individuals are less amenable to prevention because of the number, severity, and intractability of criminogenic influences in their lives. To be effective in these "overdetermined cases" prevention efforts need to be more comprehensive and intensive than is possible in preclusive prevention approaches.

Secondary Corrective Prevention

The limitations of preclusive prevention constitute part of the rationale of corrective prevention. Secondary corrective prevention is directed toward groups and individuals who are at risk of becoming involved in delinquency—the ones who "fall through the cracks" of preclusive prevention. It is more remedial in nature but is designed to correct causal processes before delinquent adaptations emerge or become well established.

The evaluation of outcomes is somewhat more straightforward since groups or individuals within a larger social group are targeted for intervention. Baseline data can be collected by measures of individual-level indicators of causal processes and of predelinquent behavior, that is, behavior which resembles delinquency but which may not be serious enough to initiate action by juvenile justice agencies. By randomly assigning high-risk youths to experimental and control groups it becomes possible to achieve rigorous evaluation of both the intervention strategy and the prediction method used to select intervention recipients.

The advantages of secondary corrective prevention include the following:

1. The costs of offenses and of intervention by the juvenile justice system are averted.
2. The process of delinquent development is interrupted at an early stage, before conventional social development (e.g., schooling) is seriously jeopardized or rendered ineffective.
3. Most feasible interventions are designed to deal with problems which are of intrinsic concern, so secondary corrective prevention has positive effects in addition to delinquency prevention.
4. Since groups or individuals are targeted, interventions can be tailored to address their specific social developmental problems.

The limitations of secondary corrective prevention are the following:

1. There are numerous correlates and presumed causes of delinquency and, depending on the criteria for determining who is sufficiently at risk to warrant intervention, the numbers of persons considered at risk can be very large. Consequently, many persons may be targeted for intervention, at perhaps relatively high costs per recipient. At the same time, base rates of prevalence may be fairly small; thus, with current prediction techniques large proportions of false positives are to be expected.
2. Some youths become involved in serious delinquency without having been observably at risk, either because observable predictive factors are not present or because they are not detected.
3. Once groups or individuals are targeted for intervention, there is a strong tendency to approach prevention as being solely a matter of changing "problematic persons" rather than problematic social processes and relationships.

Tertiary Corrective Prevention

At present and for the foreseeable future, preclusive prevention and secondary corrective prevention will remain less than perfectly effective. Some individuals will fall through the cracks in both of these approaches, announcing their arrival at the level of tertiary corrective prevention by being officially identified as "delinquents." Adjudication by a court would be a generally adequate operational indicator.

Tertiary prevention is not limited to intervention that is intensive or custodial—these are subtypes of tertiary prevention which are usually imposed only after a youth has "qualified" several times over. Therefore, not all candidates for tertiary prevention are chronic delinquents who usually reach this stage after the failure of several attempts at corrective prevention.

Since by definition tertiary corrective prevention is undertaken primarily in response to an individual's actual commission of offenses, the method of prediction necessarily includes extrapolation—"behavior predicts behavior." Unfortunately, the predictive power of one or two officially recognized delinquent acts is not impressive. As the data from Wolfgang et al. show, 35% of Philadelphia boys born in 1945 ever had a police contact and 54% of those were ever contacted at least one additional time. And over 80% desisted completely after the second offense. Thus, while juveniles with a first offense become candidates for tertiary intervention, and are more likely than juveniles with no record to come to the attention of authorities for a subsequent delinquent act, they are only slightly more likely than not to recidivate. Any interventions based solely on an entry contact, or even a second one, would be directed largely at false positives. It is not until the third offense of record that a purely extrapolative prediction would produce a false positive rate less than 33%.

Strictly speaking, tertiary prevention is not prevention but "control" because it is directed at officially designated delinquents and is intended to correct and control their future behavior. Its only advantage relative to the more purely preventive interventions lies in the smaller numbers of individuals who qualify for intensive intervention (assuming selection criteria are not too inclusive).

The disadvantages of tertiary "prevention" are best conceptualized as overreliance on the tertiary approach at the expense of the more bona fide prevention approaches. And such overreliance clearly has been the present and past norm in juvenile justice in the United States:

1. The cost of identifying individuals is large since an offense record is the usual criterion. In practice, a considerable number of offenses may be committed by an individual before officials decide to impose substantial intervention.
2. Tertiary corrective prevention is almost entirely directed at individuals and is remedial, if not merely incapacitative, in its effects. Factors in the social environment which contribute to the delinquency of targeted persons are left unabated to continue operating on them as well as on other youths who are not (yet) delinquent.
3. The social developmental processes which contribute to an individual's delinquency are left undisturbed until they are well advanced. For instance, a youth may have dropped out of school, established positive relations with other delinquents, and developed a public and self-identity as a delinquent.

To take advantage of all three types of prevention, and to avoid the disadvantages of relying on one or the other, prevention needs to be carried out at all three levels if serious delinquency is ever going to be minimized. Failure to "optimize effort" at one level (e.g., preclusive prevention) only adds to the overload at other levels (e.g., corrective prevention), with socially harmful behaviors as a by-product of prevention failure. The situation at present then consists of (a) weak traditional socialization institutions in communities (and in many communities, prodelinquent competition from gangs and other law-violating groups) and (b) reliance on prevention (and control) methods based on a logic which neutralizes the possibility of dealing with the social developmental processes through which youths become and remain involved in delinquency. While juvenile crime and contagious diseases are by no means perfectly comparable, it is fair to say that if we handled diseases the way we handle delinquency, bubonic plague would still be part of everyday life.

WHAT TO PREVENT?

Obviously, what is being prevented is crucial to any consideration, analysis, or operationalization of juvenile delinquency prevention. Juvenile delinquency is an ambiguous term. Juvenile courts have had jurisdiction over juveniles who commit crimes, engage in status offenses, or who find themselves in a dependent state of being. These disparate categories of youth have often been referred to and treated collectively as "juvenile delinquents." However, a legalistic definition of juvenile delinquency (cf. Sellin and Wolfgang, 1964:71-86) seems best-suited to considerations of delinquency prevention. Juvenile delinquency is crime committed by persons under the statutorily defined minimum age. Delinquent behavior is juvenile criminal behavior. A delinquent is a juvenile who has committed a crime; an official delinquent is a juvenile who has committed a crime which becomes known to the juvenile justice system. Ideally, the focus of prevention should first be the reduction of delinquent behavior and then of official delinquency. If programs are not directed at preventing initial involvement in delinquent behavior, the proportion of the youth population which engages in crime and may become officially delinquent will not be reduced, and the already enormous social and economic costs of juvenile delinquency will remain high.

In general, the data on delinquent behavior—both official and self-report measures—

show that juveniles are involved in both serious property and violent crimes, typically with much more involvement in the former than the latter. These types of serious delinquent acts are intercorrelated, meaning that youngsters who are involved in serious crime are involved in a variety of serious crimes, as well as less serious crimes, rather than specializing in single offense types or in property crime or violent crime categories. If there is specialization, it is not behavioral but differentiated in terms of frequency and seriousness of offenses. One category of juvenile offenders engages in less serious offenses and the other engages in more serious offenses, and the former does not predict the latter. Rather, those youngsters who commit serious crimes begin their delinquent careers with more serious crimes. The data do not support the popular notion of a unique pattern of juvenile violence, where the offender can be characterized or typified as a "violent offender" on the basis of the variety, frequency, or seriousness of his delinquent behavior.

Who Are They?

The characteristics of the juveniles who engage in serious crimes are not particularly unique—they are, in fact, similar in many ways to those of other juvenile offenders. Studies of serious and/or violent offenders consistently report a similar set of characteristics. These juvenile delinquents are predominantly male; disproportionately represented among minority youths, particularly blacks and Hispanics; more likely to have school problems, including lower potential to achieve, poor academic performance, and interpersonal difficulties and conduct problems; characterized by high residential mobility; typically come from economically disadvantaged origins; experiencing employment problems; more likely to come from families characterized by disorganization and instability, inadequate supervision, conflict and disharmony, and poor parent-child relationships; early starters in delinquency but are usually older than most delinquents, especially

those who engage in violence; and are typically involved in group offenses, with gang membership playing an important role.

What is striking about these characteristics of serious juvenile delinquents is first, they do not typically include the abnormal biological or psychological characteristics which are often attributed to these offenders. Even among officially designated violent juvenile offenders the proportion characterized or diagnosed as disturbed or mentally disordered is much smaller than is often assumed to be the case.

Second, the role of gangs is increasingly prominent, as recent evidence confirms. This first national survey of "collective youth crime" discovered that almost 50% of the 36 Standard Metropolitan Statistical Areas with at least 1 million population have "delinquent gang problems." Although in 10 intensively investigated cities with gang problems probably less than 5% of eligible boys actually belong to gangs, they "account for a disproportionate share of serious youth crime." However, one of the central findings of the research is that problems with "law-violating groups" other than gangs are generally considered to be more serious and prevalent than gang problems. The distinctions between the two types of groups are that gangs have more formal, hierarchical organization and leadership, a "turf," a recognized identity within the community, and violation of the law as a more central feature of its value system. Law-violating groups involve perhaps up to 20% of eligible boys in cities with greater than 10,000 residents, and of all law-violating groups, delinquent gangs represent only 2% and delinquent gang members only 7% of all members. When compared to the criminal behavior of other juveniles, the "paramount difference" is the "far greater tendency of gang members to engage in violent forms of crime" (Miller). And the more regular use of guns as weapons has made some of the violence a greater threat and danger than ever before.

Along with the prominence of law-violating groups other than gangs, especially in cities that are not among the very largest in the country, there have been other significant changes in the demography and ecology of these groups. First, gang problems are more apparent in smaller communities. Second, gangs are not confined as before to "inner-city" neighborhoods or areas because the ghettos, barrios, and slums have spread to the "outer city" and suburbs. Third, one cannot accurately assess the seriousness of delinquency or gang problems for a whole city—there is too much variation by district, community, or neighborhood. Gangs tend to occupy social areas within cities, and it is as incorrect to generalize gang problems from some neighborhoods to a whole city as it is to commit the same kind of ecological fallacy the other way by characterizing the delinquency problem (or rate of crime) in a neighborhood by a city's delinquency problem (or rate of crime).

Third, the characteristics of these youths personify the social areas, neighborhoods, or communities where they live—communities with high rates of crime and a plethora of related other problems. They are communities very much like those studied by Shaw and McKay in the 1920s and 1930s in Chicago and more recently by other urban ethnographers. They are often the communities with the worst delinquency and gang problems, and with diminished capacity of social service agencies and of the traditional institutions of family, school, church, and the law to help keep their children out of trouble.

Fourth, the characteristics of serious juvenile delinquents reflect the strongest general correlates of juvenile delinquency, which include the demographic variables of sex, race, and age and the more causal variables that operate within those traditional "front-line" institutions of socialization within any community, the family, school, peer relationships, employment opportunities, the law, and community dynamics.

THEORY-BASED CRITERIA FOR DELINQUENCY PREVENTION

Since the empirical evidence suggests that past efforts at delinquency prevention can be characterized as largely ineffective, one cannot propose that exemplary programs simply be replicated and generalized as the preferred approach to delinquency prevention. Rather, the apparently most valid correlates, causes, and theories of delinquent behavior, in conjunction with the best available evidence on prevention programs, should be used to establish criteria for the most promising techniques of prevention. What follows is a discussion of the strongest correlates of delinquent behavior, the apparently most important theoretically derived causal variables, and a theoretical model—the social development model—which holds promise for explaining and preventing delinquent behavior.

THEORIES

Among the major theoretical perspectives of delinquency, control theory (Nye; Reiss; Toby; Briar and Piliavin; Matza; Reckless; and Hirschi) and cultural deviance theory (Sutherland and Cressey; Miller; Wolfgang and Ferracuti; and Burgess and Akers) seem to have the most to offer theoretically, as well as for the prevention of delinquency. There are a number of reasons for this conclusion.

First, control theory and cultural deviance theory take into account and best explain the apparently strongest correlates of delinquency. The former is not class specific and focuses directly on the role of the family, school, and law in preventing delinquent behavior, while the latter is primarily a theory of peer influence on crime and of the role of community influences on crime rates.

Second, and related, control theory focuses on individual-level correlates and the impact of major institutions of socialization on individual delinquent behavior, while cultural deviance theory focuses primarily on aggregate-level correlates and the impact of community organization on community rates of delinquency and secondarily on the impact of community culture and associations on the processes of learning criminal behavior. In short, together the theories address both aggregate- and individual-level correlates of delinquency, the former by cultural deviance theory and the latter by control and cultural deviance theories.

Third, and most important, control theory has received the most empirical support of the major theoretical perspectives, with cultural deviance theory running a respectable second.

Fourth, the configuration of "causes" specified in these theories, particularly in control theory, is very similar to the public's perception of the causes of delinquency. It is also clear from a national survey of prevention program practitioners that those people who are involved directly in providing services to youth agree most with the propositions of control theory, followed by cultural deviance and then psychological theoretical perspectives. Normally, this kind of criterion—the beliefs of various publics—would be meaningless in assessing the validity of a theory of delinquency, but given that the general public and prevention practitioners should believe in and support the rationale of delinquency prevention, it suggests the prospect of easier acceptance, support, and implementation of prevention programs based on these particular theories of delinquent behavior.

Fifth, control theory is basically a theory of prevention rather than of causes of delinquency. Rather than attempt to explain why delinquency occurs, it attempts to explain why delinquency is not prevented. Consequently, as a theory, it seems to have direct and implementable implications for delinquency prevention.

Sixth, control theory has not been implemented systematically and comprehensively in a delinquency prevention program, whereas the other major theoretical perspectives have been implemented in both control and prevention efforts, and with little success. This is not a reflection of the validity or utility of control theory but rather of its relative youth compared to other theories and, perhaps, of the simple and straightforward implications for prevention at the organizational and institutional levels of intervention.

Seventh, the implications for delinquency prevention of control and cultural deviance theories are for primary preclusive prevention and secondary corrective prevention—the theories primarily inform those aspects of prevention which are carried on outside of the juvenile justice system and in the community.

Eighth, control and cultural deviance theories are particularly suitable for theoretical integration. The two theoretical perspectives can be complementary, and there have been a number of recent syntheses. This merger was hinted at by Hirschi as a way to "supplement rather than seriously modify the control theory," especially in the area of "companionship" and "group processes important in the causation of delinquency."

Control theory does not take into account the role of peers, particularly within informal group processes, nor does it take into account the role of community characteristics or context in affecting the bonding processes within the family, school, or among peers; cultural deviance theory does both, and it is here that the two theories have most to offer each other. A theoretical integration of control and cultural deviance theories offers the promise of a more complete, valid, and useful theory of delinquency and its prevention.

INTEGRATING CONTROL AND CULTURAL DEVIANCE THEORIES

Control and cultural deviance theories are a good combination because each makes up for the major deficiencies in the other, and together they offer the promise of a more complete and valid explanation of delinquent behavior. Control theory suggests that youngsters become delinquent because of inadequate socialization to conformity, while cultural deviance theory suggests that youngsters become delinquent because of socialization to delinquency, particularly in social areas, neighborhoods, or communities where there is a tradition of crime and high delinquency rates. Control theory specifies the units and elements of socialization that lead to the development of a generalized "bond" to the conventional order, but it pays little attention to how the process works of making an individual moral, nor to the interplay between socialization and the community context within which it occurs. Cultural deviance theory focuses more directly on this process of socialization to criminal behavior and on the effects of the community context on this process of learning criminal attitudes and behaviors.

Control and cultural deviance theories are also complementary in another important way. Cultural deviance theory is basically a theory of peer influence, especially among juveniles. This means that the theoretical integration of the two perspectives is even more promising, given that (a) the influence of informal group processes, particularly among friends, companions, and acquaintances who are one's peers, was underestimated and falls outside the purview of control theory; (b) the empirical evidence shows that peer socialization and attachments are directly related to delinquent behavior; and (c) delinquent peer influence has an ecological anchor in the community and is particularly powerful in communities with high delinquency rates. Regarding the nature of the supplementary role of peer influence, it is suggested that "peers" be incorporated into the integrated theoretical model as another very important unit of socialization, and that the influence of peers be conceptualized as an intervening social process between an unattached, uncommitted, and disbelieving youngster and delinquent behavior. If the social process of making a youngster moral has been interrupted by uncaring parents, poor school performance, visions of occupational failure, and a questionably legitimate legal system, he or she is more free to engage in delinquent behavior and is more likely to come under the influence of peers who may be in the same situation and who provide each other the social and psychological support, rewards, and reinforcement that are not forthcoming in more conventional contexts. Otherwise put, the more inadequate the socialization to conformity, the more likely the socialization to nonconformity. ·

An integration of control and cultural deviance theories, specifically Hirschi's control theory and Akers's social learning theory, means that the units, elements, and processes of socialization are incorporated within one theoretical model which offers a major improvement in explanatory and predictive power. This particular integration has been referred to as the social development model of delinquency and prevention (see the chapter by Weis and Hawkins in this volume). It integrates the individual socialization components of each theory but does not include the community organization and context component of cultural deviance theory as an explicit part of the model, nor does it address the interaction between community organization and context and the institutions of socialization within the community. This is not a major defect in the social development model but rather reflects a difference in emphasis—one on the general case and the other on the more specific case of serious juvenile crime in high delinquency rate communities. Clearly, the latter requires a specification of the community context wherein the social development process is to unfold. Otherwise put, the social development of youths is different in the South Bronx than in Beverly Hills.

Regarding the important variations in delinquency across communities that a theory needs to take into account, "community context" needs also to be included to better specify the integrated control and cultural deviance theoretical model, or social development model. The community context is the ecological anchor of (a) the community organization which impacts opportunities for delinquency and the community delinquency rate; (b) the operation and effectiveness of the major social control or socializing institutions—of family, school, peers, and law; and (c) the extent and magnitude of delinquent peer influence. The relationships among these three factors determine the community delinquency rate and the fate of individual youths within the community.

In general, there is a positive relation between community organization and social control, and both have a negative relation with

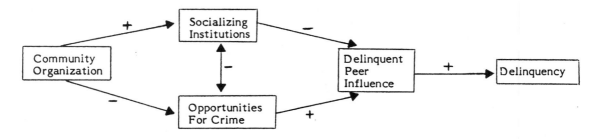

FIGURE 1 *Relationships among configurations of variables in the integrated theoretical model.*

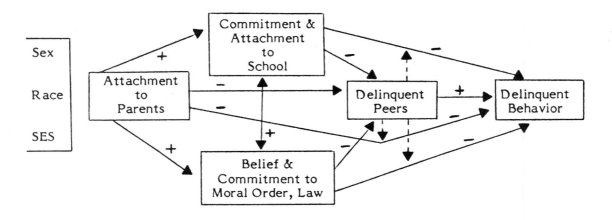

FIGURE 2 *The social development model of delinquency.*

opportunities for crime and delinquent peer influence (Figure 1).

In a community context of "disorganization," social control is less effective because the front-line socializing institutions are weakened by higher community rates of family disorganization; less adequate educational facilities and preparation; fewer material, social, and psychological resources; less respect for the law; and so on. Because of a more likely high delinquency rate or tradition of crime, there are also more opportunities to become involved in crime, which puts an even greater strain on the institutions of socialization. With the community not organized against crime and delinquency, with weakened socializing institutions, and with available illegitimate opportunities, the power

of delinquent peer influence can exert itself, often in the form of law-violating groups or delinquent gangs in these types of communities. More youths involved more frequently in more serious crime is the result of this process, which, in order to short-circuit it, must be attacked in each area—community organization, socializing institutions, and peer influence.

The social development model of delinquency which integrates control and cultural deviance theories and focuses on the roles of the institutions of socialization and peer influence is represented in Figure 2. The theoretically and empirically most important units (family, school, law, peers) and elements (attachment, commitment, belief) of socialization are depicted in the causal order of relationships among these variables. (The arrows and valences indicate the direction of the relationships, the causal chain moving from left to right with a + indicating a positive association and a – indicating a negative association between variables.) Briefly, the model shows the kinds of relationships among the units and elements of socialization as proposed in control and cultural deviance theories. Socialization within the family will be affected differentially by sociodemographic background variables, which for heuristic purposes are outside of the direct causal relationships but may influence the development of attachment to parents, and more directly by the community context. For example, research has suggested that boys and girls are socialized differently within the family, there may be cultural variation in family organization and concomitant socialization experiences, and that child-rearing practices vary across socioeconomic class. The development of attachment to parents will take place within the context of these types of sociodemographic "givens"—a child is born male or female and into a family unit with certain socioeconomic and cultural characteristics. And characteristics of the community where that family resides will interact with both the socialization of and consequences for the child.

Theoretically and empirically, the development of attachment to parents will lead to commitment to education and attachment to school and to belief in and commitment to the conventional moral order and the law. These attachments, commitments, and beliefs to conformity, or what Toby refers to as stakes in conformity, are intercorrelated and in turn directly prevent a youngster from engaging in delinquent behavior and indirectly prevent delinquent behavior by "insulating" a youngster against delinquent peer influence. Involvement with and attachment to nonconforming peers is directly related to delinquent behavior and also conditions the effects of family, school, and law on delinquent behavior by reinforcing the inclination to engage in crime among those youngsters who have low stakes in conformity.

Clearly, a dynamic multivariate causal model of delinquency is desirable for theory and prevention. A dynamic causal model and its derivative implications for prevention should be responsive to the direct and interaction effects among variables over time. In the most general sense, the different causes of delinquency have different effects at different points in time in a youngster's life. More specifically, it is clear that the causal power of the important units of socialization varies by the age of a youngster. It is not chronological age but rather institutional age that is most salient. Children move through a number of significant "institutional passages" in their social development. These passages demarcate "stages" in the life of a youngster during which different units of socialization are most important. These stages are mapped primarily by the education system: preschool, primary school, intermediate or junior high school, and high school. For preschool children the family is the most significant unit of socialization; when a child begins school in the primary grades, the school becomes an important socializing institution; beginning in junior high school, the role of peers in socialization increases and becomes even more important as a youngster moves into high school.

The first socializing institution in the sequence, the family, is of primary importance from birth until youths enter school. Opportunities for involvement in certain roles in the family plus specific parent skills lead to rewarding family involvement for children. Rewarding involvement leads to attachment to parents. This attachment influences subsequent school experiences and belief in the moral order.

School becomes an important institution during the years from school entry until graduation or dropout. Opportunities for involvement in certain school roles, consistency of expectations in the school environment, and teacher and child skills predict academic success experiences, attachment to school, and commitment to education. These, in turn, enhance belief in the moral order, inhibit association with delinquency-prone peers, and prevent delinquency. School's influence may decrease differentially depending on academic and social experiences at school. For example, for students who do not experience academic success, school may decrease in importance and employment increase in importance earlier than for students who are successful and rewarded in school.

During adolescence, peers become increasingly important to the socialization process and continue to be important through high school. The critical consideration is the extent and nature of delinquent involvement among peer groups in the school and neighborhood. For a portion of the youth population, especially those who do not experience rewarding involvement in school, employment may become an important socializing force from later adolescence on. Entry to jobs which have career prospects and which offer learning opportunities is important. The community provides the context which influences behavior throughout the process of social development.

Finally, there are important interaction effects among some of the key variables. For example, the influence of peers is most significant from the beginning of intermediate or junior high school on but is more salient for girls than boys and is more important in an explanation of less serious delinquent behavior among girls and more serious delinquent behavior among boys. Or as the family diminishes in influence from primary grades to high school, the sex difference in the role of attachment to parents in causing delinquency becomes larger—the importance of family socialization in preventing delinquency does not diminish as much for girls as it does for boys.

These types of dynamic and complex relationships among variables suggest that delinquency prevention should be responsive to the manner in which the causes of delinquency work within the social development process. If prevention efforts are to take into account and reflect the apparent complexity of causal relations, they should be directed at the causes of delinquency as they emerge and interact during the lives of youngsters, and within appropriate community contexts. Different interventions are called for at different stages in the socialization of youths. A dynamic, multivariate theoretical model suggests an equally dynamic, multifaceted model of delinquency prevention.

IMPLICATIONS OF THEORIES FOR PREVENTION

What are the theoretically derivable and empirically supportable implications for delinquency prevention of the social development model of delinquency and its prevention?

Control Theory

Control theory suggests that delinquent behavior can be prevented by increasing the effectiveness of those institutions which are primarily responsible for the socialization and control of youth. Implications for the prevention of juvenile delinquency revolve around the strategy of institutional and organizational change. If delinquent behavior is a consequence of incomplete socialization and inadequate social constraints, the family, the school, and the law must be improved. Their improvement will create more adequate outer (external, social, direct) and inner (internal, personal, internalized) controls.

The implications of control theory for the prevention of juvenile delinquency can be summarized as follows:

1. *A key to delinquency prevention is institutional and organizational change of those institutions which are primarily responsible for the socialization and control of youth—the family, the school, and the law.*

   The effectiveness of these institutions must be improved. Doing so will create more adequate outer and inner containment of potentially antisocial behavior.

2. *Efforts to improve the control effectiveness of the family should be directed at enhancing its direct control function and its ability to develop self-control among children.*

The family, rather than the predelinquent, should be the target of corrective efforts which rely on early identification and prediction. A family's direct control can be enhanced by organizing parents in supportive interaction networks. A family's ability to develop self-control in a child can be enhanced through more effective child-rearing practices, particularly those which affect the child's self-concept.

3. *Attachment to the school and commitment to education must be developed and sustained for as many students in as many ways as possible.*

Schools should organize their programs in order to improve the possibility of educational success, the relevance of curriculum to occupational careers, the commitments of youth to education and to community standards of behavior, and the means of integrating students into curricular and extracurricular activities.

4. *The juvenile court should be desocialized, or reorganized as a criminal court for juveniles, in order to strengthen belief in the law.*

School classes on the criminal justice system may improve respect for the law, but fundamental changes in the philosophy, organization, and operation of the juvenile court are necessary to suspend the sense of injustice and the claim of irresponsibility which buttress the rationalizations that neutralize belief in the moral bind of the law and of the conventional order.

5. *Enhancing the self-concept of youngsters should be part of all institutional changes directed at delinquency prevention.*

Good self-concepts are essential to effective self-control. Wherever possible, positive feedback should be encouraged and undue negative feedback discouraged in the socialization of youngsters whether in the family, school, or juvenile justice system.

In summary, juvenile delinquency can be prevented by improving the effectiveness of those institutions which are primarily responsible for the socialization and control of youth—the family, the school, and the law.

Cultural Deviance Theory

Cultural deviance theory suggests a general *community organization* approach to delinquency prevention. The research of social disorganization theorists directs prevention efforts to the community, neighborhood, or social area. Persistently high delinquency rates in certain areas of cities suggest that efforts to improve social control should be focused on the community.

Cultural disorganization theory suggests two major levels of prevention effort within the community. "Cultural conflict" (differential group organization) suggests that delinquent behavior can be controlled and prevented by organizing the community against crime. There should be a concerted, collective effort to neutralize the criminal value system and to promote conventional activities. If societies have the kind of crime they deserve, then so do communities. Local citizens must take a major share of the responsibilities for delinquency prevention. "Cultural transmission" (differential association) suggests that another focus should be the learning process through which individuals are converted to criminal values and behavior patterns.

If community organization is successful, those associations that encourage the violation of the law will be minimized, and those that discourage it will be maximized. However, more specific prevention efforts are necessary at the level of the individual association process. Encouraging youngsters to participate in the life of the community, and more specifically, in efforts to ameliorate conditions that are criminogenic has the potential to decrease the number of criminal associations and the time spent with others who might be transmitting criminal values. Additionally, participation commits youngsters to a social process of conventional value reinforcement and criminal value extinction. Involvement in anticriminal activities (e.g., a campaign to control narcotics abuse and dealing in the community) or in efforts to help others (e.g., working with children in educational or recreational contexts) engages youngsters in a process wherein they verbalize and operationalize "definitions unfavorable to the violation of the law." This may affect their behavior more than the objects of their attention.

Differential association theory also suggests that the sources of criminal values be stripped of their prestige in the community. Besides adult criminal elements, the delinquent gang should be a target of prevention efforts. The influence of older delinquent peers on children in the community can be neutralized by community co-optation of the group or by disbanding it. In effect, this minimizes the possibility of association with a social group which supports the violation of the law by its members. It also devalues the prestige attached to gang membership in the community.

The implications of cultural deviance theory for the prevention of juvenile delinquency can be summarized as follows:

1. *A key to delinquency prevention is community organization against delinquent behavior.*

   Community solidarity in the effort to prevent delinquency is essential. Social control is more effective when its source is the community rather than external forces such as law enforcement.

2. *Community control of prevention efforts and of other services for youth should be encouraged.*

   The coordination of existing social services and the development of new programs should be the responsibility primarily of community residents. Indigenous leadership is invaluable since there is a sense of responsibility to the welfare of the community and youngsters are more responsive to community leaders than to outsiders.

3. *The participation of youngsters, as well as adults, should be encouraged.*

   Increased community control should mean increased participation and power for all members of the community, particularly for the historically disenfranchised youth population. Self-help and other-help by youngsters is an effective preventive which is only possible through participation.

4. *Delinquent groups should be co-opted or disbanded.*

   One of the primary sources of criminal associations, the groups of delinquent peers in the community, should be directed into conventional behavior patterns or, if this is not possible, should be dispersed.

5. *Ties to conventional groups should be encouraged and developed.*

   Traditional social, religious, and fraternal groups for children should be supported actively within the community as a source of anticriminal associations. Less traditional civil rights, political, and nationalist groups should also be utilized, especially for older youngsters who may be seeking ways to express their alienation and discontent.

6. *A key to delinquency prevention is the expansion and equalization of access to legitimate opportunities to achieve.*

   Educational and employment opportunities, in particular, must be made accessible, regardless of socioeconomic status or race. Educational opportunities are most crucial since school performance articulates with employment prospects, and employment opportunities become most salient upon termination of formal education.

7. *Access to illegitimate opportunities should be restricted.*

   The community cultural milieu should be reorganized to remove the supports of the illegitimate opportunity structure. Community social control should be encouraged and directed at reducing the availability of delinquent adaptations.

8. *The alienation of frustrated youth should be directed into legitimate expressions of discontent.*

   Those youngsters who are discontented with their social position and who believe it is a consequence of the social injustices of class and race privilege may express this alienation from the social order in conventional or delinquent ways. Efforts to provide legitimate ideologies of alienation and opportunities for the collective expression of discontent should be made.

In summary, juvenile delinquency can be prevented by community organization against criminal values and behavior and by subverting the processes of association through which youngsters become delinquents. Overall, "The problem of prevention is partly a problem of social control and partly a problem of reorganizing the social milieu so as to reduce the visibility of a particular form of deviant behavior" (Ohlin and Cloward).

A COMPREHENSIVE MODEL OF SERIOUS DELINQUENCY PREVENTION

As discussed earlier, within any city, including some smaller cities, there may be one or more smaller communities or neighborhoods characterized by deterioration, disorganization, and high rates of crime and delinquency. In such areas, the exacerbated problems of the disorganized community and community-specific problems interact with the front-line socializing institutions of family, school, and peers and create additional problems with respect to the social development of youth who live in these areas. Therefore, there is a need for *community-based programs* in high delinquency rate neighborhoods which include additional elaborated or refined and/or new intervention program elements, including elements designed specifically to address the problems of community disorganization. The model described in this section includes elements for general community applications plus elements designed specifically for high delinquency rate neighborhoods within cities. Examples of these elements are included.

The modifications and additions for high delinquency rate communities are based on a philosophy of community-based delinquency prevention which is embodied in the well-known Chicago Area Project, which began in 1933 and continues to operate today. The basic unit of operation is the community, defined by Speigel as

a collectivity of individuals and groups, often located within a specific geographical area and variously organized and differentiated by sex, age, race, ethnicity, status, interest, need, and purpose. The area tends to be identified, both locally and externally, not always sharply and consistently, on the basis of administrative, historical, physical, political, economic, social, and cultural considerations;

or a neighborhood, defined by Sorrentino as

a small area in which the population has a similarity in educational, social, and economic levels, or in religion, race, or nationality. A strong common bond makes for easier community organization because goals and programs are more easily understood by a large proportion of the residents.

The basic philosophy and theoretical foundation of the Chicago Area Project are summarized in a set of assumptions outlined by one of its founders, Clifford R. Shaw:

(1) That the problem of delinquency in low-income areas is to a large extent the product of the social experiences to which children and young people are customarily exposed; (2) that effective treatment and prevention can be achieved only so far as constructive changes in the community life can be brought about; (3) that effective rehabilitation entails the reincorporation of the offender into some socially constructive group or groupings in the community; and (4) that in any enterprise which is likely to be effective in bringing about these changes, it is indispensable that the local residents, individually and collectively, accept the fullest possible responsibility for defining objectives, formulating policies, finding financial support, and exercising the necessary control over budgets, personnel, and programs.

Clearly, there is a general similarity between the implicit theory of delinquency in assumptions 1 through 3 and the social development theory embodied in this paper. This is not accidental. The general "program characteristics" revolve around the goal of developing the project with rather than for the community. In the Chicago Area Project, they may be summarized as including

1. Use of natural leaders: These are leaders within significant neighborhood institutions such as church leaders, professionals, students, and businessmen. Their function is to help plan, control, and give moral support to the program.
2. Staff: Recruited from the neighborhood except for a small number of trained workers as local conditions require. Some are volunteers, while others receive a small stipend. All program activities are under the supervision of the community committee. Most members of the supervisory staff have training in sociology, group work, social work, psychiatry, and law.
3. Activities: Through the community committee a program of recreational, cultural, and educational activities is carried on in conjunction with agencies already established in the community. Examples include camping, athletics and games, music, dramatics, movies, handicrafts, and various adult education and civic activities.
4. Social action: Communities carry on specific campaigns to improve the local environment, facilities, and opportunities in health, housing, employment, education, and law enforcement. These campaigns are conducted with the cooperation of local governmental, law enforcement, and service agencies as well as private business.
5. Use of natural groups: As far as possible, each child is brought into activities along with other members of the informal group to which he or she belongs, with the aim of preserving the natural relationships and controls of the group. With delinquent groups the aim is to introduce

constructive values into their actions, relying on the prestige of the group's natural leader.
6. Use of all community resources: Contributions and resources of indigenous groups as well as institutions that are initiated and sustained from outside the community are coordinated to maximize the total available resources and to limit costs by not duplicating already available resources.

Other similar projects have been attempted, notably the Midcity Project. In this project a citizen's council was formed to strengthen community organization. Interventions aimed at families and youth gangs were the other elements. The theoretical basis of the project was a version of cultural deviance theory, proposing that adherence by youths to a lower-class culture, within the context of a disorganized community, led to high rates of delinquent behavior and gangs.

PROGRAM ELEMENTS

The program elements which might constitute a truly comprehensive community delinquency prevention project, including elements which target high delinquency rate neighborhoods within the community, are listed and described below. They are divided into the five areas of intervention—community, family, school, peers, and employment—and within each area are further divided into two categories of program elements, one for "general community applications" and the other designed specifically for "high-delinquency neighborhood applications." The former includes both preclusive and secondary corrective prevention strategies, while the latter relies primarily on secondary and tertiary prevention strategies. In most communities, the program elements with general applicability would be sufficient for most prevention purposes, but in high delinquency rate communities (or high-rate neighborhoods within communities), special extra efforts need to be directed at those youths who are "falling through the cracks" of general socializing institutions and more general preclusive and secondary prevention efforts.

Community

GENERAL COMMUNITY APPLICATIONS

Community Crime Prevention Program. This is the community block-watch model which has been successful in reducing residential burglaries. This approach is included not only for its immediate and obvious deterrent potential, but more importantly for its use of a social network strategy which engages neighborhood members in shared activities around the common goal of crime prevention. This involvement can generate a sense of shared concern and power which is manifested in community norms against crime. These norms can contribute to a climate in which criminal actions are viewed by community youths as both risky and unacceptable rather than as a routine part of growing up. The community is more visibly organized against crime and delinquency.

Community Youth Development Project. Community-focused youth participation and advocacy projects may also hold some promise for delinquency prevention. In these projects community members, including youths, are organized into planning committees to mobilize community resources to provide a community environment conducive to positive youth development. The major goal here, which is clearly problematic, is the involvement of community youths who are not typically involved in leadership roles in school. If these youths are involved in planning and organizing activities and projects to improve opportunities for youths in the community, they may develop stronger stakes in conformity. Regardless of the specific activity, the major goal is to provide youths who may not have established commit-

ments to education or attachments to school with involvement in legitimate activities and ties to legitimate groups.

HIGH-DELINQUENCY NEIGHBORHOOD APPLICATIONS

Community Committee. Based on the generic Chicago Area Project model, a community committee is formed to perform overall coordination of the community-based program. Membership should reflect the population composition of the neighborhood so that no particular interest group predominates. A significant proportion of the committee should be youths; as a benchmark, less than 20% would seem insufficient. A broad-based committee is needed not just for equity and legitimacy but also to broaden the committee's familiarity with neighborhood conditions and problems, and resources in the form of contacts both inside and outside the neighborhood. In communities where youth gangs are present, the committee should include persons with close links to them. Specific community committee responsibilities would include the following:

1. Conducting an initial and ongoing crime inventory. Data should include types of crimes being committed, locations and times, identities (where known) of perpetrators and victims, and situational factors (e.g., previous conflict relationships between participants).
2. Drawing on the crime inventory and on knowledge of the community, the committee would perform a coordinated needs assessment and planning effort to identify gaps in service and to assist in the development of strategies and, if needed, services to fill those gaps. Given the multiplicity of potentially useful program elements, it is vital that long-range planning be instituted and maintained to ensure a rationally prioritized sequence of implementation and to avoid overloading the community's resource base with new projects.

3. Drawing on the crime inventory, a community crisis intervention strategy is devised and implemented. Interventions would consist of information gathering and rumor control, 24-hour hot lines, arbitration and mediation between violence-prone groups, and monitoring of high-risk situations. In general, the intervention would focus on the important socializing institutions of family, school, peers, and the law. Regarding the latter, links with local law enforcement and juvenile justice agencies are necessary and crucial components of a coordinated community effort.

4. Community committees would maximize their service delivery capabilities through the establishment and coordination of linkages with other organizations and agencies that provide or should provide specialized services to the neighborhood. Coordination of services with institutions and agencies should strengthen the variety and quality of services provided youths and the neighborhood and reduce the duplication of services.

5. The committee would engage in ongoing Development of youth service activities, with identification of and special emphasis on those program elements which are vital to the neighborhood's crime prevention program.

6. The committee would publish a community newsletter to disseminate information including program activities, calls for volunteers, victimization-avoidance information, and so on, and to provide a vehicle for area residents to communicate more effectively with each other.

Youth Committee. This is a committee of neighborhood youths, including former and present gang members where applicable, which is closely linked to the community committee and is similar in its responsibilities. The youth committees are established to provide alienated young people who may have little to no commitment to education or attachment to school with involvement in productive, conventional activities outside the school. It will maximize benefits to be gained by participating young people and the community alike by involving young people and adults in the planning of delinquency prevention/community enhancement programs through participation in the community's committee structure. Some significant number of members of the youth committee would also sit on the full community committee. A model is provided by ICRY (Inner City Roundtable of Youth) in New York City. Its function is to maximize youth involvement in the neighborhood program, in terms of initiating and participating in community projects.

Community Advocates for Youth. Community volunteers would serve as general advocates for youths, whether individuals or groups, in their relationships with organizations and institutions, including schools, law-enforcement agencies, and community business enterprises. Ideally, an advocate would have continuing responsibility for a few particular individuals or a group of youths. The advocate would serve to assist and instruct youths in finding constructive solutions to conflicts and disputes and seek fair treatment of them by youth-serving-and-controlling agencies. This could be seen as a community-based version of case management, with a distinct youth advocacy role playing a much more prominent position.

Community Improvement Project. Part of the neighborhood program would be projects to improve and augment the physical resources of the neighborhood, to enhance "safety, livability, and appearance." Youth involvement in planning and execution is required, and such projects should be used as opportunities to get youths, including gangs, involved in constructive activities. Part of the community improvement project could include "community campaigns" which would operationalize the organization of the community against delinquency or any other pressing problem. For example, there have been successful community campaigns against narcotics sales, prostitution, vandalism, littering, noise pollution, and so on, but here the focus would be on delinquency-related problems and concerns.

Family

GENERAL COMMUNITY APPLICATIONS

Parenting Training. Parenting training for delinquency prevention should seek to enhance the following characteristics of the family by teaching parents more effective child-rearing skills.

Opportunities for family involvement are partially determined by background variables, including socioeconomic status of the family and sex and age of the child, which cannot be directly addressed by prevention interventions. However, the child's role and responsibilities in the family represent opportunities for involvement which can be enhanced through training. It is hypothesized that when parents provide children with participatory roles in the family as contributors to family survival and functioning and reward children for performance in these roles, attachment to the family will be enhanced and delinquency prevented. Additionally, the greater the affection, nurture, and support shown children by parents, the greater the likelihood of attachment between parents and children and the less the likelihood of delinquency. Parenting training can provide parents with skills in showing affection and support for their children.

Parenting skills rely in good part on effective communication between parent and child. The more parents and children communicate with one another regarding thoughts, feelings, and values, the stronger the attachment between children and parents. Parents can be assisted through parenting training in opening and maintaining lines of communication with their children, in empathetic listening, and in basic interpersonal skills.

Fairness and impartiality of discipline appear related to family attachment and family control. Consistent parental discipline also appears to increase the likelihood of belief in the moral order. Parenting training can assist parents in consistent discipline practices. Parents should also consistently reinforce desired behavior and thereby develop similar skills in their children. Parenting training can provide the skills to utilize positive reinforcement to shape the life of the child. Finally, parents should be consistent as models of law-abiding behavior for their children if children are to develop belief in the legal order. Parenting training can emphasize the importance of this modeling by parents.

The general goals of parenting training for delinquency prevention are to improve parenting skills and, therefore, to increase attachment between children and parents and to improve the control effectiveness of the family. One version worth mentioning here because it targets young women who may be alienated from conventional institutions is the Mother-Infant Bonding Program in Phoenix, Arizona. It is using innovative approaches to select recipients of parenting training: Primary target groups are adolescent parents (mostly single mothers who are high school dropouts and unemployed) and parents who have been reported for child maltreatment. Continuing efforts are needed to develop ways of identifying parents in need of training and gaining their active cooperation.

HIGH-DELINQUENCY NEIGHBORHOOD APPLICATIONS

Family Crisis Intervention Services. The most promising corrective prevention approach focused on the family is crisis intervention for families with children. Family crisis intervention services which use a skill development approach to families as systems of communication and exchange have been shown effective for both preclusive and corrective prevention. Experimental evidence indicates that when both parents and children are trained in communication, contingency contracting, and negotiation skills and parents are also taught consistent and explicit rule-setting behavior, delinquency referrals are reduced among "status offenders" and minor delinquents. This approach also appears to reduce the likelihood of delinquency referrals of younger siblings in families who participate.

The family systems-oriented, skills training approach to family crisis intervention services seeks to increase effective parental supervision and family communication in families in conflict, to increase attachment between parents and children where these attachments have become weak or broken, and thereby to prevent delinquent behavior. The Family Trouble Clinic in Detroit offers immediate crisis intervention and follow-up parenting training to families who call police because of in-family violence episodes. Staff members are available on a 24-hour basis. This is an approach which not only supplements the limited crisis-intervention resources of police but uses the crisis situation to locate families in need of longer term services.

Parent Support Groups. In communities with high rates of delinquency, the ability of parents to supervise and monitor the activities of their children is more difficult, and the easy availability of illegal opportunities makes parenting even more difficult. A way to respond is to organize parents into networks and support groups in order to deal more effectively with their children, especially as youths come under the influence of peer groups. These groups of parents meet to discuss their problems as parents and to exchange ideas, perceptions, and encouragement. An appropriate organizing principle would be the formation of networks and groups of parents whose children already constitute an informal clique or belong to a neighborhood gang. This could enhance parents' ability to supervise their children and maintain knowledge of their activities, both of which act as effective deterrents to delinquency.

Surrogate Families. This is a promising but relatively undeveloped area. The idea is to provide a family-like environment within the community for children and adolescents lacking natural families. Persons filling family roles would be indigenous to the community and therefore intimately familiar with the environmental

problems of the children served. The House of Umoja in Philadelphia is an excellent model of the surrogate family concept. Originated and run by a couple whose sons were exposed to neighborhood gang influences, the program operates a residence housing a number of community youths. Affectionate, family-based "primary group" relationships and a consistent moral atmosphere are emphasized, and an assortment of services similar to those of eclectic youth service centers are provided where needed. At present, it would be difficult to replicate this program since it seems to be dependent on extraordinarily concerned and energetic natural families. However, implementation of the surrogate family concept should be a special emphasis for research and development.

School

GENERAL COMMUNITY APPLICATIONS

Personalized Instruction. Traditional methods of instruction, school curricula, and grading practices do not provide success experiences for all students. A large number of students receive poor grades in most of their subjects for all of their school careers, creating a group of students who are perpetual losers. Personalized instruction refers to a set of interrelated elements which address these issues: (a) development and implementation of curricula tailored to students' learning needs and interests; (b) establishment of clear learning goals for each student; and (c) implementation of individually paced learning programs with clear rewards for individual improvement in academic competence. Thus, a promising approach appears to be training teachers in skills necessary for personalized instruction. Teachers should be taught to develop high-interest and relevant materials; to establish realistic goals for each student; to tie clear rewards to different levels of demonstrated effort and proficiency based on student's ability and original performance rather than on competition with classmates; and to broaden available rewards beyond traditional grades.

Personalized instruction, with its contingent reward systems, should positively influence students' cognitive skills and performance levels, increase the proportion of students experiencing academic success, increase student attachment to teachers and school, and increase student commitment to education. Ultimately, delinquency will be a less likely behavioral outcome.

Student Involvement in Decision Making and Governance. The student role is largely a passive one. Commitment to education, school, and conventional lines of action can be enhanced by involving them in meaningful roles in shaping one of the institutions which affects them during this crucial period of their social development—their school and its classrooms. Student involvement in decision making and governance consists of a couple of important components. The first is classroom-based skills training in participatory governance and shared decision making. The second is student involvement in school policymaking (such as participation in formulation of the school drug policy) and in review of student violations of school rules and expectations. Attention should be given to recruitment and involvement of a broad range of "natural peer group leaders" for participation to ensure that participatory roles are available for students not typically involved in traditional student council or other student governance structures. Increasing student involvement in school policy formulation and discipline procedures and increasing student skills for fulfilling these roles should increase student attachment to school, commitment to conventional lines of action, and belief in the moral order.

Interpersonal Skills Training. Programs which seek to improve students' interpersonal skills have been broadly implemented for drug abuse prevention in the past decade. The few available rigorous evaluations have shown these interpersonal skill development approaches to be among the most promising for drug abuse prevention. These approaches propose that young people need to learn basic communication, decision-making, negotiation, and conflict resolution skills to interact effectively with family members, teachers, and peers. The premise is that schools should teach these interpersonal skills just as they teach cognitive skills. If young people have these social skills, they are more likely to find their interactions with conventional others rewarding and to develop attachments to these others. These skills may also contribute to academic success and to attachment and commitment to school. On the other hand, when these skills are absent or underdeveloped, young people may become frustrated in interaction with others, may be more susceptible to delinquent influences, and may turn to unacceptable behaviors to meet their needs. A number of interpersonal skills curricula are available.

Law-Related Education. Another preclusive intervention focused on skills development seeks ultimately to strengthen belief in the law by educating students about the functions of the law and their rights and responsibilities under it. In contrast to other law-related education approaches, this intervention combines education with power enhancement. By addressing civil and consumer law as well as criminal law, students learn how to use the law for their own protection and to achieve their goals. Rather than relying on a didactic approach emphasizing legal responsibilities, this intervention seeks to develop a more general belief in the law and related concepts, such as freedom, justice, responsibility, and authority.

Experiential Prevocational Education and Career Exploration. Another curriculum addition prepares students for the world of work while still in school. Schools should provide young people with information and experiences which will help them develop aspirations and expectations for attaining legitimate, worthwhile employment. If schools can help students make commitments to legitimate careers, delinquency should be reduced. One mechanism for achieving this goal is experiential prevocational education and career exploration, in which students are exposed to a wide range of possible career options and informed of the skills and training required to attain these. Experiential exposure to jobs and work can increase students' understanding of actual career opportunities, while contributing to placement sites, and enhancing the likelihood that involvement will be perceived as rewarding. This should, in turn, generate aspirations and commitments to conventional career roles.

Experiential prevocational education can begin as early as middle or junior high school and continue through high school. During the early years, the program should be based largely in the classroom with field trips to work sites. In subsequent years, opportunities for work or internship experiences in the community can be included and articulated with traditional course work necessary for high school graduation.

Cross-Age Tutoring. Cross-age tutoring is also a corrective prevention strategy aimed at skill development for both students in primary grades who are evidencing special difficulties in school and students in junior and senior high school who are given the opportunity to perform a productive role as tutors. The effect for both the younger student and older tutor is increased commitment to education and attachment to school. To maximize the preventive power of this intervention, selection of secondary school students as tutors should be based on teacher recommendations. To accomplish "retroflexive reformation," students whose cognitive skills are adequate for the tutoring role, but whose commitments to school appear marginal, should be included in the tutor pool along with students traditionally selected for leadership roles.

School Climate Assessment and Improvement. Research has shown that cooperation between teachers and school administrators characterizes schools with low rates of teacher victim-

ization. An approach which has shown promise for enhancing administrator and teacher cooperation is school climate assessment and improvement. This is a process in which the administrator and staff engage in a realistic assessment of program, process, and material determinants of the school's social and educational milieu. Faculty and administration collaboratively identify school climate factors in need of improvement and implement activities to address these problems. Thus, regardless of its specific focus, when properly implemented the process can enhance cooperation between administration and teachers. Additionally, where improvement activities focus on the development of a clear, common set of policies and procedures for dealing with infractions of rules, the school environment is more likely to be perceived by students as equitable and just. Consequently, students are more likely to develop stronger beliefs in the moral order of the school and, as a result, delinquent behavior should be inhibited.

Child Development Specialist as Parent Consultant. Another method for enhancing consistency of expectations and sanctions in the child's environment is to improve communication between schools and parents. Child development specialists in schools can ensure that parents are routinely contacted regarding special achievements or needs of their children. They can also coordinate recruitment of parents for volunteer involvement in classroom activities and in school decision making.

HIGH-DELINQUENCY NEIGHBORHOOD APPLICATIONS

Independent Community Alternative Schools. A corrective prevention approach aimed at academic achievement, attachment to school, and commitment to education through skill development is an alternative learning environment for junior and senior high school students who will not or cannot remain in traditional school environments because of disruptive behavior, disaffiliation, or disinterest. Alternative education programs should contain the following elements which appear important for delinquency prevention: (a) personalized instruction with curricula tailored to students' learning needs and interests, clear learning goals, and an individually paced learning program; (b) clear rewards for individual improvement in academic competence; (c) a goal-oriented learning emphasis in the classroom; (d) low student/adult ratio in the classroom; and (e) caring, competent teachers.

Alternative schools can be operated independently of public school systems to provide for the educational needs of neighborhood youths who drop out of or are expelled from public schools. Alternative schools operated by Project REAL (Return to Employment and Learning) in the Bronx, and Compton Action Center for Youth Development, Compton, California, are good examples. They serve youths who have been expelled or have dropped out of school and are typically official delinquents, and their emphasis is on occupational preparation and remedial basic education. Project REAL operates a carefully structured program to integrate students into entry-level jobs in private industry and to provide extended follow-up services. Another alternative school, actually a continuation high school, is run by SAAY (Services for Asian-American Youth) in Los Angeles. The school's program is similar to that of Project REAL but is designed to meet the needs of its particular community and its indigenous ethnic groups.

School Crisis Intervention. Activities within this element include gaining information on situations with the potential for violence, monitoring school activities which frequently are scenes of violent episodes (e.g., athletic events and dances), and negotiating solutions to conflict situations. The emphasis is on ad hoc prevention efforts in incipient violent episodes. Some exemplary programs are Sey YES (Youth Enterprise System) in Los Angeles and Community Streetwork Center and Centro de Cambio in San Francisco. All three include "in-school crisis intervention" as part of neighborhood-wide pro-

grams to control gang violence. Common features include use of indigenous staff members (sometimes former gang members), use of gang member youths, information gathering and rumor control, situation "defusing" and monitoring of high-risk activities, and maintenance of close links with police and school personnel. Another vital activity is the training of teachers, administrators, and school security personnel in techniques of crisis intervention.

In-School Suspension. This is a method of controlling youths who are violent and/or disruptive in school and is designed to avoid the counterproductive implications of suspension and expulsion. That is, if a juvenile is not in school, he will not be able to learn and he will become more detached from school and less committed to education. "Suspended" students are kept in school but are suspended only from ordinary interactions. They do individualized lesson plans in separate study carrels, usually for a few days at a time, and release from suspension is contingent on performing assigned work.

School-Community Councils. Students are probably more likely to develop attachments to school when their parents and the school staff are in agreement regarding expectations for behavior and performance. In contrast, parents' complaints about schools are not likely to inspire their children to believe in the school's authority. Collaborative cooperation between parents and school personnel and among school personnel themselves is likely to enhance student commitment to education, attachment to school, and belief in the moral order and, thereby, to prevent delinquency. This can be accomplished through a school-community council. This council would be composed of principal, teachers, parents, and other community members who are responsible for "school site management": identifying important issues, establishing common goals, and collaborating in solving problems. The council would provide a point of access and a forum for negotiation between community and school, increasing the probability that school priorities will reflect the needs of local students, as well as their parents and other community members. Promising programs under the council's purview would be (a) parents as teachers: use of parent volunteers as classroom tutors and aides; (b) home-school coordinators: school personnel with specific responsibility to act as liaison between the school and the families of students; and (c) planning, coordination, and implementation of other school-related program elements.

Peers

GENERAL COMMUNITY APPLICATIONS

Peer Leadership Groups. Peer leadership groups have been instituted in a number of middle, junior, and senior high schools across the country. The model of peer leadership which appears most promising is one in which group members are leaders of informal student cliques and groups, rather than traditional student body leaders or students in trouble. Typically, members are nominated by teachers and students, and a peer program coordinator is responsible for final selection of members. The peer leadership groups meet daily for an hour as part of their regular school activities. In contrast to therapeutic guided peer interaction programs, however, an explicit orientation of the peer leadership groups should be to identify and address school policy issues that are perceived as problems by students and to work with the school administration to develop reasonable solutions. Peer leadership groups can also serve as recruitment pools for student judicial/disciplinary bodies. Designed this way, peer leadership groups can avoid the problems of peer interventions which focus wholly on delinquent groups.

Peer leadership groups seek to encourage leaders of delinquency-prone groups to establish ties to more conventional peers. These attachments will be developed as group members work together toward common goals of institutional change in the school and as they perform judicial functions. It is also assumed that attach-

ment to school will be enhanced by performance of these functions. Finally, to the extent that informal peer group leaders are accurately selected for participation, it is hypothesized that these leaders may, in turn, influence members of their own cliques toward more positive attitudes to school. In this way, delinquency-prone groups may be co-opted.

HIGH-DELINQUENCY NEIGHBORHOOD APPLICATIONS

Gang Crisis Intervention. This is similar to in-school crisis intervention, but it operates neighborhood-wide and focuses on delinquent groups. Model programs are operated by the California Youth Authority Gang Violence Reduction Project, SAAY, Sey YES, all in Los Angeles, and by YES (Youth Enrichment System) in Detroit. Intervention strategies are similar to those employed in schools, and crisis intervention is done as part of a strategy which also includes efforts at long-term resolution of intergang conflict and redirection of gangs into nondelinquent objectives and activities. Obviously, crisis intervention on an ad hoc basis has little promise for long-term reduction of gang violence, but it is necessary to allow the operation of other cause-based program elements.

Youth Gang Councils. This intervention is directed at gangs and is intended to achieve long-term effects by addressing more basic causes. Councils are formed which include current and former gang members and leaders in order to devise solutions to gang conflicts and to create alternative objectives and activities for existing gangs. The intervention has preventive potential both in the activities of the council and in its ability to recruit gang members into a conventional structure. Model programs are operated by BUILD, Inc. (Broader Urban Involvement and Leadership Development) in Chicago, ICRY (Inner City Roundtable of Youth) in New York City, and SAAY (Services for Asian-American Youth) in Los Angeles.

Employment

GENERAL COMMUNITY APPLICATIONS

Integrated School and Work Programs. Two approaches hold promise here. One is a vocational placement service in the school. Students can use this service to assess both short- and long-term job prospects in the community. Its major function should be to link students leaving school with jobs in order to increase the likelihood that they develop commitments to conventional activities in the world of work and occupational expectations and aspirations which can inhibit delinquency. The second is a program for juniors and seniors in high school interested in vocational training. An extension of the experience-based career education program discussed earlier, this element provides academic credit for certain work experiences using learning contracts with specific individual learning goals and proficiency standards. Again, the goal is to increase attachment to legitimate school-related activities and commitment to conventional lines of action for students with marginal commitments to traditional school endeavors. This approach has been used extensively in alternative education programs.

School/Work Councils. In schools where the employment elements are implemented, school/work councils of community business people, Employment Security representatives, local Department of Labor prime sponsor representatives, and school personnel might be established. These councils oversee and coordinate the school employment elements, identify and create work exploration and placement opportunities for students, coordinate the program elements with existing and emerging school/employment transition programs, and develop and maintain linkages between the school-based employment components and the private sector. These councils also assist in the development of employment in growth industries and the expansion of job opportunities for youths not firmly attached to school or committed to education.

HIGH-DELINQUENCY NEIGHBORHOOD APPLICATIONS

Intensive Vocational Training, Expansion of Job Opportunities, and Placement. This program element is an intensive integrated corrective prevention program for school dropouts which provides training in basic work habits, job skills, and vocational assessment; recruits employers to provide job opportunities for participants; matches participants with appropriate placements; continually follows up with participants during work adjustment; and advocates for job upgrading of youths who have performed successfully on the job.

The primary target population are youths who are at risk of becoming permanently unemployable. The interventions seek to develop skills and provide roles which will enhance commitments to occupational goals and other conventional lines of action. In addition to occupational skills training, instruction is given in basic behavioral necessities (e.g., punctuality, completing work assignments, performing in a task-directed structure), in job-seeking skills, and in the distribution of job opportunities and training requirements. A phased introduction to the occupational world, as practiced by Project REAL in the Bronx, is necessary. In this project initial instruction is given in the first phase (6 months) while clients work half-time in subsidized jobs. In the second phase youths work full-time in private sector jobs (50% subsidized in this program) while their progress is monitored and counseling is available if needed. The third phase is a 12-month follow-up as clients continue to work full-time on an unsubsidized basis.

While not all prospective recipients would require the fully elaborated treatment, for a considerable number of youths the problems of ignorance or a lack of preparation for occupations require a very thorough intervention strategy. And more than other elements, this one requires the ability to locate resources—primarily employers—outside of the neighborhood in which the project is based and the youths reside.

CONCLUSIONS AND RECOMMENDATIONS

Conclusions

1. A large proportion of the serious property and violent crime in the United States is committed by juveniles.
2. A small percentage of all juvenile offenders account for a major part of serious juvenile offenses. These are defined as serious delinquents.
3. Most serious offenses do not result in arrest; serious chronic offenders are repeatedly arrested, but their arrest records usually capture only a small part of their actual delinquent behavior.
4. Most delinquents do not specialize in a particular offense type. The most useful distinction is between serious and less serious offenders.
5. Few chronic offenders are arrested repeatedly for specifically violent offenses. Their arrest records reflect the versatility of their underlying behavior, but arrest records are not useful for identifying chronically violent delinquents.
6. Gangs and other law-violating groups commit a disproportionate share of serious juvenile crimes.
7. Past efforts by the juvenile justice system to prevent delinquency have generally been ineffective.
8. Techniques for the prediction of delinquent behavior in individuals are not sufficiently developed to justify intervention strategies which concentrate only on high-risk individuals. Delinquent behavior can only be predicted somewhat confidently in individuals with an officially recorded history of repeated delinquency.
9. Intervention with individual serious delinquents can only accomplish limited remediation, and only with the individuals who are treated: It is logically impossible to attack the persisting causes of delinquency by treating individuals whose behavior is the outcome of those causes.
10. The most powerful explanatory theory of delinquency is an integrated model derived from social control and cultural deviance theories.
11. The social processes which prevent delinquency occur in social organizations and institutions (families, schools, communities) in the course of activities which are primarily directed toward positive goals (e.g., socialization of children, family interaction, education).
12. Serious offenses and offenders—including offender groups such as law-violating groups and gangs—are concentrated in particular communities and neighborhoods within cities and urban areas. These high-delinquency neighborhoods are characterized by poverty, disorganization, and weakened institutions of socialization and tend to have concentrations of minority group residents.
13. The causes of serious delinquent behavior are concentrated in these same high-delinquency neighborhoods; conversely, the social developmental processes which prevent delinquency are less effective.
14. Individuals, institutions, and organizations within communities—including high-delinquency communities—possess resources for preventing delinquency which cannot be supplied by outside agencies. These include intimate knowledge of local persons and conditions, credibility, networks of interpersonal connections, immediate personal concern with local problems, and the potential for positive effects at the cultural level.
15. Professional and governmental agencies outside neighborhoods have the potential to mobilize, direct, and support a community's resource base through theoretical, technical and organizational expertise and funding assistance.

Recommendations

1. Intervention should be directed toward the causes of serious delinquency, which includes violent delinquency: No gain in effectiveness or economy can be expected by separating violent delinquency as a special target of preventive intervention.

2. Intervention should be directed toward the social development processes which result in juveniles becoming delinquents or serious delinquents: The focus should be institutional and organizational change of the socializing institutions of family, school, peers, law, and the community.

3. Primary emphasis should be placed on developing strategies for preclusive prevention of delinquent behavior.

4. Development effort is also needed to devise strategies for secondary corrective prevention, targeted toward high-risk groups and individuals, and to devise prediction techniques for more efficient targeting of intervention.

5. Prevention efforts directed at serious delinquency should be implemented in communities with high rates of delinquency. Emphasis should be on development of community-based prevention; participation of community residents and utilization of community resources should be maximized.

6. The role of professional and governmental agencies should consist of technical and organizational assistance, specialized services which communities are unable to operate, direct and indirect funding assistance, research and development, and scientific evaluation.

7. Community-based programs should target both delinquency and one of its concomitants, the fear of crime.

8. Research and development efforts on the prevention of serious delinquency are necessary, particularly in the area of community-based strategies of prevention.

9. Primary responsibility for preventing its youths from engaging in delinquency should rest with the community.

10. Community control of prevention efforts should be encouraged.

11. Theories of and research on juvenile delinquency should be the foundation of prevention efforts.

12. In selecting strategies for community-based prevention, preference should be given to strategies which have valuable results in addition to prevention. This is especially important where the active participation of youths and their families is needed.

13. Involvement of youths in prevention efforts should be maximized, including recognized high-risk youths, delinquents, and gang members.

14. Community organizations should attempt to maximize legitimate opportunities for youth and minimize illegitimate opportunities.

QUESTIONS FOR DISCUSSION AND WRITING

1. What has historically passed as delinquency prevention? What is prevention?

2. What are three types of prevention and at whom are they directed? What is the primary aim of each?

3. Why is social control less effective in a community context of "disorganization"?

4. What are the theoretically and empirically most important units and elements in a social development model of delinquency? To what should the development of attachment to parents lead?

5. Into which five areas of intervention are the "program elements" (of a comprehensive program of serious delinquency prevention) divided, and into which categories are they further divided? What types of corrective prevention are included in the two subcategories?

Reducing Early Childhood Aggression: Results of a Primary Prevention Program

J. DAVID HAWKINS
ELIZABETH VON CLEVE
RICHARD F. CATALANO, JR.

THE research evidence suggests that prevention programs that reduce antisocial behavior, particularly aggressive behavior in boys, during the early grades of elementary school hold promise for preventing delinquency and drug use in adolescence.

Teacher and parent training have been advocated as promising approaches for reducing early antisocial behavior. The interventions tested here are based on the *social development model* and seek to enhance prosocial development, reduce aggressive antisocial behavior, and reduce the risk for delinquency and drug abuse by promoting in families and school classrooms conditions hypothesized as necessary for social bonding. These are opportunities for involvement in conventional activities, skills for successful involvement, and rewards for conventional behavior. It is hypothesized in the social development model that the levels of opportunities, the skills and rewards available in families and schools, affect youths' degree of attachment to family and school, their degree of commitment to their conventional lines of action within these settings, and their

belief in the conventional moral and legal order of society. Following Hirschi's empirically supported social control theory, the extent of social bonding to conventional socialization units of the family and school is expected to affect children's risk for delinquent and other antisocial patterns of behavior in adolescence.

This chapter describes a field experiment in which a program of parent and teacher training was tested for short-term effects on early antisocial behavior.

RESEARCH DESIGN

Eight Seattle public elementary schools participated in the study. First-grade teachers and students were randomly assigned to experimental or control classrooms in six of the eight schools. The other two schools were assigned to a full-control or full-experimental condition. In the full-experimental condition school, all first-grade students and teachers ($n = 11$) were assigned to the experimental condition. All first-grade students and teachers ($n = 10$) in the full-control school were assigned to the control condition.

All subjects entered the first grade in the fall of 1981. Of these, 520 were in project schools in the spring of 1983 when posttest data were collected.

Experimental Program

The parent and teacher training interventions tested were designed to be developmentally appropriate for parents and teachers of first- and second-grade students.

PARENT TRAINING

Poor family management practices have been identified as a factor that increases the risk that a child will become delinquent and abuse drugs. The parent training component sought to teach parents effective family management skills. It was hypothesized that improvements in parenting practices would increase bonds of attachment between parents and children and reduce the risk of later adolescent delinquency and drug abuse.

The parenting curriculum tested in this project, Catch 'Em Being Good, taught parents skills in monitoring and supervising children's behavior, in using appropriate rewards and punishments, in using consistent discipline practices, in using effective communication skills, and involving children in family activities. To increase the involvement in the activities of the family, parents also were encouraged to create age-appropriate family roles for their children and to increase family activities and family time together.

Parent training was offered in seven consecutive weekly sessions to all parents whose children were assigned to experimental classrooms. The program was offered when children were in first grade and again when children were in second grade. The program used a standard skills-training format, including the demonstration and modeling of skills, role play, feedback, and homework practice assignments.

TEACHER TRAINING

There is considerable evidence that failure in schools is positively correlated with delinquency and adolescent drug abuse and precedes delinquency. Delinquency also appears to be linked to a low degree of attachment to teachers and commitment to school and education. Teacher training designed to increase academic performance, reduce antisocial behavior, and increase bonds of attachment and commitment to school should directly affect these school-related risk factors for adolescent delinquency and drug abuse.

The experimental program tested here trained teachers in the use of proactive classroom management methods, cognitive social skills training, and interactive teaching methods. These methods of instruction are hypothesized to promote the conditions necessary for social bonding between youth and school by increasing all students' opportunities for academic success and participation in the classroom, by increasing the skills necessary for successful participation, and by providing consistent rewards for classroom participation in desired behaviors.

Proactive classroom management is designed to prevent behavioral problems before they occur by teaching basic skills for appropriate classroom participation. Teachers learn to provide clear instructions and expectations about attendance, classroom procedures, and rules. Teachers learn to use the least disruptive interventions to maintain order in the classroom without interrupting instruction. Proactive classroom management also includes the frequent use of encouragement and praise to reinforce desired behaviors in the classroom and to increase the social bonding of the student to the teacher and school. This method of instruction is expected to reduce early antisocial behavior in the classroom by giving teachers skills in extinguishing disruptive behavior without resorting to punitive sanctions and by rewarding the students for prosocial behavior.

Social skills training teaches communication, decision making, negotiation, and conflict resolution skills. The curriculum used was Interpersonal Cognitive Problem Solving developed by Spivack and Shure. This curriculum seeks to increase students' problem-solving ability as a means of improving their social adjustment. First-grade teachers were instructed in the use of the social skills lessons in this curriculum to teach children how to think through alternative solutions to problems.

Interactive teaching is based on the premise that under appropriate instructional conditions, virtually all students can succeed in school. In interactive teaching, students must master and demonstrate an understanding of clearly specified learning objectives before moving on to more advanced work. Grades are determined by this demonstration rather than by comparison to other students. It is hypothesized that the use of this instructional technique will help students develop and maintain interest in the educational material and will decrease off-task and disruptive behavior.

OUTCOME MEASURES

Subject outcomes were measured at the end of the second grade. The Teacher Report Form of the Child Behavior Checklist (CBCL) was used to assess the effects of the experimental intervention. The CBCL is a standardized instrument developed by Achenbach to measure children's antisocial and problem behaviors. It has documented reliability and validity. The teacher rating the child must have known the student being rated for a minimum of 2 months, precluding pretesting using the CBCL at first-grade entry in this study.

The 119 items of the CBCL were combined into the eight component and two composite standardized scales created by Achenbach and Edelbrock. The scales are made up of slightly different items for boys and girls. The component scales for boys are Anxious, Social Withdrawal, Unpopular, Self-Destructive, Obsessive-Compulsive, Inattentive, Nervous-Overactive, and Aggressive. The component scales for girls are Anxious, Social Withdrawal, Unpopular, Self-Destructive, Depressive, Inattentive, Nervous-Overactive, and Aggressive. The External composite scale includes the Inattentive, Nervous-Overactive, and Aggressive scale items, while the Internal composite scale includes the Anxious and Social Withdrawal scale items for both males and females.

ANALYSES

Analysis of variance procedures were used to identify significant differences in CBCL scale scores between the experimental group and control group subjects at the end of second grade. Analyses were conducted separately for boys and girls. Separate multiple analyses of variance were also conducted for race and condition within sex because of significant racial differences in scale scores. Because of the possible confounding of socioeconomic status and race, socioeconomic status, as measured by eligibility for the federal free lunch program, was controlled in all comparisons. Second, analyses were conducted to identify the proportions of experimental group and control group subjects in the clinical range on the CBCLs at the end of the second grade.

Males

Analyses for male subjects revealed lower (better) scores for the experimental group on all the CBCL scales at posttest. However, at posttest, significant differences between experimental group and control group subjects were found only on the Aggressive subscale and the Externalizing Antisocial Behavior scale. The control group subjects scored higher than the experimental group male subjects after intervention, indicating significantly more externalizing behaviors, particularly aggressiveness among the control group boys, as rated by the teachers.

To determine the possible differential effects of the intervention on black and white boys, black male members of the experimental ($n = 39$) and the control ($n = 31$) groups were compared as were white male members of the experimental ($n = 59$) and control ($n = 40$) groups. No significant differences on the CBCL scales were found for blacks, whereas white male control group subjects scored significantly higher on the Aggressive scale and the global externalized deviance scale than did experimental group subjects at posttest. The project interventions resulted in significantly lower aggressiveness among white experimental group boys when compared with the control group. The interventions did not have significant effects on the aggressiveness or the externalized deviance of black boys.

Within the experimental group, blacks scored significantly higher than whites on only two scales: Aggressive and External. Within the control group, there were no significant differences between blacks and whites. Where significant race differences were found on the CBCL scales, black males were rated more negatively by their teachers than were white males. However, this appears to reflect significantly lower rates of teacher-rated aggressiveness and external deviance among the white experimental group boys. Experimental and control group black boys were rated as having similar levels of aggressive and externalized deviant behaviors by their teachers.

Females

Analyses of the CBCL for all females revealed significant differences for experimental and control group subjects on only the Self-Destructive scale. On this scale, the female subjects of the control group were rated as more self-destructive than the girls in the experimental group by their teachers. There were no significant differences between the experimental and control groups for black females. White female subjects of the control group scored significantly higher on the Self-Destructive scale than did the subjects in the experimental group. Additionally, white female subjects in the control group were rated worse than white female subjects in the experimental group on two scales where differences approached significance: Depressive and Nervous-Overactive. Again, it appears that the project intervention had a beneficial effect for whites but not for blacks.

The control group white females were rated more anxious than were black females in the control group. Within the experimental group, blacks were rated significantly more negatively than whites on 4 of 10 scales: Depressive,

Nervous-Overactive, Aggressive, and External. Findings for females were generally consistent with those for males in that where significant differences were found, blacks were rated more negatively than whites, with the single exception of control teachers' ratings of female anxiety.

The CBCL analyses indicate that the combination of teacher and parent training offered to the experimental group subjects was followed by hypothesized differences between the experimental group and the control group for white subjects but not for black subjects. The experimental intervention appears to have had little effect on teachers' ratings of blacks. In contrast, the interventions appear associated with lower rates of externalized deviance for white subjects, particularly aggressiveness among the experimental group white boys and lower rates of self-destructiveness among the experimental group white girls as rated by the teachers at the end of Grade 2.

Clinical Range Analysis

Achenbach and Edelbrock have identified the clinical range on the Internalizing and Externalizing scales of the CBCL as the upper 11% of all scores. Students who fall into the clinical range can be considered to be at the highest risk and in need of referral for help with emotional/social or behavior problems.

A chi-square analysis was done to determine if there were significant differences in the proportions of the subjects in the experimental and control groups failing in the clinical range at the end of the second grade. Six subsamples were assessed: all males, black males only, white males only, all females, black females only, and white females only.

Only 6.8% of the experimental group white males, compared with 20% of the control group white males, fell in the clinical range on externalizing antisocial behavior. This indicates a trend after intervention toward less externally directed antisocial behavior on the part of white experimental group boys at the extreme, most antisocial, end of the behavioral spectrum when compared with white control group boys. This result is consistent with prior analyses, which found overall lower mean scores on the Aggressive scale and the composite External scale for white males.

DISCUSSION

There exist several possible threats to the conclusion that the experimental interventions tested in this study produced the observed outcomes. One threat is pretest nonequivalence. As noted earlier, it was not possible to obtain pretest scores on the CBCL before the implementation of the experimental intervention. However, a self-report baseline survey showed that the control group was either equivalent to or less antisocial than the experimental group on all available self-report baseline measures.

It is also possible that Hawthorne effects were responsible for observed posttest CBCL differences. Experimental teachers may have rated students in a more positive manner because of their awareness that these subjects were involved in an experimental project. However, the experimental group and control group teachers' posttest ratings differed significantly on only one of eight scales created from CBCL items. Hawthorne effects would be expected to appear as "halo effects," biasing the experimental group teachers' ratings on all scales in a positive direction.

The results from this study provide limited support for the hypothesis that a combination of improved teacher instructional methods and training for parents in family management and relationship-building skills can reduce early antisocial behavior. However, the lack of significant intervention effects on the experimental group teacher ratings of black subjects is a cause for concern.

Other analyses have revealed consistently higher rates of both teacher-rated and self-reported school trouble among black fifth-grade students when compared with whites. In the present study, the differences may reflect the differential perceptions of the predominantly white teachers who rated the subjects. Eaves found that white teachers tend to rate black children as more deviant and white children as less deviant. Alternatively, it is possible that the intervention is better suited to the affective and cognitive styles of white children.

The present study is part of a longitudinal investigation of the etiology and prevention of adolescent antisocial behavior. The longitudinal study will allow an assessment of the extent to which the results reported here are associated with later rates of delinquency and drug abuse in adolescence.

QUESTIONS FOR DISCUSSION AND WRITING

1. What was hypothesized in the social development model?
2. What did the analyses for male subjects reveal? Did the interventions affect black and white boys equally? What did analyses of the Child Behavior Checklist for all females reveal? Did the interventions affect white and black females equally?
3. How might Hawthorne effects have been responsible for the changes between the control and experimental groups? What finding points to the probability that Hawthorne effects were not responsible for all of the change?

LABELING, DIVERSION, AND RADICAL NONINTERVENTION

Labeling theory became a popular alternative to traditional causal theories in criminology at the same time that radical theory appeared on the criminological scene in the United States in the mid-1960s. As Schur points out in "An Overview of Labeling Theory," a relatively well-developed labeling perspective existed before it was popularized by Becker. The concepts of stigmatization, the dramatization of evil, the self-fulfilling prophecy, and secondary deviation had been around for many years. One of the most influential theoretical distinctions in labeling theory, between "Primary and Secondary Deviation," was drawn by Lemert in a book published in 1951. Kids naturally get into mischief and trouble, or "primary deviation," but some of them get caught and punished by parents, teachers, police, or the juvenile court.

As Matsueda showed in a recent refinement and test of labeling theory, "Reflected Appraisals, Parental Labeling, and Delinquency," when this happens, the identity, status, and self-concept of the publicly recognized offender may change to reflect the usually negative appraisals of the conduct and, more important, of the "self." When the juvenile accepts and incorporates those appraisals into a "delinquent role" and acts accordingly, "secondary deviation" is the consequence—the kid who occasionally got into trouble has successfully been "labeled" as a juvenile delinquent. The irony is that efforts to control relatively widespread juvenile misconduct, whether within the family or the juvenile justice system, can "backfire" and actually contribute to the problem by consolidating "official" delinquent identities, thus making it even more difficult for so-labeled kids to stay out of trouble.

Like all theories, labeling theory has its weaknesses and problems. Paternoster and Iovanni examine and assess the application of the labeling perspective to juvenile delinquency in "The Labeling Perspective and Delinquency: An Elaboration of the Theory and an Assessment of the Evidence." Contrary to earlier critical reviews of the theory and empirical evidence, they conclude that labeling theory may not be as invalid as has been suggested, and that what is called for is a revitalization, based on more precise restatements and rigorous tests, of a labeling theory that is specific to juvenile delinquency.

The implications of labeling theory for practice are straightforward and point to some relatively "radical" changes in how the juvenile justice system should operate. To whatever extent the official labeling processes of the system produce more "delinquents," and for some of them unnecessarily or unjustly, it should not try so hard but should simply leave kids alone whenever possible. Lemert refers to this policy as "judicious" nonintervention in "Diversion in Juvenile Justice." A strategy of nonintervention does not mean, literally, that nothing is to be done when juveniles commit crimes. Rather, it suggests that the full measure of official juvenile justice processing should be reserved for those offenders who commit serious crimes. Therefore, labeling theory has supported the decriminalization of status offenses (noncriminal misbehaviors); the related deinstitutionalization of status offenders; the creation of diversion programs (although Lemert cautions that diversion may lead, paradoxically, to "widening the net" of control); narrowing the jurisdiction of the juvenile court to crime only, hence "criminalizing" the juvenile justice system; and, concomitantly, returning the responsibility for all other noncriminal kids' problems—whether at home (e.g., runaway), at school (e.g., truancy), or in the community (e.g., abandonment)—to the "community" and those formal and informal social service, educational, mental health, and other institutions and agencies that should deal with kids who have not committed crimes.

An Overview of Labeling Theory

EDWIN SCHUR

THE central tenet of the labeling orientation is quite straightforward: Deviance and social control always involve processes of social definition. Howard Becker's comments, widely taken to be the most important recent statement of the position, make this point succinctly:

Social groups create deviance by making the rules whose infraction constitutes deviance, and by applying these rules to particular people and labeling them as outsiders. From this point of view, deviance is *not* a quality of the act the person commits, but rather a consequence of the application by others of rules and sanctions to an "offender." The deviant is one to whom that label has successfully been applied; deviant behavior is behavior that people so label.

KEY THEMES

At the heart of the labeling approach is an emphasis on *process;* deviance is viewed not as a static entity but rather as a continuously shaped and reshaped *outcome* of dynamic processes of social interaction. It is in this general theme of process, in concentration on deviant roles and the development of deviant self-conceptions, and in use of such concepts as "career" and "commitment" that we see most clearly the indebtedness of labeling analysis to the theoretical perspective of symbolic interactionism. Discussing George H. Mead's theory of the social self, Herbert Blumer has noted that "Mead saw

the self as a process and not as a structure." Schemes that seek to explain the self through structure alone, Blumer has pointed out, ignore the reflexive process that Mead recognized as central to social interaction.

By attending to the "social history" and ramifications of deviant behavior, rather than to the supposed basic "characteristics" of deviating acts or actors (as determined by examination of associations with standard sociological variables), the labeling approach represents a major exception to what Albert Cohen has called the "assumption of discontinuity" in deviance studies. As he has pointed out, until recently

the dominant bias in American sociology has been toward formulating theory in terms of variables that describe initial states, on the one hand, and outcomes, on the other, rather than in terms of processes whereby acts and complex structures of action are built, elaborated, and transformed.

The same point has been made perhaps even more directly by Becker, who has emphasized a distinction between simultaneous and sequential models of deviance: "All causes do not operate at the same time, and we need a model which takes into account the fact that patterns of behavior *develop* in orderly sequence."

Yet although labeling analysis represents something of a break with the rather static statistical comparisons that have tended, despite recognition of severe sampling problems, to dominate research into the "causes" of deviating behavior, it is well to keep in mind that even in the specific study of deviance and control concern with process is not entirely new. A classic statement, more explicit in its recognition of the direct impact of labeling processes, was offered by Frank Tannenbaum in his discussion of the role that early stigmatization plays in generating delinquent and criminal careers:

The process of making the criminal, therefore, is a process of tagging, defining, identifying, segregating, describing, emphasizing, making conscious and self-conscious; it becomes a way of stimulating, suggesting, emphasizing, and evoking the very traits that are complained of.

The person becomes the thing he is described as being. Nor does it seem to matter whether the valuation is made by those who would punish or by those who would reform. . . . The harder they work to reform the evil, the greater the evil grows under their hands. The persistent suggestion, with whatever good intentions, works mischief, because it leads to bringing out the bad behavior that it would suppress. The way out is through a refusal to dramatize the evil.

In his more systematic effort at theoretical elaboration, Edwin Lemert laid much of the basis for the current labeling approach. It is Lemert, furthermore, who developed the distinction between *primary* and *secondary* deviation, a distinction that has been central to the work of recent labeling analysts. At this juncture, let us simply stress the importance of always distinguishing, for purposes of analysis, between a primary or initial act of deviation, on the one hand, and deviant roles, deviant identities, and broad situations involving deviance—as shaped by societal definitions and responses—on the other.

Although we have stated that the labeling approach preeminently involves process, we have made relatively little effort so far to indicate more precisely just which processes. Very generally, as is probably already clear, the labeling school asserts that *deviance outcomes* reflect complex processes of action and reaction, of response and counterresponse. The notion of deviance "outcomes" may be useful, for it

encompasses both individual consequences of societal reactions (as represented by the secondary deviant, recently defined by Lemert as "a person whose life and identity are organized around the facts of deviance") and situational consequences for society at large (e.g., the economic consequences of labeling certain forms of deviating behavior as criminal). At times, the labeling perspective has seemed to be concerned only with the former type of outcome—that is, with the production of deviant identities or characters in individuals. There is good reason to believe, however, that a considerably broader interpretation of labeling is warranted. Processes of social definition, or labeling, that contribute to deviance outcomes are actually found on at least three levels of social action, and all three require analysis. Such processes—as they occur on the levels of *collective rule-making, interpersonal reactions,* and *organizational processing*— all constitute important concerns of the labeling school.

It should be apparent, then, that interest in labeling suggests at least several focal points for research on deviance and control. Paradoxically, this approach seems both to emphasize the individual deviator (at least his personal and social characteristics) less than did previous approaches and at the same time to focus on him more intensively, seeking the meaning of his behavior to him, the nature of his self-concept as shaped by social reactions, and so on. To the extent that the individual "offender" remains an object of direct investigation, clearly the dominant, or favored, mode of research has shifted from statistical comparison of "samples" of supposed deviants and nondeviants, aimed at unearthing the differentiating "causal factors," to direct observation, depth interviews, and personal accounts, which can illuminate subjective meanings and total situational contexts.

In line, however, with the implicit argument that "deviant" is in large measure an *ascribed status* (reflecting not only the deviating individual activities but the responses of other people as well), research attention has shifted from the deviator himself to the *reactors*. Kai Erikson has nicely described this shift:

Deviance is not a property *inherent* in certain forms of behavior; it is a property *conferred upon* these forms by the audiences which directly or indirectly witness them. Sociologically, then, the critical variable is the social *audience* . . . since it is the audience which eventually decides whether or not any given action or actions will become a visible case of deviation.

In this connection, several related but different meanings can be given to the term *audience*. Both direct and indirect "audiences" react to either a given deviating individual or a particular deviance problem-situation in a given society. All three levels of analysis mentioned come into play. One audience is the society at large, the complex of interwoven groups and interests from which emerge general reactions to (and therefore labelings of) various forms of behavior. Another audience comprises those individuals (including significant others) with whom a person has daily interaction and by whom he is constantly "labeled" in numerous ways, positive and negative, subtle and not so subtle. A third audience includes official and organizational agents of control. They are among the most significant of the direct reactors or labelers, for they implement the broader and more diffuse societal definitions through organized structures and institutionalized procedures. It is on this third audience that the labeling approach has especially focused until now, but as we shall see, this audience is only one of several important research targets suggested by a labeling orientation.

QUESTIONS FOR DISCUSSION AND WRITING

1. What is the central tenet of the labeling orientation?
2. According to Frank Tannenbaum, what is "the process of making the criminal"? How may this process backfire despite good intentions?
3. According to Kai Erikson, what is a "critical variable" in deviance?

The Labeling Perspective and Delinquency: An Elaboration of the Theory and an Assessment of the Evidence

RAYMOND PATERNOSTER
LEEANN IOVANNI

OUR concern in this paper is the relevance of labeling theory for the study of juvenile delinquency. Specifically, we will examine three issues. First we will discuss briefly the origins of labeling theory in both a conflict and a symbolic interactionist tradition. We note that these two more general theoretical traditions were separately instrumental in the development of two major premises of labeling theory: (a) that political/economic power determines *what* is labeled and *who* is labeled—the conflict tradition—and (b) that the experience of being labeled is instrumental in the creation of both a more deviant character and a more deviant lifestyle—the symbolic interactionist tradition. Second, after specifying the two major labeling theory hypotheses (and possible contingent conditions), we will suggest the form that empirical tests for its falsification should take. Finally, we will review the extant literature to determine to what extent critics are addressing these issues or instead are addressing others of their own construction.

THEORETICAL ORIGINS OF LABELING THEORY

Conflict Theory

In an early formulation of the labeling perspective, Becker noted that a critical question for any theory of deviance is "when are rules made and enforced." In seeking an answer to this two-pronged question, early labeling theorists broke from the "norm-based definition of deviance" adopted by most criminologists by considering the role of political and economic conflict in the norm creation process. The conflict orientation in labeling theory is manifested at several levels of analysis. Schur notes that conflict occurs at the levels of (a) collective rule making, (b) organizational processing, and (c) interpersonal relations. Conflict at the level of collective rule making occurs when economically and politically powerful groups use their influence to define as unlawful those behaviors which they find offensive, and direct their rule making against identified groups involved in those activities.

Conflict at the organizational level concerns the process of labeling and label negotiation in middle-level social control agencies. Here, labeling theorists argue that the powerlessness of particular groups (blacks, members of the lower class, and perhaps females) makes it more likely that they will be singled out for more severe labels (being arrested rather than dismissed by the police and being incarcerated rather than fined or put on probation by the courts).

Conflict at the level of interpersonal relations concerns the bargaining over labels in day-to-day encounters, such as between the sighted and the blind, between the deformed or the mentally ill and "normals," and between the delinquent and the court worker. At all three levels, a deviant outcome is taken to be the result of conflict between individuals or collectivities of actors with differential power.

Symbolic Interactionism

Symbolic interactionism is a second general theoretical source to which the labeling theory of deviance can be traced. In addition to focusing on the creation and enforcement of rules discussed above, labeling theorists also examine the consequences of rule enforcement for those at whom labels are directed. This concern has led labeling theorists to examine the creation and elaboration of deviant "careers." A key theme within this perspective is the idea that efforts at social control actually may have counterproductive results. Social reactions or attempts "to do something about deviance" may produce a heightened commitment to the very behavior that enforcement agents are attempting to eradicate. This idea is expressed most clearly by Lemert's now-famous notion of secondary deviance.

Contrary to many interpretations and operationalizations of this theoretical construct, the idea of secondary deviance does not imply an absolute (deterministic) position: If labeling by social control agencies occurs, then in all instances more deviance will result. Rather, it describes the conditions under which an initial flirtation with deviance may produce subsequent problems of adjustment for the individual. These problems may facilitate additional deviant involvement. Labeling theorists characterize societal reaction and the labeling process as comprising (a) a hostile social audience making negative attributions of character which also may restrict actor's access to normal activities and opportunities, (b) a supportive nondeviant audience which may make nondeviant imputations about actor and may allow actor to disavow the negative ascriptions and to keep open normal routines, and (c) a supportive deviant audience which may make actor's acceptance of a deviant role less isolating while opening up deviant routines and opportunities.

Labeling Hypotheses

The tracing of the theoretical heritage of the labeling perspective to both a conflict and a symbolic interactionist tradition serves to illuminate the origins of four labeling hypotheses as they pertain to juvenile delinquency. From the conflict tradition, we can identify and examine (1) the role of political/economic power in creating delinquency statutes or rules surrounding delinquent conduct, (2) the influence of so-called "extralegal" attributes in determining who is labeled by social control organizations, and (3) the contribution of social and physical attributes in determining face-to-face encounters. From the symbolic interactionist tradition, we can identify a fourth hypothesis: (4) that the experience of being labeled by social control agencies may result in an alteration of personal identity, an exclusion from the normal routines of everyday life, and a greater involvement in delinquent acts. In the following section, we are concerned with the first three hypotheses, although we will discuss only the second in detail. A detailed discussion of the fourth hypothesis will follow in a subsequent section.

THE STATUS CHARACTERISTICS HYPOTHESIS

Empirical research concerning Hypotheses 1 and 3 listed above is grossly limited in comparison to the volume of research on Hypothesis 2, the status characteristics hypothesis. There are only a few studies of the process of collective rule making and delinquency. There are even fewer studies concerning the use of interpersonal "interaction cues" by control agents in the processing of delinquents. Clearly, the break with criminological tradition offered by the labeling perspective is its direct consideration of other people and institutions in influencing both the form and the volume that deviance assumes in any society. Unfortunately, very little research has been conducted on the very proposition that distinguishes this perspective.

Considerable empirical research, however, has been devoted to the influence of status characteristics on labeling outcomes, and there has been some debate as to what conclusions should be drawn from this research. As we will try to demonstrate, the typical form of the status characteristics hypothesis in empirical tests is more a caricature of labeling theory than a derivative. With regard to this hypothesis, labeling theory predicts that those with less power and prestige are more likely to be processed officially (labeled) than those who occupy more privileged positions. Within an organizational context, then, labeling theorists contend that the determination of who is labeled is partially a function of extralegal or status attributes.

From this discussion we can state the following hypothesis about juvenile delinquency and organizational processing:

Given the occurrence of a deviant action (delinquency), the decision of organizational agents to sanction officially (to label) an actor is *in part* determined by the social attributes (race, sex, and social class) of the offender and/or of the offended party.

This status characteristics hypothesis can be tested by examining organizational decision making in the juvenile justice system at a number of different points (the decision to arrest, to refer to court, to place on probation or to incarcerate, and to release on parole/aftercare), and it can be determined to what extent the likelihood of a more punitive outcome is influenced by the social characteristics of the offender or the complainant. Although perhaps labeling

theorists have not always made this point clear, our construction of this hypothesis contains the implicit assumption that a more punitive sanction constitutes a more severe label than a less punitive sanction (or no sanction at all). Also implicit in our construction is the kind of evidence necessary to refute the hypothesis. If it were found that status characteristics had no effect on processing decisions among a group of juveniles who had committed a similar "infraction of the rule," the validity of this hypothesis would be in doubt.

Research Agenda: On Testing the Status Characteristics Hypothesis

What would a valid test of this hypothesis consist of? This discussion will provide an "agenda of falsification" as a basis for evaluating the extant literature, which will be reviewed in the next section of this paper. The falsification of this hypothesis would be met if, after controlling for relevant legal considerations (offense and offender history data), the social characteristics of the alleged delinquent or of the party injured by the action had no statistically significant effect on the labeling outcome.

To put such a hypothesis to systematic test would require an examination of "label application" at various levels within different types of control agencies. At the very least, the hypothesis should be tested at the police decision to arrest or to handle informally, at the court intake worker's decision to detain or to release pending a juvenile court hearing, at the decision to dispose of a case informally or to send it to a full hearing, and at the disposition and type of sentence received after a hearing. For the most part, previous tests of the status characteristics hypothesis were conducted with samples selected from the *end* of the labeling process (juveniles in court hearings or already incarcerated). The danger of this approach is that such designs minimize the possible cumulative influence of even small "labeling effects" and ignore the biasing effect of self-selected samples.

The kind of data to be collected at these points would vary with the particular context but should include, for example, the offending party's age, sex, and social class; the nature of the offense; the presence of particular aggravating or mitigating circumstances; the offender's prior delinquent history; and the family structure from which the delinquent came. In addition to the effect of the offender's race, social class position, and other social characteristics on the labeling outcome, such research also should examine the role of the victim's/complainant's social characteristics. Finally, in examining labeling effects researchers should consider seriously the estimation of sample selection models which allow for the explicit consideration of "filtering" processes.

Review of Available Literature:
Status Characteristics

Research testing the social characteristics hypothesis is neither abundant nor methodologically rigorous in the area of delinquency; most of the research was conducted on adult samples. In terms of the processing of delinquents, some data are available at each of several organizational levels. With few exceptions, the published studies (even the most recent research) consider only one of many status characteristics (and usually only of the offender). Furthermore, most of the research on status characteristics and on the labeling of delinquents was conducted at the organizational level either of the police or of the juvenile court. Our intention here is to review the data briefly and to suggest further (and we hope more fruitful) lines of research.

The evidence with respect to the influence of status characteristics on police arrest decisions is inconsistent, although more studies are contrary to the labeling hypothesis than are supportive. [Some] studies find very little or no consistent bias either by race or by social class in police decision making, while [others] find that status characteristics exhibit a moderately strong effect on that decision.

Similarly inconclusive research is found with respect to pretrial juvenile justice decision making. In an early study, Terry found that the probation officer's decision to move a case forward to a court hearing was unrelated to the offender's race, social class, or sex. Nearly identical results were found in a much more methodologically rigorous study by Cohen and Kluegel. They report that the major determinants of the intake decision and of the decision to detain a delinquent pending adjudication were the juvenile's prior record and the philosophical orientation of the court. Once these factors were taken into account, they found no evidence of a significant direct effect for race and social class. Contrary to these studies, Arnold found that even when offense seriousness and prior offense history were considered, members of racial minorities were more likely to have their case brought to trial than disposed of informally, but only for the most serious offenses. Although Arnold's data with respect to race are somewhat supportive of the labeling hypothesis, he, too, found no significant effect for social class.

Finally, the literature with respect to social characteristics and juvenile court sentencing dispositions is no more conclusive. A substantial body of data can be marshaled both to refute and to support the idea that juvenile court dispositions are influenced by extralegal variables.

There is no easy way to reconcile these divergent findings in the literature pertaining to the status characteristics hypothesis of labeling theory. The only reasonable inference that can be drawn from this literature is that there are data of uneven quality and rigor which both support and refute the hypothesis.

Regardless of the manner in which reviews of the labeling literature are conducted, it is clear that additional research is required before a more definitive assessment of the status characteristics hypothesis can be made fairly. Rather than conducting more of the same kind of research, however, we suggest two different strategies. One of these strategies would entail a consideration of the *relevant conditions* under which status characteristics would be expected to have their maximum effect. We suggest that one neglected component of most of this kind of labeling research is a consideration of the victim's or the complainant's social characteristics. The failure of almost all delinquency research to date to consider the combined effect of offender's and victim's social characteristics is a significant omission. It is entirely plausible to suspect that blacks' crimes against other blacks are treated differently by social control institutions from instances in which a black victimizes a white.

Recent empirical studies of adult justice, for example, provide evidence that although the offender's race is inconsequential, the victim's race and victim/offender racial combinations are critical in the decisions of the police, the prosecutor, and the jury. In addition to the vertical direction of law based on racial characteristics, there is evidence to suggest that participants' gender is important.

A good deal of research, then, suggests that labeling effects may vary by social context. Previous labeling research assumed simply that labeling effects would be felt equally across all groups and social conditions. In contrast, we suggest that the effect of status characteristics on labeling outcomes is not invariant but varies substantially across different social contexts. This perspective assumes that the meaning of a potential "labelee's" status characteristics depends as much on who is offended against and in what circumstances as on who is offending.

A second suggested research strategy would examine the *cumulative effects* of status characteristic variables over the *entire sequence* of juvenile justice case processing rather than at a single decision point. In previous studies, researchers generally restricted their analyses to separate points in the juvenile justice system, assuming implicitly that any discriminatory effects due to status characteristics are limited to one stage.

A more systemic approach to testing the status characteristics hypothesis along the lines suggested here would seem fruitful for two reasons. First, some research suggests that status variables are related to decisions made early in the criminal justice process. Early labeling effects may "spill over" into subsequent stages, although they may go unnoticed. For example, some research suggests that race and social class may be related to type of legal representation and to early detention decisions, which are related directly to the ultimate disposition received in court. An excellent recent example of this line of research is Sampson's study of neighborhood SES and police reaction to delinquency. Sampson reported an ecological bias with respect to police behavior in that the probability of a juvenile's having an arrest record was related inversely to the social class of the community. This social class bias at the neighborhood level resulted in an accumulated arrest record and more serious "criminal histories" for poor adolescents. It is these criminal histories which later become so strongly predictive of juvenile court disposition. An analysis of juvenile court sentencing would find that when criminal record is controlled, an individual's social class has no explanatory power; such an analysis leads to a spurious rejection of the labeling hypothesis.

Second, discrimination at early stages in the juvenile justice system may distort discrimination markedly at later stages with more "self-selected" samples. The kind of research we are suggesting here is exemplified by a study by McCarthy and Smith, who reported that social class and race become increasingly important factors at later stages of juvenile case processing.

THE SECONDARY DEVIANCE HYPOTHESIS

Consequences of Labeling

It is the symbolic interactionist tradition within labeling theory that leads to the conceptualization of the "stigmatizing" and "segregating" effects of social control efforts. Labeling theorists believe that the reaction of social control agents, through the application of a "deviant" label, results in actor's being typified or "cast" as a deviant. As a consequence of this

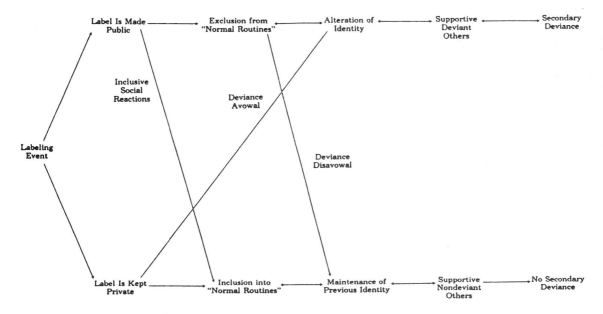

FIGURE 1 *Processes leading to greater probability of secondary deviance.*

typification process, actor's identity is *simplified* to the extent that the deviant identity comes to be of primary importance and is considered to reflect the "essential" self. Simultaneously, other properties of actor's character assume a secondary descriptive value; deviant ascription becomes a "master status" and "the deviant identification becomes the controlling one."

The central concern of labeling theorists in this tradition is "What happens to the individual after being labeled?" According to these theorists, being typified or labeled as a deviant has three main consequences: alteration of personal identity, exclusion from conventional opportunities, and an increase in the probability of further deviance. None are inevitable, however, and they are not determined solely by those who impute the label. Figure 1 portrays the process leading to possible secondary deviance effects. It shows, first of all, that the imposition of a label is unlikely to lead to secondary deviance if that fact is kept private. Not all instances of labeling are disclosed fully to others in actors' social environment: Those apprehended or arrested by the police may be released without

further action, some hearings (juvenile) may be closed to the general public, and some offenders may be able to hide their label (drunk driver and shoplifter) from all but intimate others. Consequently, these instances of labeling would be unlikely to result in exclusion from the normal routines of life. If actors' deviant status is generally broadcast, however, it becomes more likely that they will face the exclusionary practices of others.

Although exclusion from the normal routines of life is a more likely outcome of a publicly known label than of a label kept private, it is not inevitable. Rather than accepting the deviant label as indicative of actor's essential character, others instead may accept a different view (an understanding of character known and accepted before the labeling) and may attempt to neutralize the consequences of negative character attribution.

Figure 1 also suggests that even if the label is made public and one finds oneself excluded from many of the normal routines of life, the internalization of a deviant identity, though difficult to resist, is not an inevitable consequence.

Though this phenomenon is ignored in much criminological writing from the social reaction perspective, it has been noted in the general deviance literature that labeled actors may resist or refuse to concur in others' judgments about their own deviant character.

Davis refers to this process as *deviance disavowal* and defines it as a "refusal of those who are viewed as deviant to concur in the verdict"; if they do concur, "they usually place a very different interpretation on the fact or allegations than do their judges." Some of these attempts at deviance disavowal may be successful in that actors may continue to be seen and to see themselves as "essentially normal" (or at least as not deviant in the way alleged) and may maintain their previous identity. If these deviance disavowal processes are activated and are successful, secondary deviance, as a solution to problems of adjustment, would be unlikely. Secondary deviance is unlikely to occur unless actor finds the company of others who both support and exemplify the deviant status.

The contingent nature of the labeling process also can be seen in the many routes to secondary deviance. At one level, Figure 1 suggests that secondary deviance is contingent on (a) the public nature of the label, (b) exclusionary reactions by others, (c) an alteration of personal identity, and (d) support from deviant others. Each one of these contingent conditions would have to be met in order to make further rule breaking a likely outcome of imposing a deviant label.

Finally, Figure 1 reveals clearly the reciprocal nature of the labeling process. Exclusive social reactions from others are likely to lead to an alteration of personal identity and to a closer affinity with deviant others. Such closer association with supportive deviants may lead in turn to additional exclusion (likely also as a result of intentional choice on actor's part) and to a further recasting of self in line with the deviant label. This process should make clear that escalation to secondary deviance rests heavily on the subjective effects of being labeled; that is, the labeling experience serves to recast individuals *in their own eyes* as well as in the eyes of others.

Schur refers to the individual-level process of identity transformation as *role engulfment*. Being typified by others as a deviant, then, may have two distinct consequences for actor's self: One may view oneself as others do (as a deviant), and one may begin to perceive the self in a less favorable light, as less worthy. The "success" of this stigmatization or signification process as described by labeling theorists in the transformation of the individual's subjective reality is hastened and made easier by the objective effects of labeling. For labeling theory, the deviant identity is made even more plausible when actor's access to conventional (normal) roles and opportunities becomes problematic.

Even in the absence of any physical and obvious forms of separation, such as those due to incarceration, once actor is cast as generally deviant, he or she remains susceptible to exclusion from interactions with "normals." The essential character of the deviant label, then, may have the effect of curtailing actor's interactions with normal others and his access to conventional opportunities. This exclusion in turn may fix the deviant identity more securely in the individual's (and others') mind.

The interaction process ultimately may result in actor's involvement in secondary deviance; in that case, subjective reality becomes objective fact for the individual and for the larger society. For actors, secondary deviance becomes a direct response to problems created by the societal reaction to their deviance. When viewed as a problematic, contingent response to the application of a label, secondary deviance is both an attempt to cope meaningfully with the problems of a newly acquired identity and an expression of that identity.

Research Agenda:
Testing the Secondary Deviance Hypothesis

A thorough reading of labeling theory reveals a complex causal process, suggesting that the hypothesis most faithful to the theory is as follows:

Given the occurrence of a labeling experience, the individual may experience an alteration of personal identity, may find access to conventional others and opportunities barred, and as a result may exhibit a greater involvement in delinquent behavior.

Further, a review of the extant research relative to various points in this causal process reveals that we should not expect labeling effects to be invariant across societal subgroups. In an early article, Harris suggested that there is good reason to expect some subgroups to be more or less susceptible to labeling effects.

Differential susceptibility also is discussed by Lofland, one of the few labeling theorists who has given systematic attention to this issue. He identifies specific characteristics of actor which make for differential vulnerability to deviance escalation: (a) the degree of self-orientation, or the tenacity with which one holds one's personal identity (a trait which Lofland notes is associated highly with age and formal education); (b) the degree of "affective bonds" or emotional ties between actor and both normal and deviant others; and (c) the similarity between actor's and others' categories for describing an identity that is attributed to him. To the extent that actors have a weak conception of self, have positive attachments to both normal and deviant others, and use verbal categories regarding identity similar to those of the imputing others, they are more susceptible to escalation to deviant identity.

Review of Available Research:
Secondary Deviance

As mentioned previously, the causal component of labeling theory entails three main consequences: alteration of personal identity, exclusion from conventional opportunities, and an increase in the probability of further deviance. Further, these consequences constitute a causal and contingent process with stigmatizing and exclusionary effects that act as intervening variables in the escalation to secondary deviance.

The existing empirical literature, however, is limited to research that addresses these effects separately; in the case of the first two effects, tests have not necessarily been performed in a labeling context.

Some research has examined personal identity in terms of both deviant identity and self-worth. Taken as a whole, the results are inconsistent with labeling theory but not entirely contradictory. This is also true of research addressing the limitation on actor's access to conventional others and opportunities.

One example of the kind of research strategy that should be pursued further was published by Palamara, Cullen, and Gersten. The authors examined the effect of police and mental health interventions on the postintervention delinquent and problem behavior of a sample of youths who had had no prior contact with the police at the time when the study began. Controlling for preintervention behavior, these authors found that in comparison with those youths not labeled, "acquiring a criminal record significantly affects subsequent levels of both delinquency and general psychological impairment."

The theoretical import of these findings is substantial. To say that one type of label has little additional effect on secondary deviance in relation to another is not to say that it has no deviance-generating effects at all. As we have noted, it is doubtful that further increments in labeling will continue to produce further deviance; a "leveling-off" point may be reached where the process is at equilibrium. A failure to find evidence for incremental effects on secondary deviance is also to be expected theoretically. Personal identity may show continual decline, but once an actor is excluded from major conventional life situations it is not unreasonable to assume that further exclusion would have little additional meaning. This assumption would suggest that a clearly drawn conceptual distinction be maintained between absolute labeling effects (the effect of any label versus no label) and relative labeling effects (the effect of different types of labels).

THE REVITALIZATION OF A LABELING THEORY OF DELINQUENCY

What is the purpose of this extended discussion of the theoretical components of a labeling theory of delinquency and this review of the extant literature? What implications does it have for future work in this area? We hope we have shown that critics and those who work and write in the area of juvenile delinquency have understood the labeling perspective poorly and, as a result, have dismissed it prematurely. Ultimately, we argue for a revitalization of labeling theory, a renaissance of the perspective. We hope this will take the form of a reworked version of traditional labeling theory arguments and an interest in putting the resulting theoretical framework to empirical test. In this paper, we have tried to suggest some of the components that such a neolabeling theory should have and to describe some of its unavoidable complexities, but ours is certainly not the only formulation or the most elegant. It is merely intended to be a starting point.

CONCLUSIONS

In this paper, we attempted to trace the historical origins of two key labeling theory hypotheses, the status characteristics hypothesis and the secondary deviance hypothesis, to two more general theoretical traditions, conflict theory and symbolic interactionism. We then reviewed these hypotheses in detail to explicate their complexities fully as well as to provide a rationale for the importance of labeling theory within criminology. For over a decade the work of labeling theorists has been criticized as both theoretically unimportant and empirically invalid. Our review of this theory, however, suggests that the critics have formulated and tested oversimplistic labeling hypotheses—hypotheses which have invited refutation. Although much of the available empirical literature is inconsistent with labeling theory's two central hypotheses, we suggest a more theoretically valid research agenda for future work in this area. The work conducted to date says more about its critics than about labeling theory itself

QUESTIONS FOR DISCUSSION AND WRITING

1. What does the typical form of the status characteristics hypothesis predict?
2. The authors suggest that future research would entail a consideration of the relevant conditions under which status characteristics would be expected to have their maximum effect. What do the authors mean by this?
3. The authors suggest examining cumulative effects of status characteristic variables over the entire sequence of juvenile justice case processing. What have prior researchers done, and what is a more systematic approach?
4. How do labeling theorists in the "secondary deviance" hypothesis answer the question, "What happens to the individual after being labeled?"

Reflected Appraisals, Parental Labeling, and Delinquency

ROSS L. MATSUEDA

IN this article, I will draw on the writings of George Herbert Mead and the school of symbolic interactionism to conceptualize the self as being rooted in social interaction, comprising multiple dimensions, and providing a crucial link between self-control and social control. I will draw on theories of labeling and reference groups to specify the broader determinants of the self and argue that delinquency is in part determined by one's appraisals of self from the standpoint of others. I will attempt to build on prior research here by developing an explicit interactionist theory of the self and delinquency and subjecting the theory to empirical test.

SELF-CONTROL AS SOCIAL CONTROL: A CONCEPTION OF SELF BASED ON MEAD

The perspective of symbolic interactionism presupposes that social order is the product of an ongoing process of social interaction and communication. Of central importance is the process by which shared meanings, behavioral expectations, and reflected appraisals are built up in interaction and applied to behavior. These shared meanings attach to positions in society and thus link individual conduct to the organization of groups and to social structure. Social structure—the patterned regularities in soci-

ety—is an ongoing process, built up by social interactions; moreover, social structure in turn constrains the form and direction of these interactions by structuring communication patterns, interests, and opportunities. The specific mechanism linking interaction and social structure is role taking.

Role Taking and Delinquency

To analyze interaction, symbolic interactionists define the unit of analysis as the transaction, which consists of an interaction between two or more individuals. Within transactions, the important mechanism by which interactants influence each other is role taking, which consists of projecting oneself into the role of other persons and appraising, from their standpoint, the situation, oneself in the situation, and possible lines of action. With regard to delinquency, individuals confronted with delinquent behavior as a possible line of action take each other's roles through verbal and nonverbal communication, fitting their lines of action together into joint delinquent behavior.

The process by which role taking can lead to delinquent behavior is illustrated by four classic studies of delinquency. Briar and Piliavin found that boys freed from commitments to conventional lines of action are often incited into delinquency by "situationally induced motives," which are verbal motives presented by other boys. Free from considering the reactions of conventional others, these boys can take the role of each other, present delinquent motives, and

From "Reflected Appraisals, Parental Labeling, and Delinquency" by R. Matsueda, 1992, *American Journal of Sociology,* 97, pp. 1577-1611. Copyright 1992 by the University of Chicago Press. Reprinted by permission.

jointly adopt a delinquent line of action. Short and Strodtbeck noted that one's decision to join a gang fight often revolves around the risk of losing status within the gang. Gang members would take the role of the group, consider the group's negative reactions, and join in on the action for fear of losing status. Cohen argued that adolescent groups engage in a tentative probing conversation of gestures—a process best characterized as one of trial and error—and collectively innovate a new status hierarchy, a delinquent subculture. Finally, Gibbons claimed that as a result of group interactions, novel shades of norms and values emerge to influence the direction of joint behavior.

This discussion of role taking implies four major features for a theory of the self and delinquent behavior. First, the self consists of an individual's perception of how others view him or her and, thus, is rooted in symbolic interaction. Second, the self as an object arises partly endogenously within situations and partly exogenously from prior situational selves being carried over from previous experience. Thus, we can speak of a set of patterned selves that is somewhat stable over time but varies across individuals. Third, the self as an object is a *process* determined by the self at a previous point in time and by prior behavior (resolutions of problematic situations). Fourth, delinquent behavior will result in part from the formation of habits and in part from stable perceptions of oneself from the standpoint of others. Through the latter process, delinquency is controlled by one's reference groups.

Reflected Appraisals of Self and Delinquent Behavior

The self as social control is a process consisting of three components: how others actually see one (actual appraisals), how one perceives the way others see one (reflected appraisals), and how one sees oneself (self-appraisals). Thus, one's self is in part a "reflected appraisal" of how significant others appraise one.

An interactionist conception of self as social control, however, does not imply a one-to-one correspondence between reflected appraisals and actual appraisals. Clearly, reflected appraisals are the result of *selective perception* of actual appraisals, which depends on the particular problematic situations that give rise to the reflected appraisals. Thus, reflected appraisals should be only partially a function of actual appraisals. Research has also found that reflected appraisals have small effects on self-appraisals.

In light of the theoretical discussion above, I can derive a more plausible model of reflected appraisals and behavior. The revised model follows Kinch by specifying that actual appraisals by others affect behavior only by affecting one's reflected appraisals of self. The alternative hypothesis, which contradicts symbolic interactionism, posits that actual appraisals influence behavior directly, regardless of reflected appraisals. This could result if significant others are particularly proficient at appraising one and, therefore, predicting one's behavior or if other elements of the self besides reflected appraisals mediate actual appraisals. Moreover, the model diverges from Kinch's model in three ways. First, it deletes self-appraisals from the model, stipulating reflected appraisals of self as the key variable for explaining behavior. Second, it allows behavior to have a direct effect on subsequent behavior. This is consistent with our theoretical framework, which posits that institutionalized behavior occurs in nonproblematic situations and is determined not by role taking but by prior behavior. Third, it allows behavior to have a direct effect on reflected appraisals since those appraisals are formed in part from previous behavioral solutions to problematic situations. Symbolic interactionism would predict that reflected appraisals are determined more by actual appraisals of others than by past behavior.

This model can explain the relationships between parental appraisals, reflected appraisals, and delinquent behavior. It allows me to test three restrictions specified by Kinch: (a) Prior delinquency has no direct effect on later delinquency, (b) prior behavior has no direct effect on reflected appraisals, and (c) actual appraisals have no direct effect on future delinquency. To link these social psychological mechanisms to broader determinants of delinquency, I turn to labeling theory.

THE PARENTAL CONTEXT OF CONTROL: LABELING AND REFLECTED APPRAISALS

Most etiological statements of labeling theory, particularly Tannenbaum's concept of the dramatization of evil, Lemert's concept of secondary deviance, and Mead's concept of the hostile attitude of punitive justice, are rooted in the perspective of symbolic interactionism. Therefore, we can draw on labeling theory to specify the broader social determinants of the reflected-appraisals process.

Focusing primarily on the negative consequences of labeling an individual as "deviant" or "delinquent," labeling theory argues that initial acts of delinquency are relatively harmless instances of primary deviance. From the standpoint of the child, such acts are defined as "play" or "mischief"; however, from the standpoint of the larger community, they are viewed as "evil" or as a "law violation." The community's response, which initially includes reactions of parents, teachers, and peers and later encompasses reactions of the juvenile justice system, is to label the child as "bad" or "evil." The label, in turn, influences the self-image of the child, who comes to view him- or herself as bad or delinquent, which in turn increases the likelihood of future deviance. Eventually, this spiraling labeling process can leave the youth in the hands of juvenile justice officials—cut off from conventional society, stigmatized by parents and teachers, and left with a delinquent self-image. Thus, a self-fulfilling prophecy is set up: Through this process of deviance amplification, or secondary deviance, an otherwise conforming child may eventually respond to the initial labeling of harmless acts by confirming the delinquent label.

A hallmark of labeling theory is the proposition that deviant labels are not randomly distributed across the social structure but are instead more likely to apply to the powerless, the disadvantaged, and the poor. Because of existing stereotypes—which portray criminals as members of lower classes, minorities, urban dwellers, and young adults—individuals who belong to such groups are more likely than others to be labeled delinquent. Again, the result is a self-fulfilling prophecy: Members of disadvantaged groups are labeled delinquent, which alters their self-conceptions and causes them to deviate, thus fulfilling the prophecy of their initial label.

Empirical research on labeling theory has produced equivocal results. While some research has found official labeling to have trivial effects on self-image, especially when prior self-reported delinquency is controlled, other research has found official labels to have effects for some youth (whites and nonserious delinquents) but not others. In summarizing this research, Jensen concluded that official labeling may have a greater impact on delinquent self-images and attitudes among those less heavily involved in delinquency. Research on the effect of official labeling on subsequent delinquent behavior has found positive effects on delinquency, but when prior levels of self-reported delinquency are controlled the results have been inconsistent. While this research literature has led some researchers to dismiss labeling theory, others have concluded that attention should focus more on the consequences of informal rather than official labels. Menard and Morse found support for the latter proposition: Perceived informal social labels had substantial effects on delinquency and helped mediate the effect of IQ on delinquency.

Labeling theory can help specify the relationships between background characteristics, the informal labeling process, and delinquency. First, youths who have engaged in delinquent behavior should be more likely to be labeled delinquent by their parents. Second, insofar as parents act on conventional stereotypes of deviance, their appraisals of their children as either deviant or conforming may be influenced by structural conditions that reflect disadvantages.

Urban, minority, lower-class, and older adolescent youths may be more likely to be labeled by their parents as deviant and less likely labeled as conforming, in part because they engage in more objective deviance. Indeed, parents could act on stereotypes to such an extent that those parents of disadvantaged children are more likely to label their children deviant, regardless of their children's behavior. This would constitute strong evidence for a labeling perspective since the parents share the disadvantages of their children but nevertheless still act on conventional stereotypes. Third, parental appraisals of youths as deviant or conforming will influence their further delinquency, primarily by influencing youths' reflected appraisals of self as deviant or conforming.

DATA AND METHODS

The analyses that follow will examine the propositions above that are derived from both a symbolic interactionist theory of the self and a labeling theory of delinquent behavior. Such an examination requires a research design with at least three features. To examine the labeling hypothesis that parental appraisals vary by social-structural variables, a random sample of a heterogeneous population is required. To examine the joint relationships between parental appraisals, reflected appraisals, and delinquency, survey data measuring *perceptual* or subjective social psychological concepts is needed. To examine simultaneously the reciprocal effects of delinquency on parental and reflected appraisals, a longitudinal design is necessary.

Data that meet these requisites were collected by Elliott and his colleagues as part of the National Youth Survey (NYS), a longitudinal study of delinquency and drug use. Employing a multistage cluster sampling frame, the NYS obtained a national probability sample of households in the United States in 1976. Of the households, 7,998 were randomly selected, and all 2,360 eligible youths living in the households were included. Seventy-three percent of those youths (1,725) agreed to participate, signed consent forms, and along with one of their parents, completed first-wave interviews in 1977. As a result, the participating youths are reasonably representative of 11— to 17-year-olds in the United States. My analyses focus on the first three waves of data for male respondents.

The NYS used personal interviews to collect self-reports of delinquent behavior, parents' reported appraisals of their child, and youths' reflected appraisals of themselves from the standpoint of parents, friends, and teachers. The content of the appraisals cluster around four substantive dimensions: (a) sociable, measured by "well-liked" and "gets along well with others"; (b) likely to succeed, measured by a single indicator; (c) distressed, measured by "often upset" and "has a lot of personal problems"; and (d) rule violator, measured by "gets into trouble" and "breaks rules." The delinquency inventory was designed to represent the entire range of delinquent acts for which juveniles could be arrested. The analyses will focus on a 24-item scale of general delinquency since our interactionist theory does not specify a priori reasons for examining specific offenses, and empirically, recent research finds little evidence that delinquents specialize in offenses. To check the robustness of the results, however, I will also examine three subscales of delinquency: drug use, minor delinquency, and Uniform Crime Report (UCR) index offenses. Finally, the NYS also includes measures of background characteristics relevant to labeling hypotheses: age, race, urban residence, broken home, and family income.

ANALYSIS OF THE SUBSTANTIVE MODEL

Specifying the Model and Hypotheses

The substantive model, depicted in Figure 1, specifies causal relationships among the four following latent constructs: (a) a set of exogenous background variables measured at Time 1; (b) a set of endogenous parental appraisals of youths as sociable, as a success, as distressed, and as a rule violator, measured at Time 1; (c) a

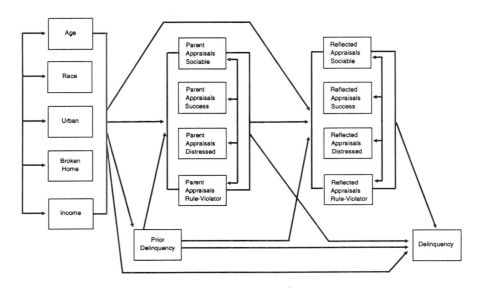

FIGURE 1 *A substantive model of parental appraisals, reflected appraisals, and delinquency.*

set of endogenous youth-reflected appraisals of self as sociable, as a success, as distressed, and as a rule violator, measured at Time 2; and (d) an outcome variable of delinquency, measured at Time 3. The causal ordering of the variables follows my theoretical specification: Parental appraisals influence reflected appraisals, which in turn influence delinquent behavior. The time ordering of the variables coincides with this causal ordering to reduce ambiguity in making causal inferences. Analyses that vary the precise timing of the variables do not change the substantive findings appreciably.

Within this model, we can identify specific hypotheses derived from labeling and symbolic interactionist theories. Consistent with labeling theory, background characteristics reflecting disadvantages should increase the likelihood of negative parental labeling and perhaps decrease the likelihood of positive labeling. Thus, parental labeling of a youth as a rule violator and as distressed may be greater for youths who have committed prior delinquent acts, who are black, and who come from urban, low-income areas and broken homes. As noted above, if disadvantages increase the likelihood of parental

labeling, net of prior delinquency, the stereotyping process specified by labeling theorists would receive strong support. Alternatively, it may be that stereotypes are used only by secondary others, such as teachers or juvenile justice officials, and that parents and other significant others use their intimate knowledge of the child in forming appraisals. Finally, parental labeling of the child, particularly as a rule violator, should have substantial total effects on future delinquency. As deviance amplification predicts, youths will commit more crimes if their parents label them as rule violators or as distressed; conversely, they may commit fewer crimes if their parents label them as sociable or as likely to succeed.

Symbolic interactionist theory implies three hypotheses concerning direct effects. First, parental appraisals should have a direct effect on their reflected counterparts, net of prior performance (delinquency). This tests the hypothesis that one's reflected appraisals of self from the standpoint of significant others is, in part, a reflection of the actual appraisals made by those significant others. Second, previous delinquent behavior should exert a direct effect on reflected appraisals of self. Prior delinquency should increase reflected appraisals as a rule violator and as distressed, and perhaps decrease reflected appraisals as sociable and likely to succeed. Third, future delinquent behavior should be directly affected by one's reflected appraisals of self. Delinquency should be substantially affected by reflected appraisals of one as a rule violator and perhaps also by reflected appraisals as distressed, sociable, and likely to succeed.

The model also allows us to test several other hypotheses. First is Kinch's hypothesis that the effect of prior behavior on reflected appraisals is entirely mediated by parental appraisals. Second is Kinch's hypothesis that the effect of prior delinquency on future delinquency is entirely mediated by the intervening reflected-appraisals process. In contrast, an interactionist theory would predict that through habit or nonreflective behavior, prior delinquency will maintain a direct effect on future delinquency. Third is the hypothesis, consistent with Kinch and symbolic interactionism in general, that parental appraisals influence delinquency only indirectly through their effects on reflected appraisals. The alternative hypothesis is that parental appraisals are sufficiently accurate to predict delinquency, even holding prior delinquency and reflected appraisals constant. Fourth is the hypothesis, consistent with labeling and interactionist theories, that the effect of background variables on delinquency works primarily indirectly through the labeling and reflected-appraisals process.

Estimation of the Model

Table 1 presents unstandardized parameter estimates of the substantive model; standardized counterparts appear in Table 2. The hypotheses derived from labeling theory involve effects of background characteristics and prior delinquent behavior on parental appraisals of youth (Tables 1 and 2, rows 2-5). As hypothesized, older youths, urban dwellers, and youths from broken homes all commit more delinquent acts on average. Consistent with labeling

theory, prior delinquent behavior substantially increases parental appraisals of a youth as a rule violator and distressed, while also slightly reducing their appraisals of a youth as sociable or likely to succeed (see rows 2-5 in column 6). Also consistent with labeling theory, the background variables exert some effect on parental appraisals, particularly rule violator ($R^2 = .13$). Parents of youths who are younger, nonwhite, and from urban areas are more likely to label their children as rule violators. This is primarily because such youths have committed delinquent acts in the past.

But the only evidence that the disadvantaged may be falsely accused by parents is a countervailing effect of race. Blacks are less likely to be labeled rule violators because they commit fewer delinquent acts; however, net of delinquency, they are more likely to be negatively labeled. Parents in nonintact families are less likely to label their children sociable and more likely to label them distressed (Tables 1 and 2, column 4). This second effect works partly indirectly through prior delinquent behavior. In general, then, these results provide limited support for the labeling hypothesis that net of their delinquent behavior, youths from disadvantaged backgrounds are more likely to be labeled negatively.

Turning to the reflected-appraisals equations, we find support for the interactionist proposition that reflected appraisals of self are partly a reflection of the objective appraisals made by others. With one exception, parental appraisals of a youth have significant effects on youths' corresponding reflected appraisals of self. This effect is particularly strong for the rule-violator appraisals, perhaps because of the salience of youths' deviant behaviors to parents, who are likely to be concerned about such behavior. The one exception is the coefficient relating parental and reflected appraisals of who is likely to succeed, which does not quite reach significance. The small size of this effect is perhaps due to the nebulous nature of the category of "likely to be a success," especially for adolescents, whose success has yet to be determined.

TABLE 1

Unstandardized parameter estimates of the substantive model: Males.

| | | | | | | | Predetermined Variables | | | | | | | | |
| | | | | | | | | Parental Appraisals | | | | Youth-Reflected Appraisals | | | |
Dependent Variables	Age (1)	Race (2)	Urban (3)	Broken Home (4)	Income (5)	Prior Delinquency1 (6)	Sociable1 (7)	Success1 (8)	Distress1 (9)	Rule Violator1 (10)	Sociable2 (11)	Success2 (12)	Distress2 (13)	Rule Violator2 (14)	R^2
1. Delinquency1	.022 (.004)	.048 (.025)	.080 (.020)	.069 (.020)	-.004 (.004)										.066
Parental appraisals:															
2. Sociable1	.022 (.012)	-.018 (.067)	.016 (.054)	-.114 (.054)	.009 (.011)	-.268 (.092)									.032
3. Success1	.088 (.011)	-.040 (.063)	.001 (.051)	-.067 (.050)	.011 (.010)	-.270 (.086)									.019
4. Distress1	.001 (.012)	-.020 (.069)	-.001 (.056)	.160 (.056)	-.017 (.011)	.513 (.100)									.077
5. Rule violator1	-.056 (.013)	-.207 (.077)	.090 (.062)	.031 (.061)	-.004 (.012)	.708 (.107)									.126
Youth-reflected appraisals:															
6. Sociable2	.000 (.007)	-.036 (.037)	.027 (.030)	-.005 (.030)	.003 (.006)	-.004 (.053)	.097 (.039)	.018 (.026)	.005 (.036)	-.037 (.041)					.068
7. Success2	-.017 (.012)	.166 (.067)	.059 (.054)	.049 (.053)	.032 (.011)	-.018 (.096)	.053 (.069)	.074 (.048)	.034 (.066)	-.180 (.075)					.101
8. Distress2	.001 (.010)	-.138 (.054)	-.038 (.043)	.016 (.043)	-.024 (.009)	.183 (.077)	-.072 (.055)	-.042 (.038)	.117 (.053)	.065 (.059)					.164
9. Rule violator2	.032 (.013)	.128 (.071)	-.056 (.056)	.016 (.056)	-.019 (.011)	.907 (.104)	-.100 (.073)	.029 (.050)	-.120 (.070)	.379 (.083)					.285
Delinquent behavior:															
10. Delinquency3	.018 (.004)	.040 (.025)	.029 (.020)	.007 (.020)	-.006 (.004)	.451 (.038)	.053 (.026)	-.019 (.017)	-.010 (.025)	.084 (.029)	.166 (.046)	.006 (.019)	-.056 (.026)	.157 (.021)	.464

Note: SEs are in parentheses, $N = 851$.

TABLE 2

Standardized parameter estimates of the substantive model: Males.

	Predetermined Variables					Prior	Parental Appraisals			Rule	Youth-Reflected Appraisals			Rule
Dependent Variables	Age (1)	Race (2)	Urban (3)	Broken Home (4)	Income (5)	Delinquency1 (6)	Sociable1 (7)	Success1 (8)	Distress1 (9)	Violator1 (10)	Sociable2 (11)	Success2 (12)	Distress2 (13)	Violator2 (14)
1. Delinquency1	.170	.071	.139	.127	−.035									
Parental appraisals														
2. Sociable1	.076	−.012	.012	.093	.037	−.119								
3. Success1	.025	−.024	.001	−.050	.042	−.110								
4. Distress1	.003	−.012	−.001	.118	−.061	.207								
5. Rule violator1	−.168	−.120	.061	.022	−.013	.275								
Youth-reflected appraisals:														
6. Sociable2	−.002	−.045	.040	−.008	.024	−.003	.185	.037	.010	−.080				
7. Success2	−.056	.105	.044	.038	.125	−.008	.051	.077	.036	−.197				
8. Distress2	.003	−.106	−.034	.015	−.112	.095	−.085	−.054	.151	.086				
9. Rule violator2	.092	.070	−.036	.011	−.065	.335	−.083	.026	−.110	.360				
Delinquent behavior:														
10. Delinquency3	.119	.051	.042	.011	−.044	.382	.101	−.039	−.021	.184	.167	.011	−.092	.361

Note: $N = 851$.

We also find support for the symbolic interactionist hypothesis that prior behavior influences reflected appraisals indirectly by influencing significant others' appraisals. Prior delinquency has a large total effect (standardized coefficient of .42) on reflected appraisals as rule violator and a moderate total effect (.17) on distressed. About 25% of the effect of prior delinquency on reflected appraisals as rule violator is mediated by parental appraisals as a rule violator. Nevertheless, contrary to Kinch's mediation hypothesis, even holding parental appraisals constant, prior delinquency significantly influences reflected appraisals as rule violator (standardized coefficient of .34) and as distressed (.09).

Overall, the model explains nearly half of the variance in delinquent behavior (Tables 1 and 2, row 10). Of the youth-reflected-appraisals variables, rule violator has by far the largest effect (a standardized coefficient of .36). Thus, persons who perceive that others view them as one who violates rules, or gets in trouble, engage in more delinquent acts. This supports the major hypothesis of an interactionist theory of delinquency: Behavior is strongly influenced by reflected appraisals. Of the remaining reflected-appraisals variables, sociable has a substantial positive effect on delinquency, and distressed a small negative effect. Net of the other variables in the model, youths who see themselves (from the standpoint of others) as sociable commit more delinquent acts, while those who see themselves as distressed commit slightly fewer delinquent acts.

Consistent with a deviance amplification hypothesis, parental appraisals of a youth as a rule violator have a substantial total effect on delinquency (a standardized coefficient of .29). Moreover, nearly one half of this effect is mediated by youth-reflected appraisals as a rule violator. This supports an important hypothesis of symbolic interactionism: Parental appraisals influence youth-reflected appraisals, which in turn influence delinquency. Nevertheless, even controlling for youth-reflected appraisals, parental appraisals of youth as a rule violator exert a substantial effect on delinquency. It appears that parents' appraisals of youths are, to some extent, more accurate than youths' perceptions of those appraisals. This finding fails to support a symbolic interactionist perspective. Parental appraisals of youths as sociable also exert a significant total effect on delinquency; however, only a small portion is mediated by youth-reflected appraisals. This effect is positive, meaning that, net of the other explanatory variables, more likable and sociable youths commit more delinquent acts. There is a small but significant indirect effect of parental appraisals as distressed on delinquency through reflected appraisals as distressed.

Prior delinquency (measured at Time 1) has a very large total effect on delinquency at Time 3 (standardized effect of .55), about 30% of which is mediated by parental and reflected appraisals as a rule violator. This implies that males between the ages of 13 and 19 are fairly stable in delinquent behavior: Those who engage in delinquency are likely to have engaged in delinquency 2 years earlier. This finding also implies that as predicted by an interactionist theory of the self, part of the stability in delinquency is due to reflected appraisals as a rule violator and part is due to habit (nonreflective behavior). Alternatively, the direct effect could reflect unmeasured mechanisms not included in the model. Finally, with one exception, the intervening mechanisms specified by the labeling and symbolic interaction process account for most of the effects on delinquency of the background variables. The one exception is age—about one half of the total effect of age on delinquency is direct.

SUMMARY AND CONCLUSIONS

In sum, these analyses yield six principal findings, which provide general support for a symbolic interactionist conceptualization of reflected appraisals and delinquency. First, youths' reflected appraisals of themselves from the standpoint of parents, teachers, and friends coalesce into a consensual self, rather than remaining compartmentalized as distinct selves.

This holds for reflected appraisals as rule violators, distressed, sociable, and likely to succeed. Second, consistent with labeling theory, parental labels of youths as rule violators are more likely among delinquents, nonwhites, and urban dwellers. Most of these effects operate indirectly through prior delinquency; thus, we find only modest evidence of disadvantaged youths being falsely accused.

Third, with the exception of likely to succeed, youths' reflected appraisals of themselves are strongly influenced by their parents' independent appraisals of them. This result is particularly strong for the rule-violator variable, the reflected appraisal most relevant to labeling and delinquency. This finding, at least with regard to rule violator, suggests that youths accurately perceive their parents' appraisals of them and that the reflected-appraisals constructs are capturing meaningful elements of self-concept. Moreover, this supports the proposition of symbolic interactionism that reflected appraisals of the self arise through role taking in transactions and, therefore, are in part a reflection of others' actual appraisals.

Fourth, previous delinquent behavior influences reflected appraisals of self. Consistent with predictions from labeling theory, this effect works partly indirectly through parental appraisals. Prior delinquency, however, also affects reflected appraisals directly. This implies that reflected appraisals are not a mirror reflection of others' appraisals but rather are the result of selective perception of others' appraisals and of previous behavior. Fifth, as predicted by symbolic interactionism, reflected appraisals as a rule violator exert a large effect on delinquent behavior and mediate much of the effect of parental appraisals as a rule violator on delinquency. Contrary to interactionism, however, parental appraisals as a rule violator still exert a direct effect on delinquency. Sixth, age, race, and urban residence exert significant total effects on delinquency, most of which work indirectly through prior delinquency and partially through the rule-violator reflected appraisal.

These findings suggest that an interactionist conception of the self as reflected appraisals provides an important cause and consequence of delinquent behavior. Viewed more broadly, these results indicate that the concept of role taking, as specified by symbolic interactionism, is important for delinquency. Unlike most previous research on the self and delinquency, which examines global self-esteem, I have examined specific meanings of the self pertaining to violating rules. I found that one aspect of the self-reflected appraisals as a rule violator has strong effects on delinquency. Furthermore, an interactionist perspective would imply that other specific meanings of the self may also influence delinquent behavior. These include specific attitudes and motives concerning delinquent and conforming alternatives, the specific reactions to and attitudes about delinquency held by significant others, and the presentation of situational motives for delinquency by significant others.

Such mechanisms could account for the finding that parental appraisals of a youth as a rule violator affect delinquency, net of the youth's reflected appraisals. Symbolic interactionism can also provide a framework for integrating the literatures on reflected appraisals, global self-esteem, and delinquent behavior. From this perspective, delinquent behavior is determined primarily by specific meanings concerning delinquency, including reflected appraisals, role identities, specific motives concerning delinquency, reactions of significant others to delinquency, and presentation of situational motives by significant others. Future research is needed to estimate relative weights of such processes and to determine whether conditional effects are involved. Such research would link traditional studies of self-esteem to our findings supporting a symbolic interactionist theory of delinquency.

QUESTIONS FOR DISCUSSION AND WRITING

1. How is the process by which role-taking can lead to delinquent behavior illustrated by four classic studies of delinquency? How does this discussion of role taking imply four major features for a theory of the self and delinquent behavior?

2. Focusing primarily on the negative consequences of labeling an individual as "deviant" or "delinquent," what does labeling theory argue? How does that process increase the likelihood of future deviance? What is a hallmark of labeling theory?

3. What six principal findings provide general support for a symbolic interactionist conceptualization of reflected appraisals and delinquency?

Diversion in Juvenile Justice

EDWIN M. LEMERT

L IKE many other academic concepts that have sifted into the public domain, diversion has been applied very loosely and sometimes indiscriminately to such a wide variety of procedures and programs that it may be a futile effort to try to define it in any useful way. I have characterized diversion as a "process whereby problems otherwise dealt with in a context of delinquency and official action will be defined and handled by other means."

At this point, two possible meanings of diversion emerge: In one instance, an officer has sufficient cause to believe an offense has taken place, but for a number of reasons he releases the suspected youth. Yet this is no more than what police have done traditionally—namely, make discretionary arrest decisions. It seems to me that in order for diversion to operate there has to be a conscious or policy-based choice to release a juvenile who otherwise would have been arrested and sent to the juvenile court. And herein, perhaps because of the variability in standards and the differing contingencies of law enforcement among jurisdictions and even among individuals within the same juvenile justice system, lies the difficulty of ascertaining whether diversion actually occurs.

Further considerations in attempting to define diversion pertain to the sequence of events following decisions not to process officially the case of a juvenile suspect. One possibility here is release of the youth without any requirement of further contact with law enforcement officials; in effect, the juvenile is sent back to whatever

activities he wants to pursue. A second ability is referral of the youth to some nonlegal or community alternative, presumably an agency providing appropriate services. A third possibility, whose relevance is somewhat more questionable, is referral of the juvenile to an outside agency without services.

THE RATIONALE FOR DIVERSION

Diversion is assumed to be a corrective for a variety of shortcomings in juvenile justice. Among these evils of the system are the denial to juveniles of civil rights or fair treatment; backlogs in the courts, making for inefficiency; labeling and stigmatization of youths; the failure of the juvenile justice system to reduce recidivism; and the failure of communities to assume responsibility for solving youths' problems. More positive rationales for diversion are to reduce the costs of processing delinquency cases and to promote the funding of needed services for youths.

A good deal has been made of the labeling and stigmatization of juveniles resulting from contacts with and processing by the juvenile court. There has been a tendency among many reformers to accept the validity of such consequences uncritically or to formulate related research in a simplistic fashion. Indeed, other research indicates that stigmatizing of a youth does not necessarily follow from his contact with the juvenile court. This should come as no surprise to those who understand that labeling and societal reaction theories of deviance rest on the importance of process. The idea that the label "delinquent" can be a cause of delinquent behavior is at best crude and naive, but unfortunately it is an all-too-common application of labeling theory, furthered by the use of mechanical cause-effect models to research the question. Our knowledge has not moved much beyond a starting assumption that the effect of exposure to arrest and court hearings on juveniles' self-conceptions and behavior is variable, particularly when the exposure happens but once.

SECONDARY DEVIANCE

The more enduring significance of stigma lies in its consequences. It must be said that in many, possibly most, cases, contact by juveniles with law enforcement agencies has minimal results—dismissal or discharge accompanied by warnings or moral injunctions of some sort.

The awakening of interest in deterrence theory reminds the thoughtful observer of juvenile justice that encounters with stigma are not necessarily negative; they may very well deter further deviance or, more likely, lead youths to modify their actions to avoid further contacts with police. A broader conception of labeling theory might allow that labels can be employed by design as part of a treatment procedure to confront youths with clear-cut alternatives, one being the punitive consequences of the label, the other being an opportunity to redefine or change status.

Granting these reservations does not necessarily destroy the validity of conceptions of secondary deviance, particularly if attention is directed away from the semantic aspects of labeling as a cause of delinquency to the consequences of instituting social control over youths. This points out the secondary problems social control creates, such as new rules to follow, whose violation subjects the juvenile to penalties unrelated to his original deviant act. Control also occasions more general secondary problems, as when youths are held in detention where schooling is interrupted, making reentry into the community more difficult and possibly leading to termination of schooling. This, in turn, can limit the youths' employability. How the contingencies of social control are related to

further deviant acts is admittedly a complex question, one having to do with the sequence in which various influences come to bear on the youths. However, the failure to develop a model to study secondary deviance cannot be a reason for disregarding strong evidence that it does occur.

Secondary deviance was never intended to be a general theory of delinquency causation; rather, it is an explanation of how casual, random, or adventitious deviance becomes redefined and stabilized through status change and self-conscious adaptation to secondary problems generated by social control. The number of youths who become secondary, career-type delinquents is not great, although the damage they do to society may be substantial. For this reason, there is still considerable justification for diversion from official control at critical points where transition to secondary deviance may otherwise occur.

Most of the reasons given as rationales for diversion tend to be discrete, pragmatic considerations not easily tied together in a more comprehensive justification, unless it be that provided by labeling theorists. As I have tried to show, it may be more meaningful to consider diversion in regard to the consequences of social control. Although these consequences have an immediate, distributive aspect, they also have a collective dimension pertaining to public policy and how far and under what conditions the state should intervene in the socialization of children and youths.

JUDICIOUS NONINTERVENTION

The rather caption-like policy recommendation that I advanced as a rationale for diversion was that of judicious nonintervention, an idea later taken up and more systematically stated by Schur. This was intended to be more than a plea for curtailing juvenile court intake; it was an effort to counter the emphasis in American policy with respect to youths, to move away from the puritanical, moralistic, "child-saving" legacy of the nineteenth- and early twentieth-century reform movements. Nonintervention meant that society or the local community would treat a great deal of deviance among the young as normal behavior, on the assumption that most youths will pass through their "deviant" or "storm and stress" stage and mature into reasonably law-abiding adults. This, of course, was not a new idea.

What was new was that nonintervention would be *judicious*, would become deliberate public policy, giving such policy a Jeffersonian twist that the best control of youths is the least control. It was also proposed that some kind of organized system for monitoring youths' behavior should be set up. Intervention would be based on an assessment of the amount and kinds of damage wrought by younger populations in society and would include a careful study of the forms it should take when deemed necessary. In retrospect, I think a term like *planned nonintervention* might have better conveyed the larger implications of such a policy.

LAW ENFORCEMENT TAKES CHARGE

A salient unintended consequence of the diversion movement has been its substantial preemption by police and probation departments. In many areas, they have set up in-house programs, hired their own personnel, and programmed cases in terms of their special ends and circumstances. This development is diametrically opposed to the main idea of diversion—that is, that diversion should be away from the juvenile justice system. The effect has been little more than an expansion in the intake and discretionary powers of police and a shuffling of such powers from one part of their organization to another.

In referring cases to other agencies, the police have been selective favoring some cases and ignoring others, usually depending on the feedback of information from the agencies. Just how this selection process influences the agencies' programs and their administration has not been described, but the programs' dependence on police for cases and ultimately for refunding is inescapable. Police influence over private agencies with diversion programs also has been exerted through the presence of police representatives on regional boards with the power of funding and refunding. Moreover, police frequently have been named to boards of directors of diversion agencies. Police even have gone to the extreme of actively supervising diversion programs outside the police department (e.g., in the schools).

Although the principle of diversion indicates that it should be used to redirect cases which otherwise would be processed through the juvenile justice system, it often has worked otherwise. Cases selected for diversion have included large numbers of youths who formerly would have been screened out or released after brief contact with police. Diversion projects appear to have included disproportionately large numbers of younger juveniles, those with minor or trivial offenses, youngsters without prior records, females, and status offenders.

Given that police ordinarily release around one half of the juveniles with whom they have contact, the differentiation of diversion clients is understandable. With pressures to produce cases for programs to justify their funding or refunding, police presumably have done what comes naturally or perhaps most easily by dipping into this reservoir of youths who otherwise would have gone free in order to make the desired referrals. In some instances, this has meant filling up diversion programs almost entirely with status offenders. Where deemed necessary, this has been accomplished by relabeling delinquents as status offenders or by reclassifying status offenders upward, as delinquents.

DEINSTITUTIONALIZATION OF STATUS OFFENDERS

The support given by federal policy and by associated funding sources for the decriminalization or decarceration of status offenders clearly is intertwined with the fate of the diversion movement in juvenile justice. Although the policy has a valid basis in the history of excessive incarceration of children alleged to be delinquent, the responses to the policy at the state and local levels have been mixed. An important reason for the uneven implementation of this policy has been the reluctance of juvenile court judges and unwillingness of the police to abandon the exercise of authority over younger children where no family is responsible. Even where police seem to have welcomed relief from the need to deal with status offenders, community and other pressures make it difficult for them to avoid action.

Although sequestered policymakers in Washington may conclude without too many second thoughts that status offenses should be abolished, a realistic assessment of the consequences of this policy may find that it has added another dimension of confusion to an already badly confused juvenile justice system. The old puritanical idea that the commonwealth is responsible for overseeing the serialization of children dies hard, along with its modern analog that children with problems should receive "treatment." Moreover, no matter how libertarian and freedom seeking adults become, the notion that no coercive measures should be employed to recover runaway children does not set well with responsible parents. Finally, when police invest time and energy to apprehend runaways, they are not content to see the children released if nothing more is done about the "problem."

DIVERSION AND THE JUVENILE JUSTICE SYSTEM

The impression is widely fostered that diversion should be evaluated according to its success in reducing recidivism or in terms of a balancing of costs and benefits. But it is more plausible that its future will hinge on sociopolitical developments in various parts of the juvenile justice system. The co-optation of the diversion movement by law enforcement leaves the rather sour conclusion that not only have the purposes of diversion been perverted, but moreover, police power has been extended over

youths and types of behavior not previously subjected to control. This untoward consequence, together with ubiquitous problems of evaluating related programs, has considerably dampened the early enthusiasm of diversion watchers. But if a conclusion is reached that diversion has failed, there remains painful choice of what should be done about it. It may be argued that police never should have been involved in the programmatic aspects of diversion and that the way to make diversion work is to take it out of the juvenile justice system.

The most extreme action to take diversion out of the justice system came in Scotland. There, procedures called for police to refer youths arrested to the procurator's office, where they were screened and sent, if deemed to be appropriate for diversion, to a Children's Panel. This was made up of professionals chosen from a larger appointed panel, who met with children and their parents and then decided on dispositions of the cases.

Something similar to lay boards has been proposed as a means of dealing with minor juvenile offenders and has been experimented with in a few American jurisdictions. Yet, despite these scattered instances of interest, Americans have remained cool or indifferent to this kind of diversion. In order for it to be successful, the local community must have faith and trust in its professional class, from which panel members are drawn. Distrust is very pronounced among Americans working in law enforcement, especially among district attorneys, who often refer to such diversionary schemes as kangaroo courts.

PRESSURES ON THE SYSTEM

A cynical view of diversion may be that it is merely a fad which will disappear—and so be it. Yet the pressures on the juvenile justice system as a whole remain substantial. One important source of such pressure is the progressive legalization of the juvenile court. Its jurisdiction has been steadily narrowed and its procedures tightened by appellate decisions and legislation so that it is more and more difficult to get cases in which the evidence is weak accepted for processing. At the same time, the juvenile court is growing more punitive, especially for older youths subject to waiver to adult criminal court. These developments are highlighted by the growing presence of the district attorney in juvenile courts. One outcome of this is a greater probability of more severe dispositions and stigmatization as juveniles graduate from juvenile to adult criminal court. In some jurisdictions, there has been a hardening of deviant categories by the creation of career criminal programs.

The net effect of mounting legalization of the juvenile court is an increase in the volume of nonprosecutable serious offenders, minor offenders, "nuisance" cases, and status offenders with whom the community must deal in some organized way. The choice seems to be to legitimate the larger measure of adjudicatory discretion claimed by probation officers and police or to divert cases out of the system altogether. From what has been said here, neither alternative is likely to find favor.

Meantime, there are indications that the movement to deinstitutionalize status offenders has succeeded mainly in stimulating a shift in their custody from public to private institutions. According to one analysis, this has been made possible through federal funding allowing categorization of delinquents as well as status offenders under Social Security, Aid to Dependent Children, child welfare, social services, Medicaid, and supplementary security income. Apparently, this has been done to an increasing degree through voluntary commitments by parents, guardians, or welfare agencies without formal commitment procedure. Presumably, this may help reduce pressures on the juvenile justice system—but with unwanted consequences, considering that abuses occur in private and contract institutional services as well as in public institutions.

CONCLUSION

That the best-laid schemes o' mice an' men gang oft agley seems well portrayed by the paradoxical transformation of diversion. What began as an effort to reduce discretion in juvenile justice became a warrant to increase discretion and extend control where none existed before. If nothing else is learned from this, it is the fearsome difficulty of trying to understand how even a segment of our highly contrived society works. But something else may have been learned, namely, the extent of the de facto power of police in the scheme of American justice.

QUESTIONS FOR DISCUSSION AND WRITING

1. Of what does the awakening of interest in deterrence theory remind the thoughtful observer of juvenile justice? What does a broader conception of labeling theory allow? Does granting these reservations necessarily destroy the validity of conceptions of secondary deviance?

2. Although the principle of diversion indicates that it should be used to redirect cases that otherwise would be processed through the juvenile justice system, has it often worked otherwise? How has this happened?

3. What is the net effect of mounting legalization of the juvenile court? Meantime, what indications are there that the movement to deinstitutionalize status offenders has succeeded mainly in stimulating a shift in their custody from public to private institutions?

Data Analysis Exercises

███████████████████████

A. An Exploration of Differential Association-Reinforcement Theory

In this data analysis exercise, we will use Wave I data from the National Youth Survey (NYS) to explore differential association-reinforcement theory, which was discussed in Part IV (in the section on social learning and behavior modification).

DESCRIPTION OF THE DATA SET

See the exercises for Part II for a description of the NYS data set. Before we start our analyses, we will need to load up a different data set from the one we have used in the past, "NYSJD." NYSJD includes only the dichotomous (i.e., coded into two categories) versions of the combined measures, some of the individual delinquent acts, and some new variables related to differential association-reinforcement theory.

EXPLORING DIFFERENTIAL ASSOCIATION-REINFORCEMENT THEORY: GETTING A HANDLE ON THE DATA AND USING CROSS-TABULATION TABLES

Part IV presents a comprehensive list of theories that have been used to explain juvenile delinquency. Although they are all valid, this exercise will focus on differential association-reinforcement theory, also called social learning theory. Although it was developed in the 1930s, differential association is still one of the most widely cited theories. In a nutshell, Edwin Sutherland argued that youths become delinquents because they associate with other delinquents and learn how to commit crimes from them. Although youths also learn good behaviors from others, it was delinquency that most interested Sutherland. Sutherland also argued that the more important a relationship is to a person, the stronger the association with what is being learned. Therefore, if I hang out with people who drink at parties, I may decide to drink at parties because there is an excess of definitions in favor of doing so. If I hang out with the campus ministry, however, I may decide to have bible-reading meetings on Friday nights while other people are out drinking at parties. The NYS is an excellent data set for testing some of the tenets of differential association.

Burgess and Akers updated Sutherland's theory to make it more useful in predicting when juveniles will engage in delinquency, relabeling it "differential association-reinforcement theory." They omitted some of Sutherland's propositions and modified the others. Despite their changes, the core elements of the theory remain untouched. Juveniles learn the techniques and motivations for delinquency from those with whom they interact. Let's test their theory.

Rather than run frequencies on the demographic factors that we have already examined (in the previous two exercises), we can turn our attention to testing differential association-reinforcement, which is discussed in detail in the article by Burgess and Akers.

When we are trying to test a theory or a part of a theory, we often face the difficulty of trying to choose variables from our data set that match the theory's propositions. We had this problem when we examined the correlates of crime because we had to use INCOME and WELFARE to measure social class. Researchers often find that the "fit" of the variables included in the data collected by others may be less than ideal. In some cases, this less than ideal fit may be beneficial because it allows us to move beyond the most basic elements in a theory into alternate measures of those elements. This form of replication can be exciting, as we will soon find out.

Therefore, we turn our attention to finding some appropriate variables. We will test two ideas: (a) Reinforcements against norm-breaking prevent delinquency and (b) the strength of good and bad influences on one's behavior have important consequences for delinquency.

If a person's close influences (i.e., parents and friends) view crime as acceptable, he or she may also lean in that direction. The stronger opinions against norm-breaking, the less likely that norm-breaking will occur. One series of questions in the NYS asked the youths how much disapproval they believed their parents and friends would feel if the respondent engaged in several delinquent actions, including using marijuana, drinking alcohol, stealing objects worth less than $5.00, and stealing objects worth $50.00 or more. These assessments, taken together, demonstrate the nature of each youth's reinforcements for his or her behavior. Before we test this tenet, run frequencies on my recoded versions of parental opinions (i.e., OP_P_MJ, OP_P_ALC, OP_P_5L, and OP_P_50M) and opinions held by friends (i.e., OP_F_MJ, OP_F_ALC,

OP_F_5L, and OP_F_50M) to get a better handle on these variables.[1] From the frequencies, we note that very few of the parents approved of delinquency at all, whereas friends were more likely to tolerate some delinquency.

If differential association-reinforcement theory is correct, parental and peer opinions will be important influences on the youths' actual delinquency. To determine if the NYS data support this idea, run cross-tabulation tables, with DIDMJ as the dependent (row) variables and OP_P_MJ and OP_F_MJ as the independent (column) variables (remember to choose "Phi and Cramer's *V*" under **Statistics** and check off "Column percentages" under **Cells**). Then, run cross-tabulation tables with DIDALCO as the dependent (row) variables and OP_P_ALC and OP_F_ALC as the independent (column) variables. We will examine only marijuana and alcohol use, leaving the two theft measures for you to explore for the Further Exploration questions.

What do you notice about the OP_P_MJ → DIDMJ table? The youths who said their parents strongly agreed that it was wrong for youth to use marijuana were less likely than their counterparts with less approving parents to smoke marijuana (only 10.6% said they had used it during the previous year compared to 29.9% of youths who reported that their parents merely agreed that it was wrong for youths to smoke marijuana). Those who reported more ambivalent parents, however, were likely to use marijuana (only 47.4% did not smoke it). To learn the strength of the relationship between parental opinion of marijuana use and youths' actual use, examine the Cramer's *V*. It is a moderate relationship and is statistically significant. We can say, therefore, that the two variables are related.

Now turn your attention to the OP_F_MJ → DIDMJ table. Notice that only 2.4% of youths whose friends strongly disapprove of marijuana use state that they themselves use the drug and also that the percentage of smokers increases as peer disapproval diminishes. In fact, it appears that marijuana smoking might be more strongly related to peer opinion than to parental opinion. To determine if that is true, check the statistics. Our suspicions are confirmed; the Cramer's *V* of .56 indicates a strong relationship, and it is statistically significant.

What do you notice about the OP_P_ALC → DIDALCO table? The youths who said their parents strongly agreed that it was wrong for youth to drink were less likely than their counterparts with more ambivalent parents to drink (only 31.3% with parents who strongly disapproved of alcohol drank compared to 85.8% of those with parents who did not disapprove of alcohol). How strong is this relationship? It is strong. Is it statistically significant? Yes. We can say, therefore, that the two variables are related.

Now turn your attention to the OP_F_ALC → DIDALCO table. The findings for this table mirror those found previously for parental opinion; the more disapproving one's friends are regarding drinking, the less likely the youths are to drink. The Cramer's *V* of .58 indicates a strong relationship, and it is statistically significant.

Taken together, these analyses support the idea that reinforcements against norm-breaking help prevent delinquency.

Regarding the second idea that we test, youths are as susceptible as, if not more susceptible than, adults to peer influences. If they find themselves in a situation in which their friends advocate norm-breaking, it is logical to assume that they may follow that lead. If the influences are good, however, then the youths may be less inclined to engage in delinquency. Let's find out if this is true.

The 1976 NYS survey asked parents about the youths' friends. The parents were asked how many of their child's friends were a "good influence on him/her" (INFGOOD) and how many were a "bad influence on him/her" (INFBAD). The parents were also asked how many of their child's friends were "good students" (GOODSTUD) and how many had broken the law (BROKELAW). The NYS also asked the youths if their friends had ever suggested that they break the law. It seems logical that such suggestions, coming from friends, could play some role in the youths' views of whether laws are inviolable or whether they are viewed as something to be broken from time to time. Together, these five variables are powerful predictors of the nature of the reinforcements youths receive daily regarding delinquency. Before we test this tenet, run frequencies on all five variables to get a better handle on them. Because very few subjects are classified in the negative extreme categories for the four parental measures, I recoded them to make the analyses more meaningful.[2]

The frequency tables show that relatively few of the youths' friends are perceived by parents to be bad influences on their children or recognized by parents as lawbreakers, and that moderate numbers are believed to be good influences on their children or good students. The majority of youths reported that none of their friends had suggested that they break the law. Now, let's determine if these independent variables are related to actual delinquency. To do this, run cross-tabulation tables with DIDMJ and DIDALCO as the dependent (row) variables and INFBAD, INFGOOD, GOODSTUD, BROKELAW, and SUGGBLAW as the independent (column) variables.

What do these 10 cross-tabulation tables show? Let's examine them one by one, beginning with INFBAD → DIDMJ. What percentage of the youths whose parents believed none of their friends were bad influences actually smoked marijuana? What is the general trend for marijuana smoking as increasingly more of the friends were bad influences? What is the strength of the relationship shown in the table? Is it statistically significant? How can we summarize this table? Does this finding support differential association-reinforcement theory?

Now, examine the INFGOOD → DIDMJ table. How many of the youths whose parents believed that none of their friends were good influences smoked marijuana? What is the general trend for marijuana smoking as increasingly more of the friends were good influences? What is the strength of the relationship shown in the table; is it statistically significant?

What about the GOODSTUD → DIDMJ table? How many of the youths whose parents believed that none of their friends were good students smoked marijuana? What is the general trend for marijuana smoking as increasingly more of the friends were good students? What is the strength of the relationship shown in the table; is it statistically significant?

What does the BROKELAW → DIDMJ table show? How many of the youths whose parents believed that none of their friends had broken the law smoked marijuana? What is the general trend for marijuana smoking as increasingly more of the friends were believed to have broken the law? What is the strength of the relationship shown in the table; is it statistically significant?

Finally, what does the SUGGBLAW → DIDMJ table show? How often is marijuana smoked by the youths who said none of their friends had suggested that they break the law? What is the general trend for marijuana smoking as increasingly more of the youths' friends suggested breaking the law? What is the strength of the relationship shown in the table? Is it statistically significant?

How can we summarize these five tables regarding marijuana use? Do our findings support differential association-reinforcement theory?

What do the five tables for alcohol use show? Again, look at them one by one, examining the percentage of the youths who reported using alcohol during the past year broken out by levels of friends who are bad influences, good influences, good students, lawbreakers, and who had suggested that the youths break the law. What is the general trend for alcohol use as increasingly more of the friends exhibit the trait under study? What is the strength of the relationships shown in the tables? Are they statistically significant? How can we summarize these tables? Do these findings support differential association-reinforcement theory?

FURTHER EXPLORATION OF DIFFERENTIAL ASSOCIATION-REINFORCEMENT THEORY

We have now explored two ideas related to differential association-reinforcement theory as they apply to smoking marijuana and drinking alcohol. If the theory is a good one, it should apply to crimes in addition to these. In the Further Exploration questions, you will apply the theory to thefts of goods valued at less than $5.00 and at more than $50.00.

DIFFERENTIAL ASSOCIATION-REINFORCEMENT THEORY ON YOUR OWN

Now that we have explored two ideas related to differential association-reinforcement theory, you could devise other ways of testing the theory. For example, you might believe that the number of friends who actually smoke marijuana (PEERMJ) is a strong predictor of whether the youths smoke it themselves. This is a difficult assignment, but try to think of other ways to measure the ideas behind differential association-reinforcement theory. If one of your ideas appears in the NYSJD data set, run some analyses to test it. Otherwise, run some tables to test the effects of number of friends who smoke marijuana and drink alcohol on marijuana and alcohol use.

While you are further examining differential association-reinforcement theory, reflect on how it helps us explain why some youths engage in delinquency. Think also about crimes or situations or both that it cannot adequately address and other weaknesses of the theory.

NOTES

1. Due to low numbers of opinions, especially for parents, in favor of delinquency, I recoded the two categories that approved or strongly approved of delinquency into the neutral "neither" category. To make direct comparisons easier, I recoded all eight variables in the same manner. Doing this ensures that all the categories have enough cases to make the analysis meaningful.
2. All four variables were recoded due to the low number of cases in the extreme categories. The lowest category ("none of them") was recoded into the next category ("few of them") for GOODSTUD and INFGOOD. For BROKELAW and INFBAD, the highest category ("all of them") was recoded into its adjoining category ("most of them").

Homework for Part IV, A: General Questions
Differential Association-Reinforcement Theory

Name: _____ Date: _____

Directions: Answer the following questions by filling in the blanks or circling the appropriate responses. Some answers have been provided for you to make sure you are on the right track. _____

EXPLORING DIFFERENTIAL ASSOCIATION-REINFORCEMENT THEORY: GETTING A HANDLE ON THE DATA AND USING CROSS-TABULATION TABLES

1. Complete the following table using percentages from the frequency tables for parental opinions (OP_P_MJ and OP_P_ALC) and peer/friend opinions (OP_F_MJ and OP_F_ALC):

	Youths' Assessment of the Degree to Which Their Parents and Friends Would Disapprove of Their Engaging in Delinquency		
	Neither (Also Includes Those Who Approve)	Disapprove	Strongly Disapprove
Marijuana use			
Parents' opinions: OP_F_MJ	2.5%	26.1%	
Friends' opinions: OP_F_MJ			
Alcohol use			
Parents' opinions: OP_F_ALC			
Friends' opinions: OP_F_ALC			

2. Complete the following table using percentages of youths who engaged in delinquency during the past year and statistics from the cross-tabulation tables for OP_P_MJ → DIDMJ, OP_F_MJ → DIDMJ, OP_P_ALC → DIDALCO, and OP_F_ALC → DIDALCO:

Category	% of Youths Who Engaged in Delinquency During the Past Year by Others' Opinion of Delinquency		
	Neither (Includes Those Who Approve)	Disapprove	Strongly Disapprove

Parents' opinions → marijuana use
    Cramer's V = .275
 	
    Sig. = .000
	52.6%	29.9%	10.6%

Friends' opinions → marijuana use
    Cramer's V = _____
 	
    Sig. = _____			

Parents' opinions → alcohol use
    Cramer's V = _____
 	
    Sig. = _____			

Friends' opinions → alcohol use
    Cramer's V = _____
 	
    Sig. = _____			

3. As parental opinion becomes more negative toward marijuana use, youths are *more/less* likely to smoke marijuana.

4. As friends' opinions become more negative toward marijuana use, youths are *more/less* likely to smoke marijuana.

5. As parental opinion becomes more negative toward alcohol use, youths are *more/less* likely to drink alcohol.

6. As friends' opinions become more negative toward alcohol use, youths are *more/less* likely to drink alcohol.

7. Overall, we can say that as opinions/reinforcements become more negative regarding delinquency, youths are *more/less* likely to engage in delinquency.

8. Complete the following table using percentages from the frequency tables for INFBAD, BROKELAW, and SUGGBLAW:

Group	Reinforcement Factors for Delinquency			
	None of Them	Few of Them	Some of Them	Most or All of Them
Friends are bad influences: INFBAD	61.9%	13.5%		
Friends break the law: BROKELAW				
Friends suggest youth break law: SUGGBLAW				

9. Complete the following table using percentages from the frequency tables for INFGOOD and GOODSTUD:

Group	Reinforcement Factors Against Delinquency			
	None or Few of Them	Some of Them	Most of Them	All of Them
Friends are good influences: INFGOOD	7.9%	12.1%		
Friends are good students: GOODSTUD				

10. Complete the following table using percentages of youths who engaged in delinquency during the past year and statistics from the cross-tabulation tables for INFBAD → DIDMJ, BROKELAW → DIDMJ, SUGGBLAW → DIDMJ, INFBAD → DIDALCO, BROKELAW → DIDALCO, and SUGGBLAW → DIDALCO:

Group	% of Youth Who Engage in Delinquency by Negative Reinforcement Factors			
	None of Them	Few of Them	Some of Them	Most or All of Them
Smoke marijuana				
Friends are bad influences (INFBAD) Cramer's V = .17 Sig. = .000	14.1%	26.2%	21.1%	50.0%
Friends break the law (BROKELAW) Cramer's V = _____ Sig. = _____				
Friends suggest youth break law (SUGGBLAW) Cramer's V = _____ Sig. = _____				
Drink alcohol				
Friends are bad influences (INFBAD) Cramer's V = .10 Sig. = .014	46.1%			
Friends break the law (BROKELAW) Cramer's V = _____ Sig. = _____				
Friends suggest youth break law (SUGGBLAW) Cramer's V = _____ Sig. = _____				

11. In general, as negative reinforcements for delinquency increase, youths are *more/less* likely to smoke marijuana and are *more/less* likely to drink alcohol.

12. Complete the following table using percentages of youths who engaged in delinquency during the past year and statistics from the cross-tabulation tables for INFGOOD → DIDMJ, GOODSTUD → DIDMJ, INFGOOD → DIDALCO, and GOODSTUD → DIDALCO:

Group	% of Youth Who Engage in Delinquency by Positive Reinforcement Factors			
	None or Few of Them	Some of Them	Most of Them	All of Them
Smoke marijuana				
Friends are good influences (INFGOOD) Cramer's V = .16 Sig. = .000				
Friends are good students (GOODSTUD) Cramer's V = _____ Sig. = _____				
Drink alcohol				
Friends are good influences (INFGOOD) Cramer's V = _____ Sig. = _____	60.2%			
Friends are good students (GOODSTUD) Cramer's V = _____ Sig. = _____				

13. In general, as positive reinforcements against delinquency increase, youths are *more/less* likely to smoke marijuana and are *more/less* likely to drink alcohol.

14. Overall, it appears that our findings using the 1976 NYS data *support/do not support* differential association-reinforcement theory.

Homework for Part IV, A: Further Exploration
Differential Association-Reinforcement Theory

Name: _____ Date: _____

TASK: Determine if the opinion measures we have developed to test differential association-reinforcement theory are statistically related to theft (i.e., DID5L and DID50M). Make sure you substitute the opinions relevant to each crime (i.e., use OP_P_5L and OP_F_5L for DID5L and OP_P_50M and OP_F_50M for DID50M).

Directions: Answer the following questions by filling in the blanks or circling the appropriate responses. Some answers have been filled in for you to make sure you are on the right track.

EXPLORING DIFFERENTIAL ASSOCIATION-REINFORCEMENT THEORY: GETTING A HANDLE ON THE DATA AND USING CROSS-TABULATION TABLES

1. Complete the following table using percentages from the frequency tables for paren-Tal opinions (OP_P_5L and OP_P_50M) and peer/friend opinions (OP_F_5L and OP_F_50M):

Group	Youths' Assessment of the Degree to Which Their Parents and Friends Would Disapprove of Their Engaging in Delinquency		
	Neither (Also Includes Those Who Approve)	Disapprove	Strongly Disapprove
Theft of items worth less than $5.00			
Parents' opinions: OP_P_5L		42.3%	
Friends' opinions: OP_F_5L			
Theft of items worth $50.00 or more			
Parents' opinions: OP_P_50M			
Friends' opinions: OP_F_50M			

2. Complete the following table using percentage~ ~~~~~
during the past year and statistics from the cross-tabula.
OP_F_5L → DID5L, OP_P_50M → DID50M, and OP_F_50M –.

Category	% of Youths Who Engaged in Delinquency During the Past ~ Others' Opinion of Delinquency		
	Neither (Includes Those Who Approve)	Disapprove	Strongly Disapprove
Parents' opinions → theft $5 or less Cramer's V = .11 Sig. = .000	27.0%	2.21%	13.8%
Friends' opinions → theft $5 or less Cramer's V = _____ Sig. = _____			
Parents' opinions → theft $50 or more Cramer's V = _____ Sig. = _____			
Friends' opinions → theft $50 or more Cramer's V = _____ Sig. = _____			

3. As parental opinion becomes more negative toward minor thefts (goods worth less than $5.00), youths are *more/less* likely to engage in them.

4. As friends' opinions become more negative toward minor thefts (goods worth less than $5.00), youths are *more/less* likely to engage in them.

5. As parental opinion becomes more negative toward major thefts ($50.00 or more), youths are *more/less* likely to engage in them.

6. As friends' opinions become more negative toward major thefts ($50.00 or more), youths are *more/less* likely to engage in them.

...say that as opinions/reinforcements become more negative regarding delinquency, youths are *more/less* likely to engage in theft.

8. Complete the following table using percentages of youths who engaged in delinquency during the past year and statistics from the cross-tabulation tables for INFBAD → DID5L, BROKELAW → DID5L, SUGGBLAW → DID5L, INFBAD → DID50M, BROKELAW → DID50M, and SUGGBLAW → DID50M:

| Group | % of Youth Who Engage in Delinquency by Negative Reinforcement Factors | | | |
	None of Them	Few of Them	Some of Them	Most or All of Them
Minor thefts (less than $5.00)				
Friends are bad influences (INFBAD) 　　Cramer's V = _____ 　　Sig. = _____	15.5%			
Friends break the law (BROKELAW) 　　Cramer's V = _____ 　　Sig. = _____				
Friends suggest youth break law (SUGGBLAW) 　　Cramer's V = _____ 　　Sig. = _____				
Major thefts ($50.00 or more)				
Friends are bad influences (INFBAD) 　　Cramer's V = _____ 　　Sig. = _____				
Friends break the law (BROKELAW) 　　Cramer's V = _____ 　　Sig. = _____				
Friends suggest youth break law (SUGGBLAW) 　　Cramer's V = _____ 　　Sig. = _____				

9. In general, as negative reinforcements for delinquency increase, youths are *more/less* likely to engage in minor thefts and are *more/less* likely to commit major thefts.

POINTS TO PONDER: Can you provide an explanation for the lack of major thefts among youths whose parents said most or all of their friends were bad influences? Could level of seriousness play a role? Note that the Cramer's *V* was not significant, so this finding could be an anomaly.

---

10. Complete the following table using percentages of youths who engaged in delinquency during the past year and statistics from the cross-tabulation tables for INFGOOD → DID5L, GOODSTUD → DID5L, INFGOOD → DID50M, and GOODSTUD → DID50M:

Group	% of Youth Who Engage in Delinquency by Positive Reinforcement Factors			
	None or Few of Them	Some of Them	Most of Them	All of Them
Minor thefts (less than $5.00)				

Friends are good influences (INFGOOD)
     Cramer's *V* = _____
 	
     Sig. = _____				

Friends are good students (GOODSTUD)
     Cramer's *V* = _____
 	
     Sig. = _____				

Major thefts ($50.00 or more)				

Friends are good influences (INFGOOD)
     Cramer's *V* = _____
 	
     Sig. = _____
	5.9%			

Friends are good students (GOODSTUD)
     Cramer's *V* = _____
 	
     Sig. = _____				

11. In general, as positive reinforcements against delinquency increase, youths are *more/less* likely to commit minor thefts and are *more/less* likely to engage in major thefts.

12. Overall, it appears that our findings using the 1976 NYS data *support/do not support* differential association-reinforcement theory.

Homework for Part IV, A: On Your Own
Differential Association-Reinforcement Theory

Name: _____ Date: _____

TASK: Try to think of other ways to measure the ideas within differential association-reinforcement theory. If one of your ideas appears in the data set, run some analyses to test it. Otherwise, run some tables for the number of peers/friends who engage in delinquent acts (i.e., PEERMJ, PEERALCO, PEER5L, and PEER50M).

Directions: Answer the following questions.

NOTE: Please print out and include your tables with these questions so your work can be graded.

DIFFERENTIAL ASSOCIATION-REINFORCEMENT THEORY
ON YOUR OWN

1. Which variable did you choose as your independent variable, and how does it relate to differential association-reinforcement theory (i.e., what does it attempt to measure)?

2. How did your independent variable affect marijuana use by the youths? Make sure to provide a description that includes the percentages, phi or Cramer's *V* value, the strength of the relationship, and the significance value.

3. How did your independent variable affect alcohol use? Make sure to provide a description that includes the percentages, phi or Cramer's *V* value, the strength of the relationship, and the significance value.

4. How did your independent variable affect thefts of goods worth less than $5.00? Make sure to provide a description that includes the percentages, phi or Cramer's *V* value, the strength of the relationship, and the significance value.

5. How did your independent variable affect thefts of goods worth more than $50.00? Make sure to provide a description that includes the percentages, phi or Cramer's *V* value, the strength of the relationship, and the significance value.

6. Can you say your idea testing supports differential association-reinforcement theory? Why/why not?

If you included other independent variables, you may summarize the findings here for future reference.

B. An Exploration of Strain Theory

In this data analysis exercise, we will use Wave I data from the National Youth Survey (NYS) to explore strain theory, which was discussed in Part IV (in the section on opportunity, strain, and rehabilitation/reintegration).

DESCRIPTION OF THE DATA SET

See the exercises for Part II for a description of the NYS data set. Before we start our analyses, we will need to load up a new data set, "NYS2JD." NYS2JD includes only the dichotomous versions of the combined measures, some of the individual delinquent acts, and some new variables related to strain theory.

EXPLORING STRAIN THEORY:
GETTING A HANDLE ON THE DATA
AND USING CROSS-TABULATION TABLES

Part IV presents a comprehensive list of theories that have been used to explain juvenile delinquency; this exercise focuses on strain theory, which argues that increased levels of strain increase the likelihood of delinquency. Financial strain, for example, might be related to thefts. Although earlier strain theories limited themselves to financial difficulties, newer strain theories such as the one posed by Agnew in his chapter recognized that youths can experience strain in many circumstances in addition to financial difficulties. We lucked out because the NYS is an excellent data set for testing some of the tenets of strain theory.

Rather than run frequencies on the demographic factors that we have already examined (in the previous exercises), we can now turn our attention to testing strain theory, which is discussed in detail in the chapter by Agnew. Now, we will operationalize strain. When we operationalize a concept, we develop indicators that will signal us when the concept is present; for example, I could decide that good students are those who do well on exams and participate in class. Both of my indicators are easily measured, so I can test their effects on whatever dependent variable I believe is appropriate. It is important for us to realize that when we operationalize a concept, our indicators might not be a perfect fit, but that they should be reasonable indicators of the concept. If I included birth month in my indicators for good students, for example, I might encounter a few raised eyebrows when I told others about my research. When we select indicators, they should always be reasonably related to the concept we are studying. In our case, we need to operationalize strain.

When I went through the data set searching for indicators, I found several that seemed good. Youths want to fit in with their friends (FIT_IN) and feel appreciated rather than lonely at home (LONELY_H). Not achieving these goals may create strain. They can also experience strain in terms of being unable to achieve the GPA they believe is necessary (GPASTRN), get the job they believe they need (WORKSTRN), or get into college when they want to (COLLSTRN). Youths may also experience a more general strain in the form of stressors (STRESSRS), such as parental divorce or moving. These negative stimuli may affect the likelihood of delinquency. All these ideas are contained in our data, so we are in business.

First, we will examine the effects of our six sources of strain on DIDANY, leaving the other combined measures for you to examine under the Further Explorations exercises. If strain theory is correct, youths who experience strain will be more likely to engage in delinquency. To determine if the NYS data support this idea, run cross-tabulation tables, with DIDANY as the dependent (row) variable and STRESSRS, FIT_IN, LONELY_H, GPASTRN, WORKSTRN, and COLLSTRN as the independent (column) variables (remember to choose "Phi and Cramer's *V*" under **Statistics** and check off "Column percentages" under **Cells**).

What do you notice about the STRESSRS → DIDANY table? In general, it appears that the more stressors the youths experienced, the more likely they were to engage in delinquency. The youths who experienced no stressors (e.g., parental divorce and separation of parents) were less likely than their more stressed counterparts to engage in delinquency.[1] The relationship is moderate and is significant, so we can say that the two variables are related. So far, strain theory seems to have predictive power.

Now turn your attention to the FIT_IN → DIDANY table. Notice that the percentage of youths classified into each FIT-IN category appears to fluctuate, decreasing and then increasing again. In fact, it appears that general delinquency might not be related to fitting in with friends. To determine if that is true, check the statistics. Our suspicions are confirmed; the Cramer's *V* is weak, and the relationship is not significant. At least for general delinquency, FIT_IN does not appear to have much predictive power.

What do you notice about the LONELY_H → DIDANY table? The youths who agreed that they felt lonely with their families were more likely to engage in delinquency than those who disagreed with the statement (strong agree, agree, and neither = higher than 90%, whereas disagree and strongly disagree = the mid-80%). The relationship is moderate and is statistically significant, so we can say that the two variables are related.

Now turn your attention to the GPASTRN → DIDANY table. Nearly all (97.1%) of the youths who experienced GPA strain, which was calculated as believing that one had not achieved a valued commodity (GPA), had engaged in delinquency during the past year. The relationship is again moderate and statistically significant, so we can say that the two variables are related.

WORKSTRN, however, does not appear to be related to general delinquency, nor does COLLSTRN. Both variables were calculated as true for those youths who valued a good job but believed they could not achieve it or who valued a college education but believed they could not obtain it. Do these findings invalidate strain theory? It is important to note that the lack of findings for a given variable or variables in one data set does not invalidate any theory. It may indicate, for example, that strain is not best measured through the measures we used in this example. In fact, researchers are often frustrated by the lack of suitable variables in data collected by others who did not have their particular theory in mind. Sometimes, concepts are difficult to measure so that 10 different researchers might have 10 different ways to measure strain. It looks like WORKSTRN and COLLSTRN might not be the best variables to use to measure strain.

It is also possible that WORKSTRN and COLLSTRN (and also FIT_IN) work for subpopulations, such as for low-income youths or males. We will discuss this idea when we learn how to add control variables.

EXPLORING STRAIN THEORY: USING CONTROL VARIABLES

By now, you should be wondering if we are ever going to be able to move beyond simple bivariate analyses (i.e., analyses that involve only two variables). You may have wanted to determine if WORKSTRN and COLLSTRN work for certain youths, such as low-income youths. It seems reasonable that low-income individuals might be more susceptible to strain regarding getting into college when they believe they need to go to college because they would feel less able to finance their education. Could income level somehow affect the relationship between COLLSTRN and delinquency? Are low-income youths more likely to be affected by COLLSTRN, whereas high-income individuals are more immune to the effects of COLLSTRN? Let's find out.

If you want to do such an analysis, there are options short of full-blown multivariate statistics. You can easily add control variables to your cross-tabulations. The third box under the Crosstabs variable boxes is used for this purpose. It allows you to feed in control variables. Although you can feed in as many control variables as you wish, it is advisable to limit yourself to one or two due to the nature of cross-tabs. Every control variable you add makes the results more difficult to interpret and increases the chance of empty cells (which affect the validity of your statistics). If you want to include more than one or two control variables, you should read about regression or other multivariate techniques that are better able to handle many variables at once. Now, back to our cross-tabs.

I do not know about you, but I want to know if adding income to our COLLSTRN → DIDANY analysis sheds any light on strain theory; lets start with an easier table and then progress into income. Run a cross-tabulation table with DIDANY as the dependent (row) variable, GPASTRN as the independent (column) variable, and MALE as the control variable (Layer 1 of 1). Mark the same statistics and cell choices we have been doing because we will need this information more than ever. Notice that the final table is much larger than our typical cross-tabulation table. In fact, it is two tables combined into one, with the statistics and probabilities for both tables appearing in the box beneath the massive table. Spend some time examining the resulting numbers to get the hang of tables that have control variables. Each category of the control variable has a minitable within it, so in our case there are two minitables, one for males and one for females. Within each of these tables is the GPASTRN → DIDANY table.

Look within the rows for males. You will see that 109 (99.1%) of the males who experienced GPASTRN had actually engaged in delinquency compared to 625 (91.2%) of those who did not experience GPA strain (they believed they were meeting their GPA goals). The phi is .101, and the relationship is significant. Moving to the rows for females, we see that 58 (93.5%) of the females who experienced GPASTRN had actually engaged in delinquency compared to 527 (82.0%) of those who did not experience GPA strain. The phi is .087, and the relationship is significant. In other words, the relationship we found between GPASTRN and DIDANY cannot be "explained away" as due to the effects of gender rather than GPA strain. Among both genders, experiencing GPASTRN increased chances of engaging in general delinquency.

Now, let's return to testing our COLLSTRN → DIDANY idea to determine if lower-income youths are affected by COLLSTRN, whereas higher-income youths are not. If this is true, the lack of a relationship for the higher-income individuals could mask or cover up a real relationship between COLLSTRN and

DIDANY. To test this idea, run a cross-tabulation table with DIDANY as the dependent (row) variable, COLLSTRN as the independent (column) variable, and INCOME_D as the control variable (Layer 1 of 1). We are using yet another measure of income to prevent low cell sizes from affecting the validity of our statistics. Remember, you will get a table for each category of the control variable; this means that there will be five separate tables, which increases the chances of small cell sizes. To address this concern, I recoded the bottom two income categories into one category and the top two categories into one. That reduces the number of tables to three, which is a good move since there are only 73 youths who experienced COLLSTRN.

Looking within the rows for the lowest income youths, we see that 45 (90%) of the low-income youths who experienced COLLSTRN had actually engaged in delinquency compared to 671 (86.1%) of those who did not experience COLLSTRN. The phi value is abysmally low, and the relationship is not significant. Moving to the rows for middle-income youths, we see that 10 (90.9%) of the middle-income youths who experienced COLLSTRN had engaged in delinquency compared to 326 (88.8%) of those who did not experience COLLSTRN. The phi for this table is also abysmally low, and the relationship is not significant. When we finally turn our attention to the rows for high-income youths, we see that 8 (100.0%) of the high-income youths who experienced COLLSTRN had engaged in delinquency compared to 210 (92.1%) of those who did not experience COLLSTRN. The phi for this table is not much better than the previous two, and the relationship is not significant. In summary, our data do not show that COLLSTRN interacts somehow with income to mask the relationship when income is not controlled. Despite our recodes, however, there were still some small cell sizes, so let's not eliminate this idea just yet.

We could run control variables forever, but we will save this for the On Your Own exercises and for the exercises for Part V.

FURTHER EXPLORATION OF STRAIN THEORY

We have explored some ideas related strain theory as they apply to general delinquency. What happens when we examine the individual combined measures? For example, it seems more logical that drug use might be related more to feelings that one did not mesh well with one's family (LONELY_H), whereas school-related delinquency might be related more to COLLSTRN and violence would be related to stressors because youths may act out due to their frustration. If the theory is a good one, it should apply to a variety of reasonable offenses and not just the general delinquency measure. For the Further Exploration questions, you will apply strain theory to thefts, drug use, and school-related delinquency to determine if the various forms of strain are tied more to a particular form of delinquency.

STRAIN THEORY ON YOUR OWN

Now that we have explored two ideas related to strain theory, you could devise other ways of testing the theory. For example, you might believe that feeling that one does not belong in school (N_BELONG) may have profound effects on doing drugs or on school-related delinquency. This is another difficult assignment, but try to think of other ways to measure the ideas behind strain theory. If one of your ideas appears in the NYSJD data set, run some analyses to test it. Otherwise, run some tables to test the effects of N_BELONG on drug use and school-related delinquency. Also, include at least one control variable to determine if the addition of other factors changes the relationship you find.

While you are further examining strain theory, reflect on how it helps us explain why some youths engage in delinquency. Think also about crimes or situations or both that it cannot adequately address and other weaknesses of the theory.

NOTE

1. The entire list included parental divorce, separation of parents, remarriage of parents, serious illness/death in the family, serious accident, school suspension or dropout, trouble with the law, father unemployed, mother unemployed, change in schools, family move, mother move in or out of home, father move in or out of home, and other relative move in or out of home. Due to the low number of youths who experienced high numbers of stressors, I recoded the 15 youths who experienced six or more stressors and added them to the youths who experienced five stressors during the past year.

Homework for Part IV, B: General Questions
Strain Theory

Name: _____ Date: _____

Directions: Answer the following questions by filling in the blanks or circling the appropriate responses. Some answers have been filled in for you to make sure you are on the right track.

EXPLORING STRAIN THEORY:
GETTING A HANDLE ON THE DATA
AND USING CROSS-TABULATION TABLES

1. In the 1976 NYS sample, _____ (_____%) youths had experienced no stressors (STRESSRS) during the past year; _____ (_____%) had experienced one, 242 (_____%) had experienced two, _____ (_____%) had experienced three, _____ (_____%) had experienced four, and _____ (_____%) had experienced five or more stressors during the past year.

2. Complete the following table using the information from the frequency tables FIT_IN and LONELY_H:

Variable	Number and % of Youths Agreeing That They Have Strain in Fitting in and/or Feeling Lonely in Their Families				
	Strongly Disagree	Disagree	Neither	Agree	Strongly Agree
FIT_IN	285 (19%)				
LONELY_H					

3. Complete the following table using the information from the frequency tables GPASTRN, WORKSTRN, and COLLSTRN:

| Category | Number and % of Youths Who Experienced Each Source of Strain | |
	Strain Absent	Strain Present
GPASTRN		
WORKSTRN		464 (30.9%)
COLLSTRN		

4. In the STRESSRS → DIDANY cross-tabulation, _____ (_____%) of the youths who experienced no stressors during the past year said they had engaged in delinquency during the previous year compared to _____ (_____%) of those who experienced one stressor, _____ (_____%) of those who experienced two stressors, _____ (_____%) of those who experienced three stressors, _____ (_____%) of those who experienced four stressors, and _____ (_____%) of those who experienced five or more stressors during the past year. It appears that as the number of stressors increases, the likelihood of general delinquency *increases/decreases*. The largest difference between the six percentages is _____%, which appears to be *negligible/potentially interesting*. This relationship is *weak/moderate/strong*. This relationship *is/is not* statistically significant.

5. Complete the following table using percentages of youths who engaged in delinquency during the past year and statistics from the cross-tabulation tables for FIT_IN → DIDANY and LONELY_H → DIDANY:

| Category | % of Youths Who Engaged in Delinquency During the Past Year by Source of Strain | | | | |
	Strongly Disagree	Disagree	Neither	Agree	Strongly Agree

FIT_IN
    Cramer's V = _____
 	
    Sig. = _____					

LONELY_H
    Cramer's V = _____
 	
    Sig. = _____					

6. Complete the following table using percentages of youths who engaged in delinquency during the past year and statistics from the cross-tabulation tables for GPASTRN → DIDANY, WORKSTRN → DIDANY, and COLLSTRN → DIDANY:

| Category | % of Youths Who Engaged in Delinquency During the Past Year by Source of Strain | |
	Strain Absent	Strain Present
GPASTRN phi = _____ Sig. = _____		
WORKSTRN phi = _____ Sig. = _____		
COLLSTRN phi = _____ Sig. = _____		

7. Youths who experience GPASTRN are *more/less/not significantly related* likely to engage in delinquency. Those who experience WORKSTRN are *more/less/not significantly related* likely to engage in delinquency. Those who experience COLLSTRN are *more/less/not significantly related* likely to engage in delinquency.

8. Overall, we can say that as strain increases delinquency, youths are *more/less* likely to engage in delinquency.

9. In the GPASTRN → DIDANY cross-tabulation with MALE as a control variable, 109 (99.1%) of the males who experienced GPASTRN had actually engaged in delinquency compared to _____ (_____%) of those who did not experience GPA strain. For males, it appears that the presence of GPA strain *increases/decreases* the likelihood of general delinquency. This relationship is *weak/moderate/strong*. This relationship *is/is not* statistically significant. When we turn our attention to the female rows, we see that _____ (_____%) of the females who experienced GPASTRN had actually engaged in delinquency compared to _____ (_____%) of those who did not experience GPA strain. For females, it appears that the presence of GPA strain *increases/decreases* the likelihood of general delinquency. This

relationship is *weak/moderate/strong*. This relationship *is/is not* statistically significant. Overall, we *can/cannot* say that controlling for gender in our model substantially changes the relationship we found between GPA strain and likelihood of engaging in general delinquency.

10. In the COLLSTRN → DIDANY cross-tabulation with INCOME_D as a control variable, <u>45</u> (<u>90.0</u>%) of the lowest income youths who experienced COLLSTRN had actually engaged in delinquency compared to _____ (_____%) of those who did not experience COLLSTRN. For the lowest income youths, it appears that the presence of GPA strain *increases/decreases* the likelihood of general delinquency, but this relationship *is/is not* statistically significant. When we turn our attention to the middle-income youths, we see that _____ (_____%) of the middle-income youths who experienced COLLSTRN had actually engaged in delinquency compared to _____ (_____%) of those who did not experience COLLSTRN. For the middle-income youths, it appears that the presence of COLLSTRN *increases/decreases* the likelihood of general delinquency, but this relationship *is/is not* statistically significant. When we turn our attention to the high-income youths, we see that _____ (_____%) of the high-income youths who experienced COLLSTRN had actually engaged in delinquency compared to _____ (_____%) of those who did not experience COLLSTRN. For the high-income youths, it appears that the presence of COLLSTRN *increases/decreases* the likelihood of general delinquency, but this relationship *is/is not* statistically significant. Overall, we *can/cannot* say that controlling for income in our model substantially changes the relationship we found between COLLSTRN and likelihood of engaging in general delinquency. In other words, it *is/is not* true that COLLSTRN interacts with income in such a way that COLLSTRN affects only youths at certain income levels.

11. Overall, we can say that our analyses *do/do not* support strain theory.

Homework for Part IV, B: Further Exploration
Strain Theory

Name: _____ Date: _____

TASK: Determine if the variety of strain has differential effects on varying types of delinquency. We will examine the effects of LONELY_H, COLLSTRN, and STRESSRS on DIDDRUG, DIDSKL, and DIDVIO.

Directions: Answer the following questions by filling in the blanks or circling the appropriate responses. Some answers have been filled in for you to make sure you are on the right track.

EXPLORING STRAIN THEORY:
GETTING A HANDLE ON THE DATA
AND USING CROSS-TABULATION TABLES

1. Complete the following table using percentages of youths who engaged in delinquency during the past year and statistics from the cross-tabulation tables for the effects of LONELY_H on DIDDRUG, DIDSKL, and DIDVIO.

Category	% of Youths Who Engaged in Delinquency During the Past Year by Loneliness Within Family Rating				
	Strongly Disagree	Disagree	Neither	Agree	Strongly Agree
Using drugs (DIDDRUG) Cramer's V = .17 Sig. = .000	7.3%				
School-related delinquency (DIDSKL) Cramer's V = _____ Sig. = _____					
Violence (DIDVIO) Cramer's V = _____ Sig. = _____					

2. On the basis of the previous table, it appears that LONELY_H is a significant predictor of (circle the correct variables): *DIDDRUG, DIDSKL, DIDVIO*. It appears to be most related to (circle one): *DIDDRUG, DIDSKL, DIDVIO*.

3. Complete the following table using percentages of youths who engaged in delinquency during the past year and statistics from the cross-tabulation tables for the effects of COLLSTRN on DIDDRUG, DIDSKL, and DIDVIO:

Category	% of Youths Who Engaged in Delinquency During the Past Year by the Presence of COLLSTRN	
	COLLSTRN Absent	COLLSTRN Present

Using drugs (DIDDRUG)
  phi = _____
 	
  Sig. = _____		

School-related delinquency (DIDSKL)
  phi = ._____
 	
  Sig. = _____
	58.5%	

Violence (DIDVIO)
  phi = _____
 	
  Sig. = _____		

4. On the basis of the previous table, it appears that COLLSTRN is a significant predictor of (circle the correct variables): *DIDDRUG, DIDSKL, DIDVIO*. It appears to be most related to (circle one): *DIDDRUG, DIDSKL, DIDVIO*.

5. Complete the following table using percentages of youths who engaged in delinquency during the past year and statistics from the cross-tabulation tables for the effects of STRESSRS on DIDDRUG, DIDSKL, and DIDVIO:

Category	% of Youths Who Engaged in Delinquency During the Past Year by Number of Stressors During the Past Year					
	0	1	2	3	4	5 or more

Using drugs (DIDDRUG)
    Cramer's V = .12 ___
 	
    Sig. = .001 ___
	62.6%					

School-related delinquency (DIDSKL)
    Cramer's V = ___
 	
    Sig. = ___						

Violence (DIDVIO)
    Cramer's V = ___
 	
    Sig. = ___						

6. On the basis of the previous table, it appears that STRESSRS is a significant predictor of (circle the correct variables): *DIDDRUG, DIDSKL, DIDVIO*. It appears to be most related to (circle one): *DIDDRUG, DIDSKL, DIDVIO*.

7. On the basis of the three previous tables, it appears that strain *does/does not* have differential effects on types of delinquency, and that those relationships are somewhat logical.

8. Overall, it appears that our findings using the 1976 NYS data *support/do not support* strain theory.

POINTS TO PONDER: Could the "direction" in our analyses be wrong (e.g., could school-related delinquency actually predict inability to get into college)? How are we sure that the direction is correct?

Homework for Part IV, B: On Your Own
Strain Theory

Name: _____ Date: _____

TASK: Try to think of other ways to measure the ideas within strain theory. If one of your ideas appears in the data set, run some analyses to test it. Otherwise, run some tables to test the effects of believing that one does not "belong" at school (N_BELONG) on doing drugs (DIDDRUG) or school-related delinquency (DIDSKL). Then, try adding a control variable to determine if the relationship you find changed by the addition of control variables.

Directions: Answer the following questions.

NOTE: Please print out and include your tables with these questions so your work can be graded.

STRAIN THEORY ON YOUR OWN

1. Which variable did you choose as your independent variable, and how does it relate to strain theory (i.e., what does it attempt to measure)?

2. What dependent variable did you choose, and why did you choose that particular variable?

3. How did your independent variable affect your dependent variable? Make sure to provide a description that includes the percentages, phi or Cramer's *V* value, the strength of the relationship, and the significance value.

4. Can you say that your idea testing supports strain theory? Why/why not?

5. Which control variable did you choose, and why did you choose to control that factor?

6. What was the relationship between the independent and dependent variables before the addition of the control variable?

7. Did the control variable change the relationship between the independent and dependent variables; that is, did the relationship between the two variables vary by control variable subcategory?

8. On the basis of your findings, what modifications or additions would you make to strain theory?

9. Can you say that your testing supports strain theory? Why/why not?

If you included more than one control variable or more than one independent or dependent variable, you may summarize the findings here for future reference.

V

JUVENILE JUSTICE REFORM

W E are in an exciting period of juvenile justice reform. For approximately the first 70 years since being heralded in 1899 as the "greatest innovation ever" in criminal justice, the juvenile court resisted substantial change in its philosophy and operation. During the past 30 years, however, there have been many changes in the juvenile court, moving away from the "traditional" social work model (organized around the rehabilitative ideal) toward a "criminalized" juvenile court model (organized around deterrence and punishment). What happened? Why did the changes occur? Are they improvements? Where is juvenile justice headed?

As Clark, in "Juvenile Court Theory and Impact in Historical Perspective," points out, the seeds of dissent and change existed in the original philosophy and implementation of the juvenile court: (a) The statutes were vague and ambiguous, leaving them open to legal attacks on constitutional grounds; (b) resources were often inadequate to implement fully and effectively the intent and philosophy of the juvenile court; and, most problematic, (c) there was an inherent, fundamental conflict in the goals of the court—on the one hand, to "save" children in trouble and in need, rehabilitate the transgressor, prevent involvement in more serious trouble, and always act in the best interests of the child, and on the other hand to "punish" young offenders, hold them accountable for their crimes, deter future criminality, and protect community safety. Those inconsistencies in ideals are difficult to reconcile conceptually, but they are even more difficult to implement—without creating substantial friction, confusion, and conflict—within the same organization. This legacy has plagued the juvenile court from its very inception.

In addition, many other factors coalesced in the late 1960s that created a greater sense of urgency that something had to be done to improve the operation and effectiveness of the juvenile justice system. First, between 1965 and 1975 there were huge increases, never seen before or since, in the juvenile crime rate that were caused in good part by the "baby boomers" moving into the crime-prone teen years and, literally, coming of age as juvenile delinquents. There was a corresponding public concern and fear about the fantastic growth in the crime problem.

Second, the accumulation of many evaluation studies, and their analyses, were concluding that the rehabilitation of both adult and juvenile offenders, whether in institutions or in community-based programs, did not seem to be working very well (or at least not as well as promised, expected, or hoped). The whole rehabilitative foundation of the juvenile court was being called into question.

Third, self-report studies confirmed, over and over again, that most juveniles commit a crime at one time or another, most of them get away with it, and a "selective" subpopulation ends up getting arrested and referred to court. The implications drawn by critics were that the juvenile justice system was not only ineffective in preventing and controlling crime but also that it was perpetrating injustices by its discriminatory selection and processing of certain types of offenders.

Fourth, labeling theory, based on the principle of discriminatory processing and labeling, became a powerful theoretical perspective and liberal critique of the juvenile justice system during this period. Its ideas suggested and then supported many of the reforms that were put into place.

Fifth, in response to the exploding juvenile crime problem and to the growing public pressure to do something about it, the President's Commission on Law Enforcement and the Administration of Justice was convened to study and recommend solutions. The commission's report in 1967 made many recommendations regarding juvenile justice issues, most of which should sound quite familiar by now, including the deinstitutionalization of status offenders, the creation of diversion programs, the decriminalization of status offenses, the use of community-based alternatives to incarceration, and the extension of "due process" protections as specified in the Constitution to children.

Sixth, in 1974 the Federal Juvenile Justice and Delinquency Prevention Act created an office with the responsibility for implementing and monitoring the deinstitutionalization of status offenders in state juvenile correctional facilities and for setting and conducting a nationwide program and research agenda on the prevention and control of juvenile delinquency.

Finally, there were many very important Supreme Court decisions on a variety of constitutional issues relating to juvenile justice. Those judicial decisions, particularly the *Gault* decision in 1967, granted most of the due process protections granted to adults in criminal proceedings, including the notification of charge, the right to an attorney, the right against self-incrimination, and the right to confront one's accuser and cross-examine witnesses. As Clark suggested, shortly after the *Gault* decision was handed down, it presented juvenile courts with the challenge to continue their commitment to the "traditional" humanitarian ideals while guaranteeing basic constitutional rights to the children coming through their doors. That challenge was met directly in what has been called a "convergence" model of the court—a more legal version of the old model, working toward the application of rehabilitative ideals within the protections of due process.

The impact of *Gault* on the juvenile court was not immediate, primarily because it called for many major organizational, operational, and procedural changes in the court as well as in police practices, probation services, and juvenile corrections, all of which cost money and took time to modify. Nor was the impact complete. Lerman, in "Beyond *Gault:* Injustice and the Child," shows in an analysis of pre— and post-*Gault* state and national data that the decision did not affect important matters of "substantive" justice, including more severe sanctions for juvenile than adult offenders who commit comparable offenses (Gerald Gault would have spent 6 years incarcerated for a misdemeanor that if committed by an adult would have carried a $50 fine or short jail time), and longer periods of detention for status offenders than juvenile criminals. In short, although there may be more "procedural" elegance and fairness in the convergence model of the juvenile court, it still does not ensure justice for the child because pre- and postjudicial decisions and practices, which *Gault* did not affect—primarily because it could not—do not guarantee equal treatment under the law for juvenile delinquents.

Disappointingly, Feld shows that even in the "judicial" phase of the juvenile justice process—ostensibly legalized and protected by *Gault*—there is less than comprehensive compliance 20 years after the decision. "In re *Gault* Revisited: A Cross-State Comparison of the Right to Counsel in Juvenile Court" focuses on the implementation of one of the due process rights, albeit the most important one, the right to counsel. If a juvenile has an attorney who is competent, other rights should be protected. In three of the six states compared, almost half of the delinquents and status offenders did not have lawyers and, most surprisingly, those juveniles who committed the most serious offenses were more likely to be represented by counsel, but even when controlling for the differences in offense severity they ended up with more harsh dispositions than those not represented. In other words, there still is not anywhere near full compliance in half of the jurisdictions studied, and it is not clear that having counsel guarantees more justice or less severe treatment by the juvenile court.

As Greenwood notes in "Responding to Juvenile Crime: Lessons Learned," the dispositional alternatives, from intake to incarceration, available to the juvenile justice system have diversified over the past 30 years. In addition, evidence has mounted on the relative effectiveness of different kinds of interventions, treatments, and programs in reducing recidivism (repeat offending). The best available evidence suggests that there may be a 10% reduction in recidivism among the hundreds of juvenile justice programs that were evaluated, with some types of interventions (particularly those that are community based, structured, and have more intense, multiple treatments) having more impact than others. He also describes the great variety of disposition options used within the juvenile justice system, beginning with the controversial increasing reliance on waivers or transfers of juveniles to adult criminal courts, detention, custodial institutionalization, wilderness programs, group homes, parole and aftercare, boot camps, community supervision, probation, and diversion programs. He concludes that the system needs this vast array of dispositions, careful monitoring of their effectiveness, and the capacity to modify the options based on research evidence.

In addition to the many evaluations of program effectiveness, there is substantial research on the operation of the juvenile justice system and decision-making processes that may produce varied disposition decisions for different types of juveniles (by sex, race, age, and economic status) or types of offenders (status offenders, violent offenders, and career delinquents). The impact of gender on decisions and dispositions has been investigated by many researchers, including Bishop and Frazier in "Gender Bias in Juvenile Justice Processing: Implications of the JJDP Act." They investigate the effects of gender of the juvenile at several points in the juvenile justice process, from intake decisions through judicial disposition. Their analyses of 3 years of data on status offenses and crimes show that the sexual double standard continues to operate even after the mandates of the JJDP Act—there are more severe sanctions for males than females who commit similar crimes but little evidence of gender bias in processing status offenses, where boys and girls receive similar dispositions. Females referred for contempt (a violation of conditions of their sentence), however, are more likely to be petitioned (prosecuted) by the court for delinquency.

The effects of the personal or sociodemographic characteristics of a juvenile on a seldom-researched stage in the juvenile justice process—prehearing detention—are examined by Kempf in "Race, Gender, and the Prehearing Detention of Juveniles." She concludes that both race and gender (other things being equal) lead to more likely detention for blacks in general and for females in suburban and rural areas. As important, it is clear that detention status affects subsequent decisions within the juvenile justice process, typically in more punitive directions and particularly for black offenders.

One of the most volatile issues in justice reform is the transfer of juvenile offenders from the juvenile court to the adult criminal court, particularly for more serious crimes committed by older criminal youths. There has been a flurry of research on this controversial reform, including Fagan's work on "The Comparative Advantage of Juvenile Versus Criminal Court Sanctions on Recidivism Among Adolescent Felony Offenders." The results, based on a comparison of a large sample of juvenile offenders in New Jersey with a matched group in New York, focus on the relative effectiveness of juvenile court versus adult criminal court processing on recidivism and reincarceration: Juveniles sentenced in criminal court are more likely to be incarcerated, but the length of confinement is similar, whether the case is heard in juvenile or criminal court. Recidivism rates, however, are lower for those sentenced in juvenile court, regardless of the type or severity of the sanction. Fagan concludes that the evidence does not support systematic transfer or efforts to eliminate separate jurisdiction for juvenile offenders.

A convergence model of the juvenile court carries with it the perception that it is "tougher" on juvenile delinquency than the traditional model. This seems to carry over even to the kinds of intervention programs that have become popular in the 1980s and 1990s—"intermediate sanctions" such as home confinement and electronic monitoring, wilderness stress-challenge programs, and boot camps. In general, as Lab and Whitehead show in "An Analysis of Juvenile Correctional Treatment," more traditional institution-based correctional treatment does not hold out much promise for preventing the future criminality of juvenile offenders. Their review of many relatively rigorous evaluation studies indicated that more than half showed either a negative or no impact on recidivism, leading them to conclude that it is "hard to reaffirm rehabilitation."

More contemporary alternatives, however, seem to offer more, although somewhat mixed, promise for changing the behavior of juvenile delinquents. In 1988, Vaughn did a "Survey of Juvenile Electronic Monitoring and Home Confinement Programs" and discovered that the first juvenile program was implemented in 1986. Since then, many other jurisdictions have started home confinement/electronic monitoring programs, primarily as an alternative to detention in an institutional setting. Vaughn concludes that they are an effective way to alleviate overcrowding and a viable, more humane alternative form of offender treatment.

"Outdoor/wilderness challenge" programs are another alternative to more traditional approaches to rehabilitation. This type of program has become very popular, as it was during the days of the "child savers" at the end of the nineteenth century, but there is little evidence regarding its effects on recidivism. One of the better studies, "Alternative Placements for Juvenile Offenders: Results From the Evaluation of the Nokomis Challenge Program" by Deschenes and Greenwood, reports on the effectiveness of a multiple-component effort to rehabilitate low- and medium-risk delinquents—a combination of short-term residential outdoor challenge programs followed by longer term community-based aftercare. There were significant cost savings but few differences in behavioral outcomes. Both the program participants and controls improved their social adjustment, which disappeared during the 2-year follow-up period. Paradoxically, the delinquents who were "challenged" and provided aftercare were more likely to be arrested more quickly when they returned to the community. They conclude that the aftercare component must be intensive and strengthened to prevent recidivism more effectively.

The evidence on bootcamps is also mixed. Salerno, in "Boot Camps: A Critique and a Proposed Alternative," reviews the available evidence, though sparse, on the effectiveness of "short-term, intensive programs of hard work, military drill, and treatment" and concludes that even though they may be the "newest and fastest growing correctional program" they should be "phased out immediately—they are doomed to fail and they can be very costly." He discusses the many reasons why and offers an alternative model of intermittent incarceration, intensive probation supervision, boot camp, and graduated freedom.

Where do we go from here? What are the prospects for the future of juvenile justice? Ohlin discusses "The Future of Juvenile Justice Policy and Research," particularly what he views as the challenges that lie ahead—beyond the characteristic contemporary juvenile court—based on the convergence of the original family court model and the post-*Gault* due process model. A small number of states have taken another step beyond the convergence model of the juvenile court and have instituted a more purely "criminalized" juvenile justice system, as in Washington State. This latest reincarnation of the juvenile court reflects very old theory, the "deterrence" principles of the eighteenth century rebottled by neoclassical criminologists such as James Q. Wilson, and very old strategies of crime control: "just deserts" tactics anchored in straightforward punishment and retribution resurrected by other neoclassical thinkers such as Andrew von Hirsch.

This "new" juvenile court is described by Feld as a "scaled-down, second-class criminal court." He sees three alternatives for the future: (a) Return to the "traditional" therapeutic juvenile court and do it right, which is unlikely given the institutionalized "constitutional domestication" of the court; (b) commit comprehensively to the "criminalized" juvenile court; or (c) abolish the juvenile court altogether, and send juvenile criminals to the adult criminal court, with perhaps extra procedural safeguards and a separate juvenile correctional system. After careful consideration, spanning many years and publications addressing this issue, Feld proposes that the juvenile court should be abolished, with some important qualifications. Judicial decisions would be made within a criminal court, but the characteristics of the offense and the offender would be taken into account in a "discount" on sentencing and the juvenile criminal would remain, in the great majority of cases, within a juvenile corrections system to be transferred at a qualifying level of maturity into the adult system.

Is this the best solution? We do not know for sure. With Feld, however, we believe that a commitment to "humanitarian justice" (i.e., trying to balance what is in the best interest of the offender, victim, and the community, protected by the constitution) and a recognition that most kids are different than adults is essential in dealing with young people who get into trouble with the law.

JUDICIAL REFORM

Juvenile Court Theory and Impact in Historical Perspective

HOMER H. CLARK, JR.

THE development of juvenile courts in the United States is quite well-known to most of us. It was preceded by some nineteenth-century attempts to treat young criminals differently from adult criminals. As you know, at common law the rule was that a child became responsible for his criminal acts at the age of 7. Between the ages of 7 and 14, the child was presumed incapable of committing a crime, but the presumption could be rebutted, and on occasion it was, there being records of children below 14 who were executed for capital crimes in England.

In America during the latter half of the nineteenth century, it began to be recognized that perhaps further distinctions between youthful and adult criminals might be made. Most of these distinctions took place in the methods of detention and punishment. Massachusetts, for example, established a reform school for juveniles about the middle of the century. There was some attempt also to avoid punishment of juveniles and to place them in various kinds of school or cottage settings. There was recognition of the desirability of keeping juvenile offenders separate from adult offenders. And finally, toward the end of the nineteenth century

there were statutes providing for separate trials for juvenile criminals in Massachusetts and in some other states.

EARLY STATUTORY DEVELOPMENTS

Illinois is normally credited with having the first juvenile court statute in the United States, in 1899. This early statute set the style for many later juvenile court acts. It set up jurisdiction over dependent, neglected, and delinquent children and as far as possible attempted to create an atmosphere and procedure that would emphasize guidance, protection, and rehabilitation of the child rather than imposition of punishment as a result of finding criminal guilt.

Both the language and the procedure created by the Illinois statute testified to its dependence on a still influential idea in the juvenile court movement. This idea is summed up by the Latin phrase *parens patriae*. The meaning of this phrase in general terms was and is that the state as the sovereign power has both a right and an obligation to step in and protect those of its citizens whose legal capacity is impaired either through lack of age and understanding, as in the case of children, or through mental incompetence or other reasons.

Very shortly after the Illinois juvenile court statute was passed, a similar statute was enacted in Colorado in 1903. It applied to children

From *GAULT: What Now for the Juvenile Court?* (pp. 1-24) V. Norris, editor, 1968, Ann Arbor, MI: Institute of Continuing Legal Education. Copyright 1968 by the Institute of Continuing Legal Education. Reprinted by permission.

16 years old and under and contained the classic nineteenth-century definition of delinquency which prevailed in this state until relatively recently. In addition to covering children who violated the law, it included those who were incorrigible or who knowingly associated with thieves or vicious or immoral persons; who grew up in idleness or crime; who knowingly visited a house of ill repute; who knowingly patronized a policy shop or operated or visited a saloon or dram shop; who patronized a public poolroom or bucket shop; who wandered about the streets at night or wandered about railroad yards or jumped or hooked onto any moving train; who habitually used obscene or indecent language; or who were guilty of any immoral conduct in any public place or near any schoolhouse.

The county courts were given jurisdiction under the statute, which went on to make it plain that the process would be civil in nature, that it would be conducted separately from adult cases, that the child would be in most cases released pending trial, that probation officers would be appointed for juvenile cases, and that commitment of such children should be to the state industrial schools. The statement of purpose in the statute was rather like that of Illinois' except that it included an admonition that "as far as practicable any delinquent child shall be treated not as a criminal but as misdirected and misguided and needing aid, encouragement, help, and assistance."

SOURCES OF REFORM

It is somewhat interesting to ask why the juvenile court movement should have started just at the turn of the century rather than earlier or later. I think this can be explained on the ground that it was a phase of the social reform movement which was becoming so influential at that time and which included divorce reform and woman suffrage. It coincided with an expansion and development in the social sciences as academic disciplines and was accompanied by a tendency to apply the learning from those disciplines to social problems. There was a very strong, optimistic feeling among these reformers that the knowledge we were acquiring in the social sciences would prove quickly and significantly effective in relieving such social problems as youthful crime.

These early juvenile court statutes showed a surprising (to us in view of the *Gault* decision) solicitude for the child's legal rights. For example, the Colorado statute provided for a jury trial. It provided for notice to the child's parent or guardian for transfer proceedings, and it assured the child of the right to bail and authorized the courts in any case to appoint counsel to appear and defend on behalf of the child. If detention of the child was necessary, it was required to be separate from that of the adult offenders.

Similar statutes were passed in the years following the enactment of those in Colorado and Illinois. There were, of course, many local variations, but it is accurate for our purposes to say that in their philosophy and general framework, they resembled the Illinois and Colorado models. Some idea of the hopefulness and optimism with which these courts were greeted can be obtained from Dean Roscoe Pound's remark to the effect that the juvenile court was the most significant advance in the administration of justice since the Magna Carta.

PHILOSOPHY OF THE JUVENILE COURT

The juvenile court movement as so conceived and as it originally was embodied in the statutes reflects not a single, logical working out of a unified philosophy but rather a large number of empirical and ethical philosophic ideas of more or less generality. It is of some help in understanding both the operations of juvenile courts and the various judicial and legislative limitations on those operations to list some of these goals and assumptions:

1. The broadest and most general of all the ideas underlying the juvenile court is a simple

humanitarian concern and sympathy for children. This is very strongly expressed in the early history of these courts and by Judge Mack in his famous article on the juvenile court:

The judge on a bench, looking down upon a boy standing at the bar, can never evoke a proper sympathetic spirit. Seated at a desk, with the child at his side, where he can on occasion put his arm around his shoulder and draw the lad to him, the judge, while losing none of his judicial dignity, will gain immensely in the effectiveness of his work.

2. Another idea that strongly influenced the development of the juvenile court emphasized that the child's environment had brought about his delinquency or dependency or neglect and that the juvenile court should so deal with the child as to change his environment. This might be done by placing the child in a foster home or by controlling his parents in some way, or ultimately by committing him to a state institution.

3. Running strongly through all delinquency statutes and discussions is the idea that the child's problem is a product of poor parental care and that one feature of the delinquency proceeding is to bring this home to the parent and to require the parent to provide better care. This idea is expressed most forcibly by the inclusion in many delinquency statutes of the offense of contributing to delinquency or contributing to dependency, an offense of which adults may be guilty and which may be tried in the juvenile court.

4. The juvenile court movement was also firmly grounded on the view that children can be rehabilitated if the appropriate legal proceeding and disposition can be found and that the adult criminal is very often a product of youthful crimes that went uncorrected. A sharp contrast is made between delinquency and crime. Crime is to be followed by punishment or retribution while juvenile delinquency should not be; rather, it should precipitate attempts at rehabilitation which should be carried on not in a spirit of revenge or even of deterring the particular conduct but rather as a means of chang-

ing both this particular child and the environment in which he lives in such a way that further crimes will not be committed by him. An aspect of this view is the related idea that each child should be treated as an individual, in the light of *his* background and personality, and that the particular act of delinquency is not determinative of the treatment.

5. Another idea that has had great influence in the juvenile court movement is the view that the courts should attack all the child's problems in a single proceeding in a single court. It is commonplace in discussions of the juvenile court to remark that a particular child who is in court because he has committed an offense which would be a crime if committed by an adult may really be more properly cared for as a dependent child or one who is in need of various kinds of medical, psychiatric, or other care. The juvenile court was visualized as a single court which could provide the entire range of child services.

6. Along with the preceding idea goes the view that the juvenile court should have at its disposal a staff representing many different disciplines, many or all of whom can be looked to for guidance in helping the particular child both by way of diagnosis and therapy. A logical corollary of this idea was that the juvenile court in entering an order of disposition respecting children before it should have a wide range of possible remedies. In the juvenile court, it has always been felt that the judge should have a much broader range of remedies than in the criminal law, and that the remedy should be very carefully framed with reference to the particular child's needs.

THE JUVENILE COURT IDEA
IN OPERATION

At least three major obstacles lay in the way of realization of the ideals on which the juvenile court was originally predicated:

1. The first of these was the loose drafting of juvenile court statutes themselves. In the first flush of enthusiasm for the new institution,

many of the details were left open by the statutes, the extent of jurisdiction was sometimes not clearly outlined, and there were ambiguities even in the very definition of children who could be brought before the court.

2. Another such obstacle lay in the lack of financial support given to juvenile courts, one feature of which was that the jurisdiction was often placed in inferior courts which did not begin to have the training, staff, or facilities to accomplish what the statute contemplated.

3. The third obstacle was a fundamental conflict among the ideals of the juvenile court itself.

Statutory Drafting

Examples of the first difficulty abound in the delinquency statutes of the various states. One of the old-fashioned terms still found in many statutes is incorrigibility. An incorrigible child is a delinquent. Usually, the statute contains no definition, and the word itself implies a certain amount of circular reasoning. A child who has not in fact been corrected by his parents is presumably incorrigible, and the reason he has not been corrected by his parents is that he is incorrigible. It is extremely difficult to develop standards which will be of much help in defining what is meant by a term like incorrigibility.

The vagueness of the statutes and the broadness of statutory language produced a certain amount of constitutional attack on the juvenile court acts in the years following their enactment. For the most part, the statutes were held constitutional. The early leading Pennsylvania case of *Commonwealth v. Fisher* is an example. It upheld the statute against attacks based on due process, equal protection, and a failure to provide various procedural safeguards. The opinion emphasized that the statute did not provide for the punishment of offenders but for the salvation of children, going so far as to say at one point that the legislature may provide for the salvation of a child, if its parents or guardians are unable to do so, by bringing it into one of the courts of the state without any process at all.

Financial Obstacles

It has been said many times that the juvenile courts in many parts of the United States are juvenile courts in name only. In Colorado before the judicial reorganization which occurred in 1965, juvenile jurisdiction was exercised in the county courts which were staffed in many counties of the state by persons who were not lawyers and who very often had no knowledge of juvenile problems nor interest in them. Even in the larger cities of the state and of other states where juvenile courts are presided over by experienced judges having an interest in and sympathy for problems of juveniles, staffs are usually quite inadequate to handle the workload and to provide the kind of services for juveniles which the juvenile court ideal originally envisaged. Still another aspect of this problem is the inadequate support given in most states to the institutional facilities for dealing with juveniles.

Inconsistencies of the Juvenile Court Ideal

The final obstacle to the working out of the juvenile court ideal is the fact that this ideal contains inconsistencies within itself. We have never really accepted the rehabilitative function of the juvenile court to its fullest extent. In many ways, the juvenile court is viewed in the community as a sort of junior-grade criminal court, and the commitment to the state industrial school by the juvenile court is almost universally viewed, at least by the juvenile who is committed, as analogous to a prison sentence. The ambivalence of ideals is not reduced by the fact that juvenile jurisdiction is invoked in the first instance very often by the commission of an act which would be a crime if committed by an adult and by the fact that the first contact of the juvenile with the law is necessarily personified by a police officer.

The result of this ambivalence has of course been not only a tension within the juvenile court itself but a confusion in the administration of juvenile courts, caused by that tension. It is often expressly reflected in conflicts between those having a social work orientation and those with traditional legal training who insist on more formal adherence to legal processes. It is also reflected in conflict between many people in law enforcement and the community, on the one hand, and those directly involved in juvenile court work, on the other.

THE *GAULT* EXPERIENCE

The best illustration of the conflict in ideals that I can give you is the opinion of the Arizona Supreme Court in the case In re *Gault*. It will be helpful to outline the facts of the case very briefly.

Gerald Gault was arrested on June 8, 1964, when he was 15 years old, on the ground that he had made an obscene telephone call to a neighbor. He was placed in the Children's Detention Home without any notice being sent to his parents, who were both away at work at the time of his arrest. His parents finally learned where he was and when they appeared at the detention center, they were told that a hearing would be held the next day. On the following day, June 9, the probation officer filed a juvenile delinquency petition containing no statements of fact but merely a general recital to the effect that Gerald Gault was a delinquent minor. No copy of the petition was ever served on the Gaults before this hearing.

The hearing on June 9 occurred in the chambers of the juvenile court judge. Present were the probation officer, Gerald Gault, his mother, and his older brother. The neighbor who supposedly received the obscene telephone call was not present. There was no sworn testimony. Neither Gerald Gault nor his mother was told that he had a right to counsel or that he had a right not to make a statement. The hearing was not recorded in any way. At the later habeas corpus hearing, there was a conflict of testimony on the issue of whether Gerald had admitted making the obscene telephone call. A probation officer and the juvenile court judge at that later hearing

testified that he had admitted it, but his mother testified that he said he had just dialed the neighbor's number and handed the telephone to a friend who did all the talking. At the end of the hearing on June 9, the judge took the case under advisement, and Gerald Gault was held in the detention center for 2 or 3 more days. When he was released, his mother received a note from a probation officer which stated that further hearings in the case would be held on June 15.

At the later hearing, Gerald and his father and mother were present as well as the probation officer, but the neighbor who supposedly received the telephone call was again not present. Later testimony at the habeas corpus hearing was likewise in conflict as to whether Gerald admitted making the statements over the telephone. The judge looked at a "probation officer's referral report," but he did not disclose the report either to Gerald or to his parents. At this hearing, the judge committed Gerald as a juvenile delinquent to the Arizona State Industrial School "for the period of his minority . . . unless sooner discharged by due process of law." Since Gerald was then 15, this sentence apparently made possible a 6-year commitment.

On August 3, 1964, Gerald's parents filed a petition for habeas corpus in the Arizona Supreme Court, which then ordered that the matter be heard by the Superior Court of Maricopa County, and this was done on August 17, 1964. At this hearing, there was not only conflict in the testimony concerning what had happened at the earlier two hearings on June 9 and June 15, but the juvenile court judge testified in such a manner as to suggest that he had no real notion of what law it was that Gerald was supposed to have violated. At one point, he stated that it consisted of disturbing the peace and at another point he indicated that he thought it consisted of using lewd language in the presence of another person, and finally he thought it might have been that the boy had been habitually involved in immoral matters. Since there was no record of the delinquency hearings, whatever did happen had to be established by the testimony of the juvenile court judge, the probation officer, and Mrs. Gault. Gerald did not testify at the habeas corpus hearing.

The Superior Court of Maricopa County dismissed the petition for habeas corpus and remanded Gerald to the Arizona Industrial School. An appeal was then taken to the Supreme Court of Arizona, which affirmed the denial of habeas corpus and upheld the action of the juvenile court.

The Supreme Court of Arizona classified the assignments of error under three main headings:

1. That the Arizona Juvenile Code was unconstitutional for failure to give notice to parents and children of specific charges; for failure to require timely, adequate, and proper notice of the hearing; and for failure to provide for an appeal
2. That the juvenile court in fact denied Gerald Gault and his parents due process of law by failing to provide proper notice of both the delinquency charge and the hearing, by failing to notify them of their constitutional rights to counsel and to remain silent, by relying on unsworn hearsay testimony, by failing to provide a proper record of the delinquency proceedings, and by removing Gerald from the custody of his parents without any showing of their incompetency or inability to care for him
3. A group of miscellaneous errors dealing with the habeas corpus hearing in Maricopa County and the original detention of Gerald

These contentions were made under both the due process clause of the Fourteenth Amendment to the United States Constitution and the corresponding provision of the Arizona constitution.

All the contentions made in support of the petition for habeas corpus were rejected. Starting with the premise that all statutes are to be found constitutional, if reasonably possible, the court cited many cases which have held in general that juvenile court statutes and juvenile codes are constitutional.

The court relied on the *parens patriae* doctrine as the conceptual basis for the juvenile court, stating that this doctrine functions to benefit and protect the delinquent and the public but that it does not justify depriving a child of due process. The court then went on to say that the power of a juvenile court is necessary in order to achieve the individualized consideration of the child which is the true objective both today and 60 years ago when the juvenile court movement began.

THE IMPACT OF *GAULT*

When the *Gault* case came to the Supreme Court of the United States, the court was faced with the claim that Gerald Gault had been denied six fundamental constitutional rights in the juvenile court proceeding. These were as follows:

1. Notice of the charges
2. Right to counsel
3. Right to confrontation and cross-examination of the witnesses
4. Privilege against self-incrimination
5. The right to a transcript of the proceedings
6. The right to appellate review

A majority of the Supreme Court did not pass on the last two claims. With respect to the first four of these claims, the Supreme Court held that the procedure in the Arizona juvenile court did not meet constitutional requirements.

In other words, the Supreme Court held

1. That specific notice of the offense charged must be given before the hearing to enable the juvenile and his parents to prepare a defense, the sort of notice which would be constitutionally adequate in a criminal proceeding
2. That the juvenile and his parents must be advised of their right to counsel where the proceedings may result in commitment to an institution, and if they are unable to afford counsel, counsel must be appointed

3. That the juvenile has a right to confront witnesses against him, to cross-examine them, and to have testimony sworn, in the absence of a valid confession adequate to support the court's determination
4. That the constitutional privilege against self-incrimination is as applicable to juveniles as to adults

The court conceded that special problems arise respecting waiver of this privilege by or on behalf of children but went no further in the solution of those problems than to say that if counsel is not present when an admission is made, then greatest care must be taken to assure that the admission is voluntary.

The rationale of the *Gault* decision is that the impact of a delinquency proceeding on the juvenile is analogous to the impact of a criminal proceeding on an adult. This being so, the juvenile is entitled to those constitutional safeguards which would be given an adult in a criminal proceeding. There may be a limitation here, although I am not sure. The court might be saying that those constitutional safeguards need not be provided which would seriously hamper working out the juvenile court ideal of individualized rehabilitation for the juvenile, but in this case the constitutional limitations concerned would not interfere with any of the legitimate goals of the juvenile court, and they must therefore be provided.

The Arizona Supreme Court, like many other state courts, was willing to be content with a pious repetition of conventional dogma. The U.S. Supreme Court differed by insisting that the dogma be given some reality in the handling of this and similar cases. This I believe epitomizes the positions taken by the U.S. Supreme Court in criminal cases over the past 10 years.

One way of assessing the impact of *Gault* is to ask what will be its relationship to the six underlying assumptions which I mentioned earlier, and to the obstacles which I suggested had prevented the full working out of the juvenile court idea. In other words, will *Gault* frustrate the goals of juvenile courts? And will it magnify or reduce the obstacles?

Humanitarian Concern for Children

The first underlying assumption, the humanitarian concern for children, is, I think, not interfered with by the *Gault* case, but in any event I believe humanitarian feelings are no longer influential in the juvenile court movement. It is extremely rare to hear the problems of delinquency discussed in humanitarian terms. I have the feeling that we find this embarrassing. More often than not, the discussion revolves around the "tough kid" and how to handle him, the inference being that we must be "realistic" rather than sympathetic. The departure of the humanitarian ideal from the juvenile court movement parallels its departure from American government generally.

Change of Environment

The second assumption, that the purpose of the juvenile court proceeding is to do something about the child's environment, may be affected by *Gault*. This is a question on which I hope to hear some opinions. The assumption is best effectuated by a careful, individualized disposition. Disposition is expressly left alone by *Gault*, but the decision has obvious implications for the dispositional stage of the delinquency proceeding.

Parental Care and Rehabilitation of the Child

The same can be said with respect to the idea that the delinquency proceeding should do something about the child's parental care. The fourth goal of the juvenile court movement was rehabilitation as opposed to punishment. So far as the *Gault* decision requires the safeguards of a criminal proceeding, it might be argued that it makes the proceeding look more like a criminal one than a civil one. It also seems to me not unlikely that some juvenile courts may feel a greater willingness to impose severe sanctions in juvenile cases because they are now required to observe many of the constitutional safeguards applicable to criminal proceedings.

Single Proceeding

It seems to me that the *Gault* case creates some problems with respect to the fifth goal of the juvenile court movement, namely, that all the child's problems should be attacked in a single proceeding. The *Gault* case was concerned with a child who was charged with committing an offense which would be criminal if committed by an adult. In several parts of the opinion, Mr. Justice Fortas limited his remarks to that situation, but conceivably the juvenile court might wish to treat a child in court on this basis as a dependent child, in which event perhaps some of the constitutional safeguards would not be required.

But this would not be known until a hearing was held. This problem may perhaps be capable of solution under a carefully drafted statute, but undoubtedly in many states the courts will have to wrestle with it without the benefit of statute.

Interdisciplinary Treatment

The sixth goal of the juvenile court movement was said to be the application to children's problems of many different disciplines. It seems to me that this is the goal which is most sharply affected by the *Gault* decision. In the *Gault* case itself a probation report was apparently relied on by the juvenile judge in determining what decision to reach in Gerald Gault's case. This report was not made available to his parents. It seems clear that under the *Gault* decision, juvenile courts will have to observe constitutional safeguards in using all such reports, certainly at the adjudicatory stage of the proceeding and perhaps also at the stage of disposition. At the adjudicatory stage, it certainly means allowing the juvenile or his counsel to see the report and to cross-examine the person who made it. Whether or not it means more than this is very hard to say. It is likewise not clear under the

Gault case to what extent such material should and can be used at the stage of intake in the juvenile court. If the decision whether to file a formal proceeding, for example, turns on such material, does this mean that the child and his counsel have the right to see this material? If such material is used in a transfer proceeding from the juvenile court to the criminal courts, the *Kent* case seems to require constitutional safeguards there.

I have referred to three obstacles which lay in the way of effective working out of the juvenile court ideal, and the question arises, what is the effect on these of the *Gault* decision? With respect to the second of these obstacles, that is, the lack of support for juvenile courts, obviously the *Gault* case has no relevance whatever. The other two obstacles I think are affected by the *Gault* decision. The first one mentioned was the loose drafting of juvenile court statutes, leaving a great deal of room for informal and sometimes arbitrary action. The *Gault* decision makes clear that under such statutes the courts either must observe constitutional requirements or expect to see their decisions reversed. This should bring about some attempts on the part of the various state legislatures to revise these statutes in the direction of more safeguards and more specific provisions protecting the rights of juveniles in these cases.

The third obstacle mentioned was a conflict within the juvenile court movement itself between the ideals of rehabilitation of the juvenile and the instinct to punish. *Gault* affects this conflict in several ways. In the first place, by imposing many constitutional safeguards, the Supreme Court goes far in the direction of characterizing the delinquency proceeding as a criminal one. At the same time, the Court is at some pains to point out that imposing the constitutional safeguards does not affect the achievement of the goals of the juvenile court. The suggestion is made in the opinion that juveniles in the court will have more respect for its processes and will be readier subjects for rehabilitation if they recognize that they have been treated fairly. Certainly, the imposition of these requirements does not interfere with the range and flexibility of remedies involved in a juvenile court proceeding, and it is there that the most important rehabilitative consequences exist.

The danger created by the decision, it seems to me, is that it will be superficially read and construed by many people as converting delinquency proceedings into criminal proceedings thereby justifying abandonment of those protections for the juvenile which are not required by the Constitution, such as the restrictions on publicity, special provisions concerning detention and arrest, and the flexibility of remedies.

Properly construed, however, the *Gault* decision should merely serve to guarantee the essential constitutional protections in children's cases. It will not be easy in some instances to work out the details of those protections, such as in the area of waiver of the right of self-incrimination. The *Gault* decision also places an additional burden on the attorney, who will now be more often drawn into delinquency proceedings. One of the problems that he will face when he is appearing in delinquency proceedings will be a difficult problem of conflict of interest. Very often he will be employed by the child's parents to represent the child under circumstances where the interests of the child and the interests of the parents are at least inconsistent and perhaps diametrically opposed.

The major effect of the *Gault* case therefore seems to be that of a challenge both to legislatures and to the practicing bar along with the juvenile courts to devise ways of carrying out the original juvenile court ideal by fair and constitutional means. If we have sufficient imagination and organizing ability to do this, then some of the optimism of the early days of the juvenile court movement will have been warranted.

QUESTIONS FOR DISCUSSION AND WRITING

1. What six goals and assumptions underlay the juvenile court?
2. What three major obstacles lay in the way of realization of the ideals on which the juvenile court was originally predicated?
3. What four claims raised by *Gault* did the United States Supreme Court rule unconstitutional? Which two did it fail to rule on?
4. What does the author believe is the danger created by the *Gault* decision?

THE LEGAL LEGACY

Beyond *Gault:* Injustice and the Child

PAUL LERMAN

ON May 15, 1967, the U.S. Supreme Court rendered a decision that highlighted the procedural defects characteristic of many juvenile courts. A majority of the Court ruled that 15-year-old Gerald Gault, accused of having placed, with a friend, an anonymous phone call to a woman and making lewd remarks to her, had been denied the following "basic rights" by the state of Arizona: (a) notice of charges, (b) right to counsel, (c) right to confront and cross-examine the complainant, and (d) protection against self-incrimination. This far-reaching decision will probably have important effects on the procedural justice accorded to juveniles throughout the United States. However, it will not restrain the 50 states from exercising enormous discretion in the detention and institutionalization of youth. Although the issues of procedural justice for juveniles have been faced, the problems of substantive justice have scarcely been addressed, legally or empirically. This chapter will not analyze problems of juvenile justice from a legal perspective; rather, we shall approach three problems empirically by using available data. The problems and the data, however, become meaningful only by using traditional standards of justice as a frame of reference. Therefore, the problems and standards will be briefly discussed before presenting evidence concerning the Court's

actual decisions concerning detention and institutionalization.

THE FIRST PROBLEM: EQUAL TREATMENT FOR COMPARABLE OFFENSES

In the *Gault* case, the Supreme Court deliberately avoided dealing with the substantive issues arising from the detention and lengthy incarceration of a 15-year-old boy. Specifically, this restriction of the issues to procedural rights governing court hearings means that the Court refrained from deciding whether young Gault had been unreasonably detained for 4 or 5 days prior to his trial; they also refrained from deciding whether the dispositional sentence of 6 years in a state institution was unreasonable as compared to the penalty for a similar offense by an adult: a fine of $5 to $50 or a jail sentence of not more than 60 days. Because of the Supreme Court decision, Gerald Gault was released from Arizona's State Industrial School for Delinquents before he had reached adulthood. But he was released because his trial was adjudged "unfair"—not because the disposition was deemed unreasonable.

Had 15-year-old Gault been accorded a "fair" trial, he might still have been sentenced to a 6-year term for a 60-day misdemeanor. Although procedural justice can have a great impact on the substantive justice rendered to suspected offenders, it is important not to confuse "fairness" and "justice." The Supreme Court has not yet ruled on how much deprivation of liberty (before and after a "fair trial") can be imposed on the juveniles of America. How soon it will rule on the "prejudicial stages" and on the "post-adjudicative or dispositional process" may depend on how sensitive the friends of the Court are to the issues of arbitrary detention and lengthy incarceration of juveniles.

Justice is not an easy concept to define, much less measure, but two central aspects of its meaning in relation to criminal adjudication can be identified as providing standards: (a) Equal punishment should be accorded to all those who commit comparable offenses, and (b) the penalties imposed should be graded according to the degree of social harm the defendant has actually done or clearly threatens to do to the community. To the extent that actual cases depart from these two tenets, our own sense of justice is affronted. Regarding the first standard, the *Gault* case affects our sense of justice because Gault did not receive treatment equal to what would have been given to an *adult* committing the same act. On the basis of an adult standard of punishment, Gault should have received a maximum sentence of 60 days—not 6 years.

THE SECOND PROBLEM: MATCHING EXTENT OF PUNISHMENT WITH DEGREE OF SOCIAL HARM

Adherence to traditional standards implies that a day's "imprisonment" in a county jail or state prison is equal to a day's "placement" in a county detention home, state training school, or residential treatment facility. Semantic differences, as well as actual differences in personnel, food, housing, programs, and general amenities, should not obscure the central fact that deprivation of liberty—even for 24 hours—is an extreme form of punishment. Both adult and juvenile facilities involve custodial management, as well as loss of liberty, as part of the judicial intervention authorized by the court. There is no logical reason to regard a stay at a "residential treatment center" as any less depriving of liberty than a stay of the same duration at a state training school. In brief, a court-imposed "treatment plan" is actually a *type of punishment*.

If we accept the fact that any deprivation of liberty is actually a punishment, then a sense of justice also requires a proportionate relationship between the seriousness of the actual or clearly potential "social harm" and the penal sanction. If traditional beliefs about justice prevailed in the juvenile system, as they do in the regular criminal court system, convicted misdemeanants like Gerald Gault would spend less time in detention and "training" than a juvenile burglar would. We are here concerned not with a comparison of the judicial outcomes of juveniles and adults but with the relative severity of judicial intervention within a juvenile offender population.

THE THIRD PROBLEM: DETENTION AND SEVERITY OF FINAL DISPOSITION

Juveniles can be legally detained (i.e., deprived of liberty) at three stages of the adjudication process, even in a "fair" jurisdiction: (a) prior to a hearing to determine whether the offender is guilty of delinquency; (b) after conviction but prior to dispositional hearing, while the court assembles information that will guide it in handing down sentence; and (c) after sentencing but prior to institutionalization, while court personnel attempt to "place" the offender in a state or private facility. Whether youngsters should be detained to the degree that they are has been widely discussed in the literature. The possibility that many juveniles may be detained at a greater rate and for longer periods of time at all stages of the adjudication process has been implicitly covered under the discussion of the disparity in the punishment of juveniles and adults. The problem with which we are here concerned focuses on the influence of detention per se on the likelihood that the offender will be found guilty and sentenced to an institution. This problem also refers to the standard of equal punishment for comparable offenses. But the problem is sufficiently important to warrant separate treatment.

AVAILABLE EVIDENCE

These three types of problems have never been studied directly. However, available evidence indicates that the juvenile court system is probably characterized by these types of unreasonable outcomes in many cases.

Unequal Punishment of Juveniles and Adults

The President's Commission on Law Enforcement and Administration of Justice had the *Gault* case and others in mind when it argued that the juvenile courts should institute fairer proceedings to avoid overly severe dispositions:

The essentials of fair procedures are most imperative in light of the fact that the juvenile court's broad jurisdiction and indefinite commitment power lead not infrequently to sanctions more severe than those an adult could receive for like behavior.

This conclusion gains further credence from the data released after a national survey conducted for the commission:

The average institutional stay before first release among the (adult) misdemeanant institutions covered by the National Survey (which excluded those handling persons sentenced for less than 30 days) was slightly less than 8 weeks, as compared to 20.9 months for adult felons and 9.3 months for juveniles.

Since it is a well-known fact that the bulk of offenses handled by the juvenile court are of a minor nature, it is difficult not to infer that many juveniles are being punished about four times as severely as adult misdemeanants. This, of course, is a gross estimate of the disparity. In cases of youngsters "placed" at private residential treatment centers (at public expense), the disparity may even be greater. One private facility studied by the author kept youngsters who completed "treatment" for an average of 2½ years, whereas those who did not complete treatment were released after 16 months. Such lengthy stays rival the average national figure for the incarceration of convicted *felons* (as revealed by the national survey). If special programs of this kind yielded higher rates of successful rehabilitation, we might be confronted by an ethical dilemma; however, there is no convincing evidence that greater success actually occurs. It appears, then, that juveniles may be institutionalized for minor offenses 4 to 16 times as long as adult misdemeanants.

These estimates of disparities in punishment, it should be noted, are based on actual sentences served—not on sentences imposed at the time of dispositional adjudication. The distinction is important, for both juveniles and adults. In New York State, for example, juveniles can be held for a maximum of 3 years under the usual sentence imposed; however, the actual length of stay at *public* institutions averages about 9 months. It is important to recognize that on a relative basis the "nontreated" felon is punished much less severely than the law allows, in comparison to the "treated" juvenile offenders "placed" for 2½ years of a maximum 3-year term. Whether we apply an absolute or a relative standard, the youngsters who probably experience the greatest disparity are those minor offenders who purportedly receive the *best* treatment. As Allen has noted, "One with reason may inquire as to the value of therapy purchased at the expense of justice."

Failure to Match Punishment and Degree of Social Harm

The criminal statutes that exist or are proposed as models attempt to establish a range of penalties based on the relative harmfulness of the criminal conduct or the probable degree of danger represented by repeated offenders.

TABLE 1

Disposition of juvenile cases at three stages of adjudication in 19 of 30 largest cities, 1965.

| | Offense Categories[a] | | |
Stage of Adjudication	Part I Type	All Other Adult Types	Juvenile-Status Offenses
Percent court petition	57	33	42
	N = (37,420)	(52,862)	(33,046)
Percent convicted—if petition	92	90	94
	N = (21,386)	(17,319)	(13,857)
Percent placed or committed—if convicted[b]	23	18	26
	N = (19,667)	(15,524)	(12,989)

Source: Juvenile Court Statistics, 1965.
a. See text for definition of each category.
b. All suspended sentences are considered as noncommitments.

Although the range and inconsistency of sentencing distinctions are often deplored, there is little doubt that in dealing with adult offenders all 50 states make some attempt to fit the penalty to the degree of social harm inflicted by the crime. However, juvenile delinquency statutes are not drawn up in this manner.

It is possible, of course, that in actual practice juvenile court personnel attempt to assess degree of social harm and to pass sentence accordingly. Available national data suggest that differences in degree of punishment probably occur at the *initial* stages of processing—where the decision to "adjust" the cases unofficially or to bring the offender before the court is made. Once the juveniles are placed on petition before the court, there do *not* appear to be any differences in the dispositional outcomes. Table 1 provides the data for these inferences. Based on a secondary analysis of information published by the Children's Bureau for 19 of the 30 largest cities reporting in detail, offenders are classified as follows: (a) *Part I type* refers to the offenses considered most serious by the FBI (homicide, rape, armed robbery, burglary, aggravated assault, and theft of more than $50); (b) *all other adult types* refers to offenses that would be crimes if committed by an adult, but not serious crimes;

and (c) *juvenile-status offenses* refers to acts deemed harmful but not criminal if committed by an adult (e.g., running away, truancy, incorrigibility, and disobedience). Three stages in the processing of juveniles are depicted in Table 1: (a) whether an official petition is drawn; (b) whether the juvenile is found guilty, if brought before the court; and (c) whether he is placed or committed to an institution, if convicted. The rates are computed for each offense type at each of the stages.

As Table 1 makes clear, the only major difference between offense categories exists at the stage of unofficial adjustment or petition (57% versus 33% and 42%). Convictions and commitment rates do not vary greatly. These data suggest that once an offender reaches the judge's bench, the relative seriousness of his offense does not influence the likelihood of his becoming an official delinquent or receiving the maximum penalty—deprivation of liberty.

The national data summarized in Table 1 do not refer to cities like New York where some differentiation of offenders has begun. Beginning in September 1962, New York's family court has been labeling juvenile-status offenders as "persons in need of supervision" (PINS) rather than as delinquents. But has this change in labels led

TABLE 2

Disposition of juvenile cases at two stages of adjudication, New York City Family Court cases, July 1, 1965-June 30, 1966 (boys and girls combined).

| | Type of Court Petition | |
Stage of Adjudication[a]	Delinquency	PINS[b]
Percent convicted	58	81
	N = (6,604)	(3,545)
Percent placed or committed—if convicted	21	26
	N = (3,832)	(2,859)

Source: State of New York, *Report of the Family Court* (Report of the Administrative Board of the Judicial Conference for the Judicial Year July 1, 1965-June 30, 1966), reprint from 12th Annual Report, pp. 52-59.
a. The following cases of both types are excluded: discharged to another petition, discharged to mental institution, and transfers.
b. PINS = persons in need of supervision.

to less severe punishment of youth? Official data of the Family Court for New York City indicate that the *reverse* appears to be occurring. Since this court has implemented "fair hearings" to the extent of providing legal counsel for virtually all court cases, the available comparisons are of some interest.

In Table 2, New York City youth are classified according to their petition labels, whether "delinquency" or PINS. As with the national data reported in Table 1, stages of the adjudication process are considered. Unfortunately, the "petition" stage has had to be omitted because this information is not available by offense category.

The conviction rate for "delinquents" shown in Table 2 is much lower than the national rate reported in Table 1, but this may occur because New York City adjusts fewer cases unofficially. However, PINS youth do not fare as well as the "delinquents": 81% are convicted as compared to only 58% of the youth who commit offenses that are regarded as crimes if committed by an adult. The actual rates of commitment disclose a 5% difference to the disadvantage of PINS youth.

If actual length of stay in the institution is considered, the comparisons again reveal that the PINS label is not a benign one. In a pilot study that focused on a 1963 random sample of officially adjudicated PINS and delinquent boys appearing in Manhattan Court, the author gathered data on the range, median, and average length of stay for institutionalized boys. The *range* of institutional stay was 2 to 28 months for delinquents and 4 to 48 months for PINS, the *median* was 9 months for delinquents and 13 months for PINS, and the *average* stay was 10.7 months for delinquents and 16.3 months for PINS. Regardless of the mode of measurement, it is apparent that more boys convicted and sentenced for juvenile offenses are actually punished for longer periods of time than juveniles convicted for criminal-type offenses.

Detention and Severity of Final Disposition

There have been many studies of juvenile detention practices in the United States. Given the strong tendency to use juvenile detention for a variety of reasons that have nothing to do with whether the accused (presumed to be innocent until proved guilty) will appear at his trial or dispositional hearing, it would not be surpris-

TABLE 3

Comparison of detention data for delinquent and PINS youth appearing in court, New York City, July 1, 1965-June 30, 1966 (boys and girls combined).

	Type of Court Petition	
Detention Data	Juvenile Delinquents	Juvenile PINS
Percent detained—if petition	31	54
	N = (6,497)	(3,849)
Percent detained more than 30 days—if detained	25	50
	N = (2,024)	(2,067)

Source: State of New York, *Report of the Family Court* (Report of the Administrative Board of the Judicial Conference for the Judicial Year July 1, 1965-June 30, 1966), reprint from 12th Annual Report, pp. 44-51.

ing to find that unequal treatment exists in comparison to adult detention practices. But comparisons of this type cannot be made with available data.

More reliable inferences can be drawn about detention and the second type of problem (i.e., failure to match punishment and degree of social harm). Table 3 indicates the proportion of New York City youth detained for any length of time, comparing those who appear in court on "delinquency" and PINS petitions; in addition, these two offender categories are compared according to the percentage detained for more than 30 days, if they are detained. It is quite evident that substantial differences exist in the detention rates of the two offender groups. Those charged with the least socially harmful offenses (i.e., noncriminal) are, in fact, detained much more often—and for longer periods of time.

Whether detention per se also makes it more likely that a youngster will be found guilty and sentenced to an institution has not been studied, except for the author's pilot study. Using the same type of sample as reported in the discussion of length of stay, data were also gathered concerning previous court appearance and detention prior to final disposition. Boys that have never appeared, or appeared once, are much more likely to be institutionalized if they have

also been detained prior to their dispositional hearing. Apparently, if boys have appeared two or more times then detention is not related to institutionalization.

TRADITIONAL STANDARDS OF JUSTICE AND JUVENILE COURT PHILOSOPHY

If the conventional standards of justice are used as a norm, there exists sufficient evidence for indicating that the current system of juvenile adjudication probably operates unreasonably in many cases. However, it is important to recognize that the type of evidence presented refers to problems of juvenile justice only if we use the standards of conventional criminal justice.

Proponents of the traditional juvenile court philosophy might suggest that these traditional standards of justice should not be employed. The juvenile court, they might argue, does not punish the offender but, rather, hands down treatment-oriented decisions according to individual need. The court's philosophy of "justice" is to treat the offender's underlying needs, irrespective of the legal distinctions among offenses. Some proponents of this philosophy might even argue that a boy who has committed a fairly trivial offense might, nevertheless, need a correctional or treatment regime of long duration, whereas another boy who has engaged in an act of serious wrongdoing might not need institutional treatment at all.

By using the conventional standards of justice, we have implicitly rejected this traditional juvenile court philosophy. On what grounds do we challenge this philosophy and adopt instead the standards of the adult system of justice?

1. It can hardly be disputed that court-imposed treatment plans are not freely chosen by juvenile offenders and their families but are based on a coercive deprivation of liberty. Therefore, court-imposed "treatment" is actually a type of punishment—however benign the intentions or rhetoric of the court personnel.

2. If probation and institutionalization—the two basic "modalities of treatment"—involve restrictions on the liberty of parents and children, then care must be taken that punishment not be meted out unfairly and unreasonably. The treatment ethos does not contain safeguards that can be consistently applied to prevent arbitrary and unreasonable "treatment" of offenders. Therefore, even benign treatment of offenders will be less arbitrary and unreasonable if rehabilitation plans are introduced *after* a fair and just adjudication limits their imposition and duration.

3. To oppose unregulated punishment implies that one adheres to a moral position in favor of reasonable standards. But morality aside, it is critically important for the juvenile court philosophy that the treatment personnel be capable of accurately diagnosing the presumed treatment needs of offenders. If their diagnoses are not reliable and valid, then the rationale for using criteria that do not contain safeguards against unregulated punishment is weakened even further. Empirical studies that test this assumption of expertise are notably absent in the delinquency literature. However, in the general field of mental health there is sufficient empirical evidence that diagnoses can be, and often are, quite unreliable and invalid. Why should the juvenile court system with its well-known personnel problems be expected to perform any

better than trained psychiatrists in providing diagnoses that are reliable and valid?

4. Practically, there appears to be substantial doubt that the juvenile court system has been able to inaugurate and sustain treatment programs that are sufficiently individualized to meet "needs" as idealized by professional treatment personnel.

5. When empirical studies attempt to evaluate the effectiveness of the actual treatment regimes provided to juveniles, the following conclusion tends to emerge: The treatment programs geared to juvenile offenders do not appear to be successful in curbing renewed delinquency.

The foregoing assessment indicates that the modern juvenile court philosophy is based on assumptions that are unreasonable and an operational system that is questionable on moral, empirical, and practical grounds. We contend, therefore, that the current system should be assessed by the traditional norms of criminal justice in regard to judicial outcomes, as well as procedures.

SUMMARY AND CONCLUSIONS

The Supreme Court has highlighted the procedural injustice associated with the juvenile court tradition; this chapter has attempted to provide evidence that substantive injustice is also associated with the juvenile court. It appears quite likely that even in fair jurisdictions—like New York City—minor juvenile offenders are deprived of their liberty for much longer periods of time than adult misdemeanants. If one is concerned about traditional standards of justice, it appears that our current juvenile court system is an unjust one; the Gerald Gaults of America have yet to be counted in their entirety.

From a theoretical perspective, the juvenile court tradition affords another example of how unintended consequences can flow from benign intentions. The juvenile court reformers were successful in taking children out of the traditional criminal court jurisdictions; however, on behalf of humanitarian motives they engaged in unregulated "treatment." In the process, they have probably caused juveniles to be detained more frequently and institutionalized for longer periods of time than adults. By paying little heed to the seriousness of the youngster's offenses, they have unwittingly been "easy" on the felonious delinquent and "hard" on the misdemeaning youngster.

Our societal response to youthful deviations has always been subject to the influence of competing interest groups. It is time to reshape that response so that professional language does not obscure punishment as a palpable fact, and benign intentions do not disguise the operation of an unjust system.

QUESTIONS FOR DISCUSSION AND WRITING

1. What three problems and standards for juvenile courts does the *Gault* case illustrate?
2. What does the author argue is difficult not to infer about unequal punishment of juveniles and adults? What about those "placed" at private residential treatment centers (at public expense)?
3. From a theoretical perspective, how can the juvenile court tradition afford another example of how unintended consequences can flow from benign intentions?

In re *Gault* Revisited:
A Cross-State Comparison of the
Right to Counsel in Juvenile Court

BARRY C. FELD

MORE than 20 years ago in In re *Gault*, the U.S. Supreme Court held that juvenile offenders were constitutionally entitled to the assistance of counsel in juvenile delinquency proceedings. The *Gault* Court mandated the right to counsel because "a proceeding where the issue is whether the child will be found to be 'delinquent' and subjected to the loss of his liberty for years is comparable in seriousness to a felony prosecution." *Gault* also decided that juveniles were entitled to the privilege against self-incrimination and the right to confront and cross-examine their accusers at a hearing. Without the assistance of counsel, these other rights could be negated.

In the two decades since *Gault*, the promise of counsel remains unrealized. Although there is a scarcity of data, in many states less than 50% of juveniles adjudicated delinquent receive the assistance of counsel to which they are constitutionally entitled. Although national statistics are not available, surveys of representation by counsel in several jurisdictions suggest that "there is reason to *think* that lawyers still appear much less often than might have been expected."

Even when juveniles are represented, attorneys may not be capable of or committed to representing their juvenile clients in an effective adversarial manner. Several studies have questioned whether lawyers can actually perform as advocates in a system rooted in *parens patriae* and benevolent rehabilitation. Indeed, there are some indications that lawyers representing juveniles in more traditional "therapeutic" juvenile courts may actually disadvantage their clients in adjudications or dispositions. Duffee and Siegel, Clarke and Koch, Stapleton and Teitelbaum, Hayeslip, and Bortner all reported that juveniles with counsel are more likely to be incarcerated than juveniles without counsel. *Regardless of the types of offenses with which they were charged*, juveniles represented by attorneys receive more severe dispositions.

THE PRESENT STUDY

The present study provides the first opportunity to analyze systematically variations in rates of representation and the impact of counsel in more than one juvenile court or even one jurisdiction. It analyzes variations in the implementation of the right to counsel in six states—California, Minnesota, New York, Nebraska, North Dakota, and Pennsylvania—as well as Philadelphia. These statistical analyses provide the first comparative examination of the circumstances under which lawyers are appointed to represent juveniles, the case characteristics associated with rates of representation, and the effects of representation on case processing and dispositions.

This study uses data collected by the National Juvenile Court Data Archive (NJCDA) to analyze the availability of and effects of counsel in delinquency and status offense cases disposed of in 1984. The six states included in this study were selected solely because their data files included information on representation by counsel.

The NJCDA's unit of count is "cases disposed" of by a juvenile court. Typically, juvenile delinquency cases begin with a referral to a county's juvenile court or a juvenile probation or intake department. Many of these referrals are closed at intake with some type of *informal* disposition: dismissal, counseling, warning, referral to another agency, or probation.

The sample in this study consists exclusively of petitioned delinquency and status offense cases. It excludes all juvenile court referrals for abuse, dependency, or neglect, as well as routine traffic violations. Only formally *petitioned* delinquency and status cases are analyzed because the right to counsel announced in *Gault* attaches only after the formal initiation of delinquency proceedings.

The filing of a petition—the formal initiation of the juvenile process—is comparable legally to the filing of a complaint, information, or indictment in the adult criminal process. Since different county intake or probation units within a state, as well as the various states, use different criteria to decide whether or not to file a formal delinquency petition, the cross-state comparisons reported here involve very different samples of delinquent populations. The common denominator of all these cases is that they were formally processed in their respective jurisdictions. The proportion of referred cases to petitioned cases differs markedly, from a high of 62.8% in Nebraska to a low of 10.7% in North Dakota.

In most jurisdictions, a juvenile offender will be arraigned on the petition. Since the constitutional right to counsel attaches in juvenile court only after the filing of the petition, it is typically at this stage, if at all, that counsel will be appointed to represent a juvenile. At the arraignment, the juvenile admits or denies the allegations in the petition. In many cases, juveniles may admit the allegations of the petition at their arraignment and have their case disposed of without the presence of an attorney.

The types of underlying offenses represented in the formally filed delinquency petitions differ substantially; the large urban jurisdictions confront very different and more serious delinquency than do the more rural, midwestern states. In this study, the offenses reported by the states are regrouped into six analytical categories. The "felony/minor" offense distinction provides both an indicator of seriousness and is legally relevant for the right to counsel. Offenses are also classified as person, property, other delinquency, and status. Combining person and property with the felony and minor distinctions produces a six-item offense scale for cross-state comparisons. When a petition alleges more than one offense, the youth is classified on the basis of the most serious charge. This study also uses two indicators of the severity of disposition: out-of-home placement and secure confinement.

DATA AND ANALYSIS

Part of these analyses treat the availability and role of counsel as a dependent variable using case characteristics and court processing factors as independent variables. Other parts treat counsel as an independent variable, assessing its relative impact on juvenile court case processing and dispositions. These analyses attempt to answer the interrelated questions regarding when lawyers are appointed to represent juveniles, why they are appointed, and what difference it makes whether or not a youth is represented.

Petitions and Offenses

Initially, the appearance of counsel must be placed in the larger context of juvenile justice administration in the respective states. The juvenile courts in the various states confront very different delinquent populations. In part, these differences reflect the nature of pre-petition screening. While California, Nebraska, and Pennsylvania courts formally petition approximately half of their juvenile court referrals, North Dakota juvenile courts only charge about 10.7% of their referrals. The numbers of petitions involved also differ substantially. The large, urban states handle far more cases than the rural midwestern states. Indeed, Philadelphia alone processes more delinquency petitions than Nebraska and North Dakota together.

The nature of the offenses petitioned also differs substantially among the states. Felony offenses against the person—homicide, rape, aggravated assault, and robbery—are much more prevalent in the large, urban states.

The states also differ markedly in their treatment of status offenders. Pennsylvania/Philadelphia juvenile courts do not have jurisdiction over status offenders. Similarly, status offenders in California appear to be referred to juvenile courts only as a last resort. By contrast, in the midwestern states, status offenses are the second most common type of delinquency cases handled.

Rates of Representation

Although *Gault* held that every juvenile was constitutionally entitled to "the guiding hand of counsel at every step of the process," *Gault's* promise remains unrealized in half of these jurisdictions.

The large, urban states are far more successful in assuring that juveniles receive the assistance of counsel than are the midwestern states. Overall, between 85% and 95% of the juveniles in the large, urban states receive the assistance of counsel as contrasted with between 37.5% and 52.7% of the juveniles in the midwestern states. In every jurisdiction and regardless of the overall rate of representation, public attorneys handle the vast bulk of delinquency petitions by ratios of between 3:1 and 10:1.

It is possible to provide very high levels of defense representation to juveniles adjudicated delinquent. More than 95% of the juveniles in Philadelphia and New York State, and 85% or more in Pennsylvania and California, were represented. Since the large, urban states process a greater volume of delinquency cases, their success in delivering legal services is all the more impressive. While it may be more difficult to deliver legal services easily in all parts of the rural midwestern states, county-by-county analysis in Minnesota shows substantial disparities within the state; even the largest county in the state with a well-developed public defender system provides representation to less than half the juveniles. These variations suggest that rates of representation reflect deliberate policy decisions.

One pattern that emerges in all of the states is a direct relationship between the seriousness of the offense and the rates of representation. Juveniles charged with felonies—offenses against person or property—and those with offenses against the person generally have higher rates of representation than the state's overall rate.

A second and similar pattern is the appearance of larger proportions of private attorneys on behalf of juveniles charged with felony offenses—person and property—and offenses against the person than appear in the other offense categories. Perhaps the greater seriousness of those offenses and their potential consequences encourage juveniles or their families to seek the assistance of private counsel. Conversely, private attorneys are least likely to be retained by parents to represent the status offenders with whom the parents are often in conflict.

Offense and Disposition

There is extensive research on the determinants of juvenile court dispositions. However, "even a superficial review of the relevant literature leaves one with the rather uncomfortable feeling that the only consistent finding of prior research is that there are no consistencies in the determinants of the decision-making process."

In general, the seriousness of the present offense and the length of the prior record—the so-called legal variables—explain most of the variance that can be accounted for in juvenile sentencing, with some additional influence of race.

Although this cross-state comparison cannot identify fully the determinants of dispositions, the data lend themselves to an exploration of the relationships among offenses, dispositions, and representation by an attorney. The states differ markedly in their overall use of out-of-home placements and secure confinement, ranging from a high of 30.8%/14.5% in California to a low of 10.3%/1.1% in Philadelphia. The ratio of out-of-home placement to secure confinement also varies from 17:1 in Pennsylvania to about 2:1 in California.

As expected, the seriousness of the present offense substantially alters a youth's risk of removal and confinement. In every state, felony offenses against the person garner both the highest rates of out-of-home placement and secure confinement, typically followed either by minor offenses against the person or felony offenses against property, for example, burglary. Conversely, minor property offenses—primarily petty theft and shoplifting—and status offenses have the lowest rates of removal or confinement.

Offense and Disposition by Counsel

When juveniles commit felonies against the person in California, 39.5%/20.4% receive out-of-home placement and secure confinement dispositions. Youths *with counsel* were somewhat more likely to receive severe dispositions than those *without counsel*—40% versus 35.5% out of home and 21.0% versus 15.4% secure confinement.

Youths with lawyers receive more severe dispositions than do those without lawyers. With 12 possible comparisons in each state—six offense categories times two dispositions—represented, youths received more severe dispositions than unrepresented youth in every category in Minnesota, New York, and Pennsyl-vania, in all but one in California and Philadelphia, and in all but two in Nebraska. Even in the highest representation jurisdictions—New York and Philadelphia—this pattern prevails; there was virtually no secure confinement of unrepresented juveniles in these locales.

While the relationship between representation and more severe disposition is consistent in the different jurisdictions, the explanation of this relationship is not readily apparent. It may be that the presence of lawyers antagonizes traditional juvenile court judges and subtly influences the eventual disposition imposed. However, the pattern also prevails in the jurisdictions with very high rates of representation where the presence of counsel is not unusual. Perhaps judges discern the eventual disposition early in the proceedings and appoint counsel more frequently when an out-of-home placement or secure confinement is anticipated. Conversely, judges may exhibit more leniency if a youth is not represented. Or, still another possibility is that other variables besides the present offense may influence both the appointment of counsel and the eventual disposition.

Detention by Offense

Detention, as used here, refers to a juvenile's custody status following referral but prior to court action. It is important to note, however, that detention is coded differently in various jurisdictions. Regardless of the jurisdictional definition of detention, its use follows similar patterns. Juveniles committing felonies against the person are the most likely to be detained, followed either by those committing minor offenses against the person or felony offenses against property. Since the evidentiary distinctions between a felony and a minor offense against the person, for example, the degree of injury to the victim, may not be apparent at the time of detention, these patterns are not surprising.

Detention and Counsel

Detention, particularly if it continues for more than a day, is a legally significant juvenile court intervention that also requires the assistance of counsel. Every jurisdiction provides for a prompt detention hearing to determine the existence of probable cause, the presence of grounds for detention, and the child's custody status pending trial.

In Minnesota, 66.1% of the juveniles charged with felony offenses against the person were represented, and 24.6% of them were detained. However, 75.0% of those who were detained were represented as contrasted with 63.8% of those who were not detained.

For each state, a comparison reveals a consistent pattern—youths who were held in detention had higher rates of representation than did juveniles who were not. In four of the six states at every level of offense, detained youths were more likely to be represented. In Nebraska, in five of the six levels of offenses, detained youths were more likely to be represented. Again, only in North Dakota, with its small numbers and low rates of representation, does the pattern break down.

Detention and Dispositions

Several studies have examined the determinants of detention and the relationship between a child's pretrial detention status and subsequent disposition. These studies report that while several of the same variables affect both rates of detention and subsequent disposition, after appropriate controls, detention per se exhibits an independent effect on dispositions.

The results are remarkably consistent; in five of the six jurisdictions and at every offense level, youths who were detained received more severe dispositions than those who were not. Even in North Dakota with its small numbers, the relationship between detention and secure confinement appears in most offense categories.

The same factors that determine the initial detention decision appear to influence the ultimate disposition as well. However, when one compares the zero-order relationship between offense and disposition with the relationship between offense/detention and disposition, it is apparent that detained youths are significantly more at risk for out-of-home placement and secure confinement than are nondetained youths. Generally, pretrial detention more than doubles a youth's probability of receiving a secure confinement disposition.

Counsel, Detention, and Disposition

A detained youth who is represented by counsel is more likely to receive a severe disposition than a detained youth who is not represented. In New York, California, and Pennsylvania, which had very high rates of representation, the represented/detained youths consistently received more severe dispositions than the small group of unrepresented/detained juveniles, as was also the case in Nebraska. Only in Minnesota and North Dakota was the presence of counsel not an "aggravating" factor at the sentencing of detained youth. Again, this may simply be the result of dwindling numbers, or perhaps the factors that influenced the initial detention decision took precedence over the presence of counsel in those states.

Prior Referrals and Disposition

Within each offense level, there is a nearly perfect linear relationship between additional prior referrals and the likelihood of more severe dispositions. For example, in Minnesota, 35.7% of those juveniles with no prior record who commit a felony offense against the person receive an out-of-home placement, as compared with 51.9% of those with one or two priors, 84.8% of those with three or four priors, and 100.0% of those with five or more priors. The same pattern obtains for secure confinement dispositions. A similar direct relationship between prior referrals and dispositions is evident in Nebraska as well. Clearly, then, after controlling for the seriousness of the present offense, the addition of a prior record strongly influences the sentencing practices of juvenile courts.

Prior Referrals and Rates of Representation

The aggregate rates of representation are the composite of juveniles with and without prior referrals. For example, in Minnesota, in 1986, 77.3% of all juveniles charged with felony offenses against the person were represented. However, this proportion of representation consisted of 73.6% with no priors, 81.5% with one or two, 89.3% with three or four, and 100.0% with five or more priors. A similar relationship between prior referrals and rates of representation prevails in Minnesota at all offense levels. Thus, in Minnesota prior referrals increase both the likelihood of out-of-home placement and secure confinement as well as the appointment of counsel. In Nebraska, by contrast, the relationship between prior referrals and rates of representation is not nearly as consistent. The major difference in rates of representation occurs between youths with no prior referrals and those with one or two priors.

Disposition by Attorneys by Priors

Youths with attorneys are more likely to receive out-of-home placement and secure confinement than are those without counsel. In effect, controlling for present offense and prior record simultaneously, larger proportions of youths with lawyers receive out-of-home placements and secure confinement than do those without. In Minnesota, with 48 possible comparisons—six offenses times dispositions times four priors—represented, youths received more severe dispositions in 44 instances. In Nebraska,

represented youths received more severe dispositions in 39 comparisons.

DISCUSSION AND CONCLUSION

Nearly 20 years after *Gault* held that juveniles are constitutionally entitled to the assistance of counsel, half of the jurisdictions in this study are still not in compliance. In Nebraska, Minnesota, and North Dakota, nearly half or more of delinquent and status offenders do not have lawyers. Moreover, many juveniles who receive out-of-home placement and even secure confinement were adjudicated delinquent and sentenced without the assistance of counsel. In light of the findings from other jurisdictions, it is apparent that many juveniles are unrepresented.

Clearly, it is possible to provide counsel for the vast majority of young offenders. California, Pennsylvania and Philadelphia, and New York do so routinely. What is especially impressive in those jurisdictions is the very low numbers of uncounseled juveniles who receive out-of-home placement or secure confinement dispositions. While this study shows substantial differences in rates of representation among the different states, it cannot account for the greater availability of counsel in some of the jurisdictions than in others.

There are direct legislative policy implications of the findings reported here. In those states in which juveniles are routinely unrepresented, legislation mandating the automatic and nonwaivable appointment of counsel at the earliest stage in delinquency proceeding is necessary. As long as it is possible for a juvenile to waive the right to counsel, juvenile court judges will find such waivers. Short of mandatory and nonwaivable counsel, a prohibition on waivers of counsel without prior consultation with and the concurrence of counsel would assure that any eventual waiver was truly "knowing, intelligent, and voluntary." Moreover, a requirement of consultation with counsel prior to waiver would assure the development of legal services delivery systems that would then facilitate the more routine representation of juveniles. At the very least, legislation should prohibit the removal from home or incarceration of any juvenile who was not provided with counsel. Such a limitation on dispositions is already the law for adult criminal defendants and for juveniles in some jurisdictions, and it is apparently the informal practice in New York and Pennsylvania where virtually no unrepresented juveniles were removed and confined.

Apart from simply documenting variations in rates of representation, this research also examined the determinants of representation. It examined the relationship between "legal variables"—seriousness of offense, detention status, and prior referrals—and the appointment of counsel.

There is obviously multicollinearity between the factors producing more severe dispositions and the factors influencing the appointment of counsel. Each legal variable that is associated with a more severe disposition is also associated with greater rates of representation. And yet, within the limitations of this research design, it appears that in virtually every jurisdiction, representation by counsel is an aggravating factor in a juvenile's disposition. When controlling for the seriousness of the present offense, unrepresented juveniles seem to fare better than those with lawyers. When controlling for offense and detention status, unrepresented juveniles again fare better than those with representation. When controlling seriousness of the present offense and prior referrals, the presence of counsel produces more severe dispositions. In short, while the legal variables enhance the probabilities of representation, the fact of representation appears to exert an independent effect on the severity of dispositions.

Although this phenomenon has been alluded to in other studies, this research provides the strongest evidence yet that representation by counsel redounds to the disadvantage of a juvenile. Why? One possible explanation is that attorneys in juvenile court are simply incompetent and prejudice their clients' cases. While systematic evaluations of the actual performance of counsel in juvenile court are lacking, the available evidence suggests that even in jurisdictions where counsel are routinely appointed, there are grounds for concern about their effectiveness. Public defender offices in many jurisdictions assign their least capable lawyers or newest staff attorneys to juvenile courts to get trial experience, and these neophytes may receive less adequate supervision than their prosecutorial counterparts. Similarly, court-appointed counsel may be beholden to the judges who select them and more concerned with maintaining an ongoing relationship with the court than vigorously protecting the interests of their clients.

Perhaps, however, the relationship between the presence of counsel and the increased severity of dispositions is spurious. Obviously, this study cannot control simultaneously for all the variables that influence dispositional decision making. It may be that early in a proceeding, a juvenile court judge's greater familiarity with a case may alert him or her to the eventual disposition that will be imposed, and counsel may be appointed in anticipation of more severe consequences. In many jurisdictions, the same judge who presides at a youth's arraignment and detention hearing will later decide the case on the merits and then impose a sentence. Perhaps, the initial decision to appoint counsel is based on the same evidence developed at those earlier stages that also influences later dispositions.

Another possible explanation is that juvenile court judges may treat more formally and severely juveniles who appear with counsel than those without. Within statutory limits, judges may feel less constrained when sentencing a youth who is represented. Such may be the price of formal procedures. While not necessarily punishing juveniles who are represented, judges may incline leniency toward those youths who appear unaided and "throw themselves on the mercy of the court."

QUESTIONS FOR DISCUSSION AND WRITING

1. What is sometimes true about lawyers representing juveniles in more traditional "therapeutic" juvenile courts?
2. Although *Gault* held that every juvenile was constitutionally entitled to "the guiding hand of counsel at every step of the process," what did the author find was true in 1984? Which states were more successful in ensuring that juveniles receive the assistance of counsel? What two patterns emerged?
3. What direct legislative policy implications of the findings reported in the article does the author suggest?

THE SYSTEM LEGACY

Responding to Juvenile Crime: Lessons Learned

PETER W. GREENWOOD

UNTIL the early 1970s, the typical placement for serious or chronic delinquents in most states consisted of large congregate training schools. In 1971, Jerome Miller, then head of the Department of Youth Services (DYS) in Massachusetts, took a significant step when he abruptly removed most of the youths from that state's training schools and placed them in a variety of small community-based institutions and programs. Those youths requiring secure care were placed in a number of small (typically 20- to 30-bed) facilities.

An evaluation of the Massachusetts reforms, which compared outcomes for samples of youths committed to DYS before and after the reforms occurred, found higher average recidivism rates for the postreform youths. However, in those parts of the state where the new reforms were most successfully implemented, as indicated by the character and diversity of their programs on an objective rating scale, postreform recidivism rates appeared to be lower. A more recent attempt to evaluate the Massachusetts model compared recidivism rates for all youths

released by the Massachusetts DYS in 1985 with those reported for several other states (California, Florida, Pennsylvania, Utah, and Wisconsin) and found the Massachusetts rates to be among the lowest. However, the significance of these comparisons is obscured by systematic differences in the characteristics of youths committed to these state programs and by variations in the reporting of juvenile police and court contacts.

TRENDS IN JUVENILE CORRECTIONS POLICY

Twenty-five years after the Massachusetts experiment, the debate over the most effective method of dealing with chronic and serious juvenile offenders continues. Maryland recently attempted to copy some of the Massachusetts reforms by closing one of two state-run juvenile institutions, the Montrose Training School, which at that time had a population of approximately 320 youths. A postrelease sample of youths who probably would have been sent to Montrose had it not been closed had higher recidivism rates than groups who completed Montrose or were there when it closed. While proponents continue to urge other states to adopt Massachusetts-type reforms, a number of states, with California the most prominent example, continue to rely heavily on large

Source: Greenwood, Peter W. "Responding to Juvenile Crime: Lessons Learned." *The Future of Children* (Winter 1996) 6/3:75-85. Reprinted with permission of the David and Lucile Packard Foundation. *The Future of Children* journals and executive summaries are available free of charge by faxing mailing information to: Circulation Department (415) 948-6498.

custodial institutions for handling their most seriously delinquent youths.

The most popular recent reform in the handling of serious or chronically delinquent youths is the increasing use of waiver or transfer of juvenile cases to adult criminal court. Between 1988 and 1992, the number of juveniles waived to criminal courts increased by 68%, from 7,000 to 11,700. For less seriously delinquent youths, a number of jurisdictions are expanding their use of in-home tracking, day treatment, and family treatment programs first pioneered in Massachusetts.

DIFFICULTIES IN EVALUATION

Little is known about which correctional approaches are best suited to particular types of youths at least in part because there have been only a limited number of careful program evaluations. Although many judges and correctional practitioners appear to believe they can assess a program's effectiveness by observing and talking with its participants, such anecdotal evaluation is often clearly wrong. A youth's improved manners and respectful demeanor may quickly disappear when he returns to the influence of his old neighborhood. Moreover, the few youths who do come back to visit a program or the juvenile court are probably not representative of the typical participant.

The effectiveness of any one particular program is unknown unless it is evaluated. At a minimum, follow-up recidivism data (rearrest or self-reports) for an adequate sample of participants must be compared with those for an appropriate control group. Because the primary goal of juvenile corrections is community safety, recidivism is used as the minimal measure. Other measures, such as subsequent attainment of a general educational development certificate or employment, are used less frequently.

To be useful to policymakers and practitioners outside the program, the results of any program evaluation must include a complete description and documentation of the program's procedures and methods of treatment. Administrators tend to incorporate a variety of currently popular methods in any one program, rather than testing one single well-defined approach, creating an additional impediment to program evaluation.

To reach a definitive conclusion about the effectiveness of a particular approach, it is best if results from several individual evaluations are pooled. The positive effects observed in a particular study may be attributable to chance, an unusually effective program administrator, staff, or particularly ineffective programming applied to the comparison group. The preferred method for assessing results from a number of studies involves the statistical techniques of meta-analysis, which allow the reviewer to compare results across programs in a common framework while controlling for differences in sample characteristics and research methods. Results from several recent meta-analyses of juvenile corrections evaluations are discussed later in this article.

WHAT WORKS IN CHANGING DELINQUENT BEHAVIOR

One of the primary goals of the juvenile justice system has always been the salvation of the minor from a self-destructive life of crime. While public protection has always been an implicit goal of the system, in recent years many state legislatures have also explicitly included it as one of the system's primary goals. Both of these objectives require the juvenile justice system to pursue the difficult task of changing individual behavior patterns. Changes in delinquent behavior are pursued by the juvenile justice system through the competing mechanisms of deterrence and rehabilitation.

Deterrence refers to the discouraging effect that threatened punishments have on potential offenders. Research efforts to date have not supplied compelling evidence that increasing the severity of sanctions deters more crime, but available evidence suggests that the certainty with which sanctions are applied is much more important than their severity. This finding is often used to justify the imposition of more consistent sentencing and requiring some sanctions for all offenders, regardless of their prior record.

Rehabilitation refers to the process of attempting to change the propensity of individual offenders to commit crimes through training, education, and other services. The rehabilitative role of juvenile correctional programs was set back considerably by a series of scholarly reviews of the evaluative literature in the late 1970s which were interpreted as saying that "nothing worked" or, more precisely, that there was insufficient evidence to conclude that treatment worked or that any one particular method of treatment was more effective than any other.

A number of critics responded to the generally defeatist tone of the "nothing works" reviews by pointing out that each of the reviews contained numerous references to programs that did work and that a more rigorous screening on therapeutic integrity and program quality could identify programs that were effective.

When reviewers began using the new technique of meta-analysis, systematic reviews of the evaluation literature began turning up evidence of consistent positive effects for particular intervention strategies. The most thorough of these meta-analyses for juveniles was conducted by Mark Lipsey and covers more than 400 published and unpublished evaluations of juvenile programs conducted since 1945. Lipsey's study also goes beyond most of the others in coding the characteristics of the interventions, the context in which they were administered, the population that received them, and the evaluation methodology. At this time, Lipsey's findings serve as the baseline from which all observations about the treatment of juvenile offenders are made. The findings from the review which pertain to this article are summarized below.

THE OVERALL EFFECTIVENESS OF CORRECTIONAL TREATMENT

Starting from a baseline recidivism rate of 50%, Lipsey reports an average 5-percentage-point reduction in recidivism or a 10% improvement for all the programs evaluated. Because effect sizes are attenuated by the unreliability of the outcome measures used (recorded arrests), it is likely that the actual effects of treatment are closer to 10 percentage points, or a 20% reduction in recidivism from the comparison groups. As might be expected, Lipsey found that evaluations in which control groups received some intervention showed less contrast (smaller effect size) than those in which the comparison group received no treatment at all.

The remainder of this section summarizes some of the other key variables that appear to be associated with effect size.

- Institutional versus community placements: Treatment in public facilities, custodial institutions, and the juvenile justice system were associated with smaller effect sizes than treatment in community-based programs.
- Treatment modality: Structured approaches that attempt to train subjects in new behaviors and skills were associated with larger effect sizes than less structured programs such as counseling and general supervision.
- Intensity and exposure: A "modest positive relationship" was found between effect size and treatment intensity and duration.
- Risk level of clients: There was a slight tendency for studies of juveniles with higher risk levels, as indicated by their prior records or the recidivism rate of the control group, to show larger effects of treatment when compared with those whose risk levels were lower, but this difference was not statistically significant.
- Organization, staffing, and management: Higher levels of involvement by the researcher in the treatment program were associated with higher effect sizes, suggesting that operating the program in a manner consistent with its original intent and design is important.

- Methodological factors: Greater attrition from treatment or control groups was associated with smaller effects sizes, as were larger samples and more outcome variables. Any significant attrition from either experimental or control groups within an evaluation study can affect the comparability of the two groups and make the interpretation of outcome results problematic. Some researchers question the appropriateness of including nonrandomized studies in meta-analyses.

ASSESSING THE PRIMARY JUVENILE JUSTICE DISPOSITIONAL ALTERNATIVES

Once a youth is adjudicated delinquent, the central task of the juvenile court is to order and oversee the appropriate disposition. The principal dispositional alternatives available in the juvenile justice system are discussed below.

Waiver or Transfer to Adult Court

The increased use of transfers of juveniles to adult court is usually justified on the grounds that the criminal courts can impose more severe sanctions than the juvenile court. Studies conducted in the late 1970s and early 1980s found that the majority of juveniles sentenced in adult courts received probation or some other alternative to incarceration. A study of juvenile and young adult robbery and burglary cases disposed of in three California cities found that juvenile court dispositions were more severe, after controlling for offense severity and prior record. A similar study in an East Coast jurisdiction found no significant differences in the minimum and maximum terms imposed on similar juvenile and young adult defendants in juvenile and adult court.

However, a more recent study by the General Accounting Office found that the majority of juvenile offenders now being transferred to criminal courts and convicted of serious offenses are receiving prison terms. The study did not report any results on time served, conviction rates, or recidivism—all factors that need to be considered in assessing the impacts of waiver.

Custodial Institutions

Despite intensive lobbying efforts to close large juvenile training institutions, many states continue to operate these facilities, some of which were built before 1900. The primary criticisms leveled against traditional state training schools have been that they offered sterile and unimaginative programs, were inappropriate places to run rehabilitative programs, and fostered abuse and mistreatment of their charges. Critics seek to replace them with community-based programs because such programs provide a more realistic setting in which youths can learn and practice social skills and because they allow youths to develop or maintain contacts with their families, schools, and employers. The large institutions are defended on the grounds that community programs have not been shown to be more effective and/or that their institutional programs offer more protection to the public.

In terms of postrelease arrest rates, the Lipsey analysis described in the previous section found a significant advantage in favor of community programs. Whether or not this advantage is sufficient to justify the somewhat greater risk created by letting youths reside in the community while participating in rehabilitative programs is a function of the specific risks represented by the population under consideration, the intensity of their supervision while in the community, and the community's tolerance for the kind of risk they represent. The large growth in private community placements over the past 10 years demonstrates that many communities believe the risks are worth it.

Where large custodial institutions continue to operate, the Lipsey analysis provides guidance concerning effective programming within these settings. Some of the advantages of community programs can be obtained by breaking a large institution's population and staff down into small self-contained units which more closely parallel the size of community programs. For example, in Massachusetts and Utah, secure institutions are built to accommodate client populations of no more than 20 or 30 youths. Other strategies include involving community members in the daily activities of the institution and simulating the social and economic systems that are found on the outside.

Wilderness Programs

A number of private providers who are willing to take the kind of serious delinquents who are usually placed in state training schools have found that they can operate more open programs in isolated wilderness camps, where the remoteness of the location provides the necessary security and overcoming the challenges of the environment becomes an aspect of the program. An evaluation based on 90 youths committed to VisionQuest, a prominent provider of this type of program, found that a significantly smaller fraction were rearrested during the first 6 to 18 months after their release than a similar group who had participated in a probation department camp program (emphasizing primarily custody, classroom education, and recreation) the previous year.

Group Homes

For youths who need to be placed out of their homes but do not represent such a risk that they need to be placed in a secure program, group homes are the placement of choice. They can be designed to provide as much structure as necessary, while allowing youths to attend school and/or participate in other community programs. Because group homes can take advantage of existing community resources such as education, job training, and medical services, they are less costly to the juvenile justice system.

Aftercare and Parole

Assistance with community reintegration, relapse prevention, service advocacy, and surveillance are just a few of the many justifications cited to support the provision of aftercare services to graduates of institutional programs. In spite of these arguments, very few jurisdictions provide aftercare for any significant fraction of their youth, and there is little in the way of evaluative research. A recent evaluation of intensive follow-up supervision in Pennsylvania found that this effort was effective in reducing postrelease arrests, primarily by reincarcerating failing youths sooner than would be likely without such supervision. Another evaluation of efforts to provide intensive postrelease supervision and assistance to both youths and their families in Detroit, Michigan, and Pittsburgh, Pennsylvania, found no effect of such efforts on recidivism or self-reported delinquency. The Lipsey meta-analysis found little or no effectiveness associated with traditional parole.

Boot Camps

Boot camps for either juveniles or adults have recently attracted wide political support. Both politicians and the public appear to be impressed by the strict discipline, physical labor, and military drill that such programs entail. Since their inception in 1983, more than 29 states, the Federal Bureau of Prisons, 9 juvenile systems, and 10 local jurisdictions have initiated such programs, without any evidence as to their effects on recidivism. In addition, these programs are supposed to cost only a fraction of a regular prison or training school commitment because they require just 90 days in a residential setting. Many boot camp programs also involve extensive aftercare components.

A recently completed evaluation of eight state boot camp programs for young adult offenders concluded that four of the programs had no effect on recidivism, one resulted in higher recidivism rates (possibly because it put little emphasis on treatment), and three showed improvements in some recidivism measures. Boot camp programs are difficult to evaluate because of the high washout or dropout rate of program participants. In the three programs found to be effective by MacKenzie and colleagues, the average dropout rate was 38%.

A recent evaluation of a 90-day juvenile wilderness boot camp in Michigan, where challenging outdoor activities were used to support teamwork and increase self-confidence, found that youths assigned to the challenge camp had higher recidivism rates than similar youths assigned to regular training schools. The program included an ambitious 9-month aftercare component run by private providers. In the Michigan program, 22% of participating youths were escalated to regular training school placements during the residential phase, and another 47% were escalated or went absent without leave during the community aftercare phase. Instead of participating in a 90-day residential program with 9 months of aftercare, youths assigned to the Michigan challenge program averaged 322 days in some form of custody during the first 2 years after placement in the program.

Community Supervision and Programming

Jurisdictions serious about working with youths have developed a wide array of programs offering varying degrees of supervision and services. At the low-intensity end of the spectrum are performance contracts and higher-than-usual frequencies of contact with volunteer case manager/trackers. At the high-intensity end are dawn-to-dusk education and training programs such as those run by Associated Marine Institutes (AMI) in more than a dozen (mostly southern) states. These programs provide meals, work with parents, arrange supplementary recreational or work experience activities on weekends, and can lead to certification as a scuba diver. It is primarily evaluations of the early forerunners of these rapidly spreading nonresidential programs, which were often developed or initiated by academic researchers, that provide the basis for Lipsey's finding that

noncustodial, nonjuvenile justice programs are more effective than other forms of treatment.

Lipsey argues that no one approach is clearly better than the others. In addition to private sponsorship and community setting, the more effective programs all appear to have multiple modes of intervention, higher levels of intensity and duration, and greater structure in common. They are more theoretically rigorous, ambitious, and tightly executed.

Probation and Diversion

Probation or diversion is the most frequent disposition for all juvenile arrests because it is inexpensive. Because the majority of juveniles who are arrested one or two times are never arrested again, as a practical matter, probation or diversion is the most reasonable option in most cases. However, for youths with multiple risk factors (several prior arrests, arrests at an early age, drug or gang involvement, or parental problems) probation and diversion are not effective options.

Probation and diversion cover a range of low-level services, monitoring, and performance obligations. Probation is supervised by the juvenile justice department once a youth is adjudicated delinquent, while diversion is overseen by social services or a community agency in cases where prosecution was suspended. As a condition of probation or diversion, a youth may be required to refrain from certain activities and complete certain programming, community service, or restitution obligations. In both instances, there is an implied threat of a harsher sanction for any subsequent offense. In some jurisdictions, such as the state of Washington, the diversion process is highly formalized, with specific guidelines for sanctions to be imposed by a community board. In other jurisdictions, it is routine and informal with little effort at customizing or enforcing sanctions.

In reality, an overworked probation officer who sees a client only once a month has little ability either to monitor the client's behavior or to exert much of an influence over his life.

Augmented forms of probation can be effective. Probation combined with intensive supervision, restitution, or other types of enhancement was found by Lipsey to have had positive effects, albeit considerably fewer than the more ambitious and structured multimodal methods.

The Lipsey meta-analysis also suggests that more intensive behavioral and skill-oriented interventions might be more effective than routine probation or diversion with high-risk delinquents if these interventions focus on solving problems with both the youths and their families. This is the strategy represented by Eight Percent Solution, a program established by the probation department in Orange County, California, which targets the 8% of juvenile arrestees who account for 50% of their arrests.

Treatment Methods That Do More
Harm Than Good

Some intervention methods appear to have negative effects—that is, to lead to worse outcomes than no treatment at all. Follow-up studies of the Cambridge-Somerville project, which provided trained volunteer mentors to at-risk youth, have clearly shown that even well-intended interventions can have harmful effects. In Lipsey's analysis, nonjuvenile justice individual counseling, vocational programs, and deterrent schemes such as Scared Straight produced negative average effects. Another method, or possible side effect, often cautioned against by delinquency researchers, is bringing delinquents together in any unsupervised or unstructured setting. Negative peer pressure appears to be particularly strong in supporting continued delinquency.

CONCLUSION

To achieve an optimal balance between effective treatment, accountability, and community protection, the available evidence suggests that juvenile courts require access to a broad array of dispositional options. These extend from formal diversion to local accountability boards or social services, through in-home supervision and day treatment, to a variety of out-of-home placements providing different levels of security and types of treatment. Methods that concentrate on changing individual behavior patterns which lead to delinquency and improving pro-social skills are likely to be 10% to 20% more effective in reducing subsequent delinquency than less structured programs that emphasize individual counseling or general education.

The evidence also suggests that a certain degree of skill and experience is required to develop and run both institutional and community-based correctional programs that are effective in changing behaviors. While effective programs can be run by either public or private agencies, meta-analyses and program surveys suggest that such programs are more likely to be developed by private providers, probably because they are usually held to higher standards of performance and accountability and are more free to innovate.

As courts determine appropriate individual dispositions, considerations of public safety and appropriate treatment should not be confused. While a youth's instant offense may be a useful indicator of his potential risk to the community, it is not a good indicator of what kind of programming is required to change his behavior. All things being equal, treatment programs run in community settings are likely to be more effective in reducing recidivism than similar programs provided in institutions. Whether or not the risk of additional crime posed by allowing particular categories of youths to remain in the community can be justified by the reduction in their recidivism rate can be determined only by assessing both of these parameters and weighing them carefully. This same calculation can be made for youths who are considered for transfer to adult criminal courts, although no state appears to be doing it explicitly. There is currently no direct evidence regarding whether increases in potential punishment and immediate community protection achieved through adult court are accomplished at the cost of higher recidivism rates.

There are no simple solutions or magic cures for the juvenile court to apply to problems of juvenile delinquency. The most effective systems and processes will be flexible and continuously experimental in their approach, provide a wide range of treatment and placement options, and be accountable for their results.

QUESTIONS FOR DISCUSSION AND WRITING

1. What six key variables were associated with effect size for the overall effectiveness of correctional treatment?
2. What did research on waiver or transfer to adult court find in the 1970s and 1980s? More recently?
3. What are some intervention methods that appear to lead to worse outcomes than no treatment at all?

Gender Bias in Juvenile Justice Processing: Implications of the JJDP Act

DONNA M. BISHOP

CHARLES E. FRAZIER

THE criminological literature has traditionally depicted female juvenile misconduct as sexual or "relational" in nature. Increasingly, however, commentators have recognized that this picture is distorted and inaccurate, reflecting biases in American culture and in the juvenile justice system.

Over the last 30 years there have been numerous studies of how the juvenile justice system deals with male and female offenders. A historical review of their findings reveals an interesting pattern. With few exceptions, the findings of analyses of data collected more that 15 years ago are remarkably consistent and can be briefly summarized. The findings of this body of research suggest that females were considerably more likely than males to be referred to the juvenile justice system for status offenses—that is, for "juvenile only" offenses, which would not constitute crimes if committed by adults (e.g., runaway, incorrigibility, and truancy). Moreover, once referred, female status offenders were more likely than their male counterparts to be petitioned to formal court processing, to be placed in preadjudicatory detention, and to be incarcerated upon the judicial disposition of their cases.

In contrast, when we consider acts of delinquency (offenses that would be crimes if committed by adults), research for this same time period indicates that delinquent males frequently received harsher treatment than delinquent females. Consistent with the so-called "chivalry" or "paternalism" hypothesis, police were less likely to arrest females suspected of person or property crimes. Moreover, postarrest processing decisions appeared to amplify the gender differential apparent in the arrest findings: Young female offenders were less likely than their male counterparts to be formally charged with criminal offenses; and, if charged, they were less likely than males to be institutionalized for these offenses.

In sum, the findings of early studies of the influence of gender on juvenile justice processing suggest that police officers, intake personnel, judges, and other court officials supported a sexual double standard. Compared to their male counterparts, female status offenders were singled out for especially harsh protectionist treatment. At the same time, male delinquents (that is, those who committed criminal-type offenses) received harsher and more punitive penalties than their female counterparts.

In the past decade, this picture has begun to change. Recent studies have challenged the traditional understanding of the role that gender plays in juvenile justice decision making. For example, two relatively recent studies of the court referral and judicial disposition stages of processing report no difference in the treatment accorded male and female status offenders. In addition, while some recent studies report that males charged with criminal-type offenses are treated more harshly than their female counterparts, several other studies find no evidence that gender influences delinquency case outcomes.

At the very least, these more recent studies suggest that the role of gender in juvenile case processing is less clear today than it was 15 years ago, when studies consistently reported substantial gender differentials. Conservatively, one might conclude only that the impact of gender has become more equivocal: There are about as many recent studies reporting that gender plays no significant role in justice decision making as there are studies reporting significant gender effects. Even in those recent studies that report significant gender differences, however, the magnitude of these differences is considerably smaller than typically found in earlier years. Thus, the record seems to suggest that gender plays a less significant role in juvenile justice processing today than it did in the past.

This observation lends itself to several possible interpretations. One explanation is that sociocultural changes—chief among them, the feminist movement—may have produced attitudinal changes that have in turn prompted more egalitarian treatment of male and female offenders.

A second explanation for the apparently diminishing role of gender in the processing of status offenders is that significant legal changes have forced more evenhanded treatment of males and females, even in the absence of changes in the attitudes of juvenile justice officials. One such legal change was brought about by the passage of the Juvenile Justice and Delinquency Prevention Act of 1974 (hereinafter "the JJDP Act" or "the Act"), which mandates the deinstitutionalization of status offenders. Under the JJDP Act, participating states may not place status offenders in any secure facility, including jails, police lockups, juvenile detention centers, or training schools. One consequence of this change in the law may be that it has become difficult for justice officials to practice differentially protectionist policies toward female status offenders. That is, to the extent that females were disadvantaged in the past by practices now forbidden, the legal reforms of the last 15 years may have tended to equalize the treatment accorded male and female status offenders.

Finally, there is the possibility that no significant changes have occurred in the treatment of males and females, but that differential treatment is now hidden in one or more ways. Justice officials may have redefined many status offenses as criminal-type offenses in order to render girls eligible for the kinds of protectionist sanctions which had traditionally been applied.

Gender bias may be obscured in other ways as well. Certain provisions of the JJDP Act permit practices that might allow justice officials to circumvent the spirit of the law and its mandate of deinstitutionalization. Of particular concern is a 1980 amendment to the Act, which provides that status offenders found in contempt of court for violating a valid court order may be placed in secure detention facilities, thus permitting the juvenile courts to use their contempt power to incarcerate repeat status offenders. Contempt proceedings may be initiated based on either a subsequent status offense or a failure to comply with an earlier court order.

If the juvenile courts applied their contempt power differentially more often to female status offenders, the effect would be a concealment of the continuation of traditional patterns of gender bias. In that case, non-status offense data would include female status offenders (subsequently held in contempt), who traditionally have received harsher protectionist treatment than their male counterparts, in addition to male delinquents (charged with criminal-type offenses), who traditionally have received harsher penalties than their female delinquent counterparts. Because these effects pull in opposite directions, failure to distinguish between contempt and other criminal-type offenses might obscure real gender differences in processing.

THE PRESENT RESEARCH

This study examines the effects that the reform initiatives mandated by the JJDP Act have had on the juvenile justice system to determine whether the system's past pattern of unequal treatment of male and female status offenders and delinquents has been corrected or merely masked. Fresh analysis is needed in part because the JJDP Act's mandate to deinstitutionalize status offenders may have reduced both the motivations and the opportunities to treat females differently from males. In addition, as suggested above, the Act may also have had the unintended consequence of encouraging practices that make gender differentials in juvenile justice processing more difficult to detect.

Using the records of status and non-status offense referrals processed in Florida over a 3-year period, we evaluate the extent to which gender affects decisions made at several stages in juvenile justice processing, from initial intake through judicial disposition. We conduct multivariate analyses that include controls for a number of legal and extralegal variables of potential relevance to processing decisions. In addition to exploring the main effects of gender in additive models, we estimate interactive models to determine whether the effect of gender is conditioned by levels of other predictor variables. Given the possibility, noted above, that gender effects are contingent upon offense, interactions between gender and offense type are of special interest.

The Sample

Data for this research are drawn from records of the total population of cases referred to the juvenile justice system in Florida from January 1, 1985, to December 31, 1987. Florida has a statewide juvenile justice information system well suited to the questions we wished to address. From this information system we obtained a data set consisting of cases referred to juvenile justice intake units throughout the state. Florida

law requires that all juvenile complaint reports be processed through intake offices located in each county. Thus, the data include records of all police contacts (except those that resulted in informal field adjustments) as well as referrals from parents, school officials, and other non-police sources. The data set is quite comprehensive—it includes cases closed without action and cases disposed of informally (e.g., through diversion to a community service agency), as well as cases formally petitioned to and processed in juvenile court or transferred to adult court jurisdiction. We were able to organize the records so that we could trace the movement of youths through several processing stages in the juvenile justice system. In delinquency (non-status offense) cases, the sequence of processing stages included intake screening, detention, court referral, adjudication, and judicial disposition. Because of structural differences within the juvenile justice system, status offense cases included only three processing stages: court referral, adjudication, and judicial disposition.

Because prior research suggests that processing decisions are affected by youths' prior records of offending and by the dispositions of youths' prior cases, controlling for offense and processing histories is important. Accordingly, we restricted our analyses to the last referral in 1987 for each youth in the data set. This procedure allowed us to capture at least two full years of prior offense and prior disposition information. The total number of youths included in the analyses is 137,671.

Dependent Variables

We examined five dependent variables for delinquency cases and three for cases involving status offenses. All of the dependent variables were encoded dichotomously.

DELINQUENCY CASES

Intake Screening. For delinquency cases, intake screening begins the official juvenile justice process. In Florida, intake officers review the facts of the case, interview the juvenile and (where possible) the juvenile's parents or guardians, and make nonbinding recommendations to state's prosecuting attorneys regarding the preferred method of handling each referral. Intake officers may recommend that a case be closed without action, that it be diverted from the juvenile justice system for informal handling, or that it be referred to the juvenile court for formal processing. Intake Screening outcomes are coded as follows: either 0 if closed without action or handled informally or 1 if referred for formal processing.

Detention Status. Decisions regarding detention status are made in all delinquency cases shortly after a referral is received. Detention decisions are made jointly by intake staff, law enforcement officials (when the referral is police initiated), and prosecutors. For Detention Status, cases that resulted in preadjudicatory detention are coded 1; those released are coded 0.

Court Referral. After reviewing intake recommendations, Florida prosecutors decide whether a delinquency case will proceed to formal court processing. Court Referral is coded to distinguish between cases in which no petition was filed or in which a petition was filed and subsequently withdrawn (coded 0) and cases in which a petition was filed that resulted in formal court processing (coded 1).

Adjudication. The next stage of delinquency case processing involves judicial decision making. In the first of two major court decisions, judges decide whether to adjudicate a youth delinquent (i.e., to find him or her guilty of the charge[s]) or to dismiss the case, find the youth not guilty, or withhold adjudication. Adjudication is coded to distinguish between youths who, for any of the aforementioned reasons, were not adjudicated delinquent (coded 0) and those who were formally adjudicated delinquent (coded 1).

Judicial Disposition. The second major court decision involves the equivalent of sentencing

in a criminal court. Youths found to have committed delinquent offenses may receive a number of alternative judicial dispositions, ranging from community-based sanctions and services (e.g., probation and intensive probation) to commitment to residential facilities (e.g., youth camps and training schools). Additionally, youths may be transferred to criminal court for trial as adults, arguably the most severe sanction available to the juvenile justice system. In this study, Judicial Disposition is coded to distinguish between those ordered into some kind of community-based program (coded 0) and those committed to a residential facility or transferred to criminal court (coded 1).

STATUS OFFENSES

Court Referral and Adjudication. Status offenders in Florida, like criminal-type offenders (delinquents), enter the justice system at the intake screening stage. Because status offenders are legally defined as dependents rather than delinquents, however, their processing differs somewhat from that of youths charged with offenses that would be crimes if committed by adults. First, intake officers decide, rather than merely recommend, whether there should be formal court action for status offenders. In contrast to their advisory role in delinquency cases, the intake officers make the *final* decision whether or not to petition these cases to juvenile court. The first stage in status offender processing, then, is Court Referral, which is coded to distinguish between cases closed without action or handled informally (coded 0) and those petitioned to juvenile court (coded 1). The second stage in the processing of status offenders is Adjudication, which is coded in the same manner as was the analogous stage of delinquency case processing, described above.

Judicial Disposition. The third stage in the processing of status offenders is judicial disposition. In a general sense, status offenders who are adjudicated dependent by the court risk the same fate as delinquent offenders, viz., placement outside the home in some residential or institutional facility such as a foster home or a group home. At the most severe end of the continuum of dispositional alternatives, however, status offenders are not subject to the two harshest sanctions reserved for delinquent offenders, incarceration in a training school and transfer to criminal court. Outcomes of Judicial Disposition are coded to distinguish between youths ordered by the court to receive some community-based service or treatment (coded 0) and those made wards of the court and removed from their homes (coded 1).

Independent Variables

SOCIAL CHARACTERISTICS

The independent variables examined in this study include social characteristics of offenders and attributes of their current offenses, offense histories, and case processing outcomes. The offender characteristics are Gender, Race and Age.

CURRENT OFFENSES

Offense Seriousness. In the analysis of delinquency cases, a measure of offense seriousness was constructed by scoring the most serious offense with which each youth was charged.

Contempt Status. In light of our discussion of contempt and its potential importance as a vehicle for circumventing federal mandates to deinstitutionalize status offenders, we introduced contempt status as a variable in this analysis. In Florida, juvenile contempt proceedings, which are legally recognized as delinquency proceedings, are initiated by intake officers and proceed through the system in the same manner as do other delinquency offenses. Contempt referrals involve instances in which an intake officer is notified that a juvenile has violated a condition of supervision previously imposed by the court. A petition is then filed initiating a delinquency contempt proceeding, rather than a dependency action for a repeat status offense. State

law allows judges to place juveniles found in contempt into secure detention for up to 5 months and 29 days at the judicial disposition of their cases. Contempt Status is coded to distinguish between cases referred for contempt (coded 1) and all other delinquency cases (coded 0).

OFFENSE HISTORY

Prior Record. Prior record is measured in terms of the severity of the youth's previous offenses. To construct this variable, we summed the severity scores of all previous referrals during the 3-year study period. In cases where a youth's offense history included a status offense, the status offense was assigned a value equivalent to the most minor misdemeanor offense.

Prior Disposition. Because previous research suggests that the disposition of prior referrals has a significant impact on the outcome of subsequent referrals, we also constructed a measure of prior disposition that scored the most severe disposition that each youth had previously received.

ANALYSIS

The analysis proceeds from an examination of bivariate relationships to multivariate regression models. Because each of the dependent variables is a dichotomous contrast, we selected logistic regression as the method of estimation. In addition to estimating main effects in additive models, we also estimated models that included all two-way interactions including gender. These latter models allow us to consider whether the covariation of gender with other independent variables influences case outcomes at each processing point.

Inclusion of an individual in the analysis of any stage of processing is conditional on the individual's having reached that stage. This conditioning results in a selected sample, which could in turn, if not compensated for, produce biased estimates. Biased estimates may occur when the analyst makes inferences to a population that is not sampled. Since we wanted our estimates of gender effects to apply to the entire cohort, we included a correction for sample selection to adjust for differences in the probability of reaching a particular stage. In other words, the estimates adjust for the individual's probability of reaching the stage under consideration.

FINDINGS

The data indicate that, in delinquency cases, gender is weakly but significantly related to four of the five case processing outcomes. When referred to the juvenile justice system for criminal-type offenses, males are more likely than females to be recommended for formal processing, to be held in secure detention facilities, to be petitioned to court by prosecutors, and to be incarcerated or transferred to criminal court at the judicial disposition of their cases. Adjudication is the only outcome that is apparently unrelated to gender.

In status offense cases, gender is weakly but significantly correlated with court referral decisions. In contrast to their delinquent counterparts, female status offenders are more likely than males to be petitioned to court. At both the adjudicatory and judicial disposition stages, however, gender appears to be unrelated to the outcome of status offense cases.

In the logistic regression analyses we modeled the first three stages in the processing of delinquency cases: intake screening, detention status, and court referral. Consistent with the findings of other studies of juvenile justice processing, both the seriousness of the current offense and the seriousness of the youth's prior record weigh heavily in intake decision making. Intake officials also consider the prior dispositions that youths have received and, all other things being equal, are more likely to recommend formal processing in cases involving youths with histories of previous court inter-

ventions. In addition, sociodemographic characteristics (i.e., age, race, and gender) of youths influence intake referral decisions. Older youths, blacks, and males are significantly more likely to be recommended for formal processing than younger adolescents, whites, and females. Of these variables, gender has the greatest impact on referral decisions—being male has approximately one and one-half times the effect on the likelihood that a youth will be recommended for formal processing as does being black, and it has about the same effect as a 2-year increment in age. Although the results show that contempt cases are more likely to be recommended for formal processing than are noncontempt cases, there is no indication that contempt cases involving females are more likely to be recommended for formal processing by intake officers than are contempt cases involving males.

Detention decisions are influenced only minimally by gender when other important variables are controlled. Given the large sample size, even small effects may be statistically significant. In terms of *substantive* significance, gender appears to have very little impact on detention decisions: In the typical referral, the probability of being detained is 13% for males and 12% for females. The strongest predictors of detention status are the legal variables (characteristics of both current and prior offenses) and prior disposition. Youths referred for contempt are especially likely to be detained, but there is no indication that this effect is conditioned by gender. Race and age have modest effects on detention status: Blacks and older youths are more likely to be detained than are whites and younger adolescents.

As was the case with the previous stages of delinquency processing, offense seriousness, seriousness of the prior record, and prior disposition each have significant effects on prosecutorial decision making. Also noteworthy is the finding that, net of controls for other variables in the model, being detained increases the likelihood of court referral. The effects of both age and race are very modest at this stage, although it is interesting to speculate that some of the effects of both age and race may be subsumed by the effect of detention status. The effect of gender on prosecutorial filing decisions is moderate. In the typical youth referral, a male has a 37.6% probability of being referred for formal prosecution, compared to a female's 31.6% probability.

The analysis reveals a significant interaction between gender and contempt status. Among males, court referral decisions seem to be little affected by whether the offense for which a referral is made involves a substantive violation of law or an instance of contempt, such as a violation of conditions previously set by the court. The typical male not in contempt has a 37.6% probability of referral to court. The probability increases modestly, to 45.7%, if the youth is referred for contempt. Among females, however, being referred for contempt has a major impact in the direction of increasing the probability of formal processing. The typical female not in contempt has a 31.2% probability of referral to court. When referred for contempt, her likelihood of court referral increases strikingly to 69.7%, a difference of nearly 40 percentage points.

Taken together, these findings indicate that, at the court referral stage, males are somewhat disadvantaged when it comes to delinquency offenses involving the commission of offenses that would be crimes if committed by adults. Females, on the other hand, are severely disadvantaged in cases where repeat status offending results in a referral for contempt of court.

We examined the final two stages of delinquency case processing, adjudication and judicial disposition. The more severe the offense and the more severe the prior disposition, the greater the likelihood of an adjudication of delinquency. Also, black youths and those who have been detained are more likely to be adjudicated delinquent than are white youths and youths who have been released into the community pending an adjudicatory hearing. At this processing stage, there is no evidence that the offender's gender influences decision making.

As might be expected, the seriousness of the offense has a significant impact on case disposition. Even more notable is the effect of prior disposition: All other things being equal, youths who have been incarcerated or transferred in the past are much more likely to be incarcerated again. Detention also has a significant impact on disposition decisions: Those held in secure detention awaiting final disposition are more likely to receive harsh dispositions than those released to the community.

At the dispositional stage, each of the socio-demographic characteristics has a significant effect on case outcomes. Older youths, blacks, and males are more likely to be incarcerated or transferred than are younger adolescents, whites, and females. However, the effect of gender is not the same across all offense types. There is a significant interaction between gender and contempt status, the effect of which is to elevate substantially the risk of incarceration for females found in contempt. In contrast, among males, contempt status has little impact on judicial disposition. The typical male offender who is not in contempt has a 3.9% probability of incarceration. The risk is increased only slightly, to 4.4%, when he is found in contempt. In sharp contrast, the typical female offender not in contempt has a 1.8% probability of incarceration, which increases markedly to 63.2% if she is held in contempt. In short, females referred to juvenile court for contempt following an earlier adjudication for a status offense receive harsher judicial dispositions than their male counterparts.

Finally, we examine adjudicatory and judicial disposition outcomes for status offenders. As was the case with adjudicatory outcomes in delinquency cases, none of the variables is a significant predictor of judicial decisions to adjudge youths as status offenders. Similarly, the results reveal that none of the independent variables reaches statistical significance for judicial disposition. We can only speculate that considerations such as parental cooperation and quality of the child's family environment—

potentially important factors not measured here—provide some predictability to these case outcomes.

DISCUSSION

Our findings provide a fairly complex portrait of the effects of gender in juvenile justice processing. On the one hand, we have found that, when referred to the system for criminal-type offenses, male delinquents are substantially more likely than females (a) to be recommended for formal processing (prosecution) by intake officials, (b) to be petitioned to court by prosecutors for adjudication, (c) to be detained in secure facilities until adjudication, and (d) to receive judicial dispositions (sentences) that involve incarceration or similar liberty constraints. This is consistent with the pattern of gender bias in the juvenile justice system's handling of delinquents that has been documented in the research literature over several decades.

Our analyses of status offense cases, on the other hand, detected little evidence of gender bias. Youths referred to the justice system for status offenses tend to be younger than the average delinquency referral, and they are typically first-time offenders. The decision to refer these youths to court, as well as the decision to place them in foster care or group homes or to return them to their natural homes, was unaffected, for the most part, by the variables included in our models. Females were somewhat more likely than males to be referred to court for status offenses, but they had approximately the same probability as males of being adjudicated dependent and returned to their natural homes.

The finding that female status offenders do not receive harsher treatment than comparable males may be a result of the restrictions imposed by the JJDP Act. We must be cautious in this interpretation, however, because we do not have comparable data for the period prior to the enactment of the JJDP Act. Nonetheless, it seems reasonable to ask whether reforms encouraged by the JJDP Act may have reduced opportunities within the juvenile justice system for differential treatment of dependent females. Like most other states participating in programs under the JJDP Act, Florida has enacted laws prohibiting the secure detention and institutionalization in training schools of status offenders. Our findings are consistent with the notion that, at least insofar as first-time status offenders are concerned, this prohibition may have had a salutary impact upon females.

Finally and importantly, our analyses of contempt cases demonstrate that considerable gender bias remains in the handling of repeat status offenders. We found that females referred for contempt are more likely to be petitioned to court than females referred for other criminal-type offenses and are substantially more likely to be petitioned to court than males referred for contempt. Moreover, females found in contempt are much more likely than their male counterparts to be sentenced to a period of up to 6 months' incarceration in secure detention facilities. These differences in the treatment of male and female offenders are striking and dramatic.

CONCLUSION

Our findings point to the conclusion that the traditional sexual double standard continues to operate. Both female status offenders and male delinquents are differentially disadvantaged in the juvenile justice system. This state of affairs appears to reflect the continuation of protectionist policies toward female status offenders, as well as an attitude toward non-status offenders (delinquents) that sanctions differentially harsher penalties for males and more leniency toward females. It is important to highlight the fact that, had we not introduced contempt status as a variable in our analyses and looked for interaction effects, our findings would have suggested that gender bias in juvenile justice processing had diminished considerably.

QUESTIONS FOR DISCUSSION AND WRITING

1. What does research during the past 30 years show for "status offenses" and "acts of delinquency"?
2. What has happened in the past decade?
3. What do the data indicate in delinquency cases? What about in status offenses? [Note: These are bivariate analyses.] In the logistic regression analyses of intake decision making, how did sociodemographic characteristics influence intake referral decisions?
4. What significant interaction between gender and contempt status was revealed? What significant interaction between gender and contempt status was revealed at the dispositional stage?

Race, Gender, and the Prehearing Detention of Juveniles

KIMBERLY KEMPF-LEONARD

RECENTLY called "the underbelly of the juvenile justice system," the detention process is the juvenile justice counterpart to jailing in the criminal justice system. Detention most often occurs prior to the resolution of a case, although for some youths detention is the final disposition. Regrettably, there has been little research on detention. What we do know comes primarily from studies on other aspects of juvenile justice processing. This chapter addresses difficulties resulting from inadequate attention to detention. Its specific concern is with changes in federal support that inadvertently expand the purposes and opportunities to detain. Given the discretion and the informal nature of traditional juvenile justice processing, there is a very real danger that expanded use of juvenile detention will frequently be arbitrary or, worse, intentionally discriminatory. In addition to these more general concerns, the chapter discusses the particular problems of race and gender disparities.

BENEFICIAL REFORMS ARE IN JEOPARDY

Many beneficial detention reforms enacted by previous Congresses are now in jeopardy. Be-

From *Race, Gender, and the Prehearing Detention of Juveniles* by K. Kempf-Leonard, n.d. Copyright Kimberly Kempf-Leonard. Adapted with permission.

An earlier version of this paper was presented to the National Research Council Panel on Juvenile Crime: Prevention, Treatment, and Control.

ginning in 1974 with passage of the Juvenile Justice and Delinquency Prevention Act (JJDP Act), Congress initiated five reforms which currently affect prehearing detention. The JJDP Act required states first to remove status offenders and nonoffenders from secure confinement and also to separate adults and juvenile offenders within correctional settings as a condition of states receiving federal funds. In addition to sight and sound separation of all youths from adults, the act made the deinstitutionalization of status offenders and nonoffenders, known as the DSO mandate, an important second objective for states. Although reauthorization of the JJDP Act in 1980 weakened the requirements for states to receive federal funds by allowing confinement of habitual runaways, juveniles who refuse court-ordered treatment, and those who violate court orders, the DSO requirement remains important. In 1980, removing juveniles from adult jails became a third priority, after many atrocities committed on minors were brought to public attention. Reauthorization in 1988 added the fourth requirement, known as the DMC requirement, that states investigate the disproportionate representation of minorities in confinement. Fifth, following the 1992 reauthorization hearings, states were given an opportunity to assess the adequacy of their services, particularly for girls, and to receive funding to initiate improvements through a new challenge grant program.

Although the level of state compliance with requirements of the JJDP Act varies both by specific reform and locale, better treatment of youths and improved juvenile justice processing is evident in most states from each reform effort. Unfortunately, any positive trends occurring could be radically affected by adoption of any one of many proposals now being discussed in Congress. Recent congressional debates on reauthorization of the JJDP Act do not instill confidence that more progress is likely to be forthcoming. Most congressional attention has been directed at serious, violent, and chronic juvenile offenders, to the exclusion of concerns about more typical juvenile cases. Some proposals would give states discretion in implementing the five initiatives specified in the JJDP Act, while others would dismantle altogether existing reforms aimed at separating juveniles and adults in corrections, removing minors from adult jails, and reducing minority overrepresentation. Some even advocate the abolishment of the JJDP Act altogether.

THE PURPOSES AND FUNCTIONS OF DETENTION ARE CHANGING

Children are taken into custody for all the same reasons for which adults are arrested, but also to protect runaways or remove children from situations deemed inappropriate. Though governing statutes vary, prehearing detention may be used to protect the minor, to protect others from the minor, and to make certain the minor does not abscond. Detention sometimes is used as a sanction, that is, youths are detained so that they might "learn a lesson," and finally, juvenile court officers sometimes employ detention as a form of treatment.

In theory, detention traditionally has not been intended as punitive, but rather as providing a safe haven from negative influences. The means of providing that security, however, never have been truly clear, usually have been applied inconsistently, and seldom have been effective. Recent changes in state laws convey legislative responses to heightened public fear of juvenile crime, and the result of the altered laws has been revised goals for many juvenile justice systems. The new laws typically add concern for public safety to that for the needs of the youths. Often the public safety goal becomes dominant. The public expects juvenile justice systems to enhance public safety, but new policies and explicit procedures on how to achieve safety seldom accompany the directive.

Detention can easily be adapted to comply with the new objective of enhanced public safety. Concern for the safety of others no doubt influenced detention decisions in the past, and the changes merely make this practice more explicit. In 1984, in *Schall v. Martin*, the U.S. Supreme Court affirmed the constitutionality of pretrial preventive detention for the sake of public safety. Not long ago, selective incapacitation was touted for serious chronic adult offenders, so it makes sense to some that if delinquents pose a major crime problem they should be detained.

Considerable evidence suggests that detained youths are more apt than comparable nondetainees to receive more restrictive dispositions of their cases. Research, however, has not clearly identified the reasons for harsher outcomes following detention. The significant effect of detention may indicate that prehearing decisions and case dispositions share similar factors; that is, those who are detained deserve custody, and their dispositions similarly reflect their greater needs for treatment and supervision than youths who are not detained. Alternatively, prehearing detention may result from influential decisions that are guided by criteria unrelated to the needs of youths or public safety. The latter explanation would indicate that harsher dispositions reflect a negative effect of detention at the early stages of case processing, such as inability to assist with the case or a negative stigma of detention on decisions at subsequent stages.

OPPORTUNITIES FOR DETENTION ARE INCREASING

Another concern involves the number and type of detention facilities. Minors are most often detained in secure facilities (including juvenile court detention centers, police holdover lock-ups, private institutions, and adult jails). There are fewer nonsecure shelters (including group homes, foster care, and day supervision centers), although they are often needed for status offenders and nonoffenders who need prehearing supervision or protection in order to comply with the DSO mandate. Secure facilities are expensive both to build and to operate, and especially in rural areas there is limited access to them. Secure settings tend to be more commonly used for both black and Latino youths, and nonsecure shelters tend to be more commonly used for white youths.

Somewhat similar to the growth in urban jail construction, many new detention centers have been built in recent years. Crowding and outdated facilities have been a factor in the construction; however, the detention edifice phenomenon differs from jails because many of the new facilities have been constructed where previously none existed. The implications of this growth are important. Lerman has linked detention rates to the availability of detention centers. The "capacity causes utilization" argument is further buttressed by many recent experiences with adult jails and prisons. Also, new construction is likely to continue given the federal funds to build new facilities that have recently become available.

Although costs of administering facilities varied from $1 per youth in Arkansas and South Carolina to $183 in the District of Columbia in 1988, it is worth noting that new detention centers often include security features similar to those in adult jails. They also are similar in that diagnostic and counseling services, legal and family services, and education and medical treatment, while often inadequate, are improving. The way prehearing custody is administered is especially important because juveniles have a high risk of suicide and self-mutilation, and they are vulnerable to abuse by others in custody and by bad staff. Youths also must be adequately supervised to minimize their exposure to other offenders who might use the facility as a "training ground" for crime.

Although some of the new, bigger, stronger facilities are located in cities, detention centers often are built in rural jurisdictions to appease officials who think they need them. Construction of detention centers in rural areas may change juvenile case processing in general, as urban differences in court systems now primarily reflect variations in resource allocation. Urban courts tend to have more formal bureaucratic procedures and more specialized personnel than rural courts. Urban caseloads are larger, more routinely include serious offenses, and urban courts serve populations with significant numbers of minority youths. Urban courts tend to employ attorneys and to operate their own detention facilities. These characteristics help many urban courts to expedite case processing based on the nature of the offense and due process concerns. In contrast, rural courts have smaller, less serious caseloads primarily involving white youths. Smaller staffs perform the full spectrum of case processing duties from a central location. It is not uncommon for one court officer to handle all aspects of case processing and to provide supervision based on his or her personal assessment of the youth's needs. The geographic jurisdiction is apt to be large, and access to a detention center is apt to involve travel. There is more reliance on informal and individualized case processing in rural courts.

UNSTRUCTURED DISCRETION PREVAILS IN JUVENILE JUSTICE

Finally, in considering detention generally, it is important to keep the informal nature of case processing and unstructured discretion that prevails in the juvenile court in mind. Considered fundamental to the "best interests" doctrine, most juvenile justice systems allow, encourage, even require individualized and discretionary decision making throughout the process.

Most juvenile cases are handled informally, which sometimes means that all decisions pertaining to a case are made by police officers or by court officers without consulting a judge.

Many officers may lack the qualifications and expertise required to respond effectively to juveniles. Even in cases in which a judicial decision is made, informal conversations and recommendations made outside of the hearing may nullify any potential contribution from the youth or from the actual hearing. Usually the entire court process is completed in the course of a few days, and it virtually always occurs more quickly than the criminal court process, which also sometimes means that few records are kept and appellate review is rare. Many parents advise their children to waive their rights to counsel and to accept plea bargains. When attorneys are present, observers are often concerned about the quality of their training and their ability to prepare effective representation. Parents may accept coerced agreements that result in secure custody for their children in private hospitals and group homes. The informality, swiftness of the court process, and the aura of "best interests of the child" tend to make due process a secondary concern, even in courts where it may be emphasized.

Detention as a protective device offers much more latitude than any standards applied to adults and jails. Detention also is used for its shock value as a means of exacting punishment and as a perceived treatment. Aside from the growing number of secure beds, there are few alternatives for prehearing supervision of youths. Juveniles rarely are released on their own recognizance, money bail, or a deposit option. Outright release means parental supervision, while other forms of third party, community-based, supervision are uncommon. Thus, the detention situation in most juvenile justice systems does not mirror the enhanced rationality of pretrial release decision making in criminal justice.

Within this legal venue where decisions are seldom reviewed, and independence and individualized case processing are revered, it makes sense that agents of the system would welcome dismantling of any or all of the federal restrictions. Next, I discuss specifically how race and gender disparities currently are linked to detention.

RACE, GENDER, AND DETENTION

Both race and gender are related to detention, and there is a likely interaction effect, the nature of which is not yet clear. Juvenile court data available from the National Center for Juvenile Justice show that in 1996, the last year for which information was available, 316,368 minors were held in prehearing custody pending resolution of a law violation. Data for the past decade convey some of the race and gender differences.

For all cases, the proportion with detention did not differ much from 1987 to 1996. This pattern generally held for the race and sex subgroups in the data, although a slight decline in detention use occurred among non-black youths. The decline among non-black youths and the stable detention pattern among black females changed the subgroup ranking. In 1996, black females were detained at percentages more comparable to minority males, whereas previously their rates of detention were more akin to those of other females and white males. Throughout the 10-year period, the proportion of youths detained was highest for black males and lowest for white females, which suggests that the interaction between race and sex is important and possibly quite direct.

Among cases involving offenses against persons, the proportions detained were fairly stable over the 10-year period. Black males consistently had the highest percentage of detention, followed by other non-white males. White males and black females were detained in approximately the same proportions, followed closely by other non-white females. The lowest percentage detained involved white females. The combination of race and sex again seems important in understanding detention for offenses against persons, although the relationship is less straightforward.

The percentage detained among property offenders showed a slight decline, except among black youths. Detention was highest among black males, followed by other non-white males. White males, black females, and other non-white females shared third place, with white females close behind. Thus, for property offenders, sex differences initially seem greater than race differences, with the exception of white males.

A contrary pattern favoring race differences is evident among both drug offenses and public order offenses. Among drug cases, a small increase in detention occurred across nearly all subgroups in the late 1980s and early 1990s. This temporary blip was less pronounced among white youths, as detention rates of these youths declined. Detention was consistently highest among black youths, particularly males, followed by other non-white youths, and lowest among white youths.

Detention also declined for youths whose cases involved public order offenses, except among black youths, for whom it remained stable and highest. The proportions of white males and females detained for public order offenses remained nearly equivalent. The sharpest decline occurred among other non-white females, and in 1996 only 7% of this group was detained. The decline was not as steep for other non-white males.

Thus, these data show that while the overall rate of detention has remained fairly stable at about one fifth of delinquency cases overall, it involved nearly one third of African American males. When offense type was controlled, detention was always highest for African American males. Sometimes gender differences seemed to prevail, such as among property offenses, in which regardless of race, detention was higher among boys. In contrast, race seemed more important for drug offenses and public order violations, with detention of minority girls sometimes higher than that of white boys.

These differences are interesting, but the aggregated descriptive data preclude anything beyond speculation about why they exist. While the nature of interactions between race and gender is not always clear, Federele and Chesney-Lind suggested that the DSO serves to keep white boys out of detention, to lock girls in private mental health facilities, and to free bed space to warehouse many more minority children—all for essentially the same types of behaviors.

Race, Gender, and the Purposes of Detention

Returning to the purposes of detention, there is evidence of differential processing of both minority youths and females, linked to the reasons for which they are detained. Stereotypes manifest themselves as direct institutional biases, accounting for a large proportion of the disparities.

Racial stereotypes hold that minorities are more in need of preventive detention. Austin reported results from focus groups with agency personnel who were in a good position to provide insight on juvenile justice processing. He noted stereotypes and institutional racism, including perceptions that African Americans are more violent, less controllable, and have less family support than whites. In another study, following interviews, one judge commented that detention of minority males is not an indication of discrimination, but rather it is an opportunity for treatment, safety, and support that often is not routinely available. Finally, in still another study, juvenile justice officials reported in phone surveys that black youths are less able than white youths to obtain private counsel, to access private mental health services, to have their parents appear in court, and that their single-parent homes are "more broken" than others. Noting these stereotypes, the researchers concluded that the bias that causes racial differentials in juvenile justice is embedded in institutional structure and practice.

In contrast, gender stereotypes take the form either of shunning girls because officials consider them deceitful, manipulative, and difficult to work with or of detaining them as an expression of more paternalistic protection for girls. This paternalistic response reflects, at least in part, the traditional concern for restricting the sexuality of girls. Yet, most detention centers do not provide a protective, nurturing environment. In addition to the ample security and stark environment, intrusive pelvic examinations were routinely administered to all girls in detention for health assurances until the mid-1970s. Although no longer routine, body cavity searches by police and court officers now are often justified for security reasons and sometimes conducted merely to humiliate the girl.

The "gendered" nature of court referrals is another manifestation of the stereotype that girls are more in need of protection than are boys. Offenses are "gendered" in that status offenses accounted for more than one fourth of arrests of girls in 1995 but less than 10% of arrests of boys; this pattern has held for several years. Girls have lower rates of detention overall, but among alleged status offenders detention is more likely for girls than for boys and gender-based expectations are a likely reason. Dealing with runaways is a specific concern because they often are detained, and many runaways are girls.

Given their prominence as status offenders, females may have benefited most from the important DSO reforms, and they may be most at risk from current efforts to reverse them. For example, before passage of the JJDP Act in 1974, about three fourths of all girls, compared to only one fourth of all boys, were incarcerated for status offenses. By 1979, the number of girls detained had dropped by 40% and has since remained stable. However, juvenile justice officials are not lacking creativity, and their paternalistic motives appear quite virile; thus, this also may be a situation in which even worse experiences accompany the perceived cure.

There are not enough alternatives to secure detention, and frustrated juvenile justice officials have circumvented the DSO in three important ways. One pattern involves reclassifying status offenses as minor crimes, as a means of "bootstrapping" juveniles into detention. Another pattern involves making a court order so strict and limiting that it is almost a certainty that a nonoffender will violate a court order citation. That violation is an offense for which detention is possible. These strategies were both made possible with the relaxed standards accompanying reauthorization of the JJDP Act in 1980. The final pattern involves essentially hiding the fact of a youth's detention within a privately operated facility. This may result from a direct court order, or it may involve an element of coercion with the court officer and parents "negotiating" no sustained court record if the family "voluntarily" commits the youth.

We know very little about the extent to which these types of circumvention occur. Given the recent growth in number of facilities and bed space available in private juvenile facilities and treatment centers, hidden detention may well be fairly common. It is likely that girls are disproportionately affected because of the nature of the behaviors that bring them to court, their growing numbers, and because inadequate public-run bed space for girls is a major problem. Although Medicaid may cover some costs of hospitalization and "psychiatric care," poor youths are less likely than those who can afford health insurance to be in a position to accept these bargains. Because minority youths are disproportionately poor, this may help explain their overrepresentation in public-run facilities. Whether treatment in private institutions is better is debatable, but some do provide youths with longer stays (or until insurance expires), secure settings, and overmedication. The extent to which this is problematic is unknown because the monitoring requirements of the DSO currently do not include such facilities.

Race, Gender, and More Opportunities for Detention

Next, I discuss the implications of increased access to detention centers on differing rates of detention based on race and gender. As I noted earlier, much of the new construction is making secure detention more accessible to less populated areas, and this change is likely to have an effect on both race and gender differences in detention.

In terms of gender, "justice by geography" may mean something very different from its racial implications. If detention of girls is greater in cities, the serious problems in rural areas entail responding to the small numbers of females, their involvement in status offending, and administrative decisions that allocate most resources to boys. However, Frazier and Cochran found that detention was more likely for youths who were black, rural, and females than for those white, urban, and male. Similarly, Feld observed that not only were girls more likely than boys to be detained, particularly for minor offenses, but he also found evidence that paternalistic responses from judges occurred less often in urban courts. It was in the more rural courts, those with caseloads of predominantly minor offenses, where girls received more restrictive interventions.

Thus, is appears that while higher numbers of youths are detained in urban courts, both minorities and girls are disadvantaged at detention by court processing outside of cities. More important, these geographic race and gender differences in detention are likely to escalate as rural and ex-urban systems find new funding for detention and federal support for female-specific interventions.

Race, Gender, and Unstructured Discretion

Bias and discrimination can be direct, indirect, cumulative, and/or geographical. The cause of disparate treatment is difficult to determine because the race and gender variables can interact with each other, and both also may interact with other factors, such as offense type, prior record, social class, or neighborhood. Aspects of juvenile justice that are informal, discretionary, and hidden from public view make understanding the difficulties even more problematic.

We know little about the effects of gender on detention, but there is no doubt that racial minorities, especially black males, are detained at higher rates than white youths. Most states have tried to comply with the new requirement addressing the disproportionate confinement of minority youths (the DMC) of the JJDP Act and in doing so have identified significant overrepresentation of minorities in detention. Of the 44 states that could assess the situation in secure detention facilities, 43 identified a problem. Only 22 states could assess the situation in adult jails, but 19 of them reported a problem. Only 10 states assessed police lockup facilities, but 9 of them reported a problem.

What is not clear is whether ethnicity or color is solely responsible for minority overrepresentation. Hindelang suggested that disproportionate representation of minorities probably mirrors real behavioral differences, and, to varying degrees, other authors have echoed this suggestion of race-specific behavioral differences. Still others offer the opposite view. The problem might occur prior to detention, with police disproportionately patrolling minority neighborhoods or racial bias at charging. A similar concern may exist for girls because girls are at greater risk of having their parents initiate the court referral and of having their families refuse to allow them to return home. Feld reported that private legal counsel was retained three times more often by white youths than by black youths in cases involving serious felony offenses against persons and twice as frequently in property offense cases.

In response to the DMC mandate, much rigorous research on this issue is under way. Thus far, many findings show that race continues to be a factor in the decision making, even after controlling for many other relevant variables. According to Feld,

It is readily apparent that proportionately more black and minority youths than white youths are detained for the same offenses. For juveniles charged with a felony offense against a person appearing in juvenile court for the first time, more than twice as many blacks as whites are detained, 52.8% vs. 24.1%.

The race effect on detention has been identified by Kempf-Leonard as more important than offense, personal problems, family or school problems, or the type of court in which the case was handled, and more important than prior record or prior commitment to a juvenile correctional facility. This appearance of direct institutional racism, regardless of whether it is intentional, suggests that juvenile justice officials target minorities for detention.

Race, Gender, and the
Consequences of Detention

Perhaps most important, a harsher disposition for youths with prehearing detention is a recurrent finding. Almost without exception, the percentage adjudicated between 1987 and 1996 was higher for cases in which youths were detained. When this pattern was slight or did not hold, at issue were recent drug offenses involving black males or other non-white females, or recent public order offenses involving black youths or other non-white females. Some gender differences were quite pronounced. For example, the percentage adjudicated for males who had not been detained more closely resembled the percentages for females who had been detained, particularly among person and property offenses.

Detention can pose an indirect effect on the outcome of the case. As we reported in 1995, a consistent finding since the mid-1980s regarding the juvenile justice process is that the effect of race on disposition may be masked by prior detention. More recently, I observed a detention effect on placement for both girls and boys—not only was prehearing detention the single best predictor of commitment but also detained girls were three times as likely as other girls to be removed from their homes. Detention also improved the likelihood that treatment services were ordered for youth; detention status made treatment 11 times more likely for girls and 6 times more likely for boys. Feld found that the effect of detention on case outcome was comparable to that of the actual offense, and sometimes even more important.

This indirect effect may even amplify disparities or serve to cumulatively disadvantage certain categories of youth later in the process. In one study, we observed that the cumulative disadvantage was especially strong for black youths. This finding was supported by Wordes and Bynum, who reported that the further

youths were processed into the system, the greater the extent of minority overrepresentation. Austin observed that the overrepresentation of African American youths escalated until the final stage of commitment to the California Youth Authority. By contrast, he found that white youths were disproportionately screened out at earlier stages of the process and little variation from the overall pattern for Latino and Asian youths.

SUMMARY AND RECOMMENDATIONS

It appears that the purpose and function of detention is thwarted by stereotypical responses to youth of color, particularly African Americans, and to girls. As authorities appear increasingly to be using detention as a preventive measure, the situation is likely to worsen for minorities, who are more often perceived as dangerous simply because of their color. Disparities also are apt to increase, particularly outside of urban environments, as many jurisdictions access funding for new secure detention facilities where none have previously existed. We also know that youths are more likely to be adjudicated and to receive harsher dispositions as a consequence of prehearing detention.

Some progress toward more equitable treatment in the prehearing stages is found among several federal initiatives, particularly deinstitutionalization of status offenders and jail removal. Even so, the unstructured discretion available to those who administer juvenile justice seems to have minimized the gains that should have been made—especially for girls, given their greater propensity to be processed as status offenders. Official discretion thwarts progress because options for prehearing interventions that do not involve secure custody have always been too few. Those deficiencies did not change with the DSO initiative. As a result of discretionary practices, many girls, some of whom were merely victims, and probably some abused boys too, have instead been reclassified as delinquents and processed more like criminals. Other youths got sent to mental hospitals and other private facilities where the true state of their care is not monitored. At least some are confined in secure, cell-like settings, medicated for the ease of supervision. Some experience these conditions for a long time.

Given current problems, the following three recommendations are warranted. First, it is important that the core requirements of the JJDP Act be retained, and the provisions that weakened them in 1980 should be removed. Second, detention decisions must be consistent, applied uniformly, and subject to review. The best method to achieve this structure is through validated guidelines instruments. It is important that detention guidelines reflect the concerns for the best interests of youths, without jeopardizing public safety. Criteria in the guidelines also must be neutral in terms of race, sex, and factors closely related to them. Implementing these new procedures would reduce disparity among youths in prehearing custody. In this area, juvenile justice could benefit significantly from similar improvements already made in pretrial release procedures in criminal justice.

Guidelines, however, cannot help overcome the frustrations of not having good options among which to choose. To overcome current deficiencies, the third recommendation is the development of more alternatives to secure detention facilities. Detention is too convenient when the facility is in-house, so even secure centers probably should not be administered by courts. In light of findings that minority youths are indirectly or cumulatively disadvantaged by prehearing detention, we certainly need more equitable access to shelter care, foster care, diversion, and other community-based opportunities and solutions. A significant number of youths could be released without jeopardizing public safety. Moreover, many nonsecure options, such as 24-hour screening and crisis intervention services, family shelter care, home detention, and group homes, are less expensive. More appropriate use of detention facilities and alternatives would likely free up space, which would both minimize the need for additional construction and create opportunities for treatment that some youth could use at this early stage in the process.

Finally, systemwide changes need to occur if juvenile justice is expected to survive as an effective means of responding to troubled youths. Improvements at the prehearing stage really need to be integrated within broader reforms. We need to recognize that juvenile justice officials—like other people familiar with independence and a comfortable routine—do not welcome or embrace change. More often, they disregard or circumvent it and render potential reforms impotent.

Discretion and lack of knowledge have hindered many important reforms in juvenile justice. First, despite a decline in the rate of juveniles in jails, attributed to the JJDP Act, the jail removal mandate has been problematic because of discretion. Rather than limited alternatives, Frazier and Bishop attributed noncompliance in one state to the location of routine processing of juveniles at jail sites, ignorance of the 1974 law, and deliberate disregard. Second, beyond jail removal, some backsliding for the DSO core requirement has been blamed on officials who want the power to arrest and detain status offenders in secure facilities. Third, when OJJDP made working to overcome disproportionate confinement of minorities a core requirement of the JJDP Act, many did not understand the complexity of even the monitoring, let alone achieving race-neutral processing. Fourth and finally, without clear knowledge of what female-specific programming should entail, the rush to expand options for girls provided by challenge grant funding may mean better etiquette and grooming but not necessarily less stereotypical responses, effective life skills, or even higher esteem for more troubled girls.

The solution is not just quota hiring because some youth of color receive harshest treatment from minority staff and women are as likely as men to express distaste for working with girls. Higher job qualifications, better pay, and more training for court staff are part of the answer, but it would be futile to expect to overcome all the biases present in society. The solution is a rational system that is held accountable for its procedures.

QUESTIONS FOR DISCUSSION AND WRITING

1. What is the Juvenile Justice and Delinquency Prevention Act, and what did it and its three reauthorizations do?
2. "Thus," what do "these data show" (i.e., detention data for 1987–1996)? What do Federele and Chesney-Lind suggest about the DSO?
3. In what three ways have frustrated juvenile justice officials circumvented the DSO?
4. What thwarts the purpose and function of detention, and what are some predictions the author makes that are tied to that thwarting?

The Comparative Advantage of Juvenile Versus Criminal Court Sanctions on Recidivism Among Adolescent Felony Offenders

JEFFREY FAGAN

THERE is a long-standing and contentious debate on the appropriate judicial forum for the adjudication and disposition of adolescent felony offenses. Critics suggest that juvenile court sanctions do not rehabilitate felony offenders, offer weak retribution for serious crimes, and are ineffective in deterring subsequent crimes. They contend that the criminal court is the most appropriate forum for adjudicating juvenile offenders whose offense and behavior patterns mandate lengthy incarceration in secure facilities. Criminal court sanctions are viewed as according greater community protection, more effective deterrence of future crime, and more proportionate, retributive responses to serious crimes. The seriousness of many juvenile crimes suggests that these adolescents can be neither controlled nor rehabilitated in the juvenile justice system.

Supporters of the juvenile court argue that violent juvenile crime is a transitory behavioral pattern, and that adolescent crime is unlikely to escalate to more serious or persistent crime. They argue that adolescent offenders can bene-fit from the treatment services of the juvenile justice system with minimal threat to public safety and avoidance of the lasting stigmatization of criminal justice processing. Also, many proponents of juvenile justice processing of violent delinquents do not accept the criticisms of rehabilitative programs, arguing instead that weak evaluation research or poor program quality mask the natural strengths of juvenile corrections.

This chapter examines these issues in a natural experiment to assess key issues in sentencing adolescent felony offenders. It compares the severity, certainty, and celerity of sanctions for 15- and 16-year-old adolescents charged with robbery and burglary in juvenile court in New Jersey with identical offenders in matched communities in New York State whose cases are adjudicated in criminal court, and it determines the effectiveness of these sanctions in reducing recidivism and reincarceration.

A comparison of the severity and effectiveness of juvenile and criminal court sanctions directly bears on the jurisdictional debate in several ways. First, there has been rapid change in statutes that determine the judicial forum to adjudicate felony crimes by adolescents. Since 1978, nearly every state has passed laws to restrict the jurisdiction of the juvenile court. Some states have lowered the age of jurisdiction for

From "The Comparative Advantage of Juvenile Versus Criminal Court Sanctions on Recidivism Among Adolescent Felony Offenders" by J. Fagan, 1996, *Law & Policy, 18*, pp. 77-115. Copyright 1996 by Blackwell Publishers Ltd. Adapted with permission of Blackwell Publishers Ltd.

criminal court, either for all offenders or for selected offense categories. Other states have expanded the basis for transfer of cases from juvenile to criminal jurisdictions, either by expanding the criteria for transfer or by shifting the burden of proof from the state to the defendant. Still others have established concurrent jurisdiction for selected offenses or offenders, giving prosecutors broad discretion in electing a judicial forum for the adjudication and sanctioning of adolescent crimes. However, there has been little systematic research to determine if the sanctions in criminal court are in fact harsher and more consistent and if punishment as an adult results in less recidivism. The resolution of these questions bears on policy and legislation on the age threshold, offense or offender eligibility criteria for criminal court, and continuing efforts to redefine the jurisdiction of the juvenile court.

Second, the comparison of sanctions in juvenile and adult courts provides empirical evidence regarding a "leniency gap" in criminal court for young offenders whose juvenile records are not disclosed in criminal court proceedings. Early research on juveniles prosecuted in criminal courts suggested that juveniles may appear less serious in the "stream of cases" in criminal court in contrast to older, more experienced offenders. The juvenile usually has had less time to accumulate a record in the criminal justice process, and accordingly, the most restrictive sentences are reserved for the older, more "dangerous" defendants. Also, the adolescent defendant's age may lead judges to impose less severe sanctions due in part to the potential dangers of incarceration of youth in prisons.

But the offense-based criminal court also may be inclined to view serious juvenile crime as a threat to public safety and deserving of the most severe sanctions. Research with chronic violent adolescents adjudicated as adults suggests that they indeed are treated with greater severity and more certain punishment compared to those retained in juvenile court. Though violent offenders in juvenile court are the most serious cases before the court, the tra-

ditional emphasis on rehabilitation, together with administrative and statutory limitations on sanction length or severity, suggests that they may be treated less harshly than similar youth in criminal court. Accordingly, this study compares the certainty, celerity, and severity of sanctions for adolescents charged with violent crimes and adjudicated in juvenile or adult court.

Third, the study examines a critical age-sanction threshold for violent crimes. Few empirical sentencing studies have focused on young offenders and optimal sanctioning patterns to reduce recidivism among this high-rate offender group. Thus, the considerable advances in sentencing research over the past decade may not be generalizable to a new, younger defendant class in criminal courts. Compared to decisions involving older offenders, criminal court judges presiding over cases involving defendants near the age of majority must make sentencing decisions without knowledge of critical factors such as prior criminal history, involvement with substances, or other salient social factors.

In these cases, judges instead must rely exclusively on the severity and context of the offense, any mitigating circumstances, and information developed in presentence investigations of defendants' social ties. Moreover, to the extent that judges retain rehabilitative ideals in their sentencing practices, adolescent offenders may receive less severe sanctions, so they may benefit from noncustodial interventions to enhance their education, work, and family ties while addressing other problems such as problematic substance use or mental health. Accordingly, this research can inform sentencing policy through analyses of the relationship between sanction severity and recidivism and develop base expectancy rates for the new class of juveniles appearing before the criminal courts.

Fourth, comparison of juvenile and criminal court sanctions reflects on the organizational context of legal decision making. In particular, holistic and working group theories of legal decision making suggest that the "going rate" for juvenile crime is not any higher in the criminal justice process than in the juvenile court, and in fact it may be lower. But this is contrary to the demands and expectations of the many legislatures who have passed laws relocating adolescent felony offenders to the criminal court. Like many other legal reforms, criminalizing delinquency may have unintended consequences, reflecting the social organization of the courts and processual contexts rather than legal statute. By analyzing the possible determinants of sentences for juveniles charged with felony offenses in the criminal and juvenile courts, public policymakers can plan more appropriately for legal reform. If bringing juveniles into the criminal court is a symbolic process for deterring crime, then it is important to determine whether these ends are better served in the less formal juvenile court.

THE EVOLUTION OF THE MODERN JURISDICTIONAL BOUNDARIES

Three criticisms motivated legislative action to narrow the jurisdiction of the juvenile court and relocate classes of adolescent offenses and offenders to the criminal court. First, sanctions in juvenile court appeared to be less certain or severe (or inappropriately lenient, based on crime severity) than in criminal court, creating the image of a leniency gap in punishment and retribution. Second, rehabilitative dispositions in juvenile court were ineffective in curtailing further crime and violence, as evidenced by growing rates of juvenile violence throughout the 1980s. Third, juvenile court sanctions posed risks to the public of (inappropriately) shorter terms of incarceration than the lengthy sentences meted out by the criminal courts.

There has been little research to address the validity of these critiques. Whether the criminalization of violent juvenile crime has resulted in more certain or severe sanctions is not at all clear. Comparisons of recidivism rates for adolescents adjudicated in juvenile versus adult court are extremely rare and often limited by selection bias. Podkopacz and Feld found that recidivism rates of adolescents waived to the

criminal court were higher (58%) compared to those retained in the juvenile court (42%), but their analysis did not control for systematic differences in the two samples. Similar analyses by Bishop et al. using a matched cases design show that youths transferred (by direct file or waiver) reoffended at a higher rate than nontransferred controls, despite more certain and severe incarceration sentences.

In sum, only these few studies have addressed the critiques of the juvenile court. Previous research on waiver has examined sanctioning patterns but has been limited by sampling bias inherent in the transfer decision. There also is little empirical evidence that reductions in the age of majority have had a general deterrent effect on aggregate adolescent crime rates. Finally, the rare tests comparing the deterrent or incapacitative effects of juvenile and criminal court sanctions for adolescent felony offenders have been severely limited by selection bias and other sampling artifacts that confound risk factors for recidivism with the criteria used in sorting adolescents for prosecution as juveniles or adults. Except for Bishop et al.'s study, no studies have compared the deterrent effects of sanctions in juvenile and criminal courts of specific, matched samples of legislatively strategic offense and offender groups of adolescent felony offenders. Most studies which have attempted to ascertain the deterrent effects of criminal court sanctions on juveniles have conceptualized deterrence broadly in terms of aggregate juvenile crime rates.

Accordingly, the specific contribution of juvenile versus criminal court jurisdiction to the deterrent effects of sanctions has yet to be examined. Yet policy decisions and laws governing the age of jurisdiction have been made in the absence of valid empirical evidence that recidivism is better reduced by punishment in the criminal system. That gap is addressed in this research.

METHODS

This research compared the deterrent effects of sanctions and court jurisdiction on recidivism rates in juvenile versus adult court. Recidivism rates were compared for $N = 800$ youths in four matched counties. Sanction and recidivism rates for adolescents (ages 15 to 16) charged in juvenile court with felony robbery and burglary in two northern New Jersey counties were compared with matched samples in matched counties in southeastern New York State, whose cases originate in the criminal court. The four counties are part of a large metropolitan area and regional economy that shares demographic, social, and cultural commonalities. Both the concentration of risk factors for delinquency and crime problems among juveniles and young adults are comparable in the four counties.

Samples

Two types of selection bias are relevant in this research: (a) selection artifacts that arise when adolescent cases are purposively channeled from juvenile to criminal court and (b) biases introduced by the legal criteria demarking juvenile and criminal jurisdictions. For example, the waiver process reflects a selection process based on subjective interpretations of statutory criteria such as "amenability to treatment" and "dangerousness." Comparisons of offenders of consecutive ages that span legal statuses, where age alone determines court jurisdiction, invite distortion due to the age threshold that is precisely the rationale for demarking the two jurisdictions.

On the other hand, comparison of age-offender groups across jurisdictions is problematic because of the difficulty of controlling for differences in social and legal contexts. The contextual influences that shape case outcomes range from political influences on legal decision makers to normative regional attitudes on crime and punishment. Hagan and Bumiller explain the importance of controlling for such contextual or aggregative influences, including not only political influences on crime control policies but also socioeconomic influences on rates of crime commission.

Offender cohorts from comparable if not identical offense and offender profiles are necessary to avoid these selection biases. The process of assignment to juvenile or criminal court should be independent of any consideration other than legislated jurisdiction. Comparisons would occur in a regional context where a legal division occurs in court jurisdiction, but within a socially and economically homogeneous area. These should be areas within regional economies and transportation systems and where crimes reflect exchanges between smaller social areas within the region. This would control for such factors as economic opportunity, availability of weapons, and other criminogenic influences (e.g., drug use, gang influences, and physical environment).

SELECTION OF JURISDICTIONS

Selecting jurisdictions and cases from the greater New York metropolitan area, including New York City and the highly urbanized northern New Jersey counties, provides an opportunity for a natural experiment. The counties of the region are interrelated economically, in transportation, media and culture, and in major social institutions, including universities, financial services, and medical centers. Because of the elaborate transportation network, crime problems also are regional, and crime serves a redistributive function. The unique legal context for juvenile offenders in New York State, combined with its contiguous location to the traditional jurisprudential setting for juveniles in New Jersey, allows for comparisons of legal jurisdiction with minimal selection effects due to spatial or individual differences.

Within states, cases were sampled from Essex and Passaic counties in New Jersey and Kings (Brooklyn) and Queens counties in New York. The counties were selected from 10 candidate counties in each state based on census and crime data for each county. Counties were matched on social structural characteristics and crime problems that influence sanctioning rates for juvenile offenders. The matching procedure identified counties that differed by no more than 10% on key crime or socioeconomic indicators. The matching criteria included crime and criminal justice, demographic, socioeconomic, labor force, and housing characteristics. Criminal justice indicators for county matching included the county's percentage contributions to state prison commitments (for adults) and juvenile corrections commitments, felony juvenile arrests (under 18 years of age) per 1,000 population, total per capita arrest rates, and per capita law enforcement expenditures. Each county has local incarceration facilities for adults and juveniles, and each has a well-developed indigent defender system for juveniles and adults.

SELECTION OF OFFENSE CATEGORIES

Analysis of New York and New Jersey cases affords a 2-year age range for comparisons of adolescent felony cases. Adolescents ages 15 and 16 charged with first- and second-degree robbery and first-degree burglary in New York were compared with similar juveniles in New Jersey. The offense categories selected were robbery and burglary. The age of criminal jurisdiction for all offenders in New York is 16, and it is 13 for selected felony offenders under the Juvenile Offender Law. Thus, cases for 15-year-old defendants charged with felonies originate in criminal court and are subject to Juvenile Offender Law provisions for disposition. In New Jersey, the age of jurisdiction remains 18 years of age, although transfer to criminal court is permitted at age 13 for selected cases. In New York, cases alleging felony robbery (first- and second-degree) and burglary (first-degree) charges originate in criminal court, whereas in New Jersey they originate in juvenile court.

Robbery events comprise the prototypical violent juvenile crime which has evoked fear of crime as well as legislative action in the past decade. Robbery also reflects the importance of violence to the debate on juvenile court jurisdiction. The inclusion of burglary addresses the broader and more complex pattern of judicial responses to property crime observed in prior research on juvenile sanctions. Property offenders comprise a significant proportion of incarcerated juveniles in each state and also those waived to criminal court.

SELECTION OF CASES

A multistage cluster sampling procedure resulted in random samples of ($N = 200$) offenders within each county during 1981 and 1982. The 1981-1982 period provided sufficient time for a significant proportion of the cohorts to have completed their sentences and accumulated at least 4 years of time at risk. Sampling parameters within age and offense categories were determined by the total population for the two charge categories combined in each county. Cases were selected after charges were filed in the court: at criminal court arraignment in New York and upon filing of juvenile court petitions in New Jersey. This procedure avoided sample attrition at the outset from prosecutorial screening or dismissals prior to arraignment.

Variables and Measures

Variables for each case included prior charges, current charge, race, gender, age at first offense and sample offense, and case processing information such as detention status. Juvenile court records were not available for the criminal court cases. Case processing times were recorded to measure the celerity of sanctions. Sanction measures included the type and length of disposition: the imposition of fines or restitution, probation supervision, out-of-home placement, and incarceration sentences (minimum and maximum terms).

Recidivism measures were constructed from subsequent juvenile and criminal history for all offenses recorded through June 30, 1989. This allowed for risk time of at least 2 years for all cases, including incarceration terms. Recidivism measures included arrests, charges, convictions, supervision or other nonincarcerative sanction, incarceration (training school, jail, or prison), and drug or weapon involvement in subsequent offenses. "Street" time for calculation of offending rates was reduced for subsequent convictions that resulted in incarceration terms. Estimates of time served were based on the same assumptions that were used to calculate sentence length in the sample case.

Criminal career variables were constructed to measure participation, timing, and frequency of subsequent offending. These measures were disaggregated for several offense categories. To minimize known errors in official records, recidivism variabl͏‍ included multiple measures of officially recorded contacts with the law: timing of rearrest, frequency of rearrest and conviction, severity of rearrest charge, and justice system penetration. This strategy reduces potential error within official records from gross recidivism measures that do not afford internal consistency checks.

RESULTS

The Certainty and Severity of Sanctions

"Guilt" in the juvenile court is based on a sustained petition alleging a specific act and penal code section. The base rate of conviction was higher for burglary cases than for robbery cases. Regardless of court jurisdiction, nearly two in three burglary cases resulted in a guilty plea or conviction (finding) compared to about half the robbery cases. Robbery cases in juvenile court were less likely to result in conviction than robbery cases in the criminal court. Even when waiver in New Jersey is combined with convictions, the rate of dismissal in juvenile court for robbery was significantly lower than in the criminal court.

Nearly half the defendants in criminal court convicted of either charge type were sentenced to incarceration in jail, adult prisons, or juvenile corrections facilities. The incarceration rates for robbery cases were significantly greater in criminal court than juvenile court: Fewer than one in five (18.3%) juvenile court defendants were placed in a training school or residential facility. In criminal court, nearly half (46.4%) of those convicted of robbery were sentenced to state prison, secure youth corrections facilities, or local jails.

For burglary convictions, incarceration rates for juveniles were slightly higher (23.8%) than for robbery cases but still were lower than the

criminal court rate for burglaries (46.5%). Incarceration rates in criminal courts were similar for burglary and robbery cases (about 46.5%). For both types of charges, most juvenile court defendants received probation sentences (nearly 6 in 10), while fewer than half the criminal court defendants received probation commitments. Suspended sentences or continuances (of previous probation sentences) were more likely in the juvenile than criminal court.

Results of analysis of variance (ANOVA) for both charge and court types in each period showed no significant differences in sentence length, by either charge type or court jurisdiction. The absence of significant interaction effects shows that the patterns were constant across charge types by court jurisdiction.

Comparative Impacts of Sanctions on Recidivism

Recidivism measures are compared for juvenile and criminal court cohorts for each offense type. For robbery offenders, rearrest rates were higher for cases adjudicated in the criminal courts. However, rearrest rates did not differ for burglary offenders by court jurisdiction. The pattern was similar for reincarceration. There were significant differences for court jurisdiction for robbery cases but not for burglary. Robbery cases in the criminal court cohort were reincarcerated more often (56.2%) than those in the juvenile court robbery cohort.

Reoffending rates were computed for offenders with at least one rearrest (for a new criminal violation). The reoffending rearrest rates were calculated by annualizing total arrests over the time at risk during the follow-up period. Time reincarcerated was excluded from the reoffending "window." Once again, the patterns for rearrest and reincarceration prevalence are mirrored for reoffending rates. There were significant differences in rearrest rates for robbery offenders. Robbery offenders in criminal court had reoffending (rearrest) rates over 50% higher than those of robbery offenders in juvenile court (2.85 vs. 1.67 arrests per year at risk). There were no significant differences in the rates for burglary offenders by court jurisdiction.

Failure time analyses present a similar trend for robbery offenders. In the juvenile court, the time to first rearrest for robbery offenders was significantly longer (553 days) compared to that in criminal court (456.5 days). For burglary offenders, there was no significant difference between juvenile and criminal court cases (the large disparity in the means is not significant due to the small Ns and large within-group variances).

The results present a consistent trend where the deterrent effects of sanctions on recidivism are greater for robbery cases in the juvenile court. For burglary offenders, the recidivism indicators are unaffected by court jurisdiction. That is, there is no comparative advantage in recidivism reduction for burglary cases disposed and sentenced in the criminal court. For robbery cases, the results at first glance suggest that there is a comparative advantage in recidivism for cases disposed in the juvenile court. Comparisons were then made to determine whether these effects remain after controlling for type of sanction. Since there were no significant differences in length of incarceration, these analyses did not control for sanction severity.

REARREST PREVALENCE

There were significant differences in rearrest prevalence only for robbery cases sentenced either to probation or incarceration terms. Nearly all those incarcerated in the criminal court for robbery charges were rearrested (90.5%), compared to fewer than three in four sentenced in juvenile court (73.0%). Fewer robbery offenders sentenced to probation in the juvenile court were rearrested (64.4%) than those sentenced in the criminal court (81.2%). There were no significant differences in rearrest prevalence by court jurisdiction for cases suspended or dismissed and no significant differences for burglary offenders for any sanction.

TIME TO FIRST REARREST

Similar to analyses of rearrest prevalence, failure rates (time to first rearrest) differed significantly only for robbery offenders who were incarcerated. The time to first rearrest for robbery offenders who were sentenced to incarceration in juvenile court was over 50% longer than that for robbery offenders sentenced in criminal court (631 vs. 392 days). There were no significant differences for any other charge-court jurisdiction analysis.

OFFENDING RATES

Annualized rearrest rates for robbery offenders did not differ significantly for incarcerated offenders. For nonincarcerative sanctions, rearrest rates were consistently lower for robbery offenders sentenced in the juvenile court. The results were significant and substantively large. Annual rearrest rates for robbery offenders sentenced in criminal court were more than 75% greater than those sentenced in juvenile court. Only for burglary offenders who were incarcerated were rearrest rates lower for offenders sentenced in criminal court (3.37 vs. 6.25 rearrests/year). Other rearrests rates for burglary offenders did not differ significantly by type of sanction.

The Effects of Sentence Length and Court Jurisdiction on Recividism

To determine whether sentence length influences recidivism rates, we estimated a competing risks model of the hazard of rearrest. Hazard models estimate the probability that an individual will fail during a given time period. Hazard analyses simultaneously estimate the likelihood of two dimensions of recidivism: its prevalence during a given time period and the interval until rearrest occurs.

The competing risks hazard model is appropriate for analyses when the occurrence of one type of event removes the individual from the risk of other event types. That is, the person is censored from the analysis of a second type of event at the point in time when the first event occurs. Each event type is analyzed separately and has its own hazard function.

Accordingly, we examined the effects of juvenile court jurisdiction (controlling for the length of incarceration sentences) on failure times for four types of crimes. It is the consistency of the results (Table 1) that depicts the substantial comparative advantage of the juvenile court in controlling recidivism. Even when disaggregated by types of crime and controlling for prior record and sentence severity, the hazards of rearrest for adolescents are far lower when they are sanctioned by the juvenile court compared to the criminal court. Of course, there may be competing explanations that reflect the differences between the two jurisdictions. These may include differences in patrol practices, arrest probabilities, the distribution of criminal opportunities, and the salience of social controls in the New Jersey communities. However, the matching procedures for the counties were designed to minimize differences in these exogenous effects. Accordingly, the contrast of court cultures and statutory contexts within one structurally integrated metroplex suggests that the allocation of effects should tip strongly toward differences in the jurisprudential forums.

CONCLUSIONS

Since 1975, legal and social institutions throughout the United States have mobilized to strengthen the punitive element of legal sanctions for adolescent offenders. Two widely held perceptions fueled these legislative efforts: that rehabilitation is ineffective, undermining the sine qua non of the juvenile court, and that punishment was discounted in the juvenile court setting. States have applied a variety of statutory mechanisms to "criminalize" adolescent crimes by bringing them under the jurisdiction of the criminal courts. These efforts have included expanded use of judicial waiver as well as statutory exclusion (legislative waiver) of classes of juvenile offenders from juvenile court jurisdiction.

The trend to remove juvenile cases to the criminal court represents a legislative and societal rejection of the *parens patriae* philosophy of

the juvenile court, its emphasis on rehabilitation and individualized justice, and the effectiveness of its dispositions in controlling the recurrence of crime or its initiation. Despite increasing emphasis in the juvenile court on the punitive dimensions of dispositions, especially for violent offenders, efforts to relocate adolescent crimes have been fueled by the expectation of greater accountability (more certain and proportionate punishment) and lengthier sentences in the criminal court. For many proponents of the criminalization of delinquency, these efforts also promised more effective punishment and lower recidivism rates.

The results of this study suggest that none of these promises has been fulfilled. Earlier efforts examining the relative likelihood of punishment in juvenile versus adult courts concluded much the same. This effort went two significant steps further, to examine sentence lengths and recidivism. If more certain, swifter, and effective punishments are not forthcoming for adolescents punished in the adult criminal courts, new questions are raised concerning efforts over the past decades to narrow the jurisdiction of the juvenile court. These issues are discussed below.

By What Standard Should Jurisdiction Be Defined?

Implicit in these trends is the stubborn perception that juvenile court dispositions are more lenient, less certain, fail to rehabilitate, are ineffective deterrents to future crime, and accordingly increase threats to community safety. In this view, the criminalization of delinquency affords not only greater retribution and proportionality in punishment but also more effective punishment that will better deter future criminal behavior.

Unstated in this debate on the appropriate jurisprudential forum for adolescent crime are decision standards to assess the wisdom and efficacy of the criminalization of delinquency. Dimensions of the debate, such as due process and equal protection gaps between juvenile and criminal court, are sideshows to the central con-

TABLE 1

Competing risk proportional hazard model for time to first rearrest by type of crime and court jurisdiction, controlling for sentence length (coefficient and exponentiated coefficient).

	Model I Any Rearrest		Model II Violent		Nonviolent		Other Felony		Model III Misdemeanor		Drug	
	B	Exp (B)	B	Exp (B)	B	Exp (B)	B	Exp (B)	B	Exp (B)	B	Exp (B)
Age	-0.02	0.98	-0.07	0.93	0.05	1.05	0.05	1.06	0.12	1.13	-0.07	0.93
Case length	-0.001	0.99	-0.001	1.00	0.0003	1.00	-0.0001	0.99	0.001	1.00	0.001	1.00
Burglary	-0.03	0.97	-0.16	0.85	0.30*	1.36	0.61**	1.85	-0.14	0.87	0.18	1.20
Priors	0.03*	1.03	0.04*	1.04	0.04*	1.04	0.01	1.01	0.03	1.03	0.02	1.02
Sentence length	-0.002	0.99	0.001	1.00	-0.0001	0.99	0.0001	1.00	0.0004	0.99	0.001	1.00
Court	0.34***	0.71	0.33*	0.72	-0.09	0.91	0.22	1.25	-0.91***	0.40	1.01**	2.75
Sentence × court	0.0002	1.00	-0.001*	0.99	0.0001	1.00	-0.001	0.99	-0.0002	1.00	0.001	1.00
N arrested	587		227		360		166		131		51	
% Arrested	72.5		28.0		44.4		20.5		16.2		6.3	
–2 Log likelihood	4849.5		2950.5		4606.2		2172.9		1692.2		650.3	
Chi-square	16.2		20.9		13.9		13.3		30.4		44.2	
p (chi-square)	.023		.004		.053		.0662		.0001		.0000	

*p < .05; **p < .01; ***p < .001.

troversy of crime control strategy. Nor is this debate about rehabilitation versus punishment, for there is nothing inherently at odds in the modern juvenile court between treatment and accountability or punishment.

Rather, the debate has unfolded in terms of punishment, community protection, and its effectiveness as crime control strategies. If the impetus for removal of adolescent felony offenders is to close the leniency gap, criteria for evaluating court reform would include the certainty and severity of punishment. If juveniles have been relocated to criminal court to enhance the deterrent effects of legal responses to juvenile crime, or to reduce the risks to the community from adolescent crime, then recidivism rates are a more appropriate standard.

Standards also are unstated with respect to specific versus general deterrence of crime. Certainly, the rhetoric and symbolism of these "reforms" have been directed at deterring adolescents as a class from crime commission by raising the perceived certainty and severity of punishment. Yet waiver statutes rarely achieve more than a symbolic role in reform, limited from larger impacts by their low base rate and uncertain outcomes in the criminal court. Accordingly, despite the widespread publicity for "get tough" measures targeted at adolescent offenders, their effects are difficult to measure at the aggregate level, and their application within a system of individualized justice suggests that they be assessed by their specific deterrent effects.

What Is Gained and Lost in Criminalization

The comparison of closely matched states and offender cohorts in juvenile and criminal courts suggests that there may be a negative return from criminalizing adolescent crime. The effects on case outcomes may actually be quite the opposite from what was intended and subject to exogenous factors that influence the makeup of court caseloads and salience of classes of offenses. Accountability for adolescent offenders in criminal courts was significantly greater than in the juvenile court, as evidenced by the higher conviction and sentencing rates. However, criminal court punishment was not a more effective strategy for crime control. Quite possibly, more harm than good resulted from the effort to criminalize adolescent crimes.

Convictions were higher in the criminal court for the 1981-1982 cohorts, and conviction rates for adolescents remained stable over the next decade as drug crimes paralyzed the criminal courts in New York. Punishment was less swift (100 days to sentencing in juvenile court compared to 145 days in criminal court). The likelihood of a severe sanction (deprivation of liberty through incarceration) was greater in the criminal court. But instead of the relatively swift half-life of juvenile court cases, criminal court cases took months longer to resolve. Neither retributive nor incapacitative effects were greater in the criminal court: For those sentenced to incarceration, sentence lengths were nearly identical. Long sentences were rare for both the juvenile and criminal court cohorts in this study.

Comparing overall crime rates for the 1981–1982 cohorts, recidivism rates appeared to be higher for criminal court cases, their rearrests occurred more quickly, and their return to jail was more likely. Recidivism among the juvenile court cohort also appeared to be no more serious than that for the criminal court cohort. Rather than affording greater community protection, the higher recidivism rates for the criminal court cohort suggest that public safety was in fact compromised by adjudication in the criminal court. Moreover, the data hint that increasing the severity of criminal court sanctions may actually enhance the likelihood of recidivism.

By neither public safety nor punishment (or just deserts) standards can claims be made that the criminal justice system affords greater accountability for adolescent felony offenders or protection for the public. If criminalization is intended to instill accountability, its effects are diluted by the lengthier case processing time. If it is intended to protect the public by making incarceration more certain and terms lengthier, it fails also on this count. While these processes may have symbolic value to the public, they seem to offer little substantive advantage in the legal response to adolescent crimes. It is only for the earlier accumulation of a criminal record, leading to lengthier terms and more severe punishments for subsequent offenses, that there is a marginal gain in the relocation of adolescent crimes to the criminal court.

Statutory Implications

The results suggest that efforts to criminalize adolescent offending, or to narrow the scope of the juvenile court to exclude these offenses, may not produce the desired results and may in fact be counterproductive. Accordingly, two primary policy implications are derived from this research. First, there should continue to be both a special jurisprudence for adolescent crimes and a separate jurisdiction for juvenile offenders. Second, the current trajectory of juvenile court reforms should continue. These reforms have increased the emphasis on proportionate and certain punishment while attending to due process considerations of offenders who now are liable for significant intervals of punishment.

MAINTAIN A SPECIAL JURISPRUDENCE OF ADOLESCENCE

This research offers no empirical support for claims that adolescent felony offenses should be removed from the jurisdiction of the juvenile court. In fact, there are other reasons not to do so. For example, Freeman's survey of adolescent males in Boston suggests that involvement of adolescents in the criminal court, with its public records and lasting stigmatization, severely limits their future labor market participation. The erection of barriers to legal work for young males in effect steers them toward illegal work as an income-generating choice.

The emerging model of the juvenile court offers a jurisprudential forum that matches the expectations of proponents of the criminal court model while retaining the advantages of the separation of juvenile crimes and the shield for those juveniles whose criminality desists as they approach adulthood. Transfer, or waiver, from juvenile to criminal court remains as a viable option for specific types of cases that require a response beyond the limits of juvenile justice or juvenile corrections.

MAINTAIN THE CURRENT TRAJECTORY OF JUVENILE COURT REFORMS

Efforts to narrow the jurisdiction of the juvenile court reflected criticisms not only of its ineffectiveness but also of the constitutionality of its proceedings. Both equal protection and due process concerns were addressed in U.S. Supreme Court decisions that formalized juvenile court proceedings. Other concerns reflected doubts about the juvenile court as an institution of social control. The evolution of the juvenile court over the past decade attempted to strengthen the juvenile court response to adolescent crimes by making punishment both more certain and severe. The quest for more proportionate punishment to reflect the severity of crimes and perceived threats to public safety from serious juvenile offenders led to changes in the going rates of punishment in the juvenile court.

The lower recidivism for juveniles sanctioned in juvenile court argues against the current trend to restrict the jurisdiction of the juvenile court. But this does not argue against the continuation and stabilization of procedural reforms. As discussed earlier, research on waiver decisions and statutes suggests informality and vagueness that challenges the commitment to fairness and equal protection. Waiver is an area where continued legislative attention is needed, not only to reinforce the boundaries and conditions for transfer of jurisdiction but also to the operational definitions and statutory criteria that inform these decisions.

QUESTIONS FOR DISCUSSION AND WRITING

1. What three criticisms motivated legislative action to narrow the jurisdiction of the juvenile court and relocate classes of adolescent offenses and offenders to the criminal court? What is true about the validity of these criticisms?
2. What was true about the certainty and severity of sanctions?
3. What did the author find with respect to the four recidivism measures: rearrest, reincarceration, reoffending, and failure time analyses?

THE PROGRAM LEGACY

An Analysis of
Juvenile Correctional Treatment

STEVEN P. LAB
JOHN T. WHITEHEAD

THE state of the evidence concerning correctional treatment prompts a vast array of differing opinions. One extreme position posits that "nothing works." The opposite view stresses that various programs have a positive effect on selected clients under certain conditions. Still another view contends that, apart from the effectiveness issue, the rehabilitation philosophy should be retained because it supports a humane correctional environment.

The claim that "nothing works" centers on the question of whether interventions reduce recidivism. A good deal of the debate revolves around the quality of the evaluations and the outcome measures of interest. Typically, the most rigorous evaluations that use control groups and random assignment fail to uncover positive results. Likewise, studies that search for changes in aggregate measures of redicivism (i.e., recidivism rates) report modest or no positive outcomes. Favorable evaluations of treatment, on the other hand, tend to focus on qualitative improvements in the behavior of subjects (e.g., self-esteem and educational achievement) apart from recidivism or on the reduction of recidivism for some (amendable) clients. In either case, the claim that some programs work for some individuals (however few) cannot be dismissed. The major concern for recidivism, however, is not addressed in these claims. The present study represents an attempt to clarify the unclear state of juvenile correctional treatment by presenting recent evidence on the effectiveness of various interventions as they affect recidivism.

LITERATURE REVIEW

A review of the literature indicates that there are three basic ways to assess the evidence on the effectiveness of correctional interventions. The first, the so-called ballot-box or voting method, has been the most frequently utilized approach. The researcher gathers as many evaluations of intervention efforts that meet certain inclusion criteria (e.g., use of a comparison group or pre-post measures) as possible and then simply adds up the findings of successes, failures, and no difference. A second approach, hereafter termed the analytical method, involves the researcher going beyond simple tabulation to appraise critically the theory, methodology, and implementation of the various interventions to extrapolate common principles or the best substantiated findings. A variant of this method is to select exemplary interventions of various types and rely on the outcomes of such exemplary projects as critical tests. The third and most current approach is meta-analysis, which calculates a statistic (effect size) that allegedly summarizes the individual statistics of each intervention into an overall measure of effectiveness.

Interestingly, the three approaches to summarizing individual evaluation studies into some sort of overall conclusion about the effectiveness of delinquency all come to the same conclusion: Many efforts do not work. This conclusion, however, must be tempered by the limits of the analyses. Many of these reviews look at only a select few studies, especially diversion and behavioral interventions. Also, in many instances only a single source is used in locating studies for inclusion in the review. In addition, meta-analyses and analytical approaches often do not allow for direct comparison between the methods and do not provide the reader the opportunity to draw his or her own conclusions.

THE PRESENT STUDY

The present effort attempted to avoid these problems by conducting a comprehensive, up-to-date ballot-box or voting method analysis of delinquency intervention programs. Our review has several strengths. First, it was not limited to a single source of studies for analysis; instead, it used several abstracts and the National Criminal Justice Reference Service Index. This review, therefore, included studies not found in other analyses. Second, it allows for comparison with previous ballot-box studies, such as that of Wright and Dixon, to determine if interventions have been more or less successful in different time periods. Third, the focus on recent research followed the suggestions of the National Academy of Sciences and Gendreau and Ross that more recent programs have been pursuing more promising intervention strategies than the ones evaluated 10 or 15 years ago. Fourth, unlike most of the other recent analyses,

this review was not limited to a single category or type of intervention. Instead of looking only at diversion or behavioral treatments, we included evaluative reports, regardless of intervention type (with few qualifications), which provided enough detail for reasonable discussion. The specific inclusion criteria are outlined below. Fifth, we focused on recidivism, whereas many of the other recent reviews looked at a variety of outcome measures (sometimes ignoring recidivism) in arriving at their conclusions. As noted earlier, recidivism appears to be the major goal and concern of most juvenile intervention programs. Sixth, unlike meta-analyses and other reviews, we have presented the actual recidivism data, as well as information on statistical significance levels and the original authors' ratings of the studies. This allows others to inspect and understand the prior evaluation results in a very direct manner. Also, presentations such as meta-analysis may be confusing to some because of their focus on the harder to interpret effect size statistics. Finally, our presentation of the basic recidivism data and significance levels allows others some opportunity to judge for themselves the validity of the claims of the original authors concerning success or failure of the particular intervention efforts, as well as our assessments of success, no impact, or negative impact. While a complete assessment of the claims of particular researchers requires a thorough inspection of the research in question, our presentation allows for a comparison of the claims of the researchers versus the data they used to make their claims.

DATA AND METHODS

This study focused on juvenile correctional treatment and subsequent recidivism. Treatment was broadly defined as an attempt to reduce the incidence of further (or initial) offending. Interventions that were strongly punishment oriented, such as corporal punishment, imprisonment, or restriction of privileges or liberty, were not considered in this context of treatment. The results incorporated programs ranging from police cautioning to restitution to residential treatment. One additional exception to this definition was the exclusion of treatment solely for drug/alcohol usage. The outcome measure of interest was recidivism. As with the definition of treatment, the measure of recidivism varied greatly and was restricted only to the extent that the study subjects had some subsequent contact with the justice system due to delinquent/criminal behavior.

The study used secondary data taken from previously published reports of juvenile correctional treatments from 1975 through 1984, inclusive. The present analysis focused only on those reports found in professional journals and excluded government documents, books, theses, and dissertations. Titles and abstracts provided initial information on the age of the subjects, the existence of control groups and data, and a clear treatment method. The study excluded those reports that lacked one of these factors. These procedures resulted in over 500 documents for inspection of which approximately 200 were professional, journal articles. Many of those 200 reports were excluded upon further examination due to the lack of data, a focus on adults, the duplication of the results in more than one forum, or the absence of other required information.

FINDINGS

The literature search resulted in 55 research reports that met our criteria and one additional criterion; the study reported the percentage of the "experimental" and "control/comparison" groups that recidivated. Studies not reporting such basic results but noting more complex statistical analyses (e.g., regression results) were not included.

The 55 research reports offered 85 comparisons between an experimental group and some sort of comparison or control group. These multiple comparisons came from different experimental interventions or multiple experimental sites within a single published report. Disregarding tests of significance and relying on the assessment of the original authors, 40 of the comparisons showed that the experimental group had less recidivism than the control/comparison group, 34 showed no difference, and 11 showed higher recidivism for the experimental group. Looking only at comparisons where the authors computed tests of statistical significance, 15 of those comparisons were in favor of the experimental group, 28 showed no difference between the experimental and control groups, and 5 revealed the experimental group to have higher recidivism than the control group.

Based on authors' evaluations without regard to tests of significance, only one subgroup, system diversion, had more positive outcomes than other outcomes; that is, only system diversion showed more findings of lower recidivism for the experimental group than findings of no difference between the groups or findings of higher recidivism for the experimental group than for the control group. As many negative or no difference results were found in nonsystem diversion programs as findings of positive impact on recidivism. The other three categories of studies all had more findings of no difference and/or higher recidivism for the experimental group.

Most studies reported tests of statistical significance for their results. Of the 48 comparisons where a test of significance was reported, only 20 represented a difference between comparison and experimental groups exceeding the author's chosen level of significance. In total, 28 of the statistical tests failed to reach significance, indicating no effect of experimental intervention. Overall, 15 of the 20 significant differences were in the positive direction: That is, the experimental group had a significantly lower recidivism rate than the control group. The remaining five statistically significant differences were in the negative direction, indicating higher recidivism by experimental subjects. System diversion fared the best when considering statistical significance, with all six significant comparisons showing a positive impact of experimental treatment. Nonsystem diversion was successful in six of eight comparisons reporting statistically significant differences. The remaining treatment categories reflected few studies reporting statistically significant differences in the results.

Parenthetically, we did not agree with all the authors' assessments of the various interventions. For example, two sets of authors claimed success even though their tests of significance showed no statistically significant differences between the experimental and control groups. Other researchers claimed success without reporting the significance levels of their results. Such differences of opinion between the authors of the research reports and ourselves were few, however, and sometimes they merely reflected our focus on the percentage of experimentals and controls recidivating, whereas the original authors included several measures as the basis for their overall assessment of the intervention.

One common basis for concern in reviews of treatment literature entails the method of assigning subjects to experimental and control groups. Evaluations using random assignment are considered to be more rigorous tests of the intervention. In the present review, only 22 of the studies used random assignment. The remaining studies relied on program selection, matching, or some other method for dividing subjects into groups (in 3 studies the method of group assignment was unknown). Based on authors' ratings without concern for statistical significance, the more rigorous evaluations (random assignment) presented 14 positive evaluations of the treatment, 12 comparisons showing no effect, and 6 instances where the control group did better than the experimental group. Comparisons from nonrigorous evaluations showed similar results with approximately half (24) of the comparisons being positive and 26 outcomes reflecting no difference between the groups or higher recidivism by the experimental subjects. Based on this review, more rigorous evaluations reported findings similar to those of studies using less rigorous methodologies. In both instances, the negative or no impact findings were greater in number than the positive results.

DISCUSSION

The results are far from encouraging for rehabilitation proponents. Disregarding tests of statistical significance, 45 of the comparisons showed no impact or negative impact for the various interventions with juvenile offenders while 40 interventions showed positive impact. Where authors reported tests of significance, only 15 comparisons were in favor of the experimental group, whereas 33 showed no impact or a negative impact. Based on these statistics, it is difficult to reaffirm rehabilitation.

Diversion programs appear to hold the most promise. Both system and nonsystem diversion interventions revealed at least as many positive findings as negative findings or findings of no differences between experimental and control groups. This held true when looking at authors' evaluations or evaluations based only on findings of statistical differences. Interestingly, system diversion programs showed the greatest positive results. This is surprising in light of the argument that system contact exacerbates delinquent tendencies. Such a "labeling" argument has formed a key part of the rationale for diversion programs that are not connected to the juvenile or criminal justice systems.

Two caveats are in order. First, critical to any analysis is the assessment of the "no difference" findings. We opted to interpret findings of no difference rather negatively. Die-hard advocates of rehabilitation might interpret such findings more optimistically, with the claim that such null findings show that the experimental interventions were no worse than the traditional interventions. A typical companion claim has been that the experimental intervention was less expensive than the traditional intervention.

A second caveat is that a direct comparison of the study results is not possible. The studies used a wide array of subjects, interventions, tests of significance, and outcome measures. We attempted to group the various studies into meaningful categories and make comparisons along similar dimensions. A more sophisticated analysis (such as meta-analysis) might have resulted in more optimistic conclusions than this traditional analysis that simply totaled comparisons. We reiterate, however, that recent examinations of evaluation research by other authors came to similar conclusions whether they used the voting, analytical, or meta-analytical techniques.

For several reasons, future research may be more optimistic than our overall assessment that offers little encouragement for rehabilitation advocates. First, the importance of treatment integrity has been emphasized, and thus current and future interventionists have no excuse for failing to ascertain that their treatment techniques are in fact implemented as intended. Unfortunately, some prior efforts, including some of the more recent efforts reported in our study, failed to check for treatment integrity and thus the evaluations of those efforts were flawed. Attention to this problem may in itself increase effectiveness.

Second, recent interventions have begun to incorporate simple but necessary rehabilitative principles, such as the abandonment of any attempt at total personality change in favor of more limited but realistic interventions and the use of somewhat coercive and intrusive intervention techniques for at least some delinquents and criminals. Interventions such as intensive supervision, house arrest, and probation detention centers are based, at least in part, on the premise that some offenders "require external controls, heavy structuring, and with respect to community programs, considerable surveillance." This does not mean that counseling, education, and training are no longer appropriate. It does point out that some past programs were too optimistic and ignored the need for basic constraints on offenders.

Finally, one trend in evaluation research is to go beyond simple, dichotomous measures of success to more complex measures such as failure-rate analysis or the analysis of suppression effects. While these more complex measures are not without their critics, they do offer some hope for uncovering effects masked by dichotomous measures of success. Thus, future evaluation studies and reviews of evaluation studies may be more optimistic than past reports. At the very least, future studies should leave less room for the claim that the research is so slipshod that it really does not clarify the issue of program effectiveness.

QUESTIONS FOR DISCUSSION AND WRITING

1. Around what does a good deal of the recidivism intervention debate revolve? Which evaluations find negative results? Which evaluations find positive results?
2. Of the 48 comparisons for which a test of significance was reported, how many were significant? How many of those differences were in the positive direction (i.e., the experimental group had a significantly lower recidivism rate than the control group)? How many were negative?
3. What was true about rigorous and nonrigorous evaluations?

Alternative Placements for Juvenile Offenders: Results From the Evaluation of the Nokomis Challenge Program

ELIZABETH PIPER DESCHENES
PETER W. GREENWOOD

JUVENILE JUSTICE REFORM

A cornerstone of the juvenile justice system is the concept of rehabilitation. Up until the early 1970s, this meant placing juvenile delinquents in small community group homes or large congregate training schools where they would receive education and perhaps job training. Over the past three decades, with overcrowding due to high arrest rates, these traditional schools have been criticized. Among the primary criticisms were allegations that they offered sterile and unimaginative programs, were inappropriate places to run rehabilitative programs, and fostered abuse and mistreatment of their charges. These criticisms have led both to the closing of some state training schools (such as those in Massachusetts and Maryland) and to the development of various community-based alternatives.

According to Palmer, these alternative programs represent the "reinvention of rehabilitation." The reform movement has focused on three basic themes: (a) improving the individual's self-concept and attitudes toward others through individual, group, and/or family counseling; (b) providing external controls/surveillance, usually through intensive supervision; and (c) developing life skills through cognitive or social skills training in addition to the more traditional educational and vocational training. Of primary concern is the effectiveness of these alternative programs. There is limited evidence regarding the impact of the individual components on delinquency or substance use.

The purpose of this study was to determine whether an integrated short-term residential/intensive community supervision program provided a more cost-effective means of controlling delinquent youths and reducing subsequent criminal behavior and drug use than did traditional residential placements.

CURRENT STUDY

The evaluation of the Nokomis Challenge Program in Michigan was a joint effort of staff from the Michigan Department of Social Services (DSS) and RAND.

At the time the Nokomis program was being developed, delinquent youths who were committed to the DSS were usually placed in state training schools or private residential facilities. Almost all the programs used group-based treatment models, similar to Positive Peer

From "Alternative Placements for Juvenile Offenders: Results From the Evaluation of the Nokomis Challenge Program" by E. Piper Deschenes and P. W. Greenwood, 1998, *Journal of Research in Crime and Delinquency, 35*, pp. 267-294. Copyright 1998 by Sage Publications, Inc. Adapted with permission of Sage Publications.

Culture or Guided Group Interaction, with individualized treatment services. The average length of stay was between 15 and 16 months. Beginning in 1990, the Michigan DSS increased its focus on the families of youths. In the training schools, youth group leaders provided family counseling sessions one or two times per month. Family services provided by a number of the private residential facilities were generally delivered in a more formal program of family therapy or counseling. Therapy sessions were held on average one or two times per month with a family therapist and once per month with a group leader. For youths placed in residential facilities, most of the postrelease supervision was, and still is, provided by the delinquency service workers from local DSS offices. The frequency of face-to-face contacts averaged about one contact per month. In general, the state training schools in Michigan have been highly regarded. However, due to concerns of overcrowding and budgetary constraints, Michigan, like other jurisdictions, has tested a variety of alternative programs, including the Nokomis Challenge Program.

THE EXPERIMENTAL NOKOMIS PROGRAM

The Nokomis Challenge Program began in 1989 as an alternative placement to the traditional training school for medium- and low-risk youths. It is a 12-month integrated treatment program combining a 3-month residential component and a 9-month community-based component. A critical feature of this program is the blending together of various highly successful treatment approaches into an extremely focused, intensive treatment modality with clearly defined program outcomes.

Eligibility for the Nokomis program is limited to youths 14 years of age and older who have none of the following conditions:

- Conviction of a Class I offense or arson
- Suicidal tendencies
- A developmental or emotional disability

- A medical condition that would limit their participation in the outdoor challenge activities

The Michigan Department of Social Services' Nokomis Challenge Program represents an ambitious effort to develop an alternative program for nonviolent juvenile offenders, adjudicated for a felony offense, who would otherwise serve an average 15 or 16 months in regular training schools. The program was designed to meet the needs of the specific client population. These needs were identified as low self-concept/self-esteem, underdeveloped socialization skills, dysfunctional thought processes, dysfunctional family systems, lacking a positive life direction, substance abuse, underdeveloped empathy skills, underdeveloped sense of community, and a history of abuse or neglect. The Nokomis program model combines relapse prevention with various specific elements from successful impact and treatment programs, such as the development of cognitive, behavioral, and social skills, self-esteem, and family functioning. It combines a short-term residential placement, in a rural wilderness setting that is somewhat similar to a boot camp, with 9 months of intensive community-based surveillance and treatment services.

EVALUATING THE NOKOMIS PROGRAM

The evaluation of the Nokomis program was designed to measure whether the program was effective in meeting three goals:

1. Increasing youths' participation in school and legitimate employment and improving the functioning of youths' families
2. Suppressing and detecting criminal activity and drug use while the youths are in the community under intensive supervision (and the comparison youths are still in residential placement)
3. Reducing the youths' level of criminal activity and drug use after they have completed the program

In addition, the study examined changes in specific program components, including cognitive skill development and coping skills. A second objective of the evaluation was to determine for what types of youths this integrated correctional programming strategy was most effective. This chapter discusses the outcomes of the Nokomis program in comparison to traditional residential programming.

Research Design

One of the difficulties in deciding how to design the evaluation of the Nokomis program in comparison to the traditional residential placements was the fact that it is a fixed length of stay program (3 months residential and 9 months aftercare), whereas the length of stay in training schools or other residential programs is variable, averaging approximately 15 months. Consequently, it was necessary to allow a minimum of 24-month follow-up from intake, the date of the youth's Case Assessment Review (CAR) hearing, to obtain comparisons of outcome measures of substance use and recidivism for both groups. Yet, to compare the program implementation and intermediate outcomes, it was necessary to obtain exit data for Nokomis youths at 3 and 12 months following intake. To standardize the comparisons, the study was designed with intake, 12-month, and 24-month follow-up interviews for both experimental and comparison groups with youths and their families.

The evaluation included youths who were assigned to Nokomis by Michigan juvenile courts and a comparison sample of similar youths who met the Nokomis eligibility criteria. The comparison group was selected from a sample of youths who were not placed in the program for one of two reasons: Either they resided in counties with judges who refused to place youths at Nokomis or they became ineligible for placement when all of the 10 Nokomis slots had been filled. Thus, the analysis sample consists of 97 youths who entered the Nokomis program and 95 similar comparison youths who were placed in a training school or private residential program during the same time period.

Data were collected from five sources: (a) official records maintained by the DSS, (b) interviews with youths, (c) interviews with the families of youths, (d) observation and interviews with staff at Nokomis and the training schools, and (e) official arrest records from the state police as well as county-level circuit and probate courts.

Intake data were coded from youths' records, and interviews were conducted with the youths and 101 of the families who agreed to participate in the evaluation. For the Nokomis experimental group, information on the residential phase of the program was obtained in an interview with the youths at the end of the 3-month residential period, and program activities were observed and videotaped. Follow-up information at 12 months was obtained in interviews with 147 youths and 110 of the youths' families. At 24 months, information was obtained from interviews with 114 youths and 116 of the primary caregivers. Official arrest records and placement information were coded for the full sample of 192 youths at 24 months.

Youth interviews included measures of personal goals, coping skills, self-esteem, family functioning, the Jesness asocial index, and program services received, as well as self-reported delinquency and substance use in the past 12 months. Family interviews included measures of family functioning and program services received. During the interviews, a status calendar was filled out for each individual that tracked the dates of placement into or release from various correctional programs. This information was augmented with data collected from official record sources, including the DSS files, the Wayne County Residential Services, and probate and circuit courts. The total number of days for each "status," for example, Nokomis or juvenile detention facility, were summed for the complete follow-up period.

There are several limitations to this study. First, the sample youths may not be representative of the total population of youths that have been admitted into the Nokomis program.

Comparison of this sample to other youths in Nokomis (both before and after this sample was drawn) showed some differences in background characteristics and outcomes. Second, because of sample attrition, the results of analyses using the interview data may be less valid and reliable than official record information, even though we did use a weighting procedure to correct for possible bias. Despite these limitations, this evaluation provides a measure of the effectiveness of the Nokomis program in terms of changes in social adjustment, family functioning, and recidivism.

Data Analysis

To analyze the outcome measures of social adjustment, that is, coping skills, family functioning, and self-esteem, differences in change scores within groups (from intake to 12 months or intake to 24 months) were statistically compared using t tests. Between-group differences were compared for both the 12-month and 24-month time periods, controlling for intake or baseline levels of these measures.

To examine differences between groups in recidivism rates, the first strategy was to compare the 24-month follow-up recidivism measures, controlling for time at risk. To have a more realistic picture of the risk of recidivism following residential placement, the second strategy was to use survival analysis to examine the time to failure (rearrest). Differences in the time until the first arrest following an intervention were graphed and statistically compared. Survival analysis marks a starting event and a terminal event for each individual. For the current study, the starting point was the date of release to the community from the residential program (or the date a youth went AWOL [absent without leave] from the residential program). Using the official record information and calendar dates mentioned above, we were able to calculate the number of days until failure (rearrest) or the end of the follow-up period at 24 months.

Different survival models were generated based on different follow-up time periods and subgroups of individuals. Twenty-four youths (5 in the experimental group and 19 in the comparison group) were excluded from the survival analysis because they had not been released from residential placement during the 24-month time frame and thus were not at risk to reoffend. For the first model, a time period of 180 days from release to the community from residential placement (Nokomis, training school, or CAR facility) was used. This was the shortest follow-up period that would allow sufficient time to measure rearrest. It maximized the comparability of the Nokomis and comparison groups in terms of time at risk and increased the number of subjects. However, selection of this time period limited the proportion of youths who were arrested (18 individuals or 11% of those at risk). Therefore, the time period was expanded to 360 days following release from residential placement into the community.

CHARACTERISTICS OF STUDY YOUTHS

The majority of study youths lived in the Detroit metropolitan area, and more than half came from a single female-headed household where the primary caregiver was unemployed. The majority were African American. For about one third of the sample, the current arrest was for a person offense, whereas most of the others had been arrested for a property offense. Fifteen percent of the youths had been arrested for a drug offense, and another 15% for some other offense, such as a program violation. On average, these youths had been arrested about three times prior to the study, their first arrest occurring when they were 14 years old. Less than 20% of the youths were known gang members, but 40% were drug dealers according to the DSS information, and over half were known drug users. In general, the statistical analyses of the official record data indicated the experimental and comparison groups were similar at intake, thus minimizing the possibility of selection bias.

The only statistically significant difference was the age of the offender at intake. Youths in the experimental group tended to be slightly older than those in the comparison group (aged 17 vs. 16). Other minor differences between youths in the experimental and comparison groups were generally in the direction of higher severity or risk for those in the experimental group (e.g., younger at first arrest and more prior arrests and adjudications). Since this is just the opposite of the usual selection bias problem, better results for the experimental group, relative to the comparison group, cannot be attributed to differences in background characteristics such as fewer arrests. However, a lack of differences in the outcome variables between the experimental and comparison groups or differences in the negative direction might be attributed to the greater severity or risk of the experimental group.

STUDY FINDINGS

Even though the Nokomis program was designed to last 12 months, not all youths followed the standard program path of 3 months residential and 9 months of community supervision. Youths in the Nokomis program who did not show signs of improvement during the residential phase were "escalated" to a training school. During the community phase, youths could fail to follow program rules and be escalated, go AWOL or truant from placement, or could be rearrested. Seventy-eight percent of youths in the experimental group completed the residential phase of Nokomis in comparison to 84% of youths placed in the training schools or private facilities. Only 40% of youths in the experimental study group successfully completed the 12-month Nokomis program.

During the 24-month study, youths in the experimental group spent an average of 16 days in detention, 73 days in the Nokomis residential phase, and 163 days in other juvenile residential placements—a total of 252 days, or about one third of the total time period in custody. By contrast, youths in the comparison group spent 20 days in detention and a much longer time—an average of 426 days—in a juvenile residential

placement (private CAR facilities or state training schools as well as other residential facilities), or well over half their time in custody. Following residential placement, the average youth in the experimental group spent 171 days in the Nokomis community component and another 20 days in a residential care center or group home, or a quarter of the total time under supervision. In contrast, those in the comparison group spent an additional 81 days in a residential care center or group home and 4 days on average in aftercare, or about 12% of the total time under community supervision. Overall, although those in the experimental group averaged more time in custody than the planned 90 days for the Nokomis Challenge Center, they still had more time at risk in the community than comparison group youths (417 days vs. 268 days).

On average, a youth placed at Nokomis who participated in our study cost the juvenile system approximately $60,500 for the 2-year period. In contrast, a youth in the comparison group placed in a state training school or private facility cost the system about $83,400. The cost savings of $10,000 per year can be attributed to the shorter time in custody.

Program Impact on Social Adjustment and Family Functioning

A major objective of the Nokomis program was to provide youths with the opportunity to change their attitudes, values, and behaviors through effective learning. To evaluate the program and measure individual changes, the data collection instruments included three psychological variables used in prior delinquency research that have been found to be related to behavioral change (personal goals, self-esteem, and the Jesness Asocial Index). In the analyses, changes within groups from intake to 12 months and intake to 24 months were examined using t tests of means. For the experimental groups, the change from intake to 3 months was measured for selected variables. Differences between experimental and comparison groups were compared at 12 months and 24 months, controlling for the scores at intake. Differences in progress during residential placement were compared using the 3-month Nokomis interview and 12-month comparison group data. Only those youths who were interviewed at all three time periods (intake, 12 months, and 24 months) were included in the analysis.

Both groups showed an increase in self-reported personal goals during residential placement, for example, between intake and 12 months for the comparison group and intake and 3 months for Nokomis, which disappeared by the end of the 24-month period. There was a significant increase in self-esteem and decrease in antisocial attitudes for the comparison group between intake and 12 months but no statistically significant change for the Nokomis group. By 24-month follow-up, however, the differences between groups and gains in self-esteem and asocial attitudes had disappeared. Neither group changed significantly in the aggregate measure of coping skills during residential placement. On the other hand, both groups showed some positive change from intake to 12 months for some of the individual measures of coping mechanisms. Both groups showed negative changes at 24-month follow-up. There were significant differences between groups in general family functioning at intake, with Nokomis youths reporting a more healthy family than those in the comparison group. Between intake and 12 months, however, there were no significant changes in family functioning, even though both groups reported a decrease in most of the dimensions. At 24 months, Nokomis youths reported a significant increase, which indicated a change for the worse. There were significant changes in problem solving, roles, and affective involvement. Nonetheless, there were no differences between groups at 24 months according to youth reports.

Several measures were gathered to assess youths' reintegration into the community, including educational and employment participation and family relationships. The results of our analysis of the 24-month follow-up interview indicate few differences between the experimental and comparison groups in social adjustment. Youths in the comparison group were more likely to have attended school in the past 12 months (77% to 56%), probably because they had been in a residential correctional program during this time period. In both groups, youths had attained a 10th-grade level of education. At 24-month follow-up, about half of the youths reported having held a job in the last 12 months.

At 24-month follow-up, youths were also asked about the impact of the program on family relationships. Of those who were released to a male or female parent or guardian, there were no significant differences between the comparison and experimental groups. A majority of youths in both groups reported that they got along better with their mother or father (or guardians) and that the program had helped them to get along better with their parents.

Thus, the impact of the programs appears mixed. Both groups showed some positive gains from intake to 12 months, yet the effects had disappeared by follow-up. Neither Nokomis nor other residential programs had a great impact on improving family functioning. On the other hand, youths perceived they got along better with family members.

Program Impact on Recidivism and Substance Use

Both official records and self-reports were used to measure delinquent behavior in the year prior to placement and following release from placement until the end of the 24-month period. Official record data indicated no difference in criminal history at intake. However, during the first 12-month follow-up period, a higher proportion of youths in the experimental group than the comparison group had a new felony arrest (26% vs. 3%), partly because they had more time free in the community. On the other hand, there was no statistically significant difference between groups at 24 months (31% of the experimental vs. 19% of the comparison group had a new arrest).

Even after controlling for time at risk in the community during the 24-month follow-up period, the Nokomis youths had higher rates of rearrest in terms of prevalence and incidence than youths in the comparison group. On the other hand, during the last 6 months of the entire follow-up period when the majority of youths were on the street, both groups had similar rearrest rates (17.3% for the experimental group and 15.8% for the comparison group). Annual arrest rates, controlling for time at risk, also failed to show a program impact on recidivism during this time period.

When the interview data were examined, there were some significant differences between groups at intake in the types of offenses reported. For example, a higher proportion of youths in the comparison group than in the Nokomis group reported involvement in property offenses (88% vs. 74%) and drug offenses (92% vs. 64%). Changes from intake to 24-month follow-up indicated a significant decrease in self-reported delinquency for both the experimental and comparison groups. At 24 months, approximately 42% of youths in the Nokomis group and 49% of youths in the comparison group reported involvement in delinquent or criminal behavior after release from the correctional programs. Youths in the Nokomis group reported significantly less involvement in drug sales than did those in the comparison group.

Measures of prevalence and incidence show these youths to be heavily involved in substance use in the year prior to intake, particularly alcohol and marijuana. No differences were found between these groups in either the type or frequency of drugs used. More than 90% of youths interviewed reported using drugs or alcohol. About 30% of the youths reported use of hard drugs (including 13% amphetamines, 13% LSD, 10% cocaine, 6% crack, and 6% barbiturates). At 24-month follow-up, approximately 75% of juveniles reported using some type of drug or alcohol since release from the residential program, most often marijuana or alcohol. There appear to be significant reductions in all other types of drug use, with less than 10% of youths reporting use of hard drugs.

To examine the issue of recidivism somewhat differently, because youth in the experimental and comparison groups had varying times at risk, we analyzed the time to failure. The survival curves for the time to first felony arrest from the date of release to the community (or AWOL from a residential placement) for the experimental and comparison groups were quite similar for the first 180-day period. Although it appears that the experimental group tended to fail somewhat faster, there were no statistically significant differences between the two groups. However, once the time period was extended to 360 days, the picture looked quite different, with the experimental youths failing at a faster rate. The statistics for the 360-day period confirm the significant difference between the two groups.

The fact that youths in the experimental group were older at intake than those in the comparison group may change these results. In addition, when youths went AWOL from placement, they were more likely to be arrested. Examining the survival curves during the 24-month period separately for those who went AWOL in comparison to those who did not confirmed this hypothesis. When the covariates of age at placement and number of priors were entered into the survival models, there was no significant impact on the time to first arrest during the first 180 days. During the 360-day time period, the covariate of number of prior arrests was significant. Those with fewer prior arrests had a longer time to failure (rearrest) than those with many prior arrests.

CONCLUSIONS AND POLICY IMPLICATIONS

The goal of the Nokomis Challenge Program was to substitute 3 months of intensive residential and wilderness challenge programming, followed up by 9 months of intensive aftercare, for the average 15.5-month residential stay in a medium-custody training school serving felony delinquents. The Nokomis residential program offered comprehensive treatment focusing on cognitive and behavioral skills and was more intensive than traditional placements. For each youth who might successfully complete the Nokomis program, without the need for any other remedial programming, it was estimated that the program would cost approximately $38,400 per year and result in savings in correctional costs of approximately $17,600 annually for a typical placement in a residential program.

However, the results of this evaluation indicated that only about 40% of the youths in this study successfully completed the 12-month Nokomis program (residential and community phases) compared to an 84% program completion rate for comparison youths assigned to the state training schools or private facilities. A substantial number of Nokomis youths were transferred/escalated to residential placements or placed in other types of custodial programs. The rate of these in-program failures was higher for the experimental group in comparison to those in traditional placements. They are perhaps a good indication of the system response to an individual's need for increased or different services. Similarly, there were several escalations during the community phase, which indicates the aftercare program was detecting and removing youths who needed additional time in placement.

Youths assigned to the experimental program spent an average of 73 rather than 90 days in the residential phase of that program, and another 240 days in some other type of placement, for a total of 313 days in custody out of the 730 days in the follow-up study period. Nonetheless, these 313 days of custody for youths initially placed in Nokomis compared favorably to the 462 days spent in custody by youths assigned to the comparison group. When the 170 days of intensive community supervision (at $75 per day) received by the typical Nokomis youth are included, the difference in total program costs between the two options is about $20,000 ($85,000 vs. $65,000) in favor of Nokomis over the 24-month time period.

However, these correctional savings were counterbalanced by the risk of increased crime in the community. The survival analysis indicated that the Nokomis youths failed at a faster rate than graduates of regular residential programs, despite the fact that they were placed in intensive aftercare following their release, whereas most youths in the comparison group had no aftercare. However, as indicated in previous research on intensive aftercare in Michigan, supervision alone is not sufficient to prevent recidivism and relapse. Within 6 months after their release from custody, 13% of the Nokomis youths had been arrested for a felony, in contrast to about 8% of the comparison group. Within a year, this difference had increased to 29% of the Nokomis group and 16% of the comparison group. If this difference in failure rates further increased or remained relatively constant over time, a higher fraction of the Nokomis youths would eventually be arrested. These findings, however, appear to be related to the higher risk of recidivism for experimental youths and the fact that these are official record data. The self-report data on delinquency and substance use showed no difference between the experimental and comparison groups in the year following placement, although both groups decreased criminal behavior and drug use.

The results of the evaluation indicated the Nokomis program was almost equally as effective as longer term residential placement in providing cognitive and behavioral skills. Both groups showed improvements while in the program in increased goals, self-esteem, and coping skills and decreased antisocial behavior, but these effects disappeared by the end of the follow-up period. Youths in Nokomis were less likely to attend school following release to the community than were youths in the comparison group. In addition, there was no difference in employment between youths in the experimental and comparison groups.

At 24 months, there appeared to be little difference between those who spent 14-16 months in a residential program and those in the Nokomis program. Both groups exhibited relapse to criminal and substance-using behavior, and most of the positive changes made during the residential program disappeared. This would seem to suggest that, regardless of the intervention, youths who are released back into the same environment face the same difficulties with readjusting to the community setting without relapse.

The current evaluation of the Nokomis Program has some limitations. First, the study sample may not be representative of the earlier and later cohorts of youths entering the Nokomis program. For example, the study sample was younger at first arrest and had significantly more prior arrests than those not in the study. Because these variables are generally correlated with recidivism, our results concerning new arrests during the 24-month follow-up may be overestimating the actual risk of new arrests for those in the Nokomis program. A second limitation is the fact that the results of this study may not be generalizable to other jurisdictions in that it was limited to one experimental program in a specific state.

Nonetheless, the study does present some evidence that short-term residential placements with aftercare may be more cost-effective than long-term residential stays for low- to medium-risk youths. Thus, it appears that efforts will continue to be made to reform the juvenile justice system and rehabilitate juvenile delinquents.

QUESTIONS FOR DISCUSSION AND WRITING

1. What three goals was the evaluation of the Nokomis program designed to measure? What other objectives existed for the evaluation?
2. Why did the authors use survival analysis, and what did it show? What happened when the authors controlled for age and prior offenses?
3. What were the cost savings for Nokomis? What counterbalanced those savings?

A Survey of Juvenile Electronic Monitoring and Home Confinement Programs

JOSEPH B. VAUGHN

PUBLIC attention on the juvenile justice system and its dispositional practices was brought to the forefront over 20 years ago when the U.S. Supreme Court decided the case In re *Gault*. The debate has continued, with the courts, criminal justice system, and public often at odds. Seemingly, we are unable to reach a consensus or develop workable alternatives. To some extent, this is due to the shifting of objectives from rehabilitation to crime control precipitated by rising crime rates and a perceived crisis in the adult correctional system. Even though the adult system typically receives more public attention, problems of the juvenile and adult systems seem to parallel each other.

In 1985, there were 1,040 publicly operated juvenile detention, correctional, and shelter facilities in the United States, housing over 51,000 youths. These institutions have been criticized for several reasons. They are viewed as expensive and archaic operations which merely allow youth gangs to flourish. Treatment programs are ineffective because they are overcrowded.

Juvenile probation practices were also subjected to public scrutiny and criticism. Officials are assigned the seemingly incompatible roles of social control and rehabilitation. There is a growing demand from the public for more

effective crime control and a corresponding decline in their willingness to accept the rehabilitative ideal.

Other alternatives were explored, including restitution, community service, prerelease programs, early parole, and intensive supervision programs. Advances in technology made possible the use of electronic monitoring and home confinement as one possible solution. Programs were first developed for use with adult offenders. As experience was gained, applications were developed for juveniles. Use of the technology has given rise to many questions and issues which remain unanswered. Because electronic surveillance is relatively new, little research has been conducted. Most of the existing literature is descriptive in nature. Even so, electronic monitoring and home confinement are gaining acceptance as viable social control strategies.

This chapter describes the existing technology which has made possible inclusion of larger numbers of offenders in home detention programs. Use by the adult system is briefly reviewed as it spawned use of the technology by juvenile programs. In November 1988, a survey of the existing juveniles programs was conducted. Results of that survey are presented along with an examination of the concerns voiced over use of the technology as an adjunct to juvenile intensive supervision programs.

ELECTRONIC MONITORING DEVICES

One of the earliest references to the use of an electronic monitoring device was reported in the literature over 20 years ago. A portable device was used to track the location of parolees, mental patients, and research volunteers in Massachusetts. The first formalized use of the technology by a criminal justice agency occurred during 1983 in Albuquerque, New Mexico.

The primary purpose of the equipment is to monitor offenders' compliance with curfew restrictions mandated in the terms of their release. Existing technology can be placed in one of two broad categories: continuously signaling/monitoring (referred to in the early literature as an active system) and programmed contact (referred to in the early literature as a passive system). A continuously signaling system is composed of a transmitter, home receiver unit, and a central computer. The transmitter, which is worn by the offender, broadcasts an encoded signal. When the person is within range of the receiver (normally within 150 feet) the transmitter's signal is received, indicating the person is at home. When he leaves the residence, reception of the signal is interrupted, and a message is sent to the computer indicating his absence. Upon the person's return, signal reception is resumed, and notification is made of the person's arrival. If the offender leaves home during an unauthorized period, a violation report is generated. If, however, the offender leaves home at an authorized time, the times of arrival and departure are noted, but no violation report is generated.

There are several variations in how the programmed-contact systems operate. In one system, the offender is required to wear an encoder device. The central office computer generates random calls to the offender's home. When the telephone call is received, he is required to insert the encoder device into a verifier box to confirm his presence. The system will generate reports which indicate if the telephone is not answered, if a busy signal is received, or if the offender fails to properly insert the encoder device into the verifier box. Other programmed-contact systems rely on the use of video telephones or voice verification techniques. When the random calls are made to an offender, the offender is required to transmit a photograph or provide a voice sample, which is then compared to information stored in the computer. Drive-by systems have been developed which require the offender to wear a transmitter. A receiver is then placed in the probation officer's car, and he makes random checks on the offender by driving past his residence or other locations the offender is supposed to be.

The primary difference between the continuous-signaling and programmed-contact systems is that one provides more information on compliance with the curfew. The continuous-signaling systems record when the offender enters and leaves the residence. The programmed-contact system can only confirm the presence of the offender in the residence at the time the random phone call is made.

ADULT PROGRAM EXPERIENCE

Electronic monitoring was believed to offer a number of benefits to correctional agencies. Initially, its hoped-for benefits included a reduction of personnel costs associated with supervising offenders, a reduction in institutional populations, and delayed or reduced need for construction of additional facilities. While it is too early to pass judgment, serious questions can be raised as to whether these benefits will be achieved. As more experience was gained, administrators began to look toward the humanistic benefits which might be achieved through its use. Programs could be designed which focused on rehabilitation in the home rather than the artificial environment of an institution. Adverse effects on the family might be reduced by using alternatives to incarceration. Staff time could be used more efficiently, allowing them to spend additional time with those offenders who needed it. While cost reduction remains the primary selling point of the technology, agencies are beginning to focus more on program aspects and the societal benefits to be achieved.

As previously mentioned, there is little experience to draw from, and evaluations are almost nonexistent. In March 1986, there were only 10 programs in the United States, 2 of which were not operational. By February 1987, less than 1 year from the original study, use of the technology had expanded to 50 plus programs in 21 states, monitoring over 800 offenders. The trend at that time was toward larger programs and the inclusion of higher risk offenders. The program failure rate remained relatively stable at about 10%.

One year later, 33 states had implemented monitoring programs and were monitoring nearly 2,300 offenders. Even with the apparent success of many adult programs, there were a number of concerns expressed over use of the technology with juveniles. No one knew whether juveniles were mature or stable enough to handle responsibilities imposed by an electronic monitoring program. Given the age of the participants and their presumed immaturity, concern was expressed that the equipment tamper rate or loss rate would be significantly higher than was experienced by the adult programs. It was feared juveniles may have less impulse control and would simply "run away," resulting in a high failure rate. Any monitoring program is intrusive by its very nature, and concern was expressed over whether it would interfere with the life of all family members, effectively resulting in their confinement as well. In the event of a dysfunctional family unit, forcing the child to remain in the home might subject the child to physical or mental abuse. Nationwide, there was some strong emotional and philosophical opposition to use of the technology with juveniles. It was feared children might be stigmatized by having to wear a monitoring device.

JUVENILE PROGRAM EXPERIENCE

In November 1988, a survey was conducted of the known juvenile programs in the United States. From information supplied by equipment manufacturers, 11 programs were identified, 9 of which participated in the telephone survey. Two of the respondents were private companies which provide monitoring services on a contract basis, and 7 were government agencies. One of the private contractors provided monitoring services for 2 of the government agencies. Agencies participating in the survey were Pulaski County, Arkansas Juvenile Court; Orange County, California Probation Department; Riverside County, California Probation Department; Opportunity House, West Palm Beach, Florida; Marion County, Indiana Juvenile Court; North Carolina Office of Court Administration's Juvenile Court Counselor Services; Dallas County, Texas Juvenile Court; Program Monitors, Inc., Dallas, Texas; and the Texas Youth Commission.

Use of electronic monitoring in juvenile programs is a relatively new phenomenon. The oldest known program was instituted by the North Carolina Office of Court Administration's Juvenile Court Counselor Services in May 1986. At the time of the survey, the programs in existence ranged in age from 5 to 31 months. Three of the programs were adapted from existing adult programs in their jurisdiction. All three began as an adjunct to the adult program, using their equipment. They later separated from the adult system and began operating their own program.

PROGRAM COMPARISON

This section draws conclusions from and summarizes the information obtained during the telephone survey.

Program Objectives

The most common reason for use of the technology was a lack of adequate detention facilities. Some agencies cited a need to enhance existing home confinement programs.

Five of the eight programs had more than one application for the technology. Most commonly, it was used as an alternative to prehearing detention. Four agencies used it as a supplement to probation, and three agencies used it for early release from an institution. One program applied the technology as an alternative sanction for parole violations. The objectives to be achieved by the programs, other than to reduce overcrowding, were not clearly documented by many of the agencies. Some, however, did set forth objectives prior to program implementation. Among these were the following:

- Increase the number of minors safely released into existing home confinement programs.
- Reduce the number of minors returned to juvenile detention for violating home confinement restrictions.
- Reduce the number of field contacts required of home confinement officers, and free them for other tasks.
- Provide a reasonably safe alternative to custody for relatively low-risk offenders.
- Provide for early reunification with the family.
- Provide reentry into the community.
- Allow for return to school.
- Increase the number of persons using the equipment in existing adult programs to increase cost-effectiveness.

Eligibility Criteria

Screening of applicants for participation in the program is done primarily by the agency responsible for providing supervision. In two programs, Marion County, Indiana, and Dallas County, Texas, participants are assigned directly by the court, and as such no screening is done by the agency. In Riverside County, California, potential participants are first identified and screened by the detention hall staff and then referred to the probation department. The private contractor, Opportunity House, identifies potential participants, conducts a screening interview, and then applies to the court for the person's release. The court has on occasion referred clients to them without prior screening. Although the private contractor may refuse to accept these individuals, he has not yet done so. Many of the program directors identified the screening process as the critical stage in the program. During the interview, the family and child must be made aware of the nature of the program and their responsibilities. The process used by the agencies ranged from use of a formal assessment instrument designed specifically for the program to reliance on the "gut feelings" of the interviewer about the probable success of the participant. During the interview, the agency is guided by its established eligibility and exclusion criteria.

All the programs surveyed required that a person would have otherwise been detained before being eligible. Some required juveniles to serve a minimum amount of time in detention prior to release.

There were a number of automatic exclusion criteria established by programs. Among the criteria used are the following:

- Living in a residence which is incompatible with equipment operation: One program specifically excludes those living in house trailers because it interferes with operation of the transmitting device.
- Those without a telephone or those who refuse to have certain features disconnected: The telephone is required for operation of all the monitoring systems. Features such as call waiting or call forwarding interfere with the equipment's operation.
- Violent offenders
- Lack of a suitable home environment or an uncooperative parental attitude
- Unwillingness of the juvenile to participate in program
- Those who pose a risk of escape or have a prior history of escape
- Mental problems
- Alcohol or drug abusers

- Those who have committed a "serious" felony: This is normally defined according to the grade of offense under a particular state's laws.
- Residential burglars
- When the victim of the crime resides in the home

Profile of Participants

A profile of those accepted into the programs is difficult to establish because statistics were not available at the time of the study. Three agencies did provide profiles based on pilot projects they had conducted or on a limited sample of offenders. In Orange County, California, the average participant is 15 years old and considered to be in the medium- to high-risk category. A breakdown of the type of offense shows 42% had committed crimes against property, 11% had committed crimes against persons, and 29% were probation violators, with unspecified "other" offenses accounting for the rest of the participants. There were more pretrial detainees (65%) than postadjudication (35%) participants.

In Riverside County, California, the average participant is a 17-year-old Caucasian or Hispanic male who has one prior arrest or adjudication for theft. Most of the juveniles (80.5%) had been placed in the program for technical violations of probation or violations of the motor vehicle code; 18.5% had been adjudicated for serious crimes consisting of assault, weapons offenses, or drugs. With only one exception, all the minors had been adjudicated prior to placement.

The North Carolina program consists predominantly of black males between the ages of 14 and 17. No other demographic information was provided by the agency. From the limited information available, it is not possible to draw any conclusions regarding the type of offender most likely to be placed in an electronic monitoring and home detention program.

Monitoring and Supervision Procedures

Once in the program, monitoring of the equipment and supervision of the client are accomplished in one of several ways. The two private contractors offer different services. Opportunity House monitors the equipment and provides supervision during participation in vocational or treatment programs but does not make home visits. Program Monitors Incorporated (PMI) monitors the equipment and makes home visits twice a week to verify it has not been tampered with. Three of the seven public agencies surveyed use the services of a private contractor to monitor the equipment. Reports are submitted to them by the private contractors, and arrangements can be made for immediate notification of violations if necessary. One agency has equipment monitored for it by another criminal justice agency. Only three of the seven public agencies surveyed actually monitor their own equipment.

All seven public agencies provide field supervision for their clients. Five provide sole supervision, although one of these, at the inception of its program, relied on officers from the adult probation department to provide field supervision. The other two public agencies provide field supervision of the juveniles and also rely on the private contractor to contact them twice a week to verify the equipment has not been tampered with. Only Opportunity House, a private contractor, does not conduct home visits or field contacts with participants. Two agencies have no set minimum number of contacts, the number varying with perceived need and staff availability. The amount of contact provided by the remaining five agencies varies from twice a day to once a month.

All participants are placed under a curfew, and some programs are more restrictive than others. While one may require a 24-hour-a-day curfew, another may establish a particular time, 7:00 p.m., for example. Depending on the program, exceptions to the curfew may be granted. All agencies allow or require the juvenile to attend school, work, or participate in treatment and vocational programs. In the event of a medical or other emergency, the juvenile is permitted to leave the house. Notification must be given the agency prior to or as soon as possible. Some programs view relaxing curfew restrictions as a reward for acceptable behavior. As the child makes satisfactory progress through the program, more freedom is allowed. Other agencies view the program as an extension of the detention facility and grant exceptions only in rare circumstances.

In the event a curfew violation is reported by the computer, the agency has a number of response options. They can respond immediately or wait until the next day and confront the juvenile. Five of the programs call the residence in an attempt to ascertain if the report was caused by an equipment problem, a momentary absence from the range of the receiver, or is an actual violation. Three programs make an immediate response to the residence (two telephone calls first) to verify the violation. The programs in Texas determine their response policy based on the perceived threat the individual poses. With some clients, they respond immediately, and with others they wait until the next business day. Three of the programs have a policy of waiting until the next day to confront the child, although one attempts to telephone the residence when the report is received.

There are problems and benefits with any policy adopted. Immediate responses and telephoning the residence allows the agency to confirm the violation. Such confirmation is believed a prerequisite to successful termination if a court hearing is required. If false alarms frequently occur, valuable staff time is consumed unnecessarily. If the problem continues, the staff will become disillusioned with the equipment. Participants may lose confidence in the equipment's ability to monitor them accurately and begin violating the program's restrictions. Some would argue that if an immediate response is necessary due to the perceived threat the child poses, the wrong individuals are being placed in the program.

Program Statistics

It is still too early to evaluate the success of these programs. Some agencies have not yet compiled adequate statistics and were able to provide only estimates. The information presented here is based on available statistics and estimates from eight responding programs.

From May 1986 through November 1988, approximately 845 juveniles have been under electronic monitoring and home detention. The average length of monitoring ranged from 16 to 90 days. All the programs are small, monitoring from 2 to 20 children on the day the survey was administered. Failure rates in the program ranged from 4.5% to 30%. Programs report most of the unsuccessful terminations resulted from commission of technical violations rather than new offenses. Although the data are incomplete, there were only five known new offenses committed while in the program. From the available data, the number of absconders is believed to be low, with only 18 reported.

Ten pieces of equipment were lost or damaged by program participants. Of the 5 lost, 4 were intentionally removed by the participant, and 1 was lost through carelessness when the strap broke. One piece of equipment was intentionally lost by the juvenile because he believed it could track his whereabouts. The other 5, although damaged, were recovered.

Comparisons were made between adult and juvenile programs by two respondents. PMI monitors both adults and juveniles. Juveniles show less judgment and often act against their own best interests. Cabin fever occurs quicker with juveniles than adults, generally within 1 month. To avoid this problem, exceptions to curfews or some alteration of routine must occur. The most critical time for preventing failures in the juvenile program is during the first 6 to 8 days. In their experience, approximately half of those who fail do so during the first week on the program. They speculate this occurs for two reasons: The initial shock of detention has worn off for pretrial detainees, and family problems are intensified by the increased amount of time spent in the home. For both juveniles and adults, parolees tend to take the program more seriously and have a better compliance record. Pretrial detainees have more violations and remain absent for longer periods of time. The company believes this occurs because the technology is being used as a reward for good behavior for parolees and as a punishment for inappropriate behavior by the pretrial detainees.

The Orange County Probation Department is responsible for supervision of both adult and juvenile offenders. While the juvenile program has higher failure rates (approximately 25%) than the adult program (5%), the department states this should not be interpreted to mean the program is less successful with juveniles than adults. The juvenile program is directed at medium- to high-risk offenders, while the adult program is used predominantly with low-risk offenders. The department also finds that juveniles on electronic monitoring have a higher success rate than normal for the target population of the three home detention programs which do not use electronic monitoring.

Program Costs

Equipment acquisition costs are most commonly paid for by the agency. Three departments do not own the equipment and are charged a user fee by the private contractor who provides the monitoring service.

Because there is no common method used to compute program costs, comparison between programs is not possible. The cost of equipment alone ranged from $3.17 to $11.00 per day, depending on whether it was leased or purchased and the amortization schedule used. Others provided a yearly program cost of $46,317 to $77,000. Alternative program costs ranged from $42 to $500 per day. Some programs estimated cost savings of $98,420 to $113,400 per year. Determining cost benefit is difficult. Merely comparing the cost of alternative programs to equipment acquisition illustrates an obvious cost saving. Before accepting claimed savings at face value, it is necessary to compute the actual costs to society.

Program Problems

Some program difficulties arose because the concept was new and the agencies had little or no experience to draw from. The problems encountered thus far can be categorized into three basic areas: administrative problems, problems with the family, and problems with the participants. Agencies soon realized the program was more labor intensive than they anticipated. Many participants are in the program for a relatively short period of time. The continual turnover in clients creates a heavy workload for those responsible for data entry and system maintenance. The amount of time spent screening applicants and installing and retrieving equipment is significantly increased if participants are in the program for a short period of time. While the equipment may allow more time for supervision officers because they can reduce the number of nightly checks, administrative time may be increased. Some agencies have found it necessary to add additional staff to maintain the program. None has decreased the number of personnel. There were a number of hidden costs involved in program implementation. The cost of telephone service is but one example; the equipment requires installation of dedicated telephone lines. One agency soon discovered its monthly telephone service charges were exceeding $300 per month.

Although it has not yet become a prevalent problem, the lack of a telephone in an offender's home has caused some difficulties. The family cannot afford the installation charge or owes past-due bills and the phone company will not provide service. In some instances, a juvenile has been placed on the program only to have the family default on their telephone bill and have service disconnected. When no phone is available, the child is denied access to the program by those agencies who do not have funds to pay for telephone services. Not all juveniles want to participate in the program, and in a few cases the juvenile or the family lied about having a telephone to avoid being placed on the equipment. This is more common if an agency operates another home confinement program without electronic monitoring.

Family problems are more acute when the person being monitored is not the head of the household. Home detention and electronic monitoring programs, in effect, place the entire family on community detention. A child does not have the control or influence necessary to require adjustments to family routine or the ability to move to another residence if necessary to make participation possible. Some families want the child placed in detention, not in the home. If returned to the home, the child becomes an inconvenience for the family. There are several known instances of parents sabotaging the child's progress. They have taken them out of the house in violation of the curfew or called the department and falsely accused them of violating the program's restrictions. Parents may rely too much on the equipment to supervise the child. In effect, the technology becomes an electronic baby-sitter.

Other than the normal difficulties of supervision, program directors identified three problems unique to juvenile programs. For many of their clients, the perception of the juvenile justice system is that it is too lenient. As one director noted, it is difficult for the offenders to take the system seriously when they receive a 90-day sentence in a halfway house for the same crime for which an adult receives a 5-year prison sentence. Escapes from the adult and juvenile programs in some areas are viewed differently. An adult who absconds is charged with felony offense of escape, while the juvenile sanction for the same activity is, at worst, a return to detention.

Summer months cause unique problems with juveniles under electronic monitoring and home detention. Adults would be leaving their home for work. Children are out of school in the summer and, absent any employment, are restricted to the house 24 hours a day. It is problematic in two ways: There may be no adults home to supervise the child during the day, and boredom quickly sets in. This leads to an increase in behavioral problems. Programs operating during the summer have found it necessary to relax

curfew restrictions and allow the child to go outdoors under parental supervision.

Program Benefits

Benefits are felt to outweigh the problems encountered in program operation. Although it has not yet been empirically demonstrated, most agencies feel the programs are successful in reducing the number of days spent in detention and are having a positive impact on institutional population. The programs allow the children who would otherwise be detained to remain in the home and participate in counseling, educational, or vocational activities, while also providing a reasonable amount of security for the community. The equipment allows for closer supervision than the staff could provide and prevents them from having to work 24 hours a day. They are now able to maintain closer supervision over larger numbers of clients without having to increase home visits.

By returning the child to the home, the agency is given an opportunity to work with the family and address problem areas. Some find there is a rehabilitative aspect which was previously unexpected. Parents report increased communication and dialogue between themselves and the child. Before, when a disagreement arose, the child would merely leave the house. Under the program, however, they are required to remain in the house. This forces the parents and child to discuss and deal with the problem.

One primary benefit for pretrial detention programs is that the department can place the child back in a natural environment with supervision. This provides the court a much clearer picture of how the child would perform on probation, allowing the court to make a more informed sentencing decision.

From the juvenile's standpoint, many have commented that "there is light at the end of the tunnel." With most programs, there is a date certain for its completion. If the child complies with the restrictions until that date, the child is removed from the program, unlike many others who have no established completion date or have one extended over a long period of time.

The additional level of supervision afforded by electronic monitoring allows the child to be given an opportunity to remain in the community. Departments believe the increased control represents a real consequence for violation of program restrictions, a necessary condition if they are to be workable.

CONCLUSIONS

One lesson learned from the adult programs is that an agency should carefully consider *why* it wants to use the technology *before* the program is implemented. Juvenile applications, for the most part, have begun in much the same way adults' programs did. The primary consideration has been reducing populations in crowded facilities. In some instances, the programs were offshoots of an existing adult program. While the technical issues were resolved during implementation of the adult program, the philosophical question has, in many instances, remained unanswered.

Clearly stated objectives are important to a program's success for many reasons. If the "why" is addressed during the planning stage, as has been done by some agencies, other objectives for use of the technology may become apparent. Besides the administrative concerns of institutional populations and efficient use of staff time, there are humanistic goals which should be explored. Some objectives which have been suggested by existing juvenile programs include early reunification with the family, reentry into the community, continuation in school, and creation of an intermediate sanction between unsupervised probation and commitment to a youth facility.

Notably absent from the stated program objectives were the issues of providing treatment programs and family counseling in the home environment rather than in the artificial setting of an institution. Experience from the adult program indicates the potential for modification of the peer group relationship, creation of better family relationships, and institution of self-discipline. While none of these benefits has been empirically validated, they have been observed in some offenders.

If the only stated objective is to reduce institutional populations, a majority, if not all, of the programs will ultimately be evaluated as failures. By searching for and identifying other reasons for its use, the technology's worth as an adjunct to a program can be determined more accurately. Continual evaluation of innovative programs is critical. It is only through evaluation that one is able to determine what is beneficial and should be continued.

There is a growing belief that alternatives to detention should be used as a means to alleviate overcrowding and as a more humane and effective form of offender treatment. Electronic monitoring and home detention programs have shown promise as a practical tool. It is premature to attempt an assessment of the impact these programs will have on the juvenile justice system. Perhaps two cautions are in order. The technology, by itself, cannot solve the problems currently faced by the system. It should not become a substitute for sound decision making by corrections officials.

QUESTIONS FOR DISCUSSION AND WRITING

1. What benefits was electronic monitoring believed to offer to correctional agencies? As more experience was gained, what happened?
2. Despite the apparent success of many adult programs, what were some of the concerns expressed regarding use of the technology with juveniles?
3. What was one lesson learned from the adult programs? What has the primary consideration been? If the only stated objective is to reduce institutional populations, how will the program fare when it is evaluated?

Boot Camps:
A Critique and a Proposed Alternative

ANTHONY W. SALERNO

THE newest thing on the correctional scene is boot camps (or, as it is called by some, shock incarceration). As presently structured in those states that have implemented them, they should be phased out immediately—they are doomed to fail and they can be very costly.

ROOTS OF THE PROGRAM

The historical basis for boot camps goes back to World War II. The British became aware of the excessively large loss of lives when ships were sunk in combat. A conclusion that the excessive losses were due to the lack of will on the part of some servicemen to fight to the last ounce of energy led the British to revamp their training regimen. Preservice training involved more rigorous and taxing activities than had heretofore been used. The developers of the World War II program believed servicemen needed more than mere knowledge of survival skills. "They also needed confidence in their physical and psychological toughness in the face of life-threatening conditions." The training henceforth included challenging physical tasks. The payoff was increased survival rates in combat at sea.

In the early 1960s in Colorado, this type of programming was adapted to treat juvenile

delinquents. It was called Outward Bound (or Wilderness Training in some jurisdictions). The theoretical underpinnings of this approach are that delinquents suffer from negative self-esteem and that if self-esteem, an internal self-evaluator, is raised, then the probability of delinquency is lessened. This theoretical assumption is questionable, and research results are mixed. For instance, negative self-esteem, school failure, and delinquency are thought to be interrelated; a negative self-image is seen as a causal factor in behavior; official processing is related to negative labeling and delinquency; and positive self-esteem is seen as an insulation against delinquency. On the other hand, several research studies question the link between self-esteem and delinquency.

Nevertheless, Outward Bound programs have flourished and continue to grow. There are at least seven such programs in the United States at this time. The core of these programs is exciting, adventurous, and challenging activities. They include outdoor camping, mountain climbing, rappelling, shooting the rapids, surviving solo in the environment, and so on. Other positive features of this kind of program are the fact that staff interact with the delinquents constantly since the group is forced into regular face-to-face interaction by its very nature. This lends itself to crisis counseling, counseling on an as-needed basis, and the development of self-reliance skills and self-confidence.

A second basis for boot camps is the shock aspect of the program, which includes incarceration in the environment within which the

From "Boot Camps: A Critique and a Proposed Alternative" by A. Salerno, 1994, *Journal of Offender Rehabilitation, 23,* pp. 147-158. Copyright 1994 by The Haworth Press. Reprinted by permission.

program operates. Antecedents for this lie in shock probation and Scared Straight programs. With respect to the former, and as pioneered by the state of Ohio, offenders who are eligible for probation but who are incarcerated may petition the court for a sentence modification. This is usually done within 120 days of commitment, and if granted, the offender is placed on probation. This brief period of incarceration presumably teaches the offender a lesson.

Scared Straight, a second type of shock, is aimed at juveniles and assumes that a single visit to a prison (during which hardened, long-term convicts scream, curse, and describe the horrors of prison life in street language) will frighten youngsters into conformity. Notwithstanding its public popularity and serving as the basis for a documentary which won an Emmy Award, its effectiveness is clearly called into question.

BOOT CAMP: A VARIATION

Boot camp is a military version of Outward Bound with elements of shock probation and Scared Straight. It ordinarily involves hard work, physical training, military drill and activities (e.g., obstacle course), counseling, and/or education programs. Participation in the program is usually restricted to young adults who have been convicted of nonviolent crimes and who have not previously been incarcerated. The underlying assumptions are that the rigorous program will act as a specific deterrent, will enhance a positive self-image, and coupled with any gains made through counseling and/or education will have a rehabilitative effect.

Georgia and Oklahoma were the first states to open boot camps (in 1983), and as of the end of 1988 there were 15 programs in nine states, 3 were scheduled to open in 1989, and at least 9 other states were considering boot camp programs.

In Georgia, the process resembles shock probation (in fact, in some jurisdictions it is referred to as shock incarceration) in that the sentencing judge determines who goes to boot camp. The usual term is 90 days and is followed by probation. In Florida, offenders committed to the Department of Corrections (DOC) who meet the criteria are selected by corrections officials and, if approved by the sentencing judge, are transferred to camps. The 90— to 120-day period is followed by probation.

A CRITIQUE

The May 22, 1989, issue of Newsweek referred to boot camp programs as "An Officer and a Gentleman" meets "Scared Straight," thus mating two desirable processes: military training and shock. The claim of this writer is that these programs will not work and are a waste of correctional resources. Why so?

The programs on which they are based have had limited or no success. Both the classic analysis of Scared Straight programs by Finckenauer and an analysis by Parent conclude that programs of this sort have achieved little effect.

Research on Outward Bound programs seems to reveal tentatively better results, but it is far from conclusive since the results have not achieved statistical significance. In fact, the obvious void in these short-term programs is to maintain the program gains once a client returns home.

Shock probation programs have fared no better. At best, there have been mixed results, and nothing conclusive can be claimed largely because of methodological flaws in the studies.

Research and Boot Camps

The two states with the longest history of boot camps are Georgia and Oklahoma. Each of them has done some preliminary tracking of program graduates. An Oklahoma group was followed for 29 months and compared to a similar group of nonviolent offenders sentenced to the DOC. At the 29-month mark, almost half of the boot camp graduates had returned to prison while 28% of the other group had. Georgia found little difference between program graduates and similar offenders released from the DOC.

But conventional wisdom tells us that beyond the preliminary results noted above, state officials should at the very least think twice before committing scarce resources to a new "panacea." As Parent warns: "In states considering programs correctional officials should make certain that political leaders are fully aware of the current lack of evidence about the ultimate impact and effectiveness of [boot camps]."

A Panoply of Criticism

A panoply of criticisms has been voiced toward programs of the boot camp variety.

1. Advocates of boot camps will of course argue that the incarceration period is short and the grueling military regimen is not the same as the brutalizing prison environment. After all, for almost two centuries military training has been associated with patriotism and defense of our nation. Yet we must be reminded that candidates for boot camps (convicted felons) have long been rejected for military service. Why so? The most probable and plausible reasons for this are the association often found between criminality and character disorder and the problems of authority often found in criminals. Indicators of this might be the fact that in the Louisiana program, about 40% withdraw before program completion, most during the first week or two. And, in New York, almost one half refuse to enter the program, although refusal means a significantly longer period of incarceration in a traditional prison setting.

2. The second point to be made in this critique relates to the voluntary aspect of boot camp programs. Do candidates really volunteer? It cannot possibly be so since the offer is a trade-off between long and short periods of incarceration. Thus, we return to one of the most contentious issues of the 1960s and 1970s: the value of coerced treatment. Although it is dressed differently, the boot camp program presents the same scenario: Play the game and you get out early.

3. One of the standard eligibility criteria is that a candidate be a first offender. This is ordinarily defined as not having served a prior period of incarceration. The reason for this is to avoid or at least minimize the prisonization process and achieve the same results with respect to contamination of boot camp inmates. Thus far, this criterion has not included pretrial detention. This is given as one reason for the high refusal rate, a presumed refusal to do hard time and a presumed degree of prisonization.

4. The degree of popularity of boot camp programs varies among criminal justice workers. Officials who tour these programs invariably come away impressed. This is especially so among those who themselves served in the armed forces. Part of Parent's study was to survey criminal justice personnel in states which had boot camp programs in operation. At the top of the list in terms of support were judges. At the bottom were DOC administrators. What is the meaning of this? During the 1960s and 1970s when community corrections was in vogue, one major criticism leveled at criminal justice decision makers was net widening, that is, placement into programs simply because programs exist. In the present case, there are some officials in Georgia and Mississippi who believe that some offenders sentenced to boot camps would have gotten straight probation if the camps had not existed. Since judges in the states with programs have much to do with who goes to camp, and since they appear to support strongly this type of sentence, then the likelihood of net widening is very plausible.

5. Cost calculations can be elusive and illusory and, like evaluations of effectiveness, have not either been undertaken or completed. The variables that would have to be taken into consideration are staff-inmate ratios, the proportion of staff allocated to treatment, camps that are "stand-alone" compared to those that are separate units of an existing prison, length of stay, comparative incarceration costs on a per annum basis, and aftercare costs (probation, parole, electronic monitoring, intensive supervision, etc.). The contention here is that boot camps will not be less costly nor more cost-effective than ordinary incarceration. Preliminary data indicate that in Georgia and Mississippi, boot camp costs are comparable to prison

costs and exceed those costs in New York and Oklahoma.

6. Professor Sean McConville recounts the British experience with boot camps. They were begun in 1948 with the same purpose and for the same type of offender as we see in the United States. They had apparently fallen into disuse previously because the Thatcher administration, in an attempt to restore them to use, commissioned a study of their efficacy. The results of the study: no reduction in recidivism.

7. Rather high refusal and dropout rates were cited above, and research should explore the reasons why. The *New York Times* ran an article on May 30, 1989, on the Forsyth, Georgia, boot camp, and among other aspects of the experience quoted a 20-year-old inmate who was referring to the barking and screaming: "Discipline is one thing. . . . But cussing you like dogs is another. It makes you have a grudge." Whether this was mere talk, or isolated in its prevalence, is not known. This writer believes that considering the clientele that stock boot camps, the quote above is not rare and isolated.

8. Last is the matter of treatment. All programs but Georgia at this time put a good deal of emphasis on various treatment techniques. Six of the eight states with boot camps provide drug/alcohol counseling and five of the eight reality therapy, among other approaches.

AN ALTERNATIVE APPROACH

A more sensible, less costly, and predictably just as effective alternative is herewith outlined. It essentially combines probation with jail, intermittent incarceration, intensive supervision, and electronic monitoring. Those eligible for the program are those who fit the ordinary profile in boot camps at this time.

The sentence handed down to these offenders is 1-year probation with special conditions. It will probably be easier to conceptualize the total program if we follow a hypothetical case from beginning to end.

Probation With Special Conditions

The first step after the sentence is handed down is 1 week's incarceration. If there were plenty of spaces in existing jails, the 1-week period would take place there, provided these special cases could be isolated from the rest of the population. A better setting, at minimal cost, would be a typical camp setting: barracks living and surrounded by a single chain-link fence. There is little to concern ourselves with security risks, given the brevity of stay and the type of offender. Also recall that in most of the present boot camps the length of stay is 90 to 120 days. A workable facility would be an unused or partially used armed services camp.

Life in this setting is simple. The offender is given food, clothing, shelter, bathing facilities, medical care, and nothing else. He is free to communicate with fellow prisoners, but the system will not supply him with morale-building or time-occupying activities like TV, radio, games, athletics, and so on.

At the end of the week, he is released to probation field services. He will be hooked to one of the new electronic monitoring devices programmed so that he may initially leave his place of residence to work or seek work. Other than these ordinary hours, he is restricted to his residence. He is also under intensive supervision which means, among other things, intensified face-to-face contacts and unannounced urine checks for drugs and/or alcohol.

When the next weekend arrives, he reports back to the camp and spends from Friday evening to Sunday evening there, under the same circumstances he experienced during his full week's stay. He does this for 4 consecutive weekends.

Rationale for Intermittent Incarceration

Why the intermittent incarceration? It is contended that the failure of Scared Straight, Outward Bound, and other such programs stems in part from the lack of follow-up. Youngsters who are truly frightened by a visit to prison during which they are screamed at by hardened criminals lose track of that experience with the passage of time. The same holds true for those who return to the troubled streets of their neighborhoods after an esteem-building experience in the wilderness.

In the case at hand, if offenders in this program are truly first offenders in the sense of having no previous incarceration experience, then that first week should provide some shock, reinforced by four more consecutive weekends. In addition, during the intervening periods between weekends his movements are severely curtailed and he is closely watched.

After the fourth weekend of incarceration, weekends spent in camp continue but at a declining rate. For 2 months it is every second weekend; for the following 3 months it is every third weekend. In addition to intensive supervision, the offender gets regularly spaced living reminders of incarceration.

At the end of approximately 6 months, the offender should have spent 1 full week in camp plus 12 weekends. At this point in time, probation officials will decide whether to continue some regimen of intermittent weekend incarceration or forgo that in favor of some level of probation supervision.

Left to the discretion of probation officials, too, are decisions that relate to the easing or tightening of the monitoring restrictions as well as the intensity of supervision. Left to them as well is the handling of rule violations. Sanctions can range from reprimands through extra and increased camp-incarceration periods to outright violation proceedings before a judge.

CONCLUSION

The writer has presented what he believes to be eight weaknesses in the current shock incarceration programs. The proposed alternative program ostensibly compensates for some of those weaknesses and potentially holds some benefits that boot camps cannot achieve. Specifically, comparison of the two should reveal the following:

1. The proposed program should not pose any greater threat to public safety.
2. The proposed program is likely to get fewer refusals and dropouts.
3. The proposed program will be far less costly to the taxpayer. This will be seen by comparing incarceration costs and then the added benefits of probationers working from almost the outset of the sentence. The benefits are obvious: taxes, restitution, fines, court costs, and fees charged for probation services. These benefits in boot camp programs cannot be realized until release comes about.
4. The proposed program is less likely to result in hardened attitudes among criminal clients.
5. In the proposed program, treatment will take place in the community, a much more fertile environment than prison, camp, or any combination of the two.

QUESTIONS FOR DISCUSSION AND WRITING

1. What is boot camp?
2. Why does the author claim that boot camp programs will not work and are a waste of correctional resources?
3. What five benefits does the author cite for his program of intermittent incarceration and intensive supervision probation?

PROSPECTS

The Future of Juvenile Justice
Policy and Research

LLOYD E. OHLIN

ONE of the most striking developments in juvenile justice over the past 20 years has been the increasing rapidity and the widening scope of change in theories, goals, and knowledge about delinquency and its prevention or control. Many competing biological, psychological, social, and cultural theories of delinquency have emerged in the past two decades, yet none is sufficient to account for the rate and forms of delinquency today.

At the same time, confidence in the ability of our institutional system to control juvenile delinquency has been steadily eroding. Public insecurity, fear, and anxiety about youth crime are now intense and widespread, despite the juvenile court and probation system and the training schools that have evolved over the past century. In recent years, all these established institutions have been threatened by severe criticism and by proposals for reform or elimination. In addition, confidence in the ability of professionals to rehabilitate youthful offenders has been repeatedly undermined by evaluations of a wide variety of treatment programs. As a result, the field of juvenile justice is experiencing "future shock." It is time, then, to take stock of the juvenile justice policies developed

From "The Future of Juvenile Justice Policy and Research" by L. E. Ohlin, 1998, *Crime & Delinquency, 44*, pp. 143-153. Copyright 1998 by Sage Publications, Inc. Adapted with permission of Sage Publications.

over the past 20 years and to determine the principal challenges of the future.

EXAMINING THE PAST

The federal government has played an increasingly dominant role in fostering policy directions during the past two decades. At the risk of oversimplifying complex social developments, we can identify three major shifts in federal policy that have been made in response to public concern about youth crime.

Federal Policy in the Early 1960s

The first federal act to focus directly on the problem of juvenile delinquency was passed in 1961 under the aegis of the President's Committee on Juvenile Delinquency and Youth Crime. This committee, which included Secretary Abraham Ribicoff of the Department of Health, Education and Welfare and Secretary Arthur Goldberg of the Department of Labor, was chaired by Attorney General Robert Kennedy. It sought a fresh initiative to deal with the emerging and potential growth of youth crime.

The committee adopted a comprehensive community development model being tested by the Mobilization for Youth project on the lower east side of Manhattan in New York City.

This model stressed prevention of delinquency through the creation of better opportunities in the world of work, school, family, recreation, and social services. It sought to build community participation and competence to deal with delinquency by more active control of the institutions for the socialization of youth. It drew on the experiences of the Chicago Area Project developed by Clifford Shaw and Henry McKay in the 1930s and on the later community organization strategies in Chicago of Saul Alinsky. In breaking with the casework treatment approach, it redirected attention to the key role of community relationship in achieving better delinquency prevention and control. The President's Committee wished to test this model of community development in the high crime rate areas of several cities. The model was to serve as a device for integrating and maximizing the impact of several federal agency programs.

Needless to say, many problems developed in the implementation of this policy. First, many community agencies believed that delinquency prevention and control was too limited a target to justify the broad scope of the proposed reforms in youth services, and they resisted adopting the committee's plan. Second, some of the assumptions underlying the committee's recommendations appear now to have been naive. We are much more aware today that juvenile justice depends on the successful operation of a broad formal and informal network of social relationships that guide youth development. We are also more aware of the need for better knowledge of how to bring about large-scale community and institutional change in the high crime rate areas of large cities. We know that providing resources and goals for change is only part of the job. There are limits to what can be achieved through a large-scale project that funds both institutional reforms from within and social movements demanding such changes from the outside. The ensuing conflict quickly becomes politically inflamed and too threatening to the funding sources.

We should also note that those early efforts at community development for youth escalated too rapidly as the delinquency programs were combined with other community programs such as the War on Poverty, housing and area development, and the model cities program. The accompanying rhetoric and the scope of redevelopment exceeded not only the resources but also the talent and knowledge available to direct changes of such complexity. The growing gap between expectation and achievable results fostered disillusionment, alienation, social unrest, and, ultimately, abandonment of the programs themselves.

However, there is much that we can yet learn from those early federal initiatives to foster community responsibility. The experiences of the early 1960s can yield lessons about the importance of indigenous leadership, the power of entrenched institutions to resist change, the political character of major reforms, and the pace of community change in relation to social movements and conditions in the nation as a whole. It is important to examine this experience objectively, for we are entering a period in which local, community effort crime prevention is assuming renewed importance under the "new federalism" policies of President Reagan's administration.

Presidential Crime Commissions:
Focusing on Control

The second major shift in national juvenile justice policy was spearheaded by a series of presidential commissions that addressed problems of crime and violence. Their agenda was set initially by the 1967 report of the President's Commission on Law Enforcement and Administration of Justice. Unlike the efforts of the early 1960s, the mandate of this commission required a much tighter focus on control of rising crime rates. Although the task force on juvenile delinquency made many broad recommendations about prevention, its primary task was to suggest better methods of controlling identified delinquents and status offenders. This focus led to six major strategies later identified as (a) decriminalization of status offenses (such as running away from home), (b) diversion of youth from court procedures into public and private treatment programs, (c) extending due process rights to juveniles (in anticipation of the *Gault* decision that guaranteed those rights), (d) deinstitutionalization (use of group homes or nonresidential treatment facilities rather than large training schools), (e) diversification of services, and (f) decentralization of control.

These strategies were variously endorsed or expanded by a series of governmental commissions dealing with such varied topics as the rise in violent crimes and riots in large cities, the unrest on college campuses, and the issues of pornography and obscenity. The second major presidential crime commission, the National Advisory Commission on Criminal Justice Standards and Goals (appointed in 1971 to address again the surging crime problem), also supported the thrust of the 1967 report.

Despite broad consensus among experts about the validity of these strategies to deal with delinquent youth, implementation has been spotty and the results difficult to assess. Statistics cited by Barry Krisberg and Ira Schwartz indicate that the decriminalization of status offenses has had a significant impact in most states. The number of status offenders committed to institutions has declined substantially in response to support from the Office of Juvenile Justice and Delinquency Prevention in the U.S. Department of Justice. There is still some question, however, that we have simply traded control by correctional officials for welfare supervision.

The diversion strategy, in which community services are substituted for correctional facilities, has also had some impact. But an assessment by James Austin and Barry Krisberg has pointed to potentially troublesome consequences of using community-based alternatives to juvenile incarceration. Austin and Krisberg call attention to three possible effects of diversion: (a) wider nets in which more youth are officially processed, (b) stronger nets that hold more youth in the system, and (c) different types of nets other than corrections (such as mental health and welfare placements).

The due process revolution is still in progress but in the direction of increased criminalization of the juvenile court process. In some instances, it has even led to suggestions that juvenile courts be abolished—a result that would go far beyond that intended by the national commissions interested in better protection of the rights of juveniles.

Efforts to deinstitutionalize juvenile treatment have met with mixed results. Greatest success was achieved under the direction of Jerome Miller in Massachusetts. Miller reorganized and ultimately closed five correctional facilities in that state, retaining only a small percentage of the beds for juveniles requiring incarceration.

Purchase of services from the private sector has increased diversification and decentralization of services in varying degrees in different states. However, there is increasing evidence that major private vendors (group and residential care facilities) are "skimming" the more treatable cases, leaving the more difficult ones to the public institutions. There is also evidence of more resistance to the location of small, diversified facilities and programs in the home communities of delinquents.

The 1970s: A "Law and Order" Reaction

The third major shift reflects a strong conservative reaction to the liberal policies advocated by the national crime commissions. This reaction has occurred in spite of recent endorsement of those policies by the Juvenile Justice Task Force of the National Advisory Commission on Criminal Justice Standards and Goals (1976) and the standards issued by the Institute of Judicial Administration and the American Bar Association (1980).

The conservative trend originated in efforts to reexamine fundamental assumptions of the adult criminal justice system by a series of special study groups beginning, ironically, with the American Friends Service Committee publication *Struggle for Justice* (1971).

The American Friends Service Committee was guided by a desire to improve the plight of prison inmates. The committee perceived rehabilitation programs as thinly disguised measures for asserting greater control over inmates. The 1971 report suggested that indeterminate sentencing and decisions about parole were capricious and, moreover, that they permitted biased judgment and improper criteria to control the length of time served by inmates.

The original motives for rejecting rehabilitation programs and indeterminate sentencing were lost as public demand increased for "just deserts" (an eye for an eye) punishment and as sentencing and imprisonment were explored as a means of incapacitating offenders and deterring others from committing similar offenses. Growing fear of crime and increasing demands for repressive action have led to more punitive sentencing and to a rapid escalation of both the number of prisoners and the time to be served.

This approach is now spreading to juvenile justice. In many states, we see increasing incarceration even as delinquency rates decline. Juvenile reform legislation now calls for more mandatory sentencing and more determinate sentences for juveniles, lowering of the upper age of juvenile jurisdiction, greater ease in obtaining waivers to adult court for juvenile prosecution, and greater access to juvenile records.

There is also a greater preoccupation with chronic, violent offenders that has led to a redirection of resources for their confinement. In the absence of reliable criteria for identifying such offenders, this preoccupation tends to stereotype all delinquents and is likely to raise the level of precautionary confinements. It is also likely that due process reforms, which make the juvenile system look much like the adult system, will also lead to the same result.

Thinking about these major shifts in juvenile justice policy inspires a fresh appreciation of the power and depth of traditional beliefs about the causes and cures of crime in our society. The system can bend for a time in the direction of new approaches to prevention and control. But implementation is likely to be tentative and skeptical. Vested interests in traditional views surface quickly as problems arise. We are now in one of those periods of conservative reaction where the prevailing views about crime express beliefs about retribution, deterrence, and incapacitation that are deeply rooted in our religious and cultural heritage.

Our policies are now being developed by those who believe that the traditional system of punishment can be fine-tuned to control offenders by increasing the predictability and certainty of punishment. My own view, however, is that our society is unwilling to sustain the levels of repression and incarceration needed to make more than limited incremental gains in crime control. Yet, I am not bitterly opposed to this effort. The process of change has a rhythmic character. Reaction and retrenchment occur as both new and old ideas are tested for their relevance to our deep-seated beliefs and values. It is time, then, to take a fresh look at the challenges and opportunities the next wave of reform must deal with when the current reaction has run its course.

THE CHALLENGE OF THE FUTURE

Confronting the Alienation of Youth

I would like to suggest six policy issues that will require new perspectives and approaches over the next decade or two. The first major challenge lies in the increasing isolation and alienation of youth in our society. Historians are beginning to document the social processes by which adolescent youth have been progressively excluded from meaningful participation in the workforce. Economic isolation becomes especially obvious in times of economic recession as unemployed men and women displace adolescents from low-paying, unskilled jobs.

The reaction of youth has found expression not only in public disorder, vandalism, and crime but in the resurgence and increasing violence of gangs. It has also led to greater use of drugs and alcohol and more chronic youth offenders—children who are in trouble with juvenile justice and other social control agencies from an early age.

In addition, the key issues in youth crime have changed. The pervasiveness of delinquent acts among all youth has shifted our attention away from attempts to distinguish delinquents from nondelinquents. Instead, we must now explain why some young people persist in delinquency while others do not. What circumstances and experiences distinguish them from one-time or occasional offenders? More important, why do most chronic offenders also eventually cease their criminal activities?

We lack adequate theories not only of persistence but of desistance from crime. To develop them will not only require fresh ideas and data but also integration of some of the current theories. Theories of social control, economic and social strain, cultural conflict, and deviance all address somewhat different aspects of the crime problem. Progress may be made by thinking of these theories as complementary rather than competing. In any case, a greater concern with issues of persistence and desistance from crime may influence policy significantly. Should we not, for example, concentrate our resources at those points where youth are making critical choices in their lives so that they will be more likely to avoid careers in crime?

Building Community Resources

The second major policy issue relates to the role of local communities in prevention and control of crime. The local community is of central importance in the socialization of youth through the formal and informal networks that help to shape behavior. What are the characteristics of a community capable of encouraging its young people in constructive behavior? And what does it take to raise a high delinquency rate community to this level of competence? We have gained significant breakthroughs in theories of organization and personality development by studying competent and healthy organizations and personalities instead of only those that break down. We should be able to make similar gains by contrasting effective communities with ineffective ones.

At our center for criminal justice in the Harvard Law School, Alden Miller and I have been examining some Boston neighborhoods as an extension of our study of the Massachusetts Department of Youth Services. We have been especially concerned about identifying any linkage between correctional programs and other youth services in high crime rate neighborhoods. Not surprisingly, we found very little connection between the two. Once a young person is in a delinquent track, it is difficult to get out. Though we have yet to examine other communities, it seems evident that training schools or group homes isolated from community life have little sustained impact on delinquent tendencies.

Clearly, we need to know much more about community responses to delinquency. We especially need to know what high crime rate communities can do without additional financial resources because this is the situation these communities are likely to face under the "new federalism" policies that reallocate responsibility but provide fewer resources.

I have been encouraged by observing the increased control of crime in a public housing project in Boston, where a tenant council has been granted primary responsibility and resources for improving conditions. Once plagued by a high vacancy rate, vandalism, and crime-ridden elevators and buildings, the project is now making progress through effective demands for prompt police service, building maintenance, citizen patrols, a crime watch, and constant attention to youth problems and needs. Well-organized residents with a stake in their neighborhood and the responsibility and authority to command essential resources are an important ingredient in constructive change.

Allocation of Federal, State, and Local Resources

The allocation of responsibility among federal, state, and local governments is in a state of uncertainty and transition. We need to learn more about the best ways to divide and coordinate these responsibilities. Over the past 20 years, the federal government provided increasing resources, although often in an erratic and unstable pattern. It now seems likely that such resources will be substantially reduced and the federal role confined to research, statistics, and dissemination of information to states and local communities. Problems of employment, education, welfare, and housing will undoubtedly require federal involvement and will affect the ability of local communities to deal with crime. However, crime control and prevention will become more of a state and local responsibility. We are now at a critical stage in defining which allocations will best bring about effective crime control.

Employment

The fourth issue concerns problems of employment and education that contribute to the isolation and alienation of youth. In the 1970s, we saw an enormous growth in the 18 to 34 age group, the population from which new workers are recruited. The 1980s will be a decade of sharp decline in the 15 to 24 age group and significant reduction in the growth of the 25 to 34 age group. We are likely to see a labor shortage and a decline in population in the high crime risk ages. This combination of factors may provide an unusual opportunity to foster more effective involvement of youth in the workforce. We should be thinking now of ways to capitalize on that situation before it is on us.

Similarly, with the reduced school population, there is more opportunity to experiment with changes that will enhance involvement by young people now estranged from traditional school practices. Over the past decade, the growing literature on educational policy has documented prospects for increasing achievement scores through changes in the organization of schools and the roles of administrators, teachers, and students and through redefining expectations, tasks, and rewards. Strategies for change involve such practices as breaking large schools down into subschools or clusters (schools-within-a-school), infusing the curriculum with work and career-oriented exercises and opportunities, instituting cooperative learning in mixed-ability groups, encouraging more democratic decisions and tasks in the classroom, and fostering changes in school governance.

These are just a few of many innovations now being tested for their impact on delinquent conduct and school achievement in a joint project funded by the Office of Juvenile Justice and Delinquency Prevention and its National Institute of Juvenile Justice and Delinquency Prevention. The project is conducted by the Westinghouse National Issues Center in Columbia, Maryland, and the National Center for the Assessment of Delinquent Behavior and Its Prevention at the Center for Law and Justice, University of Washington, Seattle, Washington. While many of the program elements have been tested in other contexts, there is reason to believe that the controlled evaluation of this project and similar experiments will yield new insights into more effective learning environments for school-age youths.

Fear of Crime

The fifth challenge for the coming years concerns the fear of crime. Public attitude surveys indicate that the link between fear of crime and actual risk is not as direct as one might assume.

Why do national survey samples show that respondents perceive juvenile crime as increasing rapidly when juvenile arrest rates are actually declining? Inaccurate information purveyed by sensationalist media sources is an oversimplified explanation. Part of the answer may lie in the national and international scope of violent crimes reported by the media. These crimes are then perceived as happening close to home as well. Furthermore, crime is now reported in areas once perceived as remote and safe.

Some studies suggest that the fear of crime by the elderly arises as much from a pervasive sense of social disorder and lack of control of youth as from objective perceptions of risk. Idle, noisy youth hanging about obstructing and harassing passersby, vandalized empty buildings, and trash-strewn lots produce a sense of communal loss of authority and inability to preserve order. The sources of fear are complex and variable, but we need to know more about them if we wish to mobilize support for community action. It is through cooperative, organized community programs to reduce crime that a sense of safety and control is restored rather than through the barriers of locks, bars, and dogs.

The relationships of class, race, and gender to crime are potentially explosive issues that we must confront directly in the years ahead. For example, the disproportionate representation of ethnic and racial minority groups throughout the criminal justice system is a cause of great concern. This era is similar to the 1920s, when the combined impact of immigration, prohibition, and the growth of organized crime caused lengthy public debate. Concern about crime led to the studies and reports in the 1930s by the National Commission on Law Observance and Enforcement, commonly known as the Wickersham Commission. This commission quieted fears that "foreigners" were creating a crime wave and pointed instead to the social and economic systems of large cities where new arrivals were forced to reside. To some extent, the crime problem today also provides a focus for unresolved racial and ethnic conflicts that once again must be sorted out and dealt with more directly.

Creating Cooperation

The sixth issue relates to the establishment of some mechanism by which a sustained attack on the problems of juvenile delinquency can be mounted. One useful possibility would involve the establishment of several centers that would pull together already assembled data, undertake carefully designed longitudinal studies and critical short-term studies, and analyze the results systematically for their policy and theoretical implications. In the past, we have looked to the federal government to provide such initiatives in addition to training, technical assistance, and dissemination of information. But it is likely that in the future, we will have to look to private initiative for policy-oriented studies of this kind.

I wish to stress the view that juvenile justice policies cannot be successfully dealt with outside the context of a more general youth policy. We have seen enough evidence of the diffuse sources of delinquency and the variety of responses to it to realize the need for a more comprehensive and coordinated youth policy to deal with youth alienation and delinquent acts. We must also think of ways to open up more challenging opportunities for youth in our society. We need a cumulative program of research and policy analysis, for there is much to be done. Like many others, I see resorting to incarceration as a confession of bankruptcy of ideas and initiative in this field. I believe there is a large body of latent public support for less repressive, more creative solutions to the problem.

QUESTIONS FOR DISCUSSION AND WRITING

1. What three major shifts in federal policy have been made in response to public concern about youth crime?
2. By whom are our policies "now being developed," and what is the author's view?
3. What six policy issues does the author suggest?

Abolish the Juvenile Court: Youthfulness, Criminal Responsibility, and Sentencing Policy

BARRY C. FELD

WITHIN the past three decades, judicial decisions, legislative amendments, and administrative changes have transformed the juvenile court from a nominally rehabilitative social welfare agency into a scaled-down, second-class criminal court for young people. These reforms have converted the historical ideal of the juvenile court as a social welfare institution into a penal system that provides young offenders with neither therapy nor justice. The substantive and procedural convergence between juvenile and criminal courts eliminates virtually all the conceptual and operational differences in strategies of criminal social control for youths and adults. No compelling reasons exist to maintain separate from an adult criminal court a punitive juvenile court whose only remaining distinctions are its persisting procedural deficiencies. Rather, states should abolish juvenile courts' delinquency jurisdiction and formally recognize youthfulness as a mitigating factor in the sentencing of younger criminal offenders. Such a policy would provide younger offenders with

From "Abolish the Juvenile Court: Youthfulness, Criminal Responsibility, and Sentencing Policy" by B. C. Feld, 1998, *Journal of Criminal Law and Criminology, 88*, p. 68. Copyright 1998 by Northwestern University School of Law. Adapted with special permission of Northwestern University School of Law, *The Journal of Criminal Law and Criminology*.

substantive protections comparable to those afforded by juvenile courts, ensure greater procedural regularity in the determination of guilt, and avoid the disjunctions in social control caused by maintaining two duplicative and inconsistent criminal justice systems.

My proposal focuses only on the criminal delinquency jurisdiction of juvenile courts because youth crime and violence provide the impetus for most of the current public anxiety and political responses. First, this article will describe briefly the transformation of the juvenile court from a social welfare agency into a deficient criminal court. Second, it will analyze the inherent and irreconcilable contradictions between attempting to combine social welfare and penal social control in the juvenile court. Finally, once a state separates social welfare from criminal social control, no role remains for a separate juvenile court for delinquency matters. Rather, a state could try all offenders in one integrated criminal court, albeit with modifications to respond to the youthfulness of younger defendants. Adolescent developmental psychology, criminal law jurisprudence, and sentencing policy provide rationale to formally recognize youthfulness as a mitigating factor when sentencing younger offenders. Moreover, the uncoupling of social welfare from criminal social control also suggests a social policy agenda more responsive to the needs of youth than the current version of the juvenile court.

In the second section, I briefly analyze the social history of the juvenile court and its subsequent constitutional domestication. I argue that in the three decades since *Gault,* legal changes have altered juvenile courts' procedures, jurisdiction, and jurisprudence and increasingly render juvenile courts indistinguishable from criminal courts. The convergence is reflected in the decriminalization of status offenders, the criminalization of serious offenders via waiver to the criminal courts, and the increased punitiveness in sentencing of ordinary delinquents. Despite juvenile courts' increasing and explicit punitiveness, however, they still provide delinquents with fewer and less adequate procedural safeguards than those available to criminal defendants. In the third section, I argue that the juvenile court's deficiencies reflect a fundamental flaw in its conception rather than simply a century-long failure of implementation. The juvenile court attempts to combine social welfare and criminal social control in one institution but inevitably subordinates the former to the latter because of its inherent penal orientation.

In the fourth part, I propose to abolish the juvenile court and to formally recognize youthfulness as a mitigating factor in criminal sentencing, thereby accommodating the lesser culpability of younger offenders. Young offenders differ from adults in their breadth of experience, temporal perspective, willingness to take risks, maturity of judgment, and susceptibility to peer influences. These generic and developmental characteristics of adolescence affect their opportunity to learn to be responsible and to develop fully a capacity for self-control and provide a compelling rationale for mitigation of sentences. I propose an explicit, age-based "youth discount," a sliding scale of developmental and criminal responsibility, as the appropriate sentencing policy mechanism to implement the lesser culpability of younger offenders.

Finally, I suggest a number of benefits that may accrue from a formal recognition of youthfulness as a mitigating factor in an integrated criminal justice system—enhanced protection of the many younger offenders already being sentenced as adults, an affirmation of responsibility, integration of records, and a more consistent sentencing policy toward chronic younger offenders, and, ultimately, honesty about the reality of criminal social control in the juvenile court.

TRANSFORMED BUT UNREFORMED: THE RECENT HISTORY OF THE JUVENILE COURT

The Juvenile Court

Ideological changes in cultural conceptions of children and in strategies of social control during the nineteenth century led to the creation of the juvenile court in 1899. The juvenile court reform movement removed children from the adult criminal justice and corrections systems, provided them with individualized treatment in a separate system, and substituted a scientific and preventative alternative to the criminal law's punitive policies. By separating children from adults and providing a rehabilitative alternative to punishment, juvenile courts rejected both the criminal law's jurisprudence and its procedural safeguards such as juries and lawyers. Judges conducted confidential and private hearings, limited public access to court proceedings and court records, employed a euphemistic vocabulary to minimize stigma, and adjudicated youths to be delinquent rather than convicted them of crimes. Under the guise of *parens patriae,* the juvenile court emphasized treatment, supervision, and control rather than punishment. The juvenile court's "rehabilitative ideal" envisioned a specialized judge trained in social science and child development whose empathic qualities and insight would enable her to make individualized therapeutic dispositions in the "best interests" of the child. Reformers pursued benevolent goals, individualized their solicitude, and maximized discretion to provide flexibility in diagnosis and treatment of the "whole child." They regarded a child's crimes primarily as a symptom of her "real needs," and consequently the nature of the offense affected neither the degree nor the duration of intervention. Rather, juvenile court judges imposed indeterminate and nonproportional sentences that potentially continued for the duration of minority.

Progressives situated the juvenile court on a number of cultural and criminological fault lines and institutionalized several binary conceptions for the respective justice systems: either child or adult, either determinism or free will, either treatment or punishment, either procedural informality or formality, and either discretion or the rule of law. Serious youth crime challenges these dichotomous constructs. The recent procedural and substantive convergence between juvenile and criminal courts represent efforts to modify the Progressives' bifurcation between these competing conceptions of children and crime control.

The Constitutional Domestication of the Juvenile Court

In *In re Gault*, the Supreme Court began to transform the juvenile court into a very different institution than the Progressives contemplated. In *Gault*, the Supreme Court engrafted some formal procedures at trial onto the juvenile court's individualized treatment sentencing schema. Although the Court did not intend its decisions to alter juvenile courts' therapeutic mission, in the aftermath of *Gault*, judicial, legislative, and administrative changes have fostered a procedural and substantive convergence with adult criminal courts. Several subsequent Supreme Court decisions furthered the "criminalizing" of the juvenile court. In *In re Winship*, the Court required states to prove juvenile delinquency by the criminal law's standard of proof "beyond a reasonable doubt." In *Breed v. Jones*, the Court applied the constitutional ban on double jeopardy and posited a functional equivalence between criminal trials and delinquency proceedings.

Gault and *Winship* unintentionally, but inevitably, transformed the juvenile court system from its original Progressive conception as a social welfare agency into a wholly owned subsidiary of the criminal justice system. By emphasizing criminal procedural regularity in the determination of delinquency, the Court shifted the focus of juvenile courts from paternalistic assessments of a youth's "real needs" to proof of commission of a crime. By formalizing the connection between criminal conduct and coercive intervention, the Court made explicit a relationship previously implicit, unacknowledged, and deliberately obscured.

In *McKeiver v. Pennsylvania*, however, the Court denied to juveniles the constitutional right to jury trials in delinquency proceedings and halted the extension of full procedural parity with adult criminal prosecutions. Without elaborating on or analyzing the distinctions, *McKeiver* relied on the rhetorical differences between juvenile courts' *treatment* rationale and criminal courts' *punitive* purposes to justify the procedural disparities between the two settings. Because *McKeiver* endorsed a treatment justification for its decision, the right to a jury trial provides the crucial legal condition precedent to punish youths explicitly in juvenile courts. Several recent juvenile justice legislative reforms provide some youths with a statutory right to a jury in order to expand the punitive sentencing options available to juvenile court judges.

The Transformation of the Juvenile Court

In the decades since *Gault*, legislative, judicial, and administrative changes have modified juvenile courts' jurisdiction, purpose, and procedures and fostered their convergence with criminal courts. These inter-related developments—increased procedural formality, removal of status offenders from juvenile court jurisdiction, waiver of serious offenders to the adult system, and an increased emphasis on punishment in sentencing delinquents—

constitute a form of criminological "triage," crucial components of the criminalizing of the juvenile court, and elements of the erosion of the theoretical and practical differences between the two systems. This triage strategy removes many middle-class, white, and female noncriminal status offenders from the juvenile court, simultaneously transfers persistent, violent, and disproportionally minority youths to criminal court for prosecution as adults, and it imposes increasingly punitive sanctions on those middle-range delinquent criminal offenders who remain under the jurisdiction of the juvenile court. As a result of these implicit triage policies, juvenile courts increasingly function similarly to adult criminal courts.

STATUS OFFENSES

Legislative recognition that juvenile courts often failed to realize their benevolent purposes has led to a strategic retrenchment of juvenile courts' jurisdiction over noncriminal misconduct such as truancy or incorrigibility, behavior that would not be a crime if committed by an adult. In the 1970s, critics objected that juvenile courts' status jurisdiction treated noncriminal offenders indiscriminately like criminal delinquents, disabled families and other sources of referral through one-sided intervention, and posed insuperable legal issues for the court. Judicial and legislative disillusionment with juvenile courts' responses to noncriminal youths led to diversion, deinstitutionalization, and decriminalization reforms that have removed much of the "soft" end of juvenile court clientele.

WAIVER OF JUVENILE OFFENDERS TO
ADULT CRIMINAL COURT

A second jurisdictional change entails the criminalizing of serious juvenile offenders as courts and legislatures increasingly transfer chronic and violent youths from juvenile to criminal courts for prosecution as adults. Transfer laws simultaneously attempt to resolve both fundamental crime control issues and the ambivalence embedded in our cultural construction of youth. The jurisprudential conflicts

reflect many of the current sentencing policy debates: the tensions between rehabilitation or incapacitation and retribution, between basing decisions on characteristics of the individual offender or the seriousness of the offense, between discretion and rules, and between indeterminacy and determinacy. Waiver laws attempt to reconcile the contradictions posed when the child is a criminal and the criminal is a child. What legal processes, crime control policies, and substantive criteria best enable decision makers to select from among the competing cultural images of youths as responsible and culpable offenders and as immature and salvageable children?

In most states, judges decide whether a youth is a criminal or a delinquent in a waiver hearing and base their discretionary assessments on a juvenile's "amenability to treatment" or "dangerousness." The inherent subjectivity of waiver criteria permits a variety of racial inequalities and geographic disparities to occur when judges attempt to interpret and apply these vague laws. When judicial waiver decisions, legislatively excluded offenses, or prosecutorial charging decisions focus on violent young offenders, these youths often receive substantially longer sentences as criminals than do their delinquent counterparts who remain in juvenile court simply because of their new-found "adult" status.

In response to the rise in youth homicide and gun violence in the late 1980s, almost every state has amended its waiver statutes and other provisions of their juvenile codes in a frantic effort to "get tough" and to stem the tide. These recent changes signal a fundamental inversion in juvenile court jurisprudence from treatment to punishment, from rehabilitation to retribution, and from immature child to responsible criminal. Legislatures increasingly use age and offense criteria to redefine the boundaries of adulthood, coordinate juvenile transfer and adult sentencing practices, and reduce the "punishment gap." The common overarching legislative strategy reflects a jurisprudential shift from the *principle of individualized justice* to the *principle of offense*, from rehabilitation to retribution, and an emphasis on the seriousness of the offense rather than judges' clinical assessments of offenders' "amenability to treatment." State legislative amendments use offense criteria either as dispositional guidelines to structure and limit judicial discretion, to guide prosecutorial charging decisions, or automatically to exclude certain youths from juvenile court jurisdiction.

Regardless of the details of these legislative strategies, the efforts to "crack down" and to "get tough" repudiate rehabilitation and judicial discretion, narrow juvenile courts' jurisdiction, base youths' "adult" status increasingly on the offense charged, and reflect a shift toward more retributive sentencing policies. Whether the legislature makes the forum decision by excluding offenses or the prosecutor does so on a discretionary basis via concurrent jurisdiction, these laws reduce or remove both discretionary judicial authority and juvenile courts' clientele. Offense exclusion rejects juvenile courts' philosophical premise that they can aid youth and denies them the opportunity to try without regard to the "real needs" of the offending youth. Finally, the legal shift to punish more young offenders as adults exposes at least some youths to the possibility of capital punishment for the crimes they committed as juveniles.

Although legislatures and courts transfer youths to criminal court so that they may receive longer sentences as adults than they could in the juvenile system, chronic property offenders constitute the bulk of juveniles judicially waived in most states, and they often receive shorter sentences as adults than do property offenders retained in juvenile court. By contrast, youths convicted of violent offenses in criminal courts appear to receive substantially longer sentences than do their retained juvenile counterparts. For youths and adults convicted of comparable crimes, both types of disparities— shorter sentences for waived youths than for retained juveniles adjudicated for property offenses and dramatically longer sentences for waived youths than for retained juveniles convicted for violent crimes—raise issues of sentencing policy fairness and justice. No coherent policy rationales justify either type of disparities. Rather, some youths experience dramatically different consequences than do other offenders simply because of the disjunction between two separate criminal justice systems.

SENTENCING DELINQUENT OFFENDERS

The same jurisprudential shifts from offender to the offense and from treatment to punishment that inspire changes in waiver policies increasingly affect the sentences that juvenile court judges impose on serious delinquent offenders as well.

The same public impetus and political pressures to waive the most serious young offenders to criminal courts also impel juvenile courts to "get tough" and punish more severely the remaining criminal delinquents, the residual "less bad of the worst." Several indicators reveal whether a juvenile court judge's disposition punishes a youth for his past offense or treats him for his future welfare. Increasingly, juvenile court legislative purpose clauses and court opinions explicitly endorse punishment as an appropriate component of juvenile sanctions. Currently, nearly half of the states use determinate or mandatory minimum sentencing provisions that base a youth's disposition on the offense she committed rather than her "real needs" to regulate at least some aspects of sentence duration, institutional commitment, or release. Empirical evaluations of juvenile courts' sentencing practices indicate that the present offense and prior record account for most of the explained variance in judges' dispositions of delinquents and reinforce the criminal orientation of juvenile courts. Finally, evaluations of conditions of confinement and treatment effectiveness belie any therapeutic "alternative purpose" to juvenile incarceration. In short, all these indicators consistently reveal that *treating* juveniles closely resembles *punishing* adults. A strong, nationwide policy shift both in theory and in practice away from therapeutic dispositions toward punishment or incapacitation of young offenders characterizes sentencing practice in the contemporary juvenile court.

Procedure and substance intertwine inextricably in juvenile courts. The increased procedural formality since *Gault* coincides with the changes in legal theory and administrative practice from therapeutic, individualized dispositions toward more punitive, offense-based sentences. Indeed, *Gault*'s procedural reforms may have encouraged these changes by legitimating punishment.

Although the formal procedures of juvenile and criminal courts have converged under *Gault*'s impetus, a substantial gulf remains between theory and reality, between the "law on the books" and the "law in action." Theoretically, the Constitution and state juvenile statutes entitle delinquents to formal trials and assistance of counsel. But, the actual quality of procedural justice differs considerably from theory; a gap persists between "rhetoric" and "reality." Despite the criminalizing of juvenile courts, most states provide neither special procedures to protect youths from their own immaturity nor the full panoply of adult procedural safeguards. Instead, states treat juveniles just like adult criminal defendants when treating them equally places youths at a practical disadvantage and use less effective juvenile court safeguards when those deficient procedures provide an advantage to the state.

Jury. Although the right to a jury trial is a crucial procedural safeguard when states punish offenders, the vast majority of jurisdictions uncritically follow *McKeiver*'s lead and deny juveniles access to juries. Because judges and juries decide cases and apply *Winship*'s "reasonable doubt" standard differently, it is easier to convict youths in juvenile court than in criminal court with comparable evidence. Moreover, *McKeiver* simply ignored the reality that juries protect against a weak or biased judge, inject the community's values into the law, and increase the visibility and accountability of justice administration. These protective functions acquire even greater importance in juvenile courts, which typically labor behind closed doors immune from public scrutiny.

On the other hand, several states have recently enacted legislation to increase the sentencing authority and punishment capacities of juvenile courts. These "blended" sentences begin with a youth's trial in juvenile court and then authorize the judge to impose enhanced sentences beyond those used for ordinary delinquents. All the variants of "blended jurisdiction" provide these "intermediate" youths with adult criminal procedural safeguards, including the right to a jury trial. Once a state provides a youth with the right to a jury trial and other criminal procedural safeguards, it preserves the option to punish explicitly, as well as to extend jurisdiction for a period of several years or more beyond that available for ordinary delinquents. Thereby the state also gains greater flexibility to treat a youth. Finally, these statutes recognize the futility of trying to rationalize social control in two separate systems. These "blended" jurisdictional provisions represent a significant procedural and substantive convergence with an erosion of the differences between juvenile and criminal courts. They provide a conceptual alternative to binary waiver statutes by recognizing that adolescence comprises a developmental continuum that requires an increasing array of graduated sanctions for youths and procedural equality with adults to reflect the reality of punishment.

Counsel. Procedural justice hinges on access to and the assistance of counsel. Despite *Gault*'s formal legal changes, the promise of quality legal representation remains unrealized for many juveniles. In several states, half or less of all juveniles receive the assistance of counsel to which the Constitution and state statutes entitle them. Moreover, rates of representation vary substantially within states and suggest that differences in rates of appointment of counsel reflect judicial policies to discourage representation. The most common explanation for why so many juveniles are unrepresented is that judges find that they waived their right to counsel. Courts typically use the adult legal standard of "knowing, intelligent, and voluntary" under the "totality of the circumstances" to gauge the validity of juveniles' waivers of rights. Because juveniles possess less ability than adults to deal effectively with the legal system, formal equality results in practical procedural inequality.

THE INHERENT CONTRADICTION OF THE JUVENILE COURT

The foregoing jurisdictional, jurisprudential, and procedural changes have transformed the juvenile court from its original model as a social service agency into a deficient second-rate criminal court that provides young people with neither positive treatment nor criminal procedural justice. It effectively punishes young offenders but uses procedures under which no adult would consent to be tried if she faced the prospect of confinement in a secure facility. The changes in procedures, jurisdiction, and sentencing policies reflect the contradictory roles of juvenile courts and ambivalence about the social control of young offenders. In this section, I contend that juvenile courts' social welfare mission cannot and should not be rehabilitated. In the next section, I advocate abolishing the juvenile court and trying all offenders in one integrated criminal court with modifications for the youthfulness of some defendants.

Social Welfare Versus Penal Social Control

The juvenile court treatment model constitutes an inappropriate policy response to young offenders. If we formulated a child welfare policy *ab initio*, would we choose a juvenile court as the most appropriate agency through which to deliver social services, and make criminality a condition precedent to the receipt of services? If we would not create a court to deliver social services, then does the fact of a youth's criminality confer upon a court any special competency as a welfare agency? Many young people who do not commit crimes desperately need social services, and many youths who commit crimes do not require or will not respond to social services. In short, criminality represents an inaccurate

and haphazard criterion on which to allocate social services. Because our society denies adequate help and assistance to meet the social welfare needs of all young people, the juvenile court's treatment ideology serves primarily to legitimate the exercise of judicial coercion of some *because of their criminality.*

Quite apart from its unsuitability as a social welfare agency, the individualized justice of a rehabilitative juvenile court fosters lawlessness and thus detracts from its utility as a court of law as well. Despite statutes and rules, juvenile court judges make discretionary decisions effectively unconstrained by the rule of law. If judges intervene to meet each child's "real needs," then every case is unique and decisional rules or objective criteria cannot constrain clinical intuitions. The *idea* of treatment necessarily entails individual differentiation, indeterminacy, a rejection of proportionality, and a disregard of normative valuations of the seriousness of behavior. But, if judges possess neither practical scientific bases by which to classify youths for treatment nor demonstrably effective programs to prescribe for them, then the exercise of "sound discretion" simply constitutes a euphemism for idiosyncratic judicial subjectivity. Racial, gender, geographic, and socioeconomic disparities constitute almost inevitable corollaries of a treatment ideology that lacks a scientific foundation. At the least, judges will sentence youths differently based on extraneous personal characteristics for which they bear no responsibility. At the worst, judges will impose haphazard, unequal, and discriminatory punishment on similarly situated offenders without effective procedural or appellate checks.

Is the discretion that judges exercise to classify for treatment warranted? Do the successes of rehabilitation justify its concomitant lawlessness? Do the incremental benefits of juvenile court intervention outweigh the inevitable inequalities and racial disparities that result from the exercise of individualized discretion? Evaluations of the effectiveness of juvenile court intervention on recidivism rates counsel skepticism about the availability of programs that consistently or systematically rehabilitate juvenile offenders. The inability to demonstrate significant treatment effects may reflect methodological flaws, poorly implemented programs, or, in fact, the absence of effective methods of treatment. In the face of unproven efficacy and inadequate resources, the possibility of an effective rehabilitation program constitutes an insufficient justification to confine young offenders "for their own good" while providing them with fewer procedural safeguards than those afforded adults charged, convicted, and confined for crimes.

The juvenile court predicates its procedural informality on the assumptions that it provides benign and effective treatment. The continuing absence or co-optation of defense counsel in many jurisdictions reduces the likelihood that juvenile courts will adhere to existing legal mandates. The closed, informal, and confidential nature of delinquency proceedings reduces the visibility and accountability of the justice process and precludes external checks on coercive interventions. So long as the mythology prevails that juvenile court intervention constitutes only benign coercion and that, in any event, children should not expect more, youths will continue to receive the "worst of both worlds."

*Failure of Implementation
Versus Conception*

The fundamental shortcoming of the juvenile court's welfare idea reflects a failure of conception rather than simply a failure of implementation. The juvenile court's creators envisioned a social service agency in a judicial setting and attempted to fuse its welfare mission with the power of state coercion. The juvenile court idea that judicial-clinicians successfully can combine social welfare and penal social control in one agency represents an inherent conceptual flaw and an innate contradiction. Combining social welfare and penal social control functions in one agency ensures that the court does both badly. Providing for child welfare is a societal responsibility rather than a judicial one. In practice,

juvenile courts subordinate welfare concerns to crime control considerations.

The conflicted impulses engendered between concern for child welfare and punitive responses to criminal violations form the root of the ambivalence embedded in the juvenile court. The hostile reactions that people experience toward other peoples' children, whom they regard as a threat to themselves and their own children, undermine benevolent aspirations and elevate concerns for their control. Juvenile justice personnel simultaneously profess child-saving aspirations but more often function as agents of criminal social control.

The juvenile court inevitably subordinates social welfare to criminal social control because of its built-in penal focus. Legislatures do not define juvenile courts' social welfare jurisdiction on the basis of characteristics of children for which they are not responsible and for which effective intervention could improve their lives. If states defined juvenile courts' jurisdiction on the basis of young people's needs for social welfare, then they would declare a broad category of at-risk children who are eligible for public assistance.

Instead, states' juvenile codes define juvenile courts' jurisdiction based on a youth committing a crime, a prerequisite that detracts from a compassionate response. Unlike disadvantaged social conditions that are not their fault, criminal behavior represents the one characteristic for which adolescent offenders do bear at least partial responsibility. As long as juvenile courts define eligibility for "services" on the basis of criminality, they highlight that aspect of youths which rationally elicits the least sympathy and ignore personal circumstances or social conditions that evoke a desire to help. Thus, the juvenile courts' defining characteristic simply reinforces the public's antipathy to young people by emphasizing that they are law violators. Recent changes in juvenile court waiver and sentencing policies to emphasize punishment, "accountability," and personal responsibility further reenforce juvenile courts' penal foundations and reduce the legitimacy of youths' claims to compassion or humanitarian assistance.

A century ago, Progressive reformers had to choose between initiating structural social reforms that would ameliorate inequality and criminogenic forces or ministering to the individual damaged by those adverse social conditions. A century later, we face similar choices between rehabilitating "damaged" individuals in a criminal justice system and initiating more fundamental social structural change. In making these choices, the juvenile court welfare idea may constitute an obstacle to child welfare reform. The *existence* of a juvenile court provides an alibi to avoid fundamental improvement. Conservatives may deprecate the juvenile court as a welfare system that fails to "crack down" or "get tough" and thereby "coddles" young criminals. Liberals may bemoan its lack of resources and inadequate options, none of which address the underlying structural causes of crime or children's poverty. But either stance is akin to sticking fingers in the dike while the flood of adverse social indicators of youth pours over the top in a torrent. Society collectively bears responsibility to provide for the welfare of its children and does so by supporting families, communities, schools, and social institutions that nurture all young people—not by cynically incarcerating its most disadvantaged children "for their own good." Neither juvenile court judges nor any other criminal justice agencies realistically can ameliorate the social ills that afflict young people or significantly reduce youth crime.

YOUTHFULNESS, CRIMINAL RESPONSIBILITY, AND SENTENCING POLICY: YOUNG OFFENDERS IN CRIMINAL COURTS

Once we uncouple social welfare from penal social control, then no need remains for a separate juvenile court for young offenders. We can try all offenders in criminal court with certain modifications of substantive and procedural criminal law to accommodate younger defendants. Some proponents of juvenile courts properly object that criminal courts suffer from profound deficiencies: crushing caseloads, ineffective attorneys, insufficient sentencing alternatives, coercive plea bargains, and assembly line justice. Unfortunately, these shortcomings equally characterize juvenile courts as well. Others argue that because no social or political will exists to reform or provide resources for criminal courts, then juvenile court abolitionists must demonstrate conclusively their irremediable bankruptcy before remitting youths to the criminal courts that inspired their creation. In short, few juvenile court proponents even attempt any longer to defend the institution on its own merits but only to justify it by comparison with criminal courts, which they contend are worse. In this article, I do not propose simultaneously to completely reform the criminal justice system but rather only to identify the sentencing policy issues raised when the criminal is a child. Because legislatures, prosecutors, and juvenile court judges already transfer increasing numbers and younger offenders to criminal courts for prosecution as adults, formulating a youth sentencing policy has considerable contemporary salience whether or not states abolish juvenile courts in their entirety.

If the child is a criminal and the "real" reason for formal intervention is criminal social control, then states should abolish juvenile courts' delinquency jurisdiction and try young offenders in criminal courts alongside their adult counterparts. But, if the criminal is a child, then states must modify their criminal justice system to accommodate the youthfulness of some defendants. Before prosecuting a child as a criminal in an integrated court, a legislature must address issues of substance and procedure. Substantive justice requires a rationale to sentence younger offenders differently, and more *leniently*, than older defendants, a formal recognition of *youthfulness as a mitigating factor in sentencing*. Procedural justice requires providing youths with full procedural parity with adult defendants and additional safeguards to account for the disadvantages of youth in the justice system. Taken in combination, these substantive and procedural modifications can avoid the "worst of both worlds," provide youths with protections functionally equivalent to those accorded adults, and do justice in sentencing.

Politically popular "sound bites"—"old enough to do the crime, old enough to do the time" or "adult crime, adult time"—do not analyze adequately the complexities of a youth sentencing policy. My proposal to abolish the juvenile court constitutes neither an unqualified endorsement of punishment nor a primitive throwback to earlier centuries' views of young people as miniature adults. Rather, it honestly acknowledges that juvenile courts currently engage in criminal social control, asserts that younger offenders in a criminal justice system *deserve* less severe consequences for their misdeeds than do more mature offenders simply because they are young, and addresses many problems created by trying to maintain binary, dichotomous, and contradictory criminal justice systems based on an arbitrary age classification of a youth as a child or as an adult.

Formulating a youth sentencing policy entails two tasks. First, I will develop a rationale to sentence younger offenders differently, and *more leniently,* than older defendants. Explicitly punishing young offenders rests on the premise that adolescents possess sufficient moral reasoning, cognitive capacity, and volitional controls to hold them responsible and accountable for their behavior, albeit not necessarily to the same degree as adults. Developmental psychological research, jurisprudence, and criminal sentencing policy provide a rationale to explain why young offenders deserve less severe consequences for their misdeeds than do older offenders and justify formal recognition of youthfulness as a mitigating factor. Second, I will propose a youth discount as a practical administrative mechanism to implement youthfulness in sentencing.

Substantive Justice—
Juveniles' Criminal Responsibility

Questions about youths' accountability or criminal responsibility arise at two different stages in the justice system—either when deciding guilt or when imposing a sentence. In the former instance, questions of responsibility focus on the minimum age at which the state may find a person guilty of an offense. In making judgments about criminal responsibility, the criminal law's *mens rea* construct focuses narrowly on cognitive ability and capacity to make choices and excludes from consideration the goals, values, emotions, or psychological development that motivate a person's choices. In the absence of insanity, compulsion, or some cognizable legal excuse, any actor who has the capacity to choose to act otherwise than the way she did possesses criminal responsibility. For questions of criminal responsibility and guilt, the common law's insanity and infancy *mens rea* defenses provide most of the answers. These doctrines excuse from criminal liability only those who lack the requisite criminal intent, the *mens rea,* because of mental illness or immaturity. Because these *mens rea* defenses effectively excuse an offender when the state cannot prove a crucial element of the offense (i.e., criminal intent), the common law employs a very low cognitive threshold—knowledge of "right from wrong"—to establish criminal guilt.

Quite apart from decisions about guilt or innocence, individual accountability and criminal responsibility also relate to questions of disposition or sentence. Even if a court finds a youth criminally responsible for causing a particular harm, should the criminal law treat a 14-year-old as the moral equivalent of a 24-year-old and impose an identical sentence, or should youthfulness mitigate the severity of the consequences? "Old enough to do the crime, old enough to do the time" provides an overly simple answer to a complex, normative, moral, and legal question. If political "sound bites" do not capture adequately the complexity of a youth sentencing policy, then on what principled bases should we distinguish between the two in sentencing?

Contemporary juvenile courts typically impose shorter sentences on serious young offenders than adult offenders convicted of comparable crimes receive. These shorter sentences enable young offenders to survive the mistakes of adolescence with a semblance of life chances intact. The juvenile court reifies the idea that young people bear less criminal responsibility and deserve less punishment than adults. Shorter sentences recognize that young people *do differ somewhat* from adults. These differences stem from physical, psychological, or developmental characteristics of young people and as by-products of the legal and social construction of youth. Youthfulness provides a rationale to mitigate sentences to some degree without excusing criminal conduct. But, shorter sentences for young people do not require a separate justice system in which to try them. Both juvenile and adult courts separate adjudication of guilt or innocence from sentencing, confine consideration of individual circumstances largely to the latter phase, and criminal courts may impose lenient sentences on young offenders when appropriate.

A variety of doctrinal and policy reasons justify sentencing young people less severely than their adult counterparts. The common law's infancy *mens rea* defense antedated positive criminology's deterministic assumptions and recognized that young people may lack criminal capacity. The classical criminal law assumed that rational actors make blameworthy choices and deserve to suffer the consequences of their freely chosen acts. The common law recognized and exempted from punishment categories of persons who lacked the requisite moral and criminal responsibility, for example, the insane and the young. It conclusively presumed that children less than 7 years old lacked criminal capacity and treated those 14 years of age and older as fully responsible. Between the ages of 7 and 14 years, the law rebuttably presumed criminal incapacity. The common law infancy gradations reflect developmental differences that render youths less *culpable* or criminally responsible than their adult counterparts and provide a first approximation of a rationale for shorter sentences for youths than for adults. Juvenile court legislation simply extended upward by a few years the general presumption of youthful criminal irresponsibility and incapacity.

The extent to which young offenders, like adults, deserve punishment hinges on the meaning of culpability. Respect for the integrity of the individual provides the underlying rationale of *deserved punishment*. Blaming a culpable actor for her voluntary choice to do wrong and giving her the consequences that her choice deserves respects her integrity as a morally responsible individual. Deserved punishment emphasizes censure and condemnation for blameworthy choices. As long as the criminal law rests on a moral foundation, the idea of blameworthiness remains central to ascribing guilt and allocating punishment. Penalties proportionate to the seriousness of the crime reflect the connection between conduct, choice, and blameworthiness.

Because commensurate punishment proportions sanctions to the seriousness of the offense, it shifts the analytical focus to the meaning of *seriousness*. Two elements—harm and culpability—define the seriousness of an offense. Evaluations of harm focus on the nature and degree of injury inflicted, risk created, or value taken. A perpetrator's age has little bearing on assessments of harmfulness. But evaluations of seriousness also include the quality of the actor's choice to engage in the criminal conduct that produced the harm. Just deserts theory and criminal law grading principles base the degree of deserved punishment on an actor's culpability. For example, a person may cause the death of another individual with premeditation and deliberation, intentionally, "in the heat of passion," recklessly, negligently, or accidentally. The criminal law treats the same objective consequence or harm, the death of another person, very differently depending on the nature of the choice made.

Youthfulness acquires special salience when gauging the culpability of choices—the blameworthiness of acting in a particular harm-producing way. In a framework of deserved punishment, it would be fundamentally unjust to impose the same penalty on offenders who do not share equal culpability. If young people are neither fully responsible nor the moral equals of adults, then they do not deserve the same legal consequences even for their blameworthy misconduct.

Responsibility for choices hinges on cognitive and volitional competence. Do young offenders make criminal choices that constitute the moral equivalents of those made by more mature actors? If one focuses narrowly only on the capacity to make instrumental choices to do wrong, then we could view even very young actors as criminally responsible. For example, a 6-year-old child can act purposively to "steal" the toy of a friend even though she "knows" and can articulate that such conduct is "wrong." When young children make voluntary and instrumental choices to engage in prohibited conduct, they possess some moral ability to understand its wrongfulness and require discipline to hold them accountable and to teach them the consequences of violating rules. However, despite their ability to make reasoned choices and engage in goal-oriented behavior, we do not regard them as full moral agents. The criminal law regards young actors differently exactly because they have not yet fully internalized moral norms, developed sufficient empathic identification with others, acquired adequate moral comprehension, or had sufficient opportunity to develop the ability to restrain their actions. They possess neither the rationality—cognitive capacity—nor the self-control—volitional capacity—to equate their criminal responsibility with that of adults.

TOWARD A YOUTH SENTENCING POLICY RATIONALE

Certain characteristic developmental differences between adolescents and adults distinguish their quality of judgment, psychosocial maturity, and self-control and justify a different criminal sentencing policy for younger offenders. Youths differ from adults on several dimensions that directly affect their degree of criminal responsibility and deserved punishment: breadth of experience, short-term versus long-term temporal perspective, attitude toward and acceptance of risk, and susceptibility to peer influences. These developmentally unique attributes affect young peoples' capacity to comprehend fully the consequences of their actions and their empathic identification with others. Moreover, it takes time and experience to develop the capacity to exercise self-control. While young offenders possess sufficient understanding and culpability to hold them accountable for their acts, their choices are less blameworthy than those of adults because of truncated self-control. Their crimes are less blameworthy not simply because of reduced culpability and limited appreciation of consequences but because their life situations have understandably limited their capacity to learn to make fully responsible choices.

When youths offend, the families, schools, and communities that socialize them bear some responsibility for the failures of socializing institutions. Human beings depend on others for nurture; this includes the ability to develop and exercise the moral capacity for constructive behavior. The capacity for self-control and self-direction is not a matter of moral luck or good fortune, but a socially constructed developmental process that provides young people with the opportunity to develop a moral character. The ability to make responsible choices is learned behavior, and the dependent status of youth systematically deprives them of chances to learn to be responsible. Inevitably, when we grant young people autonomy in order to learn to make mature judgments, they will abuse that trust. Young people's socially constructed life situation understandably limits their capacity to develop self-control, restricts their opportunities to learn and exercise responsibility, and supports a partial reduction of criminal responsibility. Adolescence itself limits opportunities fully to develop and internalize responsible adult-quality decision making. Their susceptibility to peer group influences reflects truncated development of their own capacity for autonomous and independent judgment. Thus, a youth sentencing policy must recognize youths' reduced opportunities and abilities to make responsible choices. Such a policy would entail both shorter sentence durations and a higher offense-seriousness threshold before a state incarcerates youths than for older offenders.

Administering Youthfulness as a Mitigating Factor at Sentencing: The "Youth Discount"

Implementing a youth sentencing policy entails legal, moral, and social judgments. Because of developmental differences and the social construction of adolescence, younger offenders are less criminally responsible than more mature violators. But, they are not so essentially different and inherently incompetent as the current legal dichotomy between juvenile and criminal court suggests. In view of the developmental psychological research that suggests several ways in which youths systematically differ from adults, should the criminal law adopt a "youth-blind" stance and treat 14-year-olds as the moral equivalent of adults for purposes of sentencing, or should it devise a youth sentencing policy that reflects more appropriately the developmental continuum?

Shorter sentences for reduced responsibility represents a more modest and attainable reason to treat young offenders differently than adults than the rehabilitative justifications advanced by Progressive child savers. In this context, adolescent criminal responsibility represents a global judgment about the degree of youths' deserved punishment rather than a technical legal judgment about whether or not a particular youth possessed the requisite *mens rea* or mental state defined in the criminal statute. If adolescents as a class characteristically exercise poorer judgment than do adults, then sentencing policies can reduce the long-term harm that they cause to themselves. Protecting young people from the full penal consequences of their poor decisions reflects a policy to preserve their life chances for the future when they presumably will make more mature and responsible choices. Such a policy simultaneously holds young offenders accountable for their acts because they possess sufficient culpability and yet mitigates the severity of consequences because their choices entail less blameworthiness than those of adults.

Criminal courts in some jurisdictions already consider "youthfulness" in the context of aggravating and mitigating factors and may impose shorter sentences on a discretionary basis. Although the federal sentencing guidelines explicitly reject youthfulness as a justification to sentence outside of the guidelines range, sentencing statutes in some states recognize youthfulness as a mitigating factor at sentencing. However, states that consider youthfulness as a mitigating factor simply treat it as one element to be weighed with other aggravating and mitigating factors in deciding what sentence to impose on an individual.

A statutory sentencing policy that integrates youthfulness, reduced culpability, and restricted opportunities to learn self-control with principles of proportionality would provide younger offenders with categorical fractional reductions of adult sentences. Because youthfulness constitutes a universal form of "reduced responsibility," states should treat it unequivocally as a mitigating factor without regard to nuances of individual developmental differences. Treating youthfulness as a formal mitigating sentencing factor represents a social, moral, and criminal policy judgment rather than a clinical or psychiatric evaluation. Such an approach avoids the risks of discretionary clinical subjectivity inherent in individualized adolescent culpability determinations.

This categorical approach would take the form of an explicit youth discount at sentencing. A 14-year-old offender might receive, for example, 25-33% of the adult penalty, a 16-year-old defendant 50-60%, and an 18-year-old adult the full penalty, as presently occurs. The "deeper discounts" for younger offenders correspond to the developmental continuum and their more limited opportunities to learn and exercise responsibility. A youth discount based on reduced culpability functions as a sliding scale of diminished responsibility. Just as adolescents possess less criminal responsibility than do adults, 14-year-old youths should enjoy a greater mitigation of blameworthiness than would 17-year-olds. Because the rationale for youthful mitigation rests on reduced culpability and limited opportunities to learn to make responsible choices, younger adolescents bear less responsibility and deserve proportionally shorter sentences than older youths. The capacity to learn to be responsible improves with time and experience. With the passage of time, age, and opportunities to develop the capacity for self-control, social tolerance of criminal deviance and claims for mitigation decline.

Discounted sentences that preserve younger offenders' life chances require that the maximum sentences they receive remain substantially below those imposed on adults. For youths below the age of 14, the common law infancy *mens rea* defense would acquire new vitality for proportionally shorter "discounted" sentences or even noncriminal dispositions.

The rationale for a youth discount also supports requiring a higher in/out threshold of offense seriousness as a prerequisite for imprisonment. Because juveniles depend on their families more than do adults, removal from home constitutes a more severe punishment. Because of differences in "subjective time," youths experience the duration of imprisonment more acutely than do adults. Because of the rapidity of developmental change, sentences of incarceration are more disruptive for youths than for adults. Thus, states should require a higher threshold of offense seriousness and a greater need for social defense before confining a youth than might be warranted for an older offender.

The specific discount value—the amount of fractional reduction and the in/out threshold—reflects several empirical and normative considerations. It requires an empirically informed sentencing policy judgment about adolescent development and criminal responsibility. To what extent do specific physical, social, and psychological characteristics of youth—depreciation of future consequences, risk taking, peer influences, lack of self-control, hormonal changes, and lack of opportunities to learn to make responsible choices—induce them to engage in behavior simply because they are young? How much developmental differ-ence should a state require to produce what degree of moral and legal mitigation in its sentencing policy? To what extent will severe, unmitigated adult penalties so alter youths' life course that they will be unable to survive the mistakes of adolescence with any semblance of life chances intact? Developmental psychological research provides only suggestive directions rather than definitive answers to these sentencing policy questions.

Only the states whose criminal sentencing laws provide realistic, humane, and determinate sentences that enable a judge actually to determine "real-time" sentences can readily implement a proposal for explicit fractional reductions of youths' sentences. One can only know the value of a youth discounted sentence in a sentencing system in which courts know in advance the standard or "going rate" for adults. In many jurisdictions, implementing a youth discount would require significant modification of the current criminal sentencing statutes, including presumptive sentencing guidelines with strong upper limits on punishment severity, elimination of all mandatory minimum sentences, and some structured judicial discretion to mitigate penalties based on individual circumstances. In short, a criminal sentencing system itself must be defensible in terms of equality, equity, desert, and proportionality. Attempts to apply idiosyncratically youth discounts within the flawed indeterminate or draconian mandatory minimum-sentencing regimes that currently prevail in many jurisdictions runs the risk simply of reproducing all their existing inequalities and injustices.

INDIVIDUALIZATION VERSUS CATEGORIZATION

Youthful development is highly variable. Young people of the same age may differ dramatically in their criminal sophistication, appreciation of risk, or learned responsibility. Chronological age provides, at best, a crude and imprecise indicator of maturity and the opportunity to develop a capacity for self-control. However, a categorical youth discount that uses age as a conclusive proxy for reduced culpability and a shorter sentence remains preferable to an "individualized" inquiry into the criminal responsibility of each young offender. The criminal law represents an objective standard. Attempts to integrate subjective psychological explanations of adolescent behavior and personal responsibility into a youth sentencing policy cannot be done in a way that can be administered fairly without undermining the objectivity of the law. Developmental psychology does not possess reliable clinical indicators of moral development or criminal sophistication that equate readily with criminal responsibility or accountability. For young criminal actors who possess at least some degree of criminal responsibility, relying on inherently inconclusive or contradictory psychiatric or clinical testimony to precisely tailor sanctions hardly seems worth the judicial burden and diversion of resources that the effort would entail. Thus, for ease of administration, age alone provides the most useful criterion on which to allocate mitigation.

Youthful mitigation of criminal responsibility represents a legal concept and social policy judgment that does not correspond with any psychiatric diagnostic category or developmental psychological analog about which an expert could testify. Unlike the insanity defense, a youth discount does not attempt to assess whether antecedent forces, such as a mental illness, caused or determined a young offender's behavior. Rather, it conclusively presumes that young people's criminal choices differ qualitatively per se from those of adults. Youthfulness constitutes a form of legal "partial responsibility" without need for any specific clinical indicators other than a birth certificate. A youth discount that bases fractional reductions of sentences on age as a proxy for culpability also avoids the conceptual and administrative difficulties of a more encompassing subjective inquiry into diminished responsibility, a "rotten social background," or "social adversity." The juvenile courts' treatment ideology mistakenly denies that young people are morally responsible actors whom the law may hold accountable for their behavior.

A youth sentencing policy requires formal mitigation to avoid the undesirable forced choice between either inflicting undeservedly harsh punishments on less culpable actors or "doing nothing" about the manifestly guilty. A formal policy of youthful mitigation provides a buffer against the inevitable political pressure to ratchet-up sanctions every time youths sentenced leniently subsequently commit serious offenses. The idea of deserved punishment also limits the imposition of too little punishment as well as too much. Although the overall cardinal scale of penalties for juveniles should be considerably less than that for adults, a failure to sanction when appropriate, as juvenile court treatment ideology may dictate in some instances, can deprecate the moral seriousness of offending.

YOUTH AND GROUP CRIME

Young offenders commit crimes in groups to a much greater extent than do adults. While the law treats all participants in a crime as equally responsible and may sentence them alike, young people's susceptibility to peer group influences requires a more nuanced assessment of their degree of participation, personal responsibility, and culpability. The group nature of youth crime affects sentencing policy in several ways. The presence of a social audience of peers may induce youths to participate in criminal behavior that they would not engage in if alone. Even though the criminal law treats all accomplices as equally guilty as a matter of law, they may not all bear equal responsibility for the actual harm inflicted and may deserve different sentences. To some extent, state criminal sentencing laws already recognize an offender's differential participation in a crime as a "mitigating" factor. Similarly, some states' juvenile court waiver laws and juvenile sentencing provisions also focus on "the *culpability* of the child in committing the alleged offense, including the level of the child's participating in planning and carrying out the offense." Thus, the group nature of adolescent criminality requires some formal mechanism to distinguish between active participants and passive accomplices with even greater "discounts" for the latter.

VIRTUE OF AFFIRMING PARTIAL RESPONSIBILITY FOR YOUTH

One of the principal virtues, Goldstein argues in his seminal defense of *The Insanity Defense*, is that it dramatically affirms the idea of individual responsibility. Because the criminal law emphasizes blame, the insanity defense attempts to distinguish between the "mad" and the "bad," between the "sick" and the "evil," in order to reinforce the concept of personal responsibility. The idea of personal responsibility and holding people accountable for their behavior provides an important counterweight to a popular culture that endorses the idea that everyone is a victim, that all behavior is determined and no one is responsible, and that therefore the state cannot blame wrongdoers.

The juvenile court's "rehabilitative ideal" elevated determinism over free will, characterized delinquent offenders as victims rather than perpetrators, and envisioned a therapeutic institution that resembled more closely a preventive, forward-looking civil commitment process rather than a criminal court. By denying youths' personal responsibility, juvenile courts' treatment ideology reduces offenders' duty to exercise self-control, erodes their obligation to change, and sustains a self-fulfilling prophecy that delinquency occurs inevitably for youths from certain backgrounds.

Affirming responsibility encourages people to learn the virtues of moderation, self-discipline, and personal accountability. Because a criminal conviction represents an official condemnation, the idea of "blame" reinforces for the public and provides for the individual the incentive to develop responsibility. A culture that values autonomous individuals must emphasize both freedom and responsibility.

While the paternalistic stance of the traditional juvenile courts rests on the humane desire to protect young people from the adverse consequences of their bad decisions, protectionism simultaneously disables young people from the opportunity to make choices and to learn responsibility for their natural consequences. Even marginally competent adolescents can only learn self-control by exercising their capacity for autonomy. Accountability for criminal behavior may facilitate legal socialization and moral development in ways that juvenile courts' rejection of criminal responsibility cannot.

INTEGRATED CRIMINAL JUSTICE SYSTEM

A graduated age-culpability sentencing scheme in an integrated criminal justice system avoids the inconsistencies and injustices associated with the binary either-juvenile-or-adult drama currently played out in judicial waiver proceedings and in prosecutorial charging decisions. It also avoids the "punishment gap" when youths make the transition from the one justice system to the other. Depending on whether or not a judge or prosecutor transfers a case, the sentences that violent youths receive may differ by orders of magnitude. Moreover, appellate courts eschew proportionality analyses and allow criminal court judges to sentence waived youths to the same terms applied to adults without requiring them to consider or recognize any differences in their degree of criminal responsibility. By contrast, waived chronic property offenders typically receive less severe sanctions as adults than they would have received as persistent offenders in the juvenile system. As the sentencing principles of juvenile courts increasingly resemble more closely those of criminal courts, the sentence disparities that follow from waiver decisions become even less defensible.

An integrated criminal justice system eliminates the need for transfer hearings, saves the considerable resources that juvenile courts currently expend ultimately to no purpose, reduces the punishment gap that presently occurs when youths make the passage from the juvenile system, and ensures similar consequences for similarly situated offenders. Adolescence and criminal careers develop along a continuum. But the radical bifurcation between the two justice systems confounds efforts to respond consistently and systematically to young career offenders.

A sliding scale of criminal sentences based on an offender's age-as-a-proxy-for-culpability accomplishes much more directly what the various "blended jurisdiction" statutes attempt to achieve indirectly. The variants of "intermediate" sanctions attempt to reconcile the binary alternatives of either a sentence limited by juvenile court age jurisdiction or a dramatically longer criminal sentence imposed on a youth as an adult. While those statutes attempt to smooth the juncture between the two systems, the existence of two separate systems thwarts the fusion.

INTEGRATED RECORD KEEPING

The absence of an integrated record-keeping system that enables criminal court judges to identify and respond to career offenders on the basis of their cumulative prior record constitutes one of the most pernicious consequences of jurisdictional bifurcation. Currently, persistent young offenders may "fall between the cracks" of the juvenile and criminal systems, often at the age at which career offenders approach their peak offending rates. A unified criminal court with a single record-keeping system can maintain and retrieve more accurate criminal histories when a judge sentences an offender. Although a youth discount provides appropriate leniency for younger offenders, integrated records would allow courts to escalate the discounted sanctions for chronic and career young offenders.

DECRIMINALIZE "KIDS' STUFF"

Despite juvenile courts' overcrowded dockets and inadequate treatment resources, their procedural deficiencies and informality allow them to process delinquents too efficiently. Expedited procedures, fewer lawyers and legal challenges, and greater flexibility allow juvenile courts to handle a much larger number of cases per judge than do criminal courts and at lower unit cost. Merging the two systems would introduce an enormous volume of cases into an already overburdened criminal justice system that barely can cope with its current workload. Legislators and prosecutors forced to allocate scarce law enforcement resources would use the seriousness of the offense to rationalize charging decisions and "divert" or "decriminalize" most of the "kids' stuff" that provides the grist of the juvenile court mill until it became chronic or escalated in severity. Unlike a rehabilitative system inclined to extend its benevolent reach, an explicitly punitive process would opt to introduce fewer and more criminally "deserving" youths into the system.

SENTENCING EXPERTISE

Contemporary proponents of a specialized juvenile court contend that juvenile court judges require substantial time and commitment to become familiar with youth development, family dynamics, and community resources and cite judges' dispositional expertise as a justification for a separate justice system. Whether juvenile court judges actually acquire such expertise remains unclear. In many jurisdictions, nonspecialist judges handle juvenile matters as part of their general trial docket or rotate through a juvenile court on short-term assignments without developing any special expertise in sentencing juveniles. Even in specialized juvenile courts, the court services personnel, rather than the judge herself, typically possess the information necessary to recommend appropriate sentences.

AGE-SEGREGATED DISPOSITIONAL FACILITIES AND "ROOM TO REFORM"

Questions about young offenders' criminal responsibility and length of sentence differ from issues about appropriate places of confinement or the services or resources the state should provide to them. Even explicitly punitive sentences do not require judges or correctional authorities to confine young people with adults in jails and prisons, as is the current practice for waived youths, or to consign them to custodial warehouses or "punk prisons." States should maintain separate age-segregated youth correctional facilities to protect both younger offenders and older inmates. Even though youths may be somewhat responsible for their criminal conduct, they may not be the physical or psychological equals of adults in prison. While some youths may be vulnerable to victimization or exploitation by more physically developed adults, other youths may pose a threat to older inmates. Younger offenders have not learned to "do easy time," pose more management problems for correctional administrators, and commit more disciplinary infractions while they serve their sentences. Existing juvenile detention facilities, training schools, and institutions provide the option to segregate inmates on the basis of age or other risk factors. Some research indicates that youths sentenced to juvenile correctional facilities may recidivate somewhat less often, seriously, or rapidly than comparable youths sentenced to adult facilities. However, these findings provide modest support for a separate youth correctional system rather than for an entirely separate juvenile justice system.

Virtually all young offenders return to society, and the state should provide them with resources for self-improvement on a voluntary basis because of its basic responsibility to its citizens and its own self-interest. If a state fails to provide opportunities for growth and further debilitates already disadvantaged youths, it guarantees greater long-term human, criminal, and correctional costs.

SUMMARY AND CONCLUSIONS: LET'S BE HONEST ABOUT YOUTH CRIME CONTROL

Law reforms that tinker with the boundaries of childhood or modify judicial procedures do not appear to reduce appreciably offenders' probabilities of recidivism or increase public safety. Even far-reaching justice system changes can have only a marginal impact on social problems as complex as crime and violence. Rather, a proposal to abolish the juvenile court and to try all young offenders in an integrated justice system makes no utilitarian claims but represents a commitment to honesty about state coercion. States bring young offenders who commit crimes to juvenile court for social control and to punish them. Juvenile courts' rehabilitative claims fly in the face of their penal reality,

undermine their legitimacy, and impair their ability to function as judicial agencies. Because punishment is an unpleasant topic, juvenile courts attempt to evade those disagreeable qualities by obscuring their reality with rehabilitative euphemisms, psycho-babble, and judicial "double-speak" like "sometimes punishment is treatment."

The shortcomings of the "rehabilitative" juvenile court run far deeper than inadequate resources and rudimentary and unproven treatment techniques. Rather, the flaw lies in the very idea that the juvenile court can combine successfully criminal social control and social welfare in one system. Similarly, a separate "criminal" juvenile court cannot succeed or long survive because it lacks a coherent rationale to distinguish it from a "real" criminal court. A scaled-down separate criminal court for youths simply represents a temporary way station on the road to substantive and procedural convergence with the criminal court. Only an integrated criminal justice that formally recognizes adolescence as a developmental continuum may effectively address many of the problems created by our binary conceptions of youth and social control.

Enhanced procedural protections, a youth discount of sentences, and age-segregated dispositional facilities recognize and respond to the real developmental differences between young people and adult offenders in the justice system. Because these policy proposals require state legislators courageous enough to adopt them, several thoughtful commentators question whether elected public officials in a "get tough" political climate would make explicit the leniency implicit in the contemporary juvenile court. While the public unknowingly may tolerate nominal sanctions administered to young offenders in low-visibility juvenile proceedings, politicians may balk at openly acknowledging a policy of moderation. Many elected officials prefer to demagogue about crime and posture politically to "crack down" on youth crime rather than to responsibly educate the public about the realistic limits of the justice system to control it. Some would rather fan the flames of fear for political advantage despite overwhelming evidence that escalating rates of imprisonment represent a failed policy that ultimately leads only to fiscal and moral bankruptcy.

I propose to abolish the juvenile court with trepidation. On the one hand, combining enhanced procedural safeguards with a youth discount in an integrated criminal court can provide young offenders with greater protections and justice than they currently receive in the juvenile system and more proportional and humane consequences than judges presently inflict on them in the criminal justice system. Integration may foster a more consistent crime control response than the present dual systems permit to violent and chronic young offenders at various stages of the developmental and criminal career continuum. On the other hand, politicians may ignore the significance of youthfulness as a mitigating factor and use these proposals to escalate the punishment of young people. Although abolition of the juvenile court, enhanced procedural protections, and a youth discount constitute essential components of a youth sentencing policy package, nothing can prevent legislators from selectively choosing only those elements that serve their "get tough" agenda, even though doing so unravels the threads that make coherent a proposal for an integrated court.

In either event, the ensuing debate about a youth sentencing policy would require them to consider whether to focus primarily on the fact that young offenders are young or offenders. A public policy debate about when the child is a criminal and the criminal is a child forces a long overdue and critical reassessment of the entire social construction of "childhood." To what extent do adolescents really differ from adults? To what extent do differences in competency and judgment result from physical or psychological developmental processes or from social arrangements and institutions that systematically disable young people? If politicians ultimately insist on treating young people primarily as offenders and the equals of adults, can they simultaneously maintain without contradiction

other age-graded legal distinctions such as denial of the right to vote or to exercise self-determination?

The idea of the juvenile court is fundamentally flawed because it attempts to combine criminal social control and social welfare goals. My proposal to abolish the juvenile court does not entail an abandonment of its welfare ideal. Rather, uncoupling policies of social welfare from penal social control enables us to expand a societal commitment to the welfare of all children regardless of their criminality. If we frame child welfare policy reforms in terms of child welfare rather than crime control, then we may expand the possibilities for positive intervention for all young people. For example, a public health approach to youth crime that identified the social, environmental, community structural, and ecological correlates of youth violence, such as poverty, the proliferation of handguns, and the commercialization of violence, would suggest wholly different intervention strategies than simply incarcerating minority youths. Youth violence occurs as part of a social ecological structure; high rates of violent youth crime arise in areas of concentrated poverty, high teenage pregnancy, and AFDC dependency. Such social indicators could identify census tracts or even zip codes for community organizing, economic development, and preventive and remedial intervention.

Three aspects of youth crime and violence suggest future social welfare policy directions regardless of their immediate impact on recidivism. First, it is imperative to provide a *hopeful future for all young people*. As a result of structural and economic changes since the 1980s, the ability of families to raise children, to prepare them for the transition to adulthood, and to provide them with a more promising future has declined. Many social indicators of the status of young people—poverty, homelessness, violent victimization, and crime—are negative, and some of those adverse trends are accelerating. Without realistic hope for their future, young people fall into despair, nihilism, and violence. Second, the disproportionate overrepresentation of minority youths in the juvenile justice system makes imperative the pursuit of *racial and social justice*. A generation ago, the Kerner Commission warned that the United States was "moving toward two societies, one black, one white—separate and unequal." The Kerner Commission predicted that to continue present policies was "to make permanent the division of our country into two societies; one, largely Negro and poor, located in the central cities; the other, predominantly white and affluent, located in the suburbs." Today, we reap the bitter harvest of racial segregation, concentrated poverty, urban social disintegration, and youth violence sown by social policies and public neglect a generation ago. Third, youth violence has become increasingly lethal as the proliferation of handguns transforms adolescent altercations into homicidal encounters. Only public policies that reduce and reverse the proliferation of guns in the youth population will stem the carnage.

While politicians may be unwilling to invest scarce social resources in young "criminals," particularly those of other colors or cultures, a demographic shift and an aging population give all of us a stake in young people and encourage us to invest in their human capital for their and our own future well-being and to maintain an intergenerational compact. Social welfare and legal policies to provide all young people with a hopeful future, to reduce racial and social inequality, and to reduce access to and use of firearms require a public and political commitment to the welfare of children that extends far beyond the resources or competencies of any juvenile justice system.

QUESTIONS FOR DISCUSSION AND WRITING

1. What has happened in the past three decades? What have these reforms done? Why does the author recommend abolishing juvenile courts' delinquency jurisdiction?
2. In the third section of his article, the author decries the inherent contradiction of the juvenile court and claims that the juvenile court treatment model constitutes an inappropriate policy response to young offenders. What does he mean by this?
3. In the fourth section, the author discusses the meaning of seriousness. What two elements define the seriousness of an offense, and for which is youthfulness relevant?
4. What is a "youth discount," and how is it relevant in the author's reform plan?
5. In his conclusion, the author says, "The shortcomings of the 'rehabilitative' juvenile court run far deeper than inadequate resources and rudimentary and unproven treatment techniques." On what flaw does he focus?

Data Analysis Exercise

A Look at Juveniles Processed in the Adult Criminal Courts

In this data analysis exercise, we will use the 1996 State Court Processing Statistics, Felony Defendants in Large Urban Counties (U.S. Department of Justice, 2000) data to examine juveniles who are tried in the adult criminal courts.

DESCRIPTION OF THE DATA SET

The State Court Processing Statistics (SCPS) is a unique tracking system that monitors all felony cases filed in May until the cases are either disposed or a full year elapses. The data are collected from 40 of the 75 most populous counties in the United States. Data are collected on offender characteristics, charges at arrest, prior record, trial, conviction charges, and sentencing outcomes. We will be using the 1996 statistics, which means the cases were filed in May 1996 and followed until disposition or May 1997, whichever came first. I excluded all cases involving defendants who were 18 years of age or older at the time of their arrest, leaving just the juveniles.

Due to their age at arrest, we can assume the juveniles were somehow sent to the adult criminal court, presumably through waiver or decline hearings or mandatory certification legislation (such as the laws Fagan discusses in his article comparing juveniles sentenced in New York and New Jersey). All states allow waivers to adult criminal court in at least some circumstances; some states automatically certify to adult criminal court certain serious cases committed by juveniles who have met a minimum age criterion, whereas others allow prosecutors to file motions to ask the court to certify certain cases (Puzzanchera, 2000). Excluding the adults left 605 juveniles tried in the adult criminal courts in the 40 counties.[1]

Before we start our analyses, we will need to load up a new data set, "JDCTPROC." JDCTPROC contains many defendant characteristics and some processing variables, so we can gain a clearer picture of juveniles processed in the adult criminal courts.

EXPLORING JUVENILES IN ADULT CRIMINAL COURTS: GETTING A HANDLE ON THE DATA AND USING CROSS-TABULATION TABLES

Part V presents many articles written on the modern juvenile courts, documenting the move from the rehabilitative ideal to a more punishment-oriented forum. In addition to examining waivers of juveniles to adult criminal courts, some of the articles discuss punishment options such as electronic monitoring and boot camps. Although they do not include every 1996 juvenile delinquency case that ended up in the adult criminal courts, the SCPS data do represent a sizable proportion of adult criminal court cases due to including the largest American counties. This makes the SCPS an appropriate data set for our exercise.

First, let's get a handle on our data by running some frequency tables for SEX, RACEHISP, and AGE. We can quickly see that, at least for the 40 counties included in this data set, males predominate. Racially, more than half of the juveniles were black. In addition, the majority of juveniles were 17 at the time of arrest, with about one third aged 16, fewer than 5% aged 15, and the remaining 2% were 14 years old.

Now, we do some exploring. What offenses are committed by juveniles who are tried in adult criminal courts? We know from the first exercise (for Part II) that the majority of offenses committed by juveniles are of moderate or minor seriousness. To determine if that holds for juveniles tried in adult criminal courts, run a frequency of the most serious arrest charge (OFFENSE1). What do we learn? It becomes clear that Cernkovich, Giordano, and Pugh (in their article in Part II) were correct when they lamented about the absence of serious offenders in self-report research. Scattered among the robbery and drug cases are a few murders and rapes. When we speak about juveniles tried in adult criminal courts, it appears that their charges are more serious than those committed by their counterparts who "stay" in the juvenile courts. Of course, one reason for this is that some jurisdictions (e.g., New York) mandate transfer to adult criminal court on certain serious charges, and other states make it easier to transfer serious cases out of juvenile court. Running a frequency for CONVTYPE shows us the offenses for which the juveniles were ultimately convicted.

Now, let's examine the extent of our sample's prior criminality. Because they have been transferred to adult criminal court, one might expect these juveniles to represent the worst of the worst—that is, to have serious prior records. To determine if this is true, run a frequency table for PRIARR. Instead, it appears that only about one fourth of our sample had been arrested more than once. When we run a frequency table to examine the seriousness of prior convictions (SERCONV), we see that only about 10% of the sample has even one prior felony conviction. It appears that transfer to adult criminal court is predicated more on seriousness of the instant or current charge than on prior record.

Personally, I want to know which jurisdictions contribute the most cases. To find this out, run a frequency table for STATE. Of the 40 jurisdictions in this data set, New York contributes the most juvenile cases to the adult criminal court, nearly half of our sample. This should not surprise you, after reading Fagan's article on the advantages of trying juveniles in juvenile versus adult criminal courts. New York automatically transfers many serious juvenile cases to adult criminal court.[2] Illinois also contributes a sizable number of cases to the total waivers in this data set.

What case outcomes occur when juveniles are tried in adult criminal courts? Running a frequency table for ADJTYPE will allow us to find out. The majority of cases are settled through guilty pleas, although not as many as would be expected given national averages of 85% to 95%. More than one fourth of the cases are dismissed before trial. Only 15 of the 605 cases resulted in a trial (i.e., the 2 acquittals and the 13 "guilty-trials"). A few cases were diverted, and more than 15% had not been resolved after a full year.

What sort of sentences are handed out to juveniles who are tried in adult criminal courts? Run frequency tables for SENT1, SENT2, and SENT3 (three different representations of sentence severity) to find out. From the table for SENT1, we learn that more than one fourth of the juveniles in our sample were incarcerated for their crimes. If we recalculate the percentage based on just those cases that resulted in guilty pleas or verdicts, we learn that 59.8% (i.e., 158 of 264) of the convicted juveniles for whom sentence data are available were incarcerated. Looking at the table for SENT2 shows us that prison terms were slightly more likely to be imposed over jail terms. The table for SENT3 breaks down the sentences into even further detail—relatively few juveniles tried in adult criminal court received fines or probation as their sole penalties.

Now, let's consider the cross-tabulation tables. First, we will examine the likelihood of incarceration by offense type. It is logical that more serious charges should be more likely to result in incarceration. To determine if the SCPS data support this idea, run a cross-tabulation table with INCARCER[3] as the dependent (row) variable and CONVTYP2[4] as the independent (column) variables (remember to choose "Phi and Cramer's *V*" under **Statistics** and check off "Column percentages" under **Cells**).

What do you notice about the CONVTYP2 → INCARCER table? As would be expected, it appears that those convicted of violent offenses are more likely than those convicted of other offenses (i.e., property, drug, public-order, or misdemeanor offenses) to be incarcerated. More than three fourths of violent offenders are incarcerated compared to approximately half of the property, drug, and public-order offenders, and a few more than half of misdemeanants.

Although we could run a cross-tabulation table to compare incarceration rates by state, the table would be fairly unwieldy due to the fact that data from 16 states are included in this data set. Because we are interested only in the average incarceration rates, we can run means for each state to compare them.

Box 1

How to Run Breakout Means in SPSS

1. Click on **Analyze** (on the tool bar along the top of your screen), then **Compare Means,** and then **Means.**
2. Highlight the variables you want to break out, one at a time or in groups by holding down your right mouse button and dragging your mouse pointer down until you have highlighted the whole group. If you want to pick variables further down the list, simply hit the scroll button to move around the list. To read a whole label, merely position your mouse over the visible part of the label, and you will be able to read the entire label with its variable name in parentheses at the end of the text. The variables are listed in order by variable name, but the variable labels are shown in the listing on the left-hand side of the dialog box, making it a tad tricky to negotiate the list. Do not worry; you will get the hang of it.
3. Click on the arrow near the right-hand box labeled "Dependent List" to move your selection(s) into that box. You will get breakouts for each variable listed in this box.
4. Continue selecting variables until you have all the ones you want in the "Dependent List" box.
5. If you accidentally include a variable you do not want, highlight its name and click on the arrow to move it back into the variable list. Notice that the direction of the arrow indicates the box into which your selection will be moved.
6. Highlight the variables you want to break out your dependent list by, using the process described in Step 1.
7. Click on the arrow near the right-hand box labeled "Independent List" to move your selection(s) into that box. You will break out each variable listed in the "Dependent List" box by those in the "Independent List" box.
8. Click on the **OK** button in the upper right-hand corner of the command box to run your breakouts, which will appear in the large viewer window.

Box 2

Step-by-Step Example: Running Breakout Means in SPSS

1. Click on **Analyze** (on the tool bar along the top of your screen), then **Compare Means,** and then **Means.**
2. Highlight INCARCER, and then click the arrow by Dependent List. Highlight DISMISS, and then click the arrow by Dependent List.
3. Highlight STATE, and then click the arrow by Independent List.
4. Click **OK** to run the breakout table.

To do this, follow the directions in Box 1 to run means of INCARCER and DISMISS[5] by STATE.

A cursory examination of the tables (which are printed together, side by side in column format) shows that the incarceration rates and dismissal rates for juvenile cases tried in adult criminal courts vary quite a bit. Only one state (California) that sentenced more than three juveniles had a 100% incarceration rate for juveniles tried in adult courts. New York, which contributed more than half of the cases to the total sample, incarcerated approximately half of the juveniles that were sentenced in adult criminal courts. Looking over the column for DISMISS, we see that Indiana dismisses approximately half of the cases against juveniles in adult criminal court, whereas the average for all states is .2595 (from the top of the table). Looking at California (because it had a 100% incarceration rate) shows us that fewer than 10% of the waived juvenile cases are dismissed. Reflecting on the readings in the text, what are some explanations for California's high rate of incarceration coupled with a low rate of dismissal? What about New York's relatively low incarceration rate?

EXPLORING JUVENILES IN ADULT CRIMINAL COURTS: USING CONTROL VARIABLES

Now, let's examine sentencing outcomes by race of juvenile offender. Whether or not the courts are biased against minorities is still a controversial subject in the field of criminal justice, with researchers arguing back and forth as to whether bias exists. We can use the sentencing outcomes in our data set to examine sentencing bias.

First, try the most basic method of examining sentencing by running a cross-tabulation table for WHITE → INCARCER, which will allow us to examine sentencing outcomes for whites and nonwhites. What does the table reveal? Which group is more likely to be incarcerated?

Then, run a cross-tabulation table for WHITE → INCARCER controlling for CONVTYP2 (see exercise IV, B if you need help setting up this cross-tabulation table). The first thing you should notice is that many of the subtables have very small numbers of whites, which will make comparisons of the two racial groups tricky at best. Looking at the subtable for violent crimes, we see that whites are less likely to be incarcerated, but that the significance for the finding is not quite .05 (which means that we cannot say with confidence that whites are less likely than minorities to be incarcerated for violent acts). In fact, whites appear to be less likely than minorities to be incarcerated for all five crime subtypes, but the significance is nowhere near .05 except for violent crimes and misdemeanors. This is probably due to the small number of whites in the sample. When the tables are broken down into subtables, there are not enough whites in each cell to allow for substantial analysis. Thus, we cannot say that adding seriousness of offense into our equation changes our finding that whites are less likely than minorities to draw jail terms for their offenses, at least for violent offenses and misdemeanors.

Maybe prior record drives likelihood of incarceration so that juveniles with more extensive prior records are more likely to be incarcerated when tried in the adult criminal courts. To find out, run a cross-tabulation table for WHITE → INCARCER controlling for PRIORS. When we look the first subtable, the one for juveniles without any prior arrests, what do we see? Are whites less likely to be incarcerated? What is the strength of this finding? Is the finding significant? Now, look at the subtable for juveniles who had one or more prior arrests. Are whites less likely to be incarcerated? What is the strength of this finding? Is the finding significant? Due to the significance levels, we can say only that white juveniles with prior records are less likely to be incarcerated than their minority counterparts who share the presence of prior arrests. If there were a larger number of whites, we could try breaking out offense severity by prior record to determine if our finding that prior record makes a difference in the treatment of minorities is true for the five offense types. This analysis, however, would be doomed from the beginning due to the small cell sizes for whites. Instead, we will have to remain content with the finding that prior record appears to make a difference.

FURTHER EXPLORATION OF JUVENILES IN ADULT CRIMINAL COURTS

We have explored the issue of juveniles tried in the adult criminal courts. In the Further Exploration questions, you will do more analysis with cross-tabulation tables using other variables in the data set, such as severity of prior conviction (SERCONV).

ON YOUR OWN: JUVENILES IN ADULT CRIMINAL COURTS

The next step would be to expand your horizons with reference to juveniles in the adult criminal courts. You could decide to examine which juveniles are more likely to have their cases dismissed (DISMISS) or even which juveniles are more likely to have prior records (PRIORS). If you want to really get into the data, you could compute your own variables, for example, for juveniles who receive intermediate sanctions (i.e., fine only + probation only + probation plus). To do this, you can use the **Recode** function in SPSS to recode variables, and set the target values (in this case, 1-3 for "fine only," "probation only," and "probation plus") and set all other values to 0 (in this case, 4-7). Then, recode the "not applicables" (in this case, 8) to **Sysmis** so they will not be included in your analysis. It sounds difficult, but it is simple once you have done a few recodes. If you save your data, make sure to give them a different name or your recoded variables will be permanently changed.

While you are further examining juveniles in adult criminal courts, reflect on the readings and how they help us explain how juveniles are treated in adult criminal courts.

NOTES

1. Statistics for 1997 show that 8 of every 1,000 juvenile delinquency cases were handled in adult criminal courts (Puzzanchera, 2000).
2. The state of New York contributes 7 counties to the data set; Florida contributes 7 counties, and California contributes 9 counties. The remaining 31 counties are scattered across the nation, including 1 each in Alaska and Hawaii.
3. INCARCER is a recoded version of SENT1, excluding the 277 cases for which there was no conviction. The 64 cases for which SENT1 data are missing are also coded as missing for INCARCER.
4. CONVTYP2 is a recoded version of CONVTYPE, excluding the cases for which there was no conviction.
5. DISMISS is a recoded version of ADJTYPE, in which dismissals are coded as "1" and all other outcomes are coded as "0."

REFERENCES

Puzzanchera, C. M. (2000). *Delinquency Cases Waived to Criminal Court, 1988-1997.* Washington, DC: Office of Juvenile Justice and Delinquency Prevention.

U.S. Department of Justice, Bureau of Justice Statistics. (2000). *State Court Processing Statistics, 1990, 1992, 1994, and 1996: Felony Defendants in Large Urban Counties* [Computer file]. Conducted by Pretrial Services Resource Center. 2nd ICPSR ed. Ann Arbor, MI: Inter-university Consortium for Political and Social Research [producer and distributor].

Homework for Part V: General Questions
Juveniles in Adult Criminal Courts

Name: _____   Date: _____

Directions: Answer the following questions by filling in the blanks or circling the appropriate responses. Some answers have been filled in for you to make sure you are on the right track.

EXPLORING JUVENILES IN ADULT CRIMINAL COURT: GETTING A HANDLE ON THE DATA AND USING CROSS-TABULATION TABLES

1. In the 1996 SCPS sample, _____ (_____%) of the sample were male; _____ (_____%) were female.

2. In the 1996 SCPS sample, _____ (_____%) of the sample were non-Hispanic whites; _____ (_____%) were non-Hispanic blacks; 4 (_____%) were other non-Hispanics; and _____ (_____%) were Hispanics of any race.

3. In the 1996 SCPS sample, _____ (_____%) of the sample were aged 14; _____ (_____%) were aged 15; 190 (_____%) were aged 16; and _____ (_____%) were aged 17. The majority of juveniles waived to the adult criminal court were _____ years old.

4. In the 1996 SCPS sample, the most serious arrest charge breakdown was as follows:

   _____ murder, comprising   _____% of the sample;
   _____ rape, comprising   _____% of the sample;
   _____ robbery, comprising   _____% of the sample;
   _____ assault, comprising   _____% of the sample;
   _____ other violent crimes, comprising   _____% of the sample;
   _____ burglary, comprising   _____% of the sample;
   _____ theft, comprising   _____% of the sample;
   _____ other property crimes, comprising   _____% of the sample;
   _____ drug trafficking, comprising   _____% of the sample;
   _____ other drug offenses, comprising   _____% of the sample;
   _____ weapons offenses, comprising   _____% of the sample;
   _____ other public order offenses, comprising   _____% of the sample.

   The most common offense is _____. The most serious offense is _____.

5. _____ (_____%) of the sample were convicted of violent offenses; _____ (_____%) were convicted of property offenses; _____ (_____%) were convicted of drug offenses; _____ (_____%) were convicted of public-order offenses; and _____ (_____%) were convicted of misdemeanor offenses. The most common conviction type was for _____.

6. _____ (_____%) had not been arrested before; _____ (_____%) had one prior arrest; _____ (_____%) had been arrested twice before; and _____ (_____%) had three or more prior arrests. The highest number of prior arrests for any one juvenile was _____.

7. Of those who had prior arrests, _____ (_____%) had been arrested for misdemeanors and _____ (_____%) had been arrested for felonies.

8. In the 1996 SCPS sample, the state breakdown was as follows:

   _____ Alaska, comprising   _____% of the sample;
   _____ Arizona, comprising   _____% of the sample;
   _____ California, comprising   _____% of the sample;
   _____ Florida, comprising   _____% of the sample;
   _____ Georgia, comprising   _____% of the sample;
   _____ Illinois, comprising   _____% of the sample;
   _____ Indiana, comprising   _____% of the sample;
   _____ Maryland, comprising   _____% of the sample;
   _____ Michigan, comprising   _____% of the sample;
   _____ Missouri, comprising   _____% of the sample;
   _____ New York, comprising   _____% of the sample;
   _____ Pennsylvania, comprising   _____% of the sample;
   _____ Tennessee, comprising   _____% of the sample;
   _____ Texas, comprising   _____% of the sample;
   _____ Washington, comprising   _____% of the sample; and
   _____ Wisconsin, comprising   _____% of the sample.

   The state that contributed the most cases to the sample was _____, which comprised _____% of the sample. The states which contributed the least number of cases were _____ and _____, which each contributed only one case to the total sample.

9. _____ (_____%) of the juvenile cases transferred to adult criminal court were dismissed; _____ (_____%) resulted in acquittals; _____ (_____%) were diverted or deferred; _____ (_____%) involved guilty pleas; _____ (_____%) resulted in guilty verdicts following trials; _____ (_____%) had "other" outcomes; and _____ (_____%) cases were still pending 1 year

after the case entered the criminal justice system. The most common case outcome was _____. A total of _____ cases resulted in guilty pleas or verdicts.

10. Looking at the three sentence outcome variables, _____ (_____%) of the juveniles convicted in adult criminal court were incarcerated and _____ (_____%) were not. The most severe sentence imposed on the convicted juveniles was prison for _____ (_____%) of the sample; jail for _____ (_____%); probation for _____ (_____%); and fine for _____ (_____%). Looking at SENT3, we see that _____ (_____%) of the sample were jailed, whereas _____ (_____%) were probationed in addition to being jailed; we also see that _____ (_____%) were sent to prison, whereas _____ (_____%) were probationed in addition to being sent to prison. Probation as an "add-on" to incarceration appears to be more common with *jail/prison* sentences.

11. In the CONVTYP2 → INCARCER cross-tabulation, <u>67</u> (_____%) of the juveniles convicted of violent offenses were incarcerated compared to _____ (_____%) of those convicted of property offenses, _____ (_____%) of those convicted of drug offenses, _____ (_____%) of those convicted of public-order offenses, and _____ (_____%) of those convicted of misdemeanors. It appears that violent offenders are *more/less* likely than other offenders to be incarcerated. This relationship is *weak/moderate/strong*. This relationship *is/is not* statistically significant.

MEAN BREAKOUT TABLES FOR JUVENILES WAIVED TO ADULT CRIMINAL COURTS

Complete the following table using the breakout tables for DISMISS and INCARCER broken out by state:

State	Mean Incarceration Rate	Mean Dismissal Rate
Alaska	Ignore: Too few cases	
Arizona	68.75	
California		
Florida		
Georgia	Ignore: Too few cases	
Illinois		
Indiana		
Maryland	Ignore: Too few cases	
Michigan		
Missouri		
New York		
Pennsylvania	Ignore: Too few cases	
Tennessee		Ignore: Too few cases
Texas		
Washington	Ignore: Too few cases	Ignore: Too few cases
Wisconsin		

The state with the highest rate of incarceration was _____ (which incarcerated _____% of its juveniles convicted in adult criminal court), followed by _____ (which incarcerated _____% of its juveniles convicted in adult criminal court). The state with the lowest rate of incarceration was _____ (which incarcerated _____% of its juveniles convicted in adult criminal court).

The state with the highest rate of dismissals was _____ (which dismissed _____% of its waived cases), followed by _____ (which dismissed _____% of its waived cases). The state with the lowest rate of dismissals was _____ (which dismissed _____% of its waived cases), followed by _____ (which dismissed _____% of its waived cases).

EXPLORING JUVENILES IN ADULT CRIMINAL COURTS: USING CONTROL VARIABLES

1. In the WHITE → INCARCER cross-tabulation, <u>15</u> (_____%) of the white juveniles convicted in adult criminal courts were incarcerated compared to _____ (_____%) of the minorities. It appears that white juveniles are *more/less* likely than minorities to be incarcerated following conviction in the adult criminal courts. This relationship is *weak/moderate/strong*. This relationship *is/is not* statistically significant.

2. In the WHITE → INCARCER cross-tabulation with CONVTYP2 as a control variable, <u>7</u> (58.3%) whites convicted of violent offenses were incarcerated compared to _____ (_____%) minorities. For violent offenses, it appears that whites are *more/less* likely to be incarcerated. This relationship is *weak/moderate/strong*. This relationship *is/is not* statistically significant. When we turn our attention to the rows for property offenses, <u>6</u> (_____%) whites were incarcerated, compared to _____ (_____%) minorities. For property offenses, it appears that whites are *more/less* likely to be incarcerated. This relationship is *weak/moderate/strong*. This relationship *is/is not* statistically significant. When we turn our attention to the rows for drug offenses, <u>0</u> (<u>0</u>%) whites were incarcerated compared to _____ (_____%) minorities. For drug offenses, it appears that whites are *more/less* likely to be incarcerated. This relationship is *weak/moderate/strong*. This relationship *is/is not* statistically significant. When we turn our attention to the rows for public order offenses, <u>1</u> (_____%) whites were incarcerated compared to _____ (_____%) minorities. For public order offenses, it ap-

pears that whites are *more/less* likely to be incarcerated. This relationship is *weak/moderate/strong*. This relationship *is/is not* statistically significant. Finally, when we turn our attention to the rows for misdemeanors, _1_ (_____%) whites were incarcerated compared to _____ (_____%) minorities. For misdemeanors, it appears that whites are *more/less* likely to be incarcerated. This relationship is *weak/moderate/strong*. This relationship *is/is not* statistically significant. Overall, we *can/cannot* say that controlling for CONVTYP2 in our model substantially changes the relationship we found between race and the likelihood of incarceration.

3. In the WHITE → INCARCER cross-tabulation with PRIORS as a control variable, _7_ (36.8%) whites with no prior arrests were incarcerated compared to _____ (_____%) minorities. For those without prior records, it appears that whites are *more/less* likely to be incarcerated. This relationship is *weak/moderate/strong*. This relationship *is/is not* statistically significant. When we turn our attention to the rows for juveniles with one or more prior arrests, _8_ (_____%) whites were incarcerated compared to _____ (_____%) minorities. For those with prior records, it appears that whites are *more/less* likely to be incarcerated. This relationship is *weak/moderate/strong*. This relationship *is/is not* statistically significant. Overall, we *can/cannot* say that controlling for PRIORS in our model substantially changes the relationship we found between race and the likelihood of incarceration. We can, however, say that race appears to be more important for juveniles *with/without* prior arrests.

Homework for Part V: Further Exploration
Juveniles in Adult Criminal Courts

Name: _____ Date: _____

TASK: Determine the influence of other variables on the likelihood of incarceration. If you cannot find any variables you believe are appropriate, use the severity of prior convictions (SERCONV) and whether or not the juvenile faced many charges (MANYCHGS).

Directions: Complete the following exercises by answering the questions.

NOTE: Please print out and include your tables with these questions so your work can be graded.

1. Which independent variables did you select? Why did you select these variables?

2. Run a frequency for your independent variables, and describe them in the space provided below.

3. Run cross-tabulation tables for your variables in the format: independent variable → INCARCER. How did your independent variable affect the likelihood of incarceration? Make sure to provide a description that includes the percentages, phi or Cramer's V value, the strength of the relationship, and the significance value.

4. On the basis of your analysis, what can you say about juveniles waived to the adult criminal courts?

Homework for Part V: On Your Own
Juveniles in Adult Criminal Courts

Name: _____ Date: _____

TASK: Expand your horizons with reference to juveniles in the adult criminal courts. You could determine which juveniles are more likely to have their cases dismissed (DISMISS) or which juveniles are more likely to have prior records (PRIORS). You may also use other dependent variables of your choice. Make sure to include a control variable of your choice.

Directions: Answer the following questions.

NOTE: Please print out and include your tables with these questions so your work can be graded.

1. Which dependent variable did you choose, and why did you choose that particular variable?

2. Which variables did you choose as your independent variables, and why did you select them?

3. How did your independent variables affect your dependent variable? Make sure to provide a description that includes the percentages, phi or Cramer's *V* value, the strength of the relationship, and the significance value.

4. Which control variable did you choose, and why did you choose to control that factor?

5. Did the control variable you included change the relationship between the independent and dependent variables noted in Question 3; that is, did the relationship between the two variables vary by control variable subcategory?

If you included more than one control variable or more than one independent or dependent variable, you may summarize the findings here for future reference.

Suggested Readings

Ackley, Ethel and Beverly Fliegel. 1960. "A Social Work Approach to Street-Corner Girls." *Social Work* 5:27-36.

Agnew, R. 1991. "A Longitudinal Test of Social Control Theory and Delinquency." *Journal of Research in Crime and Delinquency* 28/2:126-56.

Akers, R. 1985. *Deviant Behavior: A Social Learning Approach.* Belmont, CA: Wadsworth.

Akers, Ronald L., Marvin D. Krohn, Lonn Lanza-Kaduce, and Marcia Radosevich. 1979. "Social Learning and Deviant Behavior: A Specific Test of a General Theory." *American Sociological Review* 44: 636-55.

Andrews, Donna A., Ivan Zinger, Robert D. Hoge, James Bonta, Paul Gendreau, and Francis T. Cullen. 1990. "Does Correctional Treatment Work?" *Criminology* 28:369-404.

Arnett, J. (1992). "Reckless Behavior in Adolescence: A Developmental Perspective." *Developmental Review* 12:339-73.

Austin, David M. 1958. "The Special Youth Program Approach to Chronic Problem Families." In *Community Organization Papers.* New York: Columbia University Press.

Austin, James and Barry Krisberg. 1981. "Wider, Stronger, and Different Nets: The Dialectics of Criminal Justice Reform." *Journal of Research in Crime and Delinquency* 18:165-96.

Austin, James and Barry Krisberg. 1982. "The Unmet Promise of Alternatives to Incarceration." *Crime & Delinquency* 28: 374-409.

Bahr, Steven. 1979. "Family Determinants and Effects of Deviance." In *Contemporary Theories About the Family*, Vol. 1, edited by Wesley Burr, Rubin Hill, F. Ivan Nye, and Ira Reiss. New York: Free Press.

Bandura, A. 1969. *Principles of Behavior Modification.* New York: Holt, Rinehart & Winston.

Bandura, A. 1979. "The Social Learning Perspective: Mechanisms of Aggression." In *The Psychology of Crime and Criminal Justice*, edited by H. Toch. New York: Holt, Rinehart & Winston.

Bangert-Drowns, R. 1985. "The Effects of School-Based Substance Abuse Education: A Meta-Analysis." *Journal of Drug Education* 18:243-65.

Beck, B. M. 1969. "Mobilization for Youth: Reflections About Its Administration." In *Justice and the Law*, edited by H. H. Weissman. New York: Association Press.

Becker, Howard S. 1973. *Outsiders: Studies in the Sociology of Deviance.* New York: Free Press.

Becker, Howard. 1966. *Outsiders: Studies in the Sociology of Deviance.* New York: Free Press.

Becker, H., M. Agopian, and S. Yeh. 1992. "Impact Evaluation of Drug Abuse Resistance Education (D.A.R.E.)." *Journal of Drug Education* 22:283-91.

Bernard, T. 1987. "Structure and Control: Reconsidering Hirschi's Concept of Commitment." *Justice Quarterly* 4/3:409-24.

Bernard, T. 1992. *The Cycle of Juvenile Violence.* Oxford, UK: Oxford University Press.

Bilchick, S. 1998. "A Juvenile Justice System for the 21st Century." *Crime & Delinquency* 44:82-94.

Bishop, D. and C. Frazier. 1988. "The Influence of Race in Juvenile Justice Processing." *Journal of Research in Crime and Delinquency* 25:242-61.

Block, Kathleen and Donna Hale. 1991. "Turf Wars in the Progressive Era Juvenile Justice: The Relationship of Private and Public Child Care Agencies." *Crime & Delinquency* 37:225-41.

Bortner, M. A. 1982. *Inside a Juvenile Court: The Tarnished Ideal of Individualized Justice.* New York: New York University Press.

Braithwaite, J. 1981. "The Myth of Social Class and Criminality Reconsidered." *American Sociological Review* 46:36-57.

Bursik, Robert J., Jr. and Jim Webb. 1982. "Community Change and Patterns of Delinquency." *American Journal of Sociology* 88:24-42.

Burt, C. 1944. *The Young Delinquent*, 4th ed. London: University of London Press.

Byrne, James M. and Robert J. Sampson, eds. 1986. *The Social Ecology of Crime.* New York: Springer-Verlag.

Caldwell, Robert. 1961. "The Juvenile Court: Its Development and Some Major Problems." *Journal of Criminal Law, Criminology, and Police Science* 51:493-507.

Canter, Rachelle J. 1982. "Family Correlates of Male and Female Delinquency." *Criminology* 20:149-67.

Castellano, T. C. and Soderstrom, I. R. 1992. "Therapeutic Wilderness Programs and Juvenile Recidivism: A Program Evaluation." *Journal of Offender Rehabilitation* 17/3-4:19-46.

Cernkovich, Stephen A. and Peggy C. Giordano. 1987. "Family Relationships and Delinquency." *Criminology* 25:295-321.

Champion, D. and G. Mays. 1991. *Transferring Juveniles to Criminal Courts.* New York: Praeger.

Chandler, C. L., R. P. Weissberg, E. L. Cowen, and J. Guare. 1984. "Long-Term Effects of a School-Based Secondary Prevention Program for Young Maladapting Children." *Journal of Consulting and Clinical Psychology* 52:165-70.

Chesney-Lind, Meda. 1973. "Judicial Enforcement of the Female Sex Role: The Family Court and Female Delinquency Issues." *Criminology* 8:51-71.

Chesney-Lind, Meda and Randall G. Shelden. 1992. *Girls, Delinquency, and Juvenile Justice.* Pacific Grove, CA: Brooks/Cole.

Cicourel, Aaron. 1968. *The Social Organization of Juvenile Justice.* New York: John Wiley.

Clarke, Steven H. and Gary G. Koch. 1980. "Juvenile Court: Therapy or Crime Control, and Do Lawyers Make a Difference?" *Law and Society Review* 14:263-308.

Clelland, D. and T. J. Canter. 1980. "The New Myth of Class and Crime." *Criminology* 18:319-36.

Clinard, M. 1964. *Anomie and Deviant Behavior.* New York: Free Press.

Cloward, Richard A. and Lloyd E. Ohlin. 1960. *Delinquency and Opportunity: A Theory of Delinquent Gangs.* Glencoe, IL: Free Press.

Cloward, R. A. and F. F. Piven. 1966. "A Strategy to End Poverty." *The Nation* 2/202:510-517.

Cohen, Albert K. 1955. *Delinquent Boys.* New York: Free Press.

Cohen, Albert K. and James F. Short, Jr. 1958. "Research in Delinquent Subcultures." *Journal of Social Issues* 14:20-37.

Conger, Rand D. 1976. "Social Control and Social Learning Models of Delinquent Behavior: A Synthesis." *Criminology* 14:17-40.

Craig, M. M. and Furst, P. W. 1965. "What Happens After Treatment? A Study of Potentially Delinquent Boys." *Social Service Review* 39:165-71.

Cressey, Donald R. 1995. "Changing Criminals: The Application of the Theory of Differential Association." *American Journal of Sociology* 61:112-26.

Cullen, F. and K. Gilbert. 1982. *Reaffirming Rehabilitation.* Cincinnati, OH: Anderson.

Curry, G. and I. Spergel. 1992. "Gang Involvement and Delinquency Among Hispanic and African American Adolescent Males." *Journal of Research in Crime and Delinquency* 29:273-91.

Davidson, W. S. and E. Seidman. 1974. "Studies of Behavior Modification and Juvenile Delinquency: A Review, Methodological Critique, and Social Perspective." *Psychological Bulletin* 8/1:998-1001.

Dawson, Robert O. 1990. "The Future of Juvenile Justice: Is It Time to Abolish the System?" *Journal of Criminal Law and Criminology* 81:136-55.

DeFleur, Melvin and Richard Quinney. 1966. "A Reformulation of Sutherland's Differential Association Theory and a Strategy for Empirical Verification." *Journal of Research in Crime and Delinquency* 3:13.

Donovan J. E., Jessor, R., and Costa, F. M. 1988. "Syndrome of Problem Behavior in Adolescence: A Replication." *Journal of Consulting and Clinical Psychology* 56/5:762-65.

Elliott, Delbert and David Huizinga. 1983. "Social Class and Delinquent Behavior in a National Youth Study." *Criminology* 21:109-17.

Elliott, Delbert S. and Harwin Voss. 1974. *Delinquency and Dropout.* Lexington, MA: Lexington.

Empey, LaMar T., ed. 1979. *Juvenile Justice: The Progressive Legacy and Current Reforms.* Charlottesville: University Press of Virginia.

Empey, L. and M. Stafford. 1991. *American Delinquency.* New York: Dorsey.

Ennett, Susan T., Nancy S. Tobler, Christopher L. Ringwalt, and Robert L. Flewelling. 1994. "How Effective Is Drug Abuse Resistance Education? A Meta-Analysis of Project D.A.R.E. Outcome Evaluations." *American Journal of Public Health* 84:1394-1401.

Fagan, Jeffrey. 1990. "Treatment and Reintegration of Violent Delinquents." *Justice Quarterly* 7:244-363.

Fagan, Jeffrey and Sandra Wexler. 1987. "Family Origins of Violent Delinquents." *Criminology* 25:643-69.

Feld, B. 1991. "The Transformation of the Juvenile Court." *Minnesota Law Review* 75:691-725.

Feld, B. 1993. *Justice for Children: The Right to Counsel and the Juvenile Courts.* Boston: Northeastern University Press.

Ferdinand, Theodore. 1987. "The Methods of Delinquency Theory." *Criminology* 25:841-62.

Finckenauer, J. O. 1984. *Juvenile Delinquency and Corrections: The Gap Between Theory and Practice.* Orlando, FL: Academic Press.

Fox, S. 1970. "Juvenile Justice Reform: A Historical Perspective." *Stanford Law Review* 22:183-194.

Friel, C., J. Vaughn, and R. del Carmen. 1987. *Electronic Monitoring and Correctional Policy: The Technology and Its Application.* Washington, DC: National Institute of Justice.

Gable, R. 1986. "Application of Personal Telemonitoring to Current Problems in Corrections." *Journal of Criminal Justice* 14:167-76.

Gewirtz, Jacob L. and Donald M. Baer. 1958. "Deprivation and Satiation of Social Reinforcers as Drive Conditions." *Journal of Abnormal and Social Psychology* 57:165-72.

Glueck, Sheldon. 1960. "Ten Years of Unraveling Juvenile Delinquency: An Examination of Criticisms." *Journal of Criminal Law, Criminology, and Police Science* 51:283-308.

Glueck, Sheldon and Eleanor Glueck. 1937. *Later Criminal Careers.* New York: Commonwealth Fund.

Gold, Martin. 1987. "The Social Ecology of Delinquency." In *Handbook of Juvenile Delinquency,* edited by H. C. Quay. New York: John Wiley.

Goldstein, P. J. 1985. "The Drugs-Violence Nexus: A Tri-Partite Conceptual Framework." *Journal of Drug Issues* 15:493-506.

Gottfredson, Denise. 1986. "An Empirical Test of School-Based Environmental and Individual Interventions to Reduce the Risk of

Delinquent Behavior." *Criminology* 24: 705-30.

Gottfredson, Gary. 1987. "Peer Group Interventions to Reduce the Risk of Delinquent Behavior." *Criminology* 25:671-714.

Gove, Walter R. 1970. "Societal Reaction as an Explanation of Mental Illness: An Evaluation." *American Sociological Review* 35: 873-84.

Gove, Walter R. 1980. "The Labeling Perspective: An Overview." In *The Labeling of Deviance,* edited by Walter R. Gove. Beverly Hills, CA: Sage.

Gove, Walter R. and Robert D. Crutchfield. 1982. "The Family and Juvenile Delinquency." *Sociological Quarterly* 23:301-19.

Gove, Walter R. and Michael L. Hughes. 1980. "Reexamining the Ecological Fallacy: A Study in Which Aggregate Data Are Critical in Investigating the Pathological Effects of Living Alone." *Social Forces* 58:1157-77.

Hackler, J. C. 1966. "Boys, Blisters, and Behavior: The Impact of a Work Program in an Urban Central Area." *Journal of Research in Crime and Delinquency* 12:155-64.

Hagan, J. 1993. "The Social Embeddedness of Crime and Unemployment." *Criminology* 31:465-91.

Hakeem, Michael. 1958. "A Critique of the Psychiatric Approach to Juvenile Delinquency." In *Juvenile Delinquency,* edited by Joseph S. Roucek. New York: Philosophical Library.

Hamparian, Donna M., R. Schuster, S. Dinitz, and J. P. Conrad. 1978. *The Violent Few.* Toronto: Lexington Books.

Handler, Joel F. and Margaret K. Rosenheim. 1966. "Privacy and Welfare: Public Assistance and Juvenile Justice." *Law and Contemporary Problems* 31:377-412.

Hawkins, J. D. and J. G. Weis. 1985. "The Social Development Model: An Integrated Approach to Delinquency Prevention." *Journal of Primary Prevention* 6/2:73-97.

Hindelang, Michael. 1978. "Race and Involvement in Common Law Personal Crimes." *American Sociological Review* 43:90-104.

Hindelang, Michael J., Travis Hirschi, and Joseph G. Weis. 1979. "Correlates of Delinquency: The Illusion of Discrepancy Between Self-Report and Official Measures." *American Sociological Review* 44:995-1014.

Hindelang, Michael J., Travis Hirschi, and Joseph G. Weis. 1981. *Measuring Delinquency.* Beverly Hills, CA: Sage.

Hirschi, Travis. 1969. *Causes of Delinquency.* Berkeley: University of California Press.

Hirschi, T. and M. Gottfredson. 1983. "Age and the Explanation of Crime." *American Journal of Sociology* 89:552-84.

Huff, Ronald. 1989. "Youth Gangs and Public Policy." *Crime and Delinquency* 35:524-37.

Inciardi, J. A. 1981. *The Drug-Crime Connection.* Beverly Hills, CA: Sage.

Jackson, Toby. 1957. "Social Disorganization and Stake in Conformity: Complementary Factors in the Predatory Behavior of Hoodlums." *Journal of Criminal Law, Criminology and Police Science* 48:12-17.

Jensen, E. and L. Metsger. 1994. "A Test of the Deterrent Effect of Legislative Waiver on Violent Juvenile Crime." *Crime and Delinquency* 40:96-104.

Jensen, Gary and David Brownfield. 1986. "Gender, Lifestyles and Victimization: Beyond Routine Activities." *Violence and Victims* 1:85-101.

Jensen, Gary F. and Kevin Thompson. 1990. "What's Class Got to Do With It? A Further Examination of Power-Control Theory." *American Journal of Sociology* 95/4:1009-23.

Jessor, R. and S. L. Jessor. 1977. *Problem Behavior and Psychosocial Development: A Longitudinal Study of Youth.* New York: Academic Press.

Johnson, Richard E. 1979. *Juvenile Delinquency and Its Origins: An Integrated Theoretical Approach.* Cambridge, UK: Cambridge University Press.

Kandel, D., O. Simcha-Fagan, and M. Davies. 1986. "Risk Factors for Delinquency and Illicit Drug Use From Adolescence to Young Adulthood." *Journal of Drug Issues* 16:67-90.

Kitsuse, John I. 1962. "Societal Reactions to Deviant Behavior: Problems of Theory and Method." *Social Problems* 9:248-63.

Klein, M., C. Maxson, and L. Cunningham. 1991. "Crack, Street Gangs, and Violence." *Criminology* 29:623-50.

Kornhauser, Ruth R. 1978. *Social Sources of Delinquency*. Chicago: University of Chicago Press.

Kowalski, G. and J. Rickicki. 1982. "Determinants of Juvenile Post-Adjudication Dispositions." *Journal of Research in Crime and Delinquency* 19:66-83.

Krisberg, Barry and James Austin. 1993. *Reinventing Juvenile Justice*. Newbury Park, CA: Sage.

Krisberg, Barry and Ira M. Schwartz. 1983. "Rethinking Juvenile Justice." *Crime & Delinquency* 29:333-64.

Krisberg, Barry, Ira M. Schwartz, Paul Litsky, and James Austin. 1986. "The Watershed of Juvenile Justice Reform." *Crime & Delinquency* 32:5-38.

Krivo, L. and R. Peterson. 1996. "Extremely Disadvantaged Neighborhoods and Urban Crime." *Social Forces* 75:619-50.

Lab, Steven P. and John T. Whitehead. 1990. "From 'Nothing Works' to 'The Appropriate Works': The Latest Stop on the Search for the Secular Grail." *Criminology* 28:405-17.

Lasley, J. 1992. "Age, Social Context, and Street Gang Membership: Are Youth Gangs Becoming Adult Gangs?" *Youth and Society* 23:434-51.

Lauritsen, J., R. Sampson, and J. Laub. 1990. "The Link Between Offending and Victimization Among Adolescents." *Criminology* 29/2:265-92.

Lefstein, Norman, Vaughan Stapleton, and Lee Teitelbaum. 1969. "In Search of Juvenile Justice: Gault and Its Implementation." *Law and Society Review* 3:491-562.

Lemert, Edwin M. 1951. *Social Pathology*. New York: McGraw-Hill.

Lipsey, M. 1992. "Juvenile Delinquency Treatment: A Meta-Analytic Inquiry Into the Variability of Effects." In *Meta-Analysis for Explanation*, edited by T. Cook, H. Cooper, D. Cordray, H. Hartmann, L. Hedges, R. Light, T. Louis, and F. Mosteller. New York: Russell Sage.

Lipton, D., R. Martinson, and J. Wilks. 1975. *The Effectiveness of Correctional Treatment*. New York: Praeger.

Lundman, R. and F. Scarpitti. 1978. "Delinquency Prevention: Recommendations for Future Projects." *Crime & Delinquency* 22:207-20.

MacKenzie, Doris L., Robert Brame, David McDowell, and Claire Souryal. 1995. "Boot Camp Prisons and Recidivism in Eight States." *Criminology* 33/3:327-57.

Matsueda, R. and K. Heimer. 1987. "Race, Family Structure and Delinquency: A Test of Differential Association and Control Theories." *American Sociological Review* 52:826-40.

Matza, David. 1957. "Techniques of Neutralization: A Theory of Delinquency." *American Sociological Review* 22:664-70.

Matza, David. 1964. *Delinquency and Drift*. New York: John Wiley.

Matza, David. 1969. *Becoming Deviant*. Englewood Cliffs, NJ: Prentice Hall.

McCorkle, Lloyd W., Albert Elias, and F. Lovell Bixby. 1958. *The Highfields Story: A Unique Experiment in the Treatment of Juvenile Delinquency*. New York: Holt.

McKay, H. 1942. *Juvenile Delinquency and Urban Areas*. Chicago: University of Chicago Press.

McKay, Henry D. 1960. "Differential Association and Crime Prevention: Problems of Utilization." *Social Problems* 8:25-27.

Mennel, Robert M. 1968. *Thorns and Thistles: Juvenile Delinquents in the United States, 1825-1940*. Hanover, NH: University Press of New England.

Merton, R. 1957. *Social Theory and Social Structure* (Chapters 4 and 5). Glencoe, IL: Free Press.

Michaels, J. J. 1940. "Psychobiologic Interpretation of Delinquency." *American Journal of Orthopsychiatry* 10:501-9.

Miller, Jerome G. 1979. "The Revolution in Juvenile Justice: From Rhetoric to Rhetoric." In *The Future of Childhood and Juvenile Justice,* edited by LaMar T. Empey. Charlottesville: University Press of Virginia.

Miller, Walter B. 1957. "The Impact of a Community Group Work Program on Delinquent Corner Groups." *Social Service Review* 31:390-406.

Miller, Walter B. 1959. "Preventive Work With Street-Corner Groups: Boston Delinquency Project." *Annals of the American Academy of Political and Social Science* 322:97-106.

Miller, Walter B. 1962. "The Impact of a 'Total Community' Delinquency Control Project." *Social Problems* 10:168-91.

Moore, Joan W. 1978. *Homeboys: Gangs, Drugs, and Prisons in the Barrios of Los Angeles.* Philadelphia: Temple University Press.

Murray, C. and L. Cox. 1979. *Beyond Probation: Juvenile Corrections and the Chronic Delinquent.* Beverly Hills, CA: Sage.

Newman, Ian M. 1984. "Capturing the Energy of Peer Pressure: Insights From a Longitudinal Study of Adolescent Cigarette Smoking." *Journal of School Health* 54:146-48.

Odem, M. and S. Schlossman. 1991. "Guardians of Virtue: The Juvenile Court and Female Delinquency in Early 20th Century Los Angeles." *Crime & Delinquency* 37:186-203.

Olweus, D. 1979. "Stability of Aggressive Reaction Patterns in Males: A Review." *Psychological Bulletin* 86:852-75.

Palmer, T. 1992. *The Re-emergence of Correctional Intervention.* Newbury Park, CA: Sage.

Phillips, E. L. 1968. "Achievement Place: Token Economy Reinforcement Procedures in a Homestyle Rehabilitation Setting for Pre-delinquent Boys." *Journal of Applied Behavior Analysis* 1:213-23.

Phillips, John C. and Delos H. Kelly. 1979. "School Failure and Delinquency: Which Causes Which?" *Criminology* 17:194-207.

Pickett, Robert S. 1969. *House of Refuge—Origins of Juvenile Reform in New York State, 1815-1857.* Syracuse, NY: Syracuse University Press.

Piven, F. F. and R. A. Cloward. 1971. *Regulating the Poor.* New York: Pantheon.

Pleck, Elizabeth. 1987. *Domestic Tyranny: The Making of Social Policy Against Family Violence From Colonial Times to the Present.* New York: Oxford University Press.

Pope, C. and W. Feyerherm. 1990. "Minority Status and Juvenile Justice Processing." *Criminal Justice Abstracts* 22:327-35, 527-42.

Powers, E. and H. Witmer. 1951. *An Experiment in the Prevention of Delinquency: The Cambridge-Somervlle Youth Study.* New York: Columbia University Press.

Radzinowicz, Leon. 1966. *Ideology and Crime.* London: Heinemann.

Ray, Melvin and William Downs. 1986. "An Empirical Test of Labeling Theory Using Longitudinal Data." *Journal of Research in Crime and Delinquency* 23:169-74.

Reiss, Albert J., Jr. 1951. "Delinquency as the Failure of Personal and Social Controls." *American Sociological Review* 16:196-207.

Robins, Lee N. 1978. "Sturdy Childhood Predictors of Adult Antisocial Behavior Replications From Longitudinal Studies." *Psychological Medicine* 8:611-622.

Rubin, T. 1979. *Behind the Black Robe—Juvenile Court Judges and the Court.* Beverly Hills, CA: Sage.

Rutter, Michael. 1990. "Psychosocial Resilience and Protective Mechanisms." In *Risk and Protective Factors in the Development of Psychopathology,* edited by J. Rolf, A. S. Masten, D. Cicchetti, K. H. Neuchterlein, and S. Weintraub. Cambridge, UK: Cambridge University Press.

Salerno, Anthony. 1991. "The Child Saving Movement: Altruism or Conspiracy?" *Juvenile and Family Court Journal* 42:37-48.

Sampson, R. 1986. "Effects of Socioeconomic Context on Official Reaction to Juvenile Delinquency." *American Sociological Review* 51: 876-85.

Sampson, Robert J. and John H. Laub. 1993. *Crime in the Making: Pathways and Turning Points Through Life.* Cambridge, MA: Harvard University Press.

Sanders, Wiley B., ed. 1970. *Juvenile Offenders for a Thousand Years: Selected Readings From Anglo-Saxon Times to 1900.* Chapel Hill: University of North Carolina Press.

Schachter, S. and J. Singer. 1962. "Cognitive, Social and Physiological Determinants of Emotional State." *Psychological Review* 69:379-99.

Schlossman, Steven L. 1977. *Love and the American Delinquent.* Chicago: University of Chicago Press.

Schmidt, A. and C. Curtis. 1987. "Electronic Monitors." In *Intermediate Punishments: Intensive Supervision, Home Confinement and Electronic Surveillance,* edited by B. McCarthy. New York: Praeger.

Schwendinger, Herman and Julia Schwendinger. 1985. *Adolescent Subcultures and Delinquency.* New York: Praeger.

Sechrest, L., S. White, and E. Brown, eds. 1979. *The Rehabilitation of Criminal Offenders: Problems and Prospects.* Washington, DC: National Academy Press.

Shaw, Clifford R. 1966. *The Jack-Roller: A Delinquent Boy's Own Story.* Chicago: University of Chicago Press.

Shaw, Clifford R. and Henry D. McKay. 1942. *Juvenile Delinquency and Urban Areas.* Chicago: University of Chicago Press.

Shaw, Clifford R., Frederick M. Zorbaugh, Henry D. McKay, and Leonard S. Cottrell. 1929. *Delinquency Areas.* Chicago: University of Chicago Press.

Short, James F., Jr. and Fred Strodtbeck. 1965. *Group Process and Gang Delinquency.* Chicago: University of Chicago Press.

Siegel, Larry J. and Joseph J. Senna. 2000. *Juvenile Delinquency: Theory, Practice, and Law.* Belmont, CA: Wadsworth/Thomson Learning.

Simcha-Fagan, Ora and Joseph E. Schwartz. 1986. "Neighborhood and Delinquency: An Assessment of Contextual Effects." *Criminology* 24:667-99.

Singer, S. 1993. "The Automatic Waiver of Juveniles and Substantive Justice." *Crime & Delinquency* 39:253-61.

Skinner, B. F. 1953. *Science and Human Behavior.* New York: Macmillan.

Spergel, Irving. 1990. "Youth Gangs: Continuity and Change." In *Crime and Justice,* edited by M. Tonry and N. Morris. Chicago: University of Chicago Press.

Spergel, Irving. 1992. "Youth Gangs: An Essay Review." *Social Service Review* 66:121-32.

Stapleton, W. Vaughan and Lee E. Teitelbaum. 1972. *In Defense of Youth: A Study of the Role of Counsel in American Juvenile Court.* New York: Russell Sage.

Steffensmeier, Darrell and Renee Hoffman Steffensmeier. 1980. "Trends in Female Delinquency: An Examination of Arrest, Juvenile Court, Self-Report, and Field Data." *Criminology* 18:62-85.

Strasburg, P. 1978. *Violent Delinquents.* New York: Monarch.

Streib, Victor L. 1987. *Death Penalty for Juveniles.* Bloomington: Indiana University Press.

Thrasher, Frederic. 1927. *The Gang.* Chicago: University of Chicago Press.

Tittle, C. and D. Curran. 1988. "Contingencies for Dispositional Disparities in Juvenile Justice." *Social Forces* 67:23-58.

Tittle, C., W. J. Villemez, and D. A. Smith. 1978. "The Myth of Social Class and Criminality: An Assessment of the Empirical Evidence." *American Sociological Review* 43:643-58.

Tracy, P. E., M. E. Wolfgang, and R. M. Figlio. 1985. *Delinquency in Two Birth Cohorts.* Washington, DC: Government Printing Office.

Tracy, P. E., M. E. Wolfgang, and R. M. Figlio. 1989. *Patterns of Delinquency and Crime in the 1958 Philadelphia Birth Cohort.* Washington, DC: Government Printing Office.

Tracy, P. E., M. E. Wolfgang, and R. M. Figlio. 1990. *Delinquency Careers in Two Birth Cohorts.* New York: Plenum.

Visher, C. 1983. "Arrest Decisions and Notions of Chivalry." *Criminology* 21:5-28.

Weis, Joseph G. 1977. "Comparative Analysis of Social Control Theories of Delinquency." In *Preventing Delinquency*, Vol. 1. Washington, DC: Government Printing Office.

Werner, E. E. 1987. "Vulnerability and Resiliency in Children at Risk for Delinquency: A Longitudinal Study From Birth to Young Adulthood." In *Primary Prevention of Psychopathology*, edited by J. D. Burchard and S. N. Burchard. Vol. 10, *Prevention of Delinquent Behavior*. Newbury Park, CA: Sage.

White, H. R., R. J. Pandina, and R. LaGrange. 1987. "Longitudinal Predictors of Serious Drug Abuse and Delinquency." *Criminology* 25:715-40.

Whyte, William Foote. 1943. "Social Disorganization in the Slums." *American Sociological Review* 8:34-39.

Wiatrowski, M. and K. Anderson. 1987. "The Dimensionality of the Social Bond." *Journal of Quantitative Criminology* 3/1: 65-81.

Williams, J. R. and M. Gold. 1972. "From Delinquent Behavior to Official Delinquency." *Social Problems* 20:209-29.

Wilson, Harriett. 1980. "Parental Supervision: A Neglected Aspect of Delinquency." *British Journal of Criminology* 20:203-35.

Wise, Kathryn L., Kaarre A. Bundy, Eugene A. Bundy, and Larry L. Wise. 1991. "Social Skills for Young Adolescents." *Adolescence* 26:233-41.

Wolfgang, Marvin E., Robert M. Figlio, and Thorsten Sellin. 1972. *Delinquency in a Birth Cohort*. Chicago: University of Chicago Press.

Woodhead, M. 1988. "When Psychology Informs Public Policy: The Case of Early Childhood Intervention." *American Psychologist* 43:443-54.

Wright, J., Jr. and R. James. 1974. *A Behavioral Approach to Preventing Delinquency*. Springfield, IL: Charles C Thomas.

Wysong, F., R. Aniskiewicz, and R. Wright. 1994. "Truth in D.A.R.E." *Social Problems* 41:448-72.

Yablonsky, L. 1963. *The Violent Gang*. New York: Macmillan.

Zimring, F. 1982. *The Changing Legal World of Adolescence*. New York: Free Press.

Index

delinquency typology and, 159-160, 161 (table)
gang activity and, 155, 157
measurement methods, 157-158
patterns of and delinquency, 160-163, 162 (table), 166
peer influence and, 302-304
regression analysis of, 163-165, 164 (table)
sampling, 158
social control/learning theories and, 157-158, 165
typology of, 160
Drug-Free Schools and Communities Act of 1987, 311
DSO (deinstitutionalization of status offenders/nonoffenders) mandate, 538, 543
Due process protections, 490-491, 501
constitutional safeguards, 503-504
counsel, right to, 513-519
See also Gault decision; Juvenile court system
Dunedin Multidisciplinary Health and Development Study, 117
Durkheim, E., 323, 354, 357

E

Early childhood aggression, 420
child behavior checklist (CBCL), 422-424
clinical range analysis, 423-424
females, 423
Hawthorne effect, 424
males, 422-423
outcome measures, 422
parent training, 421
research design, 420-421
teacher training, 421-422
Early childhood intervention, 223
effectiveness analysis, 227-228
Gutelius Child Health Supervision Study, 226
Houston Parent-Child Development Center, 225-226
parent-training programs, 227
Perry Preschool Project, 223-224
snowball hypothesis, 226-227
socio-emotional development, 227
Syracuse University Family Development Research Program, 224

University of Rochester Nurse Home-Visitation Program, 226
Yale Child Welfare Research Program, 224-225
Ecological factors:
aversive environments, 333-334, 335, 336
community, 401-402
context effects, 113-114
distribution patterns, 229
early childhood intervention and, 223
human ecology model, 241-242
measures of class, 109-110, 109 (table)
See also Chicago Area Project (CAP); Ecology theory; Environmental factors
Ecological model of crime, 240-241
Ecology theory, 231-232
African American crime rates, 238
criticisms of, 237
deviance, spiral of, 232-237
Economic status, 197
Education:
disparity in, 196
juvenile crime and, 11, 114
law-related, 413
school/work integrated programs, 417
systems and social disorganization, 243
See also School performance; Schools
Electronic monitoring, 493, 582
adult program experience, 575-576
benefits of, 581-582
costs of, 580
devices in, 575
eligibility criteria, 577-578
juvenile program experience, 576
participant profile, 578
problems in, 580-581
program evaluation, 579-580
program objectives, 576-577
supervision procedures, 578-579
Elliot and Ageton inventory, 50
Emotional dynamics, 194, 197
Employment-oriented interventions, 390-391
school/work programs, 417

vocational training/placement, 417
Environmental factors, 7-8, 11
See also Ecological factors
Ethnicity. See Race
Ever variety scale, 43, 44, 44 (table)
Excitement, lower class experience, 272
Exercises. See Data analysis exercises

F

Families:
attachments and, 366, 403
child development specialist intervention, 384-385
child-saving movement and, 9, 12
Chinese social unit of, 279-280
cohesiveness of, 197
crisis intervention services, 384, 411-412
delinquency and, 90-91, 196-197
in-home support services, 383-384
parent support groups, 412
parenting training, 382-383, 411, 421
reconstituted, 128
social development and, 379, 379-380 (figure)
socialization of, 5, 6
surrogate families, 412
welfare and, 109
women's status reorganization, 8
See also Broken homes; Unraveling Juvenile Delinquency study
Family Trouble Clinic, 412
Fate/luck, 272
FBI, xvii, 26, 98, 99
Federal Juvenile Justice and Delinquency Prevention Act of 1974, 490
Felony offenders, 548
jurisdictional debate, 548-549, 550
legal decision making, 549-550
sanction comparison, 549
sentencing research and, 549
See also Recidivism
Feminist movement, 7-9, 530
Fourteenth Amendment, 501

behavior, 42-47, 43-44 (tables), 46 (figure)
validity of, 39, 40-42, 41 (figure)
See also Chronic offenders; National Youth Survey (NYS); Seattle Youth Study (SYS)
Services for Asian-American Youth (SAAY), 415, 416
Sexual identity. *See* Gender
Sexual offenses, 95
Sey YES (Youth Enterprise System), 415, 416
Shaw, C. R., 250, 256, 257-258
Situationally induced motives, 439-440
Smartness, lower-class culture, 271-272
Snowball hypothesis, 226-227
Social class, 104, 114
    age/crime and, 105
    delinquency motivation, 320
    dropouts and, 133
    ecological context effects, 113-114
    ecological measures of, 109-110, 109 (table)
    group differences in, 111-113, 111 (table)
    incarceration rates, 102-103
    individual measures of, 110-111, 110 (table)
    item analysis, 112
    juvenile crime and, 90
    offense-specific/category scales and, 112
    official crime measures and, 104, 105
    self-report studies, 105
    socioeconomic status and, 110, 111, 111 (table)
    strain theory and, 331-332
    See also Seattle Youth Study (SYS); Socioeconomic status (SES)
Social control theory, 6, 9, 157, 163, 165, 239
    attachments, 357-358, 360, 365-366
    behavior explanations, 368
    belief, 359-360, 367
    bond elements in, 357-360, 369-370
    commitment, 358, 367, 368, 369
    conceptual/operational definitions of, 365
    conventionality and, 360, 368
    empirical testing of, 364-369

generalizability, 370
involvement, 358-359, 366-367
morality and attachment, 360
socialization and, 354
strain theory and, 331
theoretical framework, 363-364, 371
See also Prevention; Social development model
Social Darwinism, 7
Social development model, 158, 355, 401
    affective/social skills training, 386-387
    alternative educational options, 388
    child development specialist intervention, 384-385, 414
    community crime prevention program, 391
    community youth development, 389-390, 391
    consistent expectations/sanctions, 388-389
    cross-age tutoring, 387-388, 414
    family crisis intervention, 384
    in-home family support, 383-384
    institutions of socialization and, 378-381, 379-381 (figure), 402-403, 402 (figure), 403-404
    moral order/law, belief in, 387, 413
    parenting training, 382-383
    peer-oriented interventions, 389, 416
    performance-based education, 385-386
    prevocational education, 387
    school climate assessment/improvement, 388-389, 414
    student involvement approaches, 386
    teacher effectiveness training, 387
    vocational training/placement, 390-391, 413-414
    See also Early childhood aggression; Prevention
Social disorganization, 239-240
    Chinese gangs and, 282
    conceptualization of, 242-243
    data collection, 243-244
    delinquency and, 240, 402
    educational systems and, 243
    family and, 243
    feedback loops in, 248

group dynamics vs. individual motivation, 240-241, 246-247
normative assumptions and, 245-246
official records, bias in, 244-245
stability, external factors, 245-246
urban dynamics of, 241-242
victimization and, 247-248
See also Chicago Area Project (CAP)
Social identification, 296
Social influence model, 291
Social integration. *See* Social control theory
Social learning theory, 139, 149, 154-155, 290
    analysis design, 153-154
    attitudes, pro-gang, 152
    crime-involvement prediction, 154
    delinquent conduct and, 149-150, 157-158, 165, 248
    differential associations, 151-152
    drug use and, 291
    drug-related crime, 155
    gang membership, 151, 154
    group-context offenses, 154, 155
    personal crime, 154, 155
    property crime, 154
    sampling, 150
    self-report delinquency (SRD) inventory, 150-151
    social reinforcers, 152, 297, 298
    See also Behavior modification; Subculture tradition
Social networks, 135, 242, 244
Social power, 117
Social psychology, 192, 198
    learning and, 292
    risk behavior and, 217-218
    See also Chicago Area Project (CAP)
Social skills training, 413, 421
Social worker role, 8, 9, 12
Socialization:
    behavior theory and, 296
    child-saving movement, 9, 10
    cultural deviance theory and, 401
    delinquency and, 157-158, 248
    institutions of, 378-381, 379-381 (figure), 402-403, 402 (figure), 403-404
    law and family, 6
    peer influence and, 401, 402-403, 402 (figure), 404

delinquency *behavior* measurement, 40-42, 41 (figure)
ethnicity and, 44
known group validity, 51, 52 (table)
official records, 39, 40
See also Seattle Youth Study (SYS); Self-report measures
Values, 6, 10, 300
conventional vs. deviant, 327-329
deviance choices and, 324
Versatility vs. specialization, 93-96, 94 (table)
Victimization, 247-248, 282
Violent crime. *See* Gang activity
VisionQuest, 525

Vocational education, 390-391, 413-414, 417

W

Washington. *See* Juvenile Justice Act of 1994
Weapons. *See* Guns
Welfare, 9
crime incidence and, 109
Juvenile Court Law of 1899 and, 15
Wilderness programs, 494, 525
Winship decision, 597
Women:
child-saving movement and, 7-9, 12
status revolution, 8, 9
Working class, 111 (table), 112

Y

Yale Child Welfare Research Program, 224-225
YES (Youth Enrichment System), 416
Youth Enrichment System (YES), 416
Youth Enterprise System (Sey YES), 415, 416
Youth in Transition survey, 334-335

Z

Zone of transition, 232